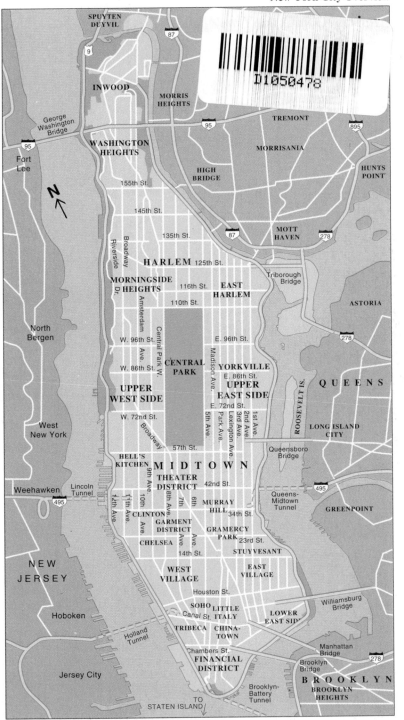

New York City Subways

Subways

Stops are not served by all trains at all times.
Refer to Transit Authority map for descriptions
of express, local, and limited service.

LEGEND

K,B   Line
168 St   Terminal

Downtown Manhattan

BLEECKER BOB'S

•— SCRAP BAR

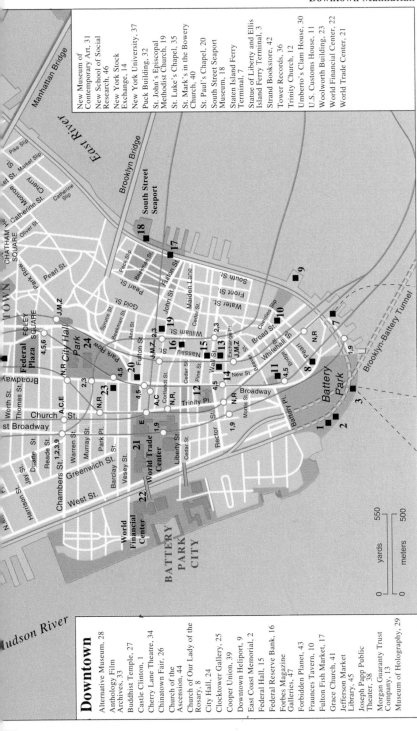

Downtown Manhattan

Downtown

Alternative Museum, 28
Anthology Film Archives, 33
Buddhist Temple, 27
Castle Clinton, 1
Cherry Lane Theatre, 34
Chinatown Fair, 26
Church of the Ascension, 44
Church of Our Lady of the Rosary, 8
City Hall, 24
Clocktower Gallery, 25
Cooper Union, 39
Downtown Heliport, 9
East Coast Memorial, 2
Federal Hall, 15
Federal Reserve Bank, 16
Forbes Magazine Galleries, 47
Forbidden Planet, 43
Fraunces Tavern, 10
Fulton Fish Market, 17
Grace Church, 41
Jefferson Market Library, 45
Joseph Papp Public Theater, 38
Morgan Guaranty Trust Company, 13
Museum of Holography, 29

New Museum of Contemporary Art, 31
New School of Social Research, 46
New York Stock Exchange, 14
New York University, 37
Puck Building, 32
St. John's Episcopal Methodist Church, 19
St. Luke's Chapel, 35
St. Mark's in the Bowery Church, 40
St. Paul's Chapel, 20
South Street Seaport Museum, 18
Staten Island Ferry Terminal, 7
Statue of Liberty and Ellis Island Ferry Terminal, 3
Strand Bookstore, 42
Tower Records, 36
Trinity Church, 12
Umberto's Clam House, 30
U.S. Customs House, 11
Woolworth Building, 23
World Financial Center, 22
World Trade Center, 21

Midtown Manhattan

Queensboro Bridge

East River

Queens-Midtown Tunnel

FDR Dr.

TURTLE BAY

United Nations

First Ave.
Second Ave.
Third Ave.
Lexington Ave.
Park Ave.
Madison Ave.
Fifth Ave.
Broadway
Seventh Ave.
Eighth Ave.
Ninth Ave.
Tenth Ave.
Eleventh Ave.
Twelfth Ave.

E. 56th St.
E. 55th St.
E. 54th St.
E. 53rd St.
E. 52nd St.
E. 51st St.
E. 50th St.
E. 49th St.
E. 48th St.
E. 47th St.
E. 46th St.
E. 45th St.
E. 44th St.
E. 43rd St.
E. 42nd St.
E. 41st St.
E. 40th St.
E. 39th St.
E. 38th St.
E. 37th St.
E. 36th St.
E. 35th St.
E. 34th St.
E. 33rd St.
E. 32nd St.

E. 60th St.
E. 59th St.
E. 58th St.
E. 57th St.

Citicorp Center

MURRAY HILL

Grand Central Terminal

New York Public Library

Empire State Building

Bryant Park
W. 40th St.

Rockefeller Center

Museum of Modern Art

Carnegie Hall

Grand Army Plaza

Central Park South

COLUMBUS CIRCLE

New York Convention & Visitors Bureau

A,B,C,D
1,2,3,9
N,R
B,Q
4,5,6
E,F
6
1,2,3,N,R,9
B,D,E
C,E
A,C,E
B,D,F,Q
B,D,F,O
4,5,6,S
7
N,R

TIMES SQUARE

HERALD SQUARE

GARMENT DISTRICT

Port Authority Bus Terminal

General Post Office

HELL'S KITCHEN

Lincoln Tunnel

Dyer Ave.

W. 60th St.
W. 59th St.
W. 58th St.
W. 57th St.
W. 56th St.
W. 55th St.
W. 54th St.
W. 53rd St.
W. 52nd St.
W. 51st St.
W. 50th St.
W. 49th St.
W. 48th St.
W. 47th St.
W. 45th St.
W. 44th St.
W. 43rd St.
W. 42nd St.
W. 41st St.
W. 39th St.
W. 38th St.
W. 37th St.
W. 36th St.
W. 35th St.
W. 34th St.
W. 33rd St.
W. 32nd St.

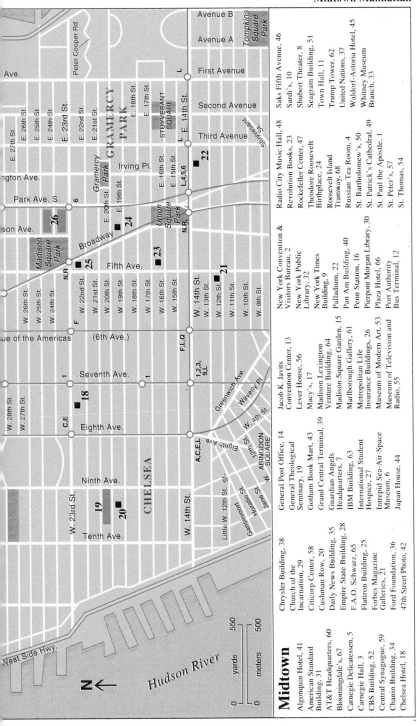

Uptown

American Museum of Natural History, 53
The Ansonia, 55
The Arsenal, 25
Asia Society, 14
Belvedere Castle, 36
Bethesda Fountain, 33
Blockhouse No. 1, 42
Bloomingdale's, 22
Bridle Path, 30
Cathedral of St. John the Divine, 47
Central Park Zoo, 24
Chess and Checkers House, 28
Children's Museum of Manhattan, 51
Children's Zoo, 26
China House, 19

Cleopatra's Needle, 38
Columbia University, 46
Conservatory Garden, 2
Cooper-Hewitt Museum, 7
The Dairy, 27
Dakota Apartments, 56
Delacorte Theater, 37
El Museo del Barrio, 1
Fordham University, 60
Frick Museum, 13
Gracie Mansion, 10
Grant's Tomb, 45
Great Lawn, 39
Guggenheim Museum, 9
Hayden Planetarium (at the American Museum of Natural History), 53
Hector Memorial, 50
Hotel des Artistes, 57

Hunter College, 16
International Center of Photography, 5
Jewish Museum, 6
The Juilliard School (at Lincoln Center), 59
Lincoln Center, 59
Loeb Boathouse, 34
Masjid Malcolm Shabazz , 43
Metropolitan Museum of Art, 11
Mt. Sinai Hospital, 4
Museum of American Folk Art, 58
Museum of American Illustration, 21
Museum of the City of New York, 3
National Academy of Design, 8
New York Convention & Visitors Bureau, 61

New York Historical Society, 54
New York Hospital, 15
Plaza Hotel, 23
Police Station (Central Park), 40
Rockefeller University, 20
7th Regiment Armory, 17
Shakespeare Garden, 35
Soldiers and Sailors Monument, 49
Strawberry Fields, 32
Studio Museum in Harlem, 44
Symphony Space, 48
Tavern on the Green, 31
Temple Emanu-El, 18
Tennis Courts, 41
Whitney Museum of American Art, 12
Wollman Rink, 29
Zabar's, 52

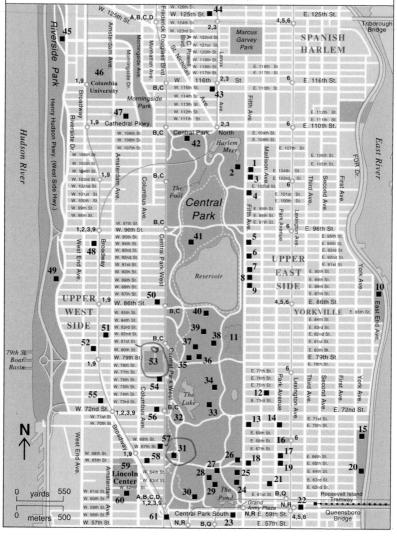

◈ Let's Go writers travel on your budget.

"Guides that penetrate the veneer of the holiday brochures and mine the grit of real life."

—*The Economist*

"The writers seem to have experienced every rooster-packed bus and lunar-surfaced mattress about which they write."

—*The New York Times*

"All the dirt, dirt cheap."

—*People*

◈ Great for independent travelers.

"The guides are aimed not only at young budget travelers but at the independent traveler; a sort of streetwise cookbook for traveling alone."

—*The New York Times*

"Flush with candor and irreverence, chock full of budget travel advice."

—*The Des Moines Register*

"An indispensible resource, *Let's Go*'s practical information can be used by every traveler."

—*The Chattanooga Free Press*

◈ Let's Go is completely revised each year.

"Only *Let's Go* has the zeal to annually update every title on its list."

—*The Boston Globe*

"Unbeatable: good sightseeing advice; up-to-date info on restaurants, hotels, and inns; a commitment to money-saving travel; and a wry style that brightens nearly every page."

—*The Washington Post*

◈ All the important information you need.

"*Let's Go* authors provide a comedic element while still providing concise information and thorough coverage of the country. Anything you need to know about budget traveling is detailed in this book."

—*The Chicago Sun-Times*

"Value-packed, unbeatable, accurate, and comprehensive."

—*Los Angeles Times*

Let's Go Publications

Let's Go: *Alaska & the Pacific Northwest 2000*
Let's Go: *Australia 2000*
Let's Go: *Austria & Switzerland 2000*
Let's Go: *Britain & Ireland 2000*
Let's Go: *California 2000*
Let's Go: *Central America 2000*
Let's Go: *China 2000* **New Title!**
Let's Go: *Eastern Europe 2000*
Let's Go: *Europe 2000*
Let's Go: *France 2000*
Let's Go: *Germany 2000*
Let's Go: *Greece 2000*
Let's Go: *India & Nepal 2000*
Let's Go: *Ireland 2000*
Let's Go: *Israel 2000* **New Title!**
Let's Go: *Italy 2000*
Let's Go: *Mexico 2000*
Let's Go: *Middle East 2000* **New Title!**
Let's Go: *New York City 2000*
Let's Go: *New Zealand 2000*
Let's Go: *Paris 2000*
Let's Go: *Perú & Ecuador 2000* **New Title!**
Let's Go: *Rome 2000*
Let's Go: *South Africa 2000*
Let's Go: *Southeast Asia 2000*
Let's Go: *Spain & Portugal 2000*
Let's Go: *Turkey 2000*
Let's Go: *USA 2000*
Let's Go: *Washington, D.C. 2000*

Let's Go *Map Guides*

Amsterdam
Berlin
Boston
Chicago
Florence
London
Los Angeles
Madrid

New Orleans
New York City
Paris
Prague
Rome
San Francisco
Seattle
Washington, D.C.

Coming Soon: *Sydney* and *Hong Kong*

Let's Go

NEW YORK CITY

2000

Lucia Brawley
Editor

Researcher-Writers:
Edward Borey
Brandee Butler
Rachel Farbiarz

St. Martin's Press ⚇ New York

HELPING LET'S GO

If you want to share your discoveries, suggestions, or corrections, please drop us a line. We read every piece of correspondence, whether a postcard, a 10-page email, or a coconut. Please note that mail received after May 2000 may be too late for the 2001 book, but will be kept for future editions. **Address mail to:**

> **Let's Go: New York City**
> **67 Mount Auburn Street**
> **Cambridge, MA 02138**
> **USA**

Visit Let's Go at **http://www.letsgo.com,** or send email to:

> **feedback@letsgo.com**
> **Subject: "Let's Go: New York City"**

In addition to the invaluable travel advice our readers share with us, many are kind enough to offer their services as researchers or editors. Unfortunately, our charter enables us to employ only currently enrolled Harvard students.

HOW TO USE THIS BOOK

Introducing NYC offers the historical, political, and cultural background of the city…and the keys to enjoying New York's offerings at the millennium.

Essentials tells you how to get to the city safely and what to expect once there. We also address travelers with specific concerns: senior citizens, disabled travelers, queer travelers, women, families and travelers with special diets. Getting Around explains the ins and outs of travel within New York and between the city and surrounding attractions. Getting Acquainted covers such necessities as health care, safety, banking, libraries, the phone system, and internet connections.

Accommodations lists budget beds, based on our R-W-tested scale of price, location, security, and comfort. **Restaurants** presents extensive listings of cheap restaurants, cafes, and shops with tasty eats throughout the city.

Once sated, rested, and ready to explore, you can flip to the **Neighborhoods** section to enrich your wanderings with well-researched local history, sights, and architectural description. **Museums** then takes that culture ball and runs with it, describing every imaginable (and unimaginable) type of, well, museum. **Galleries** does the same with galleries. **Arts & Entertainment** highlights the more gregarious arts, such as theater, film, television, opera, classical music, jazz, hip-hop, Latin, rock, punk, and electronic music. **Nightlife** offers venues of culture high and low, some very low, but all educational. **Sports** offers amenities for the athlete in you, or for the spectator you have to get in touch with and forgive. **Shopping** suggests clothing and accessory bargains through a variety of geographic areas, as well as more specialized goods listed according to category, such as record stores or bookstores. **The Queer Apple** offers specialized services, venues, nightlife, and daytrips for the queer traveler, simply because gay life plays such a prominent role in the gestalt of greater New York culture. Finally, **Daytripping from NYC** presents options for the occasional escape, either to peace (as in the case of the Hamptons beaches), to debauchery (as in the case of Atlantic City), or to good, clean fun (as in the case of Six Flags and Cooperstown).

A NOTE TO OUR READERS The information for this book was gathered by *Let's Go*'s researchers from May through August. Each listing is derived from the assigned researcher's opinion based upon his or her visit at a particular time. The opinions are expressed in a candid and forthright manner. Those traveling at a different time may have different experiences since prices, dates, hours, and conditions are always subject to change. You are urged to check beforehand to avoid inconvenience and surprises. Travel always involves a certain degree of risk, especially in low-cost areas. When traveling, especially on a budget, always take particular care to ensure your safety.

CONTENTS

MAPS

COLOR MAPS

LET'S GO PICKS

BEST SPOTS TO BOOGIE: Call for the next guerrilla electronic music happening care of **Soundlab** (p. 288); to find the beautiful gay boy trapped inside you, attend the aptly named **Kurfew** (p. 311); if you want to swing the night away, Lincoln Center offers a **Midsummer Night Swing Dancextravaganza** (p. 285); slow jams, hip-hop *and* punk play at **Arlene Grocery** in the Lower East Side (p. 285); or meet your long lost Latin lover at **The Point** (see p. 288).

BEST SMOKING PARLORS: Although *Let's Go* does not condone the dirty vice, there are several naughty places in New York that do make it look pretty good— **Circa Tabac** (see p. 277) and **Sahara East** (see p. 105).

BEST PLACES TO CUDDLE: From the Brooklyn Heights **Promenade** (see p. 202), you and your honey can gaze out at the Manhattan skyline that summons the spirit of Gershwin with its steely lyricism; or at the **Jacques Marchais Museum of Tibetan Art** (see p. 245), you two can bask in the sweet serenity of this Staten Island hilltop retreat that feels as though it's thousands of miles from this western metropolis.

THE BEST PLACES TO FISH DRUNK: Rent a rowboat, buy bait and tackle, and drink a $1 beer at **The Boat Livery, Inc.** (see p. 284) in the Bronx's City Island; or you could just slam vodka shots, while dancing to Russian disco at **Primorski Restaurant** (see p. 89), and flap your arms about in the translucent waters of Brighton Beach, Brooklyn.

RESEARCHER-WRITERS

Brandee Butler   *Queens, Brooklyn, Atlantic City, Manhattan*

Fact-checker extraordinaire, gutsy interviewer, budget seeker, and strong soul, Ms. Butler delved New York City from the point-of-view of a foreigner…well, of someone from L.A. anyway. Her objective point-of-view prevented the New Yorkers on staff from becoming too mired in native nostalgia. Her credentials range from extensive research in Africa to club-hopping in capital cities across the world. This new member of the press will soon contribute her savvy, sense of humor, and focus to the U.S. legal system, as she heads to Yale Law School in the 1999-2000 academic year. Brandee has also been known to keep it real.

Edward Borey   *Bronx, Staten Island, Liberty/Ellis Island, Fire Island, Manhattan*

A fiction writer by trade, Edward added his vivid prose style to *Let's Go: NYC 2000*, especially to the Nightlife section, which he researched in great depth. Many challenges presented themselves to Mr. Borey in the summer of 1999, including snaggletoothed strangers, rodents of unusual size, Kafka-esque cockroaches, and temperamental bathtubs.

Rachel Farbiarz   *Brooklyn, Bronx, Long Island, Manhattan*

Her unflappable humor, relentless research, passion for the arts, and profound knowledge of all things sushi, among many other gifts, contributed to this 3-year *Let's Go* veteran's stellar copy. Her enthusiasm and original spin on things inspired all who worked with her. This editor of *Let's Go: NYC 1999* brings us a new New York for the millennium.

Emily Griffin   *Cooperstown, Catskills*

ACKNOWLEDGMENTS

These books don't just put themselves together, you know. They are assembled by machine.

LUCIA BRAWLEY THANKS: My **RWs**, for their diligence, humor, and enthusiasm in the face of daunting obstacles. **Ben Harder** to whom this book really belongs. The extensive, esoteric architectural descriptions from past NYC guides. **Matt Daniels** who made everything look so pretty. **Christian Lorentzen** who worked his mojo on my technical jinx. **Elena DeCoste** and **Tom Davidson,** for their last-minute saves. **Kate Unterman, Megan Frederickson, Kaya Stone, Sonesh Chainani,** and **Adam Stein,** for their invaluable proofs. **Melissa Rudolph** for her baked goods. **Zahr Said,** for Hello Kitty. **Anne Chisholm,** for her R.S.I. therapy. **Davey D.** for understanding about litigious websters. **Matt Trent,** for his love and support, even when I didn't have time to call him back. **Ankur Ghosh** for saving the day 1,000 times and **Olivia Cowley** for the late-night act of kindness. **David Otero** and the United Colors of Eliot/Mather/South Bronx posse for being. **My parents, Ziska, Yuki, Angelica,** and my **grandparents,** who remind me who I am. **John,** for standing beautifully in the way of work.

This book is for the Cosmo Girls in the city pod. You mean the world to me.

Editor
Lucia Brawley
Managing Editor
Bentsion Harder

Publishing Director
Benjamin Wilkinson
Editor-in-Chief
Bentsion Harder
Production Manager
Christian Lorentzen
Cartography Manager
Daniel J. Luskin
Design Managers
Matthew Daniels, Melissa Rudolph
Editorial Managers
Brendan Gibbon, Benjamin Paloff, Kaya Stone, Taya Weiss
Financial Manager
Kathy Lu
Personnel Manager
Adam Stein
Publicity & Marketing Managers
Sonesh Chainani,
Alexandra Leichtman
New Media Manager
Maryanthe Malliaris
Map Editors
Kurt Mueller, Jon Stein
Production Associates
Steven Aponte, John Fiore
Office Coordinators
Elena Schneider, Vanessa Bertozzi, Monica Henderson

Director of Advertising Sales
Marta Szabo
Associate Sales Executives
Tamas Eisenberger, Li Ran

President
Noble M. Hansen III
General Managers
Blair Brown, Robert B. Rombauer
Assistant General Manager
Anne E. Chisholm

INTRODUCING NYC

There is more poetry in a block of New York than in twenty daisied lanes.
—O. Henry

Immensity, diversity, and a tradition of defying tradition characterize the city known as "the Crossroads of the World." Since its earliest days, iconoclastic New York has scoffed at the timid offerings of other American cities, striving instead to embody the American ideal at its most grand. It boasts the most immigrants, the tallest skyscrapers, and the trickiest con artists. Even the vast gray blocks of concrete have their own gritty charm. Returning from a dull vacation in rural Westchester, resident talespinner O. Henry noted, "there was too much fresh scenery and fresh air. What I need is a steam-heated flat and no vacation or exercise." However, if you wish to discover the city's more delicate offerings, fear not.

New York City *is* full of folks. The stars *are* covered with a blanket of pollution. The buildings are tall, the subway smelly, the people rushed, the beggars everywhere…BUT for every inch of grime, there's a yard of silver lining. Countless people mean countless pockets of culture—every kind of ethnicity, food, art, energy, language, attitude. Despite the crowds, there are places to be alone and reflect. However, choose to plunge into the fray and you meet the most fascinating types, full of stories, curmudgeonly humor, innovative ideas…and, yes, madness. The collage of architecture, from colonial to art deco to *Jetsons*, reveals the stratae of history that NYC embodies. Meanwhile, there's flamenco at an outdoor cafe, jazz underground at night, jungle/illbient under a bridge, Eurotechno at a flashy club. Whatever your tastes, there's something for you. If millions of penniless immigrants disembarked here and quickly learned to survive, then you, fearless budget traveler, will undoubtedly soar.

Here's a little background information to bring you up-to-date on the Gotham you're about to unravel.

Y? 2K!

The millennium may come, and it may see, but trust New York to conquer. West Village prophets put their scribes to work, and East Village paranoids turned their bugging devices on high. Financial District computer geeks grew paler as they tried to rout the 2000 bug, and persistent Staten Islanders planned their oft-frustrated secession. Partiers with extraordinary forethought have booked spots at the elegant **Rainbow Room.** In 1993, one determined man required that his reservation for the now sold-out evening be included in his will. Another 95-year-old man made a reservation because he's sure his waiting will keep him alive for the celebration. The ongoing dispute between revelers (and terrified bankers) who anxiously await 1/1/2000, and purists who point out that *2001* actually ushers in the third millennium, just means a year of unbridled celebration to New York. Budget travelers, buckle your seatbelts for the lavish festivities planned this year. Some events are free, others are exorbitant. Here are a few ideas to help you enjoy the the turn of the millennium in budget fashion.

The New York City Visitor's Convention and Visitor's Bureau are good planning resources for approaching New York's millennium. They have set up a **NYC Millennium Club** (1-800-NYC-VISIT/692-8474) that provides periodical updates on millennium-related events. Club members are also added to relevant mailing lists throughout the city. To become a member, send a check or money order for $20 to Millennium Club, NYCVB, 810 Seventh Ave., NY, NY 10019. The **websites** www.millennium.greenwich2000.com and www.everything2000.com also provide helpful information.

NEW YEAR'S EVE

While New York has always reigned as the New Year's capital of the world, New Year's 2000 has presented a welcome challenge for this city of superlatives.

Times Square 2000: For New Year's 2000, Times Square is going global, celebrating the New Year in every single time zone. The party starts at 7am on December 31, 1999 when the Fiji islands begin their New Year. With each of the 24 new years, large video screens and elaborate sound, light, and laser systems will create a display appropriate for the time zone. While Times Square usually holds a mere 500,000 people, planners are trying to think of ways to cram in even more for this global event. Contact: Times Square/Special Events, 1560 Broadway, NY NY 10023 (768-1560, ext.45).

Empire State Building: Rumors hint that there will be a free, public party at the Empire State Building, but organizers are being very mysterious. They will disclose the fruits of their labor in late 1999, when *Let's Go* goes to press.

Statue of Liberty: As *Let's Go* went to press, plans were nearing completion for a spectacular millennium event at the Statue of Liberty. Like the Empire State Building folks, these organizers are keep their plans hush-hush, but the working title of the event is "Liberty Island 2000: Celebration of a Lifetime."

2000 Celebration: The entire Jacob Javits Center (between 35th and 39th St. on the water) has been rented out for this, the most grandiose of events—with performances by Andrea Bocelli, Sting, Aretha Franklin, Enrique Iglesias, Joan Rivers, Tom Jones, and others (maybe Kool and the Gang!). Promoters advertise 5 corporate sponsors and a $20 million budget. At midnight, a spectacular fireworks display is planned to explode over the Hudson River and all the invited performers will get on stage for a "We Are the World"-type moment. To envision the scope of this event, note that the Javits Center is 5 blocks long and occupies over one million square feet.

NATIONAL AND WORLDWIDE EVENTS

Day One: Organizers are planning a huge party of 100,000+ students in 16 cities across the U.S. The event is purported to be the largest single commissioning and mobilization of students in the history of Christianity.

Earthday 2000: In the year 2000, more than 300 million people worldwide are expected to participate in the largest Earth Day ever on the day's 30th anniversary.

Leap Year 2000: A worldwide leap year festival. (!)

One Day In Peace: A global network of 1000 organizations in over 130 nations supporting the U.N.'s International Year for a Culture of Peace beginning with January 1, 2000 as a 24hr. worldwide cease-fire. See www.worldpeace2000.org.

NEW HAPPENINGS IN THE CITY

OpSail 2000: The Greatest Event in Maritime History will take place on July 3-9, 2000. President Clinton will be joined by representatives of more than 50 nations, and an anticipated fleet of 30,000 spectator vessels will accompany a 10-mile-long flotilla of tall ships through New York Harbor.

MoMA 2000: This bastion of all things contemporary opens its "Millennium Retrospective" in Oct. 1999. Will 20th century art still be modern? Only MoMA can tell us this. See **Museums,** p. 235.

Fame: This classic of kitsch opens on Broadway in January. Don't be surprised if half the cast actually *went* to the High School of Performing Arts, now part of LaGuardia High School near Lincoln Center.

Pier Show 2000: Brooklyn Waterfront Artists (BWAC) will host an extravagahn-za of painting, sculpture, photography, film, dance, and other types of installations and performance at different venues around Brooklyn between mid-May and mid-June. Includes "Dancing in the Streets," a young people's performance festival. Find out more about Brooklyn's largest artist-run organization and their events on the web at www.bwac.org or by calling their Red Hook office at 718-596-2507.

Salsa: To shake your *culo* into the millennium, see the frequently updated www.salsanew york.com/calendar.

DISCOVER NEW YORK

If these morsels whet your appetite for ambling, please see the chapter **Neighborhoods,** p. 126, which expands on the myriad historical, cultural, evangelical, nutrious, delicious, and educational offerings the city serves up as you wander through its many districts.

EARLY MORNING EXCURSIONS IN NEW YORK. After taking New York up on its invitation to "never sleep," you can bask in the spectacular silence of broad avenues just before rush hour descends. From the Upper East Side to the crooked alleys of Greenwich Village, the city is a different place at the wee hours. And while it is not completely deserted, it *is* empty enough to make you feel that it belongs to you alone. Each of these excursions should last you a whole morning. In operation for 160 years, the **Fulton Street Fish Market,** the largest fish market in the country, opens daily at 4am; tours are also given in the mornings (see **Specialty Tours,** p. 126). From 7am to 9am a group of older Chinese men gather each morning from spring through fall to **give sun to the songbirds** in Sara Delano Roosevelt Park. Intended as a distraction from vice, this old tradition ends in a symphony from the songbirds who have just woken up with the sun (see **Who Knows Why the Caged Bird Sings?,** p. 142). For the pre-dawn riser with an unquenchable wanderlust, the **Boat Livery, Inc.,** on City Island in the Bronx rents out skiffs and, for the real sailor, offers $1 glasses of Bud at the bar. Both the bar and the boat rental open at 5am (see **Nightlife,** ironically enough, p. 284).

MULTI-ETHNIC FRIED (OR OTHERWISE UNHEALTHY) FOOD SPREE. Begin your indulgence at the pan-ethnic **McDonald's,** 160 Broadway, at Liberty St., great inventor of the use of "fry" as a noun. Trust us on this one: this Mickey D's is not to be missed (see **Restaurants,** p. 112). Move on to Chinatown where Cecilia Tam of the **Hong Kong Egg Cake Co.,** cooks up a dozen of her soft, sweet egg cakes fresh from the skillet (p. 102). Sweet-lovers will want to make a quick stop at **Veniero's,** 342 E. 11th St., between First and Second Aves., in the East Village for artery-clogging fun with Italian pastries (p. 107). *Lansman!* Get thee to a knishery! **Yonah Schimmel Knishery,** 137 E. Houston St., in the Lower East Side still serves up Rabbi Schimmel's signature knish…mmm…delish (see p. 112). Find out what finger-lickin' really means at **Copeland's,** 547 W. 145th St., between Broadway and Amsterdam Ave., in Harlem. With smothered chicken and fried pork chops, Copeland's soul food takes the cholesterol crown (see p. 109).

THE WOODY ALLEN LOVERS' TREK. Any Woody tour should begin at Woody's humble abode on Central Park East. Woody lives on the 900 block of **Fifth Avenue;** if you camp out here, you're likely to catch a glimpse of the comic guru strolling with Soon Yi or fumbling for his keys. Since the closing of **Michael's Pub** in 1997, Woody has tooted his **clarinet** on Monday nights at **Cafe Carlyle** in the Carlyle Hotel on Madison Ave. and 76th St. Those interested in the young Woody should visit **Flatbush,** Brooklyn where Woody was born Allen Stuart Konigsberg (see **Downtown Brooklyn,** p. 206). Skip the trials of a bespectacled boy's youth and head straight for Greenwich Village's **New York University,** from which Woody was suspended (see **Greenwich Village,** p. 149). He went on to finish at **City College,** at 138th St. and Convent Ave. (see **Central Harlem,** p. 193). **Classic New York scenes** from Woody's movies are as common as virgins in a convent. The famous "bridge scene" from *Manhattan* is a shot of the **59th Street Bridge;** Woody sits with Diane Keaton at 57th St., just west of Sutton Place (see **Astoria and Long Island City,** p. 215). Young Alvy Singer of *Annie Hall* grew up in the house under the **Coney Island Rollercoaster;** the house still rattles underneath (see **Coney Island,** p. 208). To round it all off, you can spend the night in **Hotel 17,** 225 E. 17th St., where Alan Alda and Diane Keaton find a body in *Manhattan Murder Mystery* (see **Accommodations,** p. 85).

4 ■ HISTORY AND POLITICS

HISTORY AND POLITICS

THE EARLY YEARS

New York's vaunted self-sufficiency began early. The **Dutch West Indies Company** founded the colony of **New Amsterdam** in 1624 as a trading post, but England soon asserted rival claims to the land. While the mother countries squabbled, the colonists went about their burgeoning business, trading beaver skins, colorful *wampum* (beads made of white or violet seashells), and silver with the neighboring Native Americans. In 1626, New York's tradition of great bargains began when Peter Minuit bought the island from "natives" for 60 guilders, or just under $24. In fact, the men he assumed were locals were actually Canarsee Delawares visiting the island, and didn't even own the property they sold.

The rich and fertile land made light work for European settlers. "Children and pigs multiply here rapidly," gloated one colonist. When the Dutch West Indies Company did try to interfere, the settlers resented it. Calvinist **Peter Stuyvesant,** the governor appointed by Holland in the middle of the 17th century, enforced strict rules on the happy-go-lucky settlement. He shot hogs, closed taverns, and whipped Quakers, sparking protest and anger among the citizenry. Inexplicably, the draconian Stuyvesant has since become a local folk hero. New York schools, businesses, even several of its neighborhoods, bear his name.

Less enthralled by Dutch rule than today's citizenry, early colonists put up only token resistance when the British finally invaded the settlement in 1664. The new British governors were less noxious, if only because they were less effective. An astounding number never even made it to the colony. Some got lost en route from England, a handful went down at sea, and others found New England a more attractive address. Between 1664 and 1776, New York experienced 22 hiatuses in governance.

Left to its own devices, the city continued to mature. In 1754, higher education came to New York in the form of **King's College** (later renamed Columbia University). By the late 1770s, the city had become a major port with a population of 20,000. The preoccupation with prosperity engendered by this early success meant that New Yorkers would be rather dull to the first whiffs of revolution. British rule was good for business—and, then as now, money ruled in the soon-to-be capital of capitalism.

The new American army, understandably, made no great efforts to protect the ungrateful city, and New York was held by the British throughout the war. As a result, the **American Revolution** was a rough time for the metropolis. The city had "a most melancholy appearance, being deserted and pillaged," wrote one observer. Fire destroyed a quarter of the city in 1776. When the defeated British finally left in 1783, most people were relieved—except for 6000 Tory loyalists, who followed the redcoats out of New York and went on to Nova Scotia.

With its buildings in heaps of rubble and one-third of its population off roaming Canada, New York made a valiant effort to rebuild. Its success set a precedent of resilience. "The progress of the city is, as usual, beyond all calculations," wrote one enraptured citizen. New York's post-Revolution comeback entailed briefly serving as the nation's capital, acquiring a bank, and establishing the **first stock exchange,** which met under a buttonwood tree on Wall Street. Indeed, much of our federal framework harks back to the centralizing fiscal policies of the first Secretary of the Treasury, New Yorker and lousy shot, **Alexander Hamilton.** Meanwhile, **The 1811 Commissioner's Plan** established Manhattan's rectilinear street grid with characteristic New Yorker ambition—at the time, the island consisted primarily of marshes and open fields, and boasted fewer than 100,000 residents. Merchants built mansions on the new streets, along with tenements for the increasing numbers of immigrants from Eastern and Northern Europe.

GREASY PALMS

Administration and services continued to lag behind irrepressible growth. Early in the 19th century, New York became the largest U.S. city, but pigs, dogs, and chickens continued to run freely. Fires and riots made streetlife precarious, while the foul water supply precipitated a cholera epidemic. The notorious corruption of **Tammany Hall,** a political machine that **"Boss" William Tweed** set in motion in the 1850s, promising money and jobs to people, often immigrants, who agreed to vote for his candidates. Under Tweed's thumb, embezzlement and kickbacks were routine. He robbed the city of somewhere between 100 and 200 million dollars. When citizens complained in 1871, Tweed said defiantly, "Well, what are you going to do about it?" Although a *The New York Times* exposé led to Tweed's downfall in 1875, Tammany continued to influence elections without him, inspiring this crack by perennial complainer George Templeton Strong: "The New Yorker belongs to a community governed by lower and baser scum than any city in Western Christendom."

Still, New Yorkers remained loyal to the city, often neglecting national concerns in favor of local interests. New York initially opposed the Civil War, as its desire to protect trade with the South outweighed abolitionist and constitutional principles. President Abraham Lincoln, *The New York Times* wrote dismissively in 1860, was "a lawyer who has some local reputation in Illinois." The attack on South Carolina's Fort Sumter rallied New York to the Northern side, but a class-biased conscription act in July of 1863 led to the infamous **New York City Draft Riots,** which cost a thousand lives.

After the war, the city entered a half-century of prosperity, during which time, New York developed the elements of urban modernity that now distinguish it. The Metropolitan Museum of Art was founded in 1870, and Bloomingdale's opened its now-venerable doors in 1872. 1883 saw the completion of the Brooklyn Bridge, an engineering marvel, considered by many to be the world's most beautiful bridge— although its construction cost the lives of many immigrant laborers. This new transportation gateway portended the incorporation of The Bronx, Brooklyn, Queens, and Staten Island into the City of New York in 1898. During this period of rapid change, **Teddy Roosevelt** headed the police department, did his part to reform New York in time for the turn of the century. Dressed in a cape, he sallied forth at night like a judicial Masked Avenger, searching for policemen who were sleeping on the job or consorting with prostitutes. At the tail end of the century, **Frederick Law Olmsted** and **Calvin Vaux** created Central Park on 843 rolling acres, and the Flatiron building, the first skyscraper, was erected in 1902. With 2000 farms still in New York and a speed limit of nine miles per hour, the city began to spread out, both horizontally and vertically. "It'll be a great place if they ever finish it," O. Henry quipped. Despite entrepreneurial optimism among the powers-that-were, 70% of New York's population dwelled in substandard tenement housing in 1900.

THE "NEW METROPOLIS"

A turn-of-the century war on slums swept in a new stage of renewal. Colonel George E. Waring's army of "White Wings" put "a man instead of a voter behind every broom," thus creating the double benefit of jobs and cleaner streets. New York's most famed photographer of the era, Jacob Riis, elegized, "It was Colonel Waring's broom that first let light into the slum. The first thirty years of the century saw a Beaux-Arts construction boom, the building of the **Williamsburg Bridge**—then the longest suspension bridge in the world—and a brand new infrastructure. Perhaps the city's greatest development during this era was the opening of its world-renowned subway system. On Friday October 28th, 1904, *The New York Times* described the previous night's event thusly: "With a silver controller Mayor McClellan started the first train, the official train, which bore John B. McDonald, the contractor who dug the subway; William Barclay Parsons, Chief Engineer of the Rapid Transit Commission, and most of the other men who made the subway a possibility and a reality. The Mayor liked his job as motorman so well that he stayed at the controller until the train reached Broadway and One Hundred and Third Street."

New York's innovations reached such glamorous proportions that the city began to feature prominently in the young art form of cinema. Early films, with such apt titles as "The Cheat" (1915), portrayed the city as the "new" or "great" metropolis, emphasizing a booming business world that portended the Roaring Twenties.

During the 1920s, New York City revitalized still other media. After the 1917 NAACP protest—during which thousands of African-Americans marched down Fifth Avenue, crying out against lynchings and countless other denials of rights—the "New Negro" appeared. In the 1920s, the Harlem Renaissance reached full swing, its books and music announcing a changing world.

MID-CENTURY REFORM

Bent on healing New York's social ills, **Fiorello LaGuardia,** the city's immensely popular mayor from 1933-45 said, "Nobody wants me but the people," as he reorganized the government and revitalized the city. Laguardia's leadership engendered a fierce civic pride that saw New Yorkers through the hardships of The Great Depression. Post-World War II prosperity brought more immigrants and businesses to the city. In this era, **Robert Moses** became the most powerful man in New York. An unelected official, this urban planner steam-rolled over dissenting politicians and councils to create the physical landscape of New York as we now know it, adding twelve bridges and tunnels, 36 parks, and 35 major roads to the greater metropolitan area (see **Long Island,** p. 314). But even as the world celebrated New York as the capital of the 20th century, cracks in the city's foundations became apparent. By the 1960s, crises in public transportation, education, and housing exacerbated racial tensions and fostered criminal activity.

John V. Lindsay ran for mayor in 1965 with the slogan, "He is fresh and everyone else is tired," but even his freshness wilted under the barrage of crime, racial problems, labor unrest, and drought. City officials raised taxes to provide more services, but higher taxes drove middle-class residents and corporations out of the city. As a series of recessions and budget crises swamped the government, critics deplored **Mayor Robert Wagner's** "dedicated inactivity." By 1975, the city was pleading with the federal government to rescue it from impending bankruptcy—and was rebuffed. *The Daily News* headline the next day read "Ford to New York: Drop Dead."

However, resilient NYC rebounded on an attitude of streetwise hope. The city's massive (if goofy) **"I Love New York" campaign** spread cheer via bumper stickers. Large manufacturing, which had gone south and west of New York, was supplanted by fresh money from high finance and infotech, the big Reaganomic growth industries. In the 1980s Wall Street was hip again, or at least grotesquely profitable, and the upper middle class face of the city recovered some of its lost vitality. In poorer areas, meanwhile, discontent pervaded, manifesting itself in waves of crime and vandalism that scared off potential tourists. With a New Yorker's armor of curmudgeonly humor, **Ed Koch** defended his city's declining reputation, becoming America's most visible mayor. Koch appeared on Saturday Night Live, providing an endless stream of quotables, most notably, his catchphrase, "How'm I doing?" (If you want to know how *post-mayoral* Ed's doing, checkout www.daveyd.com which lists, "You cried the day Ed Koch took over for Wapner [on the television show People's Court]" as the twentieth of "20 Signs You're From New York").

THE LAST DECADE

The financial flurry of the 1980s faded to the gray recession of the early 1990s, aggravating class tensions. Racial conflict, in particular, reached an all-time high in the late 80s and early 90s, with bigoted beatings erupting in "the Boroughs" and a nationally publicized riot in Crown Heights, Brooklyn, sparked by a hit-and-run incident, in which an Orthodox Jewish man killed a young boy from a West Indian family. **David Dinkins,** the city's first black mayor, elected 1989 on a platform that glorified New York's "Gorgeous Mosaic," fought hard to encourage unity between the city's myriad ethnic groups and to dismantle bureaucratic corruption. Dinkins' term saw the abolition of the Board of Estimate system of municipal government, under which each borough's president had one vote. (This system was blatantly unfair, as borough populations differ vastly.) An expanded 35-member City Council replaced the old system. Now, each borough can initiate zoning, propose legislation, and deal with contractors independently.

Mounting fiscal crises and a persistent crime rate, however, led to Dinkins' defeat at the hands of **Rudy Giuliani** in the 1993 mayoral election. The election was strongly divided along racial lines. Many moderate whites who had supported Dinkins in 1989 defected to the side of the Republican Giuliani, who addressed a number of intertwining fears with a campaign that could be summed up in two words: Safety First. Some New Yorkers adore Mayor Giuliani for having cracked down on crime and having cleaned up formerly murky areas, such as Times Square. Critics believe the Mayor cares only about beautifying tourist-heavy Manhattan, at the expense of "the Boroughs" and their largely minority populations. Some say his budget cuts have damaged **The New York City Board of Education,** headed by the more charismatic of the Rudies, **Schools Chancellor, Rudy Crew.** Still others assert that Giuliani's war on crime has translated into an overzealous police force. Accusations of dire police brutality reached a fever pitch in 1997-98, when the story of **Abner Louima** broke, revealing how one Officer Volpe, aided by colleagues, sexually assaulted an innocent Haitian man with a toilet plunger. In June 1999, Federal prosecutors concluded a 20-month investigation of the New York City Police Department's indulgent attitude toward the violence of its officers.

The **Million Youth March** that took place over Labor Day Weekend 1998 in Harlem's Morningside Park addressed, among many other issues pertaining to black America's youth, the racially biased aggression of the NYPD and, by association, that of the Mayor. Emotions ran high, as many New Yorkers opposed the openly anti-white and anti-Semitic remarks of Nation of Islam spokesperson, **Kallid Muhammed,** while others decried Giuliani's refusal of a permit to the event's organizers and his shutting down of the march before the last speaker had finished speaking.

Despite a "no-apologies" stance that may outrage many New York liberals, Giuliani often defies classification. Indeed, the mayor took a big risk for the city when he crossed party lines to support **Governor Mario Cuomo** in his bid for re-election. Cuomo subsequently lost to **George Pataki,** the candidate favored by conservative upstate New York, who made a point of snubbing the mayor for several days after the election. Nonplussed, Giuliani deviated from the Republican camp again in 1996 to berate GOP Presidential candidate Bob Dole on his rigid immigration policies and refused to attend the party's August nominating convention. Priding himself on never taking a vacation and resting only five hours a night, tenacious Rudy Giuliani pursues his anti-crime campaign and Quality of Life Initiative with increasing vigor. No doubt, he hopes his hard-line attitude will earn voters' confidence in his 2000 Senate campaign against U.S. First Lady, **Hillary Rodham Clinton.**

ETHNIC NEW YORK

Jesuit missionary Isaac Jogues described one lively New Amsterdam fort in which mingled artisans, soldiers, trappers, sailors, and slaves—all together, speaking no fewer than 18 languages. New Yorkers have always claimed a wide range of national origins. The slave-owning Dutch had a sizeable African population with them, and the first black settlement began in today's SoHo in 1644. Germans and Irish came over in droves between 1840 and 1860; in 1855, European-born immigrants constituted nearly half of New York's population.

After the Civil War, a massive wave of immigration began, cresting around the turn of the century. Europeans left famine, religious persecution, and political unrest in their native lands for the perils of seasickness and the promise of America. Beginning in 1890, Italians, Lithuanians, Russians, Poles, and Greeks joined German and Irish immigrants *en masse*.

An influx of rural Southern blacks during and after World War I led to the creation of **Harlem.** In the early 20th century, real estate mavericks built hundreds of Harlem tenements in hope of renting to whites once the subway arrived; the plan backfired as whites bypassed Harlem and moved further uptown. Working at a failing real estate office, black janitor **Philip Payton** realized the business African-Americans would bring and transformed himself into the entrepreneur who created modern Harlem by convincing renters to open their buildings to blacks. The cultural and literary **Harlem Renaissance** of the 1920s stands as testament to the upsurgent vitality and creativity that the new settlement brought. Nevertheless, people of color were charged more than their white counterparts for the unhealthy tenement rooms, and the Cotton Club, Harlem's famous jazz nightclub, didn't even allow blacks inside, unless they were performing (see **Neighborhoods,** p.195).

European immigrants worked long hours in detestable and unsafe conditions for meager wages; only the **Triangle Shirtwaist Fire** of 1911, which killed 145 female factory workers, brought about enough public protest to force stricter regulations on working conditions (see **Neighborhoods,** p.151). Meanwhile, Tammany Hall-based "ward bosses" stepped in to take care of the confused new arrivals, helping them find jobs and housing and providing them with emergency funds in case of illness or accident, all in exchange for votes. The U.S. Congress restricted immigration in the 1920s, and the Great Depression, begun in 1929, brought the influx to a halt. The encroaching terrors in Europe in the late 1930s, however, brought new waves of immigrants, particularly Jews seeking escape from Hitler's persecution.

Today the melting pot simmers with more than seven million people speaking over 80 languages. New York boasts more Italians than Rome, more Irish than Dublin, and more Jews than Jerusalem. The cultural diversity resulting from past and present immigration has made whites a minority in the city. In recent years the pace of immigration has picked up. In the early 1990s, immigration was 32% higher than it was in the 1980s, with the top five sources being the Dominican Republic, the former Soviet Union, China, Jamaica, and Guyana. With immigration policies under fire nationwide, Mayor Giuliani has countered this trend, staunchly defending immigrants as the lifeblood of New York City. Giuliani expressed his views on the city's legacy of immigration, when he fought to keep Winnie the Pooh in New York, not losing him to Pooh Bear's native England: "Like millions of other immigrants, Winnie the Pooh and his friends…came to America and to New York to build a better life for themselves and they want to remain here in the Capital of the World." Who knew Rudy had a poetic side?

Harlem, Chinatown, and Little Italy spring to mind as the most reputed ethnic enclaves of New York. However, lesser-known ethnic communities thrive throughout the five boroughs. With their festivals, markets, and civic services (see calendar on p. 21) they provide an insight into the vibrancy of New York life. In Queens, Astoria (especially along Ditmars and 23rd Ave.) hosts a large **Greek** community; at Flushing's Main St., you could be stepping into **Korea; Israeli** eateries pepper Queens Blvd. in Forest Hills; and Jackson Heights bustles with large **Indian** and **South American** populations. In Brooklyn, an **Arab** community centers around Atlantic Ave. in Brooklyn Heights; **West Indians** and **Hassidim** rub elbows in Crown Heights; Brighton Beach, dubbed "Little Odessa" boasts a lively **Russian** enclave; and Bensonhurst presents a more vivid portrait of **Italian-American** life than does Manhattan's Little Italy. In the Bronx, Belmont also hosts an **Italian** community, while the South Bronx, the birthplace of Hip Hop, is home to many **African-Americans** and **Latinos.** In Manhattan, the hub of **Jewish** life has shifted from the Lower East Side to the Upper West Side (especially around Broadway and 72nd St.), and during business hours to the Diamond District around 47th St. between 5th and 6th Avenues.

This vast melange of cultures has by no means led to racial harmony. Ethnic divisions caused much of the city's strife, dating back as far as the 17th and 18th centuries. In the past few decades, ethnic conflict has led to, and been the result of, extreme segregation and distrust among neighboring communities. The 1960s saw rioting in Harlem, Bedford-Stuyvesant, and the South Bronx as angry African-Americans railed against injustices by the government and the police. In the late 1980s, racially related deaths in Bensonhurst and Crown Heights in Brooklyn, and Howard Beach in Queens, demonstrated the lethal potential of ethnic tensions.

Despite these inherent conflicts, New York's lasting cultural ferment reflects how the city still symbolizes opportunity to thousands of immigrants. And, while it takes years or lifetimes to assimilate into other cities, newcomers become New Yorkers almost instantly.

ARCHITECTURE

A hundred times have I thought "New York is a catastrophe" and fifty times: "It is a beautiful catastrophe."

—Le Corbusier, architect

Capricious New York has always warmed to the latest trends in architecture, hastily demolishing old buildings to make way for their stylistic successors. In the 19th century, the surging rhythm of endless destruction and renewal seemed to attest to the city's vigor and enthusiasm. Walt Whitman praised New York's "pull-down-and-build-over-again spirit," and *The Daily Mirror* was an isolated voice when, in 1831, it criticized the city's "irreverence for antiquity."

By the 20th century, many found that irreverence troubling. New York's history was quickly disappearing under the steamroller of modernization. Mounting public concern climaxed when developers destroyed gracious **Penn Station** in 1965, and the **Landmarks Preservation Commission** was created in response. Since then, the LPC has successfully claimed and protected 21,000 individual sites as "landmarks." However, developers seek loopholes and air-rights (the rights to scrape a specific plot of sky), in order to expand the skyline. Furthermore, efforts in the past few years to revitalize old theaters in **Times Square** and to rid this area of its once pornographic motif have aroused anger in those who resent the "Disney-fication" of this formerly gritty area and a subsequent hike in local rents. Most egregious to those who cherish the charming seediness of the Square, the much-hyped 860-room hotel designed by the Arquitectonica firm, will feature a light shooting out from its roof like a "meteor," and a "postcard" wall featuring New York icons such as the Statue of Liberty.

THE EARLY YEARS AND EUROPEAN INFLUENCE

Despite the reactive efforts of the LPC, traces of Colonial New York are hard to find. The original Dutch settlement consisted mostly of traditional homes with gables and stoops. One example from 1699, the restored **Vechte-Cortelyou House,** stands near Fifth Avenue and 3rd St. in Brooklyn. The British, however, built over most of these with imposing, Greek-influenced, Federal-style buildings like **St. Paul's Church** on Broadway.

Even after the British had been forced out, their architectural tastes lingered, influencing the townhouses built by their prosperous colonists. Through the early 19th century, American architects continued to incorporate such Federal details as dormer windows, stoops, and doors with columns and fan lights. Federal houses still line Charlton St., Vandam St., and the South St. Seaport area, while the old **City Hall,** built by D.C. mastermind Pierre L'Enfant in 1802, employs Federal detailing on a public building.

The **Greek Revival** of the 1820s and 30s added porticoes and iron laurel wreaths to New York's streets. If you see a house with uneven bricks, it probably predates the

1830s, when bricks became machine-made. Greek Revival prevails on **Washington Square North,** Lafayette St., and W. 20th St. Gray granite **St. Peter's,** built in 1838, was the first Gothic Revival church in America.

While learning from the old country and the classical tradition, Americans did manage to introduce some architectural innovations. Beginning in the 1850s, thousands of brownstones made from cheap stone quarried in New Jersey sprang up all over New York. Next to skyscrapers, the **brownstone townhouse** may be New York's most characteristic structure. Although far beyond most people's means today, the houses were once middle-class residences—the rich lived in block-long mansions on Fifth Avenue, while apartments were for the poor. Brownstones sport an essential element of New York residential architecture—the raised **stoop.** An innovation brought over by the Dutch in the 17th century to elevate the best rooms in the house above street-level, the stoop today has its own urban culture of "stoop ball," checker-playing, and intense neighbor-watching associated with it.

In 1884, the construction of the luxurious **Dakota** apartment house (later John Lennon's home), disrupted New York's architectural hierarchy. The building's name derives from its location on the far side of Central Park, so far removed from the era's social center of town that locals joked it might as well be in Dakota Territory. However, the cheap, sumptuously appointed apartments offered an alternative to the soaring real estate prices of Midtown. Soon, similar apartment buildings, like the **Ansonia,** were built on the Upper West Side and in Harlem.

In the 1890s, American architects studying abroad brought the **Beaux-Arts** style back from France and captivated the nation. Beaux Arts, which blended Classical detail with lavish decoration, stamped itself on structures built through the 1930s. Especially fine examples are the **New York Customs House,** built by Cass Gilbert, and the **New York Public Library.** Dutifully guarding the library's marble steps hover two mighty lions, aptly named Patience and Fortitude. In addition to the imposing pussycats, Grecian urns, sculptural groups, and fountains (the one on the right representing Truth, the other Beauty), all reflect the importance attached to this warehouse of culture. Inside, the grandeur of the rotating exhibits coupled with the immensity and intricacy of the architecture should remind any visitor that these folks take reading seriously (see p.170).

Architects lavished Beaux Arts flourishes on the first specimens of New York's quintessential structure—the skyscraper. Made possible by combining new technologies—the elevator and the steel frame—skyscrapers allowed the city to explode into the sky and to assuage the growing pains associated New York's spectacular commercial and human growth rate.

THE SKYSCRAPER: AN AMERICAN AESTHETIC

The city's first skyscraper, the **Flatiron Building,** sprouted up on 23rd Street in 1902. Triangular in shape and only six feet wide at its point, it stirred winds that blew women's skirts up, inspiring onlookers whom cops shooed with the now famous "23 Skidoo." For additional reasons, tall buildings proved a useful invention in a city forever short on space, and other monoliths soon joined the Flatiron.

In 1913, Cass Gilbert gilded the 55-story **Woolworth Building** with Gothic flourishes, piling terracotta salamanders onto antique "W"s and dubbing it "Cathedral of Commerce." The **Empire State Building** and the **Chrysler Building,** fashioned from stone and steel and built like rockets, stand testimony to America's romance with science, space, and atmospheric lighting.

Just 14 years after the first skyscraper came the nation's first zoning resolution, which restricted the height and bulk of the dizzying buildings. Knowledge of the changes in the zoning codes throughout the decades is the key to understanding and dating the city's architectural quirks.

Does the building have a ziggurat on top? Look like a wedding cake? Zoning restrictions of the late 1940s stipulated that tall buildings had to be set back at the summit. New York's first curtain of pure glass was the 1950 **United Nations Secretariat Building,** a nightmare to air-condition. The building quickly inspired **Lever House,** a 24-story glass box. Then, in 1958, Ludwig Mies Van der Rohe and Philip Johnson created the **Seagram Building,** a glass tower set behind a plaza on Park Avenue. Crowds soon gathered to mingle, sunbathe, and picnic, much to the surprise of planners and builders. A delighted planning commission began offering financial incentives to every builder who offset a highrise with public open space. Over the next decade, many architects stuck empty plazas next to their towering office complexes. Some of them looked a little too empty to the picky planning commission, which changed the rules in 1975 to stipulate that every plaza should provide public seating. By the late 70s, plazas moved indoors, when high-tech atriums with gurgling fountains and pricey cafes began to flourish.

The leaner skyscrapers date from the early 1980s, when shrewd developers realized they could get office space, bypass zoning regulations, *and* receive a bonus from the commission if they hoisted up "sliver" buildings. Composed largely of elevators and stairs, the disturbingly anorexic newcomers provoked city-wide grumbles. Those tired of living in the shadow of shafts altered zoning policy in 1983 so that structural planning would encourage more room for air and sun.

Builders have finally recognized the overcrowding problem in East Midtown and expanded their horizons somewhat. New residential complexes have risen on the Upper East Side above 95th St., while Donald Trump, the City's most notorious real-estate guru, recently erected the second of his muscular and gaudy towers in Columbus Circle near the Upper West Side. Some developers have even ventured into the outer boroughs, like those who created 1989's **Citicorp Building** in Queens.

The planning commission that oversees the beautiful catastrophe now takes overcrowding and environmental issues into account when making decisions. As an added safeguard, the Landmarks Preservation Commission lurks ever-vigilant, ensuring that New York does not destroy its past as it steamrolls into the future.

NEW YORK IN MUSIC

I lay puzzle as I backtrack to earlier times
Nothing's equivalent, to the New York state of mind
—Nas, "N.Y. State of Mind"

Between the extremes of Nas' rap lyrics and Frank Sinatra's crooning plea that "It's Up to You New York," lies a world of quick cadence, lyrical meandering, and pleasing dissonance all of that owe their inspiration to New York City. **Leonard Bernstein** captured the bleeding heart of the city in his musicals *West Side Story*, while **George Gershwin** used the rhythms of his train rolling into New York for the musical skeleton of his *Rhapsody in Blue*.

From sweet vibrations to killer beats, New York is *the* place to catch new music. Nearly every performer who comes to the States plays here, and thousands of local bands and DJs compete to make a statement and win an audience. Venues range from stadiums to concert halls to back-alley sound-systems. Every day of the year, clubs, bars, and smaller venues serve up sounds from open-mic folk singers to "eclectronic" DJ recombination. Annual festivals abound, such as summertime's **Next Wave Festival** that takes over the Brooklyn Academy of Music with spectacular, offbeat happenings, crackpot fusions of classical music, theater, and performance art. Whatever your inclination, New York's expansive musical scene should be able to satisfy it. (See **Arts and Entertainment,** p. 266 to p. 273.)

JAZZ

From the beginning, Jazz has expressed the sound of the big city. The Big Band sound thrived here in the 1920s and 30s, when Duke Ellington set the trend in clubs around the city. **Minton's Playhouse** in Harlem was home to **Thelonious Monk** and one of the birthplaces of bebop, a highly sophisticated jazz variant. Miles Davis, Charlie Parker, Dizzy Gillespie, Max Roach, Tommy Potter, Bud Powell, and many others contributed to the New York sound of the late 1940s and 1950s, when beatniks, hepcats, and poor old souls filled 52nd St. clubs. Today, at the Fez Cafe, one can tap into the legacy of this revolutionary era with the **Mingus Big Band,** dedicated to playing the works of the virtuoso bassist and band-leader of the 1940s, Charles Mingus. Free-jazz pioneer Cecil Taylor and spaceman Sun Ra set up shop in NYC during the 1960s and 70s. Today, skilled experimentalists like John Zorn and James Blood Ulmer destroy musical conventions at clubs like the **Knitting Factory.**

PUNK AND POST-PUNK

True to the grit of city living, the New York rock sound has always had a harder edge than its West Coast or Southern counterparts. The **Velvet Underground,** Andy Warhol's favorite band and a seminal 1960s rock group, combined jangling guitars with disconcerting lyrics on sex, drugs, and violence that deeply influenced the next generation of bands. In 1976, ambitious avant-garde poets and sometime musicians took over the campy glam-rock scene in downtown barroom clubs like **CBGB's** and Max's Kansas City. Bands and performers like the Ramones, Patti Smith, Blondie, and the Talking Heads brought venom, wit, and a calculated stupidity to the emerging **punk** scene. Ever since, New York has convulsed with musical shocks. In the 1980s, angry kids imported **straight-edge** from Washington, D.C.: a bevy of fast-rocking, non-drinking, non-smoking bands packed Sunday all-ages shows at CBGB's. In the 1980s and early 1990s the **post-punk** scene crystallized around bands such as Sonic Youth and Pavement. Obscure vinyl can be found in the city's many used record stores; prices can be absurd, but the selection surpasses that of any other North American city (see **Shopping,** p. 300). As the millennium approaches, **post-rock** proliferates. Locals Bowery Electric and Ui incorporate drum machines and dub techniques in efforts to keep rock radical, while native Brooklynites and indie-rockers extraordinaire, Lady Bug Transistor, make effete rock sexy with flutes, organs, and trumpets.

STREET POETS

Rap and **hip-hop** also began on New York's streets, and the list of NYC artists reads like a History of Urban Music, including such heavyweight emcees as KRS-1, Chuck D, LL Cool J, Run-DMC, EPMD, and Queen Latifah (who leapt across the river from Jersey). Bronx DJs **Grandmaster Flash** and **Afrika Bambaataa** laid the foundations in the late 70s and early 80s with records rooted deeply in electronic processing, scratching, and sampling. In 1979, the **Sugarhill Gang** released *Rapper's Delight,* widely considered the first true rap record.

Predominant in the East Coast hip-hop hierarchy are the **Native Tongues,** a loose collection of New York (OK—some are Long Islanders) acts which includes A Tribe Called Quest, De La Soul, and Black Sheep. Straight outta Staten Island came the ol' dirty Wu-tang Clan, whose dense, brooding beats and clever use of kung-fu samples have made names for several of its coterie, including **Method Man** and the **GZA.** Pampered young funsters like the Beastie Boys and Luscious Jackson transcended racial lines to broaden the national appeal of the hip-hop genre, incorporating jazz loops, hardcore thrash, and funk samples into their stylistic repertoire. Other recent NYC area acts to climb the charts include Nas, Mobb Deep, and the Fugees (including Wyclef Jean and 1999 Grammy winner, **Lauryn Hill,** who also have powerful solo personas). And, although too commercial, Puff Daddy's protégé, Mase, put Harlem back on the map with his 1998 release, "Harlem World," before retiring to devote himself to his new-found commitment to Christianity.

For a clearer glimpse of the hip-hop scene in New York (and across the country) pick up a copy of New York-based *The Source,* the genre's premier publication, or check out Davey D's Hip Hop Corner on the web (www.daveyd.com). In Brooklyn, the **Crooklyn Dub Consortium** eschews commercial success to create otherworldly dubhop where crooked beats fuse with third world instrumentation and Jamaican dub styles. Williamsburg record label and guerrilla think tank **Wordsound** acts as the Consortium's subterranean base. As the litany of the city's hip-hop greats reveals, Gotham's soundtrack is laid to a fat beat. At the same time, the beat itself echoes New Yorkers' feet pounding pavement.

THE ELECTRONIC WAVE

Although the Big Apple may have pioneered the hip-hop sound, it lags a bit behind Europe on the **techno** frontier. Nevertheless, New York City serves as ground zero for the east coast stage of the **rave** revolution that took hold of European and L.A. club culture. Deeelite and Moby first got the city grooving where **disco** left off with their toe-tapping amalgamation of ambient and techno-funk, and now home-grown superstar DJs like Junior Vasquez, Frankie Bones, and DB keep the crowds dancing to the newest **house, trance, jungle,** and **trip-hop.** Downtown's kitsch-hungry partygoers now groove to "loungecore," a sexy, shmaltzy revival of 1970s soft porn soundtracks and exotica records that goes great with polyester.

The newest aural concoction New York has to offer is **illbient,** a mix attitude that values sonic experiments over smooth dance mixes. At an illbient happening you might hear a hardcore rock single spliced with a minimalist piano piece, or a DJ cutup of two identical Sherlock Holmes records which fades into Moroccan *gnawa* music. Illbient sessions often incorporate video, performance art, and dance in a commitment to "cultural alchemy." Illbient resonates with the density of cultures that only New York City can provide, and can be heard at **SoundLab** (212-726-1724). Illbient performers to watch out for include Lloop, DJ Olive, the Bedouin, **/rupture,** We, Sub Dub, Byzar, and media soluble DJ Spooky.

LITERARY NEW YORK

Since **William Bradford** was appointed America's first public printer in 1698 and went on to found the country's first newspaper, the *New York Gazette,* in 1725, New York City has been the literary capital of the Americas. The epicenter of the city's literary vanguard may have shifted with each successive movement, but the Big Apple has never been at a loss for prolific pens.

The area surrounding Columbia University witnessed one of the most vibrant and important moments in American literary history, the **Harlem Renaissance,** which took place in the 1920s. Novels like George Schuyler's *Black No More* and Claude McKay's *Home to Harlem* are energized accounts of the exoticized underworld of speakeasies and nightclubs that white folks found so fascinating. **Zora Neale Hurston,** then an anthropology student at Columbia, helped create the hypercreative buzz up in Harlem. Poet **Langston Hughes** and his circle founded radical journals that proposed the idea of a "New Negro." The next generation of black talent, such as **Ralph Ellison** and **James Baldwin,** expanded the scope of African-American literary discourse, dealing with issues of whiteness and ideas of America alongside nuanced social critique. Ellison's *Invisible Man* offers an epic excursion into the complexities of black and white life in Manhattan, while Baldwin's work wields a grittier, gayer edge.

The **Gotham Book Mart,** 41 W. 47th St., established in 1920, has long been one of New York's most important literary hangouts. The store, famous for its second-story readings, has hosted some of the biggest writers of the century and once attracted all of literary New York. During the years when **Ulysses** was banned in the U.S., those in-the-know came to Gotham to buy imported copies of Joyce's magnum opus under the counter. Check out the memorabilia and old photographs that document the bookstore's history. **Columbia University** has long been the intellectual magnet of the Upper West Side. The roving Beat crowd swamped the area in the late 1940s when Ginsberg and Kerouac studied at the college. During its controversial late 60s stage, Brooklyn resident Paul Auster also honed his writing chops there. Though not an Ivy League college, Public School #6, also on the Upper West Side, boasts such prestigious alums as *Catcher in the Rye* author, **J.D. Salinger.**

A LITERARY VILLAGE. Even before it became the publishing
center of the country (supplanting Boston around the mid-19th century), New York
could claim as residents many pioneers of a national literature.

THE STARVING. Some writers, such as **Herman Melville,** born in 1819 at 6 Pearl St.
in lower Manhattan, was so disheartened by the critics' response to *Moby Dick* that he
took a job at a New York customs house and died unrecognized and unappreciated. To
top it off, the *Times* called him Henry in his obituary. **Washington Irving** knew better how
to work a room. Born at 131 William St., the author of *Knickerbocker's History of New
York* made a name for himself penning satirical essays on New York society "from the
beginning of the world to the end of the Dutch dynasty," and even gave New York its
enduring pen-name, Gotham City. Walt Whitman hung around for a while to work on the
magazine *Aurora* and wax democratic in free verse on the Brooklyn Bridge and "Mana-
hatta." **Edgar Allan Poe** was so brutally poor, living all the way out in the rural Bronx, that
he used to send his aging mother-in-law to scour nearby fields for edible roots. Among
the early 20th century's young, poor, and literarily gifted Greenwich Villagers were **Willa
Cather,** John Reed, and Theodore Dreiser—parents of the modern American novel. For
over 50 years the Village prevailed as one of America's most important neighborhoods,
hosting a full spectrum of poets, essayists, and novelists, including Marianne Moore,
Hart Crane, **e.e. cummings, Edna St. Vincent Millay,** and Thomas Wolfe.

THE STERLING. Too expensive for most Village writers, Washington Square—immortalized by **Henry James's** book of that name and by **Edith Wharton's** *Age of Innocence*—fostered a more effete literary scene. Sherwood Anderson called the
cobblestoned Washington Mews home.

THE DRUNKEN. To the south of the Square once stood the boarding houses where
O. Henry and **Eugene O'Neill** lived, and 133 MacDougal is the spot where O'Neill
revved up his Provincetown Players. Down Bleecker and MacDougal you'll find some
of the coffee houses the **Beats** made famous. **Thomas Wolfe** lived at 263 West 11th
St. And **Dylan Thomas** was not the only one of the lot who tanked up at the White
Horse Tavern., 567 Hudson St. None, however, shared the misfortune of Thomas,
who, after pumping a purported 18 shots of whiskey through his shredded gut,
lapsed into a fatal coma.

Later in the 20th century, the East Village became American literature's head-
quarters, when the nomadic Kerouac and Ginsberg moved in next to neighbors
Amiri Baraka (Le Roi Jones) and W.H. Auden (who spent a couple of decades at 77
St. Mark's Place, basement entrance). Many a writer whiled away his or her dying
days in relative obscurity at the **Chelsea Hotel,** on 23rd St. between Seventh and
Eighth Ave. Among the surviving tenants are **Arthur Miller** and **Vladimir Nabokov.**
Midtown contains the legendary **Algonquin Hotel,** 59 W. 44th St. In 1919 the wits of
the **Round Table**—writers like Robert Benchley, Dorothy Parker, Alexander
Wollcott, and Edna Ferber—chose this hotel as the site of their famous weekly
lunch meetings, making the Algonquin the site of inspiration for much of the *New
Yorker* magazine.

Some must-reads involving the city of dreams:

Age of Innocence or *House of Mirth*, Edith Wharton. Two tales of turn-of-the-century
romance and woe among the New York gentry.

Another Country, James Baldwin. Interracial lovers and same-sex couples uncover beauty
and tremendous pain trying to relate to one another in 60s Manhattan.

A Tree Grows In Brooklyn, Betty Smith. An Irish woman's coming-of-age in early 20th-cen-
tury Brooklyn. Also a 1945 film by Elia Kazan.

Bonfire of the Vanities, Tom Wolfe. A Wall Street financier takes a wrong turn off the Tri-
Boro Bridge. Hijinks ensue. For your own sake, miss the movie.

Bright Lights, Big City, Jay MacInerney. 1980s New York. A columnist for the *New Yorker* divides his time between clubs and cocaine. Michael J. Fox starred in the film. Also see *Story of My Life,* another tale of Manhattan self-indulgence.

Catcher in the Rye, J.D. Salinger. A now-classic fable of alienated youth. Prep-schooler Holden Caulfield visits the city and falls from innocence.

Eloise, Kay Thompson. A classic children's book. Young Eloise lives in the Plaza Hotel, wreaking havoc on every elegant floor and combing her hair with a fork.

The Great Gatsby, F. Scott Fitzgerald. An incisive commentary on the American Dream, vis-a-vis the rise and fall of would-be New Yorker Jay Gatsby.

Jazz, Toni Morrison. Morrison wrote this Nobel prize-winning novel in a jazz form: sensual, cerebral, and experimental. It examines love, murder, and the magical potency of the city in 1920s Harlem.

New York Trilogy, Paul Auster. Three playfully literary short stories riff on the conventions of detective fiction, and are set in Brooklyn Heights and Manhattan.

JOURNALISM

New York, the premiere society of information abundance, is a sounding board for the rest of the global village. ABC, CBS, NBC, two wire services, umpteen leading magazines, and more newspapers than anywhere else in the world have taken up residence here. The intense concentration of media amplifies every sound. Broadsheets, graffiti, posters, and billboards provide public spaces for high-profile subversion. Meanwhile, a bizarre (and often pornographic) underground world awaits on **public-access television,** if you can find a friend with cable.

New York's romance with the media began almost three centuries ago. The city's first newspaper, the **Gazette,** appeared in 1725. Ten years later, **John Peter Zenger,** editor of the **New York Weekly Journal,** was charged with libel for satirizing public officials. His description of the city recorder as "a large spaniel...that has lately strayed from his kennel with his mouth full of fulsome panegyrics" was seen as especially offensive. The governor threw Zenger into jail and burned copies of his paper in public. Zenger's acquittal set a precedent for what would become a great U.S. tradition—the freedom of the press.

The city soon became the center of the nation's rapidly developing print network. Horace Greeley's **Tribune,** based in New York, became America's first nationally distributed paper. Despite his love for the city, Greeley's advice to young men around the country (echoed in the 1970s by The Village People) was to "Go West." Home to the *Tribune* and its rivals, Nassau Street was dubbed "Newspaper Row" in the mid-19th century. Later in the 19th century, the competition between Joseph Pulitzer's *New York World* and **William Randolph Hearst's** *New York Journal* resorted to the sensationalist reporting soon to be dubbed "Yellow Journalism." New York characteristically led the vanguard of both the naughty and the nice.

Today, New York supports over 100 different newspapers, reflecting the diversity of its urban landscape. Weekly ethnic papers cater to the black, Hispanic, Irish, Japanese, Chinese, Indian, Korean, and Greek communities, among others. Candidates for local office frequently court voters by seeking endorsements from their community papers. Failure to appease community publications can damage political careers. The **New York Amsterdam News** has published, to date, 13 editorials entitled "While We Were Sleeping: Giuliani must be removed"

The highly political **El Diario/La Prensa** has been stirring up controversy since 1914. Founded originally with Puerto Ricans (or Nuyoricans) in mind, the journal now reaches over 53,000 Spanish-speaking New Yorkers from a vast array of Latin-American origins.

The **New York Post** and the **Daily News,** the city's two major tabloid dailies, infamously flaunt less-than-demure sensibilities. The *News,* recently "rescued" by now-dead Robert Maxwell, has slightly better taste—it doesn't use red ink, and it reports fewer grisly murders. Some readers think the *Post* headlines, often printed in lettering three inches high, can have a nasty ring. One of the *Post*'s more brilliant offerings read "Headless Body Found in Topless Bar." Both papers have editorial opinions more conservative than their headlines, as well as comics, advice pages, gossip columns, and horoscopes. The *Post* has a great sports section, and both have good metropolitan coverage. **Newsday** offers thorough local coverage by a youngish staff, some entertaining columnists, and a special Sunday section just for the kids. In the 80s *Newsday* began printing a New York City edition, a liberal alternative to the other tabloids, only to shut it down in 1995 when its impatient parent company, Times Mirror, pulled the plug a year before it would have begun garnering profit.

The New York Times looks down upon its tabloid companions from its vantage point as distinguished elder statesperson of all city papers. While the recent introduction of color to its photographs belies the *Times*'s moniker of "the Gray Lady," this grandmama of newspapers still soberly claims to be the authority on "all the news that's fit to print." Its editorial page provides a nationally respected forum for policy debates, coveted political endorsements, and the rantings of demi-celebrity columnists such as Maureen Dowd, William Safire, and Frank Rich. Praise from its Book Review section can revitalize living authors and immortalize dead ones, and its Sunday crossword puzzles enliven brunches from Fresno to Tallahassee. While the *Times*'s "National Editions" court audiences outside the city, the paper remains staunchly centered on New York. The new *Styles* section confirms this regional loyalty by indulging in the (hopefully) self-conscious absurdities and triumphs of upper-middle class New York life. Theater directors, nervous politicians, and other fervent readers often make late-night newsstand runs to buy the hefty, definitive Sunday *Times* around midnight on Saturday.

The Village Voice, the largest weekly newspaper in the country, captures a spirit of the city each Wednesday that you won't find in the dailies. Don't search here for syndicated advice columnists, baseball statistics, or the bikini-clad woman *du jour*. The left-leaning *Voice* prefers to stage lively political debates and print quirky reflections on New York life. It also sponsors some excellent investigative city reporting—and the city's most intriguing set of personal ads. Many New Yorkers read Michael Musto's gossip column religiously. The real estate and nightlife listings are some of the most substantial, and most considered, in the nation. Best of all, it is free to Manhattanites and can be picked up at any street corner midweek. The **New York Press,** another free weekly, also has good club and nightlife listings, in addition to entertaining articles on politics and culture.

The **Wall Street Journal** and the Upper East Side's **New York Observer** fill out the newspaper spectrum. The *Journal* gives a quick world-news summary on page one for breakfasting brokers more interested in the market pages. With its pen-and-ink drawings, conservative bent, market strategies, and continual obsession with the price of gold, the *Journal* offers to all a Wall Street insider's world perspective. The *Observer* prints articles and commentary on city politics on its dapper pink pages.

On the glossy side, New York is undoubtedly the magazine publishing capital of the country; most national periodicals have their headquarters somewhere in the city. While old staples like **Time, Newsweek,** and **Rolling Stone** have resided here for decades, other New York mainstays have not always been so venerable. **Vanity Fair** originally made its fame by publishing content that was considered by some to be scandalous by the standards of the time, and **Vogue** was a weekly digest of the trivialities and whims of New York's high society before it became the definitive fashion arbiter. A bastion of respectability, the **New Yorker** publishes fiction and poetry by well known authors and the occasional fledgling discovery. Former *Vanity Fair* editor Tina Brown handed over her short-lived reign as *New Yorker* editor-in-chief to join Miramax in creating the multi-media magazine *Talk*. During her tenure at the *New Yorker*, she brought the magazine a new style, with bimonthly articles by black intellectual Henry Louis Gates, Jr., occasional cartoons by Art Spiegelman, photographs by Annie Leibowitz, and themed issues. Despite these innovations, some rejoice in Brown's departure;

one writer has summed up the sentiments of such critics, saying, "I assume we can now look forward to Miramax becoming the shallow, celebrity obsessed money loser she made the *New Yorker*." The editorial fate of the magazine is now in the hands of David Remnick.

New York magazine prints extensive entertainment listings but, unlike the *New Yorker*, focuses more on the city's "wealthy" lifestyle than its "pretentious" literati. The spring and fall fashion issues set the standard with beautiful models and *very* cool clothes. The amazingly fast-selling *Best of New York* issue, which comes out in late spring, is a definitive guide to the city's hippest new spots. **Time Out: New York** is the most recent weekly player in the local newsprint rivalry. Read primarily for its vastly helpful entertainment listings, rumor has it that *Time Out* includes colorful, well-written articles, too.

LIGHTS, CAMERA, NEW YORK!

Always a ham, the Big Apple has shown off its pretty face on the silver screen since the birth of the genre. It's not unusual, on your mid-morning stroll down Fifth Avenue, to encounter production assistants and camera crews in mirrored sunglasses waving their hands and shouting in California-ese. The city encourages film production by granting free permits to those filmmakers who want to shoot on location; there is even a special police task force—the New York Police Movie and Television Unit—to assist with traffic re-routing and scenes involving guns or uniformed police officers. As a testament to how seriously this city takes its film industry, Mayor Giuliani proclaimed May 18, 1998 "Godzilla Day" in honor of the opening of this gargantuan flick which was shot in New York. "The industry," in turn, has rewarded Gotham well; in 1997, 213 films were shot in New York with anywhere between 60 to 90 productions on location in a given day.

If your stay in New York inspires you to create your very own urban movie cityscape, contact **The Mayor's Office of Film, Theater, and Broadcasting,** 1697 Broadway #602 (489-6710; www.ci.nyc.ny.us/html/filmcom) Their extraordinarily helpful website provides a daily schedule of the films being shot in the city. To access never-produced scripts written by the Writers' Guild of New York, at least 70% of which are set in New York, contact Vivian Cannon at the **Script Library** (489-6710, ext. 214) for an appointment. If you just want to sit back and catch a flick, call 777-FILM for movie listings-- you can even order tickets. However, you might want to VCR it, as most theaters here have hiked their prices to a whopping $9.50.

Here is a smattering of quintessential New York films:

Annie Hall (1977). Woody Allen and Diane Keaton play tennis, flirt, court, and squabble in this funny and romantic ode to the city that crystallizes his image as a neurotic Upper West Side intellectual.

Basquiat (1996). Chronicles the tragic rise to fame of Gotham street artist Jean-Michele Basquiat, protege of an aging Andy Warhol played with great nuance by David Bowie.

Breakfast at Tiffany's (1961). Audrey Hepburn frolics through Upper East Side society.

Brighton Beach Memoirs (1986). Neil Simon's—imagine it—semi-autobiographical comedy about growing up Jewish in Brooklyn with baseball and sex on the brain.

A Bronx Tale (1993). Robert DeNiro's directing debut: a tale of a boy torn between his Pop and the temptations of mob life. Shot in Brooklyn and Queens.

Coming to America (1988). Eddie Murphy emerges from his utopian jungle community in search of independence in Queens.

Crossing Delancey (1990). Amy Irving dates New York's premier pickle man.

The Daytrippers (1997). A clan of Long Islanders trek into the Big City to confront a philandering husband. Or is he?

Desperately Seeking Susan (1985). A bored housewife finds excitement when she assumes the identity of that hippest of East Village hipsters, Madonna.

Die Hard with a Vengeance (1995). Bruce Willis is forced to visit various NYC locales by the machiavellian Jeremy Irons. Watch the first half, then turn it off.

Do the Right Thing (1989). Spike Lee's explosive look at one very hot day in the life of Brooklyn's Bed-Stuy. Colorful, stylized cinematography. Racial tensions at boiling point.

Empire (1968). Master icon-manipulator Andy Warhol brings you eight hours of the Empire State Building, shot from dawn to dusk on a stationary camera.

The Fisher King (1991). Shock-jock Jeff Bridges and homeless dude Robin Williams seek redemption in the fantastical dimension of New York.

The French Connection (1971). One of the all-time great chase scenes: Gene Hackman vs. the B train.

Ghostbusters (1984). Bill Murray and Dan Ackroyd try to rid the city (and Sigourney Weaver) of ghosts. Note the New York Public Library, among other landmarks.

The Godfather I, II, and III (1972-1990). Coppola's searing study of one immigrant family and the price of the American Dream. Based on a bestseller by Mario Puzo.

Goodfellas (1990). Scorsese's look at true-life gangster Henry Hill. Great location shots in the city, especially the Bamboo Lounge in Canarsie.

Hair (1979). The love-child musical brought to the screen, complete with hippies tripping in Sheep Meadow in Central Park. Nell Carter sings a solo.

James and the Giant Peach (1996). Young James Henry Trotter travels to the Big Apple via a Big Peach. Note Richard Dreyfuss as a Brooklynite centipede.

Kids (1995). Larry Clark's study of some baaaaaad NY kids. Not for the queasy.

King Kong (1933). Single giant ape seeks female atop symbol of phallic power.

Little Odessa (1995). Tim Roth in a thriller about the emerging Russian-American mafia in Brooklyn's Brighton Beach. From the book by Joseph Koenig.

Manhattan (1979). Woody Allen's hysterically funny love-note to New York. Glimmering skyline, to the tune of Gershwin's *Rhapsody in Blue*.

Marathon Man (1976). Dustin Hoffman flees from Laurence Olivier's Nazi dentist, only to confront him at the Central Park reservoir.

Mean Streets (1973). Harvey Keitel and Robert DeNiro cruise around Little Italy looking for trouble. This film put Scorsese on the map.

Men In Black (1997). Aliens among us? Intergalactic roaches, baby extraterrestrials. Will Smith and Tommy Lee Jones save the world at the Unisphere in Queens.

Metropolitan (1990). Whit Stillman chronicles the dying Park Avenue debutante scene: a tale of east (side) meets west (side), conversation, and cocktails.

Midnight Cowboy (1969). Jon Voight, as a would-be hustler and Dustin Hoffman, as street rodent Ratso Rizzo in this devastating look at the seedy side of NY.

Moonstruck (1987). Cher falls in love with baker Nicholas Cage in this romantic comedy set in Carroll Gardens. Watch for the scene in Lincoln Center.

The Muppets Take Manhattan (1986). Kermit, Piggy, and the gang look to make it in the Big City. Hey, in this town, even Gonzo fits right in.

New York Stories (1989). Martin Scorsese, Francis Ford Coppola, and Woody Allen grind their cinematic axes on the Big Apple, to varying success.

On the Town (1949). Start spreading the news—Gene Kelly and Frank Sinatra are sailors with time and money to burn in New York City.

On the Waterfront (1954). Marlon Brando coulda been a contenda, if he'd left Hoboken.

Saturday Night Fever (1977). John Travolta shakes his polyester-clad booty.

Serpico (1973). Al Pacino fights the power in this true tale of NYPD corruption.

The Seven-Year Itch (1955). Marilyn Monroe and subway grates—perfect together.

Smoke (1995) and its less successful sequel "Blue in the Face." Wayne Wang and Paul Auster conjure up poignant and painfully funny stories that showcase some of America's best actors, including Brooklyn native Harvey Keitel.

Taxi Driver (1976). DeNiro is Travis Bickle, a taxi driver with issues. Don't look him in the eye...and tip him well.

West Side Story (1961). Romeo and Juliet retold à la fire escape.

When Harry Met Sally (1989). Meg Ryan and Billy Crystal continually emote about their foibles against a New York backdrop. The ultimate date movie.

ETIQUETTE

Like the French and the Visigoths, New Yorkers have a widespread reputation for rudeness. For most of them, lack of politeness is not a matter of principle, but a strategy for survival. Nowhere does the anonymous rhythm of urban life hammer the tenant than in New York City. Cramped into tiny spaces, millions of people find themselves confronting one another every day, struggling for space and sanity. People react by developing thick skins and keeping to themselves, especially in public. If you find the city intolerably unfriendly, remember the small humanitarian gestures that appear in the unlikeliest of places, then grit your teeth and prepare to take on the urban jungle. To begin bushwhackin', just look to New York's international language of love...

THE 411 ON (GLOSSARY OF) NEW YAUWK SLANG:

A'ight- expression of agreement

to Ax - (v.) to ask

da Bomb - (n.) something excellent; (adj.) without the "da," meaning excellent

BQE - (proper n.) Brooklyn Queens Expressway

to Book - (v.) to hightail it out of there

Boricua - (adj., n.) Puerto Rican

to Bounce/to Roll - (v.) to be out, to leave

the D.L. - (n.) the down-low, the low-down, the scoop; adj. "on the D.L. tip"

Dope - (adj.) excellent; good looking

Ecksetera - et cetera

Esscuse Me? - "you better not have said what I think you said."

Fly - (adj.) Dope

Front/Get Over - (v.) to feign; to affront

Gimme - "May I please have a . . ."

Hype - (adj.) Dope

I'm sayin' - expression of agreement

In the mix - expression meaning "involved" or "present at . . ."

Keep it real - what true New Yorkers do

the Lex - (proper n.) the 4,5 or 6 Subway that goes up Lex(ington Ave.)

the L.I.E. - (proper n.) the Lawnguyland Expressway

Lox and Shmear - (n.), a bagel with smoked salmon and cream cheese

Mami - (n.) exclamation remarking a woman's hotness

Not Tryin' To - don't want to

Peep - (v.) to look at

Phat; Phatty-Phat - (adj.) excellent; most excellent

Pie - (n.) a pizza

Putz - (n.) a small member; a wimpy jerk

Schmuck - (n.) a jerk

Tar Beach - (n.) a rooftop for sunbathing

Tight - (adj.) Dope

Wack - (adj.) bad; the opposite of dope

Yous - much like the French second person plural or "y'all"

ESSENTIALS

WHEN TO GO

New York is expensive to visit in any season, but coming in the off-season may leave you more comfortable, less overwhelmed by crowds, and slightly less at the mercy of price-gouging establishments. In May and September the weather improves, waves of tourists recede, and prices descend. Most facilities and sights stay open all winter—after all, New York is the city that never sleeps, and it certainly doesn't hibernate. Here are some preliminary tips to help you through this gateway to the USA, whatever the time of year.

First of all, consider your address book a supplementary travel guide; staying with relatives, friends, enemies, or acquaintances greatly alleviates the cost of living in New York. If you stay in hostels and prepare your own food, expect to spend anywhere from $40-75 per person per day, depending on your eating habits and other needs. Transportation and/or dining will increase these figures.

Keep an eye out for news of special events. Whether celebrating an American national holiday or commemorating a local ethnic figure, New York has a special talent for impressive annual celebrations. Catching any such events is likely to make for a memorable trip, and numerous millennium events are expected to be no exception. Below is a table of annual holidays and events that occur in New York, with the dates for late 1999 and all of 2000 given. See p. 1 for millennium-related events.

DATE	FESTIVAL	INFORMATION
November 28	Thanksgiving Day	Find a family; eat their turkey. Or attend Macy's Thanksgiving Day Parade. A 75-year tradition. Begins at E. 77th St., runs along Central Park West, and goes south on Broadway to 34th St. Huge balloon floats assembled the night before at 79th St. and Central Park West. See yourself on television!
Late-November to January	*Nutcracker* Season	The New York City Ballet performs its timeless classic. Contact: 870-5570
December 2	Tree Lighting	At Rockefeller Center. Contact: 332-6868.
December 4	Channukah	Jewish celebration lasts 8 days.
December 25	Christmas	Businesses closed.
December 31	New Year's Eve Celebrations	As New York ushers in the Millennium, this New Year's promises over the top. For information events see **Y? 2K.**, p. 1.
January 1	New Year's Day	Massive hangovers, massive confetti clean-up. Businesses closed.
January 2-10	National Boat Show	Nautical paraphernalia galore. At Jacob Javits Convention Center.
January 15-17	International Motorcycle Show	At the Jacob Javits Center.
January 17	Martin Luther King, Jr.'s Birthday	City offices closed.
February 14	Valentine's Day	Snuggle up to that sweetie in your hostel or eat a candlelit dinner by the Hudson River.
February 21	Washington's Birthday	Businesses closed.
March 4-8	Art Expo	At the Jacob Javits Convention Center.
April 1-9	Passover	Jewish holiday celebrating freedom.
April 4	Easter	Businesses closed, bunny.
April	Greater New York Orchid Show	At the World Financial Center (see p. 134).
April	St. Patrick's Day Parade	Along Fifth Avenue, everything's green—even the bagels.
April 3-11	International Auto Show	At the Jacob Javits Convention Center.

ESSENTIALS

DATE	FESTIVAL	INFORMATION
May 2	Bike New York	A springtime tradition for 22 years—bike through all 5 boroughs on traffic-free roads with 28,000 other cyclists. Contact: Bike NY (932-2453); email info@bikenewyork.org.
May 29	Memorial Day	Concerts and fireworks at the South Street Seaport. Businesses closed.
June	Music in the Anchorage	Rock concert series at the base of the Brooklyn Bridge. Contact: 206-6674, ext. 252.
June to August	World Financial Center Festival	A full entertainment schedule throughout the summer. Contact: 945-0505. Mostly free.
June to August	Summerstage	Performances in Central Park. Top acts! Contact: 360-2777; www.summerstage.org. Free.
Mid-June to Mid-August	Celebrate Brooklyn	Outdoor performing arts festival at the Park Slope Bandshell. Free.
Mid-June	Welcome Back to Brooklyn Homecoming Festival	Family festival celebrating the borough. Brooklyn natives who have made it big return home to the fanfare of bands, writers' readings, and family activities. Starts at Grand Army Plaza. Contact: 718-855-7882, ext. 54; www.brooklynx.org/welcome. Free.
Late June to Late July	Midsummer Night Swing Dancextravaganza	Dance under the stars at Lincoln Center to live music. Contact: 875-5000. Free.
Late June to August	Shakespeare in the Park	Quality Shakespeare in Central Park's Delacorte Theater. Free.
June 8	Museum Mile Festival	Fifth Avenue is closed from 82nd to 104th St. from 6 to 9pm; the museums along this strip are free and provide entertainment.
June 19-26	JVC Jazz Festival	Prestigious jazz festival with venues across the city. Contact: 496-9000.
June 25	Puerto Rican Independence Day	Parade along Fifth Ave. and festivities in El Barrio (Spanish Harlem).
June 26	Mermaid Parade	At Coney Island. A festival of fabulous fishies.
Late June	New York Restaurant Week	New York City's top restaurants allow you to partake of their fine eats for the mere price of the year (i.e., $20.00 in the year 2000).
July 4	Independence Day	Macy's fireworks display around Lower Manhattan or you can watch works over the river at the Battery Park esplanade.
Late July to August	Mostly Mozart	A celebration of Mozart. Contact: 875-5030.
Late August	Tap-A-Mania	Sponsored by Macy's, thousands of tap dancers congregate on 34th St. and Broadway. Contact: 695-4400.
September 4	Labor Day	Businesses closed.
September 5	U.S. Open	Tennis championship held in the USTA's center in Flushing Meadows, Queens. Contact: 718-760-6200.
September 6	Labor Day/Labor Day Caribbean Festival	Labor Day commemorates U.S. workers. Caribbean festival includes a Children's Carnival at St. John's Place in Brooklyn and a Labor Day Parade starting at Eastern Parkway in Brooklyn. Contact: 718-625-15115 or 773-4052. Free.
October 9	Columbus Day	Businesses closed.
Mid-October	Ice Skating begins	Rockefeller Center. Contact: 332-6868.
October 31	Halloween Parade	Ooo...inventive costumes and debauched fun. Sixth Ave. from Spring St. to 23rd St.
November 7	New York City Marathon (Election Day)	See skinny people sweat. Contact: NY Roadrunner's Club (423-2233).
November 10	Veterans' Day observed	Businesses closed.
November 23	Thanksgiving Day	Macy's Thanksgiving Day Parade begins at E. 77th St., runs along Central Park West, and goes south on Broadway to 34th St.
December 25	Christmas Day	Businesses closed.

CLIMATE

New York's weather is the worst of both worlds: summers are hot and sticky, while winters compete with neighboring New England for cold and snow. Winter snowfalls are common, but the city usually clears streets (thus clogging sidewalks) within a day. In the spring and fall, frequent impromptu showers make carrying an umbrella a good idea.

The U.S. uses the Fahrenheit temperature scale rather than the Celsius scale. To convert Fahrenheit to Celsius temperatures, subtract 32, then multiply by 5 and divide the result by 9. The freezing point of water is 32°F, its boiling point 212°, and room temperature usually hovers around 70°. See inside back cover for Farenheit and Celsius conversions.

January: 3.2" rain/snow		April: 3.8"		July: 3.8"		October: 3.4"	
High	Low	High	Low	High	Low	High	Low
38	26	61	44	95	68	66	50

INFORMATION FOR FOREIGN VISITORS

Entrance requirements for foreign visitors to the U.S. include a **valid passport** (see details below) and, generally, a **visa**. See p. 26 for more specific visa information.

OVERSEAS U.S. EMBASSIES AND CONSULATES

Contact the nearest U.S. embassy or consulate to obtain information regarding visas and passports to the United States. The U.S. **State Department** provides contact information for U.S. overseas stations, which can be found at www.state.gov/www/about_state/contacts/index.html.

U.S. Embassies: In **Australia,** Moonah Place, Canberra, ACT 2600 (02 6214 5600; fax 6270 5970); in **Canada,** 100 Wellington St., Ottawa, ON K1P 5T1 (613-238-5335 or 238-4470; fax 238-5720); in **Ireland,** 42 Elgin Rd., Ballsbridge, Dublin (016 687 1 22); in **New Zealand,** 29 Fitzherbert Terr., Thorndon, Wellington (04 472 2068; fax 47 2 3537); in **South Africa,** 877 Pretorius St., Arcadio 0083; P.O. Box 9536, Pretoria 0001 (012 342 1048; fax 342 2244); in the **U.K.,** 24/31 Grosvenor Sq., London W1A 1AE ((020) 7 499 9000; fax 7 409 1637).

U.S. Consulates: In **Australia,** MLC Centre, 19-29 Martin Pl., 59th fl., Sydney NSW 2000 (02 9373 9200; fax 9373 9125); 553 St. Kilda Rd., P.O. Box 6722, Melbourne, VIC 3004 (03 9526 5900; fax 9510 4646); 16 St. George Terr., 13th fl., Perth, WA 6000 (08 9231 9400; fax 9231 9444); in **Canada,** P.O. Box 65, Postal Station Desjardins, Montréal, QC H5B 1G1 (514-398-9695; fax 398-0973); 2 Place Terrasse Dufferin, CP939, Québec, QC G1R 4T9 (418-692-2095; fax 692-4640); 360 University Ave., Toronto, ON M5G 1S4 (416-595-1700; fax 595-0051); 1095 W. Pender St., Vancouver, BC V6E 2M6 (604-685-4311); in **New Zealand,** 4th fl., Yorkshire General Bldg. 4th fl., corner of Shortland and O'Connell St., Auckland (09 303 2724; fax 366 0870); in **South Africa,** Broadway Industries Centre, Heerengracht, Foreshore, Capetown (021 214 280; fax 254 151); Kine Centre, 11th fl., P.O. Box 2155, Johannesburg (011 331 1327; fax 838 3920); in the **U.K.,** Queen's House, 14 Queen St., Belfast, N. Ireland, BT1 6EQ (0123 232 8239; fax 224 8482); 3 Regent Terr., Edinburgh, Scotland EH7 5BW (0131 556 8315; fax 557 6023).

FOREIGN EMBASSIES AND CONSULATES IN THE U.S.

All foreign embassies in the U.S. are in Washinton, D.C. **Foreign consulates** in New York City include: **Canadian** Consulate General, 1251 Avenue Of The Americas (596-1700); Consulate General Of Consulate General Of **France,** 934 Fifth Ave. (606-3600)/10 E. 74th St. (472-8110); Consulate General Of **Ireland,** 345 Park Ave. (319-2555); **Israel,** 800 Second Ave. (499-5000); Consulate Of **The Commonwealth,** 820 Second Ave, New York (599-8478); **South African** Consulate, 333 E. 38th St. 9th fl. (213-4880); N.Y. Consulate General, 520 Twelfth Ave. (629-8749)

ESSENTIALS

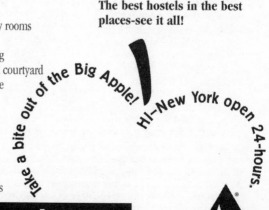

PASSPORTS

Citizens of Australia, Ireland, New Zealand, South Africa, and the U.K. need valid passports to enter the U.S. and to re-enter their own country. Only citizens of Canada do not need a passport to enter the U.S. The U.S. does not allow entrance if the holder's passport expires in less than six months; returning home with an expired passport is illegal, and may result in a fine. If you plan an extended stay, register your passport with the nearest embassy or consulate.

It is a good idea to photocopy the page of your passport that contains your photograph, passport number, and other identifying information, along with other important documents such as visas, travel insurance policies, airplane tickets, and traveler's check serial numbers, in case you lose anything. Carry one set of copies in a safe place apart from the originals and leave another set at home. Consulates also recommend that you carry an expired passport or an official copy of your birth certificate in a part of your baggage separate from other documents.

LOST PASSPORTS. If you lose your passport, immediately notify the local police and the nearest embassy or consulate of your home government. To expedite its replacement, you will need to know all information previously recorded and show identification and proof of citizenship. In some cases, a replacement may take weeks to process, and it may be valid only for a limited time. Any visas stamped in your old passport will be irretrievably lost. In an emergency, ask for immediate temporary traveling papers that will permit you to re-enter your home country.

NEW PASSPORTS. All applications for new passports or renewals should be filed several weeks or months in advance of your planned departure date—remember that you are relying on government agencies to complete these transactions. Demand for passports is highest in most nations between January and August, so apply as early as possible around these months. A backlog in processing can spoil your plans. Most passport offices do offer rush passport services for an extra charge. Citizens residing abroad who need a passport or renewal should contact their nearest embassy or consulate.

Australia: Citizens must apply for a passport in person at a post office, a passport office, or an Australian diplomatic mission overseas. Passport offices are located in Adelaide, Brisbane, Canberra, Darwin, Hobart, Melbourne, Newcastle, Perth, and Sydney. New adult passports cost AUS$126 (for a 32-page passport) or AUS$188 (64-page), and a child's is AUS$63 (32-page) or AUS$94 (64-page). Adult passports are valid for 10 years and child passports for 5 years. For more info, call toll-free (in Australia) 13 12 32, or visit www.dfat.gov.au/passports.

Canada: Citizens may cross the U.S.-Canada border with only proof of citizenship, either birth certificate or passport. Canadian citizens under 16 need notarized permission from their parents to cross the border.

Ireland: Citizens can apply for a passport by mail to either the Department of Foreign Affairs, Passport Office, Setanta Centre, Molesworth St., Dublin 2 (tel. (01) 671 1633; fax 671 1092; www.irlgov.ie/iveagh), or the Passport Office, Irish Life Building, 1A South Mall, Cork (tel. (021) 27 25 25). Obtain an application at a local Garda station or post office, or request one from a passport office. Passports cost IR£45 and are valid for 10 years. Citizens under 18 or over 65 can request a 3-year passport that costs IR£10.

New Zealand: Application forms for passports are available in New Zealand from most travel agents. Applications may be forwarded to the Passport Office, P.O. Box 10526, Wellington, New Zealand (tel. 0800 22 50 50; www.govt.nz/agency_info/forms.shtml). Standard processing time in New Zealand is 10 working days for correct applications. The fees are adult NZ$80, and child NZ$40. Children's names can no longer be endorsed on a parent's passport—they must apply for their own, which are valid for up to 5 years. An adult's passport is valid for up to 10 years.

South Africa: South African passports are issued only in Pretoria. However, all applications must still be submitted or forwarded to the applicable office of a South African consulate. Tourist passports, valid for 10 years, cost around SAR80. Children under 16 must be issued their own passports, valid for 5 years, which cost around SAR60. Time for the completion of an application is normally 3 months or more from the time of submission. For further information, contact the nearest Department of Home Affairs Office (www.southafrica-newyork.net/passport.htm).

United Kingdom: Full passports are valid for 10 years (5 years if under 16). Application forms are available at passport offices, main post offices, and many travel agents. Apply by mail or in person to one of the passport offices, located in London, Liverpool, Newport, Peterborough, Glasgow, or Belfast. The fee is UK£31, UK£11 for children under 16. The process takes about four weeks, but the London office offers a five-day, walk-in rush service; arrive early. The U.K. Passport Agency can be reached by phone at (0870) 521 04 10, and more information is available at www.open.gov.uk/ukpass/ukpass.htm.

VISAS

Most visitors obtain a **B-2**, or "pleasure tourist," visa at the U.S. consulate or embassy nearest their home, which normally costs $45 and is usually valid for six months. For general visa inquiries, consult the Bureau of Consular Affair's web page (travel.state.gov/visa_services.html). Don't lose your visa. If you do lose your I-94 form (arrival/departure certificate attached to your visa upon arrival), you can replace it at the nearest **U.S. Immigration and Naturalization Service (INS)** office, though it's very unlikely that the form will be replaced within the time of your stay.

Extensions for visas are sometimes attainable with a complete I-539 form; call the forms request line 800-870-3676. For more info, contact the INS at 800-755-0777 or 202-307-1501 (www.ins.usdoj.gov). Travelers from certain nations may enter the U.S. without a visa through the **Visa Waiver Pilot Program.** Visitors qualify as long as they are traveling for business or pleasure, are staying for 90 days or less, have proof of intent to leave (e.g., a returning plane ticket), a completed I-94W, and enter aboard particular air or sea carriers. Twenty-six countries participate in this program, and countries are added frequently; contact a U.S. consulate for more info. For information on work or study visas, see **Longer Stays,** p. 72.

By law, **HIV-positive persons** are not permitted to enter the U.S.; however, HIV testing is conducted only for those planning to immigrate permanently. Travelers from areas with particularly high concentrations of HIV-positive persons or persons with AIDS might be required to provide details when applying for a visa.

WORK VISAS. You must apply for a work visa in order to be employed while visiting the U.S. Get specific info on the jungle of paperwork surrounding work visas at your nearest U.S. embassy or consulate. Working or studying in the U.S. with only a B-2 (tourist) visa is grounds for deportation.

STUDY VISAS. Foreign students who wish to study in the United States must apply for either a M-1 visa (vocational studies) or an F-1 visa (for full-time students enrolled in an academic or language program). An F-1 allows you to work part-time in an on-campus position. In order to apply for an F-1, you must have a Form I-20, which is an official endorsement by your prospective educational institution, verification of your proficiency in English (unless you are entering a language program), and proof of your financial capability to reside in the U.S. for a certain period of time. To apply for a visa you will also need the OF-156, available from U.S. consular offices, a valid passport, and one 37 by 37mm photo. Visas are processed with a $64 fee.

If you are studying in the city, you can take any on-campus job to help pay the bills once you have applied for a social security number and have completed an **Employment Eligibility Form (I-9).** If you are studying full-time in the U.S. on an F-1 visa, you can take any on-campus job provided you do not displace a U.S. resident. On-campus employment is limited to 20 hours per week while school is in session, but you may work full-time during vacation if you plan to return to school. For further info, contact the international students office at the institution you will be attending.

If English is not your native language, you will likely be required to take the Test of English as a Foreign Language (TOEFL), which is administered in many countries. Requirements are set by each school. Contact the **TOEFL/TSE Publications,** P.O. Box 6154, Princeton, NJ 08541-6154 (609-771-7100; www.toefl.org).

CUSTOMS

Upon re-entering your home country, you must declare certain items from abroad and pay a duty on the value of those articles that exceed the allowance established by your country's customs service. Keeping receipts for purchases made in the U.S. will help establish values when you return. It is wise to make a list, including serial numbers, of any valuables that you carry with you from home; if you register this list with customs before your departure and have an official stamp it, you will avoid import duty charges and ensure an easy passage upon your return. Be especially careful to document items manufactured abroad, and don't try to bring perishable food over the border.

Upon returning home, you must declare all articles acquired abroad and pay a **duty** on the value of articles that exceed the allowance established by your country's customs service. Goods and gifts purchased at **duty-free** shops abroad are not exempt from duty or sales tax at your point of return; you must declare these

ESSENTIALS

items as well. "Duty-free" merely means that you need not pay a tax in the country of purchase. For more specific information on customs requirements, contact the following information centers:

Australia: Australian Customs National Information Line 1 300 363; www.customs.gov.au.

Canada: Canadian Customs, 2265 St. Laurent Blvd., Ottawa, ON K1G 4K3 (tel. (613) 993-0534 or 24hr. automated service 800-461-9999; www.revcan.ca).

Ireland: The Collector of Customs and Excise, The Custom House, Dublin 1 (tel. (01) 679 27 77; fax 671 20 21; email taxes@revenue.iol.ie; www.revenue.ie/customs.htm).

New Zealand: New Zealand Customhouse, 17-21 Whitmore St., Box 2218, Wellington (tel. (04) 473 6099; fax 473 7370; www.customs.govt.nz).

South Africa: Commissioner for Customs and Excise, Private Bag X47, Pretoria 0001 (tel. (012) 314 99 11; fax 328 64 78).

United Kingdom: Her Majesty's Customs and Excise, Custom House, Nettleton Road, Heathrow Airport, Hounslow, Middlesex TW6 2LA (tel. (0181) 910 36 02/35 66; fax 910 37 65; www.hmce.gov.uk).

IDENTIFICATION

When you travel, always carry two or more forms of identification on your person, including at least one photo ID. A passport combined with a driver's license or birth certificate usually serves as adequate proof of your identity and citizenship. Some establishments, especially banks, require several IDs before cashing traveler's checks. Never carry all your forms of ID together, however; you risk being left entirely without ID or funds in case of theft or loss. It is useful to carry extra passport-size photos to affix to various ID you may acquire.

ESSENTIALS

STUDENT AND TEACHER IDENTIFICATION. The **International Student Identity Card (ISIC)** is the most widely accepted form of student identification. Flashing this card can procure you discounts for sights, theaters, museums, accommodations, meals, train, ferry, bus, and airplane transportation, and other services. Present the card wherever you go, and ask about discounts even when none are advertised. Cardholders have access to a toll-free 24hr. ISIC helpline whose multilingual staff can provide assistance in medical, legal, and financial emergencies (tel. 800-626-2427 in the U.S. and Canada; elsewhere call Britain collect 44 181 666 90 25.

Many student travel agencies around the world issue ISICs, including STA Travel in Australia and New Zealand; Travel CUTS in Canada; USIT in Ireland and Northern Ireland; SASTS in South Africa; Campus Travel and STA Travel in the U.K.; Council Travel and STA Travel in the U.S. ISIC cards are also available at www.counciltravel.com/idcards/index.htm. When you apply for an ISIC, request a copy of their *International Student Identity Card Handbook*, which lists by country certain available discounts. You can also write to Council for a copy. The card is valid from September of one year to December of the following year and costs $20. Applicants must be at least 12 years old and degree-seeking students of a secondary or post-secondary school. Because of the proliferation of phony ISICs, many airlines and some other services require additional proof of student identity, such as a signed letter from the registrar attesting to your student status that is stamped with the school seal or your school ID card. The **International Teacher Identity Card (ITIC)** offers the same insurance coverage, and similar but limited discounts; the fee is $20. For more information on these cards, contact the **International Student Travel Confederation (ISTC),** Herengracht 479, 1017 BS Amsterdam, Netherlands (from abroad call 31 20 421 28 00; fax 421 28 10; email istcinfo@istc.org; www.istc.org).

YOUTH IDENTIFICATION. The International Student Travel Confederation also issues a discount card to travelers who are not students but are still under the age of 26. Known as the International Youth Travel Card (IYTC; formerly the GO25 Card), this one-year card offers many of the same benefits as the ISIC, and most organizations that sell the ISIC also sell the IYTC. Since it is good from January to December, it can sometimes be strategic to purchase an IYTC even if you are a student, although this is not usually the case for travel in New York. A brochure that lists discounts is free when you purchase the card. To apply, you will need either a passport, valid driver's license, or copy of a birth certificate, and a passport-sized photo with your name printed on the back. The fee is $20.

MONEY

In Boston they ask, How much does he know? In New York, How much is he worth?

—Mark Twain

No matter how tight your budget, you won't be able to carry all your cash with you. Even if you can, don't: non-cash reserves are a necessary precaution in the big bad city. Unfortunately, out-of-state personal checks aren't readily accepted in NYC. No matter how low your budget, if you plan to travel for more than a couple of days, you will need to keep handy a large amount of cash. Carrying it around with you, even in a money belt, is risky.

Before you arrive in New York, you might want to find out if your home bank is networked with any NYC banks; **Cirrus** (800-424-7787) and **Plus** (800-843-7587; www.visa.com) both maintain extensive **Automatic Teller Machine (ATM)** networks in New York. If you're coming to stay for a while, open a savings account at one of the local banks and get an ATM card, which you can use at any time all over the city (see **Managing Money in the City,** p. 35).

ESSENTIALS

Money From Home In Minutes.

If you're stuck for cash on your travels, don't panic. Millions of people trust Western Union to transfer money in minutes to 165 countries and over 50,000 locations worldwide. Our record of safety and reliability is second to none. For more information, call Western Union: USA 1-800-325-6000, Canada 1-800-235-0000. Wherever you are, you're never far from home.

www.westernunion.com

The fastest way to send money worldwide.

New York **banks** are usually open Monday through Friday from 9am to 5pm. Some may also be open Saturdays from 9am to noon or 1pm. All banks, government agencies, and post offices are closed on **legal holidays:** New Year's Day (January 1), Martin Luther King, Jr. Day (January 17), Presidents' Day (February 15), Memorial Day (May 29), Independence Day (July 4), Labor Day (September 3), Columbus Day (October 9), Veterans' Day (November 11), Thanksgiving Day (November 23 in 2000), Christmas Day (December 25).

CURRENCY AND EXCHANGE

The main unit of currency in the U.S. is the **dollar** (symbol $; also known as a 'buck'), which is divided into 100 **cents** (symbol ¢). Dollars circulate almost exclusively as paper money. The green bills come in denominations of $1, $5, $10, $20, $50, and $100. U.S. coins come valued at 1¢ (penny), 5¢ (nickel), 10¢ (dime), and 25¢ (quarter). The conversions below are based on exchange rates in August 1999.

THE GREENBACK (THE U.S. DOLLAR)

CDN$1=US$0.67	US$1=CDN$1.49
UK£1=US$1.62	US$1=UK£0.62
IR£1=US$1.37	US$1=IR£0.73
AUS$1=US$0.66	US$1=AUS$1.52
NZ$1=US$0.54	US$1=NZ$1.86
SAR1=US$0.16	US$1=SAR6.15

Convert your currency infrequently and in large amounts to minimize exorbitant exchange fees. Try to buy traveler's checks in U.S. dollars so that you won't have to exchange currency in the process of cashing them. Be sure to observe commission rates closely and check newspapers to get the standard rate of exchange. A good rule of thumb is to go only to places which have a 5% margin between their buy and sell prices. Anything more, and they are making too much profit. Be sure that both prices are listed. Most banks will not cash personal checks unless you open an account with them, a time-consuming affair.

Banks generally have better rates than tourist offices or exchange kiosks, but there is no guarantee. ATM cards with low international transaction fees may actually offer the best exchange rates on withdrawals in U.S. currency—and **ATM withdrawals** are also completely convenient. As a general rule, it's cheaper to convert money once you arrive in New York than in your home country. However, it's important to have enough U.S. currency to last for the first 24 to 72 hours in the city in case you arrive after banking hours or on a holiday.

TRAVELER'S CHECKS

Traveler's checks are one of the safest and least troublesome means of carrying funds, since they can be refunded if stolen. Several agencies and banks sell them, usually for face value plus a small percentage commission. (Members of the American Automobile Association, and some banks and credit unions, can get American Express checks commission-free; see **Driving Permits and Insurance**). **American Express** and **Visa** are the most widely recognized. If you're ordering checks, do so well in advance, especially if you are requesting large sums.

Each agency provides refunds if your checks are lost or stolen, and many provide additional services, such as toll-free refund hotlines in the countries you're visiting, emergency message services, and stolen credit card assistance.

In order to collect a **refund for lost or stolen checks,** keep your check receipts separate from your checks and store them in a safe place or with a traveling companion. Record check numbers when you cash them, leave a list of check numbers with someone at home, and ask for a list of refund centers when you buy your checks. Never countersign your checks until you are ready to cash them, and always bring your passport with you when you plan to use the checks.

Aladdin hotel

The Aladdin Hotel & Hostel offers rates from $22 (tax included)

All rates are subject to change

317 West 45th Street, New York City 10036 We are also on
the internet: www.aladdinhotel.com Email: aladdinhot@aol.com
Phone: 212-977-5700 Fax: 212-246-6036

American Express: In Australia call 800 251 902; in New Zealand 0800 441 068; in the U.K. (0800) 52 13 13; in the U.S. and Canada 800-221-7282. Elsewhere, call U.S. collect 1-801-964-6665; www.aexp.com. Checks can be purchased for a small fee (1-4%) at American Express Travel Service Offices, banks, and American Automobile Association offices. AAA members (see p. 68) can buy the checks commission-free. American Express offices cash their checks commission-free (except where prohibited by national governments), but often at slightly worse rates than banks. *Cheques for Two* can be signed by either of two people traveling together. The booklet *Traveler's Companion* lists travel office addresses and stolen check hotlines for each European country.

Citicorp: Call 800-645-6556 in the U.S. and Canada; in Europe, the Middle East, or Africa, call the London office at 44 171 508 7007; from elsewhere, call U.S. collect 1-813-623-1709. Commission 1-2%. Guaranteed hand-delivery of traveler's checks when a refund location is not convenient. Call 24hr.

Thomas Cook MasterCard: From the U.S., Canada, or Caribbean call 800-223-7373; from the U.K. call (0800) 622 101; from elsewhere, call the U.K. at 44 1733 318 950 and reverse the charges. Checks available in 13 currencies. Commission 2%. Thomas Cook offices cash checks commission-free.

Visa: Call 800-227-6811 in the U.S.; in the U.K. (0800) 895 078; from elsewhere, call 44 1733 318 949 and reverse the charges. Any of the above numbers can tell you the location of their nearest office.

CREDIT CARDS

In New York City, you are your credit rating. There are so many opportunities to purchase various one-of-a-kind consumer goods that you're going to want as much money at your disposal as possible. Few establishments in the city reject all of the major cards, but occasionally you'll come across a restaurant or bar who solely esteems cold, hard cash. However, credit cards are invaluable in an emergency—an unexpected hospital bill or the loss of traveler's checks—which may leave you temporarily without other resources. Other services depend completely on the issuer—some even cover car rental collision insurance. Major credit cards—**MasterCard** and **Visa** are the most welcomed—instantly extract cash advances from associated banks and ATMs throughout the United States in local currency. This can be a great way to make fast cash, but be careful when using this service—you will be charged massive interest rates if you don't pay off the bill quickly. **American Express** cards also work in some ATMs, as well as at AmEx offices and major airports. All such machines require a **Personal Identification Number (PIN).** You must ask American Express, MasterCard, or Visa to assign you one; without this PIN you will be unable to withdraw cash with your credit card. Keep in mind that MasterCard and Visa have different names elsewhere ("EuroCard" or "Access" for MasterCard and "Carte Bleue" or "Barclaycard" for Visa); some cashiers may not know this until they check their manuals.

CREDIT CARD COMPANIES. Visa (U.S. tel. 800-336-8472) and **MasterCard** (U.S. tel. 800-307-7309) are issued in cooperation with individual banks and some other organizations. **American Express** (U.S. tel. 800-843-2273) has an annual fee of up to $55, depending on the card. Cardholder services include the option of cashing personal checks at AmEx offices, a 24-hour hotline with medical and legal assistance in emergencies (tel. 800-554-2639 in the U.S.), and the American Express Travel Service. Benefits include assistance in changing airline, hotel, and car rental reservations, baggage loss and flight insurance, sending mailgrams and international cables, and holding your mail at one of the more than 1700 AmEx offices around the world. The **Discover Card** (U.S. tel. 800-347-2683; outside U.S., call 1-801-902-3100) offers small cashback bonuses on most purchases. **Diner's Club** (U.S. tel. 800-234-6377; outside U.S., call collect 1-303-799-1504) is another popular option.

CASH CARDS

Cash cards—**ATM** (Automated Teller Machine) cards—are widespread through-out New York. Depending on the system of your home bank, you will probably be able to access your personal bank account whenever you're in need of funds. Happily, the ATMs get the same wholesale exchange rate as credit cards. Despite these perks, do some research before relying too heavily on automation. There is often a limit on the amount of money you can withdraw per day, and computer network failures are not uncommon. *If your PIN is longer than four digits, be sure to ask your bank whether the first four digits will work, or whether you need a new number.*

The two major international money networks are **Cirrus** (U.S. tel. 800-4-CIRRUS or 800-424-7787) and **PLUS** (U.S. tel. 800-843-7587 for the "Voice Response Unit Locator"). To locate ATMs around the world, use www.visa.com/pd/atm or www.mastercard.com/atm. Remember, however, that ATMs that do not belong to your home bank may have a minimum charge of $1-5 with every withdrawal.

GETTING MONEY FROM HOME

AMERICAN EXPRESS. Cardholders can withdraw cash from their checking accounts at any of AmEx's major offices and many of its representatives' offices, up to $1000 every 21 days (no service charge, no interest). AmEx also offers Express Cash at any of their ATMs in New York City. Express Cash withdrawals are automatically debited from the Cardmember's checking account or line of credit. Green card holders may withdraw up to $1000 in a seven day period. There is a 2% transaction fee for each cash withdrawal, with a $2.50 minimum/$20 maximum. To enroll in Express Cash, Cardmembers may call 800-CASH-NOW (227-4669) in the U.S.; outside the U.S. call collect 1-336-668-5041.

WESTERN UNION. Travelers from Canada and the U.K. can wire money abroad through Western Union's international money transfer services. In the U.S., call 800-325-6000; in the U.K., call (0800) 833 833; in Canada, call 800-235-0000. To cable money within the U.S. using a credit card (Visa, MasterCard, Discover), call 800-CALL-CASH (225-5227). The rates for sending cash are generally $10-11 cheaper than with a credit card, and the money is usually available at the place you're sending it to within an hour.

MANAGING MONEY IN THE CITY

Large banks—including **Citibank** (627-3999, or 800-627-3999 from outside New York State), and **Chase Manhattan** (800-935-9935)—blanket the city with subsidiary branches and ATMs, and fall all over each other claiming to be the largest, nicest bank in town. Other companies specialize in providing foreign exchange services up to seven days a week, often quoting rates by phone.

American Express: Multi-task agency providing tourists with traveler's checks, gift checks, cashing services, you name it. Branches in Manhattan include: American Express Tower, 200 Vesey St. (640-2000), near the World Financial Center (open M-F 8am-6pm); Macy's Herald Square, 151 W. 34th St. (695-8075), at Seventh Ave. inside Macy's on the balcony level (open M-Sa 10am-6pm); 420 Lexington Ave. (687-3700), at 43rd St. (open M-F 8:30am-6pm); 822 Lexington Ave. (758-6510), near 63rd St. (open M-F 9am-6pm, Sa 10am-4pm).

Bank Leumi, 579 Fifth Ave. (343-5000), at 47th St. An account is not required to buy or sell foreign currencies and traveler's checks, although the Bank does charge for its services. For its customers Bank Leumi issues foreign drafts and makes payments by wire. Latest exchange rates are available by phone (343-5343). Open M-F 9am-3pm.

Cheque Point USA, 1568 Broadway (869-6281), near 47th St., with other branches throughout the city (call for locations). Wires foreign currency from major foreign cities at low rates. Open daily 8:30am-10pm.

TAXES AND TIPPING. The prices quoted throughout *Let's Go* do not include New York sales tax, which is 8.25%. Hotel tax is also 8.25%.

Remember that service is never included on a New York tab, unless you're in a large party at a restaurant (seven or more people). Tip cab drivers 15%; when tipping waiters, most New Yorkers just "double the tax"; exceptional waiters—or those who work at exceptional restaurants—are often tipped 20% of the tab. Tip hairdressers 10% and bellhops around $1 per bag. Bartenders usually expect between 50¢ and $1 per drink.

SAFETY AND SECURITY

Despite the recent dramatic decreases in crime levels throughout the city, personal safety and security should always be a consideration when visiting New York City.

IN AN EMERGENCY DIAL 911.

Police: 374-5000. Use this for inquiries that are not urgent. 24hr.

TDD Police (for the hearing impaired): 374-5911.

Fire: 999-2222.

ON FOOT

Acting like a tried-and-true New Yorker is your best defense. The New Yorker walks briskly; tourists wander absently. Be discreet with street maps and cameras; address requests for directions to police officers or store-owners. Consider covering your flagrantly yellow *Let's Go* guide with plain paper. Stay out of public bathrooms if you can; they tend to be filthy and unsafe. Instead, try department stores, hotels, or restaurants; even those with a "Restrooms for Patrons Only" sign on the door will usually allow you in if you look enough like a customer. If, despite your confident swagger, you suspect you're being followed, duck into a nearby store or restaurant. A good self-defense course will give you more concrete ways to react to different types of aggression. **Impact, Prepare and Model Mugging** can refer you to local self-defense courses in the United States (800-345-5425). Workshop (2-3 hours) start at $50 and full courses run $350-500. Both women and men are welcome.

ESSENTIALS

Rip-off artists seek the wealthy as well as the unwary, so hide your riches, especially in neighborhoods where you feel uncomfortable. Carrying a shoulder bag is better than having a backpack; in the midst of a crowd, it is easy to for pickpockets to quietly unzip backpack pockets and remove items. Grip your handbag tightly and wear the strap diagonally. If you keep the bag and the strap on one side, it can easily be pulled off—or a clever thief with scissors may cut the strap so adeptly that you don't even notice. Statistically speaking, men are mugged more often than women, and while this fact shouldn't put female travelers at ease, it should at least warn men that they are just as vulnerable.

Tourists make especially juicy prey because they tend to carry large quantities of cash—hence *Let's Go*'s advocacy of traveler's checks. Don't count your money in public or use large bills. Tuck your wallet into a less-accessible pocket and keep an extra 10 bucks or so in a more obvious one. Keep an extra bill for emergencies in an unlikely place, such as your shoe or sock. Some people even carry "mug money," in order to appease angry robbers.

Con-artists run rampant on New York's streets. Beware of hustlers working in groups. If someone spills ketchup on you, someone else may be picking your pocket. Be distrustful of sob stories that require a donation from you. (And remember that no one ever wins at three-card monte.)

Pay attention to the neighborhood that surrounds you. A district can change character dramatically in the course of a single block (e.g., 96th St. and Park Ave.). Many notoriously dangerous districts have relatively safe sections; look for children playing, women walking in the open, and other signs of an active community. If you feel uncomfortable, leave as quickly and directly as you can, but don't allow your wariness to close off whole worlds to you. Careful, persistent exploration will build confidence, strengthen your emerging New York attitude, and make your stay in the city that much more rewarding.

At night, of course, it's even more important to keep track of your environment. For example, feel free to catch after-hours jazz in Harlem or to greet dawn in a scenester bar in Alphabet City, but go in groups and exercise special caution, for these nightlife areas have sections where drug activity occurs. Late-night subways run infrequently, but stations have an "Off-Hours Waiting Area" where a crowd gathers under the watch of a subway worker. On the weekends, major subway lines may even remain crowded into the wee hours. However, if you feel uncomfortable about the neighborhood or subway, spend the extra money on a cab. (To learn the truth about the subway, as opposed to the hype you may have heard, please see p. 62.)

West Midtown and the lower part of East Midtown, both well-populated commercial centers during the day, can be unpleasant at night. Follow the main thoroughfares; try to walk on avenues rather than streets. Residential areas with doormen are relatively safe even in the twilight.

Central Park, land of frisbees and Good Humor trucks by day, becomes dangerous and forbidding after sunset. If you find yourself penniless, tokenless, and on the wrong side of the park, walk around it by Central Park South rather than north of it or through it. If you're Uptown, walk through the 85th St. Transverse near the police station. Avoid the deserted wooded areas far from the main path. If you are visiting the gay bars near the West Side docks along the Hudson River, stay away from the abandoned waterfront area. Although the bars are trendy, the surrounding areas are not safe. Bars and clubs in the Village may be a better bet. The areas around Times Square and Penn Station can be unsafe at night. (For more on safety, see **Getting Around,** p.27.)

Looking for drugs in New York City is a sure way to invite danger. Out-of-towners seeking (or on a) high are walking targets—not just for cops, but for thieves, as well. Illegal transactions are never a good idea, not just in desolate areas, but in bustling ones like Washington Square Park.

IN VEHICLES

If you take a car into the city, try not to leave valuable possessions—such as radios or luggage—in it while you're off rambling. Radios are especially tempting. In fact, many thieves in New York actually make their living solely by stealing radios. If your tape deck or radio is removable, hide it in the trunk or take it with you. If it isn't, at least conceal it under a lot of junk. Similarly, hide baggage in the trunk—although some savvy thieves can tell if a car is heavily loaded by the way it is settled on its tires. Park your vehicle in a garage or well-traveled area. Even the most committed budget traveler should rule out any consideration of sleeping in a car or van. Steering wheel "claw" locks are a popular deterrent against auto theft and cost roughly $40.

Some prefer bus travel over the subway because the driver can see you, stops are more frequent, and you stay above-ground. However, bus routes are localized and often confusing. Many New Yorkers are fluent in the subway system and rarely use buses.

Alternatively, you can treat yourself to a taxi; although more expensive, they are probably the safest mode of late night travel. A taxi's dangers are more fiscal than physical. Don't let the driver, well, take you for a ride. Cab fares can be paid only at the end of the ride. New York taxis must drop off individuals and charge a bulk fare at the end; any driver who tries to charge you per person or by location has no business doing so. Take a yellow cab with a meter and a medallion on the hood rather than an illegal "gypsy" cab, which usually isn't yellow and doesn't have a meter. The driver's name should be posted, and when you get out you can request a receipt with a phone number to call about complaints or lost articles. State your destination with authority and suggest the quickest route if you know it. If you hesitate or sound unsure, the driver will probably know that you can be taken out of your way without noticing.

When disembarking from a plane or train, be wary of unlicensed taxi dispatchers. At Grand Central or Penn Station, a person may claim to be a porter, carry your bags, hail you a cab, and then ask for a commission or share of the fare. Don't fall for this baggage-carrying scam—give directions to the driver as fast as you can and drive off in style. Official dispatchers do not need to be paid.

ALCOHOL AND DRUGS

You must be 21 years old to purchase alcoholic beverages legally in New York State. The more popular drinking spots, as well as more upscale liquor stores, are likely to card—and ruthlessly.

Possession of marijuana, cocaine, crack, heroin, methamphetamines, MDMA ("ecstasy"), hallucinogens, and most opiate derivatives (among many other chemicals) is punishable by stiff fines and imprisonment. But that doesn't stop New York's thriving **drug trade,** whose marketplaces are street corners, club bathrooms, and city parks throughout the city, most conspicuously the Village's Washington Square Park. Whiffs of marijuana smoke are commonplace throughout the city, for this drug is low on the NYPD's list of problems. Trying to acquire drugs brings increasing levels of personal danger (both from the police and sketchy dealers). Often people risk their necks buying "heroin" to discover that they've purchased powdered soap. To be blunt, attempting to purchase illegal drugs of any sort is a **very bad idea.**

If you carry **prescription drugs** when you travel, it is vital to have a copy of the prescriptions themselves readily accessible at U.S. Customs. Check with the U.S. Customs Service before your trip (see **Customs,** p. 27) for more information on questionable drugs.

HEALTH

Before you leave, check whether your insurance policy covers medical costs incurred while traveling (see **Insurance,** p. 43). Always have proof of insurance as well as policy numbers with you. If you choose to risk traveling without insurance, you may have to rely on public health organizations and clinics that treat patients without demanding proof of solvency. Call the local hotline or crisis center listed in this book under Help Lines and Medical Care. Operators at these organizations have numbers for public-health organizations and clinics that treat patients without demanding proof of solvency. If you require **emergency treatment,** call **911** or go to the emergency room of the nearest hospital.

If you have a chronic medical condition that requires **medication** on a regular basis, be sure to consult your physician before you leave. Carry copies of your prescriptions and always distribute medication or syringes among all your carry-on and checked baggage in case any of your bags is lost. If you wear glasses or **contact lenses,** carry an extra prescription and a spare pair.

Those with medical conditions (e.g., diabetes, epilepsy, heart conditions, allergies to antibiotics) may want to obtain a **Medic Alert Identification Tag.** The internationally recognized tag (first year $35, thereafter $15 annually) identifies the bearer's problem and provides the number for Medic Alert's 24-hour collect-call information number. Contact Medic Alert Foundation, 2323 Colorado Ave., Turlock, CA 95382 (800-825-3785; www.medicalert.org). The **American Diabetes Association,** 1660 Duke St., Alexandria, VA 22314 (800-232-3472), provides copies of the article "Travel and Diabetes" and a diabetic ID card that describes the carrier's diabetic status in 18 languages.

All travelers should be concerned about **Acquired Immune Deficiency Syndrome (AIDS),** which is transmitted through the bodily fluids of an infected (i.e., HIV-positive) individual. New York City has struggled with the epidemic for well over a decade now. Remember there is no assurance that someone is not infected; HIV tests show antibodies only after a six-month incubation period, and there is no way to determine through physical inspection whether or not a person carries the HIV virus. *Do not have sex without using a latex condom*, and don't share intravenous needles with anyone. The Centers for Disease Control's 24-hour **AIDS Hotline** provides AIDS information in the U.S. (800-342-2437), including how to get a test. Council's brochure, *Travel Safe: AIDS and International Travel*, is available at all Council Travel offices (see p. 51).

Although reliable **contraception** is easily obtainable in New York City, women taking birth control pills should bring enough to allow for extended stays. Condoms can be found in any pharmacy, either behind the main counter or right on the shelves. Many of the city's pharmacies, conveniently, stay open all the time.

If you are in the New York area and need an abortion, contact the **National Abortion Federation,** a professional association of abortion providers. Call its toll-free hotline for information, counseling, and the names of qualified medical professionals in the area (800-772-9100; open M-F 9:30am-5:30pm). The NAF has informational publications for individuals and health-care clinics alike. Clinics they recommend must maintain certain safety and operational standards. In New York the NAF will refer you to the Planned Parenthood clinics (274-7200).

FURTHER READING: WOMEN'S HEALTH.

Handbook for Women Travellers, Maggie and Gemma Moss. Piatkus Books ($15).

A Journey of One's Own, by Thalia Zepatos. Interesting and full of good advice, plus a specific and manageable bibliography of books and resources. Available from The Eighth Mountain Press, 624 Southeast 29th Ave., Portland, OR 97214 (503-233-3936; fax 233-0774; email soapston@teleport.com). ($17)

LOCAL HOSPITALS

Most hospitals will bill you later if you aren't covered by insurance, and most have multilingual (at least Spanish) services as well.

DOWNTOWN AND MIDTOWN

Bellevue Hospital Center, 462 First Ave. (562-4141), at 27th. St. Emergency Room 562-3015 (adult), 562-3025 (pediatric).

Beth Israel Medical Center (420-2000), First Ave., at E. 16th St. Emergency Room 420-2840.

Eastern Women's Center, 44 E. 30th St. (686-6066), between Park and Madison Ave. Gynecological exams and surgical procedures for women, by appointment only.

New York University Medical Center, 550 First Ave. (263-7300). Emergency Room, 560 First Ave. (263-5550), on E. 33rd St.

New York Infirmary Beekman Downtown Hospital, 170 William St. (312-5000) between Beekman St. and Pace University.

Walk-in Clinic, 57 E. 34th St. (252-6000), between Park and Madison Ave. Open M-Th 8am-8pm, F 8am-7pm, Sa 9am-3pm, Su 9am-2pm. Affiliated with Beth Israel Hospital.

Kaufman's Pharmacy, 557 Lexington Ave. (755-2266), at 50th St. Free delivery within 10 blocks; otherwise customer pays two-way taxi fare. Open 24hr.

Planned Parenthood (274-7200), Margaret Sanger Center at 26 Bleecker St. Clinics also in Brooklyn and the Bronx.

UPTOWN AND HARLEM

Columbia-Presbyterian Medical Center (305-2500), Fort Washington Ave. and W. 168th St. Emergency Room, 21 Audubon Ave. and 166th St. (342-4700).

Mount Sinai Medical Center (241-6500), Madison Ave. and 100th St. Emergency Room (241-7171). Affiliated with CUNY Medical School.

OUTER BOROUGHS

Bronx-Lebanon Hospital Center, 1276 Fulton Ave. (718-590-1800). 2 Emergency rooms: 1650 Fulton Ave. (718-518-5120), and Fulton Ave. (718-901-8700).

Brooklyn Hospital Center, 121 DeKalb Ave. (718-250-8000). Emergency Room on DeKalb and Ft. Greene (718-250-8075).

Interfaith Medical Center, 555 Prospect Pl., Brooklyn (718-935-7000). 2 Emergency Rooms: on St. Marks (718-935-7110) and on Atlantic Ave. (718-604-6110).

Jacobi Medical Center, 1400 Pelham Parkway South, the Bronx (718-918-5000). Emergency Room on Pelham Parkway South and Eastchester Rd. (718-918-5800).

Jamaica Hospital Medical Center, 8900 Van Wyck Expressway (718-206-6000), in Jamaica, Queens. Emergency Room also on Van Wyck (718-206-6066).

HELP LINES

AIDS Information (807-6655). Run by the Gay Men's Health Crisis. M-F 10am-9pm, Sa noon-3pm. Also walk-in information clinic M-F 11am-8pm.

AIDS Hotline, NYC Dept. of Health (447-8200 or 1-800-TALK HIV/825-5448). Open daily 9am-9pm; 24hr. recording.

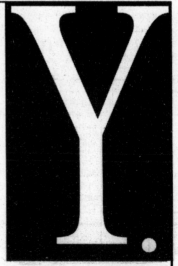

Alcohol and Substance Abuse Information Line, 800-274-2042. 24hr. info and referrals on all drug-related problems.

Crime Victims' Hotline (577-7777). 24hr. counseling and referrals for victims of crime or domestic violence.

Department of Consumer Affairs (487-4444). Handles consumer complaints. Open M-F 9:30am-4:30pm.

Help Line (532-2400). Crisis counseling and referrals. Open daily 9am-10:30pm.

Poison Control Center (764-7667). Open 24hr.

Samaritans (673-3000). Suicide prevention. Confidential counseling. Open 24hr.

Sex Crimes Report Line, New York Police Department (267-7273). 24hr. information and referrals.

Venereal Disease Information, NYC Dept. of Health (427-5120). Open M-F 8:30am-4:30pm. Provides referrals for clinics in all 5 boroughs.

Women's Health Line, New York City Department of Health (230-1111). Information and referrals concerning reproductive health. Open M-F 8am-6pm.

INSURANCE

Beware of buying unnecessary travel coverage—your regular insurance policies may well extend to many travel-related accidents. **Medical insurance** (especially university policies) often cover costs incurred abroad, but check with your provider. Your **homeowners' insurance** (or your family's coverage) often covers theft during travel. Homeowners are generally covered against loss of travel documents (passport, plane ticket, etc.) up to $500.

ISIC and **ITIC** provide basic insurance benefits, including $100 per day of in-hospital sickness for a maximum of 60 days, and $3000 of accident-related medical reimbursement (see **Youth, Student, and Teacher Identification,** p. 29). Cardholders have access to a toll-free 24-hour helpline whose multilingual staff can provide assistance in medical, legal, and financial emergencies overseas (800-626-2427 in the U.S. and Canada; elsewhere call the U.S. collect 1-713-267-2525). **Council** and **STA** offer a range of plans that can supplement your basic insurance coverage, with options covering medical treatment and hospitalization, accidents, baggage loss, and even charter flights missed due to illness. Most **American Express** cardholders receive automatic car rental (collision and theft, but not liability) insurance and travel accident coverage ($100,000 in life insurance) on flight purchases made with the card. AmEx Customer Service is 800-528-4800.

Remember that insurance companies usually require a copy of the police report for thefts, or evidence of having paid medical expenses (doctor's statements, receipts) before they will honor a claim and may have time limits on filing for reimbursement. Always carry policy numbers and proof of insurance. Check with each insurance carrier for specific restrictions and policies.

INSURANCE PROVIDERS. Council and **STA** (see p. 51 for complete listings) offer a range of plans that can supplement your basic insurance coverage. Other private insurance providers in the **U.S. and Canada** include: **Access America** (tel. 800-284-8300; fax (804) 673-1491); **Berkely Group/Carefree Travel Insurance** (tel. 800-323-3149 or (516) 294-0220; fax 294-1095; info@berkely.com; www.berkely.com); **Globalcare Travel Insurance** (800-821-2488; fax (781) 592-7720; www.globalcare-cocco.com); and **Travel Assistance International** (tel. 800-821-2828 or (202) 828-5894; fax (202) 828-5896; email wassist@aol.com; www.worldwide-assistance.com). Providers in the **U.K.** include **Campus Travel** (tel. (020) 7 730 3402) and **Columbus Travel Insurance** (tel. (020) 7 375 0011; fax 7 375 0022). In **Australia** try **CIC Insurance** (tel. (02) 9202 8000; fax 9202 8220).

KEEPING IN TOUCH

TELEPHONES

ESSENTIALS

Most of the information you will need about telephones—including area codes for the U.S., foreign country codes, and rates—is in the front of the local **white pages** telephone directory. The **yellow pages,** published at the end of the white pages or in a separate book, is used to look up the phone numbers of businesses and other services. Federal, state, and local government listings are provided in the blue pages at the back of the directory. To obtain local phone numbers or area codes of other cities, call **directory assistance** at 411. Calling "0" will get you the **operator,** who can assist you in reaching a phone number and provide you with general information. For long-distance directory assistance, dial 1-(area code)-555-1212. The operator will help you with rates or other info and give assistance in an emergency. Calls to directory assistance or the operator are free from any pay phone.

Telephone numbers in the U.S. consist of a three-digit area code, a three-digit exchange, and a four-digit number, written as 123-456-7890. Only the last seven digits are used in a **local call. Non-local calls within the area code** from which you are dialing require a "1" before the last seven digits, while **long-distance calls outside the area code** from which you are dialing require a "1" and the area code. Due to New York City's size, a call into another borough will be local in terms of price, but you'll need to dial a "1" and the area code. For example, to call the Brooklyn Museum from Manhattan, you would dial 1-718-638-5000, but it would only cost $0.25. Generally, discount rates apply after 5pm on weekdays and Sunday and economy rates every day between 11pm and 8am; on Saturday and on

Sunday until 5pm, economy rates are also in effect. Numbers beginning with area code 800 or 888 are **toll-free calls** requiring no coin deposit. Numbers beginning with 900 are **toll calls** and charge you (often exorbitantly) for whatever "service" they provide.

Pay phones are plentiful, most often stationed on street corners and in public areas. Be wary of private, more expensive pay phones—the rate they charge per call should be printed on the phone. Put your coins ($0.25 for a local call in NYC) into the slot and listen for a dial tone before dialing. If there is no answer or if you get a busy signal, you will get your money back after hanging up, unless you connect to an answering machine.

TELEPHONE CODES

TELEPHONE CODES			
Manhattan	212	Queens	718
Brooklyn	718	Staten Island	718
The Bronx	718	Hoboken	201
		Long Island	516

INTERNATIONAL CALLING CODES

You can place **international calls** from any telephone. To call direct, dial the universal international access code (011) followed by the country code, the city/area code, and the local number. Country codes and city codes may sometimes be listed with a zero in front (e.g., 033), but when dialing 011 first, drop succeeding zeros (e.g., 011-33). Rates are cheapest on calls to the United Kingdom and Ireland between 6pm and 7am (Eastern Time), to Australia between 3am and 2pm, and to New Zealand between 11pm and 10am.

COUNTRY CODES			
Australia	61	Ireland	353
Austria	43	New Zealand	64
Canada	1	South Africa	13
Italy	39	United Kingdom	44
		United States	1

Please note that all phone numbers listed without an area code are Manhattan numbers, all of which have the area code (212).

CALLING NEW YORK FROM HOME

To call direct, dial:

1. The international access code of your home country, unless calling from the U.S. or Canada. **International access codes** include: Australia 0011; Ireland 00; New Zealand 00; South Africa 09; U.K. 00.

2. 1 (USA country code).

3. The appropriate New York area code (212 or 718, depending on which part of the city you are calling; 516 for Long Island). If no area code is listed in *Let's Go*, assume 212.

4. Local number, always seven digits.

CALLING HOME FROM NEW YORK

A calling card is probably your best and cheapest bet. Calls are billed either collect or to your account. MCI WorldPhone also provides access to MCI's Traveler's Assist, which gives legal and medical advice, exchange rate information, and translation services. Other phone companies provide similar services to travelers. To **obtain a calling card** from your national telecommunications service before you leave home, contact the appropriate company below:

USA: AT&T (tel. 888-288-4685; www.att.com/traveler); **Sprint (Global One)** (tel. 800-877-4646; www.globalone.net/calling.html); or **MCI (Worldphone)** (tel. 800-444-4141; from abroad dial the country's MCI access number; www.mci.com/worldphone/english/accessnoalpha/shtml).

Canada: Bell Canada **Canada Direct** (tel. 800-565-4708; www.stentor.ca/canada_direct/eng/travel/cardform.htm).

U.K.: British Telecom **BT Direct** (tel. (800) 34 51 44; www.chargecard.bt.com/html/access.htm).

Ireland: Telecom Éireann (becomes Eircom in September 1999) **Ireland Direct** (tel. (800) 250 250; www.telecom.ie/eircom).

Australia: Telstra **Australia Direct** (tel. 13 22 00).

New Zealand: Telecom New Zealand (tel. (800) 000 000; www.telecom.xtra.co.nz/cgi).

South Africa: Telkom South Africa (tel. 09 03; www.telkom.co.za/international/sadirect/access.htm).

To call home with a calling card, contact the North American operator for your service provider by dialing:

BT Direct: tel. 800-445-5667 AT&T, 800-444-2162 MCI, 800-800-0008 Sprint.

Australia Direct: tel. 800-682-2878 AT&T, 800-937-6822 MCI, 800-676-0061 Sprint.

Telkom South Africa Direct: tel. 800-949-7027.

Wherever possible, use a calling card for international phone calls, as the long-distance rates for national phone services are often exorbitant. You can usually make direct international calls from pay phones, but if you aren't using a calling card you may need to drop your coins as quickly as your words. Where available, prepaid phone cards and occasionally major credit cards can be used for direct international calls, but they are still less cost-efficient. Although incredibly convenient, in-room hotel calls invariably include an arbitrary and sky-high surcharge (as much as $10).

The expensive alternative to dialing direct or using a calling card is using an international operator to place a **collect call.** An English-speaking operator from your home nation can be reached by dialing the appropriate service provider listed above, and they will typically place a collect call even if you don't possess one of their phone cards.

CALLING WITHIN THE U.S.

The simplest way to call within the country is to use a coin-operated phone. You can also buy prepaid phone cards, which carry a certain amount of phone time depending on the card's denomination. The time is measured in minutes or talk units (e.g. one unit/one minute), and the card usually has a toll-free access telephone number and a personal identification number (PIN). To make a phone call, you dial the access number, enter your PIN, and at the voice prompt, enter the phone number of the party you're trying to reach. A computer tells you how much time or how many units you have left on your card. Be very careful as to the type of card you buy: some operate with a PIN number you must know beforehand, while others contain the pin on the card itself.

MAIL

Individual offices of the U.S. Postal Service are usually open Monday to Friday from 9am to 5pm and sometimes on Saturday until about noon. All are closed on national holidays. **Postcards** mailed within the U.S. cost 20¢ and **letters** cost 33¢ for the first ounce and 23¢ for each additional ounce. To Canada, it costs 30¢ to mail a postcard, and 40¢ to mail a letter for the first ounce and 23¢ for each additional ounce. It costs 30¢ to mail a postcard to Mexico; a letter is 35¢ for a half-ounce, 45¢ for an ounce, and 10¢ for each additional half-ounce up to two pounds. Postcards mailed overseas cost 40¢, and letters are 50¢ for a half-ounce, 95¢ for an ounce, and 39¢ for each additional half-ounce up to 64 ounces. **Aerogrammes,** printed sheets that fold into envelopes ready to be airmailed, are sold at post offices for

45¢. Most U.S. post offices offer an **International Express Mail** service, which is the fastest way to send an item overseas. (A package under 8 ounces can be sent to most foreign destinations in 40- 72 hr. for around $13.)

The U.S. is divided into postal zones, each with a five- or nine-digit **ZIP code** particular to a region, city, or part of a city. Writing this code on letters is essential for delivery. The normal form of address is as follows:

Mary Had Alittlelamb(name)

18 Central Park West, Suite 1111 (address, apartment number)

New York, NY 10027 (city, state abbreviation, ZIP

USA (country, if mailing internationally)

RECEIVING MAIL. Depending on how neurotic your family and friends are, consider making arrangements for them to get in touch with you. Mail can be sent **General Delivery** to a city's main post office branch. Folks can send *Poste Restante* letters to you labeled like this:

Bustafa JONES (capitalize & underline last name for accurate filing)

c/o General Delivery

Main Post Office

James A. Farley Building

390 Ninth Ave.

New York City, NY 10001

The envelope should also say "Please hold until (...)," the blank filled in with a date a couple weeks after your correspondent expects you to pick up the letter. When you claim your mail, you'll have to present ID; if you don't claim a letter within two to four weeks, it will be returned to its sender.

Throughout the U.S., **American Express** acts as a mail service for cardholders if you contact them in advance. Under this free **Client Letter Service**, they will hold mail for 30 days, forward upon request, and accept telegrams. Address the envelope the same as you would for General Delivery. Some offices offer these services to non-cardholders (especially those who have purchased AmEx Travelers Cheques), but you must call ahead to make sure. For a complete explanation, call 800-528-4800.

New York's **central post office branch,** at 421 Eighth Ave. (330-2902), occupying the block between Eighth and Ninth Ave. and 33rd and 32nd St., handles General Delivery mail, which should be sent to 390 Ninth Ave. address above; you must collect your General Delivery mail at the Ninth Ave. entrance as well. The branch is open 24 hours. C.O.D.s, money orders, and passport applications are also processed at some branches. If you have questions concerning services, branch locations, or hours, call the Customer Service Assistance Center (967-8585; open M-F 8:30am-6pm). For speedier service at any time, dial 1-800-725-2161 for the 24-hour info line which provides information on branch hours and locations, postal rates, and zip codes and addresses.

EMAIL (ELECTRONIC MAIL)

If you're spending a year abroad and want to keep in touch with friends or colleagues in a college or research institution, **electronic mail (email)** is an attractive option. With a minimum of computer knowledge and a little planning, you can beam messages anywhere for no per-message charges. One option is to befriend college students as you go and ask if you can use their email accounts. Travelers who have the luxury of a laptop with them can use a **modem** to call an internet service provider. Long-distance phone cards specifically intended for such calls can defray normally high phone charges. Check with your long-distance phone provider to see if they offer this option.

If you don't have a portable cyber companion, remember: **Traveltales.com** (www.traveltales.com) provides free, web-based email for travelers and maintains a list of cybercafes, travel links, and a travelers' chat room. Other free, web-based email providers include **Hotmail** (www.hotmail.com), **Yahoo! Mail** (www.yahoo.com), **RocketMail** (www.rocketmail.com), and **USANET** (www.usa.net). Many free email providers are funded by advertising and some may require subscribers to fill out a questionnaire. You may want to consult www.**cyberia**cafe.net/cyberia/guide/ccafe.htm where you can find a list of **cybercafes** to call your own. **Public libraries** offer free internet connections; however, there is often a wait and you are limited to 15-30 minutes (see p. 74). The following are joints from which you can email your buds.

alt.coffee, 139 Ave. A (529-2233), between 8th and 9th St., across from Thompkins Sq. Park. No sign out front. Chill atmosphere: comfy couches, dim lighting, and sour bohemians. Computer time $10 per hr., $5 for 30 min. $2.50 for 15 min. Open Su 10am-1:30am, M-Th 8:30am-1:30am, F-Sa 8:30am-3am.

Canal Jean Co., 504 Broadway (226-3663), between Prince and Broome St., in SoHo. You read it right—on the second floor, Canal offers free iMac use (that means access to the internet) for an unlimited amount of time with an ID, credit card, or $20 deposit (these precious items are returned to you when you return the keyboard and mouse). Open Su-Th 10:30am-8pm, F-Sa 10:30am-9pm. Open in summer daily 9:30am-9pm.

Cybercafe, 273 Lafayette St. (334-5140; fax 334-6436), at the corner of Prince St. Exactly as one might imagine a cybercafe to look—a virtual cybercafe if you will. New light wood, metal chairs, and soothing music surround you as you ride the electronic wave and sip a cup of joe. Computer time $12.80 per hr., Mac Design Station $24 per hr. You can also fax, scan, or take computer lessons. Discounted 6 pack of 30min. Open M-F 9am-10pm, Sa 11am-10pm, Su 11am-8pm.

Kinko's, 14 locations throughout Manhattan; call 800-254-6567 for the one you want; or visit www.kinkos.com. Internet time generally $12 per hr.; 20¢ per min. Many other office related services: laminate, collate, and copy to your heart's content. Open 24hr.

READER MAIL HELPS US MAKE EVERY EDITION BETTER.
Let's Go may be reached by email at "feedback@letsgo.com".

GETTING TO NEW YORK

The Americans are justly very proud of it, and its residents passionately attached to it. A young New Yorker, who had been in Europe for more than a year, was in the same sleigh with me. "There goes the old city!" said he in his enthusiasm, as we entered Broadway; "I could almost jump out and hug a lamp-post!

—Alexander Mackay, The Western World, 1849

BY PLANE

If you're planning to fly into New York, you will have to choose not only a carrier but an airport as well. Three airports serve the New York metropolitan region. The largest, **John F. Kennedy Airport,** or JFK (718-244-4444), is 12 mi. from midtown Manhattan in southern Queens and handles most international flights. **LaGuardia Air-**

port (718-533-3400), 6 miles from midtown in northwestern Queens, is the smallest, offering domestic flights as well as hourly shuttles to and from Boston and Washington, D.C. **Newark International Airport** (973-961-6000), 12 mi. from Midtown in Newark, NJ, offers both domestic and international flights at budget fares often not available at the other airports (though getting to and from Newark can be expensive). Bi-monthly free *Airport Guides* by the Port Authority have comprehensive information on all flights arriving and departing from New York. Fax your request to Airport Customer Services (fax 435-4838; telephone 435-4878).

DETAILS AND TIPS

Timing: Airfares to the U.S. peak between mid-June and early September; holidays are also expensive periods in which to travel. Midweek (M-Th morning) round-trip flights run $40-50 cheaper than weekend flights, but the latter are generally less crowded and more likely to permit frequent-flier upgrades. Return-date flexibility is usually not an option for the budget traveler; traveling with an "open return" ticket can be pricier than fixing a return date when buying the ticket and paying later to change it.

Route: Round-trip flights are by far the cheapest; "open-jaw" (arriving in and departing from different cities) and round-the-world, or RTW, flights are pricier but reasonable alternatives. Patching one-way flights together is the least economical way to travel. Flights between capital cities or regional hubs will offer the most competitive fares.

Boarding: Whenever flying internationally, pick up tickets for international flights well in advance of the departure date, and confirm by phone within 72 hours of departure. Most airlines require that passengers arrive at the airport at least two hours before departure. One carry-on item and two pieces of checked baggage is the norm for non-courier flights. Consult the airline for weight allowances.

BUDGET AND STUDENT TRAVEL AGENCIES

A knowledgeable agent specializing in flights to the U.S. can make your life easy and help you save, too, but agents may not spend the time to find you the lowest possible fare—they get paid on commission. Students and under-26ers holding **ISIC and IYTC cards** (see **Identification**, p. 28), respectively, qualify for big discounts from student travel agencies. Most flights from budget agencies are on major airlines, but in peak season some may sell seats on less reliable chartered aircraft.

Campus/Usit Youth and Student Travel, 52 Grosvenor Gardens, **London** SW1W 0AG (in London call (020) 730 34 02, in North America call 44 171 730 21 01, worldwide call 44 171 730 81 11; www.campustravel.co.uk). Other offices include: 19-21 Aston Quay, O'Connell Bridge, **Dublin** 2 (tel. (01) 677-8117; fax 679-8833); New York Student Center, 895 Amsterdam Ave., **New York,** NY, 10025 (tel. 212-663-5435; email usitny@aol.com). Additional offices in Cork, Galway, Limerick, Waterford, Coleraine, Derry, Belfast, and Greece.

Council Travel (www.counciltravel.com). U.S. offices include: Emory Village, 1561 N. Decatur Rd., **Atlanta,** GA 30307 (tel. 404-377-9997); 273 Newbury St., **Boston,** MA 02116 (tel. 617-266-1926); 1160 N. State St., **Chicago,** IL 60610 (tel. 312-951-0585); 10904 Lindbrook Dr., **Los Angeles,** CA 90024 (tel. 310-208-3551); 205 E. 42nd St., **New York,** NY 10017 (tel. 212-822-2700); 530 Bush St., **San Francisco,** CA 94108 (tel. 415-421-3473); 1314 NE 43rd St. #210, **Seattle,** WA 98105 (tel. 206-632-2448); 3300 M St. NW, **Washington, D.C.** 20007 (tel. 202-337-6464). **For U.S. cities not listed,** call 800-2-COUNCIL (226-8624). Also 28A Poland St. (Oxford Circus), **London,** W1V 3DB (tel. (020) 7 287 3337), **Paris** (144 41 89 89), and **Munich** (089 39 50 22).

CTS Travel, 44 Goodge St., W1 (tel. (020) 7 636 00 31; fax 637 53 28; email ctsinfo@ctstravel.com.uk).

STA Travel, 6560 Scottsdale Rd. #F100, Scottsdale, AZ 85253 (tel. 800-777-0112 fax 602-922-0793; www.sta-travel.com). A student and youth travel organization with over 150 offices worldwide. Ticket booking, travel insurance, railpasses, and more. U.S. offices include: 297 Newbury Street, **Boston,** MA 02115 (tel. 617-266-6014); 429 S. Dearborn St., **Chicago,** IL 60605 (tel. 312-786-9050); 7202 Melrose Ave., **Los Ange-**

les, CA 90046 (tel. 323-934-8722); 10 Downing St., **New York,** NY 10014 (tel. 212-627-3111); 4341 University Way NE, **Seattle,** WA 98105 (tel. 206-633-5000); 2401 Pennsylvania Ave., Ste. G, **Washington, D.C.** 20037 (tel. 202-887-0912); 51 Grant Ave., **San Francisco,** CA 94108 (tel. 415-391-8407). In the U.K., 6 Wrights Ln., **London** W8 6TA (tel. (020) 7 938 47 11 for North American travel). In New Zealand, 10 High St., **Auckland** (tel. (09) 309 04 58). In Australia, 222 Faraday St., **Melbourne** VIC 3053 (tel. (03) 9349 2411).

Travel CUTS (Canadian Universities Travel Services Limited), 187 College St., Toronto, Ont. M5T 1P7 (tel. 416-979-2406; fax 979-8167; www.travelcuts.com). 40 offices across Canada. Also in the U.K., 295-A Regent St., **London** W1R 7YA (tel. (020) 7 255 19 44).

Other organizations that specialize in finding cheap fares include:

Cheap Tickets (tel. 800-377-1000) flies worldwide to and from the U.S.

Travel Avenue (tel. 800-333-3335) rebates commercial fares to or from the U.S. and offers low fares for flights anywhere in the world. They also offer package deals, which include car rental and hotel reservations, to many destinations.

COMMERCIAL AIRLINES

The commercial airlines' lowest regular offer is the **APEX** (Advance Purchase Excursion) fare, which provides confirmed reservations and allows "open-jaw" tickets. Generally, reservations must be made 7 to 21 days in advance, with 7- to 14-day minimum and up to 90-day maximum-stay limits, and hefty cancellation and change penalties (fees rise in summer). Book peak-season APEX fares early, since by May you will have a hard time getting the departure date you want.

Although APEX fares are probably not the cheapest possible fares, they will give you a sense of the average commercial price, from which to measure other bargains. Specials advertised in newspapers may be cheaper but have more restrictions and fewer available seats. Popular carriers include:

American, (800-433-7300; www.americanair.com). P.O. Box 619612, Dallas-Ft. Worth International Airport, TX 75261. Offers "College SAAvers" fares for full-time college students.

Continental, (800-525-0280; www.flycontinental.com). Great deals for senior citizens in the "Freedom Club;" call 800-441-1135.

Delta, (800-2414141; www.delta-air.com)

TWA, (800-221-2000; www.twa.com). Customer Relations, 1415 Olive St., St. Louis, MO 63103. Offers last minute "TransWorld specials" via e-mail.

United, (800-241-6522; www.ual.com). P.O. Box 66100, Chicago, IL 60666. Major airline that offers good frequent flyer plans.USAir, (800-428-4322; www.usair.com). Office of Consumer Affairs, P.O. Box 1501, Winston-Salem, NC 27102-1501.Other cheap Alternatives

AIR COURIER FLIGHTS

Couriers help transport cargo on international flights by guaranteeing delivery of the baggage claim slips from the company to a representative overseas. Generally, couriers must travel light (carryons only) and deal with complex restrictions on their flight. Most flights are round-trip only with short fixed-length stays (usually one week) and a limit of a single ticket per issue. Most of these flights also operate only out of the biggest cities, like New York. Generally, you must be over 21 (in some cases 18), have a valid passport, and procure your own visa, if necessary. Groups such as the **Air Courier Association** (tel. 800-282-1202; www.aircourier.org) and the **International Association of Air Travel Couriers,** 220 South Dixie Hwy., P.O. Box 1349, Lake Worth, FL 33460 (tel. 561-582-8320; email iaatc@courier.org; www.courier.org) provide their members with lists of opportunities and courier brokers worldwide for an annual fee. For more information, consult *Air Courier Bargains* by Kelly Monaghan (The Intrepid Traveler, $15) or the *Courier Air Travel Handbook* by Mark Field (Perpetual Press, $10).

CHARTER FLIGHTS

Charters are flights a tour operator contracts with an airline to fly extra loads of passengers during peak season. Charters can sometimes be cheaper than flights on scheduled airlines, some operate nonstop, and restrictions on minimum advance-purchase and minimum stay are more lenient. However, charter flights fly less frequently than major airlines, make refunds particularly difficult, and are almost always fully booked. Schedules and itineraries may also change or be cancelled at the last moment (as late as 48 hours before the trip, and without a full refund), and check-in, boarding, and baggage claim are often much slower. As always, pay with a credit card if you can, and consider traveler's insurance against trip interruption.

Discount clubs and **fare brokers** offer members savings on last-minute charter and tour deals. Study their contracts closely; you don't want to end up with an overnight layover.

STANDBY FLIGHTS

To travel standby, you will need considerable flexibility in the dates and cities of your arrival and departure. Companies that specialize in standby flights don't sell tickets but rather the promise that you will get to your destination (or near your destination) within a certain window of time (anywhere from 1-5 days). You may only receive a monetary refund if all available flights which depart within your date-range from the specified region are full, but future travel credit is always available.

Carefully read agreements with any company offering standby flights, as tricky fine print can leave you in the lurch. To check on a company's service record, call the **Better Business Bureau of New York City** (tel. 212-533-6200). It is difficult to receive refunds, and clients' vouchers will not be honored when an airline fails to receive payment in time.

Airhitch, 2641 Broadway, 3rd fl., New York, NY 10025 (tel. 800-326-2009 or 212-864-2000; fax 864-5489; www.airhitch.org) and Los Angeles, CA (tel. 310-726-5000). In Europe, the flagship office is in Paris (tel. 147 00 16 30) and the other one is in Amsterdam (tel. 312 06 26 32 20). Travel within the USA and Europe is possible, with rates ranging from $79-$139.

AirTech.Com, 588 Broadway #204, New York, NY 10012 (tel. 212-219-7000, fax 219-0066; email fly@airtech.com; www.airtech.com). AirTech.Com arranges courier flights and regular confirmed-reserved flights at discount rates.

TICKET CONSOLIDATORS

Ticket consolidators, or **"bucket shops,"** buy unsold tickets in bulk from commercial airlines and sell them at discounted rates. The best place to look is in the Sunday travel section of any major newspaper, where many bucket shops place tiny ads. Call quickly, as availability is typically extremely limited. Not all bucket shops are reliable establishments, so insist on a receipt that gives full details of restrictions, refunds, and tickets, and pay by credit card. For more information, check the website **Consolidators FAQ** (www.travel-library.com/air-travel/consolidators.html).

TO AND FROM THE AIRPORTS

Travel between each of the airports and New York City without a car of your own becomes simpler as cost increases; you pay in time or money. Though **public transportation** is generally the cheapest option, it can be time-consuming and usually involves changing mid-route from a bus to a subway or train (especially tricky if

> ### FURTHER READING: BY PLANE.
> *Consolidators: Air Travel's Bargain Basement,* Kelly Monaghan Intrepid Traveler ($8).
> *The Worldwide Guide to Cheap Airfare,* Michael McColl. Insider Publications ($15).
> *Discount Airfares: The Insider's Guide,* George Hobart. Priceless Publications ($14).
> *The Official Airline Guide,* an expensive tome available at many libraries, has flight schedules, fares, and reservation numbers.
> *Travelocity* (www.travelocity.com). A searchable online database of published airfares. Online reservations.
> *Air Traveler's Handbook* (www.cs.cmu.edu/afs/cs.cmu.edu/user/mkant/Public/Travel/airfare.html).
> *TravelHUB* (www.travelhub.com). A directory of travel agents that includes a searchable database of fares from over 500 consolidators.

you're loaded with baggage). **Private bus companies** will charge slightly more, but will take you directly from the airport to any one of many Manhattan destinations: Grand Central Station (42nd St. and Park Ave.), the Port Authority Bus Terminal (41st St. and Eighth Ave.), or the World Trade Center (1 West St.), along with several prominent hotels. Private companies run frequently and according to a set schedule (see individual listings below). Some services peter out or vanish entirely between midnight and 6am. If you want to set your own destination and schedule, and if you're willing to pay, you can "hail" (i.e., flag down) one of New York's infamous **yellow cabs.** Heavy traffic makes the trip more expensive: traveling during rush hour (7:30-10am and 4-7:30pm) can devastate your wallet and your patience. You are responsible for paying **bridge** and **tunnel tolls.**

For the most up-to-date guide to reaching the airports, call **AirRide** (800-247-7433), the Port Authority's airport travel hotline. It's an automated interactive system offering very detailed information on how to reach any of the three airports by car, public transportation, or private bus line. Also try the **MTA/New York City Transit Center** (718-330-1234) for similar information. Finally, if you make lodging reservations ahead of time, be sure to ask about limousine services—some hostels offer transportation from the airports for reasonable fares.

JFK AIRPORT

The cheapest route into the city is on the **subway.** Catch a free brown-and-white JFK long-term parking lot bus from any airport terminal (every 10-15min.) to the **Howard Beach-JFK Airport subway station.** You can take the **A train** from there to the city ($1.50, exact change only; 1hr.); the A stops several times in lower Manhattan, as well as at Washington Sq., 34th St.-Penn Station, 42nd St.-Port Authority, and 59th St.-Columbus Circle. Heading from Manhattan to JFK, take the Far Rockaway A train. Or you can take one of the local **buses** (Q10 or Q3; $1.50, coins, tokens, Metro cards only) from the airport into Queens. The Q10 bus heads to Lefferts Blvd., where it connects with the A train, and to Kew Gardens, where it connects with the E and F trains. You can then transfer to the subway into Manhattan ($1.50). The Q3 connects JFK with the F and R train at 179th St./Jamaica and 169th St. Ask the driver where to get off, and be sure you know which subway line you want. Although these routes are safer during the day, nighttime travelers should check with the information desk to find the safest way into the city.

Those willing to pay a little more can take the **New York Airport Service** (1-800-769-7004 or 718-706-9658), a private line that runs between JFK (also LaGuardia, see below), Grand Central Station, Penn Station and Port Authority, and various midtown hotels; the trip is approximately one hour. Before 1pm buses leave every 30min.; after 1pm they leave every 15min. *(From Grand Central daily 5am-10pm. From Penn Station daily 7:40am-8:10pm. From Port Authority daily 5:50am-9:10pm. $13; roundtrip only available at airports and Grand Central $23. Student discount only available at Grand Central*

$6.) The **Gray Line Air Shuttle** (800-451-0455) will drop you off (ask ahead—it may pick you up too) at any hotel in Manhattan between 23rd and 125th St. ($14). Inquire at a Ground Transportation Center in JFK. A **taxi** from JFK to Manhattan costs $30 (plus tolls and tip, of course).

If you are heading to JFK from Manhattan, the **Gray Line Express** (800-451-0455), has pick-up points at major hotels from 23rd to 63rd St. Pickups are every hour from 5am to 7pm daily. The trip to JFK costs $19 (as well as the trip to the city). There is also a **JFK Flyer** bus service available from certain points in Long Island to JFK airport ($1.50; 516-766-6722).

LAGUARDIA AIRPORT

The journey to LaGuardia takes about half as long as the trek from JFK. If you have extra time and light luggage when leaving the airport, take the **M60 bus** (daily 4:15am-12:55am; $1.50). The M60 connects to the following subways in Manhattan: the #1 or 9 at 116th St. and Broadway, the #2 or 3 at 125th St. and Lenox Ave., and the #4, 5, or 6 at 125th St. and Lexington Ave. In Queens the M60 connects to the N train at Astoria Blvd. and 31st St. Alternatively, you can take the MTA **Q33 bus** or the **Q47 bus** ($1.50) to the 74th St./Broadway-Roosevelt Ave./Jackson Hts. subway stop in Queens. From there, transfer to the #7, E, F, G, or R train into Manhattan ($1.50). You can catch the Q33 bus from the lower level of the terminal. Allow at least 1½ hours travel time. Be especially careful traveling these routes at night. The **New York Airport Service** also runs to and from LaGuardia every 30 minutes before 1pm and every 15 minutes after 1pm. stopping at a number of locations in Manhattan (see JFK airport for times and locations; 30-45min.; $10)

If you can't afford a cab but you still crave door-to-door service, the **Gray Line Air Shuttle** (800-451-0455) also provides service to LaGuardia between the hotels from 23rd to 63rd St. (5am-7pm; $16). A **taxi** to Manhattan costs $16-$26, a sum not all that unreasonable if split between two or more people.

NEWARK AIRPORT

The trip from New Jersey's Newark Airport takes about as long as from JFK. For the same fare, the Olympia Trails Coach (212-964-6233) travels between the airport and Grand Central, Penn Station, Port Authority, or the World Trade Center (every 30min. generally daily 5am-11pm with extended service from certain pick-up points; 25min.-1hr. travel time; $10; tickets may be purchased on the bus). New Jersey Transit Authority (NJTA) (973-762-5100) runs an **Air Link bus #302** ($4) between the airport and Newark's Penn Station (not Manhattan's). From there you can take bus #108 ($3.25, exact change) or the local #62 ($1.55, exact change) into New York City. **PATH trains** ($1) also run from Newark Penn Station into Manhattan, stopping at the World Trade Center, Christopher St., Sixth Avenue, 9th St., 14th St., 23rd St. and 33rd St. Expect to travel 15 to 30 minutes. For PATH information, call 800-234-7284. A **taxi** should run you about $45, but be sure to negotiate the price with the driver before departing.

Getting in and out of New York can be less expensive and more scenic by bus or train than by plane. The hub of the Northeast bus network, New York's **Port Authority Terminal,** 41st St. and Eighth Avenue (435-7000; subway: A, C, E to 42nd St.-Port Authority), is a tremendous modern facility with labyrinthine bus terminals. The Port Authority has good information and security services, but the surrounding neighborhood is somewhat deserted at night, when it pays to be wary of pickpockets and to call a cab. Exercise caution in the terminal's bathrooms.

Greyhound (800-231-2222; www.greyhound.com) operates the largest number of lines, departing to New York from Boston (4½hr.; $34, $60 round-trip), Philadelphia (2hr.; $19, $32 round-trip), Washington, D.C. (4½hr.; $34, $60 round-trip), and Montreal (8hr.; $69, $74 round-trip). The fares listed require no advance purchase, but significant discounts off these fares can be had by purchasing tickets 3, 7, 14, or 21 days in advance. Some buses to these cities take longer (up to 2hr. more) due to additional stops or time of travel. A number of **discounts** are available on Greyhound's standard-fare tickets: students ride for 15% off with the Stu-

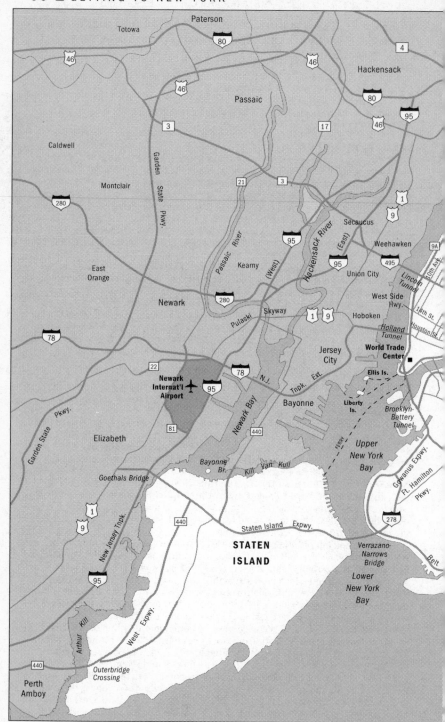

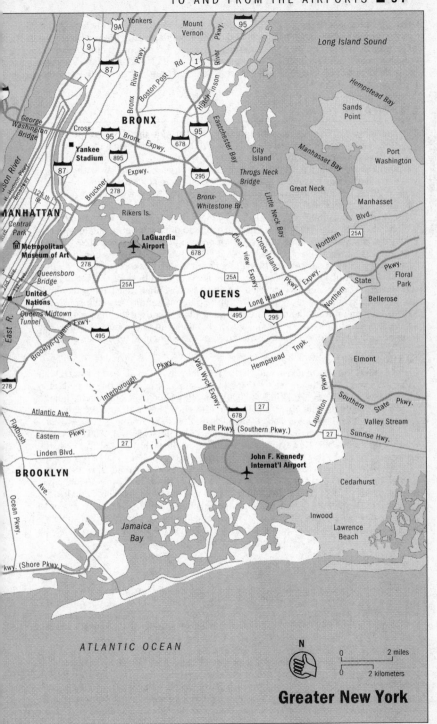

Long Island Sound

Yonkers

Mount
Vernon

95

9A

9

87

Hempstead Bay

Sands
Point

Port
Washington

George
Washington
Bridge

Cross

BRONX

95

678

95

Yankee
Stadium

895

87

Bruckner

278

Expwy.

Bronx Expwy.

Expwy.

295

Little Neck Bay

Bronx-
Whitestone Br.

Throgs Neck
Bridge

City
Island

Eastchester Bay

Manhasset Bay

Great Neck

Manhasset

Blvd.

25A

Rikers Is.

MANHATTAN

Central
Park

Metropolitan
Museum of Art

278

LaGuardia
Airport

678

Clear view Expwy.

Cross Island Pkwy.

Northern

State

Pkwy.

Floral
Park

Bellerose

Queensboro
Bridge

25A

QUEENS

25A

Long Island

495

Northern

United
Nations

Queens Midtown
Tunnel

Brooklyn-Queens Expwy.

495

295

Elmont

Pkwy.

Interborough

Hempstead Tnpk.

Van Wyck Expwy.

Laurelton Pkwy.

Southern

State

Pkwy.

Atlantic Ave.

678

27

Belt Pkwy. (Southern Pkwy.)

27

Valley Stream

Sunrise Hwy.

Eastern

Pkwy.

27

Linden Blvd.

BROOKLYN

Ave.

John F. Kennedy
Internat'l Airport

Cedarhurst

Ocean Pkwy.

Flatbush

Inwood

Lawrence
Beach

Jamaica
Bay

kwy. (Shore Pkwy.)

ATLANTIC OCEAN

N

0   2 miles

0   2 kilometers

Greater New York

dent Advantage Card (800-962-6875 to purchase), senior citizens ride for 10% off, children under 11 ride for half-fare, and children under 2 ride for free in the lap of an adult. A traveler with a physical disability may bring along a companion for free, and active and retired U.S. military personnel and National Guard Reserves (and their spouses and dependents) may take a round-trip between any two points in the U.S. for $169.

BY TRAIN

The train is one of the most comfortable ways to travel in the U.S. You can stretch your legs, buy overpriced victuals, and shut out the sun to sleep in a reclining chair (avoid paying unnecessarily for a roomette or bedroom). Travel light; not all stations will check baggage and not all trains carry large amounts. As with airlines, you can save money by purchasing your tickets as far in advance as possible. Keep in mind that discounted air travel, particularly for longer distances, may be cheaper than train travel.

For **Amtrak,** call (800) USA-RAIL (872-7245); or check out www.amtrak.com, which lists up-to-date schedules, fares, arrival and departure info, and allows reservations. **Discounts on full rail fares:** senior citizens 15% off; students 15% off with a Student Advantage Card call 800-96-AMTRAK (962-6875) to purchase a card; $20); travelers with disabilities 15% off; children under 15 accompanied by a parent 50% off; children under age two, free; current members of the U.S. armed forces, active-duty veterans, and their dependents, 25% off. Circle trips and holiday packages can also save money. Call for up-to-date info and reservations. The **Air-Rail Travel Plan** on Amtrak and United Airlines allow you to travel in one direction by train and return by plane, or to fly to a distant point and return by train. The train portion of the journey can last up to 30 days and include up to 3 stopovers.

TRAIN STATIONS

Grand Central Station, 42nd St. and Park Ave. (subway: #4, 5, 6, 7 or S to 42nd St.-Grand Central), handles more than 550 trains a day. It handles the three **Metro-North** (800-638-7646; in NYC 212-532-4900) commuter lines to Connecticut and the New York suburbs (the Hudson, Harlem, and New Haven lines). Longer train routes run out of the smaller **Penn Station,** 33rd St. and Eighth Avenue (subway: #1, 2, 3, 9, or A, C, E to 34th St.-Penn Station); the major line is **Amtrak** (800-872-7245), which serves upstate New York and most major cities in the U.S. and Canada, especially those in the Northeast (to Washington, D.C., 3¾hr., $61-76 one-way, $122-152 round-trip; Boston 4-5hr., $44-53 one-way, $88-106 round-trip). Penn Station also handles the **Long Island Railroad (LIRR)** (718-217-5477 or 516-822-5477; fares range $3-14 with service extending to the eastern tip of the island and including Belmont and Shea Stadium; see **Daytripping,** p. 314) and the **NJ Transit** service to New Jersey (973-762-5100; in NJ 800-772-2222). **PATH** trains (800-234-7284) operate between Newark, NJ and various locations in downtown New York, including the World Trade Center and 33rd St. and 6th Ave., near Penn Station.

BY CAR

There are several major approaches to driving into New York. From New Jersey there are three choices, each costing $4 a pop (you can pay by credit card at E-Z Pass booths). The **Holland Tunnel** connects to lower Manhattan, exiting into the SoHo area. From the NJ Turnpike you'll probably end up at the **Lincoln Tunnel,** which exits in midtown in the West 40s. The third and arguably easiest option is the **George Washington Bridge,** which crosses the Hudson River into northern Manhattan, offering access to either Harlem River Drive or the West Side Highway. If you are coming from New England or Connecticut on I-95, follow signs for the **Tri-Boro Bridge.** From there get onto the FDR Drive, which runs along the east side of Manhattan and exits onto city streets every 10 blocks or so. Or look for the Willis Avenue Bridge Exit on I-95 to avoid the toll, and enter Manhattan farther north on

FDR Drive. The **speed limit** in New York State, as in most other states, is 55 miles per hour. For information on renting a car, see **Getting Around,** below.

HITCHHIKING

Let's Go strongly discourages hitchhiking as a means of transport. Hitching is extremely dangerous in the New York area, *especially* for women. Hitchhiking is illegal in New York State, and the law is usually strictly enforced within New York City. If someone you don't know offers you a free ride, don't take it.

GETTING AROUND

To equip yourself for the New York City navigation experience, you will need to know how to use the **public transportation system.** Get a free subway or bus map from station token booths or the visitors bureau, which also has a free street map (see **Tourist Information,** p. 74). For a more detailed program of travel, find a Manhattan Yellow Pages, which has detailed subway, PATH, and bus maps. Since bus routes vary for each of the boroughs, you may want to get other bus maps; send a self-addressed, stamped envelope to **NYC Transit Customer Assistance,** 370 Jay St., Room 712K, Brooklyn, NY 11201 (718-330-3322). Then wait about a month. The **NYC Transit Information Bureau** (718-330-1234) dispenses subway and bus info (open daily 6am-9pm).

ORIENTATION

Contrary to popular belief, **five boroughs** compose NYC: Brooklyn, the Bronx, Queens, Staten Island, and Manhattan. Pervading Manhattan-centrism has deep historical roots. The island's original inhabitants, the Algonquin, called it "Man-a-hat-ta" or "Heavenly Land." The British were the first to call the island "New York," after James, Duke of York, the brother of Charles II. In 1898, the other four boroughs finally joined the city's government. Therefore, each of the other boroughs really does have a right to share the name.

Flanked on the east by the "East River" (actually a strait) and on the west by the Hudson River, Manhattan is a sliver of an island, measuring only 13 mi. long and 2½ mi. wide. Sizeable Queens and Brooklyn look onto their smallish neighbor from the other side of the East River, and pudgy, self-reliant Staten Island averts its eyes in the south. **Queens,** the city's largest and most ethnically diverse borough, is dotted with light industry, airports, and stadiums. **Brooklyn,** the city's most populous borough (with 2.3 million residents), is even older than Manhattan. Founded by the Dutch in 1600, the borough today cradles several diverse residential neighborhoods, from wealthy black-owned brownstones to struggling Russian immigrant communities. **Staten Island** has remained a staunchly residential borough, similar to the suburban bedroom communities of eastern Long Island. North of Manhattan sits the **Bronx,** the only borough connected by land to the rest of the U.S. Supposedly, the whole borough was once a Dutch estate owned by Jonas Bronck; an excursion to his family's farm was referred to as a visit to "the Bron-cks'." Today's Bronx encompasses both the genteel suburb of Riverdale and the economically depressed South Bronx.

DISTRICTS OF MANHATTAN

Despite the unending urban chaos within its borders, Manhattan can be broken down into manageable neighborhoods, each with a history and personality of its own. As a result of city zoning ordinances, quirks of history, and random forces of urban evolution, boundaries between these neighborhoods can often be abrupt.

The city began at the southern tip of Manhattan, in the area around **Battery Park** where the first Dutch settlers made their homes. The nearby harbor, now jazzed up with the touristy **South Street Seaport,** provided the growing city with the commercial opportunities that helped it succeed. Historic Manhattan, however, lies in the shadows of the imposing financial buildings around **Wall Street** and the civic offices around **City Hall.** A bit farther north, neighborhoods rich in the ethnic culture brought by late 19th-century immigrants rub elbows below Houston Street—**Little Italy, Chinatown,** and the southern blocks of the **Lower East Side.** Formerly home to Russian Jews, Delancey and Elizabeth Streets now offer pasta and silks. To the west lies the fashionable **TriBeCa** ("Triangle Below Canal Street"). **SoHo** ("South of Houston"), a former warehouse district west of Little Italy, has transformed into a pocket of gleaming art galleries, pricey boutiques, and people straining to be beautiful. Above SoHo huddles **Greenwich Village,** whose lower buildings and jumbled streets have for decades been home to intense political and artistic activity. To its east the **East Village** and **Alphabet City** are bohemian and anarcho-punk hangouts, with crowded streets and an active (though sometimes seedy) nightlife.

A few blocks north of Greenwich Village, stretching across the west teens and twenties, lies **Chelsea,** rapidly gentrifying into a playground for young gay professionals and dotted with galleries driven out by SoHo's high rents. East of Chelsea, presiding over the East River, is **Gramercy Park,** a pastoral collection of elegant brownstones. **Midtown Manhattan** towers from 34th to 59th St., where skyscrapers support over a million offices and department stores outfit New York. The nearby **Theater District** attempts to entertain the world, or at least people who like musicals. Adjacent **Times Square** pulses in neon as the city's energy center, although Disney's invasion adds a cosmetic surreality that is pushing the sordid Times Square sex industry westward.

North of Midtown, **Central Park** slices Manhattan into East and West. On the **Upper West Side,** the gracious residences of Central Park West neighbor the chic boutiques and sidewalk cafes of Columbus Avenue and the hubbub of Broadway. On the **Upper East Side,** the museums scattered among the elegant apartments of Fifth and Park Avenue create an even more elegant, old-money atmosphere.

Above 97th St., the Upper East Side's opulence ends with a whimper where commuter trains emerge from the tunnel and the *barrio* of Spanish Harlem begins. Above 110th St. on the Upper West Side sits majestic **Columbia University,** an urban member of the Ivy League. The communities of **Harlem, East Harlem,** and **Morningside Heights** produced the Harlem Renaissance of black artists and writers in the 1920s and the revolutionary Black Power movement of the 1960s. Although torn by crime, **Washington Heights,** just north of St. Nicholas Park, is nevertheless somewhat safer and more attractive than much of Harlem and is home to Fort Tryon Park, the Met's Medieval Cloisters museum, and a quiet community of Old and New World immigrants. Manhattan ends in a rural patch of wooded land with caves inhabited at various times by the Algonquin and homeless New Yorkers.

MANHATTAN'S STREET PLAN

The city of right angles and tough, damaged people.

—Pete Hamill

Most of Manhattan's street plan was the result of an organized expansion scheme adopted in 1811—from then on, the major part of the city grew in straight lines and at right angles. Above 14th St., the streets form a grid that a novice can quickly master. In the older areas of lower Manhattan, though, the streets are named rather than numbered. Here, the orderly grid of the northern section dissolves into a charming but confusing tangle of old, narrow streets. Bring a map; even long-time neighborhood residents may have trouble directing you to an address.

Above Washington Square, avenues run north-south and streets run east-west. Avenue numbers increase from east to west, and street numbers increase from south to north. Traffic flows east on most even-numbered streets and west on most odd-numbered ones. Two-way traffic flows on the wider streets—Canal, Houston, 14th, 23rd, 34th, 42nd, 57th, 72nd, 79th, 86th, 96th, 110th, 116th, 125th,

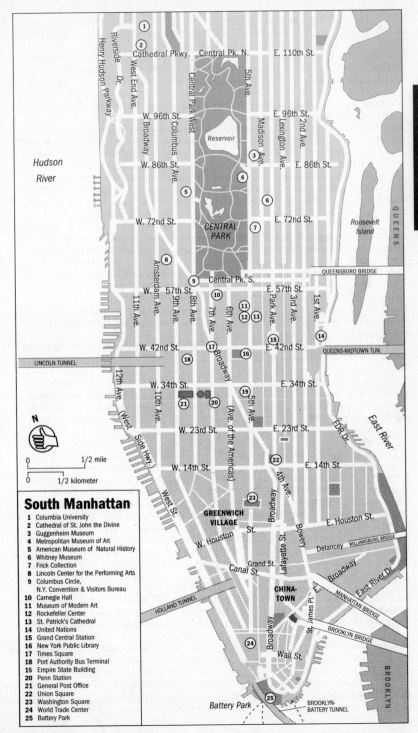

ESSENTIALS

Hudson
River

QUEENS

Roosevelt
Island

East River

BROOKLYN

LINCOLN TUNNEL

QUEENSBORO BRIDGE

QUEENS-MIDTOWN TUN.

WILLIAMSBURG BRIDGE

MANHATTAN BRIDGE

BROOKLYN BRIDGE

HOLLAND TUNNEL

BROOKLYN-
BATTERY TUNNEL

Battery Park

CHINA-
TOWN

GREENWICH
VILLAGE

N

0   1/2 mile

0   1/2 kilometer

South Manhattan

1 Columbia University
2 Cathedral of St. John the Divine
3 Guggenheim Museum
4 Metropolitan Museum of Art
5 American Museum of Natural History
6 Whitney Museum
7 Frick Collection
8 Lincoln Center for the Performing Arts
9 Columbus Circle,
   N.Y. Convention & Visitors Bureau
10 Carnegie Hall
11 Museum of Modern Art
12 Rockefeller Center
13 St. Patrick's Cathedral
14 United Nations
15 Grand Central Station
16 New York Public Library
17 Times Square
18 Port Authority Bus Terminal
19 Empire State Building
20 Penn Station
21 General Post Office
22 Union Square
23 Washington Square
24 World Trade Center
25 Battery Park

145th, and 155th. Four **transverses** cross Central Park: 65/66th St., 79th/81st St., 85/86th and 96/97th St. Most avenues are **one-way.** Tenth, Amsterdam, Hudson, Eighth, Sixth, Madison, Fourth, Third, and First Ave. are northbound. Ninth, Columbus, Broadway below 59th Street, Seventh, Fifth, Lexington, and Second Avenues are southbound. Some avenues allow **two-way traffic:** York, Park, Central Park West, Broadway above 59th St., Third below 24th St., West End, and Riverside Dr.

New York's east/west division refers to an address's location in relation to the two borders of Central Park—**Fifth Avenue** along the east side and **Central Park West** along the west. Below 59th St. (where the park ends), the West Side begins at Fifth Ave. Looking for adjectives to describe where you are relative to something else? Uptown is anywhere north of you, downtown is south, and crosstown means to the east or the west. Want to use nouns? Uptown (above 59th St.) is the area north of Midtown. Downtown (below 34th St.) is the area south of Midtown.

Now for the discrepancies in the system. You may hear **Sixth Avenue** referred to by its new name, **Avenue of the Americas,** though using this moniker is a surefire way to be identified as an out-of-towner. Lexington, Park, and Madison Ave. lie *between* Third and Fifth Ave., where there is no Fourth Ave. On the Lower East Side, there are several avenues east of First Avenue that are lettered rather than numbered: **Avenues A, B, C,** and **D.** Finally, above 59th St. on the West Side, Eighth Avenue becomes Central Park West, Ninth Avenue becomes Columbus Avenue, Tenth Avenue becomes Amsterdam Avenue, and Eleventh Avenue becomes West End Avenue. **Broadway,** which follows an old Algonquin trail, cavalierly defies the rectangular pattern and cuts diagonally across the island, veering west of Fifth Ave. above 23rd St. and east of Fifth Ave. below 23rd St.

Tracking down an address in Manhattan is easy. When given the street number of an address (e.g. #250 E. 52nd St.), find the avenue closest to the address by thinking of Fifth Ave. as point zero on the given street. Address numbers increase as you move east or west of Fifth Ave., in stages of 100. On the East Side, address numbers are 1 at Fifth Ave., 100 at Park Ave., 200 at Third Ave., 300 at Second Ave., 400 at First Ave., 500 at York Ave. (uptown) or Avenue A (in the Village). On the West Side, address numbers are 1 at Fifth Ave., 100 at Avenue of the Americas (Sixth Ave.), 200 at Seventh Ave., 300 at Eighth Ave., 400 at Ninth Ave., 500 at Tenth Ave., and 600 at Eleventh Ave. In general, numbers increase from south to north along the avenues, but you should always ask for a cross street when you are getting an avenue address.

SUBWAYS

Operated by **New York City Transit** (English speakers 718-330-1234, non-English speakers 718-330-4847; open daily 6am-9pm), the 238-mile New York subway system operates 24 hours a day, 365 days a year. It moves 3.5 million people daily, and has 468 stations. The fare for Metropolitan Transit Authority (MTA) subways is a hefty $1.50, so groups of four may find a cab ride to be cheaper and more expedient for short distances. Long distances are best traveled by subway, since once inside a passenger may transfer onto any of the other trains without restrictions. A free (and newly designed) copy of the subway map is available at any subway token booth.

The subway network integrates the **IRT, IND,** and **BMT** lines, now operated by NYC Transit. The names of these lines are still used, although they are no longer of functional significance. The IRT (#1, 9) and the IND (A, C, D, E, F, Z) are two groups of lines that run through Manhattan; the BMT (B, J, L, M, N, Q, R) runs mostly from lower Manhattan to Queens and Brooklyn. Certain routes also have common, unofficial names based on where they travel, such as the "7th Ave. Line" or the "Broadway Line" for the #1, 2, 3, or 9; the "8th Ave. Line" for the A and C; the "Lexington Line" for the #4, 5, or 6; and the "Flushing Line" for the #7.

The omnipresent **MetroCard** now serves as the dominant form of currency for subterranean and surface transit in New York. The card, containing a magnetic strip, can be used at all subway stations and on all public buses. Subway and bus

MASS (TRANSIT) CONFUSION For the first several decades of their operation, there were three independent subway lines in New York City—all competing with one another for customers. It was impossible to get a map of all three until 1940! Nowadays, the map is clear (well, it's hard to be clear with over 200 mi. of track and nearly 2 dozen lines) and comprehensive—a far cry from the "abstract" map of 1972, whose designer admitted its simplified geometric shapes were "difficult for users to understand."

ESSENTIALS

fare is still $1.50 per ride with the MetroCard, but purchasing a $15 card gets you one free ride. Moreover, MetroCards can be used for subway-bus, bus-subway, and bus-bus transfers. When you swipe the card on the initial ride, a free transfer is electronically stored on your MetroCard and is good for up to 2hrs. **Without the MetroCard, bus-subway or subway-bus transfers are not free**. A single MetroCard can store up to four transfers, good for people traveling in a group. There are certain restrictions on bus-bus transfers (i.e. passengers on a north-south bus can generally only transfer to a bus going east-west).

Recently, the Transit Authority has introduced the **"Unlimited Rides" MetroCard** (as opposed to "Pay-Per-Ride" cards); this card is sold in seven-day ($17) and 30-day ($63) denominations and is good for unlimited use of the subway during the specified period. **The Unlimited Rides Card is highly recommended for tourists who plan on visiting many sights.** Those with disabilities or over 65 qualify for a Reduced Fare card; call 878-7294 (TDD 878-0165) for information. The card can be purchased in all subway stations and at any newsstand, pharmacy, or grocery store bearing a MetroCard sticker in the storefront window. The card itself can be used at all subway stations and on all public buses within New York City. The city has set up a helpful information line (800-638-7622; in NYC 638-7622) to answer any questions about this new technology. The Transit Authority's website also provides comprehensive information on the card (www.metrocard.citysearch.com). An unlimited daily pass is available for $4 at select grocery stores and certain subway stations in New York City.

Although by far the quickest means of transportation in Manhattan, the subways are much more useful for traveling north-south than east-west, as there are only two crosstown shuttle trains (42nd and 14th St.). In upper Manhattan and in Queens, Brooklyn, and the Bronx, some lines become "El" trains (for "elevated") and ride above street level to the city's outer regions.

"Express" trains run at all hours and stop only at certain major stations; "locals" stop everywhere. Be sure to check the letter or number and the destination of each train, since trains with different destinations often use the same track. When in doubt, ask a friendly passenger or the conductor, who usually sits near the middle of the train. Once you're on the train, pay attention to the often garbled announcements—trains occasionally change mid-route from local to express or vice-versa, especially when entering or leaving Manhattan.

Efforts at aesthetic sterility in the trains have by no means erased the perils of subway crime, though the numbers are rapidly shrinking. In crowded stations (most notably those around 42nd St.), pickpockets find work; violent crimes, although infrequent, tend to occur in stations that are deserted. Always watch yourself and your belongings, and try to stay in well-lit areas near a transit cop or token clerk. Most stations have clearly marked "off-hours" waiting areas that are under observation and significantly safer. When boarding the train, pick a car with a number of other passengers in it, or sit near the middle of the train, in the conductor's car. These are not reasons to avoid the amazingly convenient subways—just keep your wits about you always.

For safety reasons, try to avoid riding the subways between midnight and 7am, especially above E. 96th St. and W. 120th St. and outside Manhattan. Try also to avoid rush-hour crowds, where you'll be fortunate to find air, let alone seating—on an average morning, more commuters take the E and the F than use the entire rapid-transit system of Chicago (which has the nation's second-largest system). Further, very crowded subways also present the danger of sexual molestation;

unfortunately, some ride the cars during rush hour to "brush up" against unsuspecting riders. If someone tries to molest you on a subway, be vocal and *loudly* ask them to move or leave you alone; concerned riders will often come to your assistance. If you must travel at rush hour (7:30-9:30am and 5-6:30pm on every train in every direction), the local train is usually less crowded than the express. Buy a MetroCard or a bunch of tokens at once at the booth. You'll see glass globes outside of most subway entrances. If the globe is green it means that the entrance is staffed 24 hours a day. A red globe indicates that the entrance is closed or restricted in some way; read the sign posted above the stairs.

BUSES

Because buses are often mired in traffic, they can take twice as long as subways, but they are almost always safer, cleaner, and quieter. They'll also get you closer to your destination, since they stop every two blocks or so and run crosstown (east-west), as well as uptown and downtown (north-south). For long-distance travel (over 40 north-south blocks) buses can be a nightmare (except at night and on weekends, when traffic is manageable), but for shorter and especially crosstown trips, buses are often as quick as, and more convenient than, trains. The MTA transfer system provides north-south travelers with a paper slip, valid for a free ride east-west, or vice-versa, but you must ask the driver for a transfer when you board and pay your fare. Make sure you ring when you want to get off.

Bus stops are indicated by a yellow-painted curb, but you're better off looking for the blue sign post announcing the bus number or for a glass-walled shelter displaying a map of the bus's route and a schedule of arrival times. A flat fare of $1.50 is charged at all times when you board; either a MetroCard (see above for more information), exact change, or a subway token is required—dollar bills are not accepted. If you use a MetroCard, within two hours afterward you can transfer without charge from the bus to the subway and vice versa.

Queens is served in addition by five bus lines: **MTA/Long Island Bus** (516-766-6722; covers mainly Nassau County, Long Island) and four private companies: **Green Bus Lines** (718-995-4700; covers mainly Jamaica and central Queens), **Jamaica Buses, Inc.** (718-526-0800; covers mainly Jamaica and Rockaway in Queens), **Queens Surface Corp.** (718-445-3100), and **TriBoro Coach Corp.** (718-335-1000; covers Forest Hills, Ridgewood, and Jackson Hts.). The Bronx has two extra lines: **Liberty Lines Express** (718-652-8400) and **New York Bus Service** (718-994-5500). Rates for these companies vary; some accept MTA tokens and MetroCard. Most of these bus routes do not appear on MTA schedules.

TAXIS

With drivers cruising at warp speed along near-deserted avenues or dodging through bumper-to-bumper traffic, cab rides can give you painful ulcers. And even if your stomach survives the ride, your budget may not. Still, it's likely that you'll have to take a taxi once in a while, in the interest of convenience or safety. Rides are expensive: the meter starts at $2 and clicks 30¢ for each additional one-fifth of a mile; 30¢ is tacked on for every 75 seconds spent in slow or stopped traffic, a 50¢ surcharge is levied from 8pm to 6am, and passengers pay for all tolls. Don't forget to tip 15%; cabbies need and expect the dough. Before you leave the cab, ask for a receipt, which will have the taxi's identification number (which can be either its meter number or its medallion). This number is necessary to trace lost articles or to make a complaint to the **Taxi Commission** (221-8294; 221 W. 41st St., between Times Sq. and the Port Authority Bus Terminal; open M-F 9am-5pm). Since some drivers may illegally try to show the naive visitor the "scenic route," quickly glance at a street map before embarking so you'll have some clue if you're being taken to your destination, or just being taken for a ride. Use only yellow cabs—they're licensed by the state of New York. Cabs of other colors are unlicensed "gypsy" cabs and are illegal in NYC. In hailing a cab, refer this rule of thumb: if the center light on the cab's roof is lit, then the

Downtown Bus Routes

— North-South routes

— East-West routes

15 All numbers are Manhattan lines, which carry M-prefix on bus display.

15 15 15 "Q" are Queens lines;
"B" are Brooklyn lines
"X" are express lines

cabbie is picking up fares, if it is dark, the cab is already taken. If you can't find any-thing on the street, commandeer a radio-dispatched cab (see the Yellow Pages under "Taxicabs"). Use common sense to make rides cheaper—catch a cab going your direction and get off at a nearby street corner. When shared with friends a cab can be cheaper, safer, and more convenient than the subway, especially late at night. But you can't cram more than four people into a cab.

DRIVING

Driving in New York is not something to look forward to. Most New Yorkers only learn to drive in order to escape from the city, and some Manhattanites never learn to drive at all, terrified by the prospect of learning to make wide right turns in mid-town traffic. When behind the wheel in New York, you are locked in combat with aggressive taxis, careless pedestrians, and crazed bicycle messengers.

Once in Manhattan, traffic continues to be a problem, especially between 57th and 34th St. The even greater hassle of parking joins in to plague the weary. Would-be parallel parkers can rise to this challenge in one of three ways. **Parking lots** are the easiest but the most expensive. In Midtown, where lots are the only option, expect to pay at least $25 per day and up to $15 for two hours. The cheapest parking lots are downtown—try the far west end of Houston St.—but make sure you feel comfortable with the area. Is it popu-lated? Is the lot guarded? Is it well-lit?

The second alternative is short-term parking. On the streets, **parking meters** cost 25¢ per 15 minutes, with a limit of one or two hours. Competition is ferocious for the third option, **free parking** at spots on the crosstown streets in residential areas. Read the signs carefully; a space is usually legal only on certain days of the week. The city has never been squeamish about towing, and recovering your car once it's towed will cost $100 or more. Break-ins and car theft are always possibilities, par-ticularly if you have a radio. The wailing of a car alarm is such a familiar tune to New Yorkers that you may hear them sing along. For information on how to obtain the **International Driving Permit (IDP)**, contact the one of the following organizations in your home country:

Australia: Contact your local Royal Automobile Club (RAC) or the National Royal Motorist Association (NRMA) if in NSW or the ACT (tel. (08) 9421 4298; www.rac.com.au/travel). Permits AUS$15.

Canada: Contact any Canadian Automobile Association (CAA) branch office in Canada, or write to CAA, 1145 Hunt Club Rd., Suite 200, K1V 0Y3 Canada. (tel. 613-247-0117; fax 247-0118; www.caa.ca/CAAInternet/travelservices/internationaldocumentation/idptravel.htm). Permits CDN$10.

Ireland: Contact the nearest Automobile Association (AA) office or write: The Automobile Association, International Documents, Fanum House, Erskine, Renfrewshire PA8 6BW (tel. (990) 500 600). Permits IR£4.

New Zealand: Contact your local Automobile Association (AA) or their main office at Auckland Central, 99 Albert St. (tel. (9) 377 4660; fax 302 2037; www.nzaa.co.nz.). Permits NZ$8.

South Africa: Contact your local Automobile Association of South Africa office or the head office at P.O. Box 596, 2000 Johannesburg (tel. (11) 799 1000; fax 799 1010). Per-mits SAR28.50.

U.K.: Visit your local AA Shop. To find the location nearest you that issues the IDP, call (0990) 50 06 00. More information available at www.theaa.co.uk/motoring/idp.asp). Permits UK£4.

U.S.: Visit any American Automobile Association (AAA) office or write to AAA Florida, Travel Related Services, 1000 AAA Drive (mail stop 100), Heathrow, FL 32746 (tel. 407-444-7000; fax 444-7380). You do not have to be a member of AAA to receive an (IDP/IADP). Permits $10.

Uptown Bus Routes

— North-South routes

East-West routes

36 All numbers are Manhattan lines, which carry M-prefix on bus display.

BX 36 "BX" are Bronx lines
X 36 "X" are express lines

CAR INSURANCE. Most credit cards cover standard insurance. If you rent, lease, or borrow a car, you will need a **green card,** or **International Insurance Certificate,** to prove that you have liability insurance. Obtain it through the car rental agency; most include coverage in their prices. If you lease a car, you can obtain a green card from the dealer. Some travel agents offer the card. Verify whether your auto insurance applies abroad. If you have a collision abroad, the accident will show up on your domestic records if you report it to your insurance company. Rental agencies may require you to purchase theft insurance in countries that they consider to have a high risk of auto theft.

CAR RENTAL

All agencies maintain varying minimum-age requirements and require proof of age as well as a security deposit. Agencies in Queens and Yonkers are often less expensive than their Manhattan counterparts, especially for one-day rentals. Most auto insurance policies will cover rented cars, and some credit cards like American Express and Chase VISA take care of your rental insurance costs if you've charged the vehicle to their card (but be sure to ask about all the particulars from the companies themselves; as always, "restrictions apply"). Many smaller local rental car companies allow drivers 21 years or older (most companies only rent to customers 25 or older); some even allow drivers 18 years or older. Most require a young driver surcharge in these cases, so check first! **Dollar** and **Enterprise** rent-a-car companies have offices in New York. (Dollar at JFK: 718-656-2400 Dollar at LaGuardia: 718-244-1235. For Enterprise: In the U.S. and Canada call 1-800-566-9249; in French speaking Canada 1-800-Loc-Auto; in the U.K. call 0-800-800227 to verify that your desired location rents to younger drivers. To check for locations near you in the U.S. call 1-800-566-9249).

Nationwide, 241 W. 40th St. (867-1234), between Seventh and Eighth Ave. Reputable nationwide chain. Mid-sized domestic sedan $33-59 per day, $289 per week, 150 free mi. per day, 1000 free mi. per week. Open M-F 7:30am-6:30pm. Vehicle return 24hr. Must be 23 with a major credit card.

AAMCAR Rent-a-Car, 315 W. 96th St. (222-8500), between West End Ave. and Riverside Dr. Compacts $50 per day, 200 free mi., 25¢ each additional mi.; $330 per week with 1000 free mi. Must be 23 to rent; surcharge for drivers under 25. Open M-F 7:30am-7:30pm, Sa 9am-5pm, Su 9am-7pm. No one-day rentals June-Aug. Sa-Su.

BICYCLING

Weekday biking in commuter traffic poses a mortal challenge even for veterans. But on weekends, when the traffic thins, cyclists who use helmets and caution can tour the Big Apple on two wheels. From January to October, Central Park (except the lower loop) is closed to traffic on weekdays from 10am-3pm and 7-10pm, and from Friday at 7pm to Monday at 6am. Otherwise, Sunday mornings are best. For a challenging and aesthetic traffic-free course, try the 3.5 mi. path in Central Park. If you must leave your bike unattended, use a strong "U" lock. Thieves laugh at (then cut through) chain locks. Don't leave quick-release items unattended; you will find them very quickly released. For more info on cycling in and around Manhattan see **Sports,** p. 292. To rent a bike check out **Pedal Pushers,** 1306 Second Ave. (288-5592), between 68th and 69th St. They rent 3-speeds for $4 per hr., $10 per day, $13 overnight; 10-speeds for $5 per hr., $14 per day, $19 overnight; mountain bikes for $6 per hr., $17 per day, $25 overnight. Overnight rentals require a $150 deposit on a major credit card, but regular rentals just need major credit card, passport, or a NYS drivers license (open Su-M 10am-6pm, W 10am-7pm, Th-Sa 10am-8pm).

WALKING, JOGGING, AND IN-LINE SKATING

Walking is the cheapest, arguably the most entertaining, and often the fastest way to get around town. During rush hours the sidewalks are packed with suited and sneakered commuters. In between rush hours, sidewalks are still full of street life. Twenty street blocks (north-south) make up a mile; one east-west block from one avenue to the next is about triple the distance of a north-south, street-to-street block. New York distances are short: a walk from the south end of Central Park to the World Trade Center, through all of Midtown and downtown Manhattan, for example, should take under 1½ hours.

If you plan to jog along the street, be prepared to dodge pedestrians and to break your stride at intersections. A better alternative to the sidewalk are paths along the rivers or in Central Park—most are pavement, but there is a 1.58 mi. cinder loop that circles the **Jacqueline Kennedy Onassis Reservoir** (between 84th and 96th St.). Joggers pack this path from 6-9am and 5-7pm on weekdays and all day on weekends. If you can, run between 9am and 5pm to avoid the night-time crime and rush-hour collisions on the narrow strip. For information on running clubs, call the **New York Roadrunner's Club,** 9 E. 89th St. (860-4455), between Madison and Fifth Ave. The Roadrunner's Club hosts races in Central Park on summer weekends and the New York City Marathon every fall.

For those who prefer speed without pounding the pavement, **in-line skates** are available at **Peck and Goodie Skates,** 917 Eighth Ave. (246-6123), between 54th and 55th St. They'll hold your shoes while you whiz past your favorite New York sights (Sa-Su $10 per 2hr., $20 per day; M-F $10 per day). Rates include all protective gear. $200 deposit or credit card is required. As with any rental agreement, be sure to read the details carefully before you sign—you may face hefty repair fees when you come back for your shoes and deposit. Private lessons are available for a fee (open M-Sa 10am-8pm, Su 10am-6pm). In-line skates are also available for rental in Central Park (see p. 180).

SPECIFIC CONCERNS
WOMEN TRAVELERS

Women exploring on their own inevitably face additional safety concerns. Always trust your instincts: if you'd feel better somewhere else, move on. Always carry extra money for a phone call, bus, or taxi. Consider staying in hostels which offer single rooms that lock from the inside or in religious organizations that offer rooms for women only; avoid any hostel with "communal" showers. Stick to centrally located accommodations and avoid late-night treks or subway rides. Hitching is never safe for lone women, or even for two women traveling together. Choose the subway in the middle of the train, where the conductor is—you'll see his face from the platform.

Look as if you know where you're going (even when you don't) and consider approaching women or couples for directions if you're lost or feel uncomfortable. Your best answer to verbal harassment is no answer at all. Wearing a conspicuous wedding band may help prevent such incidents. Don't hesitate to seek out a police officer or a passerby if you are being harassed.

In crowds, you may be pinched or squeezed—especially in summer; the look on the face is the key to avoiding unwanted attention. If harassment persists and you are in a crowded place (i.e. a subway during rush hour), make your discomfort understood LOUDLY, and the harassment probably will stop.

Carry a **whistle** or an airhorn on your keychain, and don't hesitate to use it in an emergency. A **Model Mugging** course will perhaps not only prepare you for a potential mugging, but may also raise your level of awareness of your surroundings as well as your confidence (see **Safety and Security,** p. 35). Women also face additional health concerns when traveling (see **Health,** p. 40). All of these warnings and suggestions, however, should not discourage women from traveling alone.

ESSENTIALS

For general information, contact the **National Organization for Women (NOW),** whi ch has branches across the country that refer women travelers to rape crisis centers and counseling services, and provide lists of feminist events. The Headquarters is 1000 16th St. NW, #700, **Washington D.C.** 20036 (202-331-0066, www.now.org), 105 W. 28th St., #304, **New York,** NY 10010 (212-627-9895; fax 627-9891; www.nownyc.org); and 3543 18th St., Box 27, **San Francisco,** CA 94110 (415-861-8960; fax 861-8969).

Directory of Women's Media, available from the National Council for Research on Women, 11 Hanover Sq., 20th fl., New York, NY 10005 (785-7335; fax 785-7350). The publication lists women's publishers, bookstores, theaters, and news organizations (mail order, $30, plus shipping).

Women's Travel in Your Pocket, Ferrari Guides, P.O. Box 37887, Phoenix, AZ 85069 (602-863-2408; email ferrari@q-net.com; www.q-net.com), an annual guide for women (especially lesbians) traveling worldwide ($14, plus shipping).

OLDER TRAVELERS

Senior citizens are eligible for a wide range of discounts on transportation, museums, movies, theaters, concerts, restaurants, and accommodations throughout New York City. If you don't see a senior citizen price listed, it's certainly worth it to ask. Agencies for senior group travel are growing in enrollment and popularity. For example, seniors now have access to a reduced fare MetroCard. Here are a few helpful options for the aging traveler in New York City.

New York City Department for the Aging Infoline: 212-442-1000

The MTA Reduced Fare Line: 718-243-4999 M-F 9am-5pm.

Elevators and escalator accessibility hotline: 1-800-734-6772, 24hr.

Access-A-Ride: toll-free at 1-877-337-2017

FURTHER READING: OLDER TRAVELERS.
No Problem! Worldwise Tips for Mature Adventurers, Janice Kenyon. Orca Book Publishers ($16).
A Senior's Guide to Healthy Travel, Donald L. Sullivan. Career Press. ($15).
Unbelievably Good Deals and Great Adventures That You Absolutely Can't Get Unless You're Over 50, Joan Rattner Heilman. Contemporary Books ($13).

DISABLED TRAVELERS

Particularly since President George Bush signed the Americans with Disabilities Act in 1992, New York City has slowly but surely removed many of the impediments to disabled travel. The city's **buses** all have excellent wheelchair access. Call the Transit Authority Access (718-596-8585) for information on public transit accessibility. Access-A-Ride door-to-door service is available for some; call 212-632-7272 to apply. In general it is advisable to inform airlines and hotels in advance of a disability when making arrangements for travel; some time may be needed to prepare special accommodations.

Arrange transportation well in advance to ensure a smooth trip. Hertz, Avis, and National **car rental agencies** have hand-controlled vehicles at some locations. In the U.S., both **Amtrak** and major airlines will accommodate disabled passengers if notified at least 72 hours in advance. Hearing-impaired travelers may contact Amtrak using teletype printers (800-872-7245). **Greyhound** buses will provide free travel for a companion; if you are without a fellow traveler, call Greyhound (800-752-4841) at least 48 hours before you leave and they will make arrangements for you. The following organizations provide useful publications.

Access-Able Travel Source, LLC, P.O. Box 1796, Wheat Ridge, CO 80034 (tel. 303-232-2979, fax 239-8486; www.access-able.com, e-mail bill@access-able.com). A data-base on travelling around the U.S. for disabled travellers, started by two avid disabled travellers. Provides information on access, transportation, accommodations, rentals, and various other resources.

Mobility International USA (MIUSA), P.O. Box 10767, Eugene, OR 97440 (tel. 541-343-1284 voice and TDD; fax 343-6812; email info@miusa.org; www.miusa.org). Sells *A World of Options: A Guide to International Educational Exchange, Community Service, and Travel for Persons with Disabilities* ($35).

Moss Rehab Hospital Travel Information Service (tel. 215-456-9600; www.mossresourcenet.org). A telephone and internet information resource center on international travel accessibility and other travel-related concerns for those with disabilities.

Society for the Advancement of Travel for the Handicapped (SATH), 347 Fifth Ave., #610, New York, NY 10016 (tel. 212-447-1928; fax 725-8253; email sathtravel@aol.com; www.sath.org). Advocacy group publishing a quarterly color travel magazine *OPEN WORLD* (free for members or $13 for nonmembers). Also publishes a wide range of information sheets on disability travel facilitation and accessible destinations. Annual membership $45, students and seniors $30.

Resource Directory for the Disabled, by Richard Nell Shrout. Facts on File ($45).

The following organizations arrange tours or trips for disabled travelers:

Directions Unlimited, 720 N. Bedford Rd., Bedford Hills, NY 10507 (tel. 800-533-5343; in NY 914-241-1700; fax 914-241-0243; email cruisesusa@aol.com). Specializes in arranging individual and group vacations, tours, and cruises for the physically disabled. Group tours for blind travelers.

The Guided Tour Inc., 7900 Old York Rd., Suite 114B, Elkins Park, PA 19027-2339 (tel. 800-783-5841 or 215-782-1370; email gtour400@aol.com; www.guidedtour.com). Organizes travel programs for persons with developmental and physical challenges around the U.S., including tours to the greater New York area at places like Atlantic City, the mountains around New York, and in the Poconos.

TRAVELERS WITH CHILDREN

Many attractions in New York offer discounts for children. Children under two generally fly for 10% of the adult airfare on international flights (this does not necessarily include a seat). International fares are usually discounted 25% for children from two to 11. Restaurants often have children's menus and discounts. Virtually all museums and tourist attractions also have a children's rate. Be sure that your child carries an ID in case of an emergency or he or she gets lost. And arrange a reunion spot in case of separation when sight-seeing (e.g., next to the Temple of Dendur at the Met). If you pick a B&B or a small hotel, call ahead and make sure it's child-friendly. If you rent a car, make sure the rental company provides a car seat for younger children. Consider using a papoose-style device to carry a baby on walking trips. Finding a private place for **breast feeding** is often a problem while traveling, so pack accordingly.

The website www.nycvisit.com/visit/visit_family.html provides good info on what to do with your kids in NYC. Some of the following publications also offer more general tips for adults traveling with children.

 FURTHER READING: TRAVELERS WITH CHILDREN.
How to take Great Trips with Your Kids, Sanford and Jane Portnoy. Harvard Common Press ($10).
Have Kid, Will Travel: 101 Survival Strategies for Vacationing With Babies and Young Children, Claire and Lucille Tristram. Andrews and McMeel ($9).
Adventuring with Children: An Inspirational Guide to World Travel and the Outdoors, Nan Jeffrey. Avalon House Publishing ($15).
Trouble Free Travel with Children, Vicki Lansky. Book Peddlers ($9).

VEGETARIAN, KOSHER, AND HALAL TRAVELERS

Vegetarians won't have any problem eating cheap and well in New York. Excellent vegetarian restaurants abound (see **Restaurants,** p. 91). Travelers who keep **kosher** should contact New York synagogues for information about kosher restaurants; your own synagogue or college Hillel office should have lists of Jewish institutions in New York. The *Jewish Travel Guide*, which lists Jewish institutions, synagogues, and kosher restaurants, is available from Vallentine-Mitchell Publishers, Newbury house 890-900, Eastern Ave., Newbury Park, Ilford Park, Essex, U.K. IG2 7HH (tel.(020) 599 88 66; fax 599 09 84). It is available in the U.S. ($16) from ISBS, 5804 NE Hassallo St., Portland, OR 97213-3644 (tel.800-944-6190). ChaBad houses (centers for Lubavitch Hassidim and outreach) should also be able to either provide kosher food or direct you to it. NYU's ChaBad is at 566 La Guardia #715 (998-4945), and the Upper East Side's ChaBad *shuckles* at 311 E. 83rd St., Ste. B (717-4613). Muslim travelers seeking **halal** foods should check the local *Yellow Pages* listings under "halal."

LONGER STAYS

Sometimes a vacation in New York can last a lifetime…literally. This city is one of the most "moved-to" cities in the world. If you do decide to grow roots here, either as a student or as a member of the city's infinite work force, many housing and employment options lie open to you.

ACCOMMODATIONS

Several hostels offer long term stays; Gísele at the Uptown Hostel even helps hostelers find cheap apartments (see **Accommodations,** p. 79). Subletting an apartment, however, may be your best bet. When New Yorkers feel the need to escape, they will rent out their (usually furnished) apartments for a month or more. Check the *Village Voice* for listings early Wednesday mornings (the day it comes to press). Their website (www.villagevoice.com) is another resource that can get the information to you a night before those poor, misguided seekers who wait in line the next morning for a hard copy. The *New York Times* also has a helpful classified section with real estate options (online at www.nytimes.com). While it is cheaper to find an apartment through your own resources, sometimes an exhausting search may make you feel that you need a little help from your corporate friends. **New York Habitat,** 307 Seventh Ave., #306 (255-8018; fax 627-1416; rent@nyhabitat.com; www.nyhabitat.com), finds sublets and apartment rentals as well as helping with roommate shares. The **Gamut Realty Group,** 301 E. 78th St. (800-437-8353 or 879-4229; fax 517-5356), also assists in finding sublets as well as short-term (and longer term) rooms and apartments (open M-F 9am-6pm, Sa-Su 10am-4pm). You can also **Manhattan Lodgings** (677-7616), a network that puts visitors in contact with New York apartment tenants who want to rent out their respective pads for a few days or weeks.

Act fast, but always thoroughly investigate the apartment and surrounding neighborhood to make sure you feel comfortable living there. Finding an apartment in Brooklyn or Queens will be cheaper and less competitive than Manhattan. However, if you're only here for a brief time you may want to pay extra and avoid the inter-borough subway commute. Hoboken or Jersey City, across the Hudson, however, offer more for your money, a view of the Manhattan skyline and a quick $1 (cheaper than the subway) commute to the center of everything. A great site listing many home exchange companies can be found at www.aitec.edu.au/~bwechner/Documents/Travel/Lists/Home Exchange-Clubs.html. One free New York City home exchange service is located at Vacation-Inc.com at the website **www.vacation-inc.com** with offices at 220 West 19th Street, 2nd fl. (800-700-9549; 253-4010; email: info@vacation-inc.com). Home rentals, as opposed to exchanges, are much more expensive. However, they can

EMPLOYMENT ■ 73

be cheaper than comparably-serviced hotels. Both home exchanges and rentals are ideal for families with children, or travelers with special dietary needs; you often get a kitchen, maid service, TV, and telephones.

HomeExchange, P.O. Box 30085, Santa Barbara, CA 93130 (tel. 805-898-9660; email admin@HomeExchange.com; www.homeexchange.com.

The Invented City: International Home Exchange, 41 Sutter St., 1090, San Fransisco, CA 94104 (tel. 800-788-2489 in the U.S. or (415) 252-1141 elsewhere; fax 252-1171; email invented@aol.com; www.inventedcity.com). For $75, you get your offer listed in 1 catalog and unlimited access to the club's database containing thousands of homes for exchange.

ESSENTIALS

EMPLOYMENT

Hordes of young folk flock to this city of opportunity in their post-college years to just "*be* in the city;" and while *be*-ing is a noble profession, still there are bills to pay. So, these *be*-ings will invariably intern, wait tables, serve as bike couriers, act, model, bartend, read manuscripts for a publishing firm, work in "the biz" (whatever the "biz" may be), and wait tables some more. Competition is steep here, but jobs do exist. Keep your chin up and your resume handy, and you're sure to find some gainful employment. When finding a job in New York, the **internet** will be your best friend; numerous websites are devoted to placing folks like you in swanky joints throughout the city.

Council also runs a summer travel/work program designed to provide students with the opportunity to spend their summers working in the U.S.; check your local Council agency (see p. 76).

The following is a list of head-hunting agencies working to find companies that special employee, or organizations which provide employment information/opportunities:

Careerpath.com (www.careerpath.com). Promises "the Web's largest number of the most current job listings."

Creative Freelancers (www.freelancers.com). On-line service specializing in "creative" jobs in design, photography, illustration, and the fine arts.

Monster Job Search (www.monster.com). Comprehensive on-line service that helps find jobs and internships through the help of cartoon icon Thwacker.

National Association of Temporary Staffing Services, New York Chapter (718-793-6711; www.natss.org/ny). Large organization with branches in New York City as well as Westchester and Long Island.

Oliver Staffing Inc., 350 Lexington Ave. (634-1234). Temporary employment agency serving the gay and lesbian business community.

Paladin Staffing Services, 270 Madison Ave. (545-7850; fax 689-0881; email newyork@paladinstaff.com; www.paladinstaff.com). Specializing in marketing, advertising, communications, and creative temporary placements.

Seven Staffing, 36 E. 12th St. (254-8600; fax 475-3591; www.sevenstaffing.com). Places proud computer geeks in choice jobs.

Tech List (www.ci.nyc.ny.us/html/filmcom/pdf/tech.pdf). For acting and tekkie hopefuls: gives info on productions being filmed in NY on a week-by-week basis. Contact the Mayor's Office of Film, Theater, Broadcasting (see **Film,** p. 17).

Wall Street Services, 11 Broadway, #930 (509-7200; fax 943-1507; www.wallstservice.com). Finds opportunities in the financial sector.

Yahoo! (www.ny.yahoo.com/Employment). The omniscient search-engine can find you a job, baby! Great links to specific agencies in NY.

OTHER RESOURCES FOR TRAVELERS

TOURIST INFORMATION

Times Square Visitors Center, 1560 Broadway (869-5453; fax 997-4021), between 46th and 47th St. Subway: #1, 9 or 2, 3 or 7 or N, R, S to Times Square. The newly restored Embassy Theater is the new hub of Big Apple tourism. The Center features four Fleet ATM machines, an MTA booth, a Gray Line/Circle Line counter, an automated currency exchange machine, a Broadway Show ticket center, free phone calls to hotels, free internet access (if the place is crowded enough), an NYC memorabilia booth. In addition to a ladies room, there is a unisex bathroom à la Ally McBeal. The multilingual staff at the Information Counter can meet many of your needs, including hotel listings, restaurants, entertainment ideas, and safety tips. There are also tons of maps and pamphlets giving you the low-down on a number of entertainment and touring options (open daily 9am-6pm). **Other locations:** Grand Central terminal, south side of the main concourse; Penn Station terminal, south side of the Amtrak rotunda at 34th St. between Seventh and Eighth Ave.; Manhattan Mall information booth at 33rd and 6th St.

New York Convention and Visitors Bureau, 810 Seventh Ave. at 53rd St.(484-1222, for literature 800-692-8474). Subway: #1, 9 to 50th St. Multilingual staff will help you with directions, hotel listings, entertainment ideas, safety tips, and "insiders'" city neighborhood descriptions. The recently opened Visitors Center features electronic information kiosks, ATM access, NYC memorabilia, and ticket sales to top cultural events.Very helpful website at www.nycvisit.com.

New York State Department of Economic Development, 633 Third Ave. between 40th and 41th St. Subway: #1, 9 or 2, 3 or 7 or N, R, S to 42nd St./Times Sq. Tourist Division (803-2200) open M-F 9am-5pm. Plenty of brochures on events and sights around the city. Or call their toll-free *I Love New York* number 800-CALL-NYS (225-5697) for information about sights and events.

Travelers' Aid Society: Located at JFK International Airport (718-656-4870), in the International Arrivals Building. Specializes in crisis intervention services for stranded travelers or crime victims. Open M-Th 10am-7pm, F 10am-6pm, Sa 11am-6pm, Su noon-6pm. In an emergency, call the **Victims Services Agency,** 166 W. 75th St. at Amsterdam Ave. (**24hr. hotline** 577-7777, office number 874-0724). Open M, W 9:30am-8pm; Tu, Th-F 9:30am-5:30pm.

LIBRARIES

New York Public Library, 11 W. 40th St. (930-0830 or 869-8089 for a recorded listing of exhibitions and events), entrance on Fifth Ave. at 42nd St. Non-lending central research library. Wide variety of exhibits on display. Their website (www.nypl.org) has useful information about all NY libraries. Open M and Th-Sa 10am-6pm, Tu-W 11am-7:30pm.

New York Public Library for the Performing Arts, (870-1630), relocated until Lincoln Center location renovations are completed in 2001. Circulating collection has moved to the Mid-Manhattan Library, 4th floor (see above). Call for detailed automated information about holdings locations and hours, or check out the general website (www.nypl.org).

Mid-Manhattan Library, 455 Fifth Ave. (340-0849), at 40th St. Largest branch of the circulating libraries; specialized sections include Folklore and Women's Studies. Occasional exhibitions and presentations; pick up a free events calendar at any NYPL location. Identification and proof of local address required to take out books. Free Internet access on each floor, but be sure to sign up early! Open M and W 9am-9pm, Tu and Th 11am-7pm, F-Sa 10am-6pm.

Donnell Library Center, 20 W. 53rd St. (621-0618), between Fifth and Sixth Ave. Across the street from the Museum of Modern Art. Central Children's Room for "Curious George" fans. Largest circulation of foreign-language books. Call ahead for hours, but most sections are open M, W, and F 10am-6pm, Tu and Th 10am-8pm, Sa 10am-5pm.

Schomburg Center for Research in Black Culture, 515 Lenox Ave./Malcolm X Blvd. (491-2200), on the corner of 135th St. Largest collection of books by and about African-Americans anywhere in the world. Large, quiet reading rooms on the basement and 2nd floor. Films and art exhibits shown regularly; call for schedule. Library open M-W noon-8pm, Th-Sa 10am-6pm; archives department open M-W noon-5pm and F-Sa 10am-5pm.

The other boroughs' head branches are: the **Bronx Reference Center,** 2556 Bainbridge Ave. (718-579-4200); the **St. George Library Center,** 5 Central Ave., Staten Island (718-442-8560); the **Queensborough Public Library,** 89-11 Merrick Blvd., Jamaica, Queens (718-990-0700); and the **Brooklyn Public Library,** Grand Army Plaza, Brooklyn (718-230-2100).

INTERNET RESOURCES

There are a number of ways to access the **Internet.** Most popular are commercial internet providers, such as **America On-Line** (800-827-6364) and **Compuserve** (800-433-0389). Many employers and schools also offer gateways to the Internet, often at no cost (unlike the corporate gateways above). Of most interest to Internet-surfing budget travelers are the World Wide Web and Usenet newsgroups.

THE WORLD WIDE WEB (WWW)

The **World Wide Web** provides its users with graphics and sound, as well as textual information. **Search engines** (services that search for web pages under specific subjects) aid make sifting through massive amounts of information easier. **Excite** (www.excite.com), and **Lycos** (a2z.lycos.com) are among the most popular. **Yahoo!** is a slightly more organized search engine with travel links at www.yahoo.com/Recreation/Travel. Check out **Let's Go's web site** (www.letsgo.com) and find our newsletter, information about our books, an always-current list of links, and more. Or, try some of our favorites sites directly:

Big World Magazine (www.bigworld.com), a budget travel 'zine, has a web page with a great collection of links to travel pages.

Expedia (www.expedia.com) everything budget.

Rent-A-Wreck's Travel Links (www.rent-a-wreck.com/raw/travlist.htm) is a very complete list of excellent links.

Shoestring Travel (www.stratpub.com) is a budget travel e-zine, with feature articles, links, user exchange, and accommodations information.

TravelHUB (www.travelhub.com) is a great site for cheap travel deals.

Travelocity (www.travelocity.com) more marvelous travel info and deals.

If you're looking for **New York-specific web sites,** you won't have to look too far; many organizations of interest to NYCers have their own web pages. Check for gopher and web sites maintained by ECHO ("East Coast HangOut"). ECHO is an internet service-provider based in Greenwich Village with a New York-centric world-view. Some other interesting sites:

Citysearch (newyork.citysearch.com). Like Sidewalk, this site provides huge amounts of New York info. Easy to navigate through.

Echo (www.echonyc.com). Well-designed, with comprehensive listings, links, and services. A great place to begin.

Internet Café (www.bigmagic.com).Virtual version of one of NYC's several internet cafés.

Mayor's Homepage (www.ci.nyc.ny.us/html/om/home.html). Read Rudy's press releases and see his smiling face.

New York Times (www.nytimes.com). The granddaddy of all newspapers is now both in color and on-line. What's the world coming to?!

Parks and Recreation Info (www.ci.nyc.ny.us/html/dpr/html/boomer.html). Find out what's up in the patches of greenery that dot this here beautiful city.

Sidewalk.com (newyork.sidewalk.com). Listings and info on New York happenings. Brought to you by...Microsoft.

totalny.com (www.totalny.com). Funky, with good nightlife info.

Tourist Info (www.nycvisit.com). The website of the New York Convention and Visitor's Bureau. Amazingly comprehensive...a travel guide in its own right. Links to myriad cool New York sites.

Village Voice (www.villagevoice.com). Primarily used for its lengthy real estate listings, the Voice offers articles and entertainment suggestions as well.

TRAVEL ORGANIZATIONS

American Automobile Association (AAA) Travel Related Services, 1000 AAA Dr. (mail stop 100), Heathrow, FL 32746-5063 (407-444-7000; fax 444-7380). Provides road maps and many travel guides free to members. Offers emergency road and travel services and auto insurance (for members). For emergency road services, call (800) 222-4357; to become a member, call (800) 222-4357.

Council on International Educational Exchange (CIEE), 205 East 42nd St., New York, NY 10017-5706 (888-COUNCIL/268-6245; fax 212-822-2699; www.ciee.org). A private, not-for-profit organization, Council administers work, volunteer, academic, internship, and professional programs around the world. They also offer identity cards (including the ISIC) and a range of publications, among them the useful magazine *Student Travels* (free). Call or write for further information.

Federation of International Youth Travel Organizations (FIYTO), Bredgade 25H, DK-1260 Copenhagen K, Denmark (tel. (45) 33 33 96 00; fax 33 93 96 76; email mailbox@fiyto.org; www.fiyto.org), is an international organization promoting educational, cultural and social travel for young people. Member organizations include language schools, educational travel companies, national tourist boards, accommodation centers, and other suppliers of travel services to youth and students. FIYTO sponsors the GO25 Card (www.go25.org).

International Student Travel Confederation, Herengracht 479, 1017 BS Amsterdam, The Netherlands (tel. (31) 20 421 2800; fax 20 421 2810; email istcinfo@istc.org; www.istc.org). Nonprofit confederation of student travel organizations whose focus is to promote and facilitate travel among young people and students. Member organizations include International Student Surface Travel Association (ISSA), Student Air Travel Association (SATA), IASIS Travel Insurance, the International Association for Educational and Work Exchange Programs (IAEWEP), and the International Student Identity Card Association (ISIC).

USEFUL PUBLICATIONS

In addition to this lovely volume, Let's Go offers travelers the slim, sleek fold-out maps and textual highlights of *Let's Go Map Guide: New York City*. The following businesses and organizations also specialize in keeping travelers informed:

Hippocrene Books, Inc., 171 Madison Ave., New York, NY 10016 (212-685-4371; orders 718-454-2366; fax 454-1391; email hippocre@ix.netcom.com; www.netcom.com/~hippocre). Free catalogue. Publishes travel reference books, travel guides, foreign language dictionaries, and language learning guides that cover over 100 languages. Titles include *The U.S.A. Guide to Hispanic America* and *The U.S.A. Guide to Black New York*.

Rand McNally, 150 S. Wacker Dr., Chicago, IL 60606 (800-333-0136; www.randmc-nally.com), publishes one of the most comprehensive road atlases of the U.S., Canada, and Mexico, available in their stores throughout the country, and most other bookstores for US $10. Headquarters located at 8255 N. Central Park Ave., Skokie, IL 60076. Phone orders are also available.

MEASUREMENTS

Although the metric system has made considerable inroads into American business and science, the British system of weights and measures continues to prevail in the U.S. The following is a list of U.S. units and their metric equivalents:

MEASUREMENT CONVERSIONS

1 inch (in.) = 25.4 millimeters (mm)	1 millimeter (mm) = 0.039 in.
1 foot (ft.) = 0.30 m	1 meter (m) = 3.28 ft.
1 yard (yd.) = 0.914m	1 meter (m) = 1.09 yd.
1 mile = 1.61km	1 kilometer (km) = 0.62 mi.
1 ounce (oz.) = 28.35g	1 gram (g) = 0.035 oz.
1 pound (lb.) = 0.454kg	1 kilogram (kg) = 2.202 lb.
1 fluid ounce (fl. oz.) = 29.57ml	1 milliliter (ml) = 0.034 fl. oz.
1 gallon (gal.) = 3.785L	1 liter (L) = 0.264 gal.
1 acre (ac.) = 0.405ha	1 hectare (ha) = 2.47 ac.
1 square mile (sq. mi.) = 2.59km^2	1 square kilometer (km^2) = 0.386 sq. mi.

ACCOMMODATIONS

If you know someone who knows someone who lives in New York, get that person's phone number. The cost of living in New York can rip the seams out of your wallet. At true full-service establishments, a night will cost around $125. Hotel tax is 13.4%. Many reasonable choices are available for under $60 a night, but it depends on your priorities. People traveling alone may want to spend more to stay in a safer neighborhood. The young and the outgoing may prefer a budget-style place crowded with students. Honeymooning couples may not.

Hostels offer fewer amenities than more commercial establishments yet manage to preserve a greater feeling of homeyness and camaraderie. Cheap YMCAs and YWCAs offer another budget option, but young backpackers may miss the intimacy and social life a hostel can offer. All of these places advise you to reserve in advance—even once you get to New York, you should call to make sure there are rooms available prior to making the trek there with your bags. Cheap hotels lasso hapless innocents and ingenues around the Penn Station and Times Square areas of Midtown, but you may want to avoid these sketchy spots—the hotel rooms often rent by the hour. Budget hotels also concentrate in the lower part of East Midtown, south of the Empire State Building. These joints, around Park Avenue South in the 20s, can vary widely in quality.

Crime-free neighborhoods in the city exist only in dreams; never leave anything of value in your room. Most places have safes or lockers available, some for an extra fee. Don't sleep in your car, and never, ever sleep outdoors, anywhere in New York. The city has a hard enough time protecting its vast homeless population—tourists simply would not stand a chance.

The internet often expedites find New York accommodations. Many of the accommodations listed below have websites and some offer discounts for internet reservations. There are also a number of online sites which list accommodations or help you search for them. **New York City Reference** (www.panix.com/clay/nyc/query.cgi?H3), the **Hotel Guide** (www.HOTELGUIDE.COM), and **New York city-search.com**(www.newyork.citysearch.com/New_York/Visiting_the_City/Hotels/).

Let's Go lists prices excluding tax, unless otherwise noted.

HOSTELS

Hostels offer unbeatable deals on indoor lodging and are great places to meet budget travelers from all over the world. Hostels are generally dorm-style accommodations where the sexes sleep apart in large rooms with bunk beds. Because most hostelers don't place a huge premium on luxury or privacy, hostel beds can cost as little as $14 per night. As a tradeoff, expect few frills. Guests must often rent or bring their own sheets or "sleep sacks" (two sheets sewn together); sleeping bags are usually not allowed. Many hostels make kitchens and utensils available for their guests, and some provide storage areas and laundry facilities. Some hostels are in former hotels, while others like to call themselves hotels. In most hostels, you can get a room with fewer occupants and more conveniences for a little more money. Most guests are students or of student age, often from outside the U.S., but the clientele can be surprisingly mixed. This diversity of backgrounds and experiences leads to many late-night conversations in the common room.

If you're going to travel extensively in the rest of the U.S. or Canada, you should consider joining **Hostelling International-American Youth Hostels (HI-AYH)** the leading organization of U.S. hostels. There are over 300 HI-AYH-affiliated hostels throughout North America; these are usually kept up to a higher standard than most private hostels, though they tend to be more strict and institutional. HI-AYH runs an excellent hostel in New York, with much space and many amenities (see below). Yearly **HI-AYH membership** is $25 for adults, $10 for those under 18, $35 for families, and $15 for those over 54. **Nonmembers** who wish to stay at an HI-AYH hostel usually pay $3 extra, which can be applied toward membership. For more information, contact HI-AYH, 733 15th St. NW, #840, Washington, D.C. 20005 (202-783-6161, ext. 136; fax 202-783-6171; email hiayhserv@hiayh.org; www.hiayh.org), or inquire at any HI-affiliated hostel.

Though you may not be as enthusiastic as the Village People, don't overlook the **Young Men's Christian Association (YMCA)** or the **Young Women's Christian Association (YWCA).** The rates are often better those of city hotels. Singles average $45-61 per night, rooms include use of a library, pool, and other facilities. You may have to share a room and use a communal bath or shower, however. Some YMCAs in New York (listed below) accept women and families as well as men. Reserve at least two weeks in advance, and expect to pay a refundable key deposit of about $10. For information and reservations, write or call **The Y's Way,** 224 E. 47th St., New York, NY 10017 (212-308-2899).

A very friendly alternative to hostels is **Homestay New York,** 630 E. 19th St., Brooklyn (phone and fax 718-434-2071, homestayny.com, email helayne@homestayny.com). Travelers are placed in homes of New York City residents, mostly in outer boroughs but all within 30 min. of Manhattan. Rates range from $90 per day for a standard single to $130 for a deluxe double and include some meals, a metrocard, and a phone card. Call or email for reservations at least 10 days ahead.

Let's Go lists New York's best hostels and YMCA/YWCAs, ranked according to price, safety, and location. Do check our hotel and B&B listings, however, as you may find surprising deals in a more charming ambience.

■ Banana Bungalow, 250 W. 77th St. (800-6-HOSTEL; www.bananabungalow.com), at Broadway. Subway: #1, 9 to 79th St. Banana Bungalow aspires to be the largest hostel in the world; for now, it's merely the most fun. Linens and a bathroom in each clean dorm room at no extra cost. The hostel bases its amiable atmosphere around $5 keg parties on the rooftop lounge, with its gorgeous view of the Hudson River. Also, free use of large-screen TV lounge and kitchen, innumerable outings and tours, and discounts at local pubs, restaurants, and movie theaters. Fax service. Internet access. Common refrigerator. Half-price Sony movie theater tickets. 10-bed dorms $24; 6-bed dorms $25; 4-bed dorms $30. Prices about 20% lower in winter. Passport or out-of-state ID required. $10 key deposit. Breakfast included. 14-day max. stay. Check-in and check-out anytime. No curfew.

■ New York International HI-AYH Hostel, 891 Amsterdam Ave. (932-2300; fax 932-2574; www.hinewyork.org; reserve@hinewyork.org), at 103rd St. Subway: #1, 9 or B, C to 103rd St.; just one block from the #1, 9 subway. In a block-long, landmark building, resides the mother of all youth hostels—the largest in the U.S., with 90 dorm-style rooms and 480 beds. It shares its site with the **CIEE Student Center** (666-3619), an information depot for travelers, as well as a **Council Travel** office and supply store where you can buy everything from a money pouch to your next *Let's Go* guide. Spiffy new soft carpets, blonde-wood bunks, and spotless bathrooms. Members' kitchens and dining rooms, coin-operated laundry machines ($1), communal TV lounges, and a large outdoor garden. Walking tours and outings. Internet access. Key-card entry to individual rooms. Nov.-Apr.: 10- to 12-bed dorms $22, 6- to 8-bed dorms $24, 4-bed dorms $27. May-Oct.: dorms $2 more. Nonmembers pay $3 more. Groups of 4-9 may get private rooms ($120); groups of 10 or more definitely will. Linen and towels included. Secure storage area and individual lockers. 29-night max. stay, 7-night in summer. Open 24hr. Check-in any time. Check-out 11am (late check-out fee $5). No curfew. Excellent wheelchair access.

■ Uptown Hostel, 239 Lenox (Malcolm X) Ave. (666-0559; fax 663-5000), at 122nd St. Subway: #2, 3 to 125th St. Run by the knowledgeable and friendly Gisèle, who helps long-term travelers find uptown apartments and temporary jobs. Bunk beds; clean, comfy rooms. Spacious hall bathrooms. Wonderful new common room, kitchen, and recently sanded floors add to the family atmosphere. Sept.-May: singles $15; doubles $23; June-Aug.: singles $17; doubles $23. Key deposit $10. Check-in 10am-8pm. Lockout June-Aug. 11am-4pm. Call as far in advance as possible for summer, otherwise at least 2 days is enough.

De Hirsch Residence, 1395 Lexington Ave. (415-5650 or 800-858-4692; fax 415-5578; dehirsch@92ndsty.org), at 92nd St. Subway: #6 to 96th St. Affiliated with the 92nd St. YMHA/YWHA, De Hirsch has some of the larger, cleaner, and more convenient hostel housing in the city. Air-conditioned rooms near huge hall bathrooms, kitchens, and laundry machines on every other floor give this hostel a collegiate feel. Single-sex floors, strictly enforced. 24hr. access and security. Access to the many facilities of the 92nd St. Y, including free Nautilus, 75 ft. swimming pool, and reduced rates for concerts. Organized activities such as video nights in the many common rooms and walking tours of New York. Singles $75, doubles $48. 3-day min. stay. Long-term stays from 2 months or longer for $835 per month for singles, $580-690 per month for beds in doubles. Application required at least a month in advance; must be a student or working in the city for long-term eligibility. Group rates available. Wheelchair accessible.

International Student Center, 38 W. 88th St. (787-7706; fax 580-9283), between Central Park West and Columbus Ave. Subway: B, C to 86th St. Open only to foreigners aged 18-30; you must show a foreign passport or valid visa to be admitted. An aging brownstone on a tree-lined street noted for frequent celebrity sightings. No-frills bunk rooms include showers and linens. Single and mixed-sex rooms available. Large basement TV lounge with kitchen, fridge, and affable atmosphere. 8- to 10-bed dorms $15. Key deposit $10. 7-night max. stay (flexible in winter). Open daily 8am-11pm. No curfew. No reservations, and generally full in summer, but call after 10:30am on the day you wish to stay and they'll hold a bed for you until you arrive. No wheelchair access; lots of stairs.

Sugar Hill International House, 722 Saint Nicholas Ave. (926-7030; email infohostel @aol.com; www.hostels.com/rabbit), at 146th St. Subway: A, B, C, D to 145th St. Located on Sugar Hill in Harlem, across from the subway station. Reassuring, lively neighborhood. Converted brownstone with comfortable and enormous rooms, many of them with large windows that provide views of the wide avenue in front. The friendly staff is practically a living library of Harlem knowledge; ask Jim anything about the city that you've ever wanted to know. Rooms for 2 to 10 people. All-female room available. Internet access $2 per 30min. Facilities include kitchens, stereo, and paperback library. Just up the street the owners of Sugar Hill also run the 4-floor **Blue Rabbit Hostel,** 730 Saint Nicholas Ave. (491-3892). Similar to Sugar Hill, but with more doubles and hence more of a sense of privacy. Friendly kitty-cats, common room, and kitchen. Amazingly spacious rooms. All of the following prices and info apply to both hostels. Rooms $18-22. Key deposit $10. 2-week max. stay. Check-in 9am-10pm. Check-out 11am. No lockout. No curfew. Call one month in advance during off-season. No reservations accepted July-Sept. Passport ID required. No smoking.

International Student Hospice, 154 E. 33rd St. (228-7470), between Lexington and Third Ave. Subway: #6 to 33rd St. Up a flight of stairs in an inconspicuous converted brownstone with a brass plaque saying "I.S.H." You'll never forget the friendly, helpful, owner and collector of all manner of things, Art. Despite its toney Murray Hill location, this crash pad better resembles grandpa's house than a hostel. The tiny rooms, usually occupied by European backpackers, cram bunk beds, antiquated television sets, Old World memorabilia, cracked porcelain tea cups, and clunky oak night tables. The ceilings are crumbling and the stairs slant precariously, but the house is slowly being restored by willing residents. Rooms for 1-4 people and tiny hall bathroom. $28 per night, including tax. Some weekly discounts.

Jazz on the Park, 36 W. 106th St. (932-1600; www.Jazzhostel.com; jazzonpark @aol.com), at Central Park West. Subway: B, C to 103rd St. New to the hostel scene, the Jazz riffs to the tune of friendly dorms in a renovated building right next to Central Park. Chic, clean, modern decor. Lockers and A/C make you a real cool cat. Internet access. Pretty terrace. Java bar hosts live bands and other assorted hepcats. 12- to 14-bed dorms $27; 6-to 8-bed dorms $29; 4-bed dorms $30; 2-bed dorms $37. Taxes, linens, towels, and breakfast included. Check-out 11am. No curfew. No wheelchair access.

Chelsea International Hostel, 251 W. 20th St. (647-0  www.chelseahostel.com), between Seventh and Eighth Ave. to 23rd St. Located in Chelsea on a block with a police preci dreads characterize the clientele of this 300-bed hostel overf pean youth. The congenial staff offers pizza on Wednesday windows and a sink, and guests have access to a backyard able. Internet access. Smallish but adequate 4- and 6-person $25; private rooms $55, with A/C $60. Key deposit $10. 24hr. Reservations recommended.

Aladdin Hotel, 317 W. 45th St. (246-8580; fax 246-6036), between Eighth and Ninth Ave. Subway: #1, 2, 3, 9, A, C, E, N, or R to 42nd St. Purple, yellow, green, and red decor makes it look like either a trendy club or a circus. Strong presence of international travelers on the rooftop garden. 4-bed dorms $30 per bed. Singles and doubles with shared bath $75-85. Accepts AmEx, V, MC. Reserve at least one week in advance. No wheelchair access.

Chelsea Center Hostel, 313 W. 29th St. (643-0214; fax 473-3945; chelcenter @aol.com), between Eighth and Ninth Ave. Subway: #1, 2, 3, 9, A, C, or E to 34th St. To enter, ring the labeled buzzer at the door of an inconspicuous brownstone. Gregarious, knowledgeable, multi-lingual staff will help you out with New York tips. Room for 22 guests—16 of whom stay in a spacious basement room with a summer camp feel. One of the more friendly and accommodating around, this hostel even boasts a lovely back garden. 2 showers. Dorm beds in summer $27, in winter $25. Linen provided. Light breakfast included. 2-week max. stay. Check-in 8:30am-11pm. Flexible lockout 11am-5pm. Be sure to call ahead; it's usually full in summer. Cash and traveler's checks only.

Big Apple Hostel, 119th W. 45th St. (302-2603; fax 302-2605; www.concentric.net/ ~bigapple), between Sixth and Seventh Ave. Subway: #1, 2, 3, 9, N, or R to 42nd St.; or B, D, or E to Seventh Ave. Centrally located, this hostel offers clean, comfortable, carpeted rooms, full kitchen with refrigerator, big back deck, luggage room, barbecue grill, common rooms, and laundry facilities. Lockers in some rooms, but bring your own lock. In-house cafeteria. There's even a playful cat, Caesar. Americans accepted with out-of-state photo ID or some other convincing means of proving themselves tourists. Bunk in dorm-style room with shared bath $28. Singles and doubles $75. Reception open 24hr. Accepts V, MC. No reservations accepted Aug.-Sept., but they'll hold a bed if you call after 11:30am on the day of arrival. Reservations accepted Oct.-June by email (go through the website) or fax—send your credit card number. No wheelchair access.

YMCA—Vanderbilt, 224 E. 47th St. (756-9600; fax 752-0210), between Second and Third Ave. Subway: #6 to 51st St.; or E, F to Lexington/Third Ave. Five blocks from Grand Central Station. Convenient and well-run, with reasonable prices and security. Clean, brightly lit lobby bustles with jabbering international backpackers. Each small room has A/C and cable TV; pretty low bathroom-to-people ratio, but aah, the perks! Lodgers get free use of the well-equipped gym (StairMasters, aerobics classes, Nautilus machines, pool, and sauna) and safe-deposit boxes. Five shuttles per day to the airports. Singles $68; doubles $81, with sink $83. Key deposit $10. 25-night max. stay. Check-in 3pm. Check-out 11am; luggage storage until departure $1 per bag. Make reservations 2-3 weeks in advance and guarantee with a deposit. Accepts AmEx, V, MC. Wheelchair accessible.

YMCA—West Side, 5 W. 63rd St. (787-4400; fax 875-1334), off West End Ave. Subway: #1, 9 or A, C, E or B, D, Q, to 59th St./Columbus Circle. Small, well-maintained rooms, bustling cafeteria, and spacious lounges in a popular Y with an impressive Moorish facade. Free access to pool, indoor track, racquet courts, and Nautilus equipment. Showers on every floor and spotless bathrooms. Coded locks on all bathrooms add a sense of security. A/C and cable TV in every room. 24hr. security and safe deposit boxes. Singles $68, with bath $95; doubles $80, with bath $110. 25-day max. stay. Check-out noon. No curfew. Reservations recommended. A few stairs at entrance; otherwise wheelchair-friendly.

McBurney, 206 W. 24th St. (741-9226; fax 741-8724), between Seventh and ghth Ave. Subway: #1, 9 or C, E to 23rd St. A busy YMCA with a lot of activity on the ground floor. No-frills rooms upstairs are livable and clean. Mix of elderly locals, students, and other travelers. All rooms have TV. Free access to pool and athletic facilities. Singles $59-61; doubles $71; triples $91; quads $102. With A/C add $5. Key deposit $5. 25-day max. stay. 24hr. door security. Office open daily 8am-11pm. Check-out noon. Usually has vacancies, but reservations are advisable and require a credit card or $59 money order. Wheelchair accessible.

YMCA—Flushing, 138-46 Northern Blvd., Flushing, Queens (718-961-6880; fax 718-461-4691), between Union and Bowne St. Subway: #7 to Main St.; from there, walk about 10min. north on Main St. (the Ave. numbers should get smaller), and turn right onto Northern Blvd. This branch has recently gone co-ed, opening a limited number of rooms on one floor to women. The area between the Y and Flushing's nearby shopping district is lively and well populated, but the neighborhood deteriorates north of Northern Blvd. Carpeted, small but clean rooms, with TV and A/C. Bathrooms and public telephones are in the hall. Daily maid service provided. Gym, Nautilus, squash, and swimming facilities included. Singles $46; doubles $65. 25-night max. stay (longer stays possible with advance arrangements). Key deposit $10. 2 forms of photo ID required. Make reservations at least a month in advance for summer, otherwise one week in advance. Accepts AmEx, V, MC.

DORMITORIES

Miss that two-by-four dorm ambience? Now you can experience it while traveling, too. Some colleges and universities open their residence halls to conferences and travelers, especially during the summer. You may have to share a bath, but rates are often low and facilities are usually clean and well maintained. If you hope to stay at a school, contact its housing office before you leave.

Columbia University, 1230 Amsterdam Ave. (678-3235; fax 678-3222), at 120th St. Subway: #1; 9 to 116th St. Whittier Hall sets aside 10 rooms for visitors year-round. Rooms are clean. Generally tight 24hr. security. Not the safest neighborhood, but well-populated until fairly late at night. Singles $45; doubles with A/C and bath (some with kitchen) $75. Reserve in Mar. for May-Aug., in July for Sept.-Dec. Credit card deposit required—AmEx, V, MC, and Discover accepted.

New York University, 14a Washington Pl. (998-4621; www.nyu.edu\housing\summer). NYU's Summer Housing Office rents rooms only to enrolled NYU summer school students.

HOTELS

No chocolate dainties for you—consider yourself lucky if you've found a reasonably priced room. A single in a cheap hotel should cost $45-60. Most hotel rooms can (and should) be reserved in advance. Ask the hotel owner if you can see a room before you pay for it. You should be told in advance whether the bathroom is communal or private. Most hotels require a key deposit when you register. Check-in usually takes place between 11am and 6pm, check-out before 11am. You may be able to store your gear for the day even after vacating your room and returning the key, but most proprietors will not take responsibility for the safety of your belongings. Some hotels require a *non-refundable* deposit for reservations. However, the hotel may allow you to use your deposit on a future stay at the hotel.

Let's Go has found the best budget hotels and ranked them in order of value, based on price, facilities, safety, and location.

Carlton Arms Hotel, 160 E. 25th St. (679-0680; www.carltonarms.com), between Lexington and Third Ave. Subway: #6 to 23rd St. Stay inside a submarine and peer through portholes at the lost city of Atlantis, travel to Renaissance Venice, or sleep with 3 naked ladies suspended from your walls. Each room has a different motif by a different avant-garde artist. "I sought to create a resounding rhythm that echoed wall-to-wall, layer upon layer, to fuse our separate impressions into one existence," writes the artist of room 5B. Um. Although aggressive adornment can't completely obscure the age of these budget rooms, it does prove a playful distraction for those who don't mind the shared baths or lack of A/C. All rooms have sinks. Singles $63, with bath $75; doubles $80, with bath $92; triples $99, with bath $111. Discounts for students and foreign travelers: singles $57, with bath $68; doubles $73, with bath $84; triples $90, with bath $101. Pay for 7 or more nights up front and get a 10% discount. Check-out 11:30am. Make reservations for summer at least 2 months in advance. Confirm reservations at least 10 days in advance. Accepts MC, V.

Gershwin Hotel, 7 E. 27th St. (545-8000; fax 684-5546; gershwin@attmail.com; www.netprop.com/gershwin), between Fifth and Madison Ave. Subway: #6, or N, R to 28th St. This funky hotel full of pop art, random furniture, and artsy twenty-somethings, seems more like a live MTV show than a place to stay. Currently, the hotel offers nightly entertainment including poetry, comedy, concerts, and open-mic nights, as well as an art gallery next door that features local and professional artists. 4-bed dorms $27 per bed, tax included. Private rooms (single or double occupancy) $99-139; for triples or quads add an additional $10 per person. 21-day max. stay. 24hr. reception. Check-out 11am. No curfew. Accepts AmEx, V, MC.

Chelsea Savoy Hotel, 209 W. 23rd St. (929-9353; fax 741-6309; www.citysearch.com/nyc/chelseasavoy), between Seventh and Eighth Ave. Clean, functional, and welcoming rooms decorated in forest green. All rooms have private bath, TV with cable, A/C, irons and boards, and hair dryers. 24hr. desk and security. Singles $99-115; doubles $125-145; quad $145-185. Group rates available. Check-out 11am. Reservations recommended. Wheelchair accessible.

Portland Square Hotel, 132 W. 47th St. (382-0600 or 800-388-8988; fax 382-0684), between Sixth and Seventh Ave. Subway: B, D, F, Q to 50th St./Sixth Ave. Rooms are carpeted, clean, pink, and green. Perks include phones, cable TV, A/C, sink, and safe in every room, but the hotel's greatest asset is its location. Singles with shared bath $60, with private bath $90; doubles with shared bath $70, with private bath $115; twins $125; triples $125; quads $145. Check-in 3pm, check-out noon. Accepts AmEx, JCB, MC, V.

Herald Square Hotel, 19 W. 31st St. (279-4017 or 800-727-1888; fax 643-9208; email hersquhtl@aol.com; www.heraldsquarehotel.com), at Fifth Ave. Subway: B, D, F, or N, R to 34th St. In the original Beaux-Arts home of the original *Life* magazine. Historic magazine covers grace the hallways and each of the small, pleasant rooms. Many rooms have undergone recent renovations, but all rooms include TV with cable, safes, phones, voicemail messaging, and A/C. Singles with shared bath $60, with private bath $85; doubles $115, twins $130; triples $160; quads $175. International students get a 10% discount. Accepts AmEx, Diner's Club, JCB, MC, V. Reservations recommended 2-3 weeks in advance.

Pioneer Hotel, 341 Broome St. (226-1482; fax 266-3525), between Elizabeth St. and the Bowery. Subway: N, R to Canal and walk north several blocks to Broome. Located between Little Italy and the Lower East Side in a 100 year-old building, the Pioneer is a good, no-frills place to stay if you want to be close to the addictive nightlife of SoHo and the East Village. All rooms have TV, sinks, and ceiling fans. Rooms with private bathrooms have A/C. Generally tight security at night in a neighborhood that requires it. Tax included on all prices. Singles $53; doubles $70, with bath $82; triples $82, with bath $127. Check-out 11am. Reservations recommended, at least 6 weeks in advance during peak season. Accepts AmEx, Diner's Club, Discover, MC, V.

Pickwick Arms Hotel, 230 E. 51st St. (355-0300 or 800-742-5945), between Second and Third Ave. Subway: #6 to 51st St.; or E, F to Lexington/Third Ave. Business types congregate in this well-priced, mid-sized hotel. Chandeliered marble lobby contrasts with tiny rooms and microscopic hall bathrooms. Roof garden and airport service available. A/C, cable TV, phones, and voicemail in all rooms. Singles $70, with bath $100; doubles with bath $130; studios with double bed and sofa for 2 people $150; for 4-person family $170. Additional person in room $25. Check-in 2pm. Check-out 1pm. A credit card to guarantee room. Accepts AmEx, Diner's Club, MC, V.

Chelsea Inn, 46 W. 17th St. (645-8989; www.chelseainn.com), between Fifth and Sixth Ave. Subway: F or R to 23rd St. Charmingly mismatched antique furniture in spacious pension-style rooms with kitchenettes. Attracts a primarily European crowd. Pricey but worth a splurge, if you can swing it. Guest rooms with shared bath $99-119; studios $139-149; one-bedroom suites $179; 2-bedroom suites $209-229. 10% ISIC discount. Office open daily 9am-7pm. Check-in 3pm. Check-out noon. Prices expected to rise in 2000.

Washington Square Hotel, 103 Waverly Pl. (777-9515 or 800-222-0418; fax 979-8373; www.vyp.com/washington square), at MacDougal St. Subway: A, B, C, D, E, F, Q to W. 4th St. Fantastic location. Glitzy marble and brass lobby, with an ornate wrought-iron gate in the lobby. A/C, TV, and key-card entry to individual rooms. Clean and comfortable; friendly and multilingual staff. Now with restaurant/bar with lounge, a meeting room, and an exercise room. Singles $116-130; doubles $136-140. Two twin beds $146-155; quads $155-174. Rollaway bed $17. 10% ISIC discount. Continental breakfast included. Reservation required 2-3 weeks in advance for weekend stays. Accepts AmEx, JCB, MC, V.

Hotel Grand Union, 34 E. 32nd St. (683-5890; fax 689-7397), between Madison and Park Ave. Subway: #6 to 33rd St. This centrally located hotel offers clean, pleasant rooms furnished with cable TV, phone, A/C, a mini-fridge, and full bathroom. 24hr. security. Singles and doubles $110; triples $125; quads $150; quints $180. Accepts AmEx, Diner's Club, Discover, JCB, MC, V. Wheelchair accessible.

Hotel Stanford, 43 W. 32nd St. (563-1500 or 800-365-1114; fax 629-0043; email STANFORDNY@aol.com), between Fifth and Broadway in NY's Korean district. Subway: B, D, F, or N, R to 34th St. This glitzy Korean hotel's lobby glitters with sparkling ceiling lights and a polished marble floor. Moreover, the Stanford adjoins the **Gam Mee OK** restaurant and the **Pari Pari Ko Bakery,** which serves up Korean delicacies and pastries. Rooms are impeccably clean, with firm mattresses, plush carpeting, cable TV, A/C, small refrigerators, and complimentary continental breakfast. Singles $90-110; doubles $120-150; triples $130-150. Check-out noon; fee for late check-out. Accepts AmEx, JCB, MC, V. Reservations strongly recommended.

Hotel Wolcott, 4 W. 31st St. (268-2900; fax 563-0096; email sales@wolcott.com; www.wolcott.com), between Fifth Ave. and Broadway. Subway: B, D, F, or N, R to 34th St. Enter the lobby and step into a Rococo fantasy, where flowery floors, gold leaf, marble, chandeliers, and recessed ceilings cast a somewhat gaudy facade of luxury. Fortunately, the newly renovated rooms are far simpler and include A/C, cable TV (including pay channels, such as HBO), telephones, and voicemail. Recent additions include a business center, gym, and a money-grubbing internet kiosk (cash and credit card accepted). The hotel also offers safety deposit boxes and self-service laundry. The building boasts a history as rich as its decor: here, in the early 1900s, *Titanic* survivors wrote letters and, decades later, 50s rock-and-roll legend Buddy Holly recorded two hit albums in now-defunct studios upstairs. Singles and doubles $120-150; triples $140-170; suites (for 3) $145-190. Accepts AmEx, JCB, MC, V.

Malibu Studios Hotel, 2688 Broadway (222-2954; fax 678-6842), at 103rd St. Subway: #1, 9 to 103rd St. Renovations have brought this former Gen-X kitschhaus into the slick 1990s. Clean rooms; sink for those with shared bath. Staff doles out VIP passes to popular clubs like Webster Hall. 24hr. desk. Singles $49; doubles $69; triples $85; quads $99. Deluxe rooms include private bath, A/C, and TV: singles and doubles $99, triples $124, quads $139. Reservations required. Ask about student, off-season, and weekly/monthly discounts. No wheelchair access.

Senton Hotel, 39-41 W. 27th St. (684-5800; fax 545-1690), between Sixth Ave. and Broadway. Subway: R to 28th St. Look for the shockingly blue exterior. Comfortable beds in spacious quarters, includes A/C, TV with cable, VCR, and refrigerators in every room. A number of rooms have been renovated, more to be complete by 2000. Home to many locals. The hotel has 24hr. security, so don't try to sneak in overnight guests. Singles with hall bath $64; doubles $75; suites (2 double beds) $86; 4-bed suites $92. Cash or traveler's checks only.

Hayden Hall, 117 W. 79th St. (787-4900; fax 496-3975), off Columbus Ave. Subway: B, C to 81st St. Great location, but rooms are a bit run-down. Singles and doubles $65, with private bath $100 (2-3 people); 2-room suite with private bath $125 (maximum of 4 people). Good weekly rates. Reservations recommended.

Murray Hill Inn, 143 E. 30th St. (683-6900 or 888-996-6376; fax 545-0103; www.MurrayHill.com), between Lexington and Third Ave. Subway: #6 to 28th St. Clean, floral-print rooms with shared baths exude a Holiday Inn feel at reasonable prices. Keep your fingers crossed for a room on a lower floor, as the elevator-less journey upward can be taxing. All rooms have sink, A/C, cable TV, and phone. Singles with shared bath $75; doubles with shared bath $95, with private bath $125. Extra bed $10. 21-day max. stay. Check-in 3pm, check-out noon. Cash and traveler's checks only.

Hotel 17, 225 E. 17th St. (475-2845; fax 677-8178; www.citysearch.com/nyc/hotel17), between Second and Third Ave. Just blocks from Gramercy Park, this historic site served as the setting for Woody Allen's *Manhattan Murder Mystery;* Madonna even had her portrait done in these eccentric accommodations. Mostly foreign crowd enjoys beautiful, high-ceilinged rooms with sink and A/C. Singles $75; doubles $98. Deluxe rooms with cable, hair-dryer, and daily maid service: doubles $109-$130; triples $149. Check-in 1pm. Check-out noon. Cash or traveler's checks only.

Broadway Inn, 264 W. 46th St. (997-9200 or 800-826-6300; fax 768-2807; www.broadwayinn.com), at Eighth Ave. Subway: #1, 2, 3, 9; or 7; or N, R; or S to Times Square. Located conveniently in the heart of the theater district, the quiet, cozy rooms in this lodge have an aura of unpretentious dignity. Singles $85-95; doubles $115-195; suites (for 2 adults and 2 children 6-12 or for 3 adults) $205. Continental breakfast included. AmEx, V, MC. No wheelchair access.

Madison Hotel, 21 E. 27th St. (532-7373 or 800-962-3576; fax 686-0092; madihotel@aol.com; www.madison-hotel.com), at Madison Ave. Subway: #6, N, or R to 28th St. Precipitous stairs, harboring the occasional cockroach, or an eerie elevator, lead to actually decent rooms with color TV, A/C, and private baths—refrigerators seem to be luck of the draw. Singles $86; doubles $105. Rooms for 2-4 with 2 double beds or a sleeper sofa $126. Prices include hotel tax. 14-night max. stay. Check-in noon. Check-out 11am. $5 cable deposit. $40 phone deposit. Accepts AmEx, Discover, MC, V.

BED AND BREAKFASTS

Bed and Breakfasts (private homes that rent out one or more spare rooms to travelers) are a great alternative to impersonal hotel and motel rooms. They're hardly your stereotypical B&Bs—no sleepy New England village squares or big front porches—but Manhattan does have a wide selection. Many don't have phones, TVs, or showers with their rooms. Reservations should be made a few weeks in advance, usually with a deposit. Most apartments listed have two-night minimums. Listings are divided into "hosted"—meaning traditional B&B arrangements—and "unhosted," meaning that the people renting you the apartment will not be there. Apartments in the West Village and the Upper East Side cost the most. Most B&B agencies list accommodations in boroughs other than Manhattan; these can be an excellent budget alternative. Prices vary according to borough, neighborhood, and accommodation size (but generally run singles $70-100; doubles $80-135), so call for specifics with a neighborhood and price range in mind. **Urban Ventures** (594-5650; fax 947-9320) is the oldest and most established agency in the city, with a hopping 900 listings covering Manhattan, plus additional listings for Brooklyn and Queens. **New World Bed and Breakfast** (675-5600 or toll-free from the U.S. and Canada, 800-443-3800; fax 675-6366) specializes in short-term furnished apartments, and **Bed and Breakfast of New York** (645-8134) offers weekly and monthly rates.

🔖 **Akwaaba Mansion,** 347 Macdougal St. (718-455-5958; email akwaabainn@aol.com; www.akwaaba.com), in Bedford-Stuyvesant. Subway: A, C to Utica Ave. The exterior of the Akwaaba Mansion looks straight out of New England, but the interior looks unlike anything you've ever seen. The inn won an award from the New York Landmarks Preservation Society. Photographers come here to do fashion and advertising shoots. Each of the 4 guest rooms has its own theme, from the Ashante Suite to the Black Memorabilia Suite. Library, TV room, tree-shaded patio, wrap-around sun porch, and breakfast served in an elegant dining room. A reason to come to this much-maligned neighborhood. Rooms comfortably accommodate two people. All rooms include private bath and A/C. Deluxe rooms (jacuzzi and Southern breakfast) $135, on weekends $150. Other rooms $120, on weekends $135. Check-in 4-9pm. Check-out 11am. Cocktail hour Friday and Saturday with live jazz. Call at least a month in advance to reserve a room.

■ **Bed & Breakfast on the Park,** 113 Prospect Park West (718-499-6115; fax 718-499-1385), in Park Slope, Brooklyn, between 6th and 7th St. Subway: F to Seventh Ave./Park Slope, then 2 blocks east to the park and 2 blocks north. Perfect for putting up nervous parents who doubt the city's safety (or beauty). A magnificently restored brownstone jam-packed with Victoriana, this decadent, aromatic opiate of a hotel lacks only adequate horse stables and gas lighting. Classy furnishings (rococo armoires, oriental carpets, damask) are museum-quality, but you can touch and even fall asleep on them. Gourmet breakfast in sumptuous (not-so) common room. 7 doubles, each in a different style, range $175-275. Get out of Manhattan and splurge in Park Slope.

New York Bed and Breakfast, 134 W. 119th St. (666-0559; fax 663-5000), between Lenox and Adam Clayton Powell Ave. in Harlem. Subway: #2, 3 to 116th St. or 125th St. Run by Gisèle of the Uptown Hostel (see p. 79), this B&B features a double and single bed in every light and airy room, coffee, juice, and danishes, and an aloof black cat, Harlem. (Harlem is restricted to certain rooms, so folks with allergies need not fret.) Gisèle is knowledgeable about the neighborhood and local entertainment venues, speaks French, and will help you find an apartment or job. She is currently in the process of opening another B&B a few doors down—pretty much the same as the first, but sans the felines. Doubles $55; triples $65. 2-night min. stay. Check-in 1-7pm. No lockout. Call 3-4 weeks in advance during the summer.

Crystal's Castle Bed & Breakfast, 119 W. 119th St. (865-5522; fax 280-2061; www.concentric.net/Castlev; email castlev@concentric.net), between Lenox (Malcolm X) Ave. and Adam Clayton Powell Ave. Subway: #2 to 125th St. and Lenox Ave. Two neat rooms in a comfy brownstone belonging to Crystal and her family of professional musicians. Singles $76; doubles $97; both $409 per week (plus tax). Continental breakfast served in or near well-tended garden. 25% deposit required. Check-out 1pm. Call 2 months in advance in summer; 1 month ahead in the off-season. 1-week cancellation notice required. Accepts MC, V.

RESTAURANTS

New Yorkers' high standards in everything ensure top-notch eats. Meanwhile, the city's ethnic diversity has engendered a stupendous variety of palettes. New York's restaurants do more than the United Nations to promote international goodwill, cross-cultural exchange, and happy taste buds.

Chinese restaurants spice up every neighborhood and even fill up a town of their own. Incredible Vietnamese, Thai, Burmese, and Malaysian eateries have a high Chinatown concentration as well. For a taste of *bell'Italia*, cruise Mulberry Street in Little Italy, or, better yet, Belmont in the Bronx. For the most realistic of post-post-revolutionary Russian cuisine, make a trip to Brooklyn's Brighton Beach. Many Eastern European dishes have become New York staples: *knishes* (plump traditional dumplings), *pierogi* (Polish or Ukrainian or Russian dough creations stuffed with fruit, potato, or cheese and garnished with fried onions and sour cream), and *blintzes* (thin pancakes rolled around sweet cheese, blueberries, and other divine fillings).

Then, of course, there are always the two old favorites: **pizza** and **bagels.** New Yorkers like their pizza thin and hot, with no small amount of grease. And if you don't fold your slice in half, you're not a native. The humble bagel is Brooklyn's major contribution to Western civilization. Exiles from the city often find bagel deprivation one of the worst indignities of life outside of New York.

Street food is also a hallmark of the New York culinary experience. Smoke wafts from the carts selling sweet roasted peanuts and cashews in the winter, and vendors slather mustard over hot dogs or pretzels for a little over a dollar. In the summer flavored ice comes in all the colors of the frozen rainbow. Have fun with the food in New York; even if it bites back, you'll love it for its 'tude.

ORGANIZATION

We have prefaced the neighborhood restaurant listings with a list of the same restaurants, categorized by cuisine and by features (delivery, open late, outdoor dining, etc.). Restaurants in the *"Let's Go* Pick" category feature extraordinary combinations of low prices and high quality and are denoted by a thumb (🖐). Every restaurant listed in the **By Type of Food** and **By Feature** sections is followed by an abbreviated neighborhood label, which directs you to the section under **By Neighborhood** in which you'll find the restaurant's complete write-up. The abbreviations are as follows:

BX	Bronx	*LI*	Little Italy
BC	Central Brooklyn	*LES*	Lower East Side
BD	Downtown Brooklyn	*LM*	Lower Manhattan
BN	North Brooklyn	*MH*	Morningside Heights
BS	South Brooklyn	*NL*	NoLIta
CH	Chelsea	*Q*	Queens
CHT	Chinatown	*SH*	SoHo
EM	East Midtown	*TBC*	TriBeCa
EV	East Village	*UG*	Union Sq. and Gramercy Park
GV	Greenwich Village	*UES*	Upper East Side
HWH	Harlem and Washington Hts.	*UWS*	Upper West Side
HNJ	Hoboken, NJ	*WM*	West Midtown

BY TYPE OF FOOD

RESTAURANTS

AFRICAN
Abyssinia *SH*
Keur N'Deye *BD*
Le Grenier *HWH*
Massawa *MH*
Moroccan Star *BD*
🕏 Obaa Koryoe *MH*
🕏 Oznot's Dish *BN*

AMERICAN, STANDARD
Acme Bar and Grill *EV*
🕏 Barking Dog Luncheonette *UES*
Chat 'n Chew *UG*
First Edition *Q*
Empire K. Roaster's *Q*
EJ's Luncheonette *UES*
Good Enough to Eat *UWS*
Jackson Hole Wyoming *UES*
Jimmy's Famous Heros *BS*
Johnny Rocket's *HNJ*
Junior's *BD*
Luke's Bar and Grill *UES*
🕏 Mama's Food Shop *EV*
Moonstruck *UG*
Old Town Bar and Grill *UG*
🕏 Space Untitled *SH*
Tom's Restaurant *BC*
Tom's Restaurant *MH*
Viand *UES*

BAKERIES
Bagels on the Hudson *HNJ*
Damascus Bakery *BD*
De Lillo Pastry Shop *BX*
Ecce Panis *UES*
Egidio's Pastry Shop *BX*
🕏 Ferdinando's *BN*
Galaxy Pastry Shop *Q*
H&H Bagels *UWS*
Hammond's Finger Lickin' Bakery *BC*
🕏 Hong Kong Egg Cake Co. *CHT*
The Hungarian Pastry Shop *MH*
Lung Moon Bakery *CHT*
Sea Lane Bakery *BS*

BRITISH AND IRISH
Hourglass Tavern *WM*
St. Dymphna's *EV*
Tea and Sympathy *GV*

CAFES
Bell Café *SH*
B.M.W. Gallery and Coffee Magic *CH*
Bubby's *TBC*
Café Gitane *NL*
Café La Fortuna *UWS*
🕏 Café Lalo *UWS*
Café Mozart *UWS*
Caffè Dante *GV*
Caffè Mona Lisa *GV.*
Caffè Palermo *LI*
Caffè Raffaella *GV*
Caffè Reggio *GV*
Coffee Shop Bar *UG*
De Lillo Pastry Shop *BX*
drip *UWS*
Emporium Brasil *WM*
First Street Café *EV*
Good Enough to Eat *UWS*
Guy & Gallard *UG*
La Bella Ferrara *LI*
L Café *BN*
Le Gamin Café *SH*
Lucky's Juice Joint *SH*
National Café *EV*
Pink Pony Café *EV*
Sunburnt Espresso Bar *UG*
Sweet-n-Tart Cafe *CHT*
Tea and Sympathy *GV*
Yaffa Café *EV*
🕏 Yaffa's Tea Room *TBC*

CAJUN, CARIBBEAN, CREOLE
Brisas del Caribe *SH*
Hammond's Finger Lickin' Bakery *BC*
La Caridad 78 Restaurant *UWS*
La Isla *HNJ*
National Café *EV*
Negril *CH*

Roy's Jerk Chicken *BC*
Two Boots Restaurant *EV*

CENTRAL/EASTERN EUROPEAN
Kiev *EV*
K.K. Restaurant *EV*
Monika Restaurant *BC*
🍴 Primorski Restaurant *BS*
Stylowa Restaurant *BN*
Taste of Russia *BS*
Uncle Vanya Café *WM*
🍴 Veselka *EV*

CHINESE
🍴 Big Wong's *CHT*
East Lake *Q*
Excellent Dumpling House *CHT*
Fortune Garden *EM*
House of Vegetarian *CHT*
HSF *CHT*
Hunan Wok *BC*
Joe's Shanghai *CHT*
Little Szechuan *CHT*
Mee Noodle Shop and Grill *EV*
🍴 New York Noodle Town *CHT*
Shanghai Cuisine *CHT*
Sam Chinita Restaurant *CH*
Sam's Noodle Shop *UG*
🍴 Spring Joy *CH*
Sweet-n-Tart Cafe *CHT*
Taipei Noodle House *EM*
Tang Tang *UES*
Wong Kee *CHT*
Zen Palate *UG*

DELI
Carnegie Delicatessen *WM*
🍴 Katz's Delicatessen *LES*
🍴 Park Luncheonette *BN*
🍴 Second Ave. Delicatessen *EV*
Stage Deli *WM*

DESSERTS, SWEETS
Balducci's *GV*
Chinatown Ice Cream Factory *CHT*
🍴 Economy Candy *LES*
Eddie's Sweet Shop *Q*

🍴 The Lemon Ice King of Corona *Q*
Moishe's Bake Shop *EV*
🍴 Philip's Confections *BS*
Something Sweet *EV*
Sweet-n-Tart Cafe *CHT*
Teuscher Chocolatier *EM*
Veniero's *EV*

DINER
Bendix Diner *CH*
B&H Vegetarian Restaurant *EV*
EJ's Luncheonette *UES*
Jackson Hole Wyoming *UES*
🍴 Jackson Diner *Q*
Jerry's *SH*
Moon Dance Diner *SH*
Moonstruck *UG*
Sam Chinita Restaurant *CH*
Tom's Restaurant *BC*
Tom's Restaurant *MH*

ETHIOPIAN
Abyssinia *SH*
Massawa *MH*

FAST FOOD
Big Nick's Pizza and Burger Joint *UWS*
Burritoville *(see p. 122)*
D+S Plaza *UWS*
Europa *LM*
Frank's Papaya *LM*
McDonald's *LM*
Mike's Papaya *MH*
Papaya King *UES*
Nathan's *BS*
Tang Tang *UES*

FRENCH
Elephant and Castle *GV*
Patois *BN*

GREEK, MIDDLE EASTERN
Amir's Falafel *MH*
Caesar's *CH*
Caravan *BD*
🍴 Damask Falafel *EV*
Ferdinando's *BN*
Fountain Cafe *BD*
Mr. Falafel *BC*

RESTAURANTS

RESTAURANTS

Olive Tree Cafe *GV*
🦪 Oznot's Dish *BN*
Poseidon Bakery *WM*
🦪 Sahadi Importing Company *BD*
Sahara East *EV*
Uncle George's *Q*
Uncle Nick's Greek Cuisine *WM*
Zaytoons *BN*

IBERIAN
Spain *GV*
La Rosita Restaurant *MH*
Las Tres Palmas *BD*

INDIAN, PAKISTANI, & AFGHAN
Anand Bhavan *Q*
🦪 Ariana Afghan Restaurant *WM*
🦪 Jackson Diner *Q*
Khyber Pass Restaurant *EV*
Madras Mahal *UG*
Minar *WM*
🦪 Pakistan Tea House *TBC*
Rose of India *EV*

ITALIAN
Becco *WM*
Benito One *LI*
Cucina di Pesce *EV*
🦪 Cucina Stagionale *GV*
🦪 Da Nico *LI*
Dipalo Dairy *LI*
🦪 Dominick's *BX*
🦪 Emilia's *BX*
Intermezzo's *CH*
🦪 La Focacceria *EV*
La Mela *LI*
Lombardi's *LI*
Manganaro's *WM*
Pasquale's Rigoletto *BX*
Puglia Restaurant *LI*
Ramdazzo's Clam Bar *BS*
Red Rose Restaurant *BN*
Rocky's Italian Restaurant *LI*
Two Boots Restaurant *EV*
Zigolini's *LM*

JAPANESE AND KOREAN
🦪 Dojo *EV*
🦪 Dosanko *EM*
Kum Gang San *Q*

🦪 Go Sushi *GV*
Mill Korean Restaurant *MH*
Miyako *BN*
Obento Delight *UWS*
Sapporo *WM*
Teriyaki Boy *EV*
Yoshi *LES*

KOSHER/JEWISH
Empire K.'s Roasters *Q*
Gertel's Bake Shoppe *LES*
Guss Pickle Corp. *LES*
🦪 Katz's Delicatessen *LES*
🦪 Knish Nosh *Q*
Madras Mahal *UG*
Pastrami King *Q (see p. 217)*
Ratner's Restaurant *LES*
Yonah Schimmel Knishery *LES*

LATIN AMERICAN
El Gran Castillo de Jagua *BC*
El Gran Café Restaurant *BX*
El Pollo *UES*
Emporium Brasil *WM*
Flor's Kitchen *EV*
National Cafe *EV*
Piu Bello *Q*
Rice & Beans *WM*

MEXICAN, TEX-MEX, CAL-MEX
Benny's Burritos *EV*
🦪 El Sombrero *LES*
El Teddy's *TBC*
Fresco Tortilla Plus *BD*
🦪 Kitchen *CH*
Lupe's East L.A. Kitchen *SH*
Mama Mexico *MH*
Mary Ann's *CH*
🦪 Mary Ann's *UWS*
🦪 Original Fresco Tortillas *WM*
Vera Cruz *BN*

NEW AMERICAN
Bodega *TBC*
Brooklyn Moon *BD*
Cafe Gitane *NL*
Candela *UG*
Coldwaters *EM*
🦪 Dojo *EV*
🦪 Rice *NL*

PIZZA
- Arturo's Pizza *GV*
- Grimaldi's *B*
- John's Pizzeria *GV*
- Koronet Pizza *MH*
- Lombardi's *LI*
- Ray's Pizza *GV*
- Nick's Pizza *Q*
- The Oven *EV*
- Tony's Pizza *BS*
- Totonno Pizzeria Napolitano *BS*

SEAFOOD
- Coldwaters *EM*
- Cucina di Pesce *EV*
- Petite Crevette *BD*
- Ramdazzo's Clam Bar *BS*
- Reef Restaurant *BX*

SOUPS
- B&H Vegetarian Restaurant *EV*
- Hale and Hearty Soups *UES*
- Soups on Seventeen *CH*

SOUTHERN/BBQ
- Brother Jimmy's Carolina Kitchen *UES*
- Copeland's *HWH*
- The Pink Teacup *GV*
- Sisters *HWH*
- Sylvia's *HWH*

SOUTHEAST ASIAN
- Bali Nusa Indah *WM*
- Bendix Diner *CH*
- Bo Ky *CHT*
- Cambodia Restaurant *BD*
- Elvie's Turo-Turo *EV*
- Gia Lam *BC*
- Harden & L.C. Corp. *CHT*
- Jai-Ya *UG*
- Kelly and Ping Asian Grocery and Noodle Shop *SH*
- The Lemongrass Grill *UWS*
- Mandalay Kitchen *CHT*
- Monsoon *MH*
- Mueng Thai Restaurant *CHT*
- Nyona *CHT*
- PlanEat Thailand *BN*
- Siam Square *EV*
- Thailand Restaurant *CHT*
- Vietnam *CHT*

TIBETAN
- Lhasa *EV*
- Tibetan Kitchen *UG*
- Tibet Shambala *UWS*

VEGETARIAN
- Anand Bhavan *Q*
- B&H Vegetarian Restaurant *EV*
- Bliss *BN*
- Candle Cafe *UES*
- Coconut Grill *UES*
- Dojo Restaurant *EV*
- Eva's *GV*
- House of Vegetarian *CHT*
- Kate's Joint *EV*
- Lucky's Juice Joint *SH*
- Madras Mahal *UG*
- Quantum Leap *GV*
- Tiengarden *LES*
- Uptown Juice Bar *TBC*
- Whole Earth Bakery and Kitchen *EV*
- Zen Palate *UG*

RESTAURANTS

NOT QUITE A FREE LUNCH Most budget travelers spend their sojourn in New York City without ever stepping foot into one of the city's swankier restaurants, but there are ways to treat yourself to an *extremely* fine meal without completely busting your wallet. Every summer, many restaurants participate in **NY Restaurant Week,** during which the price of lunch corresponds to the current year. For example, the 2000 price will be $20.00. While this still might seem like a lot, at ritzy places like Lutece, Gramercy Tavern, Peter Luger, and Le Cirque, it's quite a bargain. The program has begun expanding to include the entire summer, and reservations tend to go quickly. For a list of participating restaurants, send a stamped envelope to:

NYC Restaurants
New York Convention and Visitors Bureau
2 Columbus Circle
New York, NY 10019

BY NEIGHBORHOOD

Boroughs and neighborhoods (and Hoboken, NJ) appear in alphabetical order below, and restaurants within each district are also listed alphabetically. Mind you, restaurants with Spanish names beginning with "El" or "La" appear with "E" and "L" listings; whereas a restaurant beginning with "the" will appear according to the first letter of the next word. Get it? If you don't, all will become clear as you read on.

We base our appraisals on price, quality, and atmosphere. The restaurants we'll scold you for missing are marked with our "*Let's Go* Pick" thumbs (☒): these places are a true cut above the rest. **$** signifies the $5-10 entree range, **$$** the $10-15 range, and **$$$** the $15-20 range.

THE BRONX

To get to the heart of the culinary Bronx, Arthur Ave., take subway C or D to Fordham Rd. and walk 5 blocks east; or take subway #2 to Pelham Pkwy., then Bronx bus Bx12 two stops west. See map,.

The cuisine of the Bronx reflects its diverse make-up, but the local Italian fare is the main culinary magnet of the borough. When Italian immigrants settled in the Bronx, they brought with them their recipes and a tradition of hearty communal dining. The neighborhood of **Belmont** brims with pastry shops, streetside *caffè*, pizzerias, restaurants, and mom-and-pop emporiums vending Madonna 45s and imported espresso machines, without the touristy frills of Little Italy. For a 50¢ treat, try a dixie cup of Italian ice from street vendors.

☒ **Dominick's,** 2335 Arthur Ave. (718-733-2807), near 186th St. Always packed, this small family-style Italian eatery sports an extra bar upstairs. Waiters seat you at a long table and simply ask what you want. No menu here and no set prices—locals are happy to give advice. Linguine with mussels and marinara ($7), marinated artichoke ($7), and veal *francese* ($12) are all house specials. Arrive before 6pm or after 9pm, or expect a 20min. wait. Open M and W-Sa noon-10pm, F noon-11pm, Su 1-9pm. **$-$$**

☒ **Emilia's,** 2331 Arthur Ave. (718-367-5915), near 186th St. Delicious food in large portions. The *calamari fra diavolo* ($15) and the stuffed centerloin pork chop ($15) are especially good. Appetizers $5-10, pasta $10, entrees $13-18. Lunch special $10. Open Tu-Su 11am-10pm. **$$**

Pasquale's Rigoletto, 2311 Arthur Ave. (718-365-6644). This relative newcomer to the Arthur Ave. pasta scene cooks with the best of them. Pasquale's will soothe you with luscious arias; if you have a favorite in mind, ask to have it played—or sing it yourself on amateur night (Sa). Favorite customer Joe Pesci's pictures adorn the front door. Pasta $13, meat dishes $15 and up, poultry $15, seafood $17. Open Su-Th noon-10pm, F-Sa noon-10:30pm. **$$**

El Gran Cafe Restaurant, 1024 Longwood Ave. (718-378-1016) at Southern Blvd. Among the best of the South Bronx's *cuchifritas*—cheap restaurants serving big portions of Mexican and other Latin American food. The seafood dishes can be expensive, but almost everything else is under $12. For a real deal go for the weekday lunch special between 11am and 3pm. The special changes daily, but you can always get a bowl of stew, rice, and sweet banana for under $5. Open daily 6am-midnight. **$-$$**

Reef Restaurant (a.k.a. Johnny's Reef), 2 City Island Ave. (718-885-2086). Surrounded by squawking seagulls and grease, Johnny's serves up cheap, fresh seafood. Don't expect anything fancy; you'll just get it steamed or fried. Fish and chips $8. Open Su-Th 11am-midnight, F-Sa 11am-2am. **$**

RESTAURANTS

SHOPS

De Lillo Pastry Shop, 606 E. 187 St. (718-367-8198), between Hughes and Arthur Ave. Although this small shop is often crowded, it's worth your while to sit here and sample the excellent baked goods ($1-2) along with a cappuccino ($1.85) or espresso ($1.25). Open M-F 8am-7pm, Sa-Su 8am-8pm. Closed Mondays July-Aug.

Egidio Pastry Shop, 622 E. 187th St. (718-295-6077), at Hughes. A neighborhood tradition. Since 1912, Egidio has baked up mountains of Italian pastries and cakes. The colorful cases display over 100 different fresh-baked goodies! The ever-popular cannoli ($1.25) and tiramisu ($2.50) taste divine with a steaming cappuccino ($2.75). Most desserts $1-2, homemade ices 75¢-$2.50. Open daily 7am-8pm.

BROOKLYN

Brooklyn's restaurants, delis, and cafes offer as much flavor and variety as do Manhattan's—and often at lower prices. Brooklyn Heights and Park Slope offer nouvelle cuisine but specialize in pita bread and baba ghanoush. Williamsburg has cheap eats in a funky, lo-fi atmosphere; Greenpoint is a borscht-lover's paradise; and Flatbush serves up Jamaican and other West Indian cuisine. Brooklyn also has its own Chinatown in Sunset Park and own Little Italy in Carroll Gardens. See map, .

CENTRAL BROOKLYN

Good ethnic fare abounds in central Brooklyn. Because of its growing chic, the **Park Slope** area has become home to artsy coffee shops and chi-chi restaurants, while other areas of Central Brooklyn remain a haven for international specialties. **Eighth Ave.** in Sunset Park is the heart of Brooklyn's Chinatown, and **Church Ave.** in Flatbush is the spot for Jamaican and other West Indian eateries.

El Gran Castillo de Jagua, 345 Flatbush Ave. (718-622-8700), at Carlton St. across from the subway. Subway: D, Q to Seventh Ave. A terrific place for cheap, authentic Latino food. Meat dinners with rice and beans or plantains and salad $5-12. The *mofungo* (crushed green plantains with roast pork and gravy; $3.75) is absolutely grand. Open daily 7am-midnight. Cash only. **$-$$**

Gia Lam, 5402 Eighth Ave. (718-854-8818), at 54th St. in Sunset Park. Subway: N to Eighth Ave. This popular Vietnamese restaurant serves large portions at pretty low prices. The squid with lemongrass on rice ($3.75) is an excellent lunch choice. Lunches $3-5, dinner entrees $7-10. Open M-Th 11am-10:15pm, F 11am-10:30pm, Sa-Su 10:30am-10:30pm. Cash only. **$-$$**

Hunan Wok, 106 7th Ave. (718-230-4008), between Union and President St. Subway: D, Q to Seventh Ave. Menu contains some pleasant surprises, like tangerine beef ($9) and crispy shrimp with walnuts in honey sauce ($11). A cut above the average Chinese restaurant fare. Open M-Th 11:30am-11pm, F-Sa 11:30am-midnight, Su noon-11pm. Accepts AmEx, MC, V. **$$**

Monika Restaurant, 643 Fifth Ave. (718-788-6930), between 18th and 19th St. Subway: N, R to Prospect Ave., then one block west and several blocks south. This tiny joint serves 17 different Slavic soups (including yummy cold fruit *compote*) for $1-2. Kielbasa, dumpling, and meat entrees $4-5, *pierogis* (dumplings, $3.50 for 7). Open daily noon-8pm. Cash only. Wheelchair accessible. **$**

Mr. Falafel, 226 Seventh Ave. (718-768-4961), between 3rd and 4th St. in Park Slope. Subway: D, Q to Seventh Ave. Cheap, tasty Middle Eastern food with an Egyptian emphasis. The Greek salad ($6) here stands out, as does the falafel combination ($5), served with Turkish salad, tahini, and pita. Free delivery throughout the neighborhood. Open daily 10am-11pm. Cash only. **$**

Roy's Jerk Chicken, 3125 Church Ave. (718-826-0987), between 31st and 32nd St. in Flatbush. Subway: #2 or 5 to Church Ave. and 2 blocks east. Jerk chicken is a delicious Jamaican specialty—crispy chicken roasted with a sweet and very peppery marinade and served either hot or cold. You can also sample one of the many other enticing entrees ($6-7). Open M-Th 9am-2am, F-Su 24hr. Cash only. **$**

RESTAURANTS

Tom's Restaurant, 782 Washington Ave. (718-636-9738), at Sterling Pl. Subway: #2, 3 to Brooklyn Museum. Head to Washington St. on the left side of the museum and follow it northward across the multi-lane intersection. The quintessential Brooklyn breakfast place—an old-time luncheonette complete with soda fountain and waitstaff on a first-name basis with most of the clientele. Suzanne Vega made the spot famous with her catchy folk song, *Tom's Diner*—come on, you remember the chorus: "Doo-do-doo-do..." You'll sing too, once you try specials like two eggs with fries or grits, toast, and coffee or tea ($2). Famous golden challah french toast $3. Breakfast served all day. It's crowded here, but Tom's mollifies those waiting in line with orange slices and cookies. Open M-Sa 6:30am-4pm. Cash only. **$**

SHOPS

Hammond's Finger Lickin' Bakery, 5014 Church Ave. (718-342-5770), at Utica Ave. in Flatbush. Subway: #3 or 4 to Utica Ave., then 2 blocks east. West Indian pastries all $1-2, including sweet fruit turnovers ($1.60). Open daily 8am-7pm. Cash only. Wheelchair accessible.

DOWNTOWN BROOKLYN

Brooklyn Moon, 745 Fulton St. (718-243-0424) at Lafayette St. in Fort Greene. Subway: G to Fulton St.; or C to Lafayette Ave. Comfy couches and local art hang on ochre sponge-painted walls. Delicious baked goods. Salmon burger $5.50, apple salad $3.25. But the readings are what really fill this little place up. Friday is open mic night, when aspiring bards from all over New York hold forth. In addition, the Moon hosts occasional performances and readings by authors like Jamaica Kincaid and Amiri Baraka. The preferred method of applause (preferred at least by the upstairs neighbors) is to snap your fingers. Open M-Th 7:30am-10pm, F 7:30am-1am, Sa 9:30am-11:30pm, Su 9:30am-10pm. **$**

■ **Cambodia Restaurant,** 87 S. Elliott Pl. (718-858-3262), between Lafayette and Fulton St. in Fort Greene. Subway: G to Fulton St.: or C to Lafayette Ave. True to its menu boast of "no pork, less fat," this little place serves up delicious, cheap, porkless food. *Naem chao* (cold Cambodian spring rolls with shrimp, veggies, and sweet basil, $3.50) and *ktis tao hoo* (sauteed bean curd in lemon grass sauce, $6-9) are two specialties. Open Su-Tu 11am-10pm, W-Sa 11am-11pm. Accepts V, MC. **$-$$**

Caravan, 193 Atlantic Ave. (718-488-7111), between Court and Clinton St., in Brooklyn Heights. Subway: #2, 3 or 4, 5 or M, N, R to Borough Hall, then walk 4 blocks on Court St. to Atlantic Ave. Another of Atlantic Ave.'s Middle Eastern offerings, Caravan prides itself on its couscous and tandoori oven-baked bread (evidence of the menu's Indian slant). Try the sweet *tagine* (lamb or chicken stew with onions, prunes, raisins, and cinnamon, $12). Belly-dancing Saturday nights at 8:45pm. Open M-F 11am-11pm, Sa 2pm-midnight, Su 2-10pm. Accepts AmEx, V, MC. **$$**

Fountain Cafe, 183 Atlantic Ave. (718-624-6764), in Brooklyn Heights. Subway: #2, 3 or 4, 5 or M, R to Borough Hall, then walk 4 blocks on Court St. Named for the rumbly little fountain in its center, this eatery serves up inexpensive and filling Middle Eastern food. *Shwarma* or *shish kebab* $4.65, falafel sandwich $3. Open Su-Th 10:30am-10:30pm, F-Sa 11am-11:30pm. Accepts AmEx, V, MC. Wheelchair accessible. **$**

Fresco Tortilla Plus, 113 Court St. (718-237-8898), between Schermerhorn and State St. in Brooklyn Heights. Subway: #2, 3 or 4, 5 or M, N, R to Borough Hall, then head 2 blocks down Court St. Chinese-owned Tex-Mex express that's low on ambience (unless you like fluorescent-lit mirrors) but high on flavor. Tasty eats served swiftly, including flour tortillas made from scratch. The grilled steak burrito is the most expensive thing on the menu at only $5. Open daily 11am-10:30pm. Cash only. Wheelchair accessible. **$**

■ **Grimaldi's** (formerly, Patsy Grimaldi's), 19 Old Fulton St. (718-858-4300), between Front and Water St. under the Brooklyn Bridge. Subway: A, C to High St. Delicious thin crust brick-oven pizza with wonderfully fresh mozzarella. Come early to avoid long waits. If you are stuck in line, you can admire the all-Sinatra decor or choose Ol' Blue Eyes on the jukebox. Small pies $13, large $14, toppings $2 each. Open M-Th 11:30am-11pm, F-Sa noon-midnight, Su noon-11pm. Cash only. **$**

Junior's, 386 Flatbush Ave. Extension (718-852-5257), across the Manhattan Bridge at De Kalb St. Subway: #2, 3 or 4, 5 or B, D, Q or M, N, R to Atlantic Ave. Cream, sugar, cholesterol, and the suburbanites who trek for hours to consume it. Lit up like a juke-box, Junior's feeds roast beef and brisket to hordes of loyals. 10 oz. steakburgers start at $5.75, lunch specials around $8. Justly famous for its decadent cheesecake ($3.75). Accepts AmEx, V, MC, Discover. Open Su-Th 6:30am-12:30am, F-Sa 6:30am-2am. Wheelchair accessible. **$**

Keur N'Deye, 737 Fulton St. (718-875-4937), at S. Elliott Pl. in Fort Greene. Subway: G to Fulton St.; or C to Lafayette Ave. Even in New York's culinary melting pot, there aren't many Senegalese restaurants. *Tiebou dieun* (bluefish with vegetables stewed in a tomato sauce) is Senegal's most popular dish ($8). *Yassa* (broiled or fried meat or fish in a lemon, onion, and pepper sauce), is also quite delicious ($7.50-8.50). Open Tu-Su noon-10:30pm. **$**

Las Tres Palmas, 124 Court St. (718-596-2740 or 624-9565), near Atlantic Ave. Sub-way: #2, 3 or 4, 5 or M, R to Borough Hall, then walk 3½ blocks on Court St. What this small, clean restaurant lacks in polish it makes up for with excellent, affordable food. Locals come to the self-proclaimed "best Spanish restaurant in downtown Brooklyn" to enjoy hefty bowls of soup ($2.35-3) and meat dishes like chicken *fricassee* ($6.40) or *Palomilla* steak with onions ($7.60). Entrees served with rice and beans or plantains and salad. Open daily 10am-10pm. Cash only. **$**

Moroccan Star, 205 Atlantic Ave. (718-643-0800), between Court and Clinton St., in Brooklyn Heights. Subway: #2, 3 or 4, 5 or M, N, R to Borough Hall, then walk 4 blocks on Court St. to Atlantic Ave. Delicious and reasonably cheap French-influenced Moroc-can fare. Try the *pastella* (a delicate semi-sweet chicken pie with almonds, $6). Open Tu-Th 10am-11pm, F-Sa 11am-11pm, Su noon-10pm. **$-$$**

Petite Crevette, 127 Atlantic Ave. (718-858-6660), between Henry and Clinton St., in Brooklyn Heights. Subway: #2, 3 or 4, 5 or M, N, R to Borough Hall, then walk 4 blocks on Court St. to Atlantic Ave. Half retail fish market, half restaurant, this small place serves tasty seafood dishes. Daily specials like salmon, tuna, and tilefish. Sandwiches $5-6, entrees $10-13. Open Su-Th 11am-10:30pm, F-Sa 11am-11pm. Cash only. **$-$$**

SHOPS

Damascus Bakery, 195 Atlantic Ave. (718-855-1456), in Brooklyn Heights. Subway: #2, 3 or 4, 5 or M, R to Borough Hall, then walk down 4 blocks on Court St. Friendly bakery serving up all kinds of baked goods, Middle Eastern and otherwise. Package of fresh pita bread 50¢, superior baklava $1.50, spinach and feta pies $1.20. Open daily 7:30am-7pm.

Latticini-Barese, 138 Union St. (718-625-8694), between Columbia and Hicks St., in Red Hook. Subway: F, G to Carroll St. Neighborhood cheese shop sells mouth-watering homemade mozzarella for only $5 per lb. Cash only. Open M-Sa 8am-6pm.

Sahadi Importing Company, 187 Atlantic Ave. (718-624-4550), between Court and Clinton St. in Brooklyn. Subway: #2, 3 or 4, 5 or N, R to Borough Hall/Court St. A Mid-dle Eastern emporium that draws clientele from all over the city, stocking spices and seasonings, dried fruits, 20 kinds of olives, and an array of spreads and dips like hum-mus and baba ghanoush. The *lebany*, made with yogurt and spices, is great. Open M-F 9am-7pm, Sa 8:30am-7pm. Accepts V, MC.

NORTH BROOKLYN

Bliss, 191 Bedford Ave. (718-599-2547), between 6th and 7th St. Subway: L to Bedford Ave. Full of blissed-out herbivores, this almost-vegan (they use eggs and cheese) hotspot serves up tasty specialties like a marinated-tofu sandwich with horseradish sauce ($6). BYOB. Open Su-Th 8am-11pm, F-Sa 11am-11pm. **$**

Ferdinando's, 151 Union St. (718-855-1545), between Columbus and Hicks St. This 95-year-old *focacceria* still serves the Sicilian specialties that have made it a local institution. Foremost among them are the *arancini* (breaded, fried rice balls filled with meat, peas, and sauce, $2.50 each). Open M-Th 10:30am-6pm, F-Sa 10:30am-9pm. **$**

L Café, 189 Bedford Ave. (718-302-2430). Subway: L to Bedford Ave. Typical Williamsburg cafe with plenty of flyers about local happenings, a nice garden out back, and great veggie burgers ($6.50). Good selection of inventive sandwiches $5.50-7, salads $5.50-8. Open M-F 9am-midnight, Sa-Su 10am-midnight. **$**

Miyako, 143 Berry St. (718-486-0837), at N. 6th St., in Williamsburg. Subway: L to Bedford St. Head south on Bedford St. and turn west onto N. 6th. Where the Manhattanites migrate, there too goeth the sushi; even has a special Williamsburg Roll ($6.50). Affordable sushi; most entrees under $10. Open M-F 11:30am-11pm, Sa 3:30-11:30pm. **$**

Oznot's Dish, 79 Berry St. (718-599-6596), at N. 9th St. Subway: L to Bedford Ave. From the subway, walk west to Berry St. and head north. Beautiful, beautiful, beautiful, with good food to boot. Scene: Antonio Gaudí meets ex-Manhattanite artists in laid-back Williamsburg and they build a restaurant in *kif*-dream Morocco. Try the *salas thali* ($11); lunch $6.50-8.50. Weekday dinner special with entree, soup or salad, and dessert $20. Garden out back. Open daily 11am-4:30pm and 6pm-midnight. **$-$$**

Park Luncheonette, 334 Driggs Ave., at Lorimer St., in Greenpoint. Subway: G to Nassau/Manhattan. Over 100 years old, this no-frills luncheonette has thankfully not become extinct like others of its kind. The food menu is limited to delicious frankfurters ($1.25) and other inexpensive fried sandwiches. The real draw is the to-die-for selection of fountain sodas that could make even Marty McFly salivate ($1); egg creams (vanilla and chocolate) also available ($1.40-2). Bring your sweetheart and entwine straws. Open whenever the sun is out. **$**

Patois, 225 Smith St. (718-855-1535), between DeGraw and Douglass St. in Carroll Gardens. Subway: F, G to Bergen St. A quaint French bistro that has gotten quite a bit of buzz in the past years since its opening. Entrees are a bit pricey at $12-17, but traditional starters like garlic snails, puff pastry, and spinach and chives ($7.50) can allow you to sample this delicious menu. Open Tu-Th 6-10:30pm, F-Sa 6-11:30pm, Su 11am-10pm. **$$**

PlanEat Thailand, 184 Bedford Ave. (718-599-5758). Subway: L to Bedford Ave. A restaurant that could only exist in Brooklyn: the city's best inexpensive Thai food served amidst walls decorated with high-quality graffiti. All beef dishes under $6, all chicken dishes under $7, and a killer *pad thai* for only $5.25. If you ask for spicy, they'll give you medium—it'll be enough to clear your sinuses (unlike at most eateries, hot means *hot!* and is reserved for those who know what they're getting into). Open M-Sa 11:30am-11:30pm, Su 1-11pm. **$**

Red Rose Restaurant, 315 Smith St. (718-625-0963), between President and Union St., in Carroll Gardens. Subway: F, G to Bergen St. Classic cheap Italian dining. The well-stocked menu offers pastas from $5.25-8, and there's an additional list of 27 house specials (around $8). Open M and W-Th 4:30-10:30pm, F-Sa 4:30-11:30pm, Su 2-10:30pm. Accepts AmEx, V, MC, Discover. Wheelchair accessible. **$-$$**

Stylowa Restaurant, 694 Manhattan Ave. (718-383-8993), between Norman and Nassau Ave. in Greenpoint. Subway: G to Nassau Ave. Polish cuisine at its best and cheapest. Sit among native Polish speakers and sample *kielbasa* (Polish sausage) with fried onions, sauerkraut, and bread ($4.50), or roast beef in homemade gravy with potatoes ($4). Excellent potato pancakes $3. All other entrees ($2.75-7.25) served with a glass of *compote* (pink, apple-flavored fruit drink). Open M-Th noon-9pm, F noon-10pm, Sa 11am-10pm, Su 11am-9pm. **$**

Vera Cruz, 195 Bedford Ave. (718-599-7914), between 6th and 7th St. in Williamsburg. Subway: L to Bedford Ave. Authentic central Mexican food with tasty margaritas and a lovely garden. Nachos with shrimp $5.75, roasted breast of chicken in mole sauce ($11). Don't miss the "Mexican styled corn," corn on the cob covered in Mexican cheese and sprinkled with lime and chili powder ($2.50). Happy hour M-F 4-7pm. Open M 4-11pm, Tu-Th 4-11:30pm, F-Sa 4pm-midnight, Su 11am-midnight. **$-$$**

Zaytoons, 283 Smith St. (718-875-1880), at Sackett St. Delicious Middle Eastern food has found its way west of Arthur Ave. Zaytoons is best known for their "pitza," the pizza they make on their freshly baked pita bread ($5-7). Open M-Sa 11am-11pm, Su 11am-9pm. **$**

COOL SPOTS

Brooklyn Ale House, 103 Berry St. (718-302-9811), at N. 8th St. Across the street from Teddy's. A friendly neighborhood joint that welcomes you, your inner artist, and your dog. Monday is "Cheese Night" with 5-6 types of free *fromage* from Murray's Cheese Shop in the East Village; Tuesday good pool tournament. Open daily 3pm-4am.

Galapagos, 70 N. 6th St. (718-782-5188), between Kent and Wythe St. in Williamsburg. Subway: L to Bedford; go south along Bedford and then west along N. 6th St. A bit deserted at night: go with a friend. Once a mayonnaise factory, this space is now one of the hipper cultural spots in the city. Primarily a performance space that puts up theater, performance art, dance, and music as well as hosting lectures and **Ocularis,** their weekly film series (Su 7-9:30pm). The people here *are* the Williamsburg arts scene; ask them what's up in this kinetic community. Great bar in an interesting space that boasts an eerie reflecting pool supports the artistic endeavors and a fun crowd. Call to find out what is inevitably up, on, around, and over at Galapagos. Open Su-Th 6pm-2am, F-Sa 6pm-4am.

Teddy's, 96 Berry St. (718-384-9787), at N. 8th St., in Greenpoint. Subway: L to Bedford Ave.; go 1 block west. An eclectic mix of artists and wizened Brooklynites—many of them regulars—visits Teddy's for its great jukebox and friendly atmosphere. Tuesday night is "Hillbilly-Fever-Go-Go-Rama" with the appropriate music and dancers, respectively. Great, big Bloody Marys that "bloom" with vegetables ($5). Occasional 1970s lounge night. Jazz on Thursday from Nov.-Mar. Brunch Sa-Su 11am-5pm. $2 margaritas in summer. Cheap drinks ($1-3). Open Su-Th 11:30am-2am, F-Sa 11am-4am.

SOUTH BROOKLYN

Subway: D, Q train to Brighton Beach, then 4 blocks east on Brighton Beach Ave. Coney Island: B, D, F, N to Coney Island stop. Emmons Ave.: D, Q to Sheepshead Bay, then south on Sheepshead Bay Rd.

The shores of Brooklyn present a welcome culinary quandary: endless choices. Try Russian knishes (heated, flaky dough with a choice of filling) on Brighton Beach Ave., Italian calamari (fried squid) in spicy marinara sauce along Emmons Ave. in Sheepshead Bay, or tri-colored candy on Coney Island. Eat until you feel ill—it won't make a dent in your wallet.

Jimmy's Famous Heros, 1786 Sheepshead Bay Rd. (718-648-8001), near Emmons Ave. Heros—New Yorkese for subs (from the Greek gyros)—cost about $5-5.50 and can be shared by 2. Always ask for "the works" on whatever you order; you'll thank us later. Take-out only; you can eat by the Bay. Open daily 9am-6pm. **$**

Nathan's, Surf Ave. (718-946-2206), between Stillwell and 15th, in Coney Island. 74 years ago, Nathan Handwerker became famous for underselling his competitors on the boardwalk: his hot dogs cost a nickel, theirs were a dime. His crunchy dogs have since become nationally famous. A classic frank at this crowded place—the original Nathan's—sells for $1.95; cheese-fries $2.19-2.59. Mysteriously, sauerkraut available in winter, fried onions in summer. Open M-Th 6am-2am, F-Su 6am-4am. **$**

Primorski Restaurant, 282 Brighton Beach Ave. (718-891-3111), between Brighton Beach 2nd and Brighton Beach 3rd St. Populated by Russian-speaking Brooklynites, this nautically themed restaurant serves some of the Western Hemisphere's best Ukrainian *borscht* ($2.25) in an atmosphere of a red velour Bar Mitzvah Hall. Eminently affordable lunch special (M-F 11am-5pm, Sa-Su 11am-4pm; $4) is one of NYC's great deals—your choice of among 3 soups and about 15 entrees, bread, salad, and coffee or tea. At night, prices rise slightly as the disco ball begins to spin. Russian music and disco M-Th 8pm-midnight, F-Sa 9pm-2am, Su 8pm-1am. Open daily 11am-2am. **$**

RESTAURANTS

Randazzo's Clam Bar, 2017 Emmons Ave. (718-615-0010), in Sheepshead Bay. A beautiful waterfront location and a great seafood menu account for the large crowd and slightly higher prices. Many dishes are still within budget range: fried seafood sandwiches $6-7, dozen clams $12-13, chowder $2-3. Open Su-Th 11:30am-12:30am, F-Sa 11:30am-1:30am. **$**

Taste of Russia, 219 Brighton Beach Ave. (718-934-6167). This well-kept Russian deli stocks everything from fresh-baked delicacies to mango soda. Favorites include the stuffed cabbage and the blintzes (both $4 per lb.). Great selection of fresh pickles (including pickled watermelon and tomatoes) and cole slaw that the clientele is free to sample. Open daily 8am-10pm. **$**

Tony's Pizza, 34 E. Bedford Park Blvd. (718-367-2854), right off Grand Concourse. Subway: #4 or C, D to Bedford Park Blvd. Classic, friendly pizza joint with slices so tasty that students from the nearby Bronx High School of Science often skip class to grab one. Crisp crust slathered with generous amounts of cheese. Slice $1.50, extra topping 75¢; large pie $10.50. Open M-F 11am-8pm. **$**

Totonno Pizzeria Napolitano, 1524 Neptune Ave. (718-372-8606), between 15th and 16th St. This Coney Island legend is a worthy challenger for the title of finest pizza in New York. Pies $13-14.50. No slices. Open W-Su noon-8:30pm. **Another location:** 1544 Second Ave., between 81st and 82nd St. **$**

SHOPS

🔖 **Efe International,** 243 Brighton Beach Ave. (718-891-8933). Tantalizing dry goods store that vends every kind of nut, spice, seed, dried fruit, and gummy candy that your heart could possibly desire. Prices stay below $4 per lb. Also carries delicious Turtamek juice mix from Turkey. Open daily 8am-9pm.

🔖 **Philip's Confections,** 1237 Surf Ave. (718-372-8783), at the entrance to the B, D, F, N train in Coney Island. Sate your inner child. Famous salt-water taffy (95¢ per ¼ lb.). Candy or caramel apple $1. Cotton candy $1. Lime rickeys 65¢. Open Su-Th 11am-3am, F-Sa 11am-4am.

Sea Lane Bakery, 615 Brighton Beach Ave. (718-934-8877), between 6th and 7th St. Subway: D, Q to Brighton Beach. The best Jewish bakery in Brighton. Try a little of everything (9 kinds of pastry cost 9¢ each). Then again, you can't go wrong with the strudel with mixed fruit ($4). Open daily 6am-9pm.

CHELSEA

Nestled between the trendy West Village and rapidly upscaling West Midtown, Chelsea is dotted with quality eateries specializing in food from all over the Americas. The best offerings come from the large Mexican and Central American community in the southern section of the neighborhood. From 14th to 23rd St., restaurants combine Central American and Chinese cuisine, as well as varieties of Cajun and Creole specialties. The neighborhood's visible and enthusiastic gay contingent has inspired a variety of fashionable watering holes and diners. Eighth Ave. and 23rd St. provides the best restaurant browsing. (See also **Gay and Lesbian Life,** p. 306.)

Bendix Diner, 219 Eighth Ave. (366-0560), at 21st St. A successful new hybrid—the Thai greasy spoon. Entrees around $7; burgers $4.25-6.75; sandwiches $4-8; "Thai breakfast" $3-3.50. Breakfast available all day. Open daily 8am-1am. **$**

Caesar's, 206 Seventh Ave. (366-4865), between 21st and 22nd St. No-frills Greek-Mediterranean-diner grub in a relaxed, airy joint with a blue fetish. Couch/lounge in back; open front window onto the street in summer. Shish kebab, salad, hummus platter $6; falafel sandwich $2.75. Open 24hr. **$**

Intermezzo, 202 Eighth Ave. (929-3433), between 20th and 21st St. Intimate, popular Italian restaurant that offers up ample, inventive antipasti and salads worthy of a splurge. Try the ambrosial *gamberi alla griglia* (grilled shrimp, avocado, and potato pancakes, $7) or the *insalata di aragosta* (lobster, grapefruit, avocado, and mango salad, $9). If you want a full meal for dinner, your cheapest bet is the $9.95 prix fixe menu (M-F 4-6pm). The lunch menu also offers tasty dishes for $6-8 (M-F noon-4pm). Brunch ($6) served Sa-Su noon-4pm. Su-Th noon-11pm, F-Sa noon-midnight. **$-$$**

Kitchen, 218 Eighth Ave. (243-4433), near 21st St. A real kitchen that serves Mexican food and hawks books, spices, beans, and various peppers. Most order food to go, but there are a few tables. Burrito stuffed with pinto beans, rice, and green salsa with exhaustive fillings and tortilla options $6.25-6.50. For delivery $12.50 min. Open M-Sa 9am-10:30pm, Su 11am-10:30pm. **$**

Mary Ann's, 116 Eighth Ave. (633-0877), at 16th St. Benevolent waiters serve up huge portions in this white-walled restaurant hung with *piñatas* and slung with lights. Inventive Mexican cuisine with surprising seafood combos. Popular and crowded. The enchilada stuffed with shrimp and snowcrab served in *tomatillo* sauce ($11) and the goat cheese quesadilla with salad and avocado ($11) keep the locals happy. Entrees $9-12. Margaritas $4.75. Open M-Tu noon-10:30pm, W-Th 11:30am-10:45pm, Sa 11:30am-11:15pm, Su noon-10pm. **$$**

Negril, 362 W. 23rd St. (807-6411), between Eighth and Ninth Ave. Colorful decor and excellent Jamaican food in this gay-friendly eatery. Dinner options are on the expensive side, but lunch is affordable at around $8. Open M-Th 11am-midnight, F-Sa 11am-1am, Su 2pm-11am. Lively bar stays open until 2am F-Sa. **$-$$**

Sam Chinita Restaurant, 176 Eighth Ave. (741-0240), at 19th St. A 1950s diner complete with red curtains and turquoise countertops serves up Spanish-and-Chinese cuisine (perhaps a little more Chinese than Spanish). Dozens of deals under $6. Favorites include yellow rice with Latin-style chicken ($6) and lobster Cantonese with fried rice and eggroll ($9). Daily lunch specials until 4pm come with yellow rice and beans or fried rice and wonton soup. Free delivery with $5 min. purchase. Open daily noon-11pm. **$-$$**

Soups on Seventeen, 307 W. 17th St. (255-1505), off Eighth Ave. This new eatery will liquify your mind with the astounding things it does to soup. Soup, sandwich, or salad with bread, fruit, and cookie $4-7.50. Try the taro root and coconut or the southwestern sweet potato soups (both $5 for 16 oz.). Hell, taste them all. Open M-Sa 11am-7pm. **$**

Spring Joy, 17 Eighth Ave. (243-1688), between 18th and 19th St. Although the city seems to have fallen out of love with Chinese food, Spring Joy serves up good Chinese food at even more shocking prices. Numerous lunch options under $5, dinner $5.75-8.50. Design your own dish $7; diet options $6-8.50. It only gets better from here: free white wine with your dinner. Open M-Sa 11:30am-12:30am, Su noon-12:30am. **$**

CAFES

B.M.W. Gallery and Coffee Magic Espresso Bar, 199 Seventh Ave., between 21st and 22nd St. Coffee shop and wine bar which is a step above the rest. (See **Gay and Lesbian Life,** p. 309.)

CHINATOWN

Dare to explore the labyrinth of this neighborhood's streets and Chinatown will reward you with open-air markets that spill onto the sidewalk, hole-in-the-wall shops and restaurants, and a pervasive liveliness. You can buy live turtles, eels, and crabs. For food you don't have to kill yourself, head to the shops that line Mott St. above and below Canal St., which boast some of the freshest, cheapest seafood and produce in the city.

The neighborhood's 300-plus restaurants cook up superfantastic Chinese, Thai, and Vietnamese cuisine. Better yet, these restaurants won't burn a hole through your wallet. Be prepared, however, for waiters with a poor grasp of English and for highly utilitarian ambience. Many places are cash-only and/or don't serve alcohol, but allow you to bring your own. The fierce culinary competition in Chinatown ensures rapid turn-over. The Vietnamese place where you ate last year may now serve Malaysian cuisine. Whatever fare you choose of an evening, you can always take an after-dinner stroll through neon streets, as you delight in Chinese ice cream or Vietnamese desserts—but be sure to bring a few friends, for safety's sake. See map, p. 143.

Big Wong's, 67 Mott St. (964-0540), between Bayard and Canal St. Let the cafeteria-style ambience bring you back to your eating contest days. Portions are ample and most dishes are under $5. *Chow foon* (a flat, white noodle with meat, $5-6) is always a good bet. For a snack, grab some sweet or savory Chinese-style crullers (70¢). May be a wait. Cash only. Bring your own alcohol. Open daily 9am-9pm. **$**

⬛ **Bo-Ky,** 78-80 Bayard St. (406-2292), between Mott and Mulberry St. Tourists rarely grace this quality Vietnamese joint specializing in soups (most under $5). The spartan interior is not meant to pamper, but the light, flavorful food merits a visit. The coconut-and-curry chicken soup ($5) will clear that nasty head cold instantly. *Pho,* the beef broth king of Vietnamese soups, will fill you up without emptying your wallet ($3-5). Don't forget to use the thick plum sauce and hot chili at your table for an authentic sweet-and-spicy treat. Open daily 7am-9:30pm. **$**

Excellent Dumpling House, 111 Lafayette St. (219-0212), just south of Canal St. Small, unassuming, and perennially crowded with folks enjoying splendid food and fast service. Terrific veggie and meat dumplings fried, steamed, or boiled ($4 for 8 pieces). Huge bowls of noodle soups $3.50-4 and filling $6 lunch specials (served M-F 11am-3pm). Cash only. Beer available. Open daily 11am-9pm. **$**

⬛ **Harden & L.C. Corp.,** 43 Canal St. (966-5419), near Ludlow St., may offer the best meal deal in Manhattan: a massive Malaysian dinner for only $2.50. There is a menu for this Malaysian greasy spoon, but nobody uses it: cruise in, between 11am and 10:30pm, point to the 3 sides you want, and you'll get a huge plate of rice with a heaping portion of each side. While veggie dishes are available, strict vegetarians should opt elsewhere. Mirrors, bright fluorescent lights, a TV showing low-grade kung-fu flicks and Chinese soap operas spice up the ambience. Cash only. Bring your own alcohol. Open daily 9am-10:30pm. **$**

House of Vegetarian, 24 Pell St. (226-6572), between Canal and Bayard St. All animals are ersatz on the huge menu of this small and appropriately green eatery; soy and wheat by-products, taro root, and mushroom disguise themselves as beef, chicken, and fish. Fantastic dumplings (3 for $2) should please both veggies and non-veggies alike. Most entrees $6-10. Ice-cold lotus-seed or lychee drink $2. Open daily 11am-11pm. **$**

HSF, 46 Bowery (374-1319), between Bayard and Canal St. Chinese neon placards and rotating poultry festoon the window of this large, crowded eatery. Dim sum served 7:30am-5pm ($2-7). If you want to splurge, try the "Hot Pot" buffet ($20 per person), a huge pot of boiling broth placed in the center of your table with a platter of more than 50 raw ingredients spread around it for dipping. Ingredients range from fresh shrimp, clams, and periwinkles to spinach and Chinese cabbage. Other entrees ($7.50-17) include delicacies such as prawns in Yushan garlic sauce ($13). Credit cards accepted. Beer available. Open daily 8am-midnight. **$$**

Joe's Shanghai, 9 Pell St. (233-8888), between Bowery and Mott St. From fried turnip cakes ($3.25) and mushroom-tofu "vegetarian duck" ($5.25) to crispy fried whole yellowfish ($13), this Chinatown branch of the Queens legend serves up all sorts of tasty Shanghai specialties. But the true source of Joe's acclaim is his *shiao lung bao* ($7), crab meat and pork dumplings in a savory soup. Be prepared for communal tables and long lines of *bao* addicts on weekends. Cash only. Beer available. Open daily 11am-11:15pm. **$-$$**

Little Szechuan, 5 E. Broadway (732-0796), in front of Chatham Sq. Largely Caucasian crowd chowing on some damn good Chinese food. "Healthy eating" section on the menu. Appetizers $2-5, fried rice and noodle dishes $3-8. Credit cards accepted. Beer and wine available. Open Su-Th 11:30am-10pm, F-Sa 11:30am-10:30pm. **$**

Mandalay Kitchen, 380 Broome St. (226-4218), at Mulberry St. A rare Burmese pearl washed up on the Italian shores of Mulberry St. Refined Burmese cuisine (a marriage of Indian and Thai food) served in a cozy setting. Start with the 1000-layered pancake (a delicate bread, $2.50). Entrees range from $8.50 (Burmese curry) to $12.75 (mixed seafood). Credit cards accepted. Beer and wine available. Open M-F 4-11pm, Sa-Su noon-11pm. **$-$$**

Mueng Thai Restaurant, 23 Pell St. (406-4259), between Mott St. and Bowery. An extensive veggie menu is one reason to come here; the rest of the menu is the other. Perennial *pad thai* eaters should let down their angel hair and try the *pad see ewe—* wide rice noodles with shrimp, chicken, or pork ($8). $4.50 lunch specials (served Tu-F 11am-4pm). AmEx accepted. Beer and wine. Open Tu-Su noon-11pm. **$**

New York Noodle Town, 28½ Bowery (349-0923), at Bayard St. Whether they're pan-fried or in soup, *lo mein* or the wider Cantonese-style, the noodles in the Town are incredible and cheap (most under $6.50). If you're willing to spend a bit more, try the barbecued duck ($9), or the salt-roasted flounder ($16). Often crowded at lunch and dinner; go early. Cash only. Bring your own alcohol. Open daily 9am-4am. **$-$$**

Nyona, 194 Grand St. (334-3669), between Mulberry and Mott St. This popular new-comer serves up excellent Malaysian dishes in a cool, wood-lined interior. The food is quite similar to Chinese, although dishes such as the *roti* appetizer (pancakes with sauce, $2) highlight the strong Indian influences in Malaysian cuisine. The delectably spicy *nasi lemak* ($4) combines chili anchovies and curry chicken in a bed of coconut rice. For an unusual dessert, ask for the "ABC"—an indescribable treat that's not listed on the menu. Cash only. Beer and wine available. Open daily 11am-11:30pm. **$-$$**

Shanghai Cuisine, 89-91 Bayard St. (732-8988), at Mulberry St. The house specialty, "braised soy duck with 8 treasures" ($34), must be ordered a day in advance and is perhaps the richest dish you will ever taste—attack this dish only with large groups and with plenty of white rice and vegetables, lest you feel bloated for days. The menu also offers less intense dishes like spicy pepper salt prawns ($13), and mixed vegetables ($7). Cash only. Beer and wine available. Open daily 10:30am-10:30pm. **$$**

Sweet-n-Tart Cafe, 76 Mott St. (334-8088), at Canal St. Alongside inexpensive standard Chinese fare, this crowded little purple-and-white "cafe" offers *tong shui,* sweet Chinese "tonics" (soups), each believed to have medicinal value for a specific part of the body: dry bean curd with gingko for healthy skin ($2.25), lotus seeds in herbal tea with egg for the liver and kidneys ($2.60), double-boiled Oriental pears with almonds for the lungs ($3.85). Find out for yourself what snow frog with lotus seeds does for you. Cash only. No alcohol. Open daily 9am-11:30pm. **$**

Thailand Restaurant, 106 Bayard St. (349-3132). Chinatown's first Thai restaurant has dealt well with the mushrooming competition. Simple and quiet, but head and shoul-ders above the other joints. Taste the killer *pad thai* ($5.50) and roasted duck in curry with coconut milk, bamboo shoots, onions, and bell peppers ($9.50). Known for home-made Thai desserts like sweet rice with egg custard and coconut milk ($1.50). AmEx accepted. Open daily 11:30am-11pm. **$**

Vietnam, 11-13 Doyers St. (693-0725), between Bowery and Pell St. Vietnam has all of the standards—brittle spring rolls, shrimp on sugar cane, noodle soups—and then some. Try the tasty, filling Vietnamese crepes ($6) for a distinct, assertive flavor. Ask about the more innovative items on the menu like the stir-fried salmon with black bean sauce ($7) or the shrimp papaya salad ($5). You won't find these dishes anywhere else. AmEx accepted. Beer available. Open daily 11am-9:30pm. **$**

Wong Kee, 113 Mott St. (966-1160), between Canal and Hester St. Cheap, consis-tently good Cantonese food from behind a gleaming silver storefront. For the best deals, go for the Cantonese noodles, the *lo mein,* or the fried rice dishes ($3-5). If you're willing to spend a bit more, try the bean curd with straw mushrooms ($6) or the specialty of the house, *wong kee* steak ($8.50). Cash only. No alcohol. Open daily 11am-10pm. **$**

SHOPS

Dynasty Supermarket Corp., 69 Elizabeth St. (966-4943), at Hester St. One of the most extensive markets in the area and provides an air-conditioned refuge from the tumult of the street. Find ginseng, sea cucumber, live mudskipper, chicken feet, abalone slice, and Hostess cupcakes all in one stop. Open daily 9am-8pm.

RESTAURANTS

■ **Chinatown Ice Cream Factory,** 65 Bayard St. (608-4170), at Mott St. You can satisfy your sweet-tooth here with homemade lychee, taro, ginger, red bean, or green tea ice cream. One scoop $2, two $3.60, three $4.60. Open Su-Th noon-11pm, F-Sa 11:30am-11:30pm.

■ **Hong Kong Egg Cake Co.,** on the corner of Mott and Mosco St., in a small red shack on the side of a building. Proprietress Celicia Tam will make you a dozen soft, sweet egg cakes fresh from the skillet ($1). Don't worry about finding "The Co."—just follow the line wrapping around the corner of Mott.

Lung Moon Bakery, 83 Mulberry St. (349-4945). Specializing in the happy marriage of the pastry and sweet bean paste. The sesame balls (50¢), lotus seed pies ($2), egg custard pies (50¢), and pork and beef buns (50¢ and 60¢) are good starters. Open daily 9am-6pm.

Ten Ren Tea and Ginseng Company, 75 Mott St. (349-2286), between Canal and Bayard St. Comfortable and classy, the Ten Ren shop boasts a huge selection of rare, delectable teas ranging in price from the very cheap to hundreds of dollars a pound. To beat the heat in the summer, get the Green Tea Powder ($4-7), and add a packet's worth to a cold bottle of water. Drop in some apple juice for sweetener, and you've got a very refreshing, very *green* caffeine drink. Open daily 10am-8pm.

EAST MIDTOWN

In this area, tycoons run their corporate empires by wining and dining their clients well, so the tab can add up pretty quickly. Don't despair yet—the tycoons' underpaid underlings all scour for cheap lunches here. From noon to 2pm, harried junior executives trying to eat quickly and get back to work swamp the delis and cafes. The 50s on Second Ave. and the area immediately surrounding Grand Central Station contain good, inexpensive fare. Grocery stores (see below) offer a salad and hot foot alternative to the mad deli rush. East Midtown's many public plazas and parks invite you to picnic; try **Greenacre Park,** 51st St. between Second and Third Ave., or **Paley Park,** 53rd St. between Fifth and Madison Ave. If you do want to splurge, many top restaurants offer relatively reasonable prix fixe lunch menus that include an appetizer, entree, and dessert. Try **Aureole,** 34 E. 61st St. between Madison and Park Ave. (319-1660; reservations required), one of the best restaurants in the city; between 2 and 2:30pm the prix fixe for three courses is $20.

Coldwaters, 988 Second Ave. (888-2122), between 52nd and 53rd St. Subway: #6 to 52nd; or E, F to 53rd St. This recently renovated restaurant makes quite a catch with its brunch and dinner deals. Brunch ($9; 11am-3pm) tempts daily with 2 drinks (alcoholic or non-), choice of entree, salad, and fries. Dinner entrees come with all-you-can-eat salad, fries or baked potato, and a basket of fresh garlic bread. Idaho Rainbow Trout $10, Cajun Catfish $12, or Boston Cod $10. Open daily 11am-3am. The spin-off **One Fish, Two Fish,** 1399 Madison at 97th St. (369-5677), reels in a more upscale crowd. Accepts AmEx, Diner's Club, Discover, JCB, MC, V. Wheelchair accessible. **$$**

■ **Dosanko,** 423 Madison Ave. (688-8575), between 48th and 49th St. Subway: E, F to Fifth Ave.; or #6 to 52nd St. All is tranquil at this aromatic Japanese pit-stop; the food is so tasty it seems criminal to waste time talking. The scrumptious *gyoza* ($4.50) is a favorite, as are the many varieties of *larmen* (Japanese noodle soup, $5.50-7.20). Cash only. Open M-F 11:30am-10pm, Sa-Su noon-8pm. **$$**

Fortune Garden, 845 Second Ave. (687-7471), between 45th and 46th St. Subway: #4, 5, 6, or S to Grand Central, head east on 42nd and north on Second Ave. True to its name, eating in this Chinese garden will cost you a tiny fortune ($15-20). Opt for take-out, it's much cheaper and just as good. Weekday take-out lunch (11am-3pm) special is 2 appetizers and an entree for $6.25. Accepts AmEx, MC, V. Open daily 11am-11pm. Wheelchair accessible. **$-$$$**

Taipei Noodle House, 986 Second Ave. (759-7070). Subway: #6 to 52nd; or E, F to 53rd St. Great for a quick sit-down lunch, this house o' noodles can satisfy even the pickiest of eaters. Most entrees run $6.50-9. The real deal is the weekday lunch special (M-Sa 11am-4pm), featuring entree, soup, rice, and egg roll for $4.75-6. Friendly, quick service. Accepts AmEx, V, MC. Open M-Su 11am-midnight. Wheelchair accessible. **$-$$**

SHOPS

Food Emporium, 969 Second Ave. (593-2224), between 51st and 52nd St.; **D'Agostino,** Third Ave. (684-3133), between 35th and 36th St.; or **Associated Group Grocers,** 250 E. 65th St. (421-7673). Upscale supermarket chains with branches scattered throughout Manhattan. All feature reliable, well-stocked delis, fresh fruit and salad bars, ice cold drinks, gourmet ice cream, tons of munchies, and lots more—all at reasonable prices.

Teuscher Chocolatier, 620 Fifth Ave. (246-4416), on the promenade at Rockefeller Center. Subway: #6 to 51st St.; or E to Fifth Ave./53rd St. A choco-holic's paradise, Teuscher offers the freshest chocolates flown in from Zurich weekly, and unfortunately have the prices to prove it. But don't let a little transatlantic overhead keep you from this experience—you can still savor a single piece for under $2. Accepts AmEx, V, MC.

EAST VILLAGE

In the past decade the East Village has seen an accelerating process of gentrification, replete with the inevitable sleek coffee shops and wood-paneled eateries to feed the fabulous. Still, an amazing array of immigrant cultures continue to make their homes in the East Village. The result: a culinary menagerie in which Polish pastry rubs elbows with Dominican grub, which in turn learns a bit from Fillipino cuisine. This is probably the best area in the city for the budget traveler to sample the world of New York food for under $10. **First** and **Second Avenues** have a top-notch restaurant selection. **St. Mark's Place** hosts a slew of inexpensive and popular village institutions, and at night, **Avenue A** throbs with bars and sidewalk cafes. Twenty-six competing Indian restaurants line **6th St.** between First and Second Ave., as well as First Ave. itself. If you look indecisive, the anxious managers may offer free wine or discounts on the already cheap food.

Acme Bar and Grill, 9 Great Jones St. (420-1934), between Broadway and Lafayette. Po'boys, blackened catfish, and some of the best mashed potatoes and meatloaf in the city. The down-home tone of the menu can get a little old, but the place is comfortable and serves up tasty Southern grub. "Bertha's meatloaf dinner" $11. Club downstairs plays alternative rock. Open M-Th 11am-midnight, F-Sa 11am-1am, Su 11am-12:30am. **$$**

B&H Vegetarian Restaurant, 127 Second Ave. (505-8065), between 7th and 8th St. B&H is not technically a vegetarian restaurant. They do have veggie burgers ($3.50), but they also serve up salmon ($5.50) and tuna ($4.50) sandwiches. The stars here, however, are the challah french toast ($4.25), the knishes ($2.25), and, most of all, the soups, especially the borscht, the mushroom barley, and the matzo ball ($2.50). Open daily 7am-10pm. **$**

Benny's Burritos, 93 Ave. A (254-2054), at 6th St. Colorful, shiny Cal-Mex hot spot is always hoppin' and manages to serve tastier burritos than many of the city's more upscale Mexican spots. Trendy decor, lots of windows for excellent people-watching, and great food—burritos with black or pinto beans $6-12. Fab frozen margaritas $5-15. Lunch deal (burrito, soup, and soda; $5.50). Cash only. Open Su-Th 11am-midnight, F-Sa 11am-1am. **$-$$**

Cucina di Pesce, 87 E. 4th St. (260-6800), between Second and Third Ave. Classic little Italian place with oil-paintings, rosily lit nooks, sidewalk seating. Sitting in the backyard, you'll think you're in Florence. Dishes are inexpensive and large, if not excellent. Spinach penne (macaroni with asparagus, sundried tomatoes, and fontina cheese) $7. Salmon with sauteed mushrooms and pasta $10. Free mussels at the bar as you wait for your table. Daily special 4-6:30pm; weekends 4-6pm. Full dinner with bread, soup, entree, and glass of wine $10. Open Su-Th 4pm-midnight, F-Sa 4pm-1am. **$-$$**

Damask Falafel, 85 Ave. A (673-5016), between 5th and 6th St. This closet-sized stand serves the cheapest and best falafel in the area—$1.75 for a sandwich; $3.50 for a falafel platter with tabouli, chick peas, salad, and pita bread; $1.25 for two succulent stuffed grape leaves. Banana milk shakes $1.50. Open M-F 11am-2am, Sa-Su 11am-4am. **$**

Dojo Restaurant, 24 St. Mark's Pl. (674-9821), between Second and Third Ave. Unbeatable Dojo is one of the most popular restaurants and hangouts in the East Village, and rightly so: it offers an incredible variety of vegetarian and Japanese foods that manages to combine the healthy with the inexplicably cheap and surprisingly tasty. You can even take home a container of Dojo's renowned carrot dressing. Soyburgers with brown rice and salad $3.50. "Dojo salad" $5. Beer $2.75-4; pitchers $12-15. Outdoor tables allow for interaction with passersby, though the rowdy chaos of St. Mark's might give you a headache. Another location at 14 W. 4th St. (505-8934), between Broadway and Mercer St. Open Su-Th 11am-1am, F-Sa 11am-2am. **$**

Elvie's Turo-Turo, 214 First Ave. (473-7785), between 12th and 13th St. Philippine food served cafeteria-style. There's no menu here—you just point to what you want. Choose from among dishes like *pancit* (a stir-fried rice noodle dish), chicken adobo, and pork and chicken barbecue. One dish $4, two for $5.75. Open M-Sa 11am-9pm, Su 11am-8pm. **$**

Flor's Kitchen, 149 First Ave. (387-8949), at Ninth St. Small Venezuelan restaurant serving up all sorts of *arepas* (filled corn cakes; $2.75-3.25) and *empanadas* ($2.75). The beet soup is quite good ($2.50-4). Open M-Th 11am-11pm, F-Sa 11am-midnight, Su 10am-10pm. **$**

Kate's Joint, 58 Ave. B (777-7059), between 4th and 5th St. This is good vegan. Like, groovy interior, man. This couch-lined, pastel-plastered eatery delivers nonchalant and delicious veggie fare. Beefless Jamaican patty $2.50, unturkey club $8. Open Su-Th 8:30am-11pm, F-Sa 8:30am-midnight. **$**

Khyber Pass Restaurant, 34 St. Mark's Pl. (473-0989), between Second and Third Ave. Dainty place on the East Village's main drag serves Afghani food. Retreat from St. Mark's and relax on cushy pillows and Afghan rugs. The cuisine recalls familiar Middle Eastern foods but with surprising twists and turns. Plenty of unusual vegetarian selections, such as pumpkin dumplings ($3 for 4). One can sit on pillows at a low-to-the-ground table and enjoy *bouranee baunjaun* (eggplant with mint yogurt and fresh coriander, $8) or *phirnee* (delicate rice pudding with pistachios and rosewater, $2). Free delivery. Open daily noon-midnight. **$**

The Kiev, 117 Second Ave. (674-4040), at 7th St. A funky Eastern European breakfast extravaganza. A great place to end up at 4am when you have the munchies. Great breakfast deals; lox on a bagel is a steal in the city at $6. A cup of homemade soup comes with an inch-thick slab of challah bread. Lengthy menu features sandwiches of all sorts, along with potato pancakes, *kasha varnishke,* and more *pierogi* than you could shake a schtick at. Open 24hr. **$**

K.K. Restaurant, 194 First Ave. (777-4430), between 11th and 12th St. This light-wood-paneled restaurant has a down-home feel and serves solid Polish cuisine. The $5.75 lunch special comes with a choice of soup or salad, an entree, a choice of vegetable, and coffee or soda. Dinner special also available (5-11pm; $7.85). The patio makes for great outdoor dining. Free delivery. No credit cards. Open daily 7am-11pm. **$**

La Focacceria, 128 First Ave. (254-4946), between St. Marks Pl. and 7th St. For 85 years, La Focacceria has served up light, delectable Sicilian eats. The *vesteddi* (fried ricotta and kashkaval cheese, $2) and eggplant Sicilian style ($5) sandwiches are exceptional. Open M-Th 11am-10pm, F-Sa 1-11pm. **$**

Lhasa, 96 Second Ave. (674-5870), between 5th and 6th St. Despite its recent resurgence as a radical chic cause célèbre, Tibet has yet to make a big culinary splash. Tibetan combines elements of Chinese and Indian cuisines. Serene atmosphere—outback garden is the perfect place to enjoy an order of *momo (*dumplings filled with chicken or beef, $7.25 steamed or $7.50 fried). Extensive vegetarian menu. Open M-F 4-11pm, Sa 4-11:30pm, Su 3-11:30pm. **$-$$**

Mama's Food Shop, 200 E. 3rd St. (777-4425), between Ave. A and B. Specializes in Home cooking with a capital H. See laid-back Villagers obeying Mama's strict command to "Shut up and Eat." Fried chicken or salmon (each $7), with sides ranging from honey-glazed sweet potatoes to broccoli to couscous for only $1 each. Vegetarian dinner ($7) gives you any 3 sides. Bread pudding and cobbler come by the ½ pint ($3), if you have room left for dessert. Open M-Sa 11am-11pm. Mama has recently created a doppel-ganger for herself with Step Mama's, across the street at 199 E. 3rd St. (228-2663), which sells sandwiches, soups, and sides. The nourishment continues next door at **Mama's Milk,** a new, creative smoothie shop. **$**

Mee Noodle Shop and Grill, 219 First Ave. (995-0333), at 13th St. Fresh ingredients make for very good, simple Chinese food. The noodle soups are grand and filling ($3-5.20), as are the dan-dan noodles ($4.50). Other entrees $4-8.50. AmEx only. Open daily 11am-11pm. Other location at 922 Second Ave. at 49th St. (995-0563). **$**

National Café, 210 First Ave. (473-9354), at 13th St. It would be hard to find a better Cuban lunch special in the city; from 10:30am-3pm, the National serves an entree of the day, rice and beans or salad, plantain, a cup of soup, and bread for $4.25. Even without the specials, everything on this garlic-heavy menu is well under $10. Try the *mofongo* (garlicky roast pork and chicken, $4.50). Open M-Sa 11am-10pm. **$**

The Oven (O.V.O.), 65 Second Ave. (353-1444), at 4th St. This place serves up some of the best pizza in the city by (don't shoot!) departing slightly from time-honored Italian tradition, giving their pizzas a crust with the taste and consistency of *lavosh* bread. 10-inch individual-sized pizzas $4.50-9, toppings $1-2.50. Concoctions like the goat cheese eggplant pizza ($7) and the Zaatar (with thyme, sesame seeds, sumac, plum tomato, arugula, calamata olives, and extra virgin olive oil, $6) also belie the Middle Eastern origins of the restaurant's owners. No slices. Open Su-Th noon-midnight, F-Sa noon-1am. **$**

Rose of India, 308 E. 6th St. (533-5011 or 473-9758), between First and Second Ave. Decorated like a Christmas tree turned inside out and spread across a subway car, the Rose of India demonstrates the difficulty of advertising on a block with 25 other Indian restaurants—the food, however, is a definite stand-out. Curries with rice, *dal,* and chutney $5-7. Nine different breads $1.75-3, samosas $2. On your birth-day, they throw a mini-party, replete with kitschalicious cakes and lights. Great lunch special ($5). Bring your own booze. Make reservations on weekends to beat the long lines. Open daily noon-1am. **$**

Sahara East, 184 First Ave. (353-9000), between 11th and 12th St. The decent food here—standard Middle Eastern fare like couscous and hummus and shish kebab—isn't going to win any awards, but the restaurant has other benefits. After dinner or over a drink in the outdoor garden, you and your friends can order up a hookah ($5), New York's latest fad. Puff away at the fruity tobacco blend, and imagine yourselves sitting on a giant mushroom, like Lewis Carroll's caterpillar. Belly dancing on Friday and Satur-day nights. Open M-F 9am-3am, Sa-Su 9am-4am. **$-$$**

Second Ave. Delicatessen, 156 Second Ave. (677-0606), at 10th St. Established in 1954, this is *the* definitive New York deli. People come to the city just for the *haimish* ambiance. The Lebewohl family has proudly maintained this strictly kosher joint since 1954. Meals served with an array of pickles. Try the chopped liver ($6), babka ($3.25), kasha varnishkas ($4), or chicken soup ($4)—all reputed to be among the best in the city. This was once the heart of the Yiddish theater district and Hollywood-style star plaques are embedded in the sidewalk outside. Open Su-Th 8am-midnight, F-Sa 8am-3am. **$**

Siam Square, 92 Second Ave. (505-1240), between 5th and 6th St. Cheap prices for excellent Thai food. They've got the regular choices here, such as *pad thai* ($7.75), but if you want something a little less quotidian, go for the *poh thak,* a Thai bouillabaisse ($13). The kicker: all prices reduced 15% during dinner. Open Su-Th 11:30am-11pm, F-Sa 11:30am-midnight. **$-$$**

St. Dymphna's, 118 St. Mark's Pl. (254-6636), between First Ave. and Ave. A. Classy Irish food makes dining here a bit more expensive, but the gorgeous garden out back will make you happy you came. The house salad is dapperly dressed with cheese ($5.50). The beef and Guinness casserole ($10) and the chicken, smoky bacon, and wild mushroom pie ($12.50) put average pies to shame. Open Su-W 10am-midnight, Th-Sa 10am-4am. Bar open daily until 4am. **$-$$**

Teriyaki Boy, 239 E. 9th St. (477-8140), between Second and Third Ave. Tokyo-futurism at a purple new-wave fast-food sushi/teriyaki joint. Roll and a la carte sushi $1-3.25. Daily lunch specials ($6-7) noon-4pm. Open daily noon-11pm. **$**

Two Boots Restaurant, 37 Ave. A (505-2276), at 3rd St. Which 2 boots? Italy and Louisiana. A swinging East Village mezcla of Cajun and Italian, this establishment packs locals with its hybrid pizzas ($5.50-20) and pastas ($6-12). Got so popular it spread the flavor across the street, and turned into a pizzeria/video rental store (video 254-1441, pizza 254-1919) with free screenings on Thursday nights. Two Boots also exists in Park Slope, Brooklyn (718-499-3253), and as take-out in the West Village (633-9096). Open daily noon-midnight. **$-$$**

Veselka, 144 Second Ave. (228-9682), at 9th St. A down-to-earth, soup-and-bread Polish-Ukrainian joint. Traditional food served in a friendly, non-traditional setting. Big, beautiful murals adorn everything, including the dumpster around the corner. Enormous menu includes about 10 varieties of soups, as well as salads, blintzes, meats, and other Eastern European fare. Blintzes $3.50, soup $2 a cup (try the sumptuous chicken noodle). Combination special gets you soup, salad, stuffed cabbage, and four melt-in-your-mouth *pierogi* ($8). Great breakfast specials: challah french toast, OJ, and coffee for $3.75. Open 24hr. **$**

Whole Earth Bakery and Kitchen, 130 St. Marks Pl. (677-7597), between First Ave. and Ave. A. Inspired by the owner's 87-year-old mother (who still works here everyday), Whole Earth gives home cooking and baking a strictly vegan tweak. The baked goods manage to be shockingly yummy *sans* eggs. Ask for the flavorful tofu/garlic spread to put on other items. Cookies 50¢-$2; fruit cobbler $1.50; veggie burger $3.50. The owner also custom-designs vegan wedding cakes. Open daily 9am-midnight. **$**

Yaffa Café, 97 St. Mark's Pl. (674-9302 or 677-9001), between First Ave. and Ave. A. The highest decor-to-price ratio in the Village. Diners peruse a 5-page menu offering all sorts of salads ($5-6), sandwiches ($4-5), crepes (around $6), and beer ($3.50) in an interior right out of *I Dream of Jeannie*'s bottle. Stick to the salads; many of the more complex items on the menu are underwhelming. The outdoor garden is open all summer, and is a work of art itself. Open 24hr. **$**

CAFES

First Street Cafe, 72 E. 1st St. (358-7831), by First Ave. Perfect for people-watching, this small, hip cafe serves up free music every night around 9pm—mostly jazz. Tuesday, White Trash night, offers open-mic country and rockabilly. Local art graces the walls. Slake your thirst on fresh-squeezed lemonade ($1.45) or indulge in the great 3-bean chili ($3.75). Open M-Th 8am-11pm, F-Su 9am-1am.

Pink Pony Café, 176 Ludlow St. (253-1922), between E. Houston and Stanton St. This self-consciously trendy cafe/ice cream parlor/performance space catering to the Lower East Side artistic set is located in a neighborhood that stays quiet even at night. A great place to study, read, or write over an espresso ($1.50). Try their lemon-and-ginger drink ($1.50). Performance space in back lends itself to stand-up comedy and screenings; call for schedule. Comfy chairs and couches. Open Su-Th 10:30am-midnight, F-Sa 10:30am-4am.

SHOPS

East Village Cheese, 40 Third Ave. (477-2601), between 9th and 10th St. Subway: #6 to Astor Pl. The name says it all. Actually, it doesn't, because this store sells crackers and snack foods in addition to the endless varieties of *fromage*. Check out the bargain bin. Open M-F 8:30am-6:30pm, Sa-Su 8:30am-6pm.

Moishe's Bake Shop, 115 Second Ave. (505-8555), between 6th and 7th St. For 30 years this bake shop has served up *geshmak* (that's Yiddish for tasty) breads and cookies. The budget traveler would be wise to buy a delicious challah here ($2.75). Strictly kosher. Open Su 7am-8pm, M-Th 7:30am-8:30pm, F 7am until 1hr. before sunset.

Something Sweet, 177 First Ave. (533-9986), at 11th St. Delectable and inventive sweets that give Veniero's a run for its money. Indulge in a tropical fruit tart ($2.25), a mousse tart ($2), or a chocolate-covered banana ($1.50). Open M-Sa 8am-8pm, Su 9:30am-5:30pm.

Veniero's, 342 E. 11th St. (674-7070), between First and Second Ave. This Italian pastry shop has clogged the arteries of many a blissful sweets-lover for 105 years and continues to pack in loyal followers. Open Su-Th 8am-midnight, F-Sa 8am-1am.

GREENWICH VILLAGE

The West Village's free-floating, artistic spirit spawns many creative eateries and even makes stumbling around looking for food as much fun as dining. Circuitous side streets yield many fruits—you could drop into the enchanting **Peacock Caffè,** 24 Greenwich Ave. (242-9395), or join off-Broadway theatergoers who compose informal reviews over burgers and beer. You could also wander over to **John's Pizzeria,** 278 Bleecker St. (942-7288), for some of the most respected pizza in the city.

Bleecker St., between Sixth and Seventh Ave., offers a great variety of eateries—from classy to kitschy. The **Murray Cheese Shop,** 257 Bleecker St. (243-3289), at Cornelia St., is perfect for picnickers. This aromatic establishment contains over 400 kinds of cheese. Open M-Sa 8am-8pm, Su 9am-6pm. Unless otherwise specified, establishments accept credit cards.

🍴 **Arturo's Pizza,** 106 W. Houston St. (677-3820), at Thompson St. Arturo's has served up great, cheap pizza and divey class for decades now. And it's conveniently located near the Anjelika Film Center. What could be better? Only the big, cheesey pies are divine. Entrees range from $8-26. Live jazz M-F 9pm-1am, Sa-Su 9pm-2am. Open M-Th4pm-1am, F-Sa 4pm-2am, Su 3pm-midnight. **$**

🍴 **Cucina Stagionale,** 275 Bleecker St. (924-2707), at Jones St. Italian dining in a low-key, classy environment. Packed on weekends, its lines can reach the street. The *conchiglie* (shells and sauteed calamari in spicy red sauce, $8) or the spinach and cheese ravioli ($6) will tell you why. Pasta dishes $6-8; veal, chicken, and fish dishes $8-10. If you get dessert, the bill still won't exceed $15. Cash only. No alcohol, but you may bring your own. Open daily noon-midnight. **$**

Elephant and Castle, 68 Greenwich Ave. (243-1400), near Seventh Ave. Their motto is *"j'adore les omelettes,"* and boy, are those omelettes adorable ($5-8). The sound of an apple-cheddar-walnut creation or a spinach-cheddar combo may unnerve you, but once anything from this omelette repertoire arrives, it won't disappoint. Non-omelette options include intriguing toppings on delicious chicken or pasta ($9-12). Open M-F 8:30am-midnight, Sa-Su 10am-midnight. **$$**

Eva's, 11 W. 8th St. (677-3496), between MacDougal St. and Fifth Ave. Refreshing fast-service health food. Massive veggie plate with falafel, grape leaves, and eggplant salad $5.55. Vitamin store in back adds to the anti-ambience. The menus outside often contain coupons. Open daily 10:30am-11pm. **$**

🍴 **Go Sushi,** 3 Greenwich Ave. (366-9272), at Sixth Ave. and 8th St. Clean, spacious, with magazine rack and people-watching window. Minimalist decor and cheap, delicious Japanese food unite at this no-nonsense, pay-at-the-counter gem. Bento Box with *gyoza,* rice, salad, and chicken teriyaki $6. Sushi (2 salmon, 1 tuna, 1 shrimp, 4 California, 4 cucumber) $6.50. Sashimi deluxe with rice, miso soup, and 9 pieces of fresh, delicious fish $12. No alcohol, but honeyed, iced green tea ($2.25) and fresh brewed ginger ale ($2.50) are sure to satisfy. Cash only. Open daily 11:30am-11:30pm. **$**

Olive Tree Cafe, 117 MacDougal St. (254-3480), north of Bleecker St. Standard Middle Eastern food offset by endless stimulation. If you get bored by the old movies on the wide screen, you can rent chess, backgammon, and Scrabble sets ($1), doodle with chalk on the slate tables, or sit on the patio and survey the Village nightlife. Falafel sandwich $3; chicken kebab platter with salad, rice pilaf, and vegetable $9; delicious egg creams $1.75. Open Su-Th 11am-4am, F-Sa 11am-5am. **$**

The Pink Teacup, 42 Grove St. (807-6755), between Bleecker and Bedford St. Soul food in a small, pink, and friendly environment. As multiple Martin Luther King, Jrs. gaze at you from the walls, you can sit at the table of brotherhood and swoon over tasty fried chicken. Steep dinner prices, but the $6.50 lunch special (11am-2pm) includes choice of fried chicken or stew, soup or salad, two vegetables, and dessert. Coffee, eggs, and fritters can feed two for under $10. Cash only. Bring your own booze. Open Su-Th 8am-midnight, F-Sa 8am-1am. **$-$$**

RESTAURANTS

■**Quantum Leap,** 88 W. 3rd St. (677-8050), between Thompson and Sullivan St. Brown rice galore at this aggressively veggie restaurant. Large menu full of delectable options: chock-full-of-vegetables miso soup $3, spring rolls $3.50, gargantuan veggie burrito $6. Carnivores can try any fish in black bean sauce ($10-12). Vegan desserts include a yummy tofu blueberry pie ($3.50). Open daily 11am-11pm. **$-$$**

Ray's Pizza, 465 Sixth Ave. (243-2253), at 11th St. Half the uptown joints claim the title of "Original Ray's," but here's the real McCoy. People have flown here from Europe just to bring back a few pies, while kids from neighboring P.S. 41 have had first dates here. Well worth braving lines and paying upwards of $1.90 for a cheese-heavy slice. Scant seating; get pizza to go. Open Su-Th 11am-2am, F-Sa 11am-3am. **$**

Spain, 113 W. 13th St. (929-9580), between Sixth and Seventh Ave. Enormous tureens of traditional Spanish food for $11-16. The entrees can easily satisfy 2 or even 3 people (sharing incurs an extra $2 charge). Try the *paellas* or anything with garlic. Tantalizing and *free* appetizers such as *chorizo*. Cash only. Open daily noon-1am. **$$**

Tea and Sympathy, 108 Greenwich Ave. (807-8329), between Jane and W. 13th St. An English tea house—high tea, cream tea, and good old-fashioned British "cuisine." Filled with kitschy teacups and salt shakers, fading photos of obviously English families, and beautiful chipped china. The waitresses all speak the Queen's English. Afternoon tea (the whole shebang—sandwiches, tea, scones, rarebit) for $17, delicious despite being British; cream tea (tea, scones, and jam) $4.50. Open M-F 11:30am-10:30pm. Sa-Su 10am-10:30pm. Next door at 110 Greenwich is **Carry On Tea & Sympathy,** a cozy shop for Anglophiles who wish to buy British souvenirs in Manhattan. Same hours. **$-$$**

CAFES

Caffè Dante, 79 MacDougal St. (982-5275), south of Bleecker St. A Village staple, with black-and-white photos of the Old World and atmospheric lighting. *Frutta di bosco* $5.25, coffee-based liquids $2-6, nice *gelati* and Italian ices around $5. You'll love the matchbooks. A great place to take Beatrice. Open Su-Th 10am-2am, F-Sa 10am-3am.

Caffè Mona Lisa, 282 Bleecker St. (929-1262), near Jones St. Like the coffee here, *La Gioconda*'s recurring image is strong but not overpowering. In addition to well-brewed beverages ($1.50-4) and other cafe fare, Mona Lisa's oversized mirrors, stuffed chairs, and eccentric furniture pieces will make you smile enigmatically. Open daily 11am-2am.

Caffè Raffaella, 134 Seventh Ave. (929-7247), north of Christopher St. Prominently gay atmosphere for those seeking comfort without pretension. Every chair is different. (See **Gay and Lesbian Life,** p. 309.)

Caffè Reggio, 119 MacDougal St. (475-9557), south of W. 3rd St. Celebs, wannabes, and students crowd the oldest cafe in the Village. Open since 1927, this place showcases busts and madonnas in every corner, and pours a mean cup of cappuccino ($2.25). Wide selection of pastries ($2.50-5.50). Check out that shiny vintage espresso machine! Open Su-Th 10am-2am, F-Sa 10am-4am.

SHOPS

Balducci's, 424 Sixth Ave. (673-2600), between 9th and 10th St. Come on weekends for free tastings of everything from pâtés to chocolate hazelnut tortes. Huge selection of gourmet prepared foods, cheese, breads, and desserts. Open daily 7am-8:30pm.

HARLEM AND WASHINGTON HEIGHTS

Cheap food abounds in Harlem and Washington Heights. Ethnic food is everywhere, with Jewish food in Washington Heights, various Latino and Cuban foods in the Hispanic communities and, of course, all kinds of black cuisines—East and West African, Caribbean, Creole, and some of the best soul food north of the Mason-Dixon Line. For food from the heart of Harlem, check out Lenox Ave., or 125th St. and 116th St. along Nagle Ave.

Copeland's, 547 W. 145th St. (234-2357), between Broadway and Amsterdam Ave. Excellent soul food accompanied by live music in an elegant dining room makes this place a top choice. If you're not too full from the complimentary cornbread, indulge in the Southern fried chicken, candied yams, macaroni and cheese, or collard greens (your choice of sides) for $11. Other entrees are a bit pricier so you may want to check out Copeland's "cafeteria" next door—same food, lower prices, and, of course, the ambience. Open Tu-Th 4:30-11pm, F-Sa 4:30pm-midnight, Su 11am-9:30pm. Cafeteria open Su-Th 8am-11pm, F-Sa 8am-midnight. Accepts AmEx, V, MC. **$$**

Le Grenier, 2264 Frederick Douglass Blvd. (666-0653), between 121st and 122nd St. For authentic West African cuisine try this Senegalese restaurant. Beware the bite of some of the spices and, if in doubt, ask how natives down staples like *fufu* ($7)—you may be surprised. Some dishes only served on weekends or in the evenings, such as steamed fish with salad and plantains ($10), served after 6pm. Cash only. Open M-F 1pm-2am, Sa-Su 1pm-3am. **$-$$**

Sisters, 1931 Madison Ave. (410-3000), at 124th St. Soul food from the heart. At this small family restaurant you won't be inundated by tourists or ambience, just good food. Fried chicken and most other entrees range from $6-8. Open M-F 8am-8pm, Sa-Su 8am-9pm. V, MC accepted. **$**

Sylvia's, 328 Lenox Ave. (996-0660), at 126th St. This soul-food restaurant has enticed New Yorkers for over 30 years; now European tour groups arrive in buses and crowd the joint. Sylvia accents her "World-Famous talked-about BBQ ribs special" with "sweet spicy sauce" and a side of collard greens and macaroni and cheese ($11). Lunch special of salmon croquette, pork chop, fried chicken leg, collard greens, and candied yams $7. Friday nights feature free live jazz and R&B (6-9pm). Gospel Brunch Sunday.

HOBOKEN, NJ

While Hoboken may not have the same culinary diversity and distinction as its larger cousin across the Hudson, there are a growing number of good establishments to please the palate. Unfortunately, the majority of these cater to the city's wealthier clientele. Bar food, one begins to feel, may be the best solution (see **Nightlife,** p. 283). For info on how to get to Hoboken, see p. 229.

Bagels on the Hudson, 802 Washington St. (201-798-2221). This is the place to pick up a picnic for Castle Point. Homemade turkey sandwich $4, corned beef $4, bagels 50¢. Open 24hr. **$**

Johnny Rockets, 134 Washington St. (201-659-2620), at 2nd St. Johnny Rockets takes its customers on a sentimental journey back to the 1950s with its old-school diner feel and juicy hamburgers ($3.75). Most of the red booths come equipped with a 5¢ jukebox that plays Patsy Cline, Nat King Cole, and other oldies. Even better, the soda fountain sports flavored colas. A spanking-clean floor and gracious waitstaff complete the time warp. Open Su-W 11am-11pm, Th 11am-1am, F-Sa 11am-3am. **$**

La Isla, 104 Washington St. (201-659-8197). Cuban food aficionados will love this charming diner-turned-family-restaurant. Specials change daily. The large servings are mostly under $8. Adventurous vegetarians might try the *yuca*, a tasty Caribbean potato-like vegetable (and, according to the menu, an acronym for Young Upscale Cuban American). Bring your own booze; cigars at the counter $1-3. Open M-Sa 7am-10pm. **$**

LITTLE ITALY

Perhaps no street in New York is more packed with restaurants than the three blocks of Mulberry St. between Grand and Canal St. Beneath the web of Italian flags that canopy the streets, *trattorie* and *caffè* crowd the sidewalks with tables. After 7pm, the street comes to life; arrive a bit earlier for one of the better tables. On weekends, reservations are usually a must. For the sake of thrift and ambience, dine at a *ristorante* and then move to a *caffè* to satisfy your sweet tooth. While it isn't hard to find restaurants in Little Italy, it *is* hard to find stand-out cuisine.

Three tips for choosing a restaurant or *caffè:* first, just because someone famous ate there doesn't mean it's good; second, just because it's really old doesn't mean it's good; and third, just because the waiters all have heavy Italian accents...well, you know. Most area restaurants have reasonable prices, but some really milk their old world "charm." A full meal can run $60-70, particularly when you bring a bottle of wine into the equation. Save money by dining on sizable appetizers *(anti-pasti)* or grabbing a snack at one of the many shops and groceries. Unless otherwise noted, all places take major credit cards.

Benito One, 174 Mulberry St. (226-9171), between Grand and Broome St. A small, very friendly *trattoria* featuring a menu of excellent Sicilian fare. A favorite is *pollo scarpariello,* chicken on the bone with garlic, olive oil, and basil ($11). Pasta $7-13, veal $14.50, poultry $11-13, seafood $13-20. $6.50 lunch special until 4pm. Open Su-Th 11am-11pm, F-Sa 11am-midnight. **$-$$**

🔯 **Da Nico,** 164 Mulberry St. (343-1212), between Broome and Grand St. Cheap, tasty food in a lovely environment, enhanced by a spacious, tree-shaded garden in back—frequented by Al Pacino and Johnny Depp. *Pollo marsala* ($11.50) will placate a grumbling tummy. Lunch: pasta $6-10, entrees $6.50-12.50. Dinner: pasta $10-15, entrees $11-25. Open Su-Th 11am-11pm, F-Sa 11am-midnight. **$$**

La Mela, 167 Mulberry St. (431-9493), between Broome and Grand St. Plastered with kitschy photos, postcards, and letters, La Mela is the place to come for a raucous time. The chummy, boisterous waitstaff serve up generous portions "family style"—a sort of home-style *prix fixe* selection with the dishes of the day written on a sign outside the restaurant. The wine is cheap ($18 for 1.5L), but you can also bring your own. Pasta $6-8, entrees $11-15. Open daily noon-11pm. **$$**

🔯 **Lombardi's,** 32 Spring St. (941-7994), between Mott and Mulberry St. New York's oldest licensed pizzeria (1897), credited with creating the famous New York-style thin-crust, coal-oven pizza. Indoor dining rooms and the outdoor patio provide refuge from the tumult of lower Mulberry. A large pie feeds 2 ($12.50). Toppings are pricey ($3 for one, $5 for two, $6 for three), as are the more creative assortments, like the fresh clam pie ($20 for a large)—but they're worth it. Reservations for groups of 6 or more. Cash only. Open M-Th 11am-11pm, F-Sa 11:30am-midnight, Su 11am-10pm. **$-$$**

Puglia Restaurant, 189 Hester St. (966-6006), at Mulberry St. For entertainment with your pasta come after 6pm when Puglia's own sing Italian folk favorites with a Vegas sensibility. The crowd is noisy and fun-loving, and the decent food comes in large portions. Long tables yield social equality in 3 spacious, cool dining rooms and one lounge, ranging from diner chic to grotto chic. Pastas $7-10, entrees $9-18. Monstrous plate of mussels $9.25. Open Su-Th noon-midnight, F-Sa noon-1am. **$-$$**

Rocky's Italian Restaurant, 45 Spring St. (274-9756), at Mulberry St. A true neighborhood joint, Rocky's buzzes with strains of the Old Country. Their "homestyle cooking" boast means you can ask for things that aren't on the menu. For lunch, try a pizza hero ($4) or sandwich ($4-7), served until 5pm. Pasta $6.50-11, entrees $8-15. The chicken with garlic sauce ($12) is a treat. The wine is cheap ($14 for a carafe), but you can also bring your own. Open daily 11am-11pm. Jul.-Aug. closed M. **$-$$**

CAFFÈ

Caffè Palermo, 148 Mulberry St. (431-4205), between Grand and Hester St. The best of the *caffè* offerings along Mulberry. Summers, Palermo opens onto the street with an espresso bar up front. Most pastries are $3-5. The staff takes much pride in its tasty tiramisu ($5); the cannoli ($2.75) and cappuccino ($3.25) are also quite good. Open daily 9:30am-midnight.

La Bella Ferrara, 110 Mulberry St. (966-1488). The name is cribbed from the larger, factory-like Caffè Ferrara on Grand St. and basically means "better Ferrara." If you prefer a more intimate space the title holds true. Sleek glass, checkered tile inside, and outdoor seating removed from pedestrian flow create a good cheesecake-eating ambience. Pastries $2-2.50, desserts $4-5, cappuccino $3. Cash only. Open Su-Th 9am-1am, F-Sa 9am-2am.

SHOPS

Dipalo Dairy, 206 Grand St. (226-1033), at Mott St. Even the toughest budget traveler cannot live on bread alone; enter Dipalo Dairy. The shop offers a selection of breads, meats, and pastas, but specializes in cheeses. The soft, fleshy mozzarella ($4.69 per lb.) is their mainstay, but the goat cheese and the *ricotta fresca* are also delicious. What's more...free samples! The proprieter insists: "You must not buy it unless you taste it first." Open daily 9am-6:30pm.

LOWER EAST SIDE

Pasty-faced punks and starving artists dine alongside an older generation that converses in Polish, Hungarian, and Yiddish, here on the historic Lower East Side. The neighborhood took in the huddled masses, and, in return, got lots of cool, cheap places to eat. Alongside that hunk with the eyebrow ring, you'll munch *haimish* pickles, *zare-shane* bialys, and to-*kvell*-for knishes in some of the city's finest kosher establishments. Many of the stores close in observance of the sabbath, from sundown on Friday to sundown on Saturday, so make sure you stock up on your deli delectables during the week. Farther north, Ukrainian places serve borscht, *pierogi*, and other inexpensive yet hearty foods. Here are some more of the more famed establishments, as well as a couple of less kosher alternatives.

El Sombrero, 108 Stanton St. (254-4188), on the corner of Ludlow. If the gods ate at a Mexican restaurant (and lived on a budget), they'd dine here. Vibrantly painted walls complement the animated crowd of twenty-somethings eating large portions of excellent food. Vegetable enchiladas ($8) make a satisfying meal, but you'll marvel at the Fajitas Mexicana ($10). Cash only. Beer and margaritas available. Hours vary, but closes midnightish or slightly later. **$$**

Gertel's Bake Shoppe & Luncheonette, 53 Hester St. (982-3250), near Essex St. Gertel's, a kosher hole-in-the-wall, serves great sandwiches ($2.50-5). There are only a couple of tables at which to enjoy the eats, so take your *rugulach* to go (around 50¢ each)! Open Su-Th 6:30am-5pm, F 6:30am-3pm. **$**

Katz's Delicatessen, 205 E. Houston St. (254-2246), near Orchard St. Since 1888, Katz's has remained an authentic Jewish deli. Katz's widened its appeal with its "Send a salami to your boy in the army" campaign during WWII. Every president in the last 2 decades has proudly received a Katz salami. The food is orgasmic (as Meg Ryan confirmed, when she made a loud scene here in *When Harry Met Sally*), but you pay extra for the atmosphere. Heroes $5.10, sandwiches around $9. Open Su-Tu 8am-10pm, W-Th 8am-11pm, F-Sa 8am-3am. **$$**

Ratner's Restaurant, 138 Delancey St. (677-5588), just west of the Manhattan Bridge. The most famous of the kosher restaurants, partly because of its frozen-food line. In contrast to its run-down surroundings, this popular place shines "like the top of the Chrysler Building." The chefs strictly follow Jewish dietary laws—but *oy vey!* Such *matzah brei* ($9)! Also feast on fruit blintzes and sour cream ($9) or simmering vegetarian soups ($4). Open Su-Th 6am-11pm, F 6am-3pm. **$**

Tiengarden, 170 Allen St. (388-1364). A very Zen restaurant that goes beyond vegan cuisine, refraining from including any of the five impurities that could damage your *Qi.* So...it's kind of like kosher. The spicy organic tofu ($6.50) still has plenty of flavor. Cash only. No alcohol. Open Su-F noon-4pm and 5-10pm. **$**

Yoshi, 201 E. Houston St. (539-0225), near Orchard St. Soothing green pastel and light wood interior paired with decent Japanese food at a reasonable price. Sushi-sashimi combo for $13. Beer, wine, sake available. Open daily 5pm-1am. **$$**

SHOPS

Economy Candy, 108 Rivington St. (254-1531). Imported chocolates, jams, and countless confections, all at rock-bottom prices. Treat yourself to a huge bag of gummi bears ($1), a pound of chocolate-covered espresso beans ($5), or a pound of crystallized ginger ($3). Open M-F 8:30am-6pm, Sa 10am-5pm, Su 8:30am-5pm.

■ **Guss Lower East Side Pickle Corp.,** 35 Essex St. (254-4477 or 800-252-4877). Pickles galore, as seen in *Crossing Delancey.* A vast variety of glorious gherkins, from super sour to sweet, sold individually (50¢-$2) and in quarts ($4). They also offer coleslaw, pickled tomatoes, carrots, and t-shirts ($10). Open Su-Th 9am-6pm, F 9am-4pm.

Yonah Schimmel Knishery, 137 E. Houston St. (477-2858). Rabbi Schimmel's establishment, in business since 1910, has closed the gap between the knish and art. A dozen varieties available for $1.75. Try yogurt from the 88-year-old strain for $1.50. Open daily 8:30am-6pm. Closes for sabbath.

LOWER MANHATTAN

Lower Manhattan eateries tailor their schedules to the lunch breaks of Wall St. brokers. They prepare cheap food with grease-lightning speed; it's always available as take-out, often with free delivery. Fast-food joints appear en masse at Broadway near Dey and John St., just a few feet from the overpriced offerings of the Main Concourse of the World Trade Center. In the summer, food pushcarts line Broadway between Cedar and Liberty St. In addition to the usual mystery dogs, vendors sell falafel and eggplant plates ($2.75), burritos ($4.50), and chilled gazpacho with an onion roll ($3.75). You can sup in **Liberty Park,** across the street, or in the windy concrete jungle around the Twin Towers.

At the pedestrian plaza at Coenties Slip, between Pearl and South William St., you can choose among the small budget restaurants (Chinese, Indian, or fish and chips), or trek over to nearby Chinatown for hearty cuisine. North of City Hall, food kiosks fill **St. Andrew's Plaza,** a no-frills alternative for local office workers doing lunch.

Zigolini's, 66 Pearl St. (425-7171), at Coenties Alley. One of the few places in the area where indoor air-conditioned seating abounds (although there is plenty of room outdoors) this gourmet Italian restaurant serves filling sandwiches ($5-7) and some great pasta. Dishes incorporate such delicacies as sundried tomatoes and portobello mushrooms; sizeable sandwiches on foccacia are a specialty. Build-your-own sandwiches cost more with each added ingredient. Open M-F 7am-7pm.

Europa, 199 Water St. (422-0070), a block down from the Titanic Memorial at the South Street Seaport. Smoothly decorated and high-ceilinged, this gourmet self-serve joint is a little more expensive than nearby fast-food options. Fortunately, you are paying for good taste. The grilled chicken breast sandwich on ciabatta bread, with lettuce, tomatoes, and basil pesto ($6.50), provides a delicious noonday meal. Open daily 6:30am-8:30pm. Delivery until closing.

McDonald's, 160 Broadway (385-2063), at Liberty St. Yeah, it's a McDonald's, but what a McDonald's! Step inside and witness one of New York's finest examples of postmodern shmaltz. Wall St.'s Mickey D's sports a door person in a tux, a pianist above the entrance, a stock ticker, and a McBoutique on the second floor. They keep the ketchup packets in glass and brass bowls here—a little touch of McClass to justify the slightly inflated McPrice. Open M-F 6am-9pm, Sa-Su 7:30am-9pm.

MORNINGSIDE HEIGHTS

The cafes and restaurants in Morningside Heights cater mostly to Columbia students, faculty, and their families. This usually means that hours run late and the price range fits that of a starving student. Old-fashioned coffee shops abound, and there are plenty of places to grab a reasonable meal, although you could find more to savor in other areas of the city.

Amir's Falafel, 2911A Broadway (749-7500), between 113th and 114th St. Low-priced Middle Eastern staples like *shawarma, baba ghanoush,* and *musakaa* (cold eggplant salad) for vegetarians and meat-lovers alike. Sandwiches ($4-5) and vegetarian platters ($5-7) made with care. Mirrors and paintings of belly dancers await your contemplation. Cash only. Open daily 11am-10:30pm. **$**

Koronet Pizza, 2848 Broadway (222-1566), at 110th St. Frighteningly large slices of pizza for $2.25. Also offers whole pies, lasagna, and calzones. Cash only. Open daily 7am-2am. **$**

Mama Mexico, 2672 Broadway (864-2323) at 102nd St. Wonderful Mexican food, if a bit pricey. With colored lanterns, a roaming mariachi singer, and a vivacious crowd, Mama promises a lively dinner. Amazing margaritas in 12 tropical flavors $6. Entrees $9-20. Accepts AmEx, V, MC. **$$**

Massawa, 1239 Amsterdam Ave. (663-0505), at 121st St. Make sure you washed your hands before heading here, a restaurant that specializes in cheap well-prepared Ethiopian and Eritrean cuisine—traditionally eaten by hand. The many veggie dishes ($5-6) are served with spongy *ingera* bread or rice. Between 11:30am and 3pm, they offer great lunch specials like lamb stew and collard green/potato platters ($4-6). Wine (by the glass) around $4, imported beer $3-4. Open daily noon-midnight. Accepts AmEx, V, MC, Discover. **$-$$**

Mike's Papaya, 2832 Broadway (663-5076), at 110th St. Morningside Heights' entry into Manhattan's battle for papaya-hot dog stand supremacy. This take-out joint offers 2 hot dogs and one of their fruit drinks or shakes (mango, pina colada, banana daiquiri) for $2. Cash only. Open daily 24hr. **$**

Mill Korean Restaurant, 2895 Broadway (666-7653), at 112th St. The Mill offers traditional, freshly prepared Korean food at reasonable prices. They take special pride in their *bi bim bap,* a Korean rice dish with meat and assorted vegetables ($7). For a couple extra dollars get it in a hot, stone pot where the rice at the bottom cooks at your table to a candy-like crisp. Lunch specials M-F 11am-3pm ($5-7). Complete dinners with side dishes like *kim chee* (Korean pickled vegetables) for $7-10. Open daily 11am-11pm. Accepts AmEx, V, MC. **$$-$$$**

Monsoon, 2850 Broadway (665-2700), between 110th and 111th St. Good, mid-priced Vietnamese with an appropriately bamboo-heavy decor. Staples like *ga nuong xa* (grilled lemongrass chicken with peanut sauce) $5. Large, cheap soups like *La sa* (curried shrimp soup with coconut milk, and vermicelli noodles) $6. It gets pretty crowded here on weekends; reservations accepted for parties of 4 or more. Open Su-Th 11:30am-11:30pm, F-Sa 11:30am-midnight. Accepts AmEx, V, MC. **$$**

La Rosita Restaurant, 2809 Broadway (663-7804), between 108th and 109th St. The restaurant may lack the romantic atmosphere its name implies, but genuine Spanish/ Cuban cuisine more than compensates. Daily specials range from $5-6. Try the *caldo gallega* soup, made from white beans ($2-3), or the *carne guisada,* a savory beef stew ($6). Most dinners come with a heaping portion of rice and beans. Excellent *cafè con leche* (espresso with milk) $1.10. Open daily 9am-10pm. Bar opens at 6pm. Beer $2, cocktails $3.50. Accepts AmEx, V, MC, Discover. **$$**

Obaa Koryoe, 3143 Broadway (316-2950), between 125th and La Salle St. Expect excellent West African food in a laid-back setting. Ignore the American pop songs—elaborate wood carvings and African locals provide the authentic ambience you crave. Try the bean stew and fried plantains, with *jollof* rice ($9) or chicken, bean stew, *wachey,* and *gari* ($10). Indulge in a bottle of "budget" South African wine ($13-19). Open M-Sa 11am-11pm, Su 11am-9pm. AmEx, V, MC, Discover accepted. **$$**

Tom's Restaurant, 2880 Broadway (864-6137), at 112th St. Immortalized as the storefront featured in *Seinfeld* (not the Tom's in Suzanne Vega's song "Tom's Diner," as urban legend would have it). About as cheap as it gets. If you don't mind the no-frills diner feel, stop in to enjoy luxurious milkshakes ($2.45). The most popular is the "Broadway": chocolate ice cream with coffee syrup. Greasy burgers for $3-5, dinner under $6.50. Cash only. Open M-W 6am-1:30am; from Th 6am to Su 1:30am open 24hr. **$**

SHOPS

The Hungarian Pastry Shop, 1030 Amsterdam Ave. (866-4230), at 111th St. If you don't know the difference between Fila and *phyllo,* lace up the former and head over to the West Side's worst-kept secret to experience the latter. Plain, friendly pastry shop. Eclairs, cake slices, and other goodies for around $2. Pleasant outdoor seating. Cash only. Open daily 8:30am-11:30pm.

NOLITA, FOR LACK OF A BETTER WORD

Certain clever types have honored yet another downtown area with an acronym—this time, "NoLIta" (**No**rth of **L**ittle **Ita**ly). If you're embarrassed to let this word trip three times on your tongue, just call it Northern Little Italy or consider it part of the Lower East Side (see p.152). Roughly bounded by Lafayette, Spring, the Bowery, and Houston streets, this budding pocket of sidewalk and culinary action composes the sin and the soul of Manhattan's recently fashionable. Since you'll pay the price for ambience around here, you may want to go early for drinks and an appetizer or late for drinks and dessert. If you want to eat a real meal that will satisfy more than a little-girl appetite, there exist several budget options. Credit cards accepted, unless otherwise noted.

Cafe Gitane, 242 Mott St. (334-9552), at Prince St. A focal point of NoLIta life, this cafe specializes in seeing and being seen. Retro and diner-esque with red vinyl booths, tables topped with linoleum, and full counter service. A rack of glossy fashion mags invites you to linger. Healthy salads and sandwiches ($4.25-7.50). The menu includes noodle and couscous dishes ($7.75-9). Cash only. Cheap wine and beer. Open daily 9am-midnight. **$**

Mexican Radio, 250 Mulberry St. (343-0140), between Prince and Spring St. Small new restaurant serving up fresh, delicious Mexican standards to a hip, young crowd. Though the food is Mexican, the place is unapologetically New York. Entrees $10-15. Bar. Open daily noon-11:30pm. **$$**

🖎 **Rice,** 227 Mott St. (226-5775), between Prince and Spring St. Fantastic food—and darn cheap. Standard favorites here—basmati, jasmine, sticky, Japanese. However, do explore the more exotic Thai black or Bhutanese red. The sauces range from mango chutney to Aleppo yogurt; you can also add ratatouille, shrimp coconut curry, or chicken satay, among other enticing toppings. Small $4.50-7, large (it is *large*) $7-10. Cash and checks only. Beer only. Open daily noon-midnight. **$**

QUEENS

This often overlooked borough offers visitors some of the best and most reasonably priced ethnic cuisine in town. **Astoria** specializes in discount shopping and cheap eats and has many open produce markets such as **United Brothers Fruit Market,** 32-24 30th Ave. (932-9876), at the corner of 33rd St. You will also find great bounty around Steinway St. (G or R train to Steinway St. and Broadway). Greek and Italian restaurants proliferate around the elevated station at Broadway and 31st St., where you can catch the N train north to Ditmars Blvd. for still more dining options. In **Flushing** you'll find excellent Chinese, Japanese, and Korean eateries. Restaurants here often make use of rarely seen ingredients, like skatefish, squid, and tripe, which more Americanized Asian restaurants tend to avoid. **Jackson Heights** has some of the best Indian cuisine this side of the planet. **Bell Boulevard** in Bayside, out east near the Nassau border, is the center of Queens nightlife for the borough's young and semi-affluent.

In **Jamaica** and other West Indian neighborhoods to the southeast, you can try fast food like Jamaican beef patties or West Indian *roti* (flour tortillas filled with potatoes, meat, and spices). Jamaica Ave. in downtown Jamaica and Linden Blvd. in neighboring St. Albans boast many restaurants specializing in this type of cuisine. Jamaica also holds a **farmer's market,** 159-15 Jamaica Ave. (718-291-0282; open M-Sa 7am-7pm), where a few farmers offer their bounty indoors, next to a food court that offers Caribbean and Carolina-Southern restaurants, among others. To get to Jamaica, take the E or J train to Jamaica Center; from there the Q4 bus goes to Linden Blvd. in St. Albans.

Anand Bhavan, 35-66 73rd St., Jackson Heights (718-507-1600). Subway: F, G, H, R, or #7 to 74th St./Broadway, then walk 2 blocks down 73rd St. Tasty vegetarian South Indian restaurant. Picante lunch specials (noon-4:30pm) $6-8. The Anand Bhavan special, a filling 4-course meal ($12) includes *sambar* (spicy lentil soup) and a choice of *iddly* (rice crepe with peppers and onions) or *vada* (stuffed lentil dough). Note: when they say spicy, they mean spicy. Beers, foreign and domestic $3-5. Open daily noon-9:30pm. Accepts AmEx, V, MC, Discover. $

East Lake, 42-33 Main St., Flushing (718-539-8532), at Franklin St. Subway: #7 to Main St. Flushing. Four blocks down Main St., on the left. Converted 1950s diner serves up kitsch and 148 Chinese dishes. Entrees $8-16, but are uniformly enormous. Cash only. Open Su-Th 9am-2am, F-Sa 9am-3am. $

Empire K.'s Roasters, 100-19 Queens Blvd., Forest Hills (718-997-7315). Subway: G or R to 67th Ave.; when leaving the station, head right following the sign that says "67th Ave.-North Side Queens Blvd." Cheap chicken approved by a rabbi for your spiritual satisfaction. While the zillion varieties of chicken may tempt ($5-8), the fish fare (salmon, whitefish, herring, and gefilte) all bite below $10. Open Su-Th 11am-9:30pm, F 10am-2:30pm. Accepts AmEx, V, MC, Discover. $

First Edition, 41-08 Bell Blvd. (718-428-8522), at 41st Ave., Bayside. Subway: #7 to Main St./Flushing, then the Q12 bus (catch it in front of Stern's Department Store, next to the station) along Northern Ave. to Bell Blvd., then walk north 3 blocks. Neon animal-printed bar/restaurant has cheap, filling food specials and costly drinks. Entrees $8-14. Daily half-price appetizer specials. Lively singles scene at night. Open Su-Th noon-11pm, F-Sa noon-2am. Bar noon-3am. Accepts V, MC. $-$$

■ **Jackson Diner,** 37-47 74th St., Astoria (718-672-1232), at 37th Ave. Subway: E, F, G, or R to Jackson Heights/Roosevelt Ave.; or #7 to 74th St./Broadway, then walk 2 or 3 blocks north towards 37th Ave. Possibly the best Indian food in New York, complemented by minimalist red and white decor. Savor the *saag ghost* (lamb with spinach, tomato, ginger, and cumin, $10) and don't forget the samosas ($2.50). Lunch specials $6-7.50. Cash only. Open M-F 11:30am-10pm, Sa-Su 11:30am-10:30pm. $

Kum Gang San, 138-28 Northern Blvd, Flushing (718-461-0909). Subway: #7 to Main St.; walk north on Main St. and take a right on Northern Blvd (about 10min.). Good Korean food in an efficient, elegant setting with marble floors and dark wood tables. A complete lunch special can get you chicken teriyaki with salad, noodles, a California roll, and a dumpling all for $6-9. Open 24hr. Accepts AmEx, V, MC. $

■ **Nick's Pizza,** 108-26 Ascan Ave., Forest Hills (718-263-1126), between Austin and Burns St. Subway: E, F, G, or R to Forest Hills/71st Ave., then walk 3 blocks on Queens Ave. (the numbers should be going up); take a right on Ascan Ave. Suburbany establishment serves up some of the best pizza in Queens. Flaky crust and delectable sauce and toppings ($11-12, toppings $2 extra). Great calzones. Cash only. Open M-Th 11:30am-9:30pm, F 11:30am-11:30pm, Sa 12:30-11:30pm, Su 12:30-9:30pm. $

Più Bello, 70-09 Austin St., Forest Hills (718-268-4400). Subway: E, F to 71st Rd./Continental Ave. Walk west on Queens Blvd. past 70th Rd. to 70th Ave., then take a left and walk to the corner of Austin St. A slick, family-owned restaurant where the neighborhood's cool kids hang out. The Argentine expatriate owners make their smooth *gelato* and delicious cakes on the premises. Kitschy waterfall adds to the ambience. Entrees range from $7-8. Individual pizzas from $4. More than 20 *gelato* flavors to choose from, including *lamponi* (raspberry) and *fragola* (strawberry), for $6. Open daily 9am-1am. Accepts AmEx, V, MC.

Uncle George's, 33-19 Broadway, Astoria (718-626-0593), at 33rd St. Subway: N to Broadway, then 2 blocks east; or G or R to Steinway St., then 4 blocks west. Crowded, noisy, and friendly, this popular restaurant serves hearty Greek fare around the clock. All entrees are under $12. Diehard fans feed on roast leg of lamb with potatoes ($9), or octopus sauteed with vinegar ($7). Excellent Greek salad $6. Cash only. Open 24hr. $

SHOPS

Eddie's Sweet Shop, 105-29 Metropolitan Ave., Forest Hills (718-520-8514), at 72nd Rd. Subway: E, F to 71st Rd./Continental Ave., then take the Q23 to Metropolitan Ave. or take a 15min. walk through the suburbs. Selling homemade ice cream ($2), savory cappuccino ($3), junky brass horse sculptures ($90), and porcelain wares for 30 years. Old-fashioned marble floors and wooden stools evoke parlors of the 1950s and Swensens of the 1980s. Cash only. Open Tu-F 1-11:30pm, Sa-Su noon-11:30pm.

Galaxy Pastry Shop, 37-11 30th Ave., Astoria (718-545-3181). Subway: N to 30th Ave. (Grand Ave.). Make a right on 30th Ave. and walk east to 37th St. A hangout for young locals, the Galaxy offers great pastries to ruin your diet. The baklava ($1.20) tastes like the answer to a Dionysian prayer. Open daily 6:30am-3am.

■ **Knish Nosh,** 101-02 Queens Blvd., Rego Park (718-897-5554). Subway: G or R to 67th Ave. This hole in the wall doesn't offer much seating because the owners need space for racks and racks of succulent knishes ($1.50) stuffed to plumpness with potato, kasha, broccoli, or onion. Lunch special includes large knish or kosher frank in a blanket and soda or coffee ($3). Cash only. Open M-F 9am-7:30pm, Sa 9am-7pm, Su 9am-6pm.

■ **The Lemon Ice King of Corona,** 52-02 108th St., Corona (718-699-5133), at Corona Ave. Subway: #7 to 111th St., a healthy walk back one block to 108th and south 10 blocks. Keep walking—it's worth it. One of the most famous sites in Queens, on par with the Unisphere. The Emperor of Cool scrapes up juicy frozen treats outdoors. Every flavor you could want, including bubblegum, blueberry, cantaloupe, cherry, and, of course, lemon (75¢-$1.50). Cash only. Open daily 10am-midnight.

SOHO

Food is all about image in SoHo. Down with the diners that have been relegated to the fringes of town! Food here comes in a variety of exquisite and pricey forms, precious little of it fried or served over a counter. Often the best deal in SoHo is brunch, when the neighborhood shows its most cozy and good-natured front (and puts the calorie-counter away for a while).

Abyssinia, 35 Grand St. (226-5959), at Thompson St. Terrific Ethiopian restaurant with low, hand-carved stools. Although the chairs may test your posture, they make it easy to lean in and scoop up the food with your hands, aided only by pieces of spongy *injera* bread. Vegetarian entrees $6-9, meat dishes $9-13. The *azefa wotólentils*—red onions, garlic ginger, and hot green peppers, served cold—is great in the summer (as is the St. George Ethiopian beer). Open daily 6-11pm. **$$**

Bell Cafe, 310 Spring St. (334-2355), between Hudson and Greenwich St. This relaxed restaurant/hang out in an old bell factory may be off the beaten path, but there are good reasons to walk the extra blocks. Bell sports a global-village-meets-garage-sale aesthetic with a corresponding multicultural menu of Indian, African, Mexican, Jewish, and Japanese "ethno-healthy" cuisine. Always laid back and always under $12. Seating in backyard patio. Free live music nightly from 9:30pm-midnight, and monthly receptions for the new art that goes up on the restaurant's walls. Open Su-Th noon-2am, F-Sa noon-4am. **$**

Brisas del Caribe, 489 Broadway, at Broome St. Latin-American food in a decidedly un-SoHo setting. During the day this dive is populated almost exclusively by men on break from crew-work who flock here for the very cheap food (french fries $1.50, hot sandwiches $2.35-5) and roast pork that is rumored to be the best in town ($6.50). Open generally 6am-6pm. **$**

Jerry's, 101 Prince St. (966-9464), near Mercer St. The joint is jumping at Jerry's, a trendy diner with touches of red decor. Great selection of sandwiches, like the melted Vermont cheddar with bacon and tomato on seven-grain roll ($6.50). Open M-F 11:30am-5pm and 6-11pm. **$-$$**

■ **Kelley and Ping Asian Grocery and Noodle Shop,** 127 Greene St. (228-1212), between Houston and Prince St. In a hollowed out SoHo warehouse space now decorated with its own sleek Asian food products and gorgeous deep wood, Kelly and Ping serves up tasty noodle dishes for under $8. Wraps under $5, soups $5-6, wok dishes under $7.50. Also has a tea counter for all things not Lipton. Open daily 11:30am-5pm and 6-11:30pm. **$**

Le Gamin Cafe, 50 MacDougal St. (254-4678), near Houston St. Always packed with locals, this very European cafe offers simple and tasty French-inspired fare. The *salade de chevre chaudaux noix* (goat cheese croutons, tomato, mesclun, and walnuts, $9) is a sumptuous dish. Crepes $3.50-6.50. Come on Bastille Day (July 14) to see the folks at Le Gamin do the French Independence thing. Open daily 8am-midnight. Also at: 1 Main St. in DUMBO, in Brooklyn. **$**

Lucky's Juice Joint, 75 W. Houston St. (388-0300), near W. Broadway. Sunny stop specializes in fresh juice combinations. Smoothies ($4) are made with a whole banana and a choice of everything from soy milk to peaches; a variety of other additions—from ginseng to bee pollen—can be included for a dollar more. Also serves up fresh and tasty food to the weary gallery-goer in its outdoor cafe area. Veggie sandwiches $4.50-5.50, chilled 1 oz. "shots" of wheat grass $1.50. Open M-Sa 9am-8pm, Su 10am-8pm. **$**

Lupe's East L.A. Kitchen, 110 Sixth Ave. (966-1326), at Watts St. Lupe's is a small, down-scale cantina: one of the cheaper and tastier spots around. Burritos and enchiladas ($7-9) with beer are extremely filling. The Super Vegetarian Burrito ($7.25) and the Taquito Platter ($7.50) are super-tasty, as are the *huevos cubanos*—eggs any style with black beans and sweet plantain ($5). 4 types of hot-pepper sauce are provided for those who crave fire. Brunch ($4-7.25) served Sa-Su 11:30am-4pm. Open Su-Tu 11:30am-11pm, W-Sa 11:30am-midnight. **$**

Moon Dance Diner, 80 Sixth Ave. (226-1191), at Grand St. It's the real thing—an old diner-car complete with curved ceilings and counter service. Excellent short-order breakfast served all day, but the morning specials are even more rewarding. The cheese omelette with toast and home-fries ($7) is mighty tasty. The towering $5 stack of onion rings is an architectural and culinary feat. Sandwiches $7.25-9.50. Open Su-W 8:30am-midnight, Th 8:30am-4am, F opens at 8:30am and doesn't close until Su at midnight. **$-$$**

🖌 **Space Untitled,** 133 Greene St. (260-8962), near Houston St. The best of SoHo—huge, warehouse-like space with plenty of bar stools and chairs to make yourself comfortable. Black, white, brick, and art surround you while you eat, unless you choose gourmet to go. Sandwiches and salads $3-6, fabulous desserts $1.85-3.50. Coffee $1.35-1.85, wine and beer $3-4.50. Open M-Th 8am-10pm, F 8am-midnight, Sa 9am-midnight, Su 9am-9pm. **$**

SHOPS

Gourmet Garage, 453 Broome St. (941-5850), at Mercer St. With sawdust on the floor and yumminess all over, the Garage is organic-intensive, purveying pastas, produce, salads, and teas. Shhh...the Garage's best kept secret is that you can sample olives here to your heart's content. Open daily 7am-9pm.

Dean and Deluca, 560 Broadway (226-6800), at Prince St. This shop is more gallery than grocery. The colors, smells, packaging, and presentation here are all exquisite. You might be able to afford a lollipop. Open M-Sa 10am-8pm, Su 10am-7pm.

TRIBECA

While some of the dining in TriBeCa may be funkier than the experience in SoHo, the prices have begun to match those of its northern counterpart. Most of the restaurants cater to a wealthier, chic adult set. For really cheap fare head to the borders of TriBeCa, especially around Chambers and Church St. (which happens to have a handful of **halal** eateries).

Bodega, 136 W. Broadway (285-1155), between Thomas and Duane St. Smooth lighting has upgraded the diner decor of mirrored walls and checkered tablecloths to serene elegance. Menu is nuevo-American crossed with Mexican; entrees $8.50-13. Serves brunch Sa-Su. Open M-F 11am-midnight, Sa-Su 10am-midnight. **$$**

Bubby's, 120 Hudson St. (219-0666), at N. Moore St. Rough brick walls with white woodwork, un-upholstered window benches, and two walls of windows all add to this cafe's stylish simplicity. Great scones, muffins, and pies keep this place, originally a pie company, packed with locals; lunch and dinner are also excellent. Entrees are a bit expensive, but soups and salads as well as breakfast options can fill you. Full breakfast menu. Expect a wait on weekend mornings. Open M-Tu 8am-11pm, Tu-F 8am-3am, Sa 9am-3am, Su 9am-10pm. **$$-$$$**

El Teddy's, 219 West Broadway (941-7070), between Franklin and White St. You'll definitely have no trouble finding it—the monstrous, stained-glass awning hangs over windows of light-up whirligigs. First-rate, creative Mexican cuisine conceived with a strong dose of California health food. Entrees are expensive, but soups and salads ($6-7) as well as quesadillas (around $8) are affordable. Open M-W noon-3pm and 6-11:30pm, Th-Sa 6pm-1am, Su 6-11pm. **$$-$$$**

■ **Pakistan Tea House,** 176 Church St. (240-9800), between Duane and Read St. Perennially busy hole-in-the-wall eatery simmers with Tandoori dishes and other traditional Pakistani favorites. Their combo plates ($4) are an amazing deal. All meat is **halal.** Open daily 10am-4am. **$**

Uptown Juice Bar, 116 Chambers St. (964-4316), between Church and W. Broadway. Vegetarian and vegan platters, burgers, sandwiches, salads and pastries all under $9, most under $5. 10% off with student ID. Open M-F 7am-8pm, Sa 7am-6pm. **$**

■ **Yaffa's Tea Room,** 19 Harrison St. (274-9403), near Greenwich St. Amidst an eclectic arrangement of used furniture and hipsters, Yaffa's serves a very cool high tea ($20, reservations generally required), from M-Sa 2-6pm; it includes cucumber, salmon, or watercress finger sandwiches, fresh-baked scones, a dessert sampler, and a pot of tea. Sandwiches $8-10.50, salads $7-11, and entrees $8-20. "Couscous Night" every Thursday 6:30pm-midnight. The attached bar/restaurant is less subdued, with a different menu (including tapas). Bar open Su-Th 11am-2am, F-Sa 11am-4am. Restaurant open 8:30am-midnight. **$$-$$$**

UNION SQUARE AND GRAMERCY PARK

Subway: N, R, L or #4, 5, 6 to 14th St./Union Square.

Straddling the extremes, the lower Midtown dining scene is neither fast-food commercial nor *haute cuisine* trendy. Instead, this slightly gentrified, ethnically diverse neighborhood features many places where honest meals are wed to reasonable prices. On Lexington, in the upper 20s and lower 30s, a small cluster of Pakistani and Indian restaurants battle for customers and comprise Manhattan's only significant sampling of these cuisines. Liberally sprinkled throughout are Korean corner shops that are equal parts grocery and buffet bars, where you can often fill up on prepared pastas, salads, and hot entrees, paying for them by the pound. (You may ask yourself, "Why does every Korean grocery have the same chicken wings and tofu pockets in its salad bar?" *Let's Go* does not have the answer to this question.) The area around Union Square offers an equally diverse, albeit trendier dining experience, with funky diners and a hip crowd. On 18th St. and Irving Pl., among rows of 19th-century red-brick houses, you'll run into **Pete's Tavern,** a legendary New York watering hole since 1864. Legend has it that O. Henry, who lived nearby, wrote *The Gift of the Magi* in one of the booths. Unless otherwise noted, all restaurants take credit cards.

Candela, 116 E. 16th St. (254-1600), between Park Ave. South and Irving. Cavernous and candlelit, this contemporary, stylish American eatery features expensive entrees and gracious service well worth the price. Dining outside in warmer weather can be a delight, but don't expect a view. If you're prepared to splurge, and you'll want to, try the succulent filet mignon ($22) or the tender Alaskan Black Cod ($24). Promoters are known to throw parties on Friday nights—call ahead to inquire. Open M-Sa 5:30-11pm, brunch Su 11am-3pm. Bar opens at 5pm. **$$$**

Chat 'n' Chew, 10 E. 16th St. (243-1616), between Union Sq. and Fifth Ave. This self-proclaimed "trailer park food" restaurant fills the simplest of your desires in decor and cuisinary genre. They serve up heaping plates of tasty macaroni and cheese (with a crunchy top) $7.25, a classic grilled cheese with tomato $6, and "Not your Mother's Meatloaf" $11.25. Open M-F 11:30am-11pm, Sa 10am-11:30pm, Su 10am-11pm. Accepts AmEx, V, MC. **$$-$$$**

RESTAURANTS

Jai-Ya, 396 Third Ave. (889-1330), between 28th and 29th St. Critics rave over the Thai and other Asian food, with 3 degrees of spiciness, from mild to "help-me-I'm-on-fire." The soothing great interior tango with budget prices and a decidedly upscale look (cloth napkins!). The $7.25 Thai noodles are a definite steal. Most dishes $7-10. Lunch specials M-F 11:30am-3pm. Open M-F 11am-midnight, Sa 11:30am-midnight, Su 5pm-midnight. Also at 81-11 Broadway in Elmhurst, Queens (718-651-1330). **$$**

Madras Mahal, 104 Lexington Ave. (684-4010), between 27th and 28th St. This vegetarian Indian restaurant is owned by a Catholic and has been approved as strictly kosher. Despite the spices the appetizers may be bland, but the breads ($2-5) are scrumptious. Crepes run $6-9, and curries $9. For $14, the restaurant also features several dinner specials, such as the Madras or Gujarati, which will leave you supplied with leftovers and possibly an after taste. What it lacks in space and ambience it attempts to make up for in service by the army of hovering waiters. Open M-F 11:30am-3pm and 5-10pm, Sa-Su noon-10:30pm. Wheelchair access. **$$-$$$**

Moonstruck, 449 Third Ave. (213-1100; fax 481-6136), at 31st St. This restaurant offers 4 floors of culinary pleasure in its updated diner atmosphere, with huge bay windows bathing the first floor in moon- (and streetlamp-) light. Offers a staggering array of sandwich options including the Moonstruck Burger ($7.85), as well as traditional diner fare such as Silver Dollar Griddlecakes ($5.60). Most entrees hover between $10-13, but pasta dishes are a tad cheaper ($9.25). Open Su-W 6am-1am, Th-Sa 24hr. **$-$$**

Sam's Noodle Shop, 411 Third Ave. (213-2288; fax 213-9762), at 29th St. A tad short on atmosphere, but the vast selection, tasty food, and unbeatable prices make this Murray Hill Chinese eatery a dependable stop. Entrees $8-10. "Chinatown-style" lunch special offers curry chicken or roast duck with 19 other selections over rice for a jaw-droppingly low $4.50. Open daily 11:30am-midnight. **$-$$**

Sunburnt Espresso Bar, 206 Third Ave. (674-1702), at 18th St. Cheerful red coffee place with an impressive selection of tasty snacks, but the decor walks the line between kitsch and strained trendiness. Corn and red pepper salad $5. Smoked turkey with sundried tomato, basil, and brie $5. Dreamy shakes, smoothies ($2.25-5), and fat-free muffins ($1.75) round out the dessert menu. Smallish but filling lunch special $5. Open daily 7am-11pm. **$**

Tibetan Kitchen, 444 Third Ave. (679-6286), between 30th and 31st St. This tiny place serves excellent food—meatier than Chinese, with a dollop of Indian. *Momo* (beef dumplings, $7.50), and *bocha* (buttered, salted tea) are both yummy. Veggie dishes $6.75-8. The Dalai Lama smiles serenely from the wall. Open M-F noon-3pm and 5-10:30pm, Sa 5-11pm. **$**

Zen Palate, 34 E. Union Sq. (614-9291), across from the park. A must for vegans and those who love them. Fantastic Asian-inspired vegetarian/vegan cuisine, including soothing, healthy, and fabulously fresh treats like "shredded heaven" (assorted veggies and spring rolls with brown rice) for $8, stir-fried rice fettuccini with mushrooms $7, or other concoctions on brown rice/seaweed/kale and soy tip. Fresh-squeezed juices or rice milkshakes $1.50. Open M-Sa 11am-11pm, Su noon-10:30pm. Other locations: 663 9th Ave. (582-1669), at 46th St.; 2170 Broadway (501-7768), at 76th St. **$-$$**

CAFES

Guy & Gallard, 120 E. 34th St. (684-3898), at Lexington Ave. A delightful juice/coffee bar complete with small bakery and deli sections. This bar has a little something for everyone: fruit juices ($3) and delicious frozen yogurt ($2) for the health conscious, decadent desserts ($2-3) for those who could care less, and even an internet kiosk for the email fiend in all of us (credit cards accepted). Scrumptious varieties of low-fat muffins and danishes available fresh in the mornings ($1.70). Later, a selection of appealing sandwiches go for around $5. Open daily 7am-9pm. Other locations: 475 Park Ave. South and 245 W. 38th St. Accepts AmEx, V, MC.

Coffee Shop Bar, 29 Union Sq. West (243-7969), facing Union Sq. Park. A chic diner for fashion victims, owned by 3 Brazilian models whose gorgeous friends serve updated cuisine from the homeland. Sure, it's a bar and restaurant, but more importantly, it's a spectacle. Waifs abound, but Twiggy figures aren't a likely result of the delicious food like tasty *media noche* sandwich ($9). Good for dessert ($5-6), a very late dinner ($8-17), or to watch others have dinner. Beers $4-6. Open daily 6am-5am. AmEx, V, MC.

Heartland Brewery, 35 Union West (645-3400), at 17th St. Packed, loud, and friendly brew pub with a "down home" American menu that contrasts with the after-work corporate crowd. Daytime family feel gives way to swinging singles scene at night. Beers on tap $5. "Aunt Bee's" chocolate mud cake with lightly whipped cream $5. Open M-Th noon-11pm, F-Sa noon-midnight, Su noon-10pm; bar closes 2 hours later. Accepts AmEx, V, MC, Transmedia. Other locations: 1285 Ave. of the Americas (6th Ave.) at 51st St. (582-8244).

Old Town Bar and Grill, 45 E. 18th St. (529-6732), between Park Ave. and Broadway. A quiet 104-year-old hideaway with wood, brass, and a mature clientele to match, as seen on the old "Late Night with David Letterman" opening montage. The consensus among many New Yorkers is that these are the best burgers in the city. Beware of perpetual after-work and weekend mobs. Beer on tap $4, Heineken $3.75, domestics $3. Open M-Sa 11:30am-1am, Su 3pm-midnight. Accepts AmEx, V, and MC.

UPPER EAST SIDE

Meals on the Upper East Side descend in price as you move east away from Fifth Ave.'s glitzy, mildly exorbitant museum cafes towards Lexington, Third, and Second Ave. Second Avenue, especially from the mid-70s to the mid-80s, boasts beaucoup restaurants.

▨ **Barking Dog Luncheonette,** 1678 Third Ave. (831-1800), at 94th St. Enter through the doghouse-shaped door labeled "Fido" to satisfy your hunger pangs with helpings right out of canine heaven. Take note of the "dog bar" outside from which you can quench your pooch's thirst. Big salads 5-9; sandwiches $7-8. Specials (M-F 5-7pm) come with soup or salad and dessert. Open daily 8am-11pm. **$$**

Brother Jimmy's Carolina Kitchen BBQ, 1461 First Ave. (545-7427), at 76th St. The sign advertises "BBQ and booze," and this greasy-chops Carolina kitchen serves up plenty of both—as if the large wooden drawing of a pig holding beer would have you believe otherwise. Ribs are a bit pricey ($16), but cheaper options abound. Entrees $9-12, sandwiches $6-7. Numerous promotions. Kitchen open Su-Th 5pm-midnight, F-Sa 11am-1am. Bar open until around 4am. **$$-$$$**

Candle Cafe, 1307 Third Ave. (472-0970), at 75th St. Friendly vegan restaurant proves that even ladies who lunch can dine on soy products; chic departure from typical vegan fare. Try the grilled portobello vegetable wedge ($9) or the excellent miso soup ($5 for a pint). Open M-Sa 11:30am-10:30pm, Su 11:30am-9:30pm. **$**

Coconut Grill, 1481 Second Ave. (772-6262), at 77th St. Simple white-tile decor and ornate gourmet salads and sandwiches. Salads are meals—try the cucumber, feta, tomato, olive, pepper, caper, chick-pea, and basil combo ($7). The more expensive brunch is always crowded because it's just so damned good. Open M 11:30am-midnight, Tu-Th 11:30am-12:30am, F-Sa 11:30am-1am, Su 10:30am-midnight. **$**

EJ's Luncheonette, 1271 Third Ave. (472-0600), at 73rd St. The understated American elegance and huge portions in this hip 1950s-style diner have mustered a legion of devoted Upper East Siders. The scrumptious fare (buttermilk pancakes $6, cheeseburger with fries, $7) is rumored to have attracted the late JFK, Jr. Open M-Th 8am-11pm, F-Sa 8am-11:30pm, Su 8am-10:30pm. **Other locations:** 477 Amsterdam Ave. (873-3444), between 81st and 82nd St.; 432 Sixth Ave. (473-5555), between 9th and 10th St. **$**

El Pollo, 1746 First Ave. (996-7810), between 90th and 91st St. Under-hyped Peruvian joint's 7-flavored grilled chicken dishes have locals raving in this cramped restaurant. Plump chickens marinated, spit-roasted, and topped with sauces. Peruvian delicacies like fried sweet plantains ($3) make the menu an affordable epicurean adventure. Half-chicken $5. Bring your own booze. Open M-F 11:30am-11pm, Sa-Su 12:30pm-11pm. **$**

Hale and Hearty Soups, 849 Lexington Ave. (517-7600), between 64th and 65th St. Inventive, filling soups and friendly service. Rotating menu of over 40 different varieties of soup each of which comes with a slice of fresh bread. Numerous veggie and diet-watcher options. Cups (enough for a meal) $4-7; bowls $5-8; bread bowls $6-9. Sand-wiches $5-7. Open daily 11am-5pm; summer M-Th 9am-7pm, Sa 10am-5:30pm. **$**

Jackson Hole Wyoming, 232 E. 64th St. (371-7187), between Second and Third Ave. Home of the famed 7 oz. burger. 30 different kinds of burgers and 30 chicken sand-wiches with the same toppings. Burgers and platters $6-11. Open 10am-1am. Also on 83rd St. and Columbus Ave. **$-$$**

Luke's Bar and Grill, 1394 Third Ave. (249-7070), between 79th and 80th St. Waiters bustle through the dark wood-paneled room to serve you typical pub fare. The generous burgers are juicy and delicious ($6), but many other sandwiches deserve a taste too. Start things off right with an order of chewy, breaded mozzarella sticks ($5). Open Tu-F 11:30am-2am, Sa-Su 10am-3am. **$**

Papaya King, 179 E. 86th St. (369-0648), at Third Ave. New Yorkers tolerate outra-geously long lines, sparse seating, and yellow decor at this dive all for a taste of the "tastier than filet mignon" hot dogs ($1.79). You might opt for the special: 2 hot dogs and a 16 oz. tropical fruit shake, an Upper East Side steal at $4. Open M-F 8am-mid-night, Sa-Su 8am-2am. **$**

Tang Tang, 1328 Third Ave. (249-2102), at 76th St. Lightning-quick service cuts through the dense crowds to deliver cheap, hot, and tasty Chinese noodles and dumplings. Not much ambience, so focus on the food. Noodle dishes around $6; many entrees between $6-8. Open Su-Th 11:30am-11pm, F-Sa 11:30am-11:15pm. **$**

Viand, 673 Madison Ave. (751-6622), between 61st and 62nd St. An excellent post-shopping pit stop. Pricey except for the exceptional burgers. Cheeseburger $4; with fries, cole slaw, and toppings $6. Great atmosphere and friendly staff. Open daily 6am-9:30pm. **$-$$$**

SHOPS

Ecce Panis, 1120 Third Ave. (535-2099), between 65th and 66th St. The name means "behold the bread" in Latin, and that's just what you'll do in this baked-goods mecca. Try one of the sun-dried tomato loaves, a *foccacia,* or 1 of the 4 varieties of sweet *bis-cotti*. Free chunks on the counter await nibbling. Open M-F 8am-8pm, Sa-Su 8am-7pm.

Grace's Marketplace, 1237 Third Ave. (737-0600), at 71st St. Your tongue will be plas-tered to the counter's window once you see the cornucopia of fresh goodies this deli/coffee shop has to offer. Don't be ashamed...the Chanel-suited patrons already recog-nized you as an Outsider (at least, perhaps, a West Sider) who must have slipped through security. Even if you can't afford a thing at this meticulous market, Grace's is a cultural education in Upper East Side life. Open M-F, Sa 7am-8:30pm, Su 8am-7pm.

UPPER WEST SIDE

In the summer, the Upper West Side sidewalks spill over with all sorts of eth-nic and nouveau restaurants, and in the winter, large glass windows seal them off. Upper West Side restaurants may not look fancy, but they tend to be pricey. Your best bet here may be to gorge yourself at the countless pizza joints and diners that so kindly grace the area. The **Gray's Papaya,** at 72nd St. and Broadway, can also sate your hunger with amazing deals on hot dogs— look for their never-ending "recession special." Around 72nd St. from West End all the way to Columbus, kosher travelers can find all the food they've for-gone in many other parts of the city.

RESTAURANTS

GIVE ME BURRITO OR GIVE ME DEATH

After the smoke and mirrors of the "wrap revolution" have been cleared and shattered, respectively, *los gringos* seem to have finally learned that not everything wrapped belongs to the category of good Mexican food (witness the vile swordfish-chipotle-mango-spinach wrap). In the ruins of wrap culture stands the stoic burrito, basking in the glory of New York's hungry minions. Enter **Burritoville**, a homegrown New York chain that serves up delicious and inventive burritos that still manage to keep it real. Burritoville makes their own tortillas fresh everyday, provides free bottomless chips and salsa with your huge burrito, and numerous options (including ingredient substitutions) for vegans, veggies, and health nuts. And one more thing—these tasty burritos are cheap, staying south of the $7 border. In 1998 the famed *Zagat's Survey* queried "Where did single people eat before Burritoville?" If any of our readers have an answer, *Let's Go* would like to know.

The following are the Burritoville locations throughout the city; they're open Su-Th 11am-11pm, F-Sa 11am-midnight: **144 Chambers St.**, at Hudson St. (571-1144); **36 Water St.**, north of Broad St. (747-1100); **298 Bleecker St.**, at Seventh Ave. (633-9249); **20 John St.**, between Broadway and Nassau St. (766-2020); **264 W. 23rd St.**, between Seventh and Eighth Ave. (367-7256); **141 Second Ave.**, between 8th and 9th St. (260-3300); **625 Ninth Ave.**, at 44th St. (333-5352); **166 W. 72nd St.**, at Broadway (580-7700); **1489 First Ave.**, between 77th and 78th St. (472-8800); **451 Amsterdam Ave.**, between 81st and 82nd St. (787-8181); **1606 Third Ave.**, between 90th and 91st St. (410-2255).

Big Nick's Pizza and Burger Joint, 2173 Broadway (362-9238), at 77th St. Serving the West Side's "compulsive noshers, weekend partyfolk, mellow-groovy happyfolk, dedicated loners, lovers after the afterglow" tried-and-true pizza and burgers (and breakfast dishes) since 1962. This sprawling joint is damn proud of their eats and for good reason. Free delivery. Open 24hr., "sometimes *25.*" **$**

D+S Plaza, 182 Amsterdam Ave. (579-0808), between 68th and 69th St. *Let's Go* knows that you've seen them all over the city: groceries/salad bars vending stuffed tofu, watermelon and cantaloupe slices, and pasta salad. We know these groceries have achieved near iconic status in NYC. We know you can find them on your own when you crave to assemble your own meal. But we *didn't* know that any of these salad bars had air conditioned dining halls downstairs—so, we thought we'd tell you. Vast, fresh hot and cold salad bars, $4.49 per lb. Open 24hr. **$**

Good Enough to Eat, 483 Amsterdam Ave. (496-0163), between 83rd and 84th St. This country-style cafe serves up comfort food—brunch is like a big hug from Mom. Vermont cheddar and apple omelette with buttermilk biscuits $7.25, strawberry almond waffles with real Vermont syrup $8.50. Breakfast M-F 8am-4pm, brunch Sa-Su 9am-4pm, lunch M-F noon-4pm, dinner M-Sa 5:30-10:30pm, Su 5:30-10pm. **$**

La Caridad 78 Restaurant, 2199 Broadway (874-2780), at 78th St. One of New York's most successful (and packed) Chinese-Cuban hybrids. You could eat here 160 times and never have the same dish twice. The ebullient waiters disarm in three languages. No elaborate decor, but the delicious homestyle cooking will remind you of your *abuelita*. Prices stay decidedly south of the $10 border. Lunch special M-F 11:30am-4pm, $5. Open M-Sa 11:30am-1am, Su 11:30am-10:30pm. **$**

The Lemongrass Grill, 2534 Broadway (666-0888), at 95th St. Delicious culinary mainstay of the Upper West. Admidst bamboo shoots, Thai noodles and vegetables ($6-8) sate locals. Lunch specials ($5) M-F noon-3. Open Su-Th noon-11:30pm, F-Sa noon-12:30am. Also at 494 Amsterdam Ave. and 84th (579-0344), 80 University Pl. and 11th (604-9870), 37 Barrow St. and Seventh Ave. (242-0606), and Park Slope, Brooklyn at 61 Seventh Ave. (718-399-7100). **$**

Mary Ann's, 2454 Broadway Ave. (877-0132), at 91st St. A *fiesta* anytime! Simple, well-prepared Mexican food combine with excellent service to make this one of the best dinners along Broadway. Entrees $8-15 (includes bottomless chips and salsa). Open Su-Th noon-10:30pm, F-Sa noon-11:30pm. **$$**

Matsuri, 154 W. 72nd St. (787-3333), between Broadway and Columbus Ave. An exceptional feature graces Matsuri: all-you-can-eat sushi and maki for $23.50. The catch: you pay for each piece you don't consume. Order wisely and fast before you go. Su 1-11pm, M-Th noon-11pm, F-Sa noon-midnight. **$$$**

Obento Delight, 210 W. 94th St. (222-2010), between Amsterdam and Broadway Ave. Fresh Japanese food at low prices. Don't be put off by the off-the-avenue location— Obento is a classy operation with cute little tables in beige-colored wood. Vegetable tempura $6.75, shrimp shumai (10 pieces) $6. Free delivery ($7 min.). Open daily 11:30am-11pm. **$**

Tibet Shambala, 488 Amsterdam Ave. (721-1270), between 83rd and 84th St. "Shambala" means heaven on earth, a paradise attainable only by the truly enlightened. Tasty Tibetan food just about lives up to its name with many vegetarian and truly heavenly "no-moo" dishes. Lunch specials M-F noon-4pm ($6), dinner entrees ($8-9). Enlightenment not included. Open daily noon-3:30pm and 5:30-11pm. **$**

CAFES

Café La Fortuna, 69 W. 71st St. (724-5846), at Columbus Ave. Delicious Italian pastries, coffees, and sandwiches served in an intimate grotto of a cafe. A definite local favorite and it boasts that it is the oldest cafe in the Upper West Side. Espresso $2.25; pies $3-4; sandwiches $3-5; and salads $4.75-6.75. Open Su-Th noon-midnight, F-Sa noon-1:30am. Student Advantage discounts honored.

■ **Café Lalo,** 201 W. 83rd St. (496-6031), between Broadway and Amsterdam. A wall of French windows allows live jazz (and the occasional *bon mot* from a suave *monsieur* within) to escape onto the street. Perfect cakes $5 per slice, full bar available (ooh-la-la, *aperitifs, mon cheri!*). Open M-Th 8am-2am, F 8am-4am, Sa 9am-4am, Su 9am-2am.

Café Mozart, 154 70th St. (595-9797), between Amsterdam and Columbus Ave. just off Broadway. A pleasantly unpretentious cafe, away from hurried Broadway. A perfect place for gourmet coffee, reading a free paper, and sampling one of over 50 decadent desserts. Lunch special (M-F 11:30am-4pm) includes sandwich, quiches, or omelette with soda or coffee and dessert ($5). Generously proportioned salads ($4-13), large selection of sandwiches ($6-9), and pasta. Live classical music M-F 9pm-midnight, Su 1-4pm and 9pm-midnight. Open M-Th 8am-1am, F 8am-3am, Sa 10am-3am, Su 10am-1am.

drip, 489 Amsterdam Ave. (875-1032), between 83rd and 84th St. Retro, commercial culture decor sets the backdrop for students on laptops, young ladies lounging with complimentary magazines, and single Upper West Siders nervously eyeing each other over coffee. For the true lush, a full bar opens with the coffee shop. **Dating service** has no fewer than 24,500 heart-sick participants in its database. **Psychic** readings M 7-11pm, $10. Beer $4; cocktails $4-9; coffee $1.25-2. Open M-Th 8:30am-1am, F-Sa 8:30am-3am, Su 9am-midnight.

SHOPS

H&H Bagels, 2239 Broadway (692-2435), at 80th St. H&H has nourished Upper West Siders for years with cheap bagels (75¢) that have a reputation as the best in Manhattan. Dozen bagels $9. Send a dozen home to mom—they'll ship anywhere in the world on command. Open 24hr.

La Piccola Cucina, 2770 Broadway (222-2381), between 106th and 107th St. Stock up that picnic basket at this darling gourmet shop. Get a sandwich with fresh mozzarella, arugula, and tomatoes ($6). Make the choice between Sicilian-style and Tuscan-style *biscotti*, or go with the delicious *cannolis* ($2). Open daily 11am-9pm.

■ **Zabar's,** 2245 Broadway (787-2000), between 80th and 81st St. Subway: #1, 9 to 79th St. This New York institution often featured on TV's "Mad About You" sells everything you need for a 4-star meal at home. Cheese, salmons, beautiful breads, and droves of shoppers. The adjoining cafe serves pastries and great coffee. Open M-F 8am-7:30pm, Sa 8am-8pm, Su 9am-6pm.

WEST MIDTOWN

Home to newly renovated theaters and run-down tenements, West Midtown embraces a full range of culinary flavors. Your best bets generally lie along Eighth Ave. between 34th and 59th St. in the area known as **Hell's Kitchen.** Once much more deserving of its name, within the past few years this area has prospered enough to open up a fantastically diverse array of restaurants. Those willing to spend more should try a meal on posh **Restaurant Row** on 46th St. between Eighth and Ninth Ave. The block caters to a pre-theater crowd, so arriving after 8pm will make it easier to get a table. Celebrities occasionally drift over to **Sardi's,** 234 W. 44th St. (221-8440), and take a seat on the plush red leather, surrounded by caricatures of themselves and their best friends. Traditionally, on the opening night of a major Broadway play, the main star makes an entrance at Sardi's following the show—to hearty cheers for a superb performance or polite applause for a bomb. Don't rule out the top restaurants in this area; several of the city's finest have excellent prix fixe lunch deals, which include an appetizer, entree, and dessert. **Le Beaujolais,** 364 W. 46th St. (974-7464), is a charming French bistro with a $14.25 lunch special.

Unless otherwise noted, all restaurants accept major credit cards and are handicapped-accessible.

📝 **Ariana Afghan Restaurant,** 787 Ninth Ave. (664-0123; 664-0125), between 52nd and 53rd St. This little cloister of things Afghani serves up superb, filling food. Kebab dishes ($8-10) and vegetarian platters ($6-8) come with basmati rice, salad, and homemade bread. Open M-Sa noon-3pm and 5-11pm. Open Su 3-10:30pm. **$**

Bali Nusa Indah, 651 Ninth Ave. (265-2200), between 45th and 46th St. Sheer white walls, blue tiles, red and gold tablecloths, and soothing Burmese pipe music create an atmosphere that will elevate you from the blaring midtown surroundings. Great food in plentiful portions. The lunch specials, served with salad and topped with a warm, spicy peanut dressing ($5.35; daily 11:30am-4pm) are a bargain. Try the banana crepe with a splash of rum and palm sugar for dessert ($3). Open M-Th 11:30am-11pm, F-Sa 11:30am-11:30pm, Su 11:30am-10:30pm. **$$**

Becco, 355 W. 46th St. (397-7597), between Eighth and Ninth Ave. Gourmet cuisine that makes you forget about your budget. For a $17 prix fixe lunch (dinner $24) you can have a gourmet *antipasto* platter or caesar salad, plus unlimited servings of the 3 pastas of the day. Selections as exciting as the *saltimbocca di coniglio* (rabbit with prosciutto and spinach in a reduction sauce, with a caesar salad for lunch, $18) grace the menu. Open daily noon-3pm and 5pm-midnight. **$$$**

Carnegie Delicatessen, 854 Seventh Ave. (757-2245), at 55th St. One of New York's great delis. Ceiling fans whir overhead as photos of famous and well-fed customers stare down from the walls. After waiting in line, eat elbow-to-elbow at long tables and chomp on free dill pickles. First-timers shouldn't leave without trying the cheesecake (oy, it's so good!) topped with strawberries, blueberries, or cherries ($6.45). Cash only. Open daily 6:30am-4am. **$$**

Hourglass Tavern, 373 W. 46th St. (265-2060), between Eighth and Ninth Ave. A dark, crowded triangular joint on Restaurant Row with a changing menu. Servers flip an hourglass at your table when you sit down—the 59min. time limit is strictly enforced when crowds are waiting. Dramatized in John Grisham's *The Firm* as the covert meeting place for two cloak-and-dagger types. Prix fixe entrees ($15) include soup and salad. Open M-W 5-11:15pm, Th-F 5-11:30pm. Cash only. **$$**

Manganaro's, 488 Ninth Ave. (563-5331 or 800-472-5264), between 37th and 38th St. This classy Italian grocery and restaurant retains all the authentic flavor of pre-gentrified Hell's Kitchen. The staff will construct the sandwich of your dreams, or you can select one from their vast menu ($3-12). Open M-F 8am-7pm, Sa 9am-7pm; Dec.-May also open Su 11am-5pm. **$-$$**

Minar, 9 W. 31st St. (684-2199 or 967-2727), between Fifth Ave. and Broadway. Long, narrow, and decorated like a subway platform, this Indian restaurant still manages to pack in many neighborhood South Asians for lunch and dinner. Spicy vegetable curries ($4) and "non-vegetable" curries ($4-5.25) are served at the counter with a small salad and choice of bread (the unleavened *naan* is delicious). Open Su-F 10:30am-7:15pm, Sa 10:30am-5:15pm. **$**

📷 **Original Fresco Tortillas,** 536 Ninth Ave. (465-8898), between 39th and 40th St. This tiny 4-seater could be Taco Bell's better-looking father. Excellent homemade food at fast-food prices: fajitas and tacos $1-2, quesadillas $2-4, giant burritos $4-5. No artificial or chemical spices, no MSG, no preservatives, no kidding. Cash only. Not wheelchair accessible. Open M-F 11am-11pm, Sa-Su noon-10pm. **$**

📷 **Rice & Beans,** 744 Ninth Ave. (265-4444), between 50th and 51st St. This little Brazilian restaurant offers flavorful, filling food to a *samba* beat. Chicken Ipanema with tomatoes and herbs is mildly spicy and totally sublime ($10). The tropical fruit shake ($4) tops off a meal nicely. Open M-Th 11am-10pm, F-Sa 11am-11pm, Su 1-9pm. **$-$$**

Sapporo, 152 W. 49th St. (869-8972), near Seventh Ave. A Japanese diner, with the grill partially obscured by rice paper walls. A favorite spot for Broadway cast members, corporate types, and those who can converse with the waiters in their native tongue. Items are listed on the wall in Japanese (the menu explains in English). Filling portions and astounding flavors. The *Sapporo ramen* special is a big bowl of noodles with assorted meats and veggies in a miso soup base ($7). Cash only. Open M-Sa 11am-11:30pm, Su 11am-10:30pm. **$-$$**

Stage Deli, 834 Seventh Ave. (245-7957), at 54th St. This renowned eatery serves up tremendous portions of pastrami, turkey, salami, brisket, and bologna, to name a few. Feel good and look better after ordering the "Leonardo DiCaprio" with heaping portions of pastrami, turkey, and swiss cheese ($14). Open daily 6am-2am. **$$**

Uncle Nick's Greek Cuisine, 747 Ninth Avenue (245-7992), between 50th and 51st St. This classy, popular restaurant specializes in Cretan food and boasts some of the best grilled seafood in the city. Landlubbers can satisfy their palate with a large gyro platter ($10), but all others should opt for seafood. Red snapper (seasonal) grilled with oil and lemon makes for a healthy, yet elegantly simple meal. A well-stocked bar completes the establishment. Open Su-Th noon-11pm, F-Sa noon-11:30pm. **$$-$$$**

Uncle Vanya Café, 315 W. 54th St. (262-0542), between Eighth and Ninth Ave. Marionettes hang from the ceiling, while a samovar holds court in this cheerful, yet Chekov-inspired, cafe. Try the chicken *pojharski,* a yummy mix of baked ground chicken with parsley and onions ($7.50) or the vegetarian stuffed peppers ($9.50). For a true delicacy, sample the *blini* (small pancakes with red caviar, $9.50). Undiscovered, homey, and very good. No wheelchair access. Open M-Sa noon-11pm, Su 2-10pm. **$-$$**

CAFES AND SHOPS

Emporium Brasil, 15 W. 46th St. (764-4646), between Broadway and Sixth Ave. A part of "Little Brazil Street" that runs along central 46th St., this small cafe serves excellent pastries and sandwiches. Coffee drinks served in single and double sizes ($1-3.30). Sip a double cappuccino, scan a Brazilian newspaper, or watch soccer on their big-screen TV. Open M-Sa 8am-6pm. Lunch M-Sa 11am-4pm. **$-$$**

Poseidon Bakery, 629 Ninth Ave. (757-6173), near 44th St. This 76-year-old bakery serves up authentic Greek pastries and delicacies. They even make their own *filo* dough for their sweet, gooey *baklava, kreatopita* (meat pie), *tiropita* (cheese pie), and *spanakopita* (spinach pie)—all scrumptious, for around $1.60. Open July-Aug. Tu-Sa 9am-7pm; Su 10am-4pm the week before Christmas and Easter.

NEIGHBORHOODS

When you're smack in the middle of them, the tallest skyscrapers seem like a casual part of the scenery. Not all sights stand out as obviously as, say, the Statue of Liberty. So, if you need help delving into the city's hidden treasures, please look to this chapter for guidance. Tours, architectural gems, and historical sites all feature in "Neighborhoods" and are listed according to respective geographical region. This allows for greater ease and greater insight as you explore the sometimes overwhelming, always splendid, mosaic of New York.

SIGHTSEEING TOURS

SPECIALTY TOURS

Carnegie Hall, at Seventh Ave. and 57th St. (903-9790). Opens its doors to tourists between September and June on M-Tu and Th-F at 11:30am, 2, and 3pm. The tour grants entrance to the main hall itself, discusses the history and architecture of the building, and lasts about an hour. $6, students and seniors $5, under 12 $3.

Federal Reserve Bank of New York, 33 Liberty St. (720-6130). Housing a quarter of the world's gold reserves in a sunken vault 5 stories below street level, the immense bank conducts free 40min. tours of the premises. M-F 9:30, 10:30, 11:30am, 1:30, and 2:30pm. At least 7 working days' prior notification is required. Min. age 16. Max. 30 people per group.

Fraunces Tavern Museum, 54 Pearl St. (425-1778), 2nd and 3rd floors. Subway: #4 or 5 to Bowling Green; #1 or 9 to South Ferry; or the N or R to Whitehall St. Features two period rooms, along with the room where George Washington said goodbye to his troops after the Revolutionary War. The 3rd floor has changing exhibits on the culture of early America. Open M-F 10am-4:45pm, Sa-Su noon-4pm. $2.50; seniors, students, and children $1.

Fulton Fish Market (748-8786), at the end of Fulton St. at South St. Seaport. Behind-the-scenes tours of this massive fish market are given on the 1st and 3rd Thursdays of each month from May-Oct. beginning at 6am and lasting 1¾hr. Fun, but could be more informative. $10; reservations required at least a week in advance.

Heritage Trails New York, starting at Federal Hall, between Wall and Broad St. In an attempt to capture some of the spirit of similar tours in Boston, Philadelphia, and Washington, D.C., Mayor Giuliani recently helped organize 4 walking paths exploring the history and culture of Lower Manhattan. But why pay for a tour, when you can enjoy the highly informative Trailsmap? It's available at numerous tourist stops, including visitor centers and at some sites along the trails.

Lincoln Center, between 62nd and 66th St. and Amsterdam and Columbus Ave. (875-5351). Sponsors guided tours of its theaters—you might even catch a rehearsal in progress. Tours daily at 10:30am, 12:30, 2:30, and 4:30pm; 1hr. $9.50, $8, students and seniors $7, children $4. Reservations are recommended but not required; call ahead for groups. Also **Backstage Tours of the Metropolitan Opera House,** leaving M-F 3:45pm, Sa 10am. Call 769-7020 for reservations.

Madison Square Garden (465-5800), on Seventh Ave. between 31st and 33rd St. Tours include a trip into the 20,000-seat arena and the Paramount (the Garden's concert stage), and visits into the locker rooms of the 1994 Stanley Cup-winning Rangers and the always-contending-never-ending Knicks, as well as a step up into the luxury suites. Tours offered on the hour M-Sa 10am-3pm, Su and designated holidays 11am-3pm. $14, children under 12 $12.

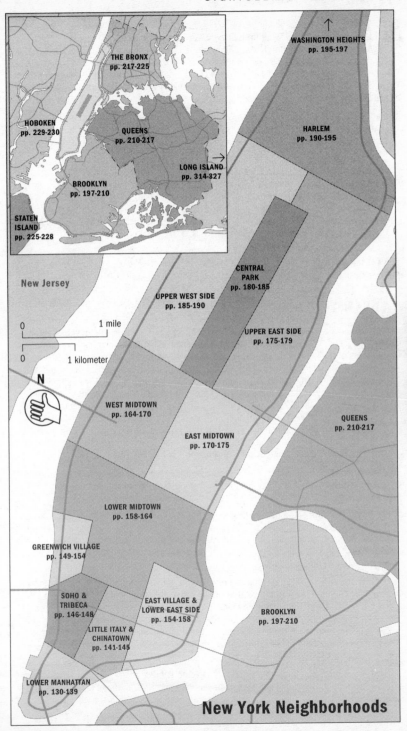

THE BRONX
pp. 217-225

HOBOKEN
pp. 229-230

QUEENS
pp. 210-217

LONG ISLAND
pp. 314-327

BROOKLYN
pp. 197-210

STATEN
ISLAND
pp. 225-228

WASHINGTON HEIGHTS
pp. 195-197

HARLEM
pp. 190-195

New Jersey

0   1 mile

0   1 kilometer

N

CENTRAL
PARK
pp. 180-185

UPPER WEST SIDE
pp. 185-190

UPPER EAST SIDE
pp. 175-179

WEST MIDTOWN
pp. 164-170

EAST MIDTOWN
pp. 170-175

QUEENS
pp. 210-217

LOWER MIDTOWN
pp. 158-164

GREENWICH VILLAGE
pp. 149-154

SOHO &
TRIBECA
pp. 146-148

EAST VILLAGE &
LOWER EAST SIDE
pp. 154-158

BROOKLYN
pp. 197-210

LITTLE ITALY &
CHINATOWN
pp. 141-145

LOWER MANHATTAN
pp. 130-139

New York Neighborhoods

NBC Studio Tour, NBC Building, 30 Rockefeller Plaza (664-4000), between 49th and 50th St. Subway: B, D, F, Q to 50th St./6th Ave.; or N, R to 49th St. You'll see *Saturday Night Live*'s famous Studio 8H and Conan O'Brien's set-up. Tours given M-Sa 8am-7pm, Su 9:30am-4pm, leaving every 30min. Extended hours for summer months and holidays. Each tour is limited to 15 people. $17.50, students and seniors $15, ages 6-16 $17.50. Tickets go on a first-come, first-serve basis from the Tour Desk in the NBC building. No one under 6 admitted.

New York Stock Exchange, 20 Broad St. (656-5168). A brief, self-directed tour includes a short film, interactive computers, and an observation deck over the frenzied main trading floor. Open M-F 9am-4:30pm; free tickets available at 8:45am and are first come, first served.

Radio City Music Hall, 1260 Sixth Ave. (632-4041), between 50th and 51st St. Subway: B, D, F, Q to 50thSt./6th Ave.; or N, R to 49th St. Behind-the-scenes tours leave every 30 to 45 minutes (M-Sa 10am-5pm, Su 11am-5pm). Billed as "the one-hour tour that will last you a lifetime," the tour grants access to the Great Stage, the 6000-seat auditorium, and the mighty Wurlitzer. In addition to getting the full history of the place, you'll talk with a current member of the Rockettes. $13.75, children under 12 $9.

■ SUPERFANTASTIC THEME TOURS. See **Discover NYC**, p. 3, for the city tour that will suit your personal whims and wildest dreams.

WALKING TOURS

Adventure on a Shoestring, 300 W. 53rd St. (265-2663). See the city with veteran guide and budget connoisseur Howard Goldberg. Detailed 1½hr. tours incorporate chats with members of the various communities. Excursions reveal some of New York's better-kept secrets; Mr. Goldberg is a walking treasure trove of information on budget eats and accommodations. Themed tours run on holidays, like the Valentine's Day Big Apple Lovers' Tour, and fascinating tours like the Haunted Greenwich Village tour run year-round. During a time of year when everyone else is jacking up prices, Shoestring offers the New Year's Eve Tour, which costs $15 total and includes a fantastic dinner in Chinatown. Other tours cost $5; the price has never increased during the organization's 36 years of existence. Some trips are open only to members ($3 per event; membership $40 per year). Tours run rain or shine, many with the option of a group meal at a local eatery.

Big Apple Greeter (669-8159; www.bigapplegreeter.org/). A goodwill program that sets you up with a New Yorker who will show you around town. Visitors can come alone, with a family, or with 2-6 friends. Free.

 Big Onion Walking Tours (439-1090; www.bigonion.com). Graduate students in American history from Columbia or NYU lead tours of historic districts and ethnic neighborhoods. Recent themed excursions include "Central Park at Twilight" and "Immigrant New York." Tours average 2-2½hr. $10-16, students and seniors $8-14. Call for automated listing of upcoming tours and prices.

Heritage Trails New York, starting at Federal Hall, between Wall and Broad St. In an attempt to capture some of the spirit of similar tours in Boston, Philadelphia, and Washington, D.C., Mayor Giuliani recently helped organize 4 walking paths exploring the history and culture of Lower Manhattan. Maps and info for the trails (red, blue, green, and orange) can be found in the free trail maps available at numerous tourists stops, including visitor centers and at some sites along the trails.

Joyce Gold's Tours, 141 W. 17th St. (242-5762; www.nyctours.com). The devoted Ms. Gold has read over 900 books on Manhattan, the subject she teaches at NYU and at the New School. On 45 pre-set days each year she and a company of adventurers give tours focusing on architecture, history, and ethnic groups within the city. Tours last approximately 3hr., depending on the subject, and cost $12.

Lower East Side Tenement Museum Walking Tours, 90 Orchard St. (431-0233). On Saturdays and Sundays in the summer at 1:30pm and 2:30pm, you can embark upon the hour-long "The Streets Where We Lived: A Multi-Ethnic Heritage Tour." $8, students and seniors $6; combination tickets available for walking tour and tenement tours. (See **Museums,** p. 246)

Municipal Art Society, 457 Madison Ave. (935-3960, tour info 439-1049; www.mas.org) near 50th St. Guided walking tours ($10, $8 for students and seniors during the week from 12:30-2pm; on weekends $30, $15 for students and seniors); destinations change with the seasons but include most major districts of Manhattan, such as SoHo, Greenwich Village, and Times Square. Their free tour of Grand Central Station meets every Wednesday at 12:30pm, at the info booth on the main concourse. Call in advance.

Museum of the City of New York, 1220 Fifth Ave. (534-1672; www.mcny.org), and 103rd St. From Apr.-Oct. the museum sponsors popular walking tours ($10) on Saturdays, starting at 1pm and lasting for a leisurely 1-2hr. Areas covered include Chelsea, the Lower East Side, and Greenwich Village, with a focus on the history and architecture of the particular district. Call to sign up a few days beforehand.

Radical Walking Tours (718-492-0069). Historian/activist Bruce Kayton leads tours that cover the alternative and underground history of New York City. For example, tours of Greenwich Village highlight radicals and revolutionaries like John Reed and Emma Goldman, as well as artistic and theatrical movements that flourished around them. Other tours include trips to Chelsea, Wall Street, the Lower East Side, and Central Park. Even lifelong locals will learn fascinating details about the city's history. All tours $10. 2-3hr. No reservations required. Call for schedule and departure sites.

Times Square Exposé, 1560 Broadway (869-1890), in the Times Square Visitors Center. This free, 2hr. walking tour unfolds the theatrical history of Times Square, along with its celebrated scandals and electronic "miracles." Tours given every Friday at noon.

92nd Street Y, 1395 Lexington Ave. (996-1100). The Y leads an astounding variety of walking tours covering all boroughs and many aspects of New York life, from the Garment District, SoHo artists, and the brownstones of Brooklyn to literary tours, museum visits, and even an all-night candlelight tour. Tours vary in length and cost $15-55. Call for the latest tours.

BOAT TOURS

Circle Line Tours, Pier 83, W. 42nd St. (563-3200), at the Hudson River and Twelfth Ave. Another location at Pier 16 on the South Street Seaport. Boats circumnavigate Manhattan Island on a 3hr. tour. Cruises run May 4 to Sept. 7 M-F 10:30, 11:30am, 1, 2, 3pm; Sa-Su every hour on the hour 10am-3pm, and one last tour at 4:30pm; off-season tours are available but not as frequent. $22, seniors $19, under 12 $12. Also conducts romantic, 2hr. "harbor lights" tours around Manhattan in the lovely light of sunset. Between June 29 and Sept. 7, tours run at 7pm; weekends only throughout the off-season. $18, seniors $16, under 12 $10. Light snacks and cocktails served. No reservations necessary; get there 30-45min. early.

NY Waterways (564-8846), on Fulton St. at South St. Seaport. Relaxing tours along NYC's waters. Open Apr.-Sept. M-W and F-Su 10am-6pm, Th 10am-8pm; Oct.-Mar. W-M 10am-5pm.

The Petrel (877-693-6131), North Cove Marina, World Financial Center. The *Petrel*, a 70 ft. pecan mahogany yacht, sails from North Cove Marina in Battery Park City and takes 40 passengers around New York Harbor, past Governor's Island, Ellis Island, and the Brooklyn Bridge or the Verrazano-Narrows Bridge—depending on Mother Nature's whims. The *Petrel* sails throughout the week with trips ranging in length (1-2hr.) and in price ($15-45). Call for reservations.

NEIGHBORHOODS

Seaport Liberty Line Cruises (748-8600), at Fulton St. in South St. Seaport. Offers tours around Manhattan. Open Su, M-Tu 10am-7pm, W-Th 10am-9:30pm, F-Sa 10am-10pm.

Staten Island Ferry (718-390-5253), at South St. near Battery Park. Offers one of the best deals in Manhattan, and round the clock to boot: it operates every 30min., 24hr. a day, 7 days a week. Amazing views of the lower Manhattan skyline, Ellis Island, the Statue of Liberty, and Governor's Island. Don't miss the trip at night, but exercise caution around the Staten Island terminal. Free! Cars $3. No reservations required.

BUS TOURS

Brooklyn Attitude, 224 W. 35th St. (718-398-0939), between Seventh and Eighth Ave. Bus tour with several walking excursions through ethnic and historic neighborhoods in Brooklyn. Departure points in both mid-Manhattan and Brooklyn. From Manhattan Sa 9am-1pm; from Brooklyn Sa 9:30am-12:30pm. $31, under 12 $21.

Gray Line Sight-Seeing, (397-2600), 42nd St. and Eighth Ave., at the Port Authority Terminal. Huge bus-tour company offering more than 20 different trips, including jaunts through Manhattan and gambling junkets to Atlantic City, conducted in English, French, German, Italian, and Spanish to name a few. Good bets include the 3 hour tour of lower Manhattan ($22, children $13) and the grand, 6hr. Night-on-the-Town tour ($55, children $50; more for a package which includes dinner). The launder-your-money unescorted voyage to Atlantic City costs $26. They also offer daylong trips to Washington, D.C., and Niagara Falls. Reservations aren't required for the in-city tours, but arrive at the terminal 30min. early.

Harlem Spirituals, 690 Eighth Ave. (391-0900), between 43rd and 44th St. Tours of upper Manhattan including the "Spirituals and Gospel" tour, which includes trips to historic homes and participation in a Baptist service ($33 for 4hr., leaves Su at 9:30am). The "Soul Food and Jazz" tour ($75, offered M, Th, and Sa 7pm-midnight) features a tour of Harlem, a filling meal at a Harlem restaurant (usually Sylvia's), and an evening at a jazz club. Reserve in advance.

Harlem Renaissance Tours (283-1297). Call ahead for a schedule and to make reservations. Tours are only offered to groups.

Kramer's Reality Tour (268-5525). If you've ever wanted to see every Manhattan locale featured in *Seinfeld*, then this multi-media bus tour, led by Kenny Kramer (the "real-life" Kramer), is for you. Life imitating art imitating life equals kinda cheesy, but it's a must for *Seinfeld* diehards. Offered Sa-Su at noon; 3hr.; $37.50. Reservations with a major credit card required.

MANHATTAN
LOWER MANHATTAN

Subway: #1 and 9 to South Ferry lands you at the southeastern tip Battery Park. Or take the #4 and 5 to Bowling Green.

Its zillion-dollar facade glistening on a thousand postcards, southernmost Manhattan's sleek financial powerhouses tower incongruously above cobblestones and antiquated edifices. Once-svelte Lower Manhattan has ballooned up and out, amassing landfill as skyscrapers reach new heights. In the midst of this expansion, the city has made commendable efforts to preserve the region's historical strata.

Lower Manhattan was the first part of the island settled by Europeans and thereafter set the stage for many U.S. firsts, including the first presidential inauguration. The area's crooked streets, below the numbers of the street grid system, remain from New York's chaotic youth. Omnipresent **Heritage Trail** markers indicate the most significant spots and provide historical information and anecdotes about the sights. For a detailed walking tour of lower Manhattan, call Heritage Trails at 888-487-2457 (see **Sightseeing Tours,** p. 135). And towering above it all, the World Trade Center plays a double role: first, as the point from which to survey the land that you're about to attack; and second, as a landmark that means "south" from almost any other point in the borough.

WORLD TRADE CENTER

Subway: #1, 9, R, or N to Cortlandt St.; A, C, or E to Chambers St. **Observation Deck,** *2 World Trade Center (323-2340). The ticket booth is located on the mezzanine. Open daily June-Aug. 9:30am-11:30pm; Sept.-May 9:30am-9:30pm. Admission $12.50, students $10.75, seniors $9.50, ages 6-12 $6.25, under 6 free.* **Branch of the Visitor Information Center** *located on the mezzanine. Open M-Sa 9am-5pm; off-season M-F 9am-5pm.* **TKTS Booth** *also on mezzanine (see p.250).*

No matter where you are in lower Manhattan, you can't help seeing the famous **Twin Towers** of the World Trade Center. The main plaza, on Church and Dey St., contains two sculptures, a large fountain, ample seating space, daily summer lunchtime entertainment, and public theater, dance and musical events (435-6600 or visit www.panynj.gov/onstage).

The tallest twin stands four feet above its sibling at 1372 ft. This sleekly striped tag team, created in 1973 by the Port Authority, dwarfs every other building in the city. The bombing of the complex in 1993 left no visible scars other than the "All visitors must carry ID" signs and the secured entry checkpoints into the office space.

Access to the glass-enclosed observatory on the 107th floor requires standing in line for tickets. Pass right by the lame exhibits on trade history and economics. Because its architects opted to place much of the skeleton of the building on the outside in order to leave open spaces in the inside, don't count on a panoramic view; the steel supports slice your sights a bit. Fear not, however—the view still astounds. The observation deck also offers a free simulated helicopter ride film, primarily for kids. In good weather, the world's tallest outdoor platform, the rooftop observation deck on the 110th floor, offers a better view. It's even romantic when the city lights up at night. Telescopes (25¢) on the roof allow you to zero in on particular parts of the city.

One level below ground at the Trade Center lurks an underground **shopping mall**—the largest in New York. If subterranean shopping isn't your "bag," follow the nearest exit signs to the World Financial Center and Battery Park City.

BATTERY PARK CITY

Subway: #1, 9, N, or R to Cortland St./World Trade Center or A, C, or E to Chambers St./World Trade Center.

The southern base of Manhattan, the area now called **Battery Park,** once lodged only fish. The spot earned its name from the forts that the American military constructed on the shallow coastal banks. Well into the 1800s, the forts were used to fend off the British, who had a rude habit of attacking American ships. Whatever was dug up to build the World Trade Center came to be dumped west of West St., and the residential Battery Park City, New York's latest and most extravagant development, was constructed upon it. Sculptures by artists such as Ned Smyth and Mary Miss line its **esplanade,** while the words of New York poets Walt Whitman and Frank O'Hara have been set into the gate bordering the harbor. Across the esplanade, you can catch a ferry to Hoboken (8min.; call 800-533-3779 for schedule; fare $2). Just inside the north gate of Batter Park, **Hope Garden,** an AIDS memorial, holds 100,000 roses. The park also contains an eclectic assortment of war monuments and memorials to various immigrants, many of whom risked everything to come to the States.

CASTLE CLINTON. Battery Park's main structure was originally located 200 feet offshore on an artificial island and served as a defense against Britain in the War of 1812. The only shots ever fired were for target practice, so by 1824 the city figured it was safe to lease the area for public entertainment. It soon became a hot spot and was the site of concerts, fireworks, scientific demonstrations, and eventually became a premier performance theater. In the next few decades, enough landfill from nearby construction had accumulated to connect Castle Clinton to the main-

NEIGHBORHOODS

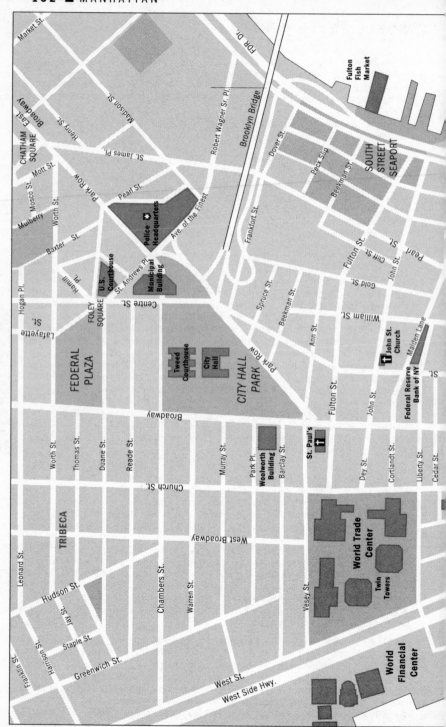

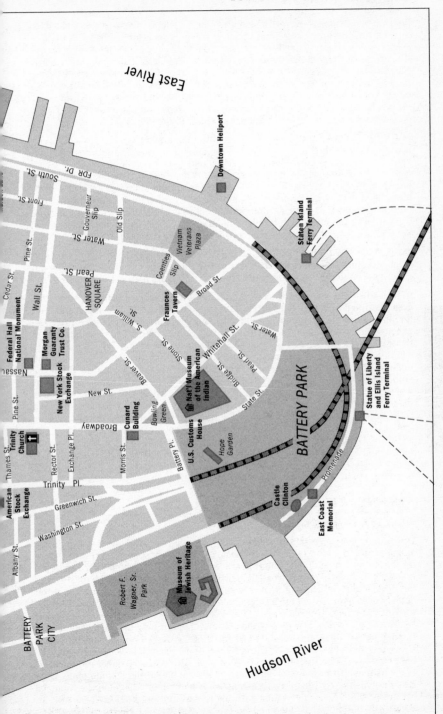

East River

FDR Dr.

South St.

Front St.

Gouverneur Slip

Old Slip

Pine St.

Water St.

Cedar St.

Wall St.

Pearl St.

HANOVER SQUARE

Coenties Slip

Vietnam Veterans Plaza

Downtown Heliport

Staten Island Ferry Terminal

Federal Hall National Monument

Morgan Guaranty Trust Co.

New York Stock Exchange

Nassau

S. William St.

Fraunces Tavern

Broad St.

Whitehall St.

Water St.

Pine St.

New St.

Beaver St.

Stone St.

Pearl St.

Bridge St.

State St.

Nat'l Museum of the American Indian

BATTERY PARK

Statue of Liberty and Ellis Island Ferry Terminal

Thames St.

Rector St.

Exchange Pl.

Trinity Church

Broadway

Cunard Building

Bowling Green

Battery Pl.

U.S. Customs House

Hope Garden

Promenade

Morris St.

American Stock Exchange

Albany St.

Trinity Pl.

Greenwich St.

Washington St.

Castle Clinton

East Coast Memorial

BATTERY PARK CITY

Robert F. Wagner, Sr. Park

Museum of Jewish Heritage

Hudson River

land, and it became New York's immigrant landing depot. Between 1855 and 1889, more than 8 million immigrants passed through its walls. When Ellis Island assumed this function, Castle Clinton turned into the site of the beloved New York Aquarium. The aquarium later moved to Coney Island, the building left vacant. The National Park Service now tends the fort, which functions as a Liberty/Ellis Island ticket booth and info center (see p.146). The vista from Castle Clinton offers a clear view of lush New Jersey, Ellis Island, Liberty Island, Staten Island, and Governor's Island, a Coast Guard command center. *(20min. walking tours of Castle Clinton. Daily every hr. 10:05am-4:05pm. Free. Castle open daily 8:30am-5pm.)*

THE WORLD FINANCIAL CENTER. This building, adjacent to the Twin Towers, boards many of the major companies we know and owe. The four granite-and-glass 40-story towers are covered by distinctive geometric copper roofs. The center's main public space is the glass-enclosed **Winter Garden,** a pretty unaffordable, but stunning, galleria replete with a sprawling marble staircase and sixteen 40-foot-tall palm trees imported from California. The garden hosts over 40 shops, restaurants, year-round festivals, and performances that are open to the public. The garden faces the magnificent, mile-long river esplanade. *(For further information call 945-0505, visit www.worldfinancialcenter.com, or see **Arts and Entertainment,** p.250.)*

MUSEUM OF JEWISH HERITAGE. "A Living Memorial to the Holocaust," this six-sided structure located in **Robert J. Wagner Park** houses impressive exhibitions and galleries recounting Jewish history of the past 150 years (see p. 134).

OTHER SIGHTS. On the northeast border of Battery Park lies **State St.** Before this area was filled in, it was the shorefront residence of wealthy merchants and their families. State St.'s glamour has dimmed, but you can still sense its former elegance in the two brick-and-wood ghosts of a bygone era: the **Church of Our Lady of the Rosary** and the adjacent **Shrine of St. Elizabeth Ann Seton,** 7-8 State St. (269-6865). Originally named James Watson House in 1792, the latter was once the home of Elizabeth Ann Seton who became the first U.S.-born saint in 1975. The adjoining church dates from 1883, when it was a shelter for Irish immigrant women. North on State St., at the rear of the courtyard adjacent to the church is the urban archaeology museum **New York Unearthed,** 207 Front St., which houses a collection of urban artifacts uncovered during construction in the downtown area (see p. 249). Right next to the museum stands the sheer, elegant, and largely empty wedge of **17 State St.** Built in 1989, this great white whale of a building stands on the site of the house in which Herman Melville was born in 1819. Melville soon left to pen masterpieces like *Moby Dick* and "Bartleby the Scrivener," a mid-19th century vision of an apathetic, soulless financial district.

FINANCIAL DISTRICT

Subway: #4 or 5 to Bowling Green

Docks of oyster harvesters once lined the water where Pearl St. now stands. Occasionally, after the workers removed the meat from the oyster and threw the waste on the streets, bystanders found pearls remaining in the shells or lying in the cracks in the road. Around Broad St., northeast of Pearl, the Dutch colonists dug a large canal in an effort to recreate the surroundings of their homeland. The water quickly turned putrid and the disappointed Dutch filled in the filthy canal to create the present street. This marriage of muck and money characterizes the Financial District to this day. On Wall St.—the cornerstone, not only of the district, but of finance as a whole—a trillion dollars of capital change hands every day. High above this and a handful of other streets, corporate masterminds negotiate the global economy. Once the northern border of the New Amsterdam settlement, it takes its name from the wall built here in 1653 to shield the Dutch colony from British invasion. By the early 19th century, it had already become the financial capital of the U.S., synonymous with big moves and big bucks. At **55 Wall St.** stands the building that once housed the Second Merchants' Exchange (1836-

1854), the predecessor of the modern stock exchange. It and the Federal Building are the two oldest buildings on Wall Street. At **68 Wall St.** lies the sight of the original stock exchange, where brokers once traded outdoors beneath a tree. At 28 Broadway, next to the Bull, is the **Museum of American Financial History,** located in the former Standard Oil building (see p. 247). The Financial District runs roughly between Battery Park City and the civic center.

NEW YORK STOCK EXCHANGE. More than 3100 companies compete on the Stock Exchange, which daily handles billions of shares. Once inside the stock exchange, you can check stock listings or ask questions at the numerous interactive computer stations, watch a brief film on the functions and hi-tech features of the exchange, and visit the observation gallery overlooking the main trading floor (which is why you really came anyway). The visitors' gallery has been enclosed ever since the 1960s, when Abbie Hoffman and fellow leftist Yippies threw dollar bills at the traders, who frantically rooted after the money, perfectly acting out the role the anti-capitalist protestors had anticipated. *(656-5165. On Broad St., between Wall St. and Exchange Pl. Admission to gallery by self-guided tour only, with interactive computers providing information along the way; last tour leaves at 3:30pm. Free tickets distributed at 20 Broad St.)*

U.S. CUSTOMS HOUSE. Completed in 1907, when the city derived most of its revenue from customs, this building now houses the Smithsonian's **National Museum of the American Indian** (see p. 248). The Customs House sits on the original Algonquin trading ground, which later became the site of the Dutch Fort Amsterdam in 1626. The magnificent Beaux-Arts building sits behind Baroque sculptures representing the supposed four continents and six races, and Mercury, the Roman god of commerce, whose face crowns each of 40 columns. Daniel Chester French, the same artist who sculpted the Lincoln Memorial in Washington, D.C., created these sculptures. *(1 Bowling Green.)*

BOWLING GREEN. The Museum of the American Indian ironically faces the site of the city's first shady business transaction—Peter Minuit's purchase of Manhattan from Native Americans for the equivalent of $24. This spot eventually became the city's first park, once used for playing the game of bowls, an ancestor of U.S. bowling. The green's tradition of controversy persisted, as colonists let the Brits know just how they felt during the tumultuous era of the Revolution. Colonists rioted here in the 1760s against King George III's Stamp Act, and after its repeal praised him by way of a larger-than-life statue erected in 1770. Upon the 1776 reading of Declaration of Independence, a passionate mob tore down the statue, ultimately converting melted bits of it into anti-British artillery in the Revolutionary War.

TRINITY CHURCH. Around the corner from the NYSE, on Broadway, this Neo-Gothic institution has the last laugh over its towering billion-dollar neighbors. Visit the modest **museum** behind the altar and the welcome center and gift shop that lie to the left of the entrance. Trinity Church owns much of the land upon which the nearby architectural giants reside, ensuring that sizable mounds of moolah support it. Its Gothic spire was the tallest structure in the city when it was first erected in 1846, and the Episcopal congregation dates from 1696. Trinity's 2½-acre yard, dating from 1681, houses the graves of Alexander Hamilton and other historical notables. In the summer, de-stressing corporate execs often come here for a shady respite from the shadier material world. From July through September, Trinity Church and St. Paul's Chapel present the Beethoven Summer Musical Festival (see **Arts and Entertainment,** p. 256). *(74 Trinity Pl. Open M-F 7am–6pm, Sa 8am-4pm, Su 7am-4pm. Welcome center open daily 10-11:45am and 1-3pm.)*

BROAD FINANCIAL CENTER. At Whitehall and Pearl St., on the east side of Bowling Green, this center contains one of New York's most whimsical lobbies. Tapering pylons topped with revolving metal globes balance on surreal spheres of marble, and a wall-sized clock face stares over a sloping pool of water.

NEIGHBORHOODS

FEDERAL HALL. A tightly pantalooned George Washington stands anachronistically on the steps of this Parthenon lookalike. After 1703, it housed the original City Hall, where the trial of John Peter Zenger helped to establish freedom of the press in 1735. Perhaps most notably, Washington was first sworn in roughly on the spot where his likeness stands today. The building served as the nation's first seat of government, and from here James Madison submitted the Bill of Rights to Congress. The original structure was demolished in 1812 and later erected to house several federal agencies including the Customs House, the Sub-Treasury, the Passport Office, and the FBI. Exhibits now include the illustrated Bible used by Washington at his inauguration, a 10-minute animated program called "Journey to Federal Hall," and several activities for children. Tours and an animated film are offered upon request. *(825-6888. 26 Wall St. Open M-F 9am-5pm; in summer, also open Sa-Su 9am-5pm. Disabled entrance at 15 Pine St.)*

CITY HALL AND THE CIVIC CENTER

Subway: #2 or 3 to Park Pl. and cross Broadway, or #4, 5, 6, J, M, or Z to Chambers St./ Brooklyn Bridge/City Hall.

Turn-of-the-century New York, bulldozed out of existence in most of the city, resides in the civic center, the nexus of city government. Most of the neighborhood's buildings derive from the late 19th-century "City Beautiful" movement that pays homage to grandiose Classical architecture. Oversized sculpture and enormous columns grace the structures that stand in the neighborhood surrounding City Hall; nearly all house some branch of city, state, or federal government, and most of them sit atop a huge flight of lime steps.

CITY HALL. John McComb, Jr. and Joseph-François Mangin (who also helped design St. Patrick's Cathedral), designed this seat of city government. In 1865, thousands of mourners filed past the body of Abraham Lincoln under the hall's vaulted rotunda. Its winding stairs lead to the **Governor's Room,** in which early portraits of Jefferson, Monroe, Jackson, Hamilton, Washington, and others adorn the walls. City Hall sits, aptly, in **City Hall Park.** Once home to a jail, a public execution ground, and a barracks for British soldiers, the park now sits more calmly amidst colorful gardens, a fountain, and local winos. Here in 1774 Alexander Hamilton led a protest against the British-imposed tea tax. On July 9, 1776, George Washington and his troops encamped here before the reading of the Declaration of Independence. This little idyll amidst stone and steel hosts a small but worthwhile **Farmer's Market.** The area along Park Row, now inhabited by a statue of journalist **Horace Greeley,** was formerly known as "Newspaper Row" because most of New York's newspapers were published near the one place they were guaranteed to find scandal. *(788-6879. Broadway at Murray St., off Park Row. Officially open to tourists M-F 10am-4pm. Public meetings often run later and can be interesting to watch. Market open Tu and F 8am-6pm; Jan.-Mar. F only.)*

AFRICAN BURIAL GROUND. As recently as 1991, archaeologists found the remains of over 20,000 slaves buried only 20 feet underground at the corner of Duane and Elk St. This is the largest known excavated African cemetery in the world. Congress declared it a national landmark, in response to protests against a new Federal Court building to be built over the site. The grassy space now stands undisturbed with plans in the works for a more elaborate memorial.

THE FEDERAL RESERVE BANK OF NEW YORK. South on Nassau St. and across Maiden Lane, this neo-Renaissance building occupies an entire block. Modeled in 1924 after the Palazzo Strozzi of a 15th-century Florentine banking family, the bank's threatening facade is meant to keep you away from one quarter of the world's known gold bullion. Storing most of her bucks at Fort Knox, the U.S. keeps only 2% of her gold in this downtown reserve. The bulk of the bullion here belongs to other nations. The vault, located 5 stories below ground, is a cell-block of 121 triple-locked compartments, each a separate storehouse, with most storehouses containing a single nation's gold. *(720-6130. 33 Liberty St. The building offers tours, but you must reservations at least a week in advance.)*

FEDERAL OFFICE BUILDING. Here, a new lobby holds breathtaking public art installations including Clyde Lynd's sculpture "America Song" and Roger Brown's commemorative mosaic depicting legions of AIDS-stricken faces descending into a sea of skulls. On the floor of the central rotunda, a work entitled "The New Ring Shout" commemorates the African burial ground. The title of this 40-foot-wide work of terrazzo and polished brass derives from a historical dance of celebration. *(290 Broadway, off Reade St., a block north of City Hall.)*

WOOLWORTH BUILDING. You can't miss this deliciously ornate 1913 construction. F.W. Woolworth purportedly paid millions in cash to house the offices of his five-and-dime store empire in what was known as the "Cathedral of Commerce." The Chrysler Building replaced it as the world's tallest structure in 1930. Its lobby boasts Gothic arches and flourishes that vault over glittering mosaics, gold painted mailboxes, and imported marble designs and carved caricatures; note the one of Woolworth himself counting change and the one of architect Cass Gilbert holding a model of the building. *(233 Broadway, south of the Federal Office Building.)*

ST. PAUL'S CHAPEL. London's St. Martin-in-the-Fields inspired this chapel's design. Constructed in 1766, with a spire and clock tower added in 1794, St. Paul's is Manhattan's oldest public building in continuous use. You can see George Washington's pew, where the first President worshipped on Inauguration Day, April 30, 1789. Above the pew hangs an oil painting of the nation's Great Seal, officially adopted in 1782. Outside the east window stands a memorial to Major General Richard Montgomery, killed in the famous 1775 attack on Quebec. The chapel offers, in conjunction with **Trinity Church,** popular classical music concerts (see p. 269). *(602-0773. A block and a half south of the Woolworth Building, near Fulton St. Chapel open M-F 9am-3pm, Su 7am-3pm.)*

SURROGATE'S COURT. Two sculpture groups—*New York in Its Infancy* and *New York in Revolutionary Times*—grace the Beaux-Arts exterior of this former Hall of Records. Meanwhile, 24 statues of notable New Yorkers enliven the building's interior. In the strangely pagan lobby, Egyptian tile mosaics and the 12 signs of the Zodiac cover the ceiling. A trip up to the balcony will give you a closer look. The court also boasts a library and a garden. *(374-8244. 31 Chambers St., near Center St.)*

TWEED COURTHOUSE. It faces City Hall from across the park like a sinister alter ego. Builders laid the foundations of the courthouse on a $150,000 budget in 1862 and finished it a decade and $14 million later. Urban legend has it that $10 million of this money actually went straight to Tweed, the corrupt boss of **Tammany Hall** (see **Introducing NYC,** p. 5). This alleged misuse of funds lead to a public outcry that marked the beginning of the end of Tweed's party rule. Politics aside, today you can admire the building's Victorian reinterpretation without paying one red cent.

OTHER SIGHTS. The **Municipal Building,** located at 1 Center St. and completed in 1914, houses a civic wedding chapel, should you desire a quick hitch. North on Center St. lies the plain and pillared **United States Courthouse,** built in 1936 and crowned by its designer with a golden roof. Next door, to the left on St. Andrew's Pl., the **Church of St. Andrew** (962-3972; open daily 8am-5:30pm), built in 1938, hides in the shadow of the Municipal Building. Head across Broadway again, then east on Ann St. to the **Nassau St. pedestrian mall** (see **Shopping, p. 294**), a little-known shopping district characterized by fabulous 19th-century architecture and cheesy discount ($10 or less!) clothing stores. This area, packed during the day, provides gritty shopping fun for the budget traveler. However, avoid the area at night, when all signs of life seem to vanish.

NEIGHBORHOODS

SOUTH STREET SEAPORT

Subway: #2, 3, 4, 5, J, Z, or M to Fulton St.; also possible: the A or C to Broadway-Nassau, or E to World Trade Center and walk east on Fulton to Water St. *Outdoor concerts* and *performances* on Ambrose Stage (sometimes free) throughout the summer; call 732-7678 for info. All above attractions open: Apr.-Sept. M-W, F-Su 10am-6pm, Th 10am-8pm; Oct.-Mar. W-M 10am-5pm.

Walking east on Fulton St. toward the East River leads you past a large strip of moderately priced restaurants that ends at the **South Street Seaport.** The shipping industry thrived here for most of the 19th century, when the city possessed the nation's most important port. After the Civil War, the South Street Seaport's shipping industry flourished, giving rise to bars, brothels, and crime. In an aggressive campaign to clean up the environs, politicians decided to place the Brooklyn Bridge directly on top of the most dangerous streets. Bigwigs continue to polish the cobbled streets to a healthy luster. Municipal decisions in the 1980s rescued the seaport from century-long debauchery. The Seaport Museum teamed up with the Rouse Corporation, which brought us Boston's Quincy Market, the St. Louis Union Station, and Baltimore's Harborplace, to design the 12-block "museum without walls." After 5pm, masses of professionals, attired in sneakers-and-skirts or trailing ties, descend upon the area for a well-deserved happy hour. The seaport also offers museums, shopping, sightseeing cruises, and street performers, in and around spacious complexes, such as the **Fulton Market Building** and the **Pier 17 Pavilion,** a shopping mall and restaurant arcade toward the river on Fulton St. You may purchase tickets for a relaxing tour around the island at the Pier 16 or NY Waterways ticket-booths (see **Sightseeing Tours,** p. 126). In the main square, on the right side of Fulton St., you may travel back in time at **Schermerhorn Row,** the oldest complete block of buildings in Manhattan, constructed mainly between 1811 and 1812.

SEAPORT MUSEUM VISITOR'S CENTER. Your first stop at the Seaport, the pretty visitor's center provides information on and sells passes to any of the galleries, ships, or other sites that constitute the museum that is a neighborhood unto itself. *(748-8600. 12-14 Fulton St. Admission: $6, students $4, seniors $5, ages 4-12 $3. Cruise and museum combination rates sometimes available. Separate ship ticket is $3.)*

FULTON FISH MARKET. The largest fresh fish market in the country, hidden beneath the overpass on South St. The city repeatedly battles the market, but it has held fast for over 160 years and still opens at 4am. After a suspicious fire, Mayor Giuliani went to town on the organized crime influences that allegedly controlled the market's activities. New York's store and restaurant owners continue to buy their fresh fish here, as they have since the Dutch colonial period. Between midnight and 8am you can see buyers making their pick from the gasping catch, just trucked in by refrigerated vehicle. Those who can stomach wriggling scaly things might get a kick out of a behind-the-scenes tour of the market given early Thursday mornings from June to October (see p. 126).

PEKING. In 1911, a Hamburg-based company constructed the *Peking*, the second-largest sailing ship ever launched. It spent most of its career on the "nitrate run" to Chile, a route that passes around Cape Horn, one of the most dangerous stretches of water in the world. You can help the current crew raise one of the ship's 32 sails or simply take a half-hour tour. *(Located on the Hudson River off Fulton St. and next to Pier 17. For a sample of this rich history, catch the 15min. 1929 film of the ship during an actual passage around Cape Horn, shown daily 10am-6pm.)*

OTHER SIGHTS. Several other ships have docked in the seaport for good. Smaller ones include the *Wavertree*, an iron-hulled, three-masted ship built in 1885. In addition, you can see the *Ambrose*, a floating lighthouse built in 1907 to mark an entrance to the New York harbor. The *Pioneer* sailing ship gives two- and three-hour cruises on which you can assist with sailing duties. Ironically named, the diminutive **Titanic Memorial Lighthouse** stands on the corner where Fulton meets Water St. To the left, on Water St., a number of 18th-century buildings have been restored and now house shops. **Bowne & Co.,** 211 Water St. (748-8660), a restored 18th-century printing shop, offers demonstrations on a working letterpress (M-Sa 10am-5pm). On the Fulton St. side of this block, you can escape to enjoy a quiet lunch in **Cannon's Walk,** a sparkling-clean back alley.

THE STATUE OF LIBERTY

> Give me your tired, your poor,
> Your huddled masses yearning to breathe free,
> The wretched refuse of your teeming shore.
> Send these, the homeless, the tempest-tossed to me.
> I lift my lamp beside the golden door!
>
> —Emma Lazarus

Contact: *363-3200; www.nps.gov/stli. Constantly updated* **video snapshot** *of Miss Liberty: www.sccorp.com/cam/.* **Ferries** *leave for Liberty Island from the piers at Battery Park about every 30min. in summer, 8:30am-4:10pm; call for winter hours. Visitors wishing to go all the way up to the crown must leave on the 8:30am ferry.* **Ferry Information:** *269-5755.* **Tickets:** *$7, seniors $6, ages 3-17 $3, under 2 free. Buy ferry tickets at Castle Clinton or across Battery Park from the South ferry terminal (see* **Lower Manhattan,** *p. 130).* **Summer wait** *to climb Liberty 1-2hr. Gift shop with essential items like $1.50 foam Liberty crowns. Cafeteria's greasy fried things $4.*

For over a century, the Statue of Liberty has represented the most noble elements of the American Dream. She has also made appearances in countless novels, television shows, and films, including *Splash, Planet of the Apes,* and alien epic *Independence Day.* For all these reasons, the Statue of Liberty has become a world-renowned tourist draw with lines as long as the green lady is tall.

Like most of the immigrants who arrived here by sea, the statue has roots in the Old World. Though today an icon of immigration, Lady Liberty began as French sculptor's Frederic-Auguste Bartholdi's large-scale tribute to Franco-American relations. The new statue commemorated the victory of the Union in the Civil War and the constitutional extension of liberty to black slaves; more pragmatically, the gift encouraged America to oppose the decidedly liberty-less government of Napoleon III in France. While his countrymen plotted against the establishment in 1870s Paris, Bartholdi, with President Grant and others, plotted production of the biggest statue the world had ever seen, *Liberty Enlightening the World.*

This monument to Franco-American relations (something few Americans, then or now, tend to get choked up about) quickly acquired a new significance: its location made it an immigrant's first sight upon pulling into the harbor. Thus, the statue became a symbol of immigration as a whole, the foundation of American culture. Joseph Pulitzer, a millionaire Hungarian immigrant who had realized the American Dream with his publishing empire, raised money for the 89 ft. pedestal by guilt-tripping ordinary New Yorkers into giving whatever they could. Locals of all ages responded to his efforts with hard-earned pennies. Once complete, the pedestal received its finishing touch, the now-famous words of welcome penned by poet Emma Lazarus.

A group of determined suffragettes chartered a boat and sailed themselves over to the statue's 1886 opening ceremonies, interrupting speakers by pointing out the irony of a female embodiment of Liberty in a country where women could neither vote nor attend the statue's inauguration. 1965 saw a more extreme protest, as four terrorists tried to sever the Lady's head and arm it with explosives.

An ideal trip to Liberty Island will entail fewer fireworks: on the first boat for Liberty at 8:30am, you should be off the island in a few hours, and over to the air-conditioned comfort of Ellis Island by noon. Ferries run in a Battery Park-Liberty-Ellis loop. The ticket costs the same no matter how long you stay and regardless of whether you want to see only the statue or the immigration station, so you might as well do both. The ferry ride is one long, tourist-pleasing photo-op, with jaw-dropping views of the Lower Manhattan skyline, the Brooklyn Bridge, and, of course, Miss Liberty.

NEIGHBORHOODS

Once you're on the island, head quickly for the statue's back entrance at Fort Wood (dating from the War of 1812), where you'll choose one of two lines. The significantly faster line on the right leads to the elevator carting folks to the observation decks atop **Richard Morris Hunt's pedestal.** The line on the left offers the only route to the crown. It's all stairs: 22 narrow, spiraling stories' worth, the last leg a precipitous staircase with lines that move at a snail's pace. Air-conditioned? No way. There are really only two reasons to go to the crown: (1) like Mt. Everest, because it's there; or (2) to glimpse Gustave Eiffel's (yes, *that* Eiffel) internal support-system. Beware—the view boasts little splendor: tiny, airplane-type windows look out not on Manhattan but on the Brooklyn dockyards. Senior citizens, young children, and anyone impatient should probably avoid the climb.

The pedestal's observation decks, on the other hand, offer enchanting views of New York, Ellis Island, and the towering statue above you. Don't bother with stealth; you can't take the elevator halfway up and climb to the top.

Some of the artifacts on display over the second entrance doors include an actual-size mold of Liberty's face, various artists' renderings of the sculpture, and evidence of Miss Liberty's lasting influence, such as the cover of Supertramp's *Breakfast in America* LP. A third-floor immigration exhibit should whet your appetite for the much more fascinating Ellis Island. Furthermore, friendly and knowledgeable rangers will answer any question you have, if they can hear you through the huddled masses of tourists. Tours, however, are sporadic and depend upon staffing availability.

Bring your own food—Liberty's costs a bundle and the climb to her crown is strenuous.

ELLIS ISLAND

*For instructions on how to get to Ellis, see **Liberty Island,** above. **Video documentary:** "Island of Hope, Island of Tears." 30min. Shown in 2 theaters, 1 with a preceding 15min. talk by a ranger. **Play:** "Ellis Island Stories," based on oral histories of those who passed through Ellis Island; performed in spring, summer, and fall. The film and play are free, but you must get **tickets** at the **info desk** near the entrance in advance of the showing. **Audio-Tour:** 1¼hr. $3.50, student and seniors $3, under 17 $2.50. **Restaurant** prices expensive (fish and fries $4).*

While the Statue of Liberty may embody the American Dream, nearby Ellis Island chronicles the harsh realities of starting over in the New World. The island reopened as a museum in 1990, after multi-million dollar renovations. During its six functional decades (1892-1954), approximately 12 million immigrants were processed here, many winding up with new names in their new homeland. During its peak years (1892-1920), Ellis Island ushered 5000 people per day into the U.S. In the spring of 1998, the island legally became New Jersey territory; the Supreme Court settled the dispute between New York and its neighbor state based on a 160-year-old claim. Ellis Island's exhibits alternate between the site's history and that of the peopling of America.

1ST FLOOR. A baggage storage area in Ellis' heyday, it now displays a colorful statistical survey of America's remarkable diversity. For those who can trace an ancestor back to Ellis, the first floor also features a computer to help track immigration records.

2ND FLOOR. "Through America's Gate" details the batteries of physical and mental tests, fitness exams, financial and criminal checks, and occasional hearings and detentions undergone by each new arrival. On the second floor you'll also find the overwhelming **Registry Room,** known as the "great hall," where most of the processing took place. Across the great hall, "Peak Immigration Years" tells the story behind the story, including depictions of ethnic immigrant neighborhoods and the poverty, racism, community, and kinship that characterized them. The exhibit includes a wall of American political cartoons on immigration (most more than a little politically incorrect) and a computer that tests your citizenship knowledge (it's harder than you might think).

3RD FLOOR. Numerous intriguing exhibits here include "Treasures from Home," a collection of artifacts and clothing that immigrants brought from the Old World. Various sculptures and large black-and-white photographs of grim-faced arrivals festoon the restored halls. Offices and an extensive library of immigration records round out the third floor (open to researchers with prior permission). There aren't any musty piles of genealogical records here, but librarians can recommend institutions that can help with tracing long-lost genetic kin.

CHINATOWN

To get to Chinatown, take subway #6, J, M, N, R, or Z or the #1 or 103 bus to Canal St., walk east on Canal to Mott St., go right on Mott, and follow the curved street toward the Bowery, Confucius Plaza, and East Broadway.

North of the Civic Center, you'll find that skyscrapers give way to exotic produce shops, herbal medicine drugstores, pagoda-topped phone booths, and multiple varieties of Asian food. Chinatown is loosely bounded by Worth St. to the south and Canal St. to the north, Broadway to the west and the Bowery to the east. A vibrant community that maintains seven Chinese newspapers, over 300 garment factories, and innumerable food shops, New York's Chinatown contains the largest Asian community in the U.S. outside San Francisco (over 300,000 estimated residents, comprising about half of the city's Asian population). Despite strict quotas on immigration, Chinatown grew up in the 1870s, as Chinese-Americans fled anti-Chinese violence out West. Although Chinese neighborhoods have since grown up in Queens' Flushing and Elmhurst and in Brooklyn's Sunset Park and Bay Ridge, Chinatown continues to grow into the surrounding streets every year, especially up through Little Italy.

Mott and Pell St., the unofficial centers of Chinatown, boil over with commercial activity. Brightly colored businesses vie for attention with everything from shelves of dried ginseng to bucketfuls of glistening baby turtles. Gift shops also line the streets, peddling miniature Buddhas, exotic swords, and spherical stress relievers. Don't let the low-priced merchandise snooker you—creative labeling abounds in several stores (those are *not* Rolexes).

During the Chinese New Year (in 2000, it begins January 5), the area's frenetic pace accelerates to a fever pitch. The Fourth of July brings dangers of its own kind. Of the numerous brands of fireworks sold, few are legal, and of their dealers, most are intimidating. In case you need further discouragement, Mayor Giuliani's "Quality of Life" crime crackdown has made many fireworks even *more* illegal.

THE ORIENTAL ENTERPRISES COMPANY. This bookstore specializes in Chinese literature. Its extensive collection includes books, tapes, CDs, and newspapers, as well as some interesting calligraphy equipment and musical instruments. *(At 13 Elizabeth St., 2nd fl. Open daily 10am-7pm.)*

BUDDHIST TEMPLE. A red-and-gold theological treat. Inside, the devout are invited to kneel and give offerings in front of a porcelain statue, while the less devout can browse through the gift shop in the rear of the same room. *(4 Pell St., off Mott St.)*

THE MUSEUM OF THE CHINESE IN THE AMERICAS. The first museum ever dedicated to the history of the Chinese-American experience. Its two small rooms contain a fascinating collection of writing, images, and artifacts. *(70 Mulberry St., corner of Bayard St. 619-4785. Open Tu-Sa noon-5pm. Admission $3, students and seniors $1.)*

MAHAYANA BUDDHIST TEMPLE. This brand-new space, with its TV screens, spotlights, and state-of-the-art sound system, might be a little jarring for those who think of Buddhism as a religion practiced in musty old monasteries in ancient Tibet. *(133 Canal St., near the Manhattan Bridge.)*

NEIGHBORHOODS

WHO KNOWS WHY THE CAGED BIRD

SINGS? Early rising ornithologists will want to take a sunrise stroll to **Sara Delano Roosevelt Park**, west of the Bowery, at the corner of Chrystie and Delancey St. There, between about 7 and 9am, a group of older Chinese men gather each morning from spring through fall to give sun to the songbirds—an old tradition intended as a distraction from vice. The men arrive with birdcages covered in cloth so that their occupants don't wake too early. After positioning the cages in a small garden at the park's northern edge, the men gingerly remove the coverings, and bid their songbirds good morning. The men do some stretching exercises and socialize as they wait for their birds to warm to the sun and begin singing. Once sufficiently bathed in light, the birds give fanfare to the day. Their songs are amazingly loud and melodic, and are easily heard over the roar of the heavy morning traffic.

FIRST SHEARITH ISRAEL GRAVEYARD. On the south side of Chatham Square, at St. James Pl. between James and Oliver St., this historical site attests to the neighborhood's previous guise as part of the Jewish Lower East Side. Indeed, the cemetery served New York City's first Jewish congregation, the Spanish-Portuguese Shearith Israel Synagogue. Some of the gravestones date from as early as 1683.

OTHER SIGHTS. At the northeast corner of Chatham Square is a statue of **Lin Ze Xi,** a Chinese official who, for his efforts in the Opium Wars, is honored as a forefather of the "Just Say No to Drugs" campaign. If you head northeast, you will find the Chatham Square branch of the **New York Public Library,** 33 East Broadway (964-6598), with a Chinese Heritage Collection boasting Chinese classics. The library also offers free art, poetry and computer classes to the community as well as live performances. At **Columbus Park,** near the Museum of the Chinese in the Americas, children play on the basketball courts and elderly Chinatown residents vie for bench space with jurors and lawyers on recess from the nearby Federal and State courthouses. Walking northeast toward where the Bowery and East Broadway meet will bring you past the grand arch and flanking colonnades that mark the entrance to the **Manhattan Bridge.** These were designed by Carrère and Hastings, the same firm that designed the New York Public Library and the Frick Mansion.

LITTLE ITALY

To get to Little Italy, take subway #4, 5, or 6, the N or R, or the J, M, or Z to Canal St.; or take the B, D, F, or Q to Broadway-Lafayette. On the bus, take #1 or 103 to Canal St. or the B51 from Brooklyn and get off at the corner of Canal and Mulberry St.

In the mind's eye of our collective psyche, Little Italy conjures up a set of stock images culled from history books and movies: laundry hanging out of windows over streets clogged with people and pushcarts and implacable *padrones* whispering orders to hot-headed wiseguys. In truth, the Little Italy experience has less to do with sights and more with tastes (for more information, see **Restaurants,** p. 91). Pasta aside, the Little Italy of the public imagination has pretty much disappeared around these parts. Even at the turn of the century, the noisy, festive parades and street fairs drew revelers from uptown. Since the 1960s, however, the neighborhood's borders have receded in the face of an aggressively expanding Chinatown. A small patch of restaurants and gift shops remains, frequented by visiting throngs. Once a year, however, Manhattan's Little Italy conjures up the old atmosphere; beginning with the second Thursday in September, Mulberry St. goes wild during the raucous 10-day **Feast of San Gennaro,** celebrating the Naples saint.

Mulberry St. remains the heart of the neighborhood. The reds, whites, and greens of the Italian flag flutter throughout its lower end, from Broome to Canal St. Come here for your very own "Kiss me, I'm Italian" t-shirt or *The Godfather* poster. The gift shop on the corner of Grand and Mulberry St., however, bears looking into even if you don't want to take home a souvenir; a conversation with

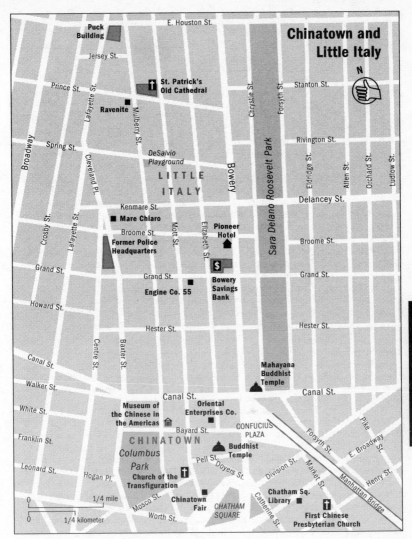

Chinatown and Little Italy

N

Puck Building

E. Houston St.

Jersey St.

Prince St.

Lafayette St.

St. Patrick's Old Cathedral

Ravenite

Mulberry St.

Spring St.

Broadway

Cleveland Pl.

DeSalvio Playground

LITTLE ITALY

Bowery

Chrystie St.

Forsyth St.

Stanton St.

Rivington St.

Eldridge St.

Allen St.

Orchard St.

Ludlow St.

Kenmare St.

Crosby St.

Lafayette St.

Mare Chiaro

Broome St.

Former Police Headquarters

Mott St.

Elizabeth St.

Pioneer Hotel

Delancey St.

Sara Delano Roosevelt Park

Broome St.

Grand St.

Grand St.

Engine Co. 55

$ Bowery Savings Bank

Grand St.

Howard St.

Hester St.

Centre St.

Baxter St.

Hester St.

Canal St.

Walker St.

White St.

Franklin St.

Canal St.

Museum of the Chinese in the Americas

Oriental Enterprises Co.

Bayard St.

Mahayana Buddhist Temple

Canal St.

CONFUCIUS PLAZA

Forsyth St.

Pike St.

E. Broadway

CHINATOWN

Columbus Park

Leonard St.

Hogan Pl.

Church of the Transfiguration

Pell St.

Buddhist Temple

Doyers St.

Division St.

Market St.

Manhattan Bridge

Henry St.

Mosco St.

Chinatown Fair

CHATHAM SQUARE

Worth St.

Catherine St.

Chatham Sq. Library

First Chinese Presbyterian Church

0   1/4 mile

0   1/4 kilometer

the proprietor, **Mr. Rossi,** may lead to an exposition of the neighborhood's history. Farther up, just below Kenmare St., sits **Mare Chiaro.** Better known as "Frank's Bar," the haunt of Ol' Blue Eyes Sinatra himself, this 90-year-old bar has hosted everyone from Gene Kelly to Madonna. As owner Tony Tenneriello will tell you, Mare Chiaro's tin walls and wood paneling have appeared in several movies, including *The Godfather III* and the steamy *9½ Weeks.*

To reach the restored **Bowery Savings Bank,** 130 Bowery St., an anomaly of un-touristed, un-Italian elegance, go east from Mulberry on Grand to the corner of Grand St. and Bowery. Designed by Stanford White, who also designed the arch in Washington Square Park and the original Madison Square Garden, and built in 1894, the building still houses the bank. It is one of the first examples of White's Neoclassical style, which features a cavernous ceiling, immense pillars, stained glass, and gold leaf.

If old-fashioned fire stations, er, set you aflame, the still-active **Engine Co. 55** stands at 363 Broome St., between Mott and Elizabeth St., dating from 1898. You can continue your tour of historic buildings devoted to civil protection by walking west on Broome St. a few blocks to Centre St. At this corner looms the massive and elegant **former police headquarters** of the city. This domed Beaux-Arts giant, built in 1909, was converted into luxury co-op apartments in the 1970s. The elegantly refurbished lobby, complete with marble columns and massive chandelier, makes it hard to imagine a more pleasant place to get booked.

Farther up Mulberry St., in the calmer reaches nearer to E. Houston St., the street feels more like a neighborhood boulevard. At the **DeSalvio playground,** on the corner of Spring St. and Mulberry, old-timers square off over checkers while children clamber over the jungle gym. On the corner of Mulberry and Prince St., reflecting this area's recent conversion of old-world grit to nouveau gritty chic is the red brick storefront that masked "Dapper Don" John Gotti's club, the **Ravenite.** It was from here that the head to the powerful Gambino crime family held court until his 1992 conviction. The club recently disappeared, replaced by the very trendy, very expensive designer boutique **Amy Chan.** The new owners kept the floor and the exposed brick walls, but the space is now filled with incredibly expensive accessories whose price tags alone are worth a gape.

St. Patrick's Old Cathedral (not to be confused with the newer uptown Cathedral of the same name), stands watch on 264 Mulberry St., near Prince St. Its facade, completed in 1815 and damaged in an 1866 fire, completes the neighborhood's old-world Italian image. Sadly, reconstruction tamed the quirky architecture of America's second oldest Gothic Revival building into a blander form. The cathedral holds regular Catholic services and administers marriages and baptisms (226-8075).

On the northern fringe of Little Italy, at the corner of Lafayette and E. Houston St., stands the beautiful red-brick **Puck Building,** built in 1885 to house the satirical *Puck* magazine. After the magazine's demise in 1916, the building served for a while as the headquarters of the magazine's descendant, *Spy.* Today, some floors function as office space while others are rented out for parties and photo shoots. To honor its namesake, the building features a cute golden Puck, who grins mischievously from his roost over the Lafayette St. door.

Fleeing the tentacles of commercialization that have introduced J. Crew and Victoria's Secret to once-avant-garde SoHo, some of the area's most tragically hip galleries and boutiques, and the beautiful people who love them, have established a toehold in an area that used to belong to Little Italy. Some pseudo-hipsters call this region—extending roughly down from Houston to Spring St. and over from Lafayette to the Bowery—**NoLIta** (**No**rth of **L**ittle **Ita**ly), but most natives wouldn't be caught dead blaspheming Nabokov. Whatever your syntactical tastes, come here to view a scene in the making, still at the tender stage before the hipper-than-thou pioneer class has moved on. The vagaries of urban fashion are on full display at the small cafes, restaurants, and bars along upper Mott and Elizabeth St. According to those in the know, this 'hood's debut as the cutting-edge ground zero will come with the conversion of the Puck Building's first floor into a retail space.

STEAL THIS RADIO Activated on Thanksgiving 1995, *Steal This Radio* (88.7 FM) is a micro-power pirate radio station that can be heard from the western edge of Williamsburg to the Bowery, with a similar North-South range centered on the Lower East Side. The brainchild of "squatters, low-income tenants, activists, and non-activists," STR serves as a "giant community drum," pounding out anarchist/grassroots music, news, politics, and radio drama, along with substantial Spanish-language broadcasting. Shows ranging from homemade music to Native American talk shows attest to the Loisaida's cultural diversity and commitment to the community. The signal is difficult to receive and the station itself is elusive—but, as with New York's anarchist paper *The Shadow,* you're likely to hear a unique take on current events. The truth is out there...

Wearmart, 229 Elizabeth St., fills its tiny boutique space with designer Martin Keehn's line of ridiculously expensive variations on hospital scrubs. **Language,** 238 Mulberry St., offers everything from clothing designed by Bella Freud (daughter of Lucien) and pashmina sweaters (a wool from the throat of Nepalese goats) to antique Amazonian feather masks and Chinese furniture. There is also a gallery with rotating shows in the back. You won't need your wallet; just try to keep a straight face when you see the prices. Farther down Elizabeth St., on a swath of grass between Spring and Prince St., resides the striking Elizabeth Street Company **sculpture garden.** Between 10am and 4pm every day (weather permitting), stop in at the corner of Elizabeth and E. Houston St. for an incredible sight. Here, **Manhattan Castles and Props,** 76 E. Houston St., sets up their enormous display of....er...junk? Old bathtubs, street signs, traffic lights, furniture, billboards, gargoyles—if it's manmade and old, they've got it. This company also rents items to movies. It's worth a visit to the area just to see this Bermuda Triangle of oddities.

LOWER EAST SIDE

Everybody ought to have a Lower East Side in their life.

—Irving Berlin

Subway: Take the G or the M, E, J, Z to Essex/Delancey St., near the Williamsburg Bridge.

Down below E. Houston lurks the trendily seedy Lower East Side, where old-timers rub shoulders with heroin dealers and twenty-somethings emulating *la vie bohème.* A huge influx of Eastern European Jews swelled the population of the Lower East Side in the span between 1850 and 1950; two million arrived in the 20 years before World War I alone, after fleeing the Czar's bloody pogroms. The Lower East Side still harbors immigrants, now mostly Asian and Hispanic. Chinatown has expanded east across the Bowery and along the stretch of East Broadway, one of the district's main thoroughfares. Here on East Broadway, cultures and eras converge. Buddhist prayer centers neighbor Jewish religious supply stores. Traces of the Jewish ghetto also persist on Orchard St., a historical shopping area that fills up, on Sundays, with salesmen hawking their discount goods in vacuum-sealed bags to multitudes of potential customers.

LOWER EAST SIDE TENEMENT MUSEUM. The museum showcases two preserved tenement houses typical of those that filled this neighborhood in the early part of the century. Admission includes a slide show, video, and guided tour. The museum gallery displays free exhibits and photographs documenting Jewish life on the Lower East Side. (For more detailed information, see p. 246.) *(97 Orchard St., between Broome and Delancey St.)*

EXPANDED ARTS. This company hosts the "94 Plays in 94 Days" festival of new theatrical work. And if you can't get tickets to Shakespeare in the Park, try Expanded Art's Shakespeare in the Parking Lot, staged in the municipal lot across the street. Locals bearing groceries march home across the "stage," cars roar by on nearby Delancey, and audience members roll in and out. But the acting is solid, and, police sirens included, watching Shakespeare outdoors for free is truly a glorious thing. Indeed this area boasts quite a thriving experimental theater scene. *(253-1813. 85 Ludlow St., between Delancey and Broome. June-Aug. W-Sa 8pm. Free. Call for schedule.)*

SYNAGOGUES. Congregation Anshe Chesed, at 172-176 Norfolk St. (780-0175; www.oresanz.org.) just off Stanton St., is New York's oldest synagogue. The red-painted Gothic Revival structure was built in 1849 to seat 1500. It now houses The Jose Oresanz Foundation. The new center for the arts has converted part of the synagogue into gallery space. On 60 Norfolk St., between Grand and Broome St., sits **Beth Hamedrash Hagadol Synagogue** (674-3330), the best-preserved of the Lower East Side houses of worship. This synagogue was purchased in 1885 by the Orthodox congregation that is still housed there; it is the oldest Orthodox congregation in New York to remain in one location.

146 ■ MANHATTAN

SUNG TAK BUDDHIST ASSOCIATION. The newly renovated grand temple of the former Congregation Sons of Israel Kalvarie, this building stood abandoned for years, dilapidated and graffiti-covered, until the Buddhist Association moved in. The house of worship now serves a new faith. The area here, though technically still the Lower East Side, is also very much a part of Chinatown. *(West of Williamsburg Bridge on East Broadway, at 15 Pike St.)*

THE FORWARD BUILDING. On the block once known as "Publishers Row," now occupied by a Chinese church, this tower once housed the offices of the Yiddish daily newspaper that bore its name (in Yiddish: *Foreverts*). At the beginning of this century, the paper was the bastion of Yiddish intellectual culture. *The Forward* now publishes weekly in English from its midtown offices. *(At 175 East Broadway, across from Seward Park.)*

OTHER SIGHTS. The Eldridge St. Synagogue (219-0903) recently completed a multi-million dollar renovation that birthed a Lower East Side historical museum. Follow Forsyth north from East Broadway to 12 Eldridge St. near Canal St. (Open Su and Tu-Th noon-4pm. Tours $4, children, students, and seniors $2. Tours are available with advance notice.) Stop in at **Schapiro's House of Kosher Wines,** 126 Rivington St. (674-4404), off of Orchard St., for a tour of the only operational winery left in NYC, famous for once giving a bottle of "the wine you can cut with a knife" to every immigrant family (tours Su 11am-4pm; you can stop in and taste the wine anytime).

TRIBECA

Walking around the **Tri**angle **Be**low **Ca**nal St., you might not guess that it has been anointed (by resident Robert DeNiro and, until his tragic death in the summer of 1999, by John F. Kennedy, Jr.) as one of the hottest neighborhoods in New York City. Hidden among hulking 19th-century cast-iron warehouses, you'll find pockets of restaurants, bars, and galleries, often maintaining SoHo's trendiness without the upscale airs. Although a street may look barren, it probably holds hidden marvels—restaurants, specialty shops, beautifully restored lofts and studios. Lacking SoHo's Rodeo Drive feel, TriBeCa has a laid-back chic that weathers well. The Institute for Contemporary Art's **Clocktower Gallery** and studio space resides in the former home of the New York Life Insurance Company on the 13th floor. To find out about community events and festivals, check out the *TriBeCa Trib,* a free newspaper available in local establishments. (233-1440. 108 Leonard St., between Broadway and Lafayette, where TriBeCa recedes into Chinatown.)

TriBeCa residents take great pride their neighborhood, and consequently, streets and community facilities are under constant renewal and improvement. At 2 White St., off the corner of W. Broadway, stands an anachronistic 1809 **Federal house,** a small brick structure whose aged exterior belies its completely refurbished interior, now a stylish bar. Continue west on White to Moore St. to see the oddly familiar building on 114 Moore St. From this firehouse, Bill Murray, Dan Ackroyd, and fellow **Ghostbusters** helped rid New York City of unwanted paranormal activity in two 1980s films. Southwest of here, on Harrison St. between Greenwich and West St., stands a row of beautifully restored 18th-century townhouses. Just to the south, in an open triangular space bounded by Greenwich, Chambers, and West St., is **Washington Market Park,** which holds a surprisingly big and green spread of grass, as well as a funky playground that attracts kids of all ages. The park hosts Thursday evening concerts each week from late June to early August in its charming blue-and-white gazebo; performances include every type of music, from jazz to R&B to country (call the Parks Dept. at 408-0100 for info, or visit the bulletin board schedule by the park's main gate). Between Chambers and N. Moore St. stands **Borough of Manhattan Community College,** part of the City University system.

NEIGHBORHOODS

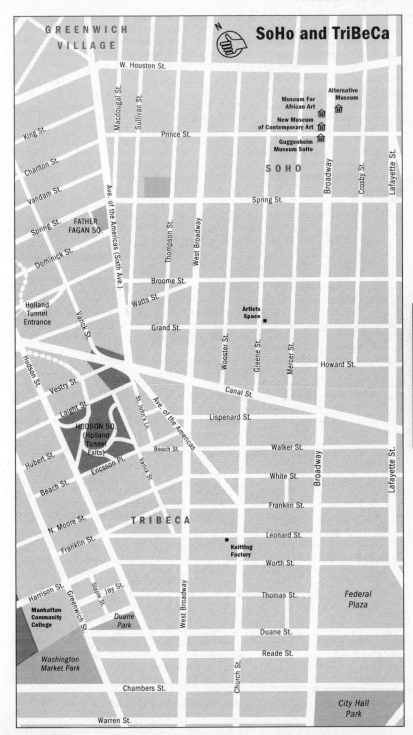

NEIGHBORHOODS

On the corner of Franklin and Greenwich St., you'll see Robert DeNiro's **TriBeCa Grill,** on the ground floor of the TriBeCa films building, in which Miramax and several other production companies work their cinematic magic. The actor-cum-entrepreneur has also opened the TriBeCa Bakery in the middle of the block, and the deeply chic, expensive and surprisingly friendly Nobu (on the corner of Franklin St. and Hudson St.), a "fusion cuisine" restaurant that attracts all types of celebrities. Rumor has it that several other neighborhood institutions belong to Mr. "You Lookin' at Me?"—but you didn't hear it here.

Southeast TriBeCa, along Broadway and Chambers St., has a more commercial feel than the rest of the area. Discount stores and cheap restaurants of all types line these streets, and with City Hall and the Financial District nearby, the area tends to get pretty busy during the day. Don't leave TriBeCa without strolling along the quieter streets, like Hudson and W. Broadway, where you'll find quite a few **second-hand stores** selling everything from furniture to vintage clothing.

SOHO

SoHo, the district **So**uth of **Ho**uston St. ("HOW-ston"), holds court between TriBeCa and Greenwich Village. In the past 10 years SoHo has solidified into a saucy dish of artsy, commercial-chic. The story of SoHo's evolution is that of an increasing number of New York neighborhoods. In the earlier part of the century, SoHo was a dark industrial zone operating factories and warehouses between its alleyways. In the mid-1940s, however, charmed by low rents and airy lofts, artists moved in; trickle roared to full-scale mass immigration by the 1960s. Until the mid-1980s, SoHo's scene, led by Jean-Michel Basquiat, Keith Haring, and Kenny Scharf, blossomed as the hotbed of artistic innovation, but as the 90s brought Victoria's Secret and J. Crew, the cutting-edge dulled. While SoHo may no longer cradle the truly avant-garde, it still boasts pockets of off-beat culture, high fashion, and meticulous design. Whether spurred on now by capitalism or the muses, those who run the restaurants, bars, shops, and galleries of SoHo put great care into the establishment's appearance and ambience: come here to reap the benefits.

An impressive collection of **galleries** remains in this area—dozens line the streets between Broadway and West Broadway. Don't be put off by snooty gallery owners unless you're interrupting a private showing to a visiting head of state. Most galleries hold interesting work behind the scenes—with the right line, you may be able to talk someone into showing you the reserve artwork. Many also host fabulous parties for openings and closings of shows; you may be able to finagle an invitation from the staff. Most close Sundays and Mondays from September to June and often close altogether through July and August. (See **Galleries,** p. 251.)

A few museums make their home amid the SoHo galleries. The **Alternative Museum** (966-4444) claims a space on the fourth floor of 594 Broadway, a building which also houses nine commercial galleries. Across the street is the **Museum for African Art,** 593 Broadway (966-1313), with changing exhibitions of African and African-American art. At 583 Broadway, just north of Prince St., you'll find the **New Museum of Contemporary Art** (219-1222), which showcases the borderline absurd of the art scene. At 575 Broadway, the Guggenheim's downtown branch, the **Guggenheim Museum SoHo** (423-3500), fills two spacious floors of a historic 19th-century building with selections from the museum's permanent collection, extensions of Uptown exhibitions, or independent shows. (See **Museums,** p. 231.)

When the conspicuous consumption begins to tug at your heartstrings, you can browse through SoHo's extensive selection of clothing boutiques, handmade stationers, and home furnishing stores. SoHo possesses a large number of **designer boutiques.** Caution: these aren't bargain designer boutiques. However, you can find deals at the district's vintage clothing stores and streetside stands. Some sales even allow those designer duds to come just within your reach. Be sure to check out the daily **"fair"** that sets up shop on a lot on Wooster at Spring St. The bargain hunt continues on Broadway with a wide selection of used clothing stores. Flea market devotees should check out the outdoor **Antiques Fair and Collectibles Market** (682-2000; open Sa-Su 9am-5pm), held year-round, hosting some 50-100 vendors on the corner of Broadway and Grand St.

GREENWICH VILLAGE

*Subway: To **West Village,** take A, C, E to W. 4th St. or 8th St.; or #1, 9 to Christopher St./ Sheridan Sq. or 14th St. To **East Village,** take #6 to Astor Pl. To **Central Village,** take N, R to 8th St.*

Greenwich Village, the area between Chelsea and SoHo on the lower West Side, has emerged from a relentless process of cultural ferment that has layered grime, activism, and artistry atop a tangle of quaint, meandering streets. In this counter-cultural capital of the East Coast, transgressions are a way of life, and very little—neither dyed hair, nor pierced foreheads, nor the rantings of Washington Square Park's soapbox prophets—seems to faze weathered "Villagers." As alternative living bleeds into the mainstream, Greenwich Village has settled into the inevitable, comfortable maturity of iconoclasm. These bustling streets take the shocking and offbeat in stride.

The area, once covered in farms and hills, developed in the mid-19th century into a staid high society playground that fostered literary creativity. Herman Melville and James Fenimore Cooper wrote American masterworks here, and Mark Twain and Willa Cather regarded the U.S. heartland from their adopted homes near Washington Square. Henry James captured the debonair spirit of his stately Village in his aptly named novel *Washington Square*.

Real estate values plummeted at the turn of the century as German, Irish, and Italian immigrants found work in the industries along the Hudson River and in pockets of the Village. Cheaper rents prompted more marginal characters to set up shop and do their own thing: John Reed, John Dos Passos, e.e. cummings, and James Agee came here to begin their writing careers in relative obscurity. The Beat movement crystallized in the Village in the 1950s, and the 1960s saw the growth of a homosexual community around Christopher St.

The Village's nonconformist ethos felt the world's intrusion in the late 60s. Violent clashes between police and homosexuals resulted in the Stonewall Riots of 1969, a powerful moment of awakening in the gay rights movement. In the 1970s the punk scene exploded and added mohawked and be-spiked rockers to the Village's diverse cast of characters. The 1980s saw the beginnings of the gentrification process that has continued through the 1990s and has made the Village a fashionable and comfortable settlement for those wealthier New Yorkers with a bit more spunk than their Uptown counterparts.

Today "the Village" primarily refers to the West Village (from Broadway west to the Hudson River), while the area east of Broadway is called the "East Village." With rising rents and the truly marginal heading eastward or to Brooklyn, many would argue that true "Village" life has shifted eastward. Still, in Greenwich Village, no matter what the hour, there's always a good time going on somewhere. If nothing else, there are few areas in the city so prime for people-watching. The Village comes out in all of its (non)traditional glory for the wild Village **Halloween Parade.** This is your chance to see people dressed as toilets or condoms. Slap on your own wig, strap on your appendage of choice, and join the crowd—no one will blink a rhinestoned eyelash.

WASHINGTON SQUARE PARK AREA

> I know not whether it is owing to the tenderness of early associations, but
> this portion of New York appears to many persons the most delectable.
> —Henry James, *Washington Square*

Washington Square Park has stood at the center of Village life for most of this century. Native Americans once inhabited the marshland here, and by the mid-17th century it had become home for black slaves freed by the Dutch. The latter half of the 18th century saw the area converted into a potter's field for the burial of the poor and unknown (around 15,000 bodies lie buried here) and then as a hanging-grounds during the Revolutionary War (people swung from trees that still stand today). In the 1820s the area metamorphosed into a park and parade ground. Soon, high-toned residences made the area the center of New York's social scene.

NEIGHBORHOODS

In the late 1970s and early 1980s, Washington Square Park became a base for low-level drug dealers, and subsequently a rough scene grew up in the area. The mid-80s saw a noisy clean-up campaign that has made the park fairly safe, though its drug traffic has not altogether vanished. After $900,000 worth of renovations completed in 1995, the park today hosts musicians, misunderstood teenagers, muttering drug dealers, sleeping homeless people, and romping children.

At the north end of Washington Square Park and the south end of Fifth Ave. stands the stolid **Washington Memorial Arch,** built in 1889 to commemorate the centennial of Washington's inauguration. Until 1964, Fifth Ave. actually ran through the arch; residents, however, complained of the noisy traffic and the city truncated the most esteemed of avenues.

The fountain in the center of the park provides an amphitheater for comics and musicians of disparate talent. In the southwest corner of the park, a dozen perpetual games of chess wind their ways toward inevitable checkmate while circles of youths engage in hours of hacky-sacking. The park also hosts bocce courts at its southern end where older men and a few upstarts compete for their honor. Like many of the city's public areas, the park turns seedier after sunset, when the drug merchants set up shop in and around the area.

Any tale of this area would not be complete without a stanza about the park's scholarly sister—**New York University.** The country's largest private university and one of the city's biggest landowners (along with the municipal government, the Catholic Church, and Columbia University), NYU is most notable for hip students, top-of-the-line communications and film departments, historic buildings, and some of the least appealing contemporary architecture in the Village. Many desperately functional-looking buildings around the Square proudly display the flaming purple NYU flag. The **NYU Admissions Office,** 22 Washington Sq. North (998-4500), offers tours of the campus (M-F 11am and 2:30pm).

Meanwhile, the north side of the park, called the **Row,** showcases some of the most elegant architecture in the city. Built largely in the 1830s, this stretch of stately Federal-style brick residences soon became an urban center populated by 19th-century professionals, dandies, and novelists. **Number 18,** now demolished, housed Henry James's grandmother and provided the setting for his novel *Washington Square.* Farther west at 29 Washington Square West stands the home in which Eleanor Roosevelt lived in the years after her husband's death. Nowadays, the Row belongs mostly to NYU administration.

The area directly south of Washington Square Park, from W. 4th St. to Houston St., may be the most heavily touristed area of the Village, since it bears the bulk of famous clubs, cafes, and bars. On MacDougal St., Sullivan St., Thompson St., and Bleecker St., one could spend weeks sipping cappuccinos, flipping through records, going to small clubs, and generally emulating bohemia. Just south of the park, at 133 MacDougal St. (info. 998-5801), the Provincetown Playhouse, joined by the young Eugene O'Neill in 1916, declares its notable presence. Farther south on **MacDougal Street** cluster the Village's finest (and most tourist-trampled) coffeehouses (see p. 88). At the intersection of MacDougal and **Bleecker Street** in particular, cafe powerhouses **MacDougal, Le Figaro,** and **Café Borgia** vie for coffee lovers' patronage. Authors Jack Kerouac and Allen Ginsberg once graced Le Figaro and Café Borgia with their Beat presences, howling out poetry with free jazz accompaniment. These sidewalk cafes still provide some of the best coffee and people watching in the city.

Parallel to MacDougal St. is **Sullivan St.,** home to the **Sullivan St. Theater** and the *Fantasticks,* the longest running show in American theater history (see p. 261).

Running perpendicular to both Sullivan and MacDougal, Bleecker St., made famous by Simon and Garfunkel, features a number of jazz clubs and bars. On the corner of Bleecker St. and LaGuardia Pl. stands a Picasso sculpture, proclaimed by the *New York Times* as the ugliest piece of public art in the city. Farther down LaGuardia Pl., a statue of sprightly former mayor and street namesake Fiorello LaGuardia (waving to passersby) appears about to cry out for justice.

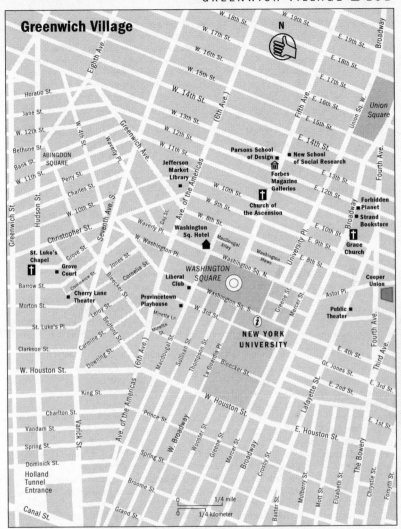

Greenwich Village

N

W. 18th St.
W. 19th St.
W. 17th St.
Eighth Ave.
W. 16th St.
Broadway
E. 19th St.
W. 15th St.
E. 18th St.
W. 14th St.
E. 17th St.
Horatio St.
W. 13th St.
(6th Ave.)
Fifth Ave.
E. 16th St.
Jane St.
W. 12th St.
E. 15th St.
Union
Square
W. 12th St.
W. 11th St.
E. 14th St.
Bethune St.
ABINGDON
SQUARE
Parsons School
of Design
New School
of Social Research
Bank St.
Jefferson
Market
Library
Fourth Ave.
W. 11th St.
Perry St.
Ave. of the Americas
Forbes
Magazine
Galleries
E. 13th St.
Charles St.
W. 10th St.
W. 9th St.
Church of
the Ascension
E. 12th St.
Hudson St.
W. 10th St.
Forbidden
Planet
Broadway
Greenwich St.
Christopher St.
Seventh Ave. S.
Waverly Pl.
Gay St.
W. 8th St.
University Pl.
E. 10th St.
E. 9th St.
Strand
Bookstore
St. Luke's
Chapel
W. Washington Pl.
Washington
Sq. Hotel
MacDougal
Alley
Washington
Mews
E. 8th St.
Grace
Church
Grove St.
Jones St.
Cornelia St.
Washington Sq. N.
Barrow St.
Grove
Court
Commerce St.
Bleecker St.
Liberal
Club
WASHINGTON
SQUARE
Cooper
Union
Cherry Lane
Theater
Provincetown
Playhouse
W. 3rd St.
Greene St.
Mercer St.
Astor Pl.
Public
Theater
Morton St.
Leroy St.
Minetta Ln.
Minetta St.
Washington Sq. S.
St. Luke's Pl.
Bedford St.
Carmine St.
MacDougal St.
Sullivan St.
Thompson St.
La Guardia Pl.
NEW YORK
UNIVERSITY
Fourth Ave.
Third Ave.
Clarkson St.
Downing St.
Bleecker St.
E. 4th St.
W. Houston St.
(6th Ave.)
Gt. Jones St.
E. 3rd St.
King St.
Ave. of the Americas
Varick St.
Prince St.
W. Broadway
Wooster St.
Greene St.
Mercer St.
Broadway
W. Houston St.
E. Houston St.
Lafayette St.
E. 2nd St.
E. 1st St.
Charlton St.
Vandam St.
Spring St.
Prince St.
Crosby St.
The Bowery
Dominick St.
Holland
Tunnel
Entrance
Spring St.
Mulberry St.
Mott St.
Elizabeth St.
Chrystie St.
Forsyth St.
Broome St.
Canal St.
Grand St.
Baxter St.

0   1/4 mile
0   1/4 kilometer

NOHO

The area dubbed "NoHo" (**No**rth of **Ho**uston) includes little more than Broadway between Houston St. and 14th St., in addition to the Washington Square Park environs—but, wow, what a "little."

On the southeast side of the park, where Washington Sq. South meets LaGuardia Pl., you'll find NYU's **Loeb Student Center,** garnished with pieces of scrap metal that purportedly represent birds in flight. The public may use the food court, phones, and bathrooms inside. Across the street looms another rust-colored bulk, the **Elmer Holmes Bobst Library,** designed by architects with the idea of unifying the severely disjointed campus through red-sandstone facades. Unfortunately the money ran out before the project was complete, so NYU opted for the cheap purple flags instead. Farther east, where Washington Sq. South and East meet, presides **NYU Information,** 50 W. 4th St. (998-4636), good for free maps, a quick air-conditioned breather, or answers to NYU-related questions.

Mere steps east of the info center sits **Gould Plaza** in front of NYU's Stern School of Business and the Courant Institute of Mathematical Sciences. A great place to eat lunch or people-watch, the plaza is home to a shiny aluminum Dadaist sculpture by Jean Arp, which bears an uncanny resemblance to a bunny rabbit.

Just around the corner are the **80 Washington Sq. East Galleries** (998-5747), featuring fascinating, exciting, and weird works by students and local pros. Just walk in to see exhibitions of student competitions and thesis projects in a variety of media and styles. The gallery closes at various times during the year to prepare for new exhibitions, so call ahead, but the window spaces always remain visible. A few doors over is the **Grey Art Gallery,** 100 Washington Sq. East (998-6780; www.nyu.edu/greyart), which features more traditional art from late 19th- and 20th-century artists (Suggested contribution $2.50; Tu and Th-F 11am-6pm, W 11am-8pm, Sa 11am-5pm.)

At Green Street and Waverly Place lies NYU's **Brown Building,** the former site of the **Triangle Shirtwaist Company** where a 1911 fire killed most of the primarily female staff—the doors had been chained shut to prevent the workers from taking too many breaks. Although the owners escaped charges of manslaughter and were instead awarded $6445 of insurance money for each victim, the ensuing uproar led to new workplace regulations and a rejuvenated worker safety movement.

A few steps north of the park, on the east side of Fifth Ave., discover **Washington Mews,** a quirky, cobblestoned alleyway. The boxy little brick buildings, originally constructed as stables for the houses facing the park, now house lucky NYU faculty, as well as University language houses. Keep northwards until you reach **8th Street,** with its eclectic mix of shops and stores from **Cassiopia Body Piercing** to **Contempo Casuals.** Here, you can fulfill your every shopping desire, from purchasing whips, leather restraints, and glow-in-the-dark bongs (for the smoking enthusiasts) to outfitting yourself in jeans and platforms. Famous residents have included Jimi Hendrix, whose **Electric Lady Studio** stood at 52 W. 8th St.

Just ahead, see 9th and 10th St., the choice residential rows among many an artist and writer in the 19th and 20th centuries. Mark Twain, author of *The Adventures of Huckleberry Finn* and other American classics, once lived at 14 W. 10th St. Forging north to Fifth Ave. and 11th St. will bring you to the site of the 1970 explosion that had esteemed actor Dustin Hoffman scrambling to save his possessions when next-door neighbors and local radicals, The Weathermen, had a bomb-making mishap at 18 W. 11th St. The townhouse currently at this site has a unique front window designed to commemorate the shape of the explosion.

A few blocks north, on the corner of Fifth Ave. and 12th St. is the eccentric **Forbes Magazine Galleries,** 62 Fifth Ave., home of Malcolm Forbes's vast collection of random objects (see **Museums,** p. 244). Up one more block, off Fifth Ave. lies the **Parsons School of Design,** 2 W. 13th St., with its own public exhibition galleries featuring daring student and professional works. Parsons has recently become one of seven divisions of the **New School,** formerly the New School for Social Research (66 W. 12th St.). Past faculty include John Dewey and W.E.B. DuBois. During World War II, the New School made itself famous by offering positions to European intellectuals fleeing the Nazis; now, it continues its tradition of progressive-minded thinking and even generates the popular Bravo cable show *Inside the Actor's Studio,* hosted by Professor James Lipton.

A few blocks east on 12th St. and Broadway lies **Forbidden Planet,** the science fiction mega-store, purportedly the world's largest. Down the street the famous **Strand** bills itself as the "largest used bookstore in the world." (For both stores, see **Shopping,** p. 304.)

Grace Church, 800 Broadway, between 10th and 11th, was constructed in 1845 using white marble mined by prisoners of the notorious New York State prison Sing Sing. Despite its dark medieval interior and creepy Gothic exterior, the church used to be *the* place for weddings and still holds a lovely Passion of St. Matthew at Easter. It shares its site with an affiliated private grammar and middle school, aptly called the Grace Church School. (Open M-Th 10am-5:30pm, F 10am-3:30pm, Sa noon-4pm, Su open for services only.)

N E I G H B O R H O O D S

Broadway to the south reveals a strange conglomeration of cheap futon stores, "antique" and "vintage" (read: used, yet expensive) clothing outlets, bars, and health food markets that mingle with electronic stores and fast-food joints. Here the styles are usually a few steps behind the truly avant-garde and a few dollars above the truly bohemian. At Broadway and 4th St., you'll find another of the Village's landmarks: **Tower Records,** much more than a chain store, with three floors and hundreds of racks full of music (but no actual records—only CDs and cassettes; see **Shopping,** p. 302). If a star is going to do a PR stint in the Village, it'll be here. At 721 Broadway and Washington Pl., NYU's **Tisch School of the Arts,** named for CBS president and NYU benefactor Larry Tisch, has produced ground-breaking filmmakers Spike Lee and Martin Scorsese, playwright Tony Kushner, and actors Marcia Gay Harden and the up-and-coming Billy Crudup, among others.

WEST OF SIXTH AVENUE

The Greenwich Village of lore lies west of Sixth Ave. Despite rising property prices, the West Village still boasts summer street activity, excellent nightlife, and the haunts of yesterday's bohemia. Street organization is equally unorthodox here—for example, W. 4th St. crosses W. 10th and W. 11th St. Beware of speeding cars desperately trying to negotiate the non-grid of "The Village." The avenues' intrusion into windy, old streets has made for very large intersections; exercise caution or follow the crowds when crossing the streets.

BALDUCCI'S. This legendary Italian grocery has grown over the years from a sidewalk stand to a gourmand's paradise (see **Food and Drink,** p. 115). Balducci's offers an orgy of aromatic cheese barrels, bread loaves, and fresh chilled vegetables. In case the food doesn't pique your interest, or you just can't afford it, you can have a staring contest with the live, bug-eyed lobsters (they'll win, but you can eat them in retaliation). (*422 Sixth Ave. at the northeast corner of the intersection of Sixth Ave. and W. 8th St.*)

JEFFERSON MARKET LIBRARY. This very visible red structure, built as a courthouse in 1874, has detailed brickwork, stained-glass windows, and a turreted clock tower. It occupies the triangle formed by the intersection of W. 10th St., Sixth Ave., and Greenwich Ave. The remarkable structure faced and beat a demolition plot in the early 1960s, and was once voted one of the 10 most beautiful buildings in the country. Carefully restored in 1967, the building reopened as a public library. A pamphlet detailing the history of the site and the restoration can be obtained at the front desk. (*243-4334. 425 Sixth Ave. Open M and Th 10am-6pm, W noon-8pm, F noon-6pm, Sa 10am-5pm.*)

SHERIDAN SQUARE. Rioters against the Civil War draft thronged here in 1863 during some of the darkest days in New York City's history; some protesters brutally murdered hundreds of free blacks. Since then, the area has become much more tolerant, as evidenced by Christopher St.'s large and very visible gay community. This is the territory of the guppie (gay urban professional), though gay males and lesbians from all socio-economic and cultural groups shop and eat here. Particularly in this part of the Village, same-sex couples walk together openly. The area of Christopher St. near Sheridan Sq. has been renamed Stonewall Place, alluding to the **Stonewall Inn,** site of the 1969 police raid that sparked the gay rights movement. A plaque marks the former site of the club at 53 Christopher St.; the bar that resides there now is not that of 30 years ago. Within Sheridan Sq., two sculptures of same-sex couples stand locked in embraces, a tribute to the vibrant gay community. Forlornly single General Sheridan stands nearby, love's looker-on. (*From W. 10th, make a left onto Seventh Ave., and follow it down to the intersection of Seventh Ave., Christopher St., W. 4th St., and Grove St.*)

CHUMLEY'S. This bar and restaurant became a speakeasy in Prohibition days, serving to literary Johns (Dos Passos and Steinbeck), Ernest Hemingway, and Thornton Wilder, among others. As if out of respect for its history of clandestine activity, no sign of any kind indicates that the neglected structure might be a commercial establishment. (*86 Bedford St. between Grove and Barrow St.*)

STAR-CROSSED LOVE. From Hudson St., it's just a few blocks over to the docks along West St., which used to handle a great deal of New York's sea traffic. In the past 10 years, it's handled a different kind of traffic: gay teenagers partying outdoors amidst in-line skaters and cyclists. From the piers, you can see Hoboken across the water, boats lit up at night, and the World Trade Center downtown. If you chill here, beware of holdover hostility from Mayor Giuliani's "quality of life" campaign, which tried to eliminate "delinquents" from these streets.

OTHER SIGHTS. At the western end of Grove St. is the **Church of St. Luke's in the Fields,** 179-485 Hudson St. The third-oldest church in Manhattan, it was named for the once-remote location at which it was built in 1821. Walking up Hudson St. will lead you to the **meat-packing district,** around W. 12th and Gansevoort St., an increasingly trendy area where lofts spring up in old factories, cafes in old garages, and clubs in old stockyards. Off 10th St. and Sixth Ave. you'll see an iron gate and a street sign that reads **"Patchin Place."** The 145-year-old buildings that line the modest path housed writers e.e. cummings, Theodore Dreiser, and Djuna Barnes during their Village sojourns. Near the corner of Commerce St. at 75½ Bedford St. you can find the narrowest building in the Village, measuring 9½ feet across. The writer Edna St. Vincent Millay lived here until 1950. In 1924, Millay founded the **Cherry Lane Theater,** 38 Commerce St. (989-2020), which has showcased Off-Broadway theater (such as Beckett's *Waiting for Godot)* ever since.

EAST VILLAGE

The East Village, the section east of Broadway and north of Houston, was carved out of the Bowery and the Lower East Side as rents in the West Village soared and its residents sought accommodations elsewhere. The eastward movement has recaptured much of the gritty feel of the old Village, and the population here boasts greater diversity than its western neighbor. Older Eastern European immigrants live alongside newer Hispanic and Asian arrivals. East Village residents embody the alternative spectrum, with punks, hippies, ravers, rastas, guppies, goths, beatniks, and virtually every other imaginable group coexisting amidst myriad cafes, bars, clubs, shops, theaters, and community centers. This multicultural compromise has not come easily; many poorer residents of the East Village feel that wealthier newcomers have pushed them out by raising rents. These tensions, however, have forged the East Village into one of the most overtly politicized regions in New York City. Residents here need little coaxing to wax poetic about the protests of the 1960s, the evils of speculating landlords, or their hatred of Mayor Giuliani.

Heterogeneity is not the only hallmark of this area. The East Village also keeps alive a vigorous tradition of creativity in the everyday. Billie Holiday sang here, and more recently, the East Village provided early audiences for Sonic Youth, the Talking Heads, Blondie, and Frank Zappa. The fashion world provides the East Village with its newest art of choice: here lurks style's avant-garde.

ST. MARK'S PLACE. Full of pot-smoking flower children and musicians in the 1960s, the street gave Haight-Ashbury a run for its hashish. In the late 1970s it taught London's Kings Road how to do punk, as mohawked youths hassled passersby from the brownstone steps off Astor Pl. Nowadays, those '60s and '70s youth still line the street—in their old-tattooed-geezer incarnations. In a way, St. Mark's Place resembles a small-town Main Street—a small town with a bad-ass history. People know one another here—sometimes, they even talk to and look after one another. Dark little restaurants and cafes rub elbows with leather boutiques and countless trinket vendors. Though many more-obscure-than-thou types now shun the commercialized and crowded areas of the street, St. Mark's remains the hub of East Village life and *the* place to start your tour of the neighborhood. *(Where E. 8th St. would be, between Third Ave. and Ave. A.)*

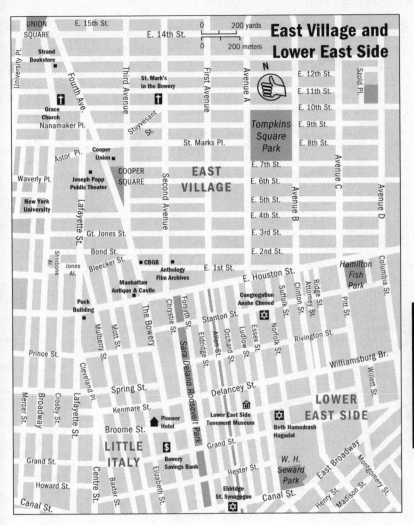

East Village and Lower East Side

ASTOR PLACE. Simultaneously a small road and a large cultural intersection, this western border of the East Village simmers with street life. Check out the ever-popular **Beaver Murals** at the Astor Subway Stop—they pay homage to Astor's prolific fur trade, seen by some Village residents as an exploitation of the Native American population. Upstairs, the subway kiosk, a cast-iron Beaux-Arts beauty, was built—believe it or not—in 1985 as part of a reconstruction of the station. A **large black cube** balanced on its corner, distinguishes Astor Place's position at the junction of Lafayette, Fourth Ave., and E. 8th St. If you and your friends push hard enough the cube will rotate, but may disturb someone sitting or sleeping underneath. "The Cube," or "the Alamo," provides a meeting point for countless rallies, marches, demonstrations, and impromptu performances, as well as for the hordes of prepubescent skaters who converge here at night. (Subway: #6 to Astor Pl.)

COLOR ME GREEN Before the flagships of hipness started moving into the East Village and Alphabet City, abandoned lots full of refrigerators, floorboards, windowpanes, and trashed carberators speckled the area. In 1973, local garden activist Liz Christy began solving the blight in a new way. She and a band that called themselves the "Green Guerrillas" began planting window boxes and tree pits in the area and threw water balloons filled with seeds into the rubbish-strewn lots. In 1974 the Green Guerrillas made the northeast corner of Bowery and Houston St. their project and rented the land from the city for $1 a month. They turned the corner into an urban oasis of serpentine paths bordered by graceful flowers, tall shady trees, and a pond populated with goldfish and turtles. In 1986 the garden was named the **Liz Christy Bowery-Houston Garden** (open year-round Sa noon-4pm; during growing season Tu 6pm-dusk). Recently, the Green Guerrillas and its sister organization, Greenthumb, encountered an even more formidable enemy than rubbish—Mayor Giuliani, whose administration sought to reclaim the lots and sell them. Luckily, Bette Midler has bought these municipal lots in order to preserve the gardens. To find out more about the Green Guerrillas, call 674-8124 or visit their offices at 625 Broadway on the 9th floor.

Other spectacular gardens in the area include:

Sixth Street and Avenue B Garden. This is the mother of all community gardens. The stunning 100 plots, trellises with grapes and raspberry bushes are not even the main attraction here. Edward Boros, a member of the garden, has constructed a 40-foot tower made of wooden slats, plastic carousel horses, and birdcages, all topped by a Puerto Rican flag. This garden is a must-see. Open generally 8am-8pm in summer.

Campos Garden, E. 12th St. between Ave. B and C. Saturnina Rios runs this beautiful space almost singlehandedly. She proudly cultivates pears, peaches, cherries, dates, roses, beans, and tomatos. When her water supply was shut off, Saturnina began carrying jugs and coolers full of water down from her sixth-floor apartment. Open Mar.-Oct. Su 3-5pm and intermittently throughout the week.

El Sol Brillante, 12th St. between Ave. A and B. Welded iron gate conceals lush mounds of hollihocks and other stunning flora.

Tenth Street Garden, 10th St. between Ave. B and C. Gorgeous geraniums, pansies, and lilies. Open M-F 6-8pm, Sa-Su noon-8pm.

Community Garden, Ave. C (Loisaida Ave.), between 8th and 9th St. Rows of chairs and blackberry trees give this nook a definite community feel. Also look for the gardens on 9th St. and Ave. C in this area.

THE COOPER UNION FOUNDATION BUILDING. Peter Cooper, the self-educated industrialist, founded the Cooper Union for the Advancement of Science and Art in 1859, as a tuition-free technical and design school. While other American universities emulated the British university system in their ideals and design, Cooper Union helped to forge a uniquely American approach toward education—as the first college intended for the underprivileged, the first coeducational college, the first racially open college, and the first college to offer free adult-education classes. The school's free lecture series has hosted practically every notable American since the mid-19th century. Both the American Red Cross and the NAACP began here. And if that's not enough history for you—Cooper Union stands as the oldest building in the U.S. to incorporate steel beams (made of old railroad rails). Appropriately enough, Cooper helped pioneer the steel rails that accelerated railroad construction. The second floor **Houghton Gallery** hosts changing exhibits on design and American history, as well as displays of work by the talented and stylish student body, but usually not during the summer. (353-4199. 7 E. 7th St. at Cooper Square in Astor Pl. Houghton Gallery open M-Th 11-7pm.)

THE JOSEPH PAPP PUBLIC THEATER. This grand brownstone structure was constructed by John Jacob Astor in 1853 to serve as the city's first public library.

After its collection moved uptown, the building became headquarters to the Hebrew Immigrant Aid Society, an organization that assisted thousands of poor Jewish immigrants in the early years of this century. In 1967, Joseph Papp's **New York Shakespeare Festival** converted the building. Look for long lines of people waiting for free tickets to **Shakespeare in the Park** (see p. 258).

ST. MARK'S IN THE BOWERY CHURCH. Erected in 1799, St. Mark's Church stands on the site of Peter Stuyvesant's estate chapel. The much-reviled, yet oft-commemorated Dutch governor lies buried here in the small cobblestone grave-yard. Restored in the mid-1970s, but burned in a 1978 fire, the building was repaired to its current state by 1986. "St. Mark's" has a long history of political activism and involvement in the arts. It hosts several community drama compa-nies, including the much-lauded **Ontological Theater,** which pioneered the non-nar-rative wackiness of playwright Richard Foreman and continues to produce some of the better small off-Broadway offerings, as well as the **Danspace Project,** and the **Poetry Project.** Call for info on upcoming events, or check the board outside; you'll need to make reservations for theater tickets and arrive 15 minutes early for the show—otherwise your seats may go to those on the waiting list. *(Church: 674-6377. 131 E. 10th St.* ***Ontological Theater:*** *533-4650.* ***Danspace:*** *674-8194; tickets $10-15.* **Poetry Project:** *674-0910; www.poetryproject.com; events are generally $7, at 8pm.)*

COLONNADE ROW. New York's most famous 19th-century millionaires—John Jacob Astor, Cornelius "Commodore" Vanderbilt, and the Delano family (as in Franklin Delano Roosevelt)— dwelled in three of these four columned houses, built in 1833. There used to exist nine of these houses; the ones that remain, at 428-434 Lafayette St., reflect the wear and tear of time. *(Lafayette and 4th St.)*

THE VILLAGE VOICE. America's largest free newspaper comprehensively lists events and advertises apartments. On Tuesday evenings, house-hunters form an immense line around the block to snatch up the first copies, which land, hot off the presses, at the kiosk in front of the Astor Pl. subway station around 8pm. *(check www.villagevoice.com for listings before they come out on paper.)*

THE SECOND AVE. DELI. This famous Jewish landmark is all that remains of the "Yiddish Rialto," the stretch of Second Ave. between Houston and 14th St. that comprised the Yiddish theater district in the early part of the (gasp) *previous* cen-tury. Stars of David embedded in the sidewalk out front contain the names of some of the actors and actresses who spent their lives entertaining the poor Jewish immigrants of the city. While this community no longer remains the Jewish enclave it once was, the historic deli stands as a loyal mainstay of that past. During the oil crisis of the 1970s, the Deli delivered its orders by horse and buggy. It still serves up the meanest pastrami sandwich in town (see p. 105). In 1996, Abe Lebe-wohl, founder of the deli and leading member of the Lower East Side/East Village community, was murdered as he deposited his daily receipts into his bank account late at night. In his honor the city renamed the small plot of land in front of St. Mark's Church **Abe Lebewohl Park** (at E. 10th St. and Second Ave.).

OTHER SIGHTS. Every Tuesday from 7am to 6pm, Abe Lebewohl Park holds a **Farmer's Market** as part of the **Greenmarket** citywide program to support regional farming. To find out other Greenmarket locations in the city call 477-3220. The **New York Marble Cemeteries,** on Second Ave. between 2nd and 3rd St., and on 2nd St. just east of Second Ave., gave the city its first two non-sectarian graveyards. You can gaze through the fences at the dilapidated tombstones, or just sit by the fence in the shade of the trees. Ukrainian-American life centers on 7th St. with cafés and several churches, the most remarkable of which rests on Taras Sevchenko Pl. (he was the "Ukrainian Shakespeare") near Cooper Sq. East. The dome of the **St. George Ukrainian Catholic Church** looms over iconic and cramped McSorley's bar. The artwork inside, visible only if you stop by Sunday after mass, eclipses even the haunting icons that ornament the outer doors.

- - -

ALPHABET CITY

East of First Ave., south of 14th St., and north of Houston, the avenues give up on numbers and adopt letters. Though the neighborhood may have been brought to you by the letters A, B, C, and D, Alphabet City's resemblance to Sesame Street stops there. The area has traditionally flaunted a thriving drug scene. In its 1960s heyday, Jimi Hendrix and the Fugs would play open-air shows to bright-eyed love children. You'll still find the residences of the East Village's "deadbeatniks" and hard-core anarchists, as well as artists and students. The local population attracts the city's most interesting poetry slams and hipster hangouts, not to mention a plethora of loud bands who have claimed Alphabet City's side streets as rehearsal space. Full of East Villagers just doin' their thang, Alphabet City is only just learning how to welcome tourists. Indeed, this notoriously seedy area has found itself squarely in the path of New York's wave of gentrification, manifest in an increasing numbers of boutiques and chic eateries.

Alphabet City is generally safe during the day. Wandering clumps of revellers, indulging in the addictive nightlife on Ave. A and B, ensure some protection, but use caution east of Ave. B after dark. Meanwhile, extremist activism (and the sometimes brutish reaction of the NYPD) has made the neighborhood chronically ungovernable in the last several years. A few years ago, police officers precipitated a riot when they attempted to forcibly evict a band of the homeless and their supporters in **Tompkins Square Park.** An aspiring video artist recorded scenes of police brutality, setting off a public outcry and further police-inspired violence. The park reopened after a two-year hiatus in the mid-90s, and officials still have high hopes for the formerly needle-ridden area.

Nevertheless, the park still reflects the collective psyche of its environs' churlish misfits. "East Side Anarchists," who hoofed down to Tompkins Square after tearing through St. Mark's Pl., incited one of many riots that erupted in New York City following the Rodney King verdict in 1992. Much to the city's chagrin, several five-foot-tall marijuana plants were found growing in the park in 1997. Officials promptly rooted out such pesky foliage.

Basketball courts and a playground in the northwest section of the park have gained popularity with the younger, less activist East Village set. You can almost always happen upon a soccer pickup game. The **dog run** in the park, a designated area for letting man's best friend romp about, provides marvelous canine-watching. In the summer, you're bound to stumble upon impromptu concerts here.

East of the park, countless memorial **murals** attest to the scars left by the drug war. Many other murals—most of them attributed to local legend "Chico"—colorfully celebrate the neighborhood. Other altruistic projects include the **community gardens** (see **Color Me Green**, p. 156) that bloom next to some of these murals and blasted buildings. At the corner of Ave. B and 2nd St., a fence made of pipes and car parts surrounds Space **2B,** an outdoor gallery and performance space.

For information on current issues and events, check for free local papers at St. Mark's Bookshop and other stores in the area. Neighborhood posters can also let you in on current happenings.

LOWER MIDTOWN
MADISON SQUARE,
UNION SQUARE, AND GRAMERCY PARK

Subway: N, R, or 6 to 23rd St.

Neither coldly commercial nor hotly trendy, lower Midtown is a hidden gem, an area yet to be trampled by most urbanites and tourists. A burgeoning population of young professionals calls this end of Midtown home, as do cafes, restaurants, and clubs that have sprung up in the past 10 years. This neighborhood has also developed into a center for graphic design and publishing.

To escape the roar of the Midtown crowds, walk downtown from the Empire State Building area. Move swiftly along, there's nothing to see where **Andy Warhol's Factory**—studio, production offices, freakhouse—once churned out Pop art with mechanical speed at the now desolate 19 E. 32nd St., between Fifth and Madison. The surrounding neighborhoods, however, have plenty to offer.

CHURCH OF THE TRANSFIGURATION. Better known as "The Little Church Around the Corner." This has been the home parish of New York's theater world ever since a liberal pastor agreed to bury Shakespearean actor George Holland here in 1870, when comic actors were considered low-lifes. The charming Cottage Gothic brick structure features peculiar green roofs, cherub-like gargoyles, and a pleasantly manicured garden out front. Check out the stained-glass windows: they may look like a scene from the Bible, but look again—the vignette is from *Hamlet.* *(29th St., between Fifth and Madison Ave. Open daily 8am-6pm.)*

MADISON SQUARE PARK. Before the park's opening, it was on this site that a game formerly known as "New York ball" was played by a group called the Knickerbockers. This game evolved to become America's "favorite pastime"—baseball. The park opened in 1847 and originally served as a public cemetery. Around it perch statues of famous Civil War generals. Annually a number of ethnic parades and cultural festivals land at the park, including the Pakistani and Filipino Parades. *(Southern end of Madison Ave. Call Parks Dept. for info at 361-8111.)*

NEW YORK LIFE INSURANCE BUILDING. Built by Cass Gilbert (of Woolworth Building fame) in 1928, this multi-tiered structure is topped by a golden pyramid shaped roof. The building is located on the former site of P.T. Barnum's "Hippodrome," which was rebuilt by Stanford White and renamed Madison Square Garden in 1879. It soon became the premier spot for New York's trademark entertainment spectacles. Star architect and man-about-town White was fatally shot here in 1906 by the unstable husband of a former mistress (the story was later fictionalized in E.L. Doctorow's *Ragtime*). *(Northeast of the park; the block between 26th and 27th St. on Madison Ave.)*

APPELLATE DIVISION OF THE SUPREME COURT. As you enter on 25th St., notice the figures representing "Wisdom" and "Force" high above the entrance. After making it past the guards, enter the courtroom to admire the original 1896 murals and to sit in on proceedings. *(Corner of Madison Ave. and 25th St.)*

METROPOLITAN LIFE INSURANCE TOWER. It surveys Madison Sq. Park from 700 ft. above ground. The hideous tower, a 1909 addition to an 1893 building, once made this building a member of New York's the-tallest-building-in-the-world club. The annex on 24th St., connected by a walkway, features an eye-catching neo-Gothic facade. *(Corner of Madison Ave. and 23rd St.)*

69TH REGIMENT ARMORY. Notable only for having hosted the infamous art exhibition in 1913 that brought Picasso, Matisse, and Duchamp to the shores of America. Teddy Roosevelt called these artists "a bunch of lunatics." Today, just the National Guard inhabits the massive eyesore, intentionally designed as a menacing refuge during riots. *(Two blocks east of Madison, on Lexington Ave. at 26th St.)*

FLATIRON BUILDING. Eminently photogenic, this historic site is yet another ex-tallest building. The intersection of Broadway, Fifth Ave., and 23rd St. forced the construction of its dramatic wedge shape. Its triangular shape resulted in stronger winds at its 23rd St. edge. In 1902 the Fuller Building, as it was originally named, was the city's first skyscraper with more than 20 stories to its glory; it was quickly dubbed "flat-iron" because of its resemblance to the clothes-pressing device. (See **Architecture,** p. 10.) *(Located off the southwest corner of Madison Sq. Park.)*

NEIGHBORHOODS

THE THEODORE ROOSEVELT BIRTHPLACE. Until he was 15, Teddy Roosevelt lived in this 1840s brownstone consisting of five elegant period rooms from Teddy's childhood. The free exhibit downstairs offers somewhat of a self-guided tour through the events of the 26th President's life. *(260-1616. 28 E. 20th St., between Broadway and Park Ave. South. Open W-Su 9am-5pm. 30min. guided tours 9am-4pm. $2.)*

GRAMERCY PARK. The gorgeous and gated private park, built in 1831, was the brainchild of Samuel B. Ruggles, a developer fond of greenery. He drained an old marsh and then laid out 66 building lots around the periphery of the central space. Buyers of his lots received keys to enter the private park; for many years, the keys were made of solid gold. Ruggles believed that the park would not only improve the quality of life for residents, but also increase property values and city tax revenues over the years. Over 150 years later, little has changed; the park, with its wide gravel paths, remains the only private park in New York, immaculately kept by its owners. The surrounding real estate is some of the choicest in the city, sporting a European flair often compared to London. Tree-lined sidewalks with conveniently placed stoops offer a breather from the traffic and noise dominating the neighborhoods east and west of the park. With its full-fledged foliage, nearby 19th St. is known as "Block Beautiful" to locals and boasts most of the one-family homes in the neighborhood. *(The foot of Lexington Ave. between 20th and 21st St.)*

THE PLAYERS CLUB. Actor Edwin Booth (brother to Lincoln's assassin) established this club where actors and actresses (then considered social outcasts) could congregate. It boasts of having one of the largest theater collections in the U.S. and an illustrious and exclusive membership. Members have included Mark Twain, Sir Laurence Olivier, Frank Sinatra, Walter Cronkite, and Richard Gere. *(16 Gramercy Park South.)*

THE BROTHERHOOD SYNAGOGUE. Formerly a Friends Meeting House, commissioned in 1859 by the Quakers. They asked the architects to design "an entirely plain, neat, and chaste structure of good taste, but avoiding all useless ornamentation." Sure enough, this building fits the bill. A rock garden outside pays homage to members and friends who died in the Holocaust. Local residents and members are known to meditate in this serene outdoor refuge. *(28 Gramercy Park South.)*

UNION SQUARE. So named because it was a "union" of two main roads, Union Square and the surrounding area sizzled with High Society aristocrats before the Civil War. Early in this century, the name gained dual significance when the neighborhood became a focal point of New York's large Socialist movement, which held its popular May Day celebrations in **Union Square Park.** On August 22, 1927, thousands gathered to protest the execution of alleged bombers and devoted anarchists Sacco and Vanzetti, a demonstration that exploded with police violence. Later, the workers united with everyone else in abandoning the park to drug dealers and derelicts, but in 1989 the city attempted to reclaim it. The park is now pleasant and generally safe, though not pristine; denizens run the gamut from homeless people to sunbathers to pigeons. Check out the sculpture of a mounted George Washington, which is said to be the finest equestrian statue in the country. The scent of herbs and fresh bread wafts through the park, courtesy of the **Union Square Greenmarket,** which makes its home here every Monday, Wednesday, Friday, and Saturday. Farmers, fisherman, and bakers from all over the state and the region come to hawk their fresh produce, jellies, and baked goods. *(Between Broadway and Park Ave. South, and 17th and 14th St. Biggest market days: F and Sa.)*

OTHER SIGHTS. Police Academy Museum, 235 E. 20th St. (477-9753), between Second and Third Ave., located on the second floor of the NYC Police Academy. This museum is open to the public and offers a history of the NYPD (see **Museums,** p. 249). On the east side of the park stands the old Neoclassical American Savings Bank at 20 Union Sq. East. Although designed by Henry Bacon, architect of the Lincoln Memorial in Washington, D.C., the building was never declared a historical landmark. The bank is now the site of the Daryl Roth Theatre, currently home

NEIGHBORHOODS

Lower Midtown

ACCOMMODATIONS

A Chelsea Center Hostel
B YMCA-McBurney
C Chelsea International Hostel
D Chelsea Pines Inn
E Chelsea Inn
F Arlington Hotel
G Hotel Stanford
H Herald Square Hotel
I Hotel Wolcott
J Hotel Grand Union
K Gershwin Hotel
L International Student Hospice
M Murray Hill Inn
N Carlton Arms Hotel
O Hotel 17

N

FDR Dr.

First Ave.

Second Ave.

Third Ave.

Lexington Ave.

Park Ave. S.

Madison Ave.

Fifth Ave.

Broadway

Avenue of the Americas (Sixth Ave.)

Seventh Ave.

Eighth Ave.

Ninth Ave.

Tenth Ave.

Eleventh Ave.

West Side Hwy.

E. 25th St.
E. 24th St.
E. 22nd St.
E. 21st St.
E. 20th St.
E. 14th St.
E. 13th St.
E. 16th St.
E. 15th St.
E. 17th St.
E. 18th St.
E. 19th St.
E. 23rd St.

GRAMERCY PARK

Gramercy Park

Stuyvesant Square

Irving Pl.

Union Square

E. 34th St.
E. 33rd St.
E. 32nd St.
E. 37th St.
E. 36th St.
E. 35th St.
E. 29th St.
E. 28th St.
E. 27th St.
E. 26th St.
E. 31st St.
E. 30th St.

Appellate Division of Supreme Court
Metropolitan Life Insurance Buildings

Church of the Transfiguration

Pierpont Morgan Library

Empire State Building

Madison Square

Flatiron Building

Theodore Roosevelt Birthplace

Forbes Magazine Galleries

Revolution Books

W. 13th St.

Macy's

HERALD SQUARE

Penn Station

Madison Square Garden

General Post Office

Chelsea Park

CHELSEA

St. Peter's

General Theological Seminary

Cushman Row

Hotel Chelsea

Lesbian and Gay Community Center

W. 23rd St.

W. 14th St.

W. 30th St.
W. 29th St.
W. 28th St.
W. 27th St.
W. 26th St.
W. 25th St.
W. 24th St.
W. 22nd St.
W. 21st St.
W. 20th St.
W. 19th St.
W. 18th St.
W. 17th St.
W. 16th St.
W. 15th St.

W. 37th St.
W. 36th St.
W. 35th St.
W. 34th St.
W. 33rd St.
W. 32nd St.
W. 31st St.

yards 0 500 550
meters 0 500

B
C
D
E
F
G
A
Q
N

of the much talked-about De La Guarda, an Argentinian performance art troupe whose show "Villa Villa" is described as a trip to the rain forest, a disco, an air show, and a circus, among other things. Tickets ($40-45) for standing space only are hot and pricey, but a limited number are sold for $20 two hours before each show. *(Call 239-6200 for info.)*

CHELSEA

Chelsea, the neighborhood which extends roughly from Sixth Ave. west to the Hudson River and from 14th to 28th St., is probably best known today for its very visible and vocal gay community. While the gay community of New York may shop for leather and lace on Christopher St., this is where it does its living. Chelsea, especially around **Eighth Avenue,** between 18th and 23rd St., is home to a large number of cafes and restaurants where the clientele consists largely of seriously buff, seriously booted men who dine in couples and then browse the numerous boutiques here for that "one of a kind" fitted white tank top. It's not only the cafes and boutiques, however, that sport the rainbow flag. Chelsea has achieved the enormous feat of normalizing the gay community here by letting the pride flag fly over laundromats, taxi cab dispatch companies, and travel agencies. Many of these local businesses are gay-owned and help to foster the feeling that Chelsea is a community like any other—albeit a bit more colorful than most. The area flaunts its most fabulous colors during **Pride Weekend** (usually the last weekend in June) when car and train loads of men and women pour into this area to celebrate and watch the Gay Pride Parade up Fifth Ave. During this weekend, Chelsea radiates a palpable joy. Indeed, the collective (very well-toned) chest of this area swells with a radiant pride.

Chelsea does not just boast a large gay community, however. Chelsea's checkered locale supports pockets of all sorts of lifestyles and backgrounds. The area boasts a large South and Latin American population; indeed, you'll hear Spanish as often as English. The area harbors residual factories and warehouses from a more industrial era. Hence, the area by the water (Ninth Ave. and higher) retains a gritty, somewhat deserted feel that stands in contrast to the busy sidewalk life of Chelsea's main drag, Eighth Ave.

The industrial spaces, in turn, hold their own surprises in Chelsea. Driven out by exorbitant rents in SoHo, gallery owners and artists in the early 1990s headed north to Chelsea in search of that most precious of New York commodities—(cheaper) space. Street level garages, entire buildings, and old warehouses have subsequently transformed into spacious highbrow **galleries** which butt up against still-functioning commercial firms. The superb galleries around **Tenth** and **Eleventh Avenues** and **22nd Street** house some of the most cutting-edge art in the city. These wide streets eventually reach the water and the **Chelsea Piers** (336-6666), a tremendous sports and entertainment complex which contains possibly the only mini-golf course in Manhattan.

Many of Chelsea's buildings date back to the mid-1800s when Clement Clark Moore (the poet who wrote *'Twas the Night Before Christmas*) owned and developed this area. There are a few exceptional examples of the 19th century architecture. **St. Peter's Church,** 356 W. 20th St., between Eighth and Ninth Ave., the oldest Gothic revival church in the U.S., towers imposingly. An example of Clement Moore's architectural work lives on at **Cushman Row,** 406-418 W. 20th St., a terrace of brownstones, complete with wrought-iron railings. These posh homes face the brick cathedral and the grounds of the **General Theological Seminary,** 125 Ninth Ave. (243-5150), between 20th and 21st St., a grassy oasis that blooms with roses in the summer. If you're lucky, you may catch some aspiring monks playing tennis. The calming, Old World grounds are open to the public. *(M-F noon-3pm, Sa 11am-3pm.)* Take in the wonder of the fancy co-op housing of the **London Terrace Apartments,** spanning an entire block, and a similarly elegant mansion at 414-16 W. 22nd St., also between Ninth and Tenth Ave.

Farther eastward, the historic **Hotel Chelsea,** 222 W. 23rd St. (243-3700), between Seventh and Eighth Ave., has housed and continues to house some of the more interesting American cultural figures. In this cavernous 400-room complex some 150 books have been penned, including works by Arthur C. Clarke, Arthur Miller, William Burroughs, Mark Twain, Eugene O'Neill, Vladimir Nabokov, and Dylan Thomas. Joni Mitchell, John Lennon, and Jasper Johns all called this hotel home at some point in their careers. Yet, despite the hype surrounding the place where Sid killed Nancy, where *9½ Weeks* was filmed, where Robert Mappelthorpe and Patti Smith rented rooms, and where Jimi Hendrix bought his guitars, the hotel is discreet and maintains a charming seediness. Ethan Hawke is rumored to live here periodically, but the doorpeople certainly aren't telling secrets. Every room is unique, with singles starting at $135 and doubles at $165.

Chelsea's **flower district** blooms on 28th St. between Sixth and Seventh Ave. Here wholesale distributors and buyers of flora congregate each morning to stock the city's florists and garden centers. The market turns your average commercial block into a fragrant and stunning oasis.

THE EMPIRE STATE BUILDING

New York impressed me tremendously because, more than any other city in the world, it is the fullest expression of our modern age.

—Leo Trotsky

279-9777; observatory 736-3100. Fifth Ave. and 34th St. at the border between Murray Hill and East Midtown. Subway: N, R to 34th St./Herald Sq.; or B, D, F, Q to 33rd St.; walk east one long block on 33rd or 34th St. to Fifth Ave. **Observatory:** *Open daily 9:30am-midnight, tickets sold until 11:30pm. Admission $6, children under 12 and seniors $3.* **Skyride:** *Open daily 10am-10pm. Admission $11.50, ages 4-12 and seniors $8.50.* **Combination Pass** *$14, children and seniors $9.*

Ever since King Kong first climbed the Empire State Building with his main squeeze in 1933, the world-renowned landmark has attracted scores of view-seeking tourists. Even alien "tourists" chose the landmark as the epicenter of their destruction in *Independence Day.* Completed in 1931, the building has become synonymous with the New York skyline and as integral to the city's image as yellow cabs, bagels, and the Statue of Liberty. Although no longer the tallest building in the world (the Petronas Twin Towers in Malaysia wins) or even the tallest in New York (the Twin Towers have several floors on it), the towering spire still dominates postcards, movies, the cover of a prestigious budget travel guide, and the hearts of city residents.

Built on the site of the original Waldorf and Astoria hotels, the limestone, granite, and stainless-steel-sheathed structure pioneered Art Deco design. Stretching 1454 ft. into the sky and containing 2 mi. of shafts for its 73 elevators, the Empire State was among the first of the truly spectacular skyscrapers. It stands in relative solitude in Midtown, proudly distinguishing itself from the forest of monoliths that has grown up around Wall St. To add to its distinctiveness, the upper 30 floors of the building light up each night in color schemes appropriate to a specific holiday or event (such as red, white, and blue for Independence Day or the Rangers' victory in the 1994 Stanley Cup hockey finals).

The lobby stands as a gleaming shrine to Art Deco interior decorating, right down to its mail drops and elevator doors. Hey, and the Empire State's arcs get the same "textured light" treatment as the Seven Wonders of the Ancient World. Follow arrows on the wall to find the escalator to the concourse level, where you can purchase tickets to the observatory. Note the sign indicating visibility level—a day with perfect visibility offers views for 80 mi. in any direction, but even on a day with a visibility of only 5 mi., one can still spot the Statue of Liberty. Prepare to wait up to an hour during peak visiting times in the summer.

NEIGHBORHOODS

Once atop the main observatory, 1050 ft. above the nearest noisy car, you can venture onto the windswept outdoor walkways or stay in the temperature-controlled interior. Either way, the breathtaking view, particularly at night, will sweep even weary feet off the ground. From this height, the reasons for the Empire State Building's romantic film career seem obvious.

As if the view didn't inspire enough awe, the Empire State tries a little too hard with **New York Skyride,** a simulation of a spaceship journey through the city, narrated by *Star Trek*'s Scotty and peppered with lousy jokes by glasnauseating has-been Yakov Smirnoff.

MURRAY HILL

Below the ruckus of East Midtown lies the sedate residential area **Murray Hill.** Lined with streets of warm brownstones and condominiums, this area is a reminder of a more genteel era when it was once the 'hood of 19th-century "robber barons." With few claims to fame, Murray Hill remains virgin to hard-core tourism, but may be worth a visit to see:

CHURCH OF THE INCARNATION. Built in 1864, the impressive church features stained glass by Tiffany, sculptures by Augustus Saint-Gaudens, and memorials by Daniel Chester French. *(Open M-F from about 11:30am-2pm, but the times vary.)*

PIERPONT MORGAN LIBRARY. In this stunning mansion, the J. Pierpont Morgan clan cultivated the concept of the book as fetish object. With regular art exhibitions and lots of rare collectibles inside, this Renaissance-style *palazzo* warrants a visit (see **Museums,** p. 241). *(685-0610. At 29 E. 36th St. at Madison Ave.)*

WEST MIDTOWN

West Midtown has undergone a bit of a revival. Neon signs and gilt window frames formerly covered with grime have renewed luster. Big companies have snatched up and renovated the old Broadway theaters, now showcasing their shiny marble stairways between 31st and 59th St. on the West Side. Still, this neighborhood has mercifully retained its own gritty character amidst the whirlwind of gentrification. West Midtown, at least for now, offers a break from the ritzy boutiques and many of the corporate multinationals that clutter East Midtown. You can find many inexpensive eateries, countless hotels, and the same old peep shows in this, the setting of *Midnight Cowboy*. Gawk as Broadway lights splash the dingy canvas of old warehouses and steamy streets, and shuffle through the West Side.

HERALD SQUARE AREA AND THE GARMENT DISTRICT

Subway: #1, 2, 3, 9 to Penn Station; A, C, E to 34th/Eighth Ave.; N, R to 34th St.; or B, D, F, Q to 33rd St.

PENNSYLVANIA STATION. This less-than-engrossing architectural offering serves as a metaphor for West Midtown in its entirety. The interior of Penn Station has been refurbished over the past few years; curved metal panels have replaced ceiling tiles covered with dripping limestone stalagmites, and antiseptic French bakeries vending rosemary bread have replaced truant-officer-filled videogame arcades. The original Penn Station, a classical marble building modeled on the Roman baths of Caracalla, was demolished in the 1960s in favor of the more practical space it made for itself 50 feet below. The railway tracks leading in and out of the station were covered with **Madison Square Garden,** New York's premier entertainment complex hosting a wide array of top acts, including the Knicks, the Rangers, and the paternal Michael Jackson. Behind-the-scenes tours of the complex, including glimpses of the locker rooms and luxury boxes, are offered daily (see **Sightseeing Tours,** p. 126). *(Located on the corner of 33rd St. and Seventh Ave.)*

ALL LIT UP One foggy night in 1945, a U.S. Army B-25 bomber crashed into the 78th and 79th floors of the Empire State Building, shooting flames hundreds of feet in the air. **Burning debris** hurled for blocks, although the steel frame swayed less than 2 in. Fourteen people lost their lives in the **bizarre accident,** but many survived thanks to New York Fire Department heroes, such as John Coletti of the 34th St. Hook and Ladder. Mind you, this was not the skyscraper's first brush with aeronautical mayhem. Its tower, originally intended as a mooring mast for airships, docked two blimps there in 1931 and, in the same year, King Kong, the **giant ape,** fought army planes from atop the famous tower.

THE JAMES A. FARLEY BUILDING. New York's immense main post office faces Madison Square Garden. Completed in 1913, the broad portico of the monumental Neoclassical building bears the motto of the U.S. Postal Service: "Neither snow nor rain nor heat nor gloom of night stays these couriers from the swift completion of their appointed rounds." During business hours, one can see the small poster of mugshots and fingerprints of the real-life "America's Most Wanted," or look around its one-room **Post Office Museum** that proudly displays such items as postal clerk ties, scales, and hats of decades past. *(421 Eighth Ave.)*

MACY'S. This titan of materialism, which occupies a full city block, recently relinquished its title as the "World's Largest Department Store" and changed its billing to the "World's Finest Department Store" when a new store in Germany was built one square foot larger. With 10 floors and some two million square feet of merchandise, Macy's has come a long way from its beginnings in 1857, when it grossed $11.06 on its first day of business. No longer in its top form as seen in *Miracle on 34th St.*, the store retains some touches of old; check out the wooden escalators on the higher floors. The store sponsors the **Macy's Thanksgiving Day Parade,** a New York tradition buoyed by helium-filled 10-story Snoopies and Barneys, as well as marching bands, floats, and general hoopla. Santa Claus glides by last in the parade, heralding the arrival of the Christmas shopping season and thereby bringing joy to kids (and merchants) everywhere. Other annual Macy sponsored events include the 4th of July fireworks extravaganza on the East River and "Tapamania," when hundreds of tap-dancers cut loose on the sidewalks of 34th St. in late August (call 695-4400 for info). Farther east along 34th St. are hundreds of **discount stores** where you can buy miscellany to your heart's content, amidst many other budget-hungry shoppers (see **Shopping,** p. 296). *(151 W. 34th St. between Broadway and 7th Ave.)*

GARMENT DISTRICT. The Garment District gained its name by once housing the bulk of the city's often inhumane clothing manufacturers. Today a small statue named *The Garment Worker*, depicting an aged man huddled over a sewing machine, sits near the corner of 39th St. to commemorate the formative era. There are still plenty of inexpensive wholesale and retail fabric, jewelry, clothing, and leather stores. *(Seventh Ave.–a.k.a. "Fashion Ave."–from 34th to 42nd St.)*

HERALD SQUARE. A bronze statue of Minerva presides over a bevy of bellringers at the center of a small asphalt triangle and park benches, offering you a break from a weary day of shopping. *(Convergence of Broadway and Sixth Ave. on 34th St.)*

TIMES SQUARE AND THE THEATER DISTRICT

You can find the Big Apple's, er, core in Times Square. At 42nd St., Seventh Ave., and Broadway, the city offers up one of the largest electronic extravaganzas in the world. In the past, admiring visitors remained completely oblivious as petty thieves stole their wallets. Indeed, Times Square may have given New York its reputation as a dark metropolis covered with strip clubs, neon, and filth, which has frightened away so many would-be tourists and residents.

NEIGHBORHOODS

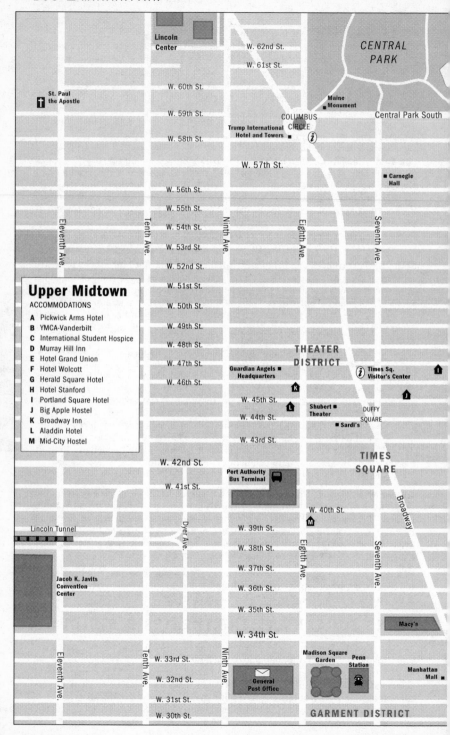

Lincoln Center

W. 62nd St.

W. 61st St.

CENTRAL PARK

W. 60th St.

W. 59th St.

St. Paul the Apostle

W. 58th St.

Maine Monument

Central Park South

COLUMBUS CIRCLE

Trump International Hotel and Towers ■

W. 57th St.

■ Carnegie Hall

W. 56th St.

W. 55th St.

W. 54th St.

W. 53rd St.

W. 52nd St.

W. 51st St.

W. 50th St.

Eleventh Ave.

Tenth Ave.

Ninth Ave.

Eighth Ave.

Seventh Ave.

Upper Midtown
ACCOMMODATIONS

A Pickwick Arms Hotel
B YMCA-Vanderbilt
C International Student Hospice
D Murray Hill Inn
E Hotel Grand Union
F Hotel Wolcott
G Herald Square Hotel
H Hotel Stanford
I Portland Square Hotel
J Big Apple Hostel
K Broadway Inn
L Aladdin Hotel
M Mid-City Hostel

W. 49th St.

W. 48th St.

W. 47th St.

W. 46th St.

THEATER DISTRICT

Guardian Angels ■ Headquarters

Times Sq. Visitor's Center

W. 45th St.

W. 44th St.

Shubert ■ Theater

DUFFY SQUARE

■ Sardi's

W. 43rd St.

TIMES SQUARE

W. 42nd St.

W. 41st St.

Port Authority Bus Terminal

Broadway

Lincoln Tunnel

Dyer Ave.

W. 40th St.

W. 39th St.

W. 38th St.

W. 37th St.

Jacob K. Javits Convention Center

W. 36th St.

Eighth Ave.

Seventh Ave.

W. 35th St.

W. 34th St.

Macy's

Eleventh Ave.

Tenth Ave.

W. 33rd St.

W. 32nd St.

Ninth Ave.

Madison Square Garden

Penn Station

Manhattan Mall ■

General Post Office

W. 31st St.

W. 30th St.

GARMENT DISTRICT

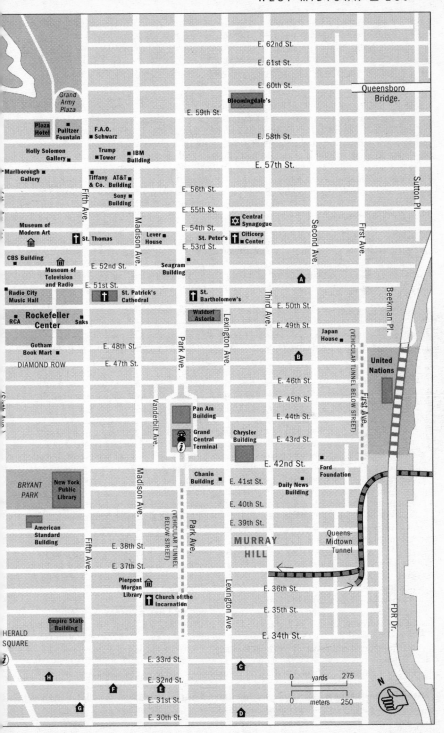

Grand Army Plaza

Queensboro Bridge.

E. 62nd St.

E. 61st St.

E. 60th St.

Bloomingdale's

E. 59th St.

Plaza Hotel

Pulitzer Fountain

F.A.O. Schwarz

E. 58th St.

Holly Solomon Gallery

Trump Tower

IBM Building

E. 57th St.

Marlborough Gallery

Tiffany & Co.

AT&T Building

E. 56th St.

Sony Building

E. 55th St.

Museum of Modern Art

St. Thomas

Lever House

E. 54th St.

Central Synagogue

St. Peter's

Citicorp Center

E. 53rd St.

CBS Building

Museum of Television and Radio

E. 52nd St.

Seagram Building

Radio City Music Hall

E. 51st St.

St. Patrick's Cathedral

St. Bartholomew's

Rockefeller Center

RCA

Saks

Waldorf Astoria

E. 50th St.

E. 49th St.

Japan House

United Nations

Gotham Book Mart

E. 48th St.

DIAMOND ROW

E. 47th St.

E. 46th St.

E. 45th St.

Pan Am Building

E. 44th St.

Grand Central Terminal

Chrysler Building

E. 43rd St.

E. 42nd St.

Ford Foundation

BRYANT PARK

New York Public Library

Chanin Building

E. 41st St.

Daily News Building

E. 40th St.

E. 39th St.

American Standard Building

MURRAY HILL

Queens-Midtown Tunnel

E. 38th St.

E. 37th St.

Pierpont Morgan Library

E. 36th St.

Church of the Incarnation

E. 35th St.

Empire State Building

E. 34th St.

HERALD SQUARE

E. 33rd St.

E. 32nd St.

E. 31st St.

E. 30th St.

Fifth Ave.

Madison Ave.

Park Ave.

Vanderbilt Ave.

Lexington Ave.

Third Ave.

Second Ave.

First Ave.

Sutton Pl.

Beekman Pl.

FDR Dr.

(VEHICULAR TUNNEL BELOW STREET)

0 yards 275

0 meters 250

N

A

B

C

D

E

F

G

H

Perhaps after a few too many people saw *Blade Runner*, the Square's laces straightened and image improved. The prime mover in this effort at urban renewal has been the Times Square Business Improvement District (BID), which began operations in 1992, funded by area residents and businesses. The BID began by putting 50 cherry-red-jumpsuited sanitation workers on the streets daily, along with 40 public safety officers. According to the Mayor's Sanitation Scorecard, the cleanliness of sidewalks nearly doubled in a year (*Let's Go* doesn't know how Rudy determined this "Sanitation Scorecard"). Robberies, purse snatchings, and the number of porn shops in the area all shot down. Large companies helped the campaign by inventing a brilliant yet succinct slogan, "New 42." The completion of Disney's entertainment complex in and around the New Amsterdam Theater, once home to the Ziegfeld Follies, has brought us a pink-and-gold wonderland in which you may see the Tony Award-winning musical, the *Lion King*. Across the street, Madame Tussaud's and AMC united to rebuild the Liberty, Empire, and Harris theaters into a wax museum and 29-screen movie megaplex. The historic Victory Theater, where Abbot met Costello and Houdini made an elephant disappear, is now the eerily Orwellian "New Victory" Theater.

Still, Times Square has not strayed *too* far from its decadent past. A recent city ordinance required new offices to cover their facades with electronic and neon glitz, which would explain the enormous stock ticker atop the Morgan Stanley building. Teens continue to roam about in search of fake IDs and, as ever, hustlers cheat suckers. One-and-a-half million people pass through Times Square every day. Theater-goers, tourists, and wanderers crowd the streets well into the night. Be sure to stop by the new **Visitors Center** (see p. 74), which offers a multitude of tourist services and two-hour walking tours of the area.

Just west of Times Square, at 229 W. 43rd St., are the offices of **The New York Times** (556-1600), founded in 1851, for which the square was named in 1904 (the *Times* then inhabited One Times Square—the big, triangular building at the head of the Square). A short trip south down Eighth Ave. to 41st St. brings you to the multi-storied **Port Authority Bus Terminal,** the departure point for an army of buses. Despite a high-profile police presence, this area and the terminal itself are a little seedier than the area north of 42nd St. and can be dangerous, especially at night: Stay on the major streets and try not to look like a tourist.

Theater Row, a block of renovated Broadway theaters, occupies 42nd St. between Ninth and Tenth Ave. The nearby **Theater District** stretches from 41st to 57th St. along Broadway, Eighth Ave., and the streets that connect them. Some of the theaters have been converted into movie houses or simply left to rot as the cost of live productions has skyrocketed. Approximately 40 theaters remain active (most of them grouped around 45th St.), 22 of which have been declared historical landmarks (see p. 257). **Shubert Alley,** originally built as a fire exit between the Booth and Shubert Theaters, now serves as a private street for pedestrians (a half-block west of Broadway between 44th and 45th St.). After shows, fans often hover at stage doors to get their playbills signed.

The **Dramatists Guild,** 1501 Broadway, suite 701 (398-9366; fax 944-0420), protects the playwrights, composers, and lyricists behind the scenes of every show. Members of the guild include luminaries Stephen Sondheim, Peter Stone, and Mary Rodgers. According to their charter, "producers, directors, agents, students, academicians, and patrons of the arts" can all become members for $50 per year. Autograph hunters prowl outside.

A few blocks uptown and to the west you will find **Hell's Kitchen** (see below), a blend of warehouses, piers, thimble-sized apartments, and theater overflow. This once crime-ridden area becomes more gentrified every day. 46th Street epitomizes the area's cultural ferment, with its **Restaurant Row** (see p. 124).

Up several blocks from the Times Square area, at 130 W. 55th St. between Sixth and Seventh Ave., **City Center Theater** replaced a mosque in 1943. Sickles and crescents still adorn each doorway, four tiny windows face Mecca (or at least the East Side) from the limestone upper stories, and a Moorish dome caps the roof. Venture inside the lobby to see the elaborate tile mosaics that surround the elevators.

This neighborhood's theatricality extends beyond the walls of its venues, however, with world-renowned ads plastering skyscrapers. Marky Mark dropped his drawers before millions for Calvin Klein, Dave Letterman broadcast segments of his show on the Sony Jumbotron, and several superheroes have hurtled into the spiraling neon Coca Cola advertisement. You'll feel a part of something extraordinary just walking the streets of the Great White Way.

CARNEGIE HALL. How do you get to Carnegie Hall? Practice, practice, practice. Carnegie Hall established in 1891, remains New York's foremost soundstage. In its illustrious career, it has hosted Tchaikovsky, Caruso, Toscanini, and Bernstein; Dizzy Gillespie, Ella Fitzgerald, and Charlie Parker; the Beatles and the Rolling Stones. Other notable events from Carnegie's playlist include the world premiere of Dvorak's Symphony No. 9 *(From the New World)* on December 16, 1893, Winston Churchill's landmark lecture *The Boer War as I Saw It* in 1901, an energetic lecture by Albert Einstein in 1934, and Martin Luther King, Jr.'s last public speech on February 28, 1968.

In the 1950s, a large office building nearly replaced Carnegie Hall, which seemed afflicted with the same "Great Music Hall Syndrome" as Radio City. Outraged citizens halted the impending demolition through special state legislation in 1960. In 1985, in commemoration of the 25th anniversary of the rescue, a $50-million restoration and renovation program gave the worn exterior a face-lift, enlarged the street-level lobby, and modernized the backstage. The stage ceiling, which had suffered during the filming of *Carnegie Hall* in 1946, was finally repaired. Legend has it that, before it was repaired, the hole in the ceiling gave Carnegie Hall better-than-perfect acoustics. Carnegie Hall's **museum** displays artifacts and memorabilia. *(903-9790. 57th St. and Seventh Ave. Subway: N, R to 57th St./Seventh Ave. Tours M-Tu and Th-F at 11:30am, 2, and 3pm. $6, students and seniors $5, under 12 $3. No tours in summer. Museum open summer M-F 11am-4:30pm, limited hours in winter. Free.)*

HELL'S KITCHEN

The **Jacob K. Javits Convention Center** (along Twelfth Ave. between 34th and 38th St.) hosts some of the grandest-scale events in the world, including international boat, car, and motorcycle shows, (see **Calendar,** p. 21), as well as a millennium extravaganza that ushers in 2000 with a plethora of bankable stars (see **Y? 2K!,** p. 2). The convention center sits at the beginning of Hell's Kitchen, the neighborhood that fostered the "Westies"—the gangs that inspired Leonard Bernstein's 1957 *West Side Story* and Marvel Comic's crimefighter Daredevil.

Hell's Kitchen (west of Ninth Ave. between 34th and 59th St.) was until recently a violent area inhabited by immigrant gangs with misleading names such as "Battle Row Annie's Ladies' Social and Athletic Club." Indeed, the area once ranked among the most dangerous areas in North America; policemen would only patrol it in groups of four or more. As the story goes, the area was named during a conversation among a group of these policemen. After a particularly brutal night, one officer told the others, "We truly are in hell's kitchen." Bernstein's Sharks and Jets sparked a brief trend of local gangs in fact dancing (perhaps a predecessor to breakdancing?).

After two children were killed by crossfire in 1959, fed-up locals tried to improve the area's reputation by renaming it **Clinton,** which, as historical irony would have it, is now an equally loaded term. With the decline of ocean travel in the 1950s and 1960s, most area docks were abandoned, and much of the housing in Hell's Kitchen was razed to build Lincoln Center and related projects. In recent years, a heterogeneous population has soaked Ninth and Tenth Avenue with restaurants, delis, and pubs; because of a recent economic upswing, the neighborhood has become one of New York's best areas for inexpensive ethnic food. The low-slung Gothic brownstone **Church of St. Paul the Apostle** (entrance on Ninth Ave.) sits placidly amid the action at 415 W. 59th St., between Ninth and Tenth Ave. A high-relief atop a sky-blue mosaic is perched above an impressive front door of carved wood, and dioramas of Christ's Passion flank the interior. Although it resembles a wishing well, be sure not to toss coins into the Baptismal Font just inside the entrance.

Student protests over tuition hikes culminated in a two-week takeover of CUNY's **John Jay College of Criminal Justice,** 899 Tenth Ave. at 58th St., in May 1990. The turmoil ended in a violent reinstatement of power by administration officials. Renovations have given the 1903 neo-Victorian building, formerly the DeWitt Clinton High School (attended by Calvin Klein), a postmodern atrium and extension.

EAST MIDTOWN

Subway: #6 to 59th St., 52nd St., or Grand Central Station.

East of Sixth Ave., from about 34th St. to 59th St., lies the bulk of East Midtown. Many tourists envision the Big Apple this way: Gucci boots and businessmen swapping loot. Here, buildings are judged by their proximity to the heavens, hotels by the size of their chandeliers, and people by the size of their credit ratings. Many tourists envision East Midtown's posh Fifth Ave., legendary 42nd St., or skyscrapers containing innumerable financiers, as epitomizing the city as a whole. Here, *Let's Go* hopes to demystify the area immortalized in *Breakfast at Tiffany's*, so that you may explore its streets with all the nonchalance of Holly Golightly.

42ND STREET

Subway: B, D, F, Q or #7 to 42nd St./Ave. of the Americas (Sixth Ave.); or #7 to 42nd and Fifth Ave.; or #4, 5, 6, 7, or S to Grand Central Station at 42nd St. and Park Ave.

NEW YORK PUBLIC LIBRARY. On sunny afternoons, throngs of people recline on the NYPL's marble steps. Featured in the hit 80s film *Ghostbusters*, two marble lions, Patience and Fortitude, dutifully guard the library from goblins. The city library's grandeur should remind any visitor that these folks take reading seriously. Unfortunately, this particular branch is solely for research purposes—you're better off across the street at the Mid-Manhattan branch for reading material (see p. 10). *(869-8089 for exhibitions and events. 42nd St. and Fifth Ave. Open M and Th-Sa 10am-6pm, Tu-W 11am-7:30pm. Free tours Tu-Sa at 11am and 2pm, leaving from the Friends Desk in Astor Hall.)*

BRYANT PARK. Spreading out against the back of the library along 42nd St. to Sixth Ave., this park set the stage for the 1853 World's Fair. Recent renovations make it a tremendously welcome break from the asphalt and steel in every direction. In the afternoon, people crowd into the grassy, tree-rimmed expanse to talk, relax, and sunbathe. The stage that sits at the head of the park's open field plays host to a variety of free cultural events throughout the summer, including screenings of classic films, jazz concerts, and live comedy. *(Park open 7am-9pm. Call the New York Convention and Visitors Bureau at 484-1222 or 517-5700 for a schedule of events.)*

GRAND CENTRAL TERMINAL. Grand Central was once the main transportation hub for visitors and commuting New Yorkers. While today its importance has been partially eclipsed by Penn Station and the airports, Grand Central is still an amazing sight. The spacious and dazzling "lobby" or Main Concourse has been known to add a little spice to the drudgery of commuting; occasional jazz and classical amateur musicians and innovative art exhibits are featured throughout the year. Jutting out from the Main Concourse, store-filled arcades snake their way underground to many of the surrounding buildings. *(East of the library and Bryant Park, on 42nd St. between Madison and Lexington Ave., where Park Ave. should be.)*

PAN AM BUILDING. Growing out of the back of Grand Central, this blue monolith looms over most of 44th and 45th St. The 59-story structure slices Park Ave. in half, much to the chagrin of many a New Yorker. Although the once-familiar Pan Am logo atop the building has been replaced by that of Met Life, the skyscraper retains its old name and vaguely aerodynamic shape. The largest commercial

N E I G H B O R H O O D S

office space ever built, the Pan Am building contains 2.4 million sq. ft. of corporate cubicles, swankier stores than Grand Central, pink rather than white marble, and a nice but unfortunately benchless atrium. Deep inside the lobby, right above the escalators, hangs an immense red-and-white Josef Albers mural.

THE CHRYSLER BUILDING. Another familiar notch in the Midtown skyline is the Empire State Building's smaller, more attractive Art Deco cousin. A spire influenced by radiator grille design tops this palace of industry—one of many details meant to evoke the romance of the automobile in the Chrysler Automobile Company's "Golden Age." Other monuments to motoring include a frieze of idealized cars in white and gray brick on the 26th floor, flared gargoyles near the top styled after 1929 hood ornaments and hubcaps, and stylized lightning-bolt designs symbolizing the energy of the new machine. During construction in 1929, the Chrysler Building engaged in a race with the Bank of Manhattan building for the title of the world's tallest structure. Work on the bank stopped when it appeared to have won. With capitalist ingenuity, devious Chrysler machinists then brought out and added the spire that had been secretly assembled inside. This elegant building stood as the world's tallest until the Empire State topped it two years later. While many consider it to be the most eye-pleasing in New York, it ruined architect William Van Alen's career. Chrysler, unsatisfied with the final product, accused Alen of bribery and refused to pay him. *(42nd St. and Lexington Ave.)*

TUDOR PARK. Near the Chrysler, between 42nd and 43rd St. on Tudor Pl., this shady park offers an ideal refuge from sizing up local architecture. The park's gravel paths, metal benches, ornate fence, and outsized oaks—congregating in a refreshingly uncluttered silence—lend a European charm to this grassy nook. Down a flight of curved stairs from Tudor Park lies **Ralph J. Bunche Park,** right in front of the United Nations. A tall sculpture, ivy-covered walls, and carved faces grace this small area. *(Tudor Park open daily 7am-11pm.)*

THE UNITED NATIONS BUILDING. Though located along what would be New York's First Ave. between 42nd and 48th St., this area is international territory and thus not subject to the laws and jurisdiction of the U.S.—as evinced by the 184 flags flying outside at equal height, in violation of American custom. An understated skyscraper and expansive lobby compose the bulk of the spot. Outside, a rose garden and a statuary park provide a lovely view of the East River (and a rather un-lovely one of Queens). Note the statue depicting a muscle-bound man beating a sword into a plowshare. The buff Socialist was a 1959 gift of the former U.S.S.R. The only way to view the imposing **General Assembly** is by the guided tour which leaves every 15min. from the U.N. visitor's entrance at First Ave. and 46th St. and is available in 20 languages. *(963-4475; General Assembly 963-7713. Tours $7.50, students $4.50, grades 1-8 $3.50, over 60 $5.50, disabled 20% discount. Children under 5 not admitted on tour. 45min. Tours leave daily 9:15am to 4:45pm.)*

UNICEF HOUSE. Up First Ave. from the U.N., this international organization is devoted to advocacy for children. The **Danny Kaye Visitors Center** opened in July 1994 with exhibits and explanations of UNICEF's mission. Recent displays included an exhibit on children's rights. A gift shop also sells cards and other paraphernalia, with all profits going to the UNICEF Children's Fund.

JAPAN SOCIETY. This is the first example of contemporary Japanese design in New York City. Designer Junzo Yoshimura created a half-Japanese, half-American amalgamation—plainly Western on the outside but completely Asian on the inside. In the spirit of a traditional Japanese home, there is an interior pool garden on the first floor, complete with stones and bamboo trees, while a gallery on the second floor exhibits traditional and contemporary Japanese art. Dedicated to bringing the people of Japan and America closer together, the Society sponsors Japanese language courses, lectures, meetings with notable leaders, a film series, and performances. *(832-1155. 333 E. 47th St. and First Ave. Society open Sept.-June Tu, Th, Sa, Su 11am-6pm, W and F 11am-6:30pm; in May M-F 11am-6pm. Suggested donation $5.)*

NEIGHBORHOODS

LEXINGTON, PARK, AND MADISON AVENUES

Subway: #4,5, 6 to Lexington Ave./42nd St. or 53rd St.

THE WALDORF-ASTORIA HOTEL. The crème de la crème of Park Avenue hotels stands regally at 301 Park Ave. between 49th and 50th St. Cole Porter's piano sits in the front lounge, while a huge chandelier and an actual red carpet greet you as you slink humbly down the hallways. The Duchess of Windsor, King Faisal of Saudi Arabia, and the Emperors Hirohito and Akihito of Japan all stayed here (as have about a million business travelers). Every U.S. President since Hoover has spent a night or two here while away from the White House. The lobby is certainly worth a peek if you have the nerve to venture in, but if you can afford to stay here then you're probably reading the wrong book.

SAINT PETER'S CHURCH. The contemporary and urban church reflects its progressive congregation. Even boasting relaxed sofa pews, this church hosts A.A. meetings, jazz services, Muslim prayer meetings, musical concerts, social groups, lectures, and drama. *(935-2200. 619 Lexington Ave. and 54th St.)*

SONY PLAZA. Sony recently leased out Philip Johnson's postmodern creation, the erstwhile AT&T Building, and renamed it. It now features two massive superstores featuring hands-on interaction with state-of-the-art products and free movie screenings of releases by Sony-owned Columbia. Sony has also answered its charge to provide free education for the children of New York with its new **Sony Wonder** technology lab, a most worthwhile interactive introduction to communications technology. *(833-8830. 530 Madison Ave. between 55th and 56th St. Lab open Tu-Sa 10am-6pm, Su noon-6pm. Free.)*

CITICORP CENTER. The Center stands on four 10-story stilts so as not to crush the temple at its base. The entire structure, sheathed in reflective grayish aluminum, radiates warmly at sunrise and sunset. The distinctive 45° angled roof was originally intended as a solar collector, but this plan never saw the light of day (heh, heh). Instead the roof supports an intriguing gadget, the so-called TMD, or Tuned Mass Damper, which senses and records the tremors of the earth and warns of earthquakes—an important feature for a building on stilts. *(The corner of 53rd St. and Lexington Ave.)*

ST. BARTHOLOMEW'S CHURCH. This Byzantine church draws heavily upon medieval European religious architecture for its inspiration. Completed in 1919, the temple features a large mosaic of the Resurrection. The life-sized marble angel in the devotional area left of the altar has been a favorite of visitors and worshippers for many years. St. Bart's hosts a summer festival of classical music on Sundays at 11am. Outside of the church is Cafe St. Bart's, a lovely, but sinfully expensive, outdoor cafe (entrees $10-22). *(378-0200. Between 50th and 51st St.)*

CENTRAL SYNAGOGUE. In 1870, Henry Fernbach built this, now the oldest continuously operating synagogue in the city. Its Moorish-revival architecture combines a lavish facade of onion domes and intricate trim with an exquisite display of stained glass within. *(652 Lexington Ave. and 55th St.)*

OTHER SIGHTS. The stylish **Madison Lexington Venture Building,** at 135 E. 57th St., is barely eight years old, but has already garnered enormous praise for its novel design. The fountain out front steals the show. Meanwhile, Stonehenge-esque Italian marble columns encircle the fountain, providing a haven from the rigors of your urban journey. On Madison Ave., between 57th and 58th St., sits the **Fuller Building,** once headquarters of the leading construction firm during the Great Depression. Inside, the Fuller contains 12 floors of art galleries (see **Galleries,** p. 253).

ROCKEFELLER CENTER

Subway: B, D, F, Q to 50th St./Sixth Ave.

Between 48th and 51st St. and Fifth and Sixth Ave. stretches Rockefeller Center, a monument to the marriage of business and aesthetics. In the American tradition of "bigger is better," Rockefeller Center is the world's largest privately owned business and entertainment complex, occupying 22 acres of Midtown including a 2-mile-long underground concourse, dozens of restaurants, plaza shops, and other amenities for the few hundred-thousand people who work and play here. Some of its tenants include NBC, the Associated Press, General Electric, and Time Warner.

TOWER PLAZA. The famous gold-leaf statue of Prometheus ("My hand's on fire!") sprawls out on a ledge of the sunken plaza, as pulsing jet streams of water taunt his burning appendage. The plaza, surrounded by over 100 flags of U.N. members, has an overpriced open-air cafe in the spring and summer and the world-famous **ice-skating rink** and sight of the Christmas tree lighting in the winter. In front of the International Building on Fifth Ave., between 50th and 51st St., stands the bronze six-pack totin' **Atlas** upholding the weight of the world with his triceps.

G.E. BUILDING. This 70-story tower on Sixth Ave., once home to RCA, remains the most accomplished artistic creation in this complex. Note the limestone pylons marking the 49th St. entrance and the mural of hulking workers (and, oddly enough, Lincoln) heaving and straining deep inside the lobby. Now, G.E. subsidiary **NBC** has its headquarters here. The network offers an hour-long tour that traces the history of NBC, from their first radio broadcast in 1926 through the heyday of TV programming in the 1950s and 60s. The tour visits the studios of Conan O'Brien and the once infamous 8H studio, home of *Saturday Night Live.* (For information on audience tickets to NBC shows, see **Arts & Entertainment,** p. 263.)

RADIO CITY MUSIC HALL. Due to public outcry this institution escaped demolition in 1979 to receive a complete interior restoration. It still thrives as a multi-program entertainment venue. First opened in 1932, the 5874-seat theater remains the largest in the world. Originally intended as a variety showcase, it ultimately functioned as a movie theater, premiering over 650 feature films between 1933 and 1979, including *King Kong* and *Breakfast at Tiffany's.* Nowadays, Radio City's world-renowned chorus line, the Rockettes, perform in annual extravaganzas, such as "The Christmas Spectacular." Its original elegance should be restored by 2000. *(Corner of Sixth Ave. and 51st St.)*

FIFTH AVENUE

Subway: B, D, F, Q to 50th St./Sixth Ave; or E, F to Fifth Ave; or N, R to 50th St., then walk east 2 blocks; or 1, 9 to 50th St. and walk east 3 blocks.

The section of Fifth Ave. between 42nd and 59th St., once the most desirable residential area among New York's elite, has been taken over by the stores and institutions that originated to serve them. The grand scale of the establishments here and the centrality of Fifth Ave. combine to make this stretch of street arguably the most famous avenue in the U.S. Protesters and celebrators from Gay Pride to Disney choose this thoroughfare for their parade routes, while parading consumers and tourists revel in unsurpassed opportunities for window-shopping. Elaborate stores and boutiques, most catering to the seven-digit crowd, line the streets here. Don't be afraid to go in and poke around—just don't break anything.

THE ALGONQUIN HOTEL. Alexander Woollcott's "Round Table," a regular gathering of the 1920s brightest theatrical and literary luminaries, made this hotel famous. The Algonquin's proximity to the offices of *The New Yorker* attracted the "vicious circle" of Robert Benchley, Dorothy Parker, and Edna Ferber, among other barbed tongues. The **Oak Room** still serves tea every afternoon, and folks say that, for better or for worse, the restaurant's menu and decor have not changed in 50 years. *(On 44th St. between Fifth and Sixth Ave.)*

ST. PATRICK'S CATHEDRAL. New York's most famous church and America's largest Catholic cathedral was completed in 1879 after 21 years of labor. The structure captures the essence of great European cathedrals while retaining its own unique spirit. The twin spires on the Fifth Ave. facade, captured in countless photos and postcards, streak 330 feet into the air. Here, F. Scott Fitzgerald, author of *The Great Gatsby*, exchanged vows with his sweetheart Zelda. *(753-2261. Southeast corner of Fifth Ave. and 51st St.)*

MUSEUM OF TELEVISION AND RADIO. The former Museum of Broadcasting spent $50 million on its recent move, expansion, and name change. The new building outsizes its predecessor by 400%, but it has only one small gallery of exhibits, and works almost entirely as a "viewing museum," allowing visitors to attend scheduled screenings or privately enjoy a TV or radio show from its library of 95,000 (see **Museums**, p. 247). *(621-6600. Just west of Fifth Ave., at 25 W. 52nd St.)*

THE CBS BUILDING. This dour spectacle that brings to mind *2001: Space Odyssey* maintains a cold watch over arch-rival NBC. For greatest dramatic effect, view the smoke-colored granite tower from the ground on Sixth Ave. (For info on tickets to CBS shows, see p. 263.) *(975-4321. 51 W. 52nd St.)*

ST. THOMAS'S CHURCH. Its lopsided left tower has slouched over this Fifth Ave. corner since 1911. From above the door, numerous saints, apostles, and missionaries gaze down at Fifth Ave.'s materialistic idolatry with expressions ranging from dispassionate to aghast. If you continue down W. 53rd St. towards Sixth Ave., you will pass the **American Craft Museum** (see **Museums**, p. 242). *(757-7013. Northwest corner of Fifth Ave. and 53rd St. Guided tours Su following the 11am service.)*

UNIVERSITY CLUB. This turn-of-the-20th-century granite palace accommodates aging, rich white guys. As indicated by its name, this organization was among the first men's clubs that required its members to hold college degrees. Twenty prestigious university crests adorn its facade. In June of 1987, the previously all-male club voted to admit women in accordance with a city ordinance. Welcome to the 21st century, boys. *(Northwest corner of Fifth Ave. and 54th St.)*

TIFFANY & CO. Marla Maples and Donald Trump named their daughter after this Fifth Ave. neighbor of their Trump Tower. Tiffany the store boasts everything beautiful. New York-related exhibitions show regularly and the window displays can be art in themselves, especially around Christmas (see **Shopping**, p. 297). *(755-8000. 727 Fifth Ave., between 56th and 57th St.)*

F.A.O. SCHWARZ. Like Tom Hanks in *Big*, you too can reclaim your inner spoiled brat. Come Christmas, the store jam packs frenzied shoppers celebrating the holiday season in a ritual that resembles the running of the bulls in Pamplona (see **Shopping**, p. 305). *(644-9400. 767 Fifth Ave. and 58th St.)*

PLAZA HOTEL. Henry J. Hardenberg's 1907 construction was built at the then-astronomical cost of $12.5 million. Its 18-story, 800-room French Renaissance interior embodies opulence, flaunting five marble staircases, countless ludicrously named suites, and a two-story Grand Ballroom. Past guests have included Frank Lloyd Wright, the Beatles, James Brown, and one eminent resident, Kay Thompson's mischievous literary heroine Eloise (whose portrait hangs downstairs just off the main lobby). When Donald Trump bought this national landmark in 1988, locals shuddered; so far, his Midas touch hasn't altered the place. Flash the doorman a charming smile as he opens the door for you and head in to have a look or a quick wee. The wealth inside amazes—marble, glass, brass, and gold—but more to the point, it's extremely well cooled and will always provide a break from summer heat, as well as a chance to stargaze at the occasional celebrity guest. *Let's Go* recommends the $15,000-per-night suite. *(Fifth Ave. and 59th St. at the southeast corner of Central Park.)*

OTHER SIGHTS. Grand Army Plaza, with its Pulitzer Memorial Fountain, double-bills as a forecourt to the Plaza Hotel and as an entrance to Central Park. Along with Karl Bitter's *Statue of Abundance* sits Saint-Gaudens' gaudy, gilt equestrian statue of *Union General William Tecumseh Sherman,* proving that war may be hell, but it definitely pays to win. **Fifth Ave. Presbyterian Church,** at the northwest corner of Fifth Ave. and 55th St., was built in 1875. The largest Presbyterian sanctuary in Manhattan, it seats 1800. If you're still in the area around sunset, check out the **Crown Building,** 730 Fifth Ave. at 57th St. Originally designed by Warren and Wetmore in 1924, the upper tier has since been overlaid with over 85 pounds of 23-carat gold leaf. As the sun sets, the reflected light creates a crown of fire. **Trump Tower** shines on 56th St. and Fifth Ave. like a beacon to excess. Inside, a ludicrous five-story waterfall washes down an atrium of orange, pink, and brown marble. The result is tacky with a capital Trump. There are enough fashion boutiques here to satisfy even the most depraved world leader (see **Shopping,** p. 297).

UPPER EAST SIDE

The Upper East Side signifies more than an area of city space. It lines the hems of well-made suits, oils the little hinges on Gucci glasses, and illuminates the cob-webbed corners of sumptuously carpeted museums. Things—etiquette, education, good family names—don't change much here. Old money and new-money-trying-hard-to-appear-old insulate the Upper East Side from the vagaries of fashion. Clean lines in its architecture and three-piece suits juxtapose the ostentation of absurdly outfitted doormen beneath curlicuing parapets. This community's vast wealth insures that its girls will become Ladies—ladies who lunch, hold poodles, serve hand-rolled ravioli, and conspicuously rule the streets between 60th and 96th and the avenues between East End and Fifth Ave. With its shockingly clean streets, occasional movie star sighting, and hordes of uniformed school children, the Upper East Side invites a tour of concentrated opulence.

The Upper East Side has held its claim for well over a century. Until the end of the Civil War, 19th-century jet-setters chose this part of town for their summer retreats, building elaborate mansions in garden settings. By the late 1860s, however, relaxing away the warm months uptown did not suffice. Landowners converted their urban villas into year-round settlements. Elevated railroads during the Gilded Age invited a swelling population. In 1896, Caroline Schermerhorn Astor built a mansion on Fifth Ave. at 65th St. The rest of high society soon followed, causing the posh East Side lifestyle to flourish until the outbreak of World War I. During this Golden Age, the old-money crowd took advantage of improvements in technology to produce mansions outfitted with everything from elevators to intercoms. Scores of gentry moved into the area and refused to budge, even during the Great Depression, when armies of the unemployed pitched their tents across the way in Central Park.

FIFTH AVENUE. Millionaires, parades, and unbearably slow buses cover a stretch once grazed by pigs. Today, the avenue boasts **Museum Mile,** which includes the Metropolitan, the Guggenheim, the International Center of Photography, the Frick, the Cooper-Hewitt, and the Museum of the City of New York, among others.

PARK AVENUE. Flanked by uniform gray-and-brown apartment buildings and the odd Gothic church, this iconic avenue sidesteps New York glitz in favor of an austere demeanor. Landscaped green islands dividing northward from southward traffic complete the scene. Gaze down this highly residential avenue until you reach the hazy outline of Midtown's skyscraping silhouettes, rising up like canyon walls.

BLOOMINGDALE'S. Enter the Upper East Side at the gateway to conspicuous consumption (see **Shopping,** p. 296). The flag-festooned store, begun by two brothers in 1872, set the stage for a number of notable firsts. Not only did Bloomingdale's invent the designer shopping bag, they also discovered many designers: Ralph Lauren, Perry Ellis, and Norma Kamali, to name a few. Try on designer clothes or sample some perfume (500 oz. sprayed each day). *(59th St. and Third Ave.)*

CARL SCHURZ PARK. Named for the German immigrant who served as a Civil War general, a Missouri senator, President Rutherford B. Hayes's Secretary of the Interior, and finally as editor of the *New York Evening Post* and *Harper's Weekly.* The park has courts for urban athletes and playgrounds for their kids and sponsors **free jazz** concerts on Wednesdays from 7 to 9pm. **Gracie Mansion,** at the northern end of the park, has housed every New York mayor since Fiorello LaGuardia moved in during World War II. Rudy Giuliani presently occupies this hottest of hot seats. *(570-4751. Between 84th and 90th St. along East End Ave. Tours W at 10, 11am, 1, and 2pm. Suggested donation $4, seniors $3. You must call in advance to receive a confirmation card before visiting.)*

CULTURAL INSTITUTES. At 22 E. 60th St., the **French Institute** (355-6100), the cultural arm of the French Embassy, offers Gallic lectures and films (open M-Th 9am-8pm, F 9am-5pm). Three cultural institutes reside at Park Ave. at 69th St.: the **Americas Society,** 680 Park Ave. (249-8950); the **Spanish Institute,** 684 Park Ave. (628-0420); and the **Italian Cultural Institute,** 688 Park Ave. (879-4242).

FASHION. The latest location of New York's fashion ground zero, **Barneys New York** rests upon its laurels at 660 Madison Ave. between 60th and 61st St. Designers such as Vera Wang, Jean-Paul Gaultier, Armani, and many more all sell here at exorbitant prices. Celeb-spotting is a sport here. Barneys has recently been joined on this block by high-fashion pals **Calvin Klein** and **Ann Taylor.** Come to ogle the eternal hipness of old money at the **Polo-Ralph Lauren** boutique, 867 Madison Ave. (606-2100), between 71st and 72nd St., which wallows in its white-columned splendor. Look wealthy or Ralph's cronies may ignore you—until you touch something. *(Open M-Sa 10am-6pm.)*

HOUSES OF WORSHIP. Note the iconic panels (taken from an old Russian church) above the altar of **Christ Church,** 520 Park Ave. (838-3036), at 60th St. *(Open daily 9am-5pm for meditation, prayer, and respectful viewing. Occasional concerts feature classical church music.)* At the corner of Fifth Ave. and 65th St. stands **Temple Emanu-El** (744-1400), the largest synagogue in the U.S. On the corner of Lexington Ave. and 76th St. sits the multi-domed **Church of St. Jean Baptiste** (open daily 10am-5pm). The **Frank E. Campbell Chapel,** 1076 Madison Ave. at 81st St., a prestigious funeral chapel, has buried the best: Robert Kennedy, John Lennon, Elizabeth Arden, James Cagney, Jack Dempsey, Tommy Dorsey, Judy Garland, Howard Johnson, Mae West, and Arturo Toscanini. Take a break from museum-going at the **Church of the Heavenly Rest,** at the corner of Fifth Ave. and 90th St., with its breathtaking stained glass window above the altar. The **Synod of Bishops of the Russian Orthodox Church Outside Russia** inhabits a 1917 Georgian mansion at Park Ave. and 93rd St. New York's most prominent mosque, the **Islamic Cultural Center,** at Third Ave. and 96th St., was precisely oriented by computer to face the holy city of Mecca. The **Russian Orthodox Cathedral of St. Nicholas** and its onion domes stand at 15 E. 97th St. The fanciful **Church of the Holy Trinity,** 316 E. 88th St. between First and Second Ave., houses a gorgeous, sloping organ and offers free classical concerts every Wednesday in July at around 7:30pm.

SARAH DELANO ROOSEVELT MEMORIAL HOUSE. The Roosevelt matriarch commissioned this pair of identical buildings from designer Charles Platt for her son Franklin's 1908 wedding. Here, FDR recovered from polio in the early 20s and launched his political career. The building is now home to the Institute for Rational-Emotive Therapy (don't ask—we don't know). *(45-47 E. 65th St., between Madison and Park Ave.)*

THE SEVENTH REGIMENT ARMORY. The regiment that once occupied this block-long armory fought in every major U.S. campaign from 1812 on—even helping the Union win the Civil War. Much of the Armory's 19th-century decoration and furnishing remain in place today. The Veterans' Room and adjoining former library, now a display room for the Regiment's silver, particularly

Upper East Side

N

0 yards 275

0 meters 250

Conservatory Garden

El Museo del Barrio

Museum of the City of New York

E. 106th St.

E. 105th St.

E. 104th St.

E. 103rd St.

E. 102nd St.

E. 101st St.

E. 100th St.

E. 99th St.

Mt. Sinai

E. 98th St.

E. 97th St.

Islamic Cultural Center

E. 96th St.

International Center of Photography

E. 95th St.

E. 94th St.

Jewish Museum

E. 93rd St.

De Hirsch Residence

E. 92nd St.

Cooper-Hewitt Museum

E. 91st St.

National Academy Museum

E. 90th St.

E. 89th St.

Gracie Mansion

Guggenheim Museum

E. 88th St.

E. 87th St.

Carl Schurz Park

Ward's Island

Fifth Ave.

Madison Ave.

Park Ave.

Third Ave.

E. 86th St.

E. 85th St.

E. 84th St.

E. 83rd St.

Second Ave.

First Ave.

York Ave.

East End Ave.

E. 82nd St.

E. 81st St.

Metropolitan Museum of Art

E. 80th St.

E. 79th St.

E. 78th St.

E. 77th St.

E. 76th St.

E. 75th St.

Whitney Museum of American Art

Lexington Ave.

E. 74th St.

E. 73rd St.

E. 72nd St.

E. 71st St.

Frick Collection

Asia Society

E. 70th St.

E. 69th St.

New York Hospital

FDR Dr.

Hunter College

E. 68th St.

E. 67th St.

Seventh Regiment Armory

Children's Zoo

Temple Emanu-El

China Institute Gallery

E. 66th St.

E. 65th St.

Rockefeller University

The Arsenal

E. 64th St.

Central Park Zoo

Museum of American Illustration

E. 63rd St.

First Ave.

Roosevelt Island

Abigail Adams Smith Museum

E. 62nd St.

Grand Army Plaza

E. 61st St.

ROOSEVELT ISLAND TRAMWAY

E. 60th St.

Bloomingdale's ■

E. 59th St.

Queensboro Bridge

Central Park

NEIGHBORHOODS

deserve a peek. The front hallway boasts a huge red plush staircase and a plethora of decomposing flags. The eerily impenetrable gloom makes it virtually impossible to see the portraits, but they can see you. The Armory still serves as a military facility. *(744-8180. Between 66th and 67th St. on Park Ave. Call to arrange a tour.)*

YORKVILLE. For Teutonic fun, head east of Lexington Ave. between 77th and 96th St. Originally settled by Germans, Yorkville welcomed immigrants from the Rhine Valley throughout the first half of this century. The 1940s saw pro-Nazi newspapers as well as anti-Nazi bookstores that carried the books Hitler banned. The heavy German flavor that once marked local restaurant menus, beer gardens, pastry shops, and deli counters has diluted in the wake of newer chain stores and pizza parlors. Today, this pleasant residential area provides a peaceful stroll. Lacking the uptight intensity of the rest of the Upper East Side, it offers a respite from the fancier avenues.

MUSEUMS. (For complete descriptions, see **Museums,** p. 231.) Between Lexington and Park Ave., at 128 E. 63rd St., stands the **Society of American Illustrators** (838-2560), and its **Museum of American Illustration.** At 1190 Second Ave. and 63rd St. resides the outdoor exhibition of a large fountain and several marble giants in the **Elizabeth Street Garden Galleries.** The newly renovated and expanded **Whitney Museum of American Art** awaits your aesthetic scrutiny at the corner of Madison Ave. and 75th St. The **Asia Society,** at 725 Park Ave. at 70th St., celebrates Asian cultural awareness with a collection assembled by John D. Rockefeller III. The **Frick Collection,** 1 E. 70th St. at Fifth Ave., kicks off Museum Mile in grand style. New York's cultural flagship, **The Metropolitan Museum of Art** holds court at 1000 Fifth Ave., near 82nd St. At Fifth Ave. and 88th St. sits the eye-catching spiral known as the **Guggenheim Museum,** designed by Frank Lloyd Wright. Down the street, the **National Academy Museum,** 1083 Fifth Ave. at 89th St., serves as both a school and a museum. After Carnegie moved up and out of his mansion at 91st St. and Fifth Ave., the Smithsonian moved in with the **Cooper-Hewitt Museum.** The **Jewish Museum,** at 92nd St. and Fifth Ave., contains the country's largest collection of Judaica. The **International Center of Photography** follows at 130 Fifth Ave. at 94th St. Museum Mile finally ends up in East Harlem with the **Museum of the City of New York,** on Fifth Ave. and 103rd St., and **El Museo del Barrio,** on Fifth Ave. and 104th St., the only museum in the U.S. specializing in Latin American and Puerto Rican art.

"OLD BOYS" CLUBS. Glide over to 60th St. and Madison Ave. to see where the sons of privilege cavort and establish networks of power. **The Metropolitan Club,** 1 E. 60th St., was built by the dynamic trio of McKim, Mead, and White on a commission from J.P. Morgan for his friends who had not been accepted at the **Union Club,** 101 E. 69th St. **The Knickerbocker Club,** 2 E. 62nd St., was founded by disgruntled Union Club men who were growing unhappy with the club's "liberal" admissions policy. At 47 E. 60th St., between Madison and Park Ave., stands the no-less-exclusive **Grolier Club.** Built in 1917 in honor of 16th-century bibliophile Jean Grolier, this Georgian structure houses a collection of fine bookbindings, a public exhibition room, and a specialized research library (open by appointment). The Richard Hunt-designed **Lotos Club,** E. 66th St. (737-7100), between Fifth and Madison Ave., is an organization of actors, musicians, and journalists.

OTHER SIGHTS. One block east of Fifth Ave., the high-art and high-fashion windows of **Madison Ave.** offer endless hours of aesthetic bliss and materialistic glee. **Lexington Ave.** contrasts with Park Ave.'s ostentation, providing shops and services not only for the upper crust and featuring **Hunter College** (772-4000). On **Third, Second,** and **First Ave.,** you'll also find vibrant crowds and necessary shops and services. **Sotheby's** (606-7171) conducts its affairs and auctions at 1334 York Ave. at 72nd St. *(Open M-F 9am-5pm; gallery open M-Sa 10am-5pm, Su 1-5pm.)*

Viewings are open to the public, though admission to a few of the big auctions requires tickets. Across the street at 1014 Fifth Ave., **Goethe House** (439-8688) imports Germanic culture in the form of films, lectures, and a library (open Tu and Th noon-7pm, W and Sa noon-5pm). Starting on 82nd St. and East End Ave., **John Finley Walk** overlooks the East River and the cars on FDR Drive. **Henderson Place** lines East End Ave. near 86th St. Although this series of Queen Anne-style houses was created in 1882 for "persons of moderate means," they nevertheless flaunt multiple turrets, parapets, and ivy-colored walls. Ghostbusters take note: rumor has it that some of these houses are haunted.

ROOSEVELT ISLAND

Subway: B, Q to Roosevelt Island; or #4, 5, 6, or N, R to 59th St. (at Lexington Ave.), then walk to 59th St. and Second Ave. and hop the tram.

"New York's Island Paradise," as Roosevelt Island's luxury apartments advertise it, has a long, sordid history. This mere slip of a thing in the East River between Manhattan and Queens was originally occupied by the Canarsie Indians and known as Minnahannock (loosely translated "It's nice to be on the island"). After the Canarsie sold the land to the Dutch in 1637, it changed hands many more times, from Dutch hog farmers to the City of New York in 1828. The city then used the island as a dumping ground for unwanted people, establishing jails, hospitals, quarantines, and a lunatic asylum. Roosevelt Island has also functioned as the city's St. Helena: Boss Tweed of the politically murky Tammany Hall was jailed here, as was Mae West (for her role, prefiguring Madonna, in a play called *Sex*). Finally, in 1969, architects Phillip Johnson and John Burgee redesigned the island as a state-sponsored utopia of mixed-income housing, security watch, and handicapped-accessibility. 1973 saw the island's name change from Welfare Island to Roosevelt Island, in an attempt to clean up its image.

An ethnically diverse mix of people, many U.N.-affiliated, live not even 300 yards away from the hustle and bustle of East Midtown and the United Nations itself. The community runs a **communal garden** and keeps fit on the plentiful running tracks, tennis courts, soccer fields, and softball diamonds. *(Garden open May-Sept. Sa-Su 8am-6pm.)* Other than these options, however, few entertainment venues exist—there's no movie theater, record store, or bowling alley. Still, public services, stores, restaurants, public schools, and cheerfully colored buses make this peaceful community a real estate hot spot.

Contributing to the general un-New-York-ness of the place, a bright red **tram** shuttles residents and tourists across the East River. *(832-4555. Cars run every 15min. Su-Th 6am-2am, F-Sa 6am-3:30am; twice as frequently during rush hour. Round-trip $3. 6min. each way.)* At the 59th St. tram stop (see transportation info above), you can pick up a handy walking tour map of the island for 25¢. The tram ride allows a grand view of the East Side. As you hover almost 250 ft. above the river, you can see the United Nations complex and the distinctive visages of the Chrysler and Empire State Buildings to your right. One of the only publicly operated commuter cable cars in the world, it generates an annual deficit of $1 million, and its future has become especially uncertain, since the subway opened to the island about 10 years ago. The Q102 bus also makes the trip—but only the tram affords a great view.

Once on the island, walk north or take the mini-bus (25¢) up Main St. and roam around a bit. A walking/skating path encircles the island, and gardens and playgrounds abound on the northern half. The southern tip of the island is currently off-limits while the city restores the ruins of the insane asylum and hospital. Lighthouse Park, at the northernmost tip of the island, is a pleasant pastoral retreat with views of the swirling East River waters.

CENTRAL PARK

> There is no greenery; it is enough to make a stone sad.
> —Nikita Khrushchev, on New York, 1960

*General Information: 360-3444; for parks and recreation info call 360-8111 (M-F 9am-5pm). The Central Park Conservancy, which runs the park and offers all kinds of public programs, has four visitors centers: the **Belvedere Castle** (772-0210), the **Charles A. Dana Discovery Center** (860-1370), **North Meadow Recreation Center** (348-4867), and the **Dairy**. The Dairy, located south of 65th St., houses the **Central Park Reception Center** (794-6564) with its brochures, calendars of events, exhibits on park history, and **free park maps**; Apr.-Oct. Tu-Su 10am-5pm, Nov.-Mar. Tu-Su 10am-4pm. **Subway:** #1, 9 to 59th St./Columbus Circle; or N to 59th St./Fifth Ave./Grand Army Plaza.*

If you miss one thing in New York, make it the Statue of Liberty. But visit Central Park, for crying out loud. This welcome oasis in the midst of the urban jungle was once an unmanicured wasteland where marginal figures—squatters—were relegated to living with wild animals. Refusing to defer to London and Paris, elite New Yorkers made a huge-to-do about building a lush park. They held a contest in 1857 for the best design. Frederick Law Olmsted's collaboration with Calvert Vaux took the prize. Out of 843 acres of bogs, cliffs, glacial leftovers, pig farms, and garbage dumps, the famed duo carved a living masterwork they called Greensward. The landscape, intended to evoke the romantic English countryside, took 15 years to build and 40 years to grow (we're talking millions of trees here). Nearly 1400 species of trees, shrubs, and flowers grow here, the work of distinguished horticulturist Ignaz Anton Pilat. In the thick of the park you can almost find serenity and forget surrounding Gotham, but for those pesky skyscrapers peeking over the tree tops. If Central Park's foliage could talk, it would recount everything from massive celebrity concerts to knee-chafing marriage proposals, from marathons to controversial gay-and-lesbian rallies. When you explore its tree-lined paths, you get lost in history.

The Reservoir marks the border between the park's northern and southern sections. Southern Central Park, surrounded by posh apartment buildings, affords more intimate settings, serene lakes, and graceful promenades; whereas the less prestigious northern end has a few ragged edges. Look to the nearest aluminum lamppost for guidance; its small metal plaque's first two digits tell you what street you're nearest (e.g., 89 = 89th St.). In order to get from East to West, or vice versa, you can use one of four transverses, spaced out conveniently at 65th St., 79th St., 85th St., and 97th St. You can also make your way across, though less directly, from either the east or west 72nd entrance. East Dr. and West Dr. both run north-south on either side of the park, from Central Park South/59th St. to Central Park North/110th St. (both between Central Park West and Fifth Ave.).

CENTRAL PARK WILDLIFE CENTER. Formerly known as the Central Park Zoo, the center has attracted flocks of visitors since its 1934 opening. A few years ago, in a sign of the times, the obsessively backstroking polar bear Gus was treated for depression. Perhaps contributing to Gus's mania, the Delacorte Musical Clock, just north of the main zoo, springs to life every half-hour. Beyond the clock lies the **Tisch Children's Zoo**, a newly reopened petting zoo. *(861-6030. E. 64th St. and Fifth Ave. Apr.-Oct. M-F 10am-5pm, Sa-Su 10:30am-5:30pm; Nov.-Mar. daily 10am-4:30pm. Last entry 30min. before closing. Combined admission $3.50, seniors $1.25, ages 3-12 50¢, under 2 free.)*

In front of the zoo at Fifth Ave. and E. 64th St. sits the ivy-covered **Arsenal** (360-8136), stalwart home to the Park's administrative offices. The 3rd-floor Arsenal Gallery hosts free park-related exhibitions. *(Open M-F 9am-4pm.)*

CHILDREN'S DISTRICT. Vaux and Olmsted designated the area south of the 65th St. Transverse as a place for the young (and the young at heart) to play, frolic on rides, and receive affordable nourishment. In the early days, the **Dairy** distributed food and purity-tested milk to poor families susceptible to food poisoning. Next to the Dairy, Olmsted and Vaux's *Kinderberg* (Children's Mountain) has become a visitor's center. With a $20 deposit you can rent equipment at the Dairy and square off at any of the 24 boards that surround the **Chess and Checkers House,** near Wollman Rink. The delightful **Friedsam Memorial Carousel** completes this rug-rat heaven. The 58-horsepower carousel, originally brought from Coney Island, was fully restored in 1983. The last scene of *Catcher in the Rye* takes place here. Another gift from George and Margarita Delacorte, **Alice in Wonderland,** along with several of her friends, lives in the Children's District. A statue of Hans Christian Andersen, a gift from Copenhagen in 1956, stands nearby. Children scramble over both statues, sitting in Andersen's lap or clinging precariously to the Mad Hatter's oversized *chapeau. (Visitor's Center: open Sa-Su 11:30am-3:45pm; Carousel: 879-0244. 65th St. west of Center Dr. Open M-F 10am-6pm, Sa-Su 10am-6:30pm, weather permitting. Thanksgiving to mid-Mar. Sa-Su 10:30am-4:30pm. $1. 340-0849. The New York Public Library sponsors **summer storytelling** at the Andersen statue Sa 11am; July Tu-W.)*

SHEEP MEADOW. This vast expanse of greenery exemplifies the pastoral ideals of the park's designers. Sheep grazed here until 1934; when lawn mowers put the flock out of work. A popular spot for love-ins in the 60s and 70s, "The Meadow" remains a countercultural enclave where alternateens gather to get high (or *did*, before Rudy's regime) alongside frisbee-tossers, picnicking families, and scoping sunbathers. On summer days, so many tanning bodies cover it that some locals morbidly call the spot "Gettysburg." Directly north of the meadow, the crowd instantly ages about 50 years. Complexions turn less bronzed under the broad straw hats and white clothes of lawn bowlers and croquet players. *(Meadow extends from about 66th to 69th St. on the western side of Central Park, directly north of the Carousel.)*

THE LAKE. Spreading out to the west from underneath Bow Bridge, the lake serves as subject for budding artists. You can watch rowers awkwardly maneuver their boats around the lake or, more fun yet, rent one yourself. The **Loeb Boathouse** supplies rowboats at reasonable rates.

CONSERVATORY WATER. To the east of the Terrace and the Lake, competitive model-yachters gather to race, even observing Olympic yachting regulations. From the Conservatory Sailboats cart, less serious yachters can rent remote-control sailboats. *(Races: Saturdays at 10am from late March to mid-November. Conservatory Sailboats: 673-1102. $10 per hr. License or credit card deposit required.)*

STRAWBERRY FIELDS. Yoko Ono's memorial to her late husband stands directly across from the Dakota Apartments where John Lennon was assassinated and where Ono still lives with their son Sean. Ono battled for this space against city-council members who had planned a Bing Crosby memorial on the same spot. Picnickers and 161 varieties of plants now adorn the rolling hills around the circular "Imagine" mosaic. On John Lennon's birthday on October 9th, thousands gather here to remember the legend. *(West of the Lake at 72nd St. and West Dr.)*

BELVEDERE CASTLE. In 1869, Vaux designed this literal high point of the Park as a whimsical fancy. The castle rises from Vista Rock, like something out of a fairy tale, commanding a view of the Ramble (a spot notorious for anonymous and dangerous gay sex at night) to the south and the Great Lawn to the north. For many years a weather station, Belvedere Castle has been reincarnated as an education and information center. *(Just off the 79th St. Transverse. Observatory open Tu-Su 11am-5pm.)*

THE GREAT LAWN. Here, near the Delacorte Theater, Paul Simon crooned and the Stonewall 25 marchers rallied (look for post-Stonewall 30 events in 2000). The New York Philharmonic and the Metropolitan Opera Company also hold summer performances here (see **Classical Music,** p. 266). When the Great Lawn isn't in the spotlight, it hosts pickup softball, touch football, and soccer games.

HARLEM MEER. The recently re-opened 11-acre lake holds the Harlem Meer Performance Festival that enlivens the shores with free jazz, reggae, and Latin music performances, as well as multicultural dance and theater. Meanwhile, at the same spot, the **Charles A. Dana Discovery Center** features exhibitions and activities pre-

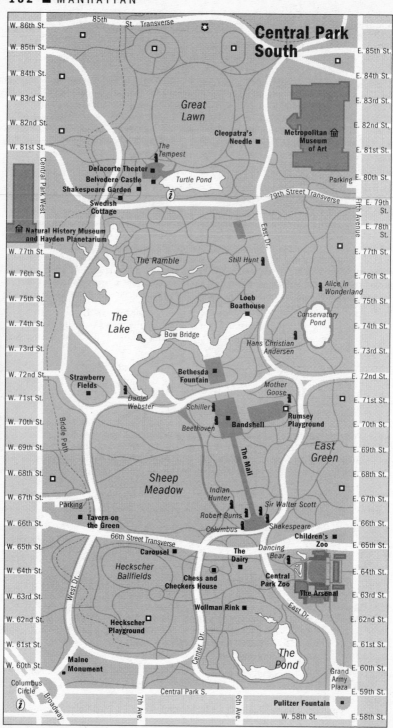

Central Park South

W. 86th St.
85th St. Transverse
W. 85th St.
E. 85th St.
W. 84th St.
E. 84th St.
W. 83rd St.
E. 83rd St.

Great Lawn

Cleopatra's Needle
W. 82nd St.
E. 82nd St.

Metropolitan Museum of Art

W. 81st St.
E. 81st St.
The Tempest

Central Park West
Delacorte Theater
Belvedere Castle
Shakespeare Garden
Turtle Pond
Parking
E. 80th St.

Swedish Cottage
79th Street Transverse
E. 79th St.

Natural History Museum and Hayden Planetarium
East Dr.
Fifth Avenue
E. 78th St.

W. 77th St.
The Ramble
Still Hunt
E. 77th St.

W. 76th St.
Alice in Wonderland
E. 76th St.

W. 75th St.
Loeb Boathouse
E. 75th St.

Conservatory Pond

The Lake
W. 74th St.
E. 74th St.

Bow Bridge
Hans Christian Andersen
W. 73rd St.
E. 73rd St.

W. 72nd St.
Bethesda Fountain
E. 72nd St.

Strawberry Fields
Mother Goose
W. 71st St.
E. 71st St.

Daniel Webster
Schiller
Rumsey Playground
W. 70th St.
E. 70th St.

Beethoven
Bandshell
Bridle Path

W. 69th St.
East Green
E. 69th St.

W. 68th St.
Sheep Meadow
The Mall
E. 68th St.

W. 67th St.
Indian Hunter
E. 67th St.

Parking
Sir Walter Scott
Robert Burns
W. 66th St.
Tavern on the Green
Columbus
Shakespeare
Children's Zoo
E. 66th St.

66th Street Transverse
Dancing Bear
W. 65th St.
Carousel
The Dairy
E. 65th St.

Heckscher Ballfields
Central Park Zoo
W. 64th St.
Chess and Checkers House
E. 64th St.

West Dr.
The Arsenal
W. 63rd St.
Wollman Rink
E. 63rd St.

W. 62nd St.
Heckscher Playground
East Dr.
E. 62nd St.

Center Dr.
W. 61st St.
E. 61st St.

The Pond
W. 60th St.
Maine Monument
E. 60th St.

Columbus Circle
Grand Army Plaza

Broadway
Central Park S.
7th Ave.
6th Ave.
E. 59th St.

Pulitzer Fountain
W. 58th St.
E. 58th St.

W. 112th St.

W. 111th St.

Lenox Ave.

Central Park North

Frederick
Douglass
Circle

Central Park North

Milbank Frawley
Circle

W.
110th St.

E. 110th St.

W. 109th St.

E. 109th St.

Harlem
Meer

W. 108th St.

E. 108th St.

West Dr.

W. 107th St.

**Lasker Rink
and Pool**

E. 107th St.

W. 106th St.

E. 106th St.

**Conservatory
Gardens**

W. 105th St.

Great
Hill

E. 105th St.

E. 104th St.

W. 104th St.

East Dr.

W. 103rd St.

The
Ravine

E. 103rd St.

E. 102nd St.

W. 102nd St.

The
Pool

W. 101st St.

E. 101st St.

W. 100th St.

North
Meadow

Fifth Avenue

Central Park West

East
Meadow

E. 98th St.

W.
97th St.

E. 97th St.

97th Street Transverse

W. 96th St.

E. 96th St.

W. 95th St.

● Tennis Courts

E. 95th St.

W. 94th St.

E. 94th St.

N

W. 93rd St.

E. 93rd St.

Bridle Path

W. 92nd St.

E. 92nd St.

W. 91st St.

| 0 | yards | 300 |

E. 91st St.

W. 90th St.

| 0 | meters | 250 |

E. 90th St.

W. 89th St.

Reservoir

East Dr.

E. 89th St.

West Dr.

W. 88th St.

□ Playgrounds
❘ Statues

E. 88th St.

W. 87th St.

E. 87th St.

W. 86th St.

85th Street Transverse

E. 86th St.

W. 85th St.

E. 85th St.

W. 84th St.

E. 84th St.

NEIGHBORHOODS

WELCOME TO THE JUNGLE It's hard to imagine a park measured in city blocks as the habitat for any wildlife besides pigeons. Central Park, however, contains quite an abundance of fauna. Especially in the denser growth of the Ramble or on the Reservoir, raccoons, groundhogs, robins, ducks, woodpeckers, herons, and kingfishers frolic. A "plan" is in the works to reintroduce owls into the park. Central Park rated among the country's 14 best bird-watching sites. The most celebrated of the city's avian inhabitants, however, don't live in the park, but on Fifth Ave. For the past five years, a pair of red-tailed hawks has nested above the top window of the building at the corner of 74th St. and Fifth Ave., across the street from the park. Dedicated birders focus their binoculars and telescopes on the nest from the southwest shore of the Conservatory Water, observing the pair court, mate (often on the balcony of Woody Allen's penthouse next door), and raise chicks. The parents make an impressive sight, swooping down into the park to snatch pigeons and rats for their brood's meals. Sneak a peek through one of the telescopes trained on the nest. Two larger, ziggurat-topped buildings (the more northerly being Woody's) flank the flat-topped home of the hawks. For more info call the Urban Park Rangers (888-697-2757), or read *Red-Tails in Love,* by Marie Winn, one of the merry bird-watching band.

senting Central Park as an environmental space to be explored by amateur and professional biologists alike. The Center also leads tours and loans out fishing rods for use in the Meer (you do have to throw the fish back, though). *(860-1370. 110th St. and Fifth Ave. at the northeast corner of the park. Shows late May to Oct., Su at 2pm. Discovery Center open Tu-Su 11am-5pm.)*

CLEOPATRA'S NEEDLE. This Egyptian obelisk was first erected at Heliopolis in 1600 BC and stolen away to Alexandria in 12 BC by those pesky Romans. New York City got hold of the ancient pylon in 1881, courtesy of the Egyptian government and William Vanderbilt, who footed the $100,000 shipping bill (and you thought CD shipping and handling was overpriced). Among other inconveniences, moving this 71 ft. granite needle required the construction of a railroad track from the Hudson River. *(Just north of Turtle Pond and east of the Great Lawn.)*

TAVERN ON THE GREEN. Supposedly the city's most profitable eatery, the tavern specializes in haphazard outdoor decor and pricey meals with a view of brilliantly illuminated greenery. Come on a warm evening to grab a drink under the Japanese lanterns. *(873-3200. West of Sheep Meadow, between 66th and 67th St. Lunch $11-26, dinner $15-37. Open M-F noon-3:30pm and 5:30-11:30pm, Sa-Su 10am-3:30pm and 5-11:30pm.)*

CONSERVATORY GARDEN. A romantic spot for cuddling or for contemplating primal causes, the garden offers a refreshing sight after navigating the park. *(860-1382. 105th St. and Fifth Ave. Free tours of the Garden every Saturday through the summer at 11am. Gates open daily spring to fall 8am-dusk.)*

OTHER SIGHTS. Off the eastern shore of the Lake, **Bethesda Fountain** presides over the end of the long **Mall** that extends from the Shakespeare Garden. Emma Stebins sculpted the fountain's 1865 statue, **Angel of the Waters,** in Rome. Benches in the sun and a central view of the lake make this an ideal spot to rest. One of the benches on the northwest shore of the Conservatory Water stars in Edward Albee's play *The Park Bench* and actors occasionally perform it here. The **Swedish Cottage Marionette Theater,** at the base of Vista Rock, puts on regular puppet shows, such as 1996's *Cinderella.* The **Shakespeare Garden,** containing plants, flowers, and herbs mentioned in the Bard's works, sits near the Cottage. The recently re-opened **Turtle Pond** stretches out adjacent to the Delacorte theater. Joggers circle the shiny, placid **Jacqueline Kennedy Onassis Reservoir** (the track around it is 1.58 miles). North of the Reservoir at the 97th St. Transverse, ballers will find the basketball courts of the **North Meadow Recreation Center** (348-4867), which sponsors boardgames, pool, wall climbing, and kite-flying. Most of these are free, but some that require equipment have a small fee.

VENUES. Central Park hosts sensational and mostly free **cultural events.** Perhaps the best known, the **Shakespeare in the Park** series often features big-name actors. A newer tradition is the free **Summerstage** performance series (see **Arts and Entertainment,** p. 272); past performers include the Metropolitan Grand Opera, Guided by Voices, and A Tribe Called Quest. In addition to music, Summerstage hosts writers such as Suzan-Lori Parks and Paul Auster reading from their latest works. For the kids, the **Swedish Cottage Marionette Theater** (988-9093) puts on puppet shows; reservations are required. *(Shows early June through Mid-Aug. M-F at 10:30am and noon; $5, children $4.)*

ACTIVITIES. Central Park is a mecca to the city folk who shed their khakis and briefcases on the weekends and turn into Extreme Sports diehards. To join the hordes of in-line skaters (and a few hold-out rollerskaters) scout out the area near Summerstage or head straight to **Wollman Rink** and rent skates for use throughout the park (see **Participatory Sports,** p. 289). You can rent bikes and rowboats on the northeast shore of the lake at **Loeb Boathouse** (see **Participatory Sports,** p. 291). Meanwhile, creative tours of the park abound. Along 59th St. (also known as Central Park South), horses chomp on oats as couples clamor for **carriage tours** of the park. *(246-0520. $34 for 1st hr.; $10 each additional 15min.).* If you disapprove of animal labor, you may find **Central Park Bicycle Tour** a healthier, more humane choice. *(541-8759. Tours leave daily at 10am, 1, and 4pm from 2 Columbus Circle. $30 for 2hr. ride, under 16 $20.)* For those adept on in-line skates, **New York Skateout** offers tours of the park with a historical slant. They also offer in-line skating classes. *(Reservations 486-1919. Tours leave daily at 9am and 5pm. $25 for 1½hr.)*

UPPER WEST SIDE

One of the friendliest areas of Manhattan, New York's frontier land of wealthy-yet-earnest types eschews the uptight pretension of the Upper East Side. Upper West Siders value a prep school education, but of a more liberal bent than that of their neighbors across Central Park. Two representative institutions roughly delineate its borders—**Lincoln Center** and **Columbia University.** Meanwhile, a recent surge of West Indian immigrants has revitalized the Upper West Side's intelligentsia. West Siders believe in midwifery and public television, freshly cut lilies, comfortable shoes, and, above all, in the fact that they don't live to the East. The Socialism (they were Trotskyites, mind you) of many a West Sider's ardent youth has given way to the more tempered passion of shopping for spinach ravioli at Zabar's. Women let their hair go gray while their partners just *love* them for it, and many treat their writer's block in a "safe-zone workshop." From posh Central Park West to the Hudson views of Riverside Dr., psychologists nod patiently while turning over evening theater plans. A non-stop sidewalk scene thrives, while nightlife and cultural options abound. The gods of organic fruit and progressive politics will reward you for wandering their domain.

While Central Park West and West End Ave. flank the Upper West with residential quietude, **Columbus Ave., Amsterdam Ave.,** and **Broadway** offer exciting dining, shopping, and people-watching at all hours. Although originally conceived as residential thoroughfares, these three colorful and energetic avenues are crammed with delis, theaters, and boutiques; on the sidewalk, hawkers peddle everything from bun dumplings to worn copies of Juggs magazine. Because of the continuous bustle, Broadway feels safe even late at night, though *Let's Go* can't say the same of the side streets that intersect it. To learn more about the long history of this former enclave of the "red diaper baby," read *Upper West Side Story: A History and Guide* (Abbeville Press, 1989). Or, put aside scholarly pursuits and just wander Upper West streets to get a feel for their eclectic offerings.

NEIGHBORHOODS

THE FRONTIER OF LUXURY Roberta Flack, Lauren Bacall, Boris Karloff, and Leonard Bernstein are just a few of the famous past residents of the Dakota. John Lennon made this luxury apartment his home, and was assassinated outside it on December 8, 1980. When constructed in 1884, the complex was surrounded by open land and shanties. So far removed from the city was the site that someone remarked, "It might as well be in the Dakota Territory." The name stuck, and architect Henry Hardenbergh even gave it a frontier flare—look for the bas-relief Native American head and the stone garnish of corn and arrowheads that adorn the "territory."

COLUMBUS CIRCLE. This bustling nexus of pedestrian and automobile traffic, on Broadway at 59th St., is where Midtown ends and the Upper West Side begins. It's also the functional entrance to Central Park West. On the west side of the circle, you'll see **New York Coliseum,** built in 1954 by the TriBoro Bridge and Tunnel Authority to serve as the city's convention center. Although the building seems to be the permanent home of the Columbus Circle Marketplace and Amish exposition, its front has become an unofficial shelter for the homeless, protecting them from the winds whipping across the circle. The city periodically evicts these homeless people in order to clean up the area for special events like the 1992 Democratic National Convention. *(Subway: #1, 9 to 59th St.)*

AMERICAN MUSEUM OF NATURAL HISTORY. J.C. Cady and Co. built the museum in 1899, though the original structure has since acquired new wings. The museum honors its patron saint, Teddy Roosevelt, with an offensive sculpture at the main entrance—Teddy rides a horse flanked by a nearly naked Native American and a black man. *(Central Park between 78th and 81st St. See **Museums,** p. 237, and The Catcher in the Rye.)*

SYMPHONY SPACE. This former skating rink has distinguished itself with brilliantly wacky programming. Their "Wall to Wall Bach" took a walk on the wild side, as did their gala birthday salute to the late avant-garde composer John Cage. Every Bloomsday (June 16), Symphony Space celebrates James Joyce's *Ulysses* with readings, lectures, and parties. The space also hosts a giant foreign-film fest each summer to complement its classical music, world-beat, and literary programs during the year (see p. 262).

DAKOTA APARTMENTS. A few blocks east are the stately apartment buildings that line Central Park West and contrast with the lively businesses of Broadway and Columbus Ave. As Manhattan's urbanization peaked in the late 19th century, wealthy residents sought tranquility in the eerily elegant building immortalized in Roman Polanski's film *Rosemary's Baby*. *(1 W. 72nd St. at Central Park West.)*

ANSONIA HOTEL. The *grande dame* of *belle* apartments bristles with ornaments, curved Veronese balconies, and towers. Its soundproof walls and thick floors enticed illustrious tenants like Enrico Caruso, Arturo Toscanini, and Igor Stravinsky. Theodore Dreiser did his own composing here, and Babe Ruth stayed just a few doors away. William Stokes, the developer of the Ansonia, used the building for an entirely different purpose—he raised chickens, ducks, and a pet bear on its roof. *(2109 Broadway between 73rd and 74th St.)*

HOTEL DES ARTISTES. A stately mass of luxury co-ops originally designed to house bohemians who had moved beyond their romantic garret stage. Built by George Mort Pollard in 1913, the building has housed Isadora Duncan, Alexander Wollcott, Norman Rockwell, and Noel Coward. Here you will also find the notoriously romantic **Café des Artistes.** The menu may be a little on the *cher* side, but the pastoral murals of reclining nudes, painted in 1934 by Howard Chandler Christy, deserve a peek. *(1 W. 67th St., between Central Park West and Columbus Ave.)*

W. 101st St.
W. 100th St.
W. 99th St.
W. 98th St.
W. 97th St.

N

Upper West Side
ACCOMMODATIONS
A International Student Center
B Hayden Hall
C Banana Bungalow Hostel
D YMCA-West Side

W. 96th St.

W. 95th St.
W. 94th St.
W. 93rd St.
W. 92nd St.
W. 91st St.
W. 90th St.
W. 89th St.

Promenade Walk

Symphony Space

Broadway

Amsterdam Ave.

A

W. 88th St.
W. 87th St.

Hector Memorial ■

Riverside Park

Soldiers and Sailors Monument ■

Henry Hudson Pkwy.

W. 86th St.

West Park Presbyterian ✝

Church of St. Paul & St. Andrew ✝

West End Ave.

Children's Museum of Manhattan 🏛

W. 85th St.
W. 84th St.
W. 83rd St.
W. 82nd St.

Central Park W.

Central Park

Riverside Dr.

W. 81st St.

Zabar's ■ W. 80th St.

Hayden Planetarium

B

Hudson River

79th St. Boat Basin

W. 79th St.
W. 78th St.
W. 77th St.
W. 76th St.
W. 75th St.

American Museum of Natural History 🏛

New York Historical Society ■

C

Ansonia Hotel ■

W. 74th St.
W. 73rd St.

Columbus Ave.

Dakota Apartments ■

W. 72nd St.

SHERMAN SQUARE

W. 71st St.
W. 70th St.

Freedom Pl.

Lincoln Square Synagogue ✡

W. 69th St.
W. 68th St.
W. 67th St.

Broadway

Hotel des Artistes ■

Museum of American Folk Art 🏛

Juilliard School

W. 66th St.
W. 65th St.

LINCOLN CENTER

W. 64th St.
W. 63rd St.

C

Damrosch Park

West End Ave.

W. 62nd St.
W. 61st St.

Bible House ■

Fordham University ■

W. 60th St.
W. 59th St.

Columbus Circle

W. 58th St.

W. 57th St.

i

New York Convention & Vistors Bureau

NEIGHBORHOODS

THE NEW YORK SOCIETY FOR ETHICAL CULTURE. Local illuminati convene here for weekly lectures, readings, and classical recitals. This venerable organization helped found many others, including the American Civil Liberties Union. Many resident yuppies favor the Ethical Culture School for the education of their young. *(874-5210. 2 W. 64th St., one block up Central Park West.)*

MUSEUM OF AMERICAN FOLK ART. The undistinguished modern facade gives way to a cool interior, where you can rest on a bench to quell the mania that 18th-century quilts inspire (see **Museums,** p. 246). *(977-7298; for group tours call 595-9533. Two Lincoln Square on Columbus Ave. between 65th and 66th St., opposite Lincoln Center.)*

BIBLE HOUSE. The American Bible Society distributes the Good Book in nearly every tongue. Its exhibition gallery showcases rare and unorthodox Bibles, plus a smattering of Gutenberg pages and an on-line Bible. *(408-1200. 1865 Broadway near 61st St. Gallery and library open M-W, F 10am-6pm, Th 10am-7pm, Sa 10am-5pm. Free.)*

NEW YORK HISTORICAL SOCIETY. In their block-long Neoclassical building, the astute staff will help you uncover obscure facts about the city's past or provide pop trivia about the present. *(873-3400. 77th St. and Central Park West.)*

WEST END COLLEGIATE CHURCH AND SCHOOL. In 1637, Dutch settlers constructed this little complex as a reproduction of a market building in Holland. Robert Gibson overhauled it in 1892, using Dutch stepped gables and elongated bricks. Collegiate now preps the sons of New York's elite for the Ivy League lifestyle; scions of the nouveau-riche stand warned by dramatic graffiti: "The Devil Lives Here." *(370 West End Ave. at 77th St. Vespers Tu 6pm. Communion W 8am.)*

APTHORP APARTMENTS. Its ornate iron gates and a spacious interior courtyard have starred in a number of New York-based films: *The Cotton Club, Heartburn, Network, Witness,* and *The Changeling.* Its simple marble facade features bas-relief vestal virgins. The apartments were built by Clinton and Russell in 1908 on commission from William Waldorf Astor, who named them after the man who owned the site in 1763. Ask the guard to let you check out the courtyard. The lopsided spires across 79th St. belong to the First Baptist Church. *(Apartments located at 2211 Broadway at 79th St.)*

ZABAR'S. The Swiss-chalet-inspired gourmet grocery store of choice. Stop in to buy a bagel and walk out with enough fancy treats to last a week (see p. 123). *(787-2000. 2245 Broadway, at 80th St.)*

CLAREMONT STABLES. The only surviving stable in Manhattan stands next to a vacant lot. The multi-story building serves as equine condos for high-pedigree horses and also gives riding lessons (see **Sports,** p. 293). Claremont riders can often be seen trotting alongside the cars on Central Park West, but the urbane West Siders seem to take it in stride. *(175 W. 89th St. at Amsterdam Ave.)*

EL DORADO APARTMENTS. The appropriately named residence on Central Park West showcases flashy Art Deco detailing in a full array of golds. The El Dorado lobby is a national landmark, and well worth a stop if you can convince the numerous security guards that you won't sneak a visit to the stars who reside there. *(Between 90th and 91st St.)*

OTHER SIGHTS. Donald Trump has laid his newest gargantuan monstrosity, **Trump International Hotel and Towers** atop Columbus Circle at 1 Central Park West. A shiny, silver globe adorns the Towers' facade, perhaps as a prediction of Trump's next real estate acquisition. A triangular plot directly across from Lincoln Center, **Dante Park,** designed in 1921, commemorates the 600th anniversary of the poet's death with a statue. Juilliard students often play jazz or chamber music here on Tuesdays at 6:30pm during the summer. A couple of blocks east, the mammoth, Moorish-style **West Side Y** (875-4100) edges Central Park, at 5 W. 63rd St. Meanwhile, one of New York City's **armories** holds down the fort at 56 W. 66th St., between Central Park West and Broadway; its turrets and battlements now defend the ABC television studios hidden behind the castle facade.

Constructed in 1970, the curvaceous, sunken **Lincoln Square Synagogue** at 69th St. and Amsterdam boasts a bustling Jewish singles social scene (and spiritual services). The large Jewish community of the Upper West Side fans out from 72 St. between Broadway and West End; this area modishly reinvents the Lower East Side. The bow-tie of **Sherman Square** knots at 72nd St. and Broadway. To the west by the river begins **Riverside Park,** where a new statue of **Eleanor Roosevelt** greets locals walking their pooches. The park, which extends to 145th St., is a bit desolate at night, but provides wonderful views and impressive architecture. On West End Ave. between 76th and 77th St. stands a block of Victorian townhouses designed in 1891 by master masons Lamb and Rich. Rumor has it that flamboyant former mayor, James "Gentleman Jim" Walker, kept his mistress on this block.

At 87th St., between Columbus Ave. and Central Park West, stands a brightly colored **graffiti mural** entitled *In Memory of Hector* (by Chico). Between 89th and 90th St., and Columbus and Amsterdam Ave., sits a sweet-smelling **West Side Community Garden,** a sanctuary with flowers, benches, and vegetable plots maintained by community volunteers. Especially verdant and bright is the **Lotus Garden** (580-4897), up a flight of stairs on 97th St. between Broadway and West End Ave. You can sit on benches and admire the fat tulips on Sundays from 1-4pm.

LINCOLN CENTER

Broadway crosses Columbus Ave. at Lincoln Center, the cultural hub of upper-crust New York, perhaps of the entire U.S. The seven facilities that constitute Lincoln Center—Avery Fisher Hall, the New York State Theater, the Metropolitan Opera House, the Library and Museum of Performing Arts, the Vivian Beaumont Theater, the Walter Reade Theater, and the Juilliard School, as well as a venue in LaGuardia High School of the Arts—accommodate over 13,000 spectators, occupying the space between 62nd and 66th St. and Amsterdam and Columbus Ave. When Carnegie Hall seemed fated for destruction in 1955, power broker Robert Moses masterminded this project. The ensuing construction forced the eviction and displacement of thousands and erased a major part of the Hell's Kitchen area (see p. 169). The complex was designed as a modern version of the public plazas of Rome and Venice, and despite its critics (the *Times* called it "a hulking disgrace"), the spacious, uncluttered architecture has made it one of New York's most admired locales. Guided tours of Lincoln Center's theaters and galleries are offered daily. (See **Sightseeing Tours,** p. 126.)

THE PLAZA. On weekend afternoons, hopeful young dancers glide across the plaza on their way to rehearsal and student musicians mill about carrying their cumbersome instrument cases. Lovers favor the plaza's impressive fountain for rendezvous. There, Cher and Nicholas Cage were *Moonstruck* and the cast of *Fame* danced at the beginning of each show. With your back to Columbus Ave., you'll find on your left an automated **info booth**—walk around to the back and touch the screen to begin your virtual odyssey.

AVERY FISHER HALL. This hall, designed in 1966 by Max Abramovitz, houses the New York Philharmonic under the direction of Kurt Masur. Previous Philharmonic directors include Leonard Bernstein, Arturo Toscanini, and Leopold Stokowski (see **Classical Music,** p. 266). Every July and August, Avery Fisher Hall hosts the **Mostly Mozart Festival,** featuring world-class musicians playing—you guessed most of it—Mozart. *(To the right of the fountain, facing away from Columbus Ave.)*

NEW YORK STATE THEATER. This wonder of modern architecture houses the New York City Ballet—founded by George Balanchine and now run by former *premier danseur* Peter Martins—and the eminent New York City Opera. December promises the City Ballet's *Nutcracker*, a yearly ritual for many New Yorkers. *(To the left of the fountain, facing away from Columbus Ave.)*

THE METROPOLITAN OPERA HOUSE. Lincoln Center's 1966 centerpiece by Wallace K. Harrison boasts a Mondrian-inspired glass facade. Chagall murals grace the plaza and lobby, where a grand, many-tiered staircase curves down to the humble opera buff. The gift shop sells erudite CDs and sneaky opera glasses. *(Shop open M-Sa 10am-5:30pm and until 6pm in summer or until 2nd intermission of performance, Su noon-6pm.)*

Damrosch Park hosts frequent outdoor concerts and the perennially popular Big Apple Circus in its Guggenheim Bandshell. The park is in the southwest corner of the center, to the left facing the opera house. In 1965, Eero Saarinen built the **Vivian Beaumont Theater,** a tidy glass box under a heavy cement helmet. Theatrical premieres here have included *Six Degrees of Separation* and *Arcadia.* Decorating the Vivian Beaumont's little front plaza, Henri Moore's 1965 *Lincoln Center Reclining Figure* lolls in the reflecting pool. Through June 2000, 14 sleek sculptures, mostly from New York City schools, populate this plaza, which one art historian calls the "greatest collection of modern art in any public space that is not a museum."

JUILLIARD SCHOOL. Prodigies eat deli sandwiches on the combined terrace and bridge leading across 66th St. from the Vivian Beaumont plaza to the halls of this prestigious school. Here Itzhak Perlman and Pinchas Zukerman fine-tuned their skills, Robin Williams tried out his first comedy routines, and Val Kilmer learned to pout dramatically. Within the Juilliard building complex, you'll find the intimate Alice Tully Hall, home to the Chamber Music Society of Lincoln Center (see **Classical Music,** p. 266). To the left and about 200 ft. away as you face Juilliard, a beige office building conceals Lincoln Center's newest offering, the **Walter E. Reade Theater.** Scan the schedule in the front window; the theater often features foreign films and special festivals (see **Film,** p. 261). *(Box office: 769-7406. Open June-Sept. M-Th 10am-5pm; Oct.-May M-F 11am-6pm. No student performances in summer.)*

NEW YORK PUBLIC LIBRARY FOR THE PERFORMING ARTS. Over eight million items, from videotapes to manuscripts, are all available for loan to anyone with a NYC library card. To accommodate renovations, from July 1998 until the fall of 2000, the collections will temporarily reside in the Mid-Manhattan Library, Fifth Ave. and 40th St., and the Library Annex, 521 W. 43rd St. (see **Essentials, p. 74**). *(Performing Arts branch: 870-1630.)*

HARLEM

Information Resources: East Harlem Chamber of Commerce (996-2288). Business Improvement District, 271 W. 125th St. (662-8999); rm. 214. For links and info on Harlem events, see www.harlem-ontime.com.

Harlem's first black population consisted of slaves belonging to 17th-century Dutch settlers. Not until a dramatic influx of rural Southerners during and after World War I, did Harlem emerge as one of the capitals of the black Western world. Between the 1920s and 30s, as Harlem's population continued to skyrocket, an artistic and literary movement known as the Harlem Renaissance announced its presence to the world. Jazz legends and Harlem residents—Louis Armstrong, Duke Ellington, and Bessie Smith—played in the area, as did greats Charles Mingus, Charlie Parker, Billie Holliday, and Ella Fitzgerald, among others. A few of the clubs they played, such as the Lenox Lounge, Apollo Theater, and Cotton Club, still display their portraits today. Literary legends, such as Langston Hughes, Zora Neale Hurston, and Jean Toomer also flourished right here in the mecca of African-American culture. Yet people of color still endured inclement conditions in Harlem. They paid more than white counterparts for unhealthy tenement rooms, for example, and places like the Cotton Club, Harlem's most famous jazz nightclub, didn't even allow black people inside unless they were performing.

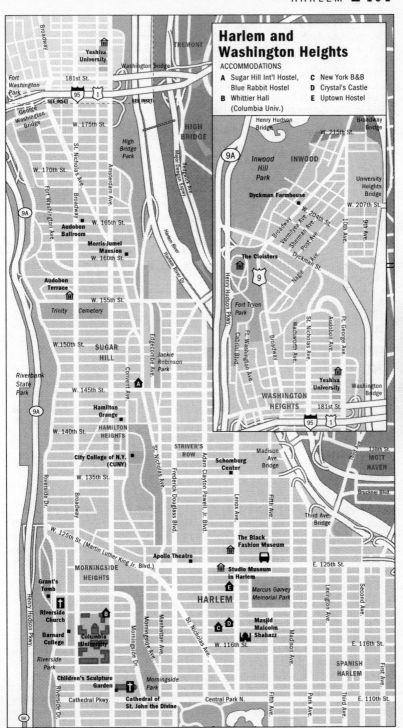

Harlem and Washington Heights

ACCOMMODATIONS

A Sugar Hill Int'l Hostel, Blue Rabbit Hostel
B Whittier Hall (Columbia Univ.)
C New York B&B
D Crystal's Castle
E Uptown Hostel

NEIGHBORHOODS

After the Depression and World War II, Harlem once again flourished culturally, if not economically. In the 1960s, riding the tidal wave of the Civil Rights movement, the radical Black Power thrived here. LeRoi Jones's The Revolutionary Theater performed consciousness-raising one-act plays in the streets, and Malcolm X, Stokely Carmichael, and H. Rap Brown spoke eloquently against racism and injustice. Recognizing the need for economic revitalization as a route to empowerment, members of the community began an attempt at redevelopment in the 1970s and 80s. This attempt continues today as the city pumps money into the area and communities join to beautify their neighborhood and resist crime. As Malcolm X's teachings of self-empowerment now gain increasing popularity, a definite strand of separatism pervades the prevailing Harlem philosophy. However, white people are hardly unwelcome here. On the contrary, many storeowners and residents take pride in receiving tourists' business and will go out of their way to make visitors feel welcome.

Today's Harlem harbors an increasingly diverse population, both ethnically and socio-economically. An influx in recent years of Dominicans has added a new Latin flavor to western Harlem. Meanwhile, you'll find students in Morningside Heights, a lot of Puerto Rican and Dominican families in Spanish Harlem, upper-middle-class black professionals in Hamilton Heights, and Orthodox Jewish families in Washington Heights and Inwood.

Much of the dangerous and poor Harlem of urban legend exists in the area south of 125th St., along Frederick Douglass Ave. and Adam Clayton Powell Blvd.; avoid this area after dark. Over the years Harlem has entered the popular psyche as the archetype of America's frayed edges, but you won't believe the hype once you've actually visited the place. Although poorer than many areas, Harlem possesses great cultural wealth.

MORNINGSIDE HEIGHTS AND COLUMBIA UNIVERSITY

Subway: #1, 9 to 110th or 116th St.

In any other city, Morningside Heights could easily serve as a major cultural and social hub—in New York, it's often overlooked. Cheap, unassuming restaurants dot this neighborhood, south of 125th St. and west of Morningside Park, where Columbia students and local Harlemites live in kooky cross-cultural coexistence.

COLUMBIA UNIVERSITY. New York City's member of the Ivy League was chartered in 1754. Now co-ed, Columbia also has cross-registration with all-female **Barnard College,** across Broadway. The campus, like a good portion of the city, was designed by McKim, Mead & White. Its centerpiece, the magisterial **Low Library,** is named after former Columbia president Seth Low. The statue of **Alma Mater** in front of the building was a rallying point during the riots of 1968. Resilient and proud, Alma survived a bomb during student protests in 1970. The steps in front of the library are great for people-watching or checking out spontaneous games of frisbee or soccer across the pedestrian walkway in the green quad. *(Morningside Dr. and Broadway, from 114th to 120th St. Group tours for prospective students from late fall through spring, but no regularly scheduled tours for the public.)*

CATHEDRAL OF ST. JOHN THE DIVINE. Already the world's largest cathedral, perpetually unfinished St. John's breaks its own record with every stone added. Its construction, begun in 1892, isn't expected to be completed any time soon. You'll probably see sculptors working on the cathedral's gargoyles as you walk by. A "living cathedral," St. John's features altars and bays dedicated not only to the sufferings of Christ, but also to such things as the experiences of immigrants and victims of genocide and AIDS. The central nave contains a 100-million-year-old nautilus fossil, a modern sculpture for 12 firefighters who died in 1966, a 2000 lb. natural quartz crystal, and a "Poet's Corner" honoring writers such as Nathaniel Hawthorne, Edith Wharton, and William Faulkner. An extensive secular schedule complements Episcopal services with concerts, art exhibitions, poetry readings, lectures, theater, and dance events. The New York Philharmonic performs here on occasion, and soprano saxophonist Paul Winter performs an annual Winter Solstice concert. The complex also contains a homeless shelter, a school, music and dance studios, a gymnasium, a Greek amphitheater (still under construction), a children's sculpture garden, a Biblical Garden, and countless other facilities available to the community. *(316-7540; tours 932-7347. Amsterdam Ave. between 110th and 113th St. Open daily 7am-5pm. Suggested donation $2, students and seniors $1. Vertical tours (you go up): noon and 2pm on the 1st and 3rd Saturdays of every month; $10; reservations necessary. Regular horizontal tours: Tu-Sa 11am, Su 1pm; $3.)*

GRANT'S TOMB. This massive granite mausoleum rests atop a hill overlooking the river. Once covered with graffiti, it now looks like a pristine monument worthy of Civil War general and 18th U.S. President Ulysses S. Grant and his wife Julia. Bronze casts of the general's cronies surround the tomb. Take a rest on the funkadelic mosaic tile benches around the monument, added in the mid-1970s. *(666-1640. Open daily 9am-5pm. Free informal ranger-guided tours on request; 5-90min., depending on how many questions you ask.)*

RIVERSIDE CHURCH. A steel-framed knock-off of France's Chartres that sprang up in only two years, thanks to John D. Rockefeller, Jr.'s deep pockets. The tower observation deck commands an amazing view both of the bells within and the expanse of the Hudson River and Riverside Park below. Best heard from the parks around the church, concerts on the world's largest carillon (74 bells) resonate on Sundays at 10:30am, 12:30, and 3pm. *(870-6792. 120th St. and Riverside Dr. Bell tower open Tu-Sa 11am-4pm, Su 12:30-4pm. Admission to observation deck Tu-Sa $2, students and seniors $1. Sunday service 10:45am. Free tours given Su 12:30pm.)*

OTHER SIGHTS. Morningside Park stretches from 110th to 123rd St. Featured in *When Harry Met Sally*, this sloping park offers rambling paths where you, too, can discuss your sexual fantasies. The wooded park is not very safe, however, especially at night. **Sakura Park** across the street from Grant's tomb provides a picnic spot complete with a little gazebo and tree-shaded benches. A walk down **Broadway** affords a wide assortment of student-filled bookstores, grocery stores, and restaurants, including the *Seinfeld*-ian **Tom's Restaurant,** 2880 Broadway (see **Restaurants,** p. 113).

CENTRAL HARLEM

Subway: #2, 3, A, B, C, or D to 125th St.

125TH STREET. Also known as **Martin Luther King, Jr. Boulevard,** this historic stretch spans the heart of Harlem. Fast-food joints, jazz bars, and the **Apollo Theater,** at 253 W. 125th St. (see **Arts and Entertainment,** p. 270), keep the street humming day and night. Street vendors, small shops, and families have combined to make this part of Harlem a lively community center and cultural hub. Many of the avenue names have changed to commemorate black leaders such as Malcolm X (Lenox or Sixth Ave.), Adam Clayton Powell, Jr. (Seventh Ave.), and Frederick Douglass (Eighth Ave.). The former **Teresa Hotel,** at the northwest corner of 125th St. and Powell Ave., has housed Malcolm X and Fidel Castro, who once preached solidarity and brotherhood from these balconies. An unconventional tourist, Castro felt safer in Harlem than in other parts of New York; still, charmingly paranoid, he brought along live Cuban chickens for his meals.

THE SCHOMBURG CENTER FOR RESEARCH IN BLACK CULTURE. This branch of the public library houses the city's archives on black history and culture. The center's namesake, avid black history scholar Arturo Schomburg, collected photographs, oral histories, and artwork, all of which now appear on exhibit here. The center also houses the **American Negro Theater,** a venue for a wide range of entertainment including concerts and plays featuring local talent and celebrities. Year-round, the center features impressive exhibits of photographs and artwork by black New Yorkers and provides a wealth of information to minority travelers (see **Essentials,** p. 75). You may want to check out the African floor mosaic, similar to the massive one in the Federal Building next to the African Burial Ground (see p. 136). Along the front of the center, a year-round exhibit features brief biographies of 100 notable black New Yorkers. *(491-2265. On 135th St. and Lenox Ave.)*

SUGAR HILL. In the 1920s and 30s, African-Americans with "sugar" (a.k.a. money) moved here. In addition to black leaders W.E.B. DuBois and Thurgood Marshall—both of whom lived at 409 Edgecombe—and musical legends Duke Ellington and W.C. Handy, some of the city's wealthiest, most notable gangsters inhabited Sugar Hill. (Wesley Snipes starred as just such a nefarious character in the film *Sugar Hill*.) Today the neighborhood has renown as the birthplace of Sugarhill Records, the rap label that created the Sugarhill Gang, whose 1979 "Rapper's Delight" became the first hip-hop song to hit the Top 40 and influenced generations to come. West of Amsterdam Ave., the neighborhood becomes predominantly Dominican, and Spanish is the dominant language. *(143rd to 155th St. between St. Nicholas and Edgecombe Ave.)*

THE STUDIO MUSEUM IN HARLEM. A fascinating collection of 19th- and 20th-century African-American, Caribbean, and African art and artifacts. In the museum gift shop you can purchase African prints, woodcarvings, posters, and cards. *(144 W. 125th St. See **Museums,** p. 249.)*

HALE HOUSE. The center's founder, the legendary "Mother" Clara Hale, pioneered the care of children born HIV-positive. Her selfless and extensive work earned the support of such influential people as Yoko Ono, Donald Trump, Patrick Ewing, and many others. Today her daughter Dr. Lorraine Hale runs the House, which now boasts a monument to the original Ms. Hale. *(For tours or to volunteer: 663-0700. 152 W. 122nd St., between Powell and Lenox.)*

THE ABYSSINIAN BAPTIST CHURCH. New York's oldest African-American church, where Adam Clayton Powell, Jr. presided over the pulpit before becoming NYC's first black congressman. His father, Adam Clayton Powell, Sr., a legendary figure credited with, among other feats, catalyzing the black migration to Harlem, preceded his son at this church. The pastor, Calvin Butts, a well-known local political leader, administers to the 4000-member congregation. *(862-7474. 132 W. 138th St. between Malcolm X and Powell Blvd. Sunday services at 9 and 11am.)*

RIVERBANK STATE PARK. In 1993 the state resolved to put a sewage plant here, an act that many considered racist, so Governor Cuomo decided that a state-run park should be built over the new plant. The popular park has year-round ice-skating, an indoor pool, tennis, tracks, roller-skating rinks, baseball diamonds, and picnic fields. The officials have, for the most part, vanquished the odor ("really, it's tidewater") problem. *(694-3643 or 694-3610. Off the West Side Highway. Subway: #9 to 145th St. Bus: M11 or Bx11.)*

STRIVER'S ROW. A group of impressive 1891 brownstones presenting a combination of architectures, from the neo-Colonial style of the south side of 139th to Stanford White's Italian Renaissance-inspired row just across the street. Originally envisioned as a "model housing project" for middle-class whites, Striver's Row acquired its nickname from lower class Harlemites who felt their neighbors were "striving" to attain "uppity" middle-class status. Now part of the St. Nicholas Historic District, the neighborhood appears in Spike Lee's *Jungle Fever*. *(138th and 139th St., between Powell and Douglass Blvd.)*

OTHER SIGHTS. Off 125th St., at 328 Lenox Ave., **Sylvia's** has reigned as "Queen of Soul Food" for over 30 years, and unfortunately everyone knows it (see **Restaurants,** p. 109). Farther south the silver dome of the **Masjid Malcolm Shabazz,** a mosque named for its first minister, Malcolm X, glitters on 116th St. at Lenox Ave. *(662-2200. Services F 1pm and Su 10am.)* The **Black Fashion Museum** is at 157 W. 125th St. between

Powell and Lenox Ave. (see **Museums,** p. 242). At 20 E. 127th St., between Madison and Fifth Ave., is the **Langston Hughes House.** Here, in his former home, a principal voice of the Harlem Renaissance lives on in photographs, manuscripts, and readings. *(862-9561. Tours by appointment only. Suggested admission $3.)* The **Liberation Bookstore,** 421 Lenox Ave., at 131st St., has a great selection of African and African-American history, art, poetry, and fiction (see **Shopping,** p. 304). Along Convent Ave. between 140th and 145th St. is **Hamilton Heights,** site of some of the city's most intricately designed brownstones. Walk down **Hamilton Terrace,** between Convent and St. Nicholas Ave., for lovely examples of these homes. Alexander Hamilton built his two-story Colonial-style country home, **Hamilton Grange,** at what is now 287 Convent Ave., at 141st St. The National Park Service wants to restore the house, currently a public museum, and make it a bona fide national landmark; if funding comes through, the house will be moved to nearby St. Nicholas Park. *(283-5154. Open F-Su 9am-4pm. Free.)*

At 749 St. Nicholas Ave. between 145th and 146th St. lies the **Ralph Ellison apartment.** He wrote Invisible Man while living in this Sugar Hill building. Farther north at Broadway and 155th St. are the four buildings in **Audubon Terrace,** the Beaux Arts complex that houses the Numismatic Society Museum, the Hispanic Society of America, the American Academy of Arts and Letters (see **Museums,** p. 242), and Boricua College, a private Hispanic liberal arts college. The Italian Renaissance courtyard has huge reliefs and sculptures. Across the street, you can wander Trinity Cemetery, between 153rd and 155th St., and Amsterdam Ave. and Riverside Dr. *(Open daily 9am-4:30pm. Subway: #1 to 157th St. or the A or B to 155th St.)*

SPANISH HARLEM

Subway: #6 to 116th or 125th St.

East Harlem, better known as Spanish Harlem or El Barrio ("The Neighborhood"), hugs the northeast corner of Central Park and extends to the 140s, as far as the Harlem River. At the main artery on E. 116th St., the streets, rollicking to a salsa beat, overflow with fruit stands, Puerto Rican eateries, and ice men selling flavored crushed ice on scorching summer days ($1). Anti-crack murals and memorials to the drug's victims adorn the walls of projects and abandoned buildings as testimony to the neighborhood's chronic and historical plight of poverty and crime. El Barrio is at its best on Puerto Rican Independence Day, June 20, when streets close off for some serious festivity. Much of Spanish Harlem north of 110th St. can be dangerous even during the day.. The northern tip of Fifth Ave.'s Museum Mile stretches up to the **Museum of the City of New York** at 103rd St. and **El Museo del Barrio** at 105th St. (see **Museums,** p. 246). On your way up the East Side, you may discover how Fifth Ave. and Park Ave. display up-close-and-personal social and cultural stratification—at E. 96th St., you'll cross from a world of doormen to a world of men sleeping in doorways.

WASHINGTON HEIGHTS

Washington Heights and neighboring Inwood can be safe on one block and plagued by crack dealers on the next. It's best to reach the neighborhood by the A train, which will bring you closer to the intriguing sights than will the #1 or 9 trains.

Up here, north of 155th St., the landscape, both geographical and ethnic, shows itself more readily than in the lower reaches of Manhattan. Here the skyline is not totally manmade, and buildings perched atop high ridges peer down hundreds of feet onto their next-door neighbors. The demarcation of ethnic enclaves can appear just as suddenly. This formerly all-Irish neighborhood now flaunts Latin, black, Greek, Armenian, and large Jewish communities. Washington Heights, therefore, has had to deal with its share of culture clashes. Recently, however, the prevalence of drugs and crime have steadily decreased, and the residents of Washington Heights take pride in their neighborhood. Pluck up your courage and explore this neighborhood's many hidden treasures.

NEIGHBORHOODS

MORRIS-JUMEL MANSION. The Georgian 65 Jumel Terrace, between 160th and 162nd St., was built in 1765 and is Manhattan's oldest existing house. Washington lived here while planning his successful (but little-known) Battle of Harlem Heights in the autumn of 1776. In 1810, Stephen and Eliza Jumel bought the house; Eliza seems to have spent most of her time primping, as seen by the vast numbers of parlors and dressing rooms in the house. Stephen died in 1832 and in 1833 Eliza up and married Aaron Burr in the front room. Don't be afraid to knock if the house seems closed. The gardens are exceptional as well, with a great view of the Harlem River. Nearby, at St. Nicholas Ave. and 161st St., more brownstones with architecturally varied facades vie for attention on **Sylvan Terrace.** *(Call the Mansion at 923-8008. Open W-Su 10am-4pm. $3, seniors and students $1. Accompanied children under 12 free. Tours by appointment. Subway: C to 163rd St.)*

AUDUBON BALLROOM. Columbia University recently ignited a controversy when it decided to buy the abandoned the site of Malcolm X's assassination, on 165th St. between St. Nicholas Ave. and Broadway. Protesters have covered the doorway with plaques calling for a memorial to the inspirational leader. Nonetheless, only the edifice remains.

GEORGE WASHINGTON BRIDGE. The corner of 181st St. and Riverside Drive provides one of the more spectacular views of the 14-lane, 3500-foot suspension bridge. Its construction coincided with the beginning of the Great Depression and the resulting lack of funds left the bridge's two towers without the granite sheathing that designer Othmar Amman's had intended. The naked steelwork creates the ultramodern, Erector-set look that so excited Le Corbusier, who pronounced it "the most beautiful bridge in the world."

LITTLE RED LIGHTHOUSE. It resides just beneath the bridge, in **Fort Washington Park,** home to remnants of the original fort. Originally constructed to steer barges away from Jeffrey's Hook, you may remember the lighthouse best from Hildegarde Hoyt Swift's children's book *The Little Red Lighthouse and the Great Grey Bridge.* To get there go north on Riverside Drive (if you're facing the water, that means taking a right onto Riverside) for about a block from the intersection with 181st, then go across the suspended walkway to your left. When you get to the other side, go south along Riverside Drive (keeping the Hudson River to your right) then follow the path as it curves down the hill and to your right. The trail winds through woods and eventually comes out right at the edge of the water. The trail is a little spooky; don't travel it alone or at night. *(Subway: A train to 181st St.; or walk up Broadway, then take a left on 181st and walk until it ends at Riverside Dr.)*

YESHIVA UNIVERSITY. Surrounded by kosher bakeries and butcher shops, the university stands on Amsterdam Ave.—six blocks over from Riverside Drive through a bustling Hispanic neighborhood—from 182nd to 186th St. This is the oldest Jewish-studies center in the U.S., dating from 1886. The **Yeshiva University Museum** (see **Museums,**) on 185th St. features exhibits focusing on the Jewish community. (Subway: #1 or 9 to 181st or 190th St.) On 186th St., the **Samuel H. & Rachel Golding Building,** formerly known as Tannenbaum Hall, provides the centerpiece of the campus, featuring Romanesque windows and colorful minarets that contrast with the drab, institutional architecture of the rest of the campus.

OVERLOOK TERRACE. Back on the west side of the island, Ft. Washington Ave. rises steeply to command a wide vista of the Hudson River on one side and the central valley of the island on the other. Take the stairs up from the east side at 187th St. The journey north along Ft. Washington Ave. takes you past a succession of mid-rise apartment buildings (c. 1920), home to many Jewish and Hispanic families. At 190th St. and Ft. Washington Ave., the **St. Francis Xavier Cabrini Chapel** shelters the remains of Mother Cabrini, the patron saint of immigrants. (Open M-Su 9am-4:30pm.) Her body lies in a crystal casket under the altar, but her smiling face is made of wax—Rome has her head. Ack. Legend has it that shortly after her death, a lock of her hair restored the eyesight of an infant who has since grown up to be a Texan priest.

FORT TRYON PARK. The official (and safest) entrance lies at Margaret Corbin Circle. Central Park's Frederick Law Olmsted lovingly landscaped this park, donated to the city by John D. Rockefeller, in exchange for permission to construct Rockefeller University. You can still see the crumbling remains of Ft. Tryon, a Revolutionary War bulwark. The park also contains a magnificent expanse of gardens, a path along the west side that offers views of the Washington Bridge and the Palisades, and **The Cloisters,** the Met's sanctuary for medieval art (see p. 243). This is one of the most peaceful sights in Manhattan and is worth the trip even if you don't have a taste for medieval art. If you're an experienced climber, or if you've completed the Central Park Conservancy's beginner course at Central Park's North Meadow Recreation Center (see **Neighborhoods,** p. 180), you can register to climb up and rappel down the 50-ft. face of the cliff on the eastern side to Ft. Tryon Park. Conservancy instructors take people up about twice a month. For information on the climbs as well as on the beginner and intermediate courses, call 360-2732. *(To get to the Cabrini Chapel or Ft. Tryon Park by subway, take the A train to 190th St., then take the elevator up from the station. Even if you're not planning to take the subway, the elevator is the best way to get down the cliff if you want to go west across town.)*

DYCKMAN FARMHOUSE MUSEUM. At Broadway and 204th St. stands a modest but charming 18th-century Dutch dwelling that belonged to a 300-acre farm. Donated to the city as a museum in 1915, the only remaining 18th-century farmhouse in Manhattan, has been restored and filled with period Dutch and English family furnishings. *(304-9422. Open Tu-Su 11am-4pm. Free. Subway: A to 207th St.)*

INWOOD HILL PARK. At the corner of Isham St. (one block north of 207th St.) and Seaman Ave., discover the entrance to the park, which boasts, with its athletic facilities and playgrounds, Manhattan's only stretch of primeval forest with a system of trails that you may use in winter for **cross-country skiing.** Perhaps the park's most interesting feature, its **caves**—once inhabited by one of Manhattan's Indian tribe—now shelter some of the city's homeless. The **nature center** (304-2365), organizes tours of the caves. *Let's Go* strongly discourages exploring the caves on your own. The neighborhood on the hill just to the east of the park is full of pretty old brownstones, and just to the northeast of the park is Columbia University's athletic facilities, **Baker Field.**

OTHER SIGHTS. You may want to bargain-shop along trinket-filled St. Nicholas Ave. or Broadway. Street vendors sell swimwear, Italian shoes, and household items for half the original price. You can find discount electronics stores here, too. Prices fall as the street numbers rise.

BROOKLYN

Our story begins, as all great stories do, in Brooklyn.

—Jon Kalish

When the Dutch settled this area in the 17th century, they called it Brooklyn, or "Broken Land." When asked to join New York in 1833, the City of Brooklyn refused, in its typical fashion, saying that the two cities shared no interests except common waterways. Not until 1898 did the citizenry decide, in a close vote, to join New York City's boroughs—a decision writer Peter Hammill calls "The Great Mistake." In the early 20th century, European immigrants flowed into the borough in great numbers. After the Depression, black Southerners also sought haven in Brooklyn, and many groups soon followed. Many visitors experience Manhattan via shopping and consuming, but folks *live* in Brooklyn.

Each of Brooklyn's neighborhoods boasts a uniquely different flavor—from the the Italian community in Bensonhurst, unflatteringly immortalized in filmmaker Spike Lee's "joints," to traditional Jewish communities in Crown Heights, and a wealthy black presence in Fort Greene. Despite their seemingly endless ethnic and religious differences, Brooklynites all share an indomitable pride in their home.

NEIGHBORHOODS

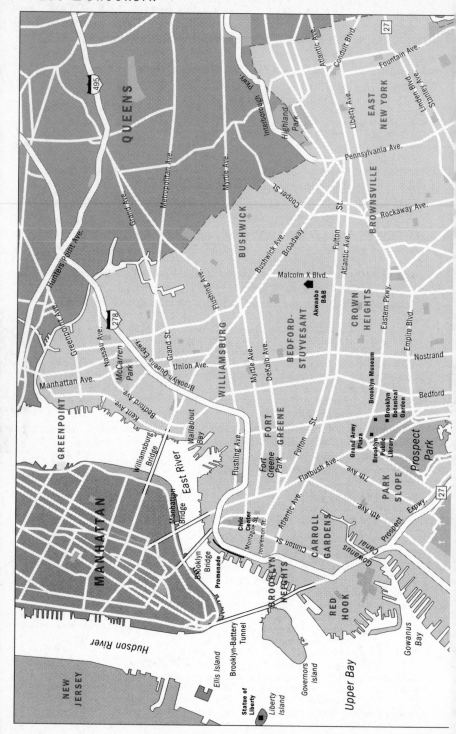

NEW JERSEY

Hudson River

Statue of
Liberty

Liberty
Island

Ellis Island

Brooklyn-Battery Tunnel

Governors
Island

Upper Bay

Gowanus
Bay

MANHATTAN

East River

Williamsburg
Bridge

Manhattan
Bridge

Brooklyn
Bridge

Promenade

BROOKLYN
HEIGHTS

Civic
Center

Montague St.

Joralemon St.

Clinton St.

CARROLL
GARDENS

RED
HOOK

Gowanus Canal

PARK
SLOPE

4th Ave.

7th Ave.

Prospect Expwy.

Prospect
Park

27

Grand Army
Plaza

Brooklyn
Public
Library

Brooklyn
Botanical
Garden

■ Brooklyn Museum

Eastern Pkwy.

Empire Blvd.

Nostrand

Bedford

CROWN
HEIGHTS

BEDFORD-
STUYVESANT

Fulton St.

Flatbush Ave.

Atlantic Ave.

Fulton

Atlantic Ave.

St.

Rockaway Ave.

BROWNSVILLE

Pennsylvania Ave.

EAST
NEW YORK

Fountain Ave.

Conduit Blvd.

Atlantic Ave.

Liberty Ave.

Linden Blvd.

Stanley Ave.

27

FORT
GREENE

Fort
Greene
Park

Flushing Ave.

DeKalb Ave.

Myrtle Ave.

WILLIAMSBURG

Union Ave.

Grand St.

Bedford Ave.

Kent Ave.

Wallabout
Bay

McCarren
Park

Brooklyn-Queens Expwy.

Flushing Ave.

Nassau Ave.

278

Manhattan Ave.

GREENPOINT

Hunters Point Ave.

Greenpoint Ave.

495

QUEENS

Grand Ave.

Metropolitan Ave.

Myrtle Ave.

Cooper St.

Highland
Park

Interborough Pkwy.

BUSHWICK

Bushwick Ave.

Broadway

Malcolm X Blvd.

Akwaaba
B&B

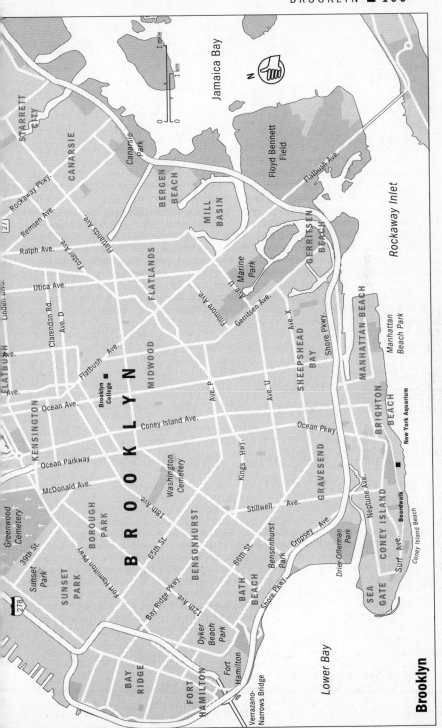

Brooklyn

BROOKLYN

Jamaica Bay

Rockaway Inlet

Lower Bay

STARRETT CITY

CANARSIE

BERGEN BEACH

MILL BASIN

Floyd Bennett Field

Flatbush Ave.

GERRITSEN BEACH

MANHATTAN BEACH

Manhattan Beach Park

Rockaway Pkwy.

Remsen Ave.

Ralph Ave.

Utica Ave.

Clarendon Rd.

Ave. D

Canarsie Park

Flatlands Ave.

Foster Ave.

FLATLANDS

Marine Park

Fillmore Ave.

Gerritsen Ave.

Ave. X

Shore Pkwy.

SHEEPSHEAD BAY

BRIGHTON BEACH

New York Aquarium

Linden Blvd.

FLATBUSH

Ave.

KENSINGTON

Ocean Ave.

Ocean Parkway

McDonald Ave.

Flatbush Ave.

Brooklyn College

MIDWOOD

Ave. P

Ave. U

Ocean Pkwy.

Kings Hwy.

Coney Island Ave.

GRAVESEND

Neptune Ave.

Boardwalk

Greenwood Cemetery

39th St.

Sunset Park

SUNSET PARK

Fort Hamilton Pkwy.

BOROUGH PARK

Washington Cemetery

18th Ave.

65th St.

BENSONHURST

Stillwell Ave.

Bensonhurst Park

Cropsey Ave.

Dreier-Offerman Park

SEA GATE

CONEY ISLAND

Surf Ave.

Coney Island Beach

BAY RIDGE

Bay Ridge Pkwy.

12th Ave.

Dyker Beach Park

86th St.

BATH BEACH

Shore Pkwy.

FORT HAMILTON

Fort Hamilton

Verrazano-Narrows Bridge

278

1 mile

1 km

N

Aged natives, even long after they've moved, still wail the Dodgers' defection to L.A. Old-time romantics often imagine Brooklyn as Woody Allen depicted it in *Annie Hall*, full of images like that of protagonist Alvy Singer in his rickety home underneath a Coney Island roller coaster. Although such nostalgia is based in truth (someone still lives in the house under Coney Island's now-defunct Thunderbolt Rollercoaster), Brooklyn has many faces, including some of the city's most forward-looking.

As New York's most populous and diverse borough, Brooklyn holds its own against Manhattan. It's a place to explore at a leisurely pace, getting a feel for the tempo and pulse of each neighborhood. For maps and other material on Brooklyn, visit the **Fund for the Borough of Brooklyn,** 16 Court St., near Montague St. (718-855-7882; subway: #2, 3 or 4, 5 or M, N, R to Borough Hall). Maps of the entire MTA system (including Brooklyn) are available in any subway station.

ORIENTATION

Brooklyn's main avenues dissect the borough. The **Brooklyn-Queens Expressway (BQE)** pours into the **Belt Parkway** and circumscribes Brooklyn. Ocean Pkwy., Ocean Ave., Coney Island Ave., and diagonal Flatbush Ave. run from the beaches of southern Brooklyn to Prospect Park in the heart of the borough. Flatbush Ave. eventually leads to the Manhattan Bridge. The streets of western Brooklyn (including those in Sunset Park, Bensonhurst, Borough Park, and Park Slope) are aligned with the western shore and thus collide at a 45-degree angle with central Brooklyn's main arteries. In northern Brooklyn, several avenues—Atlantic Ave., Eastern Pkwy., and Flushing Ave.—travel from downtown east into Queens.

Brooklyn is also spliced by **subway lines.** Most lines serving the borough pass through the Atlantic Ave. Station downtown. The D and Q lines continue southeast through Prospect Park and Flatbush to Brighton Beach. The #2 and 5 trains head east to Brooklyn College in Flatbush. The B and N trains travel south through Bensonhurst, terminating at Coney Island. The J, M, and Z trains serve Williamsburg and Bushwick and continue east and north into Queens. The Brooklyn-Queens crosstown G train shuttles from southern Brooklyn through Greenpoint into Queens.

For maps and other material on Brooklyn, visit the **Fund for the Borough of Brooklyn,** 16 Court St. (subway #2, 3, 4, 5, M, or R to Borough Hall; 718-855-7882), near Montague St. The MTA provides maps of the entire city transit system (including Brooklyn) that are available in every city station.

BROOKLYN BRIDGE

Subway: #4, 5, 6 to Brooklyn Bridge; to start in Brooklyn take subway #2, 3 to Clark St. or A, C to High St.

Walking across the Brooklyn Bridge at sunrise or sunset is one of the most exhilarating strolls New York City has to offer—especially when you're dodging the cyclists on the pedestrian path. Gracefully spanning the gap between Lower Manhattan's dense cluster of skyscrapers and Brooklyn's less intimidating shore, it is widely considered to be the world's most beautiful bridge. Georgia O'Keefe and Joseph Stella have memorialized this technological and aesthetic triumph on canvas, and Hart Crane and Walt Whitman expressed their admiration in verse. A ramp across from City Hall begins the journey from Manhattan.

Upon its 1883 completion, New York's suspended cathedral loomed far above the rest of the city. After chief architect John Augustus Roebling crushed his foot in a surveying accident and died of gangrene, his son Washington (and subsequently Washington's wife Emily Warren, after he succumbed to the bends) took over. In the end, the trio achieved a combination of delicacy and power that makes other New York bridges look either cumbersome or flimsy. Plaques at either end of the walkway commemorate the Roeblings and the 20 workers who died in the bridge's underwater chambers during construction.

Like all great bridges, the Brooklyn Bridge has had its share of post-construction deaths as well. A few days after its opening, a frantic mob feared the bridge was collapsing and trampled 12 pedestrians to death in their struggle to escape. In 1885, Robert Odlum leapt off, marking the bridge's first suicide. Locals say if he had only dived—and not belly-flopped—he might have lived. Ironically, he was a swimming instructor.

DOWNTOWN BROOKLYN

Subway #2, 3 or 4, 5 or D, Q to Atlantic Ave.; or the B, M, N, R to Pacific St.

BROOKLYN ACADEMY OF MUSIC. BAM, as New Yorkers call it, hosts a wonderful array of cultural events and film series (see **Arts and Entertainment,** p. 266).

FORT GREENE. Dubbed "Black SoHo," this vibrant neighborhood along DeKalb Ave. has enough going for it to call SoHo "White(ish) Fort Greene." Trees, hip hangouts, and elegant brownstones line the streets of this black artistic and cultural hub. Fort Greene is the home of filmmaker Spike Lee and the base of his production company, **40 Acres and a Mule,** at 124 DeKalb Ave. This area is also home to a number of other powerful art and entertainment figures who fuel Fort Greene's increasingly pan-ethnic renaissance. *(Bounded by the Navy Yard and Atlantic Ave. to the north and south, and Flatbush Ave. Extension and Clinton Ave. to the east and west.)*

FULTON MALL. Brooklyn's main commercial thoroughfare in the 1930s and 40s, the eight blocks extending from Fulton St. to Borough Hall were renamed in a 1970s effort to spark investment in the disintegrating street. Now Fulton Mall is a promenade of fast-food joints and small, cheap (and marvelously tacky) stores with bargains galore on clothes, electronics, and furniture. *(East of Ft. Greene, at Flatbush Ave. and Fulton St. Subway: #2, 3 to Fulton.)*

DUMBO. In addition to its cute nickname (an acronym for "Down Under the Manhattan Bridge Overpass"), several other traits mark this neighborhood as a real up-and-comer. For one: industrial warehouse spaces with "For Lease or Sale" signs on their doors. Some of spaces have already been taken over by Brooklyn's volunteer artist militias, who have converted them into galleries. For example, the building at 135 Plymouth St. and Anchorage St. holds several makeshift galleries, including the **Ammo Exhibitions Space.** Another gallery, the **Brooklyn Bridge Anchorage** is housed within the bridge's cavernous suspension cable storage chambers. *(718-802-1215. Corner of Hicks and Old Fulton St. Open mid-May to mid-Oct. M-Tu and Th-Su noon-8pm, W noon-7pm.)* The Anchorage features cutting-edge digital/multi-media installations that make good use of the 80 ft. high vaulted ceilings. Recently, landlords of buildings in DUMBO have tried to squeeze artists out in favor of more upscale renters. As the fear of gentrification grows, locals have banded together in a very Brooklynese attempt to maintain a low-rent atmosphere. At the northern end of Main St., between the Manhattan and Brooklyn Bridges, the **Empire-Fulton-Ferry State Park,** provides a grassy waterfront area, ripe for contemplative moments. Even during the day DUMBO is largely deserted; after dark, avoid it, unless the Anchorage is having a late-night electronic and experimental music event.

THE EAGLE WAREHOUSE AND STORAGE CO. The *Brooklyn Eagle* newspaper once produced its controversial pages in this building. The paper's editor, Brooklyn poet-laureate Walt Whitman, was fired due either to laziness or to his bold anti-slavery views—depending upon the slant of your source. The Storage Co. has since been converted into apartments. *(28 Old Fulton St. at Front St.)*

OTHER SIGHTS. Borough Hall, built in 1851, once housed the city hall of an independent Brooklyn and is now the borough's oldest building. *(209 Joralemon St., at the southern end of Fulton Mall. Tours Tu 1pm.)* If you walk to **Columbus Park** on the opposite side of the building, you can see that the statue of Justice, standing firmly with scales and sword on top of the hall, isn't wearing a blindfold. Many find this detail to be uncannily accurate. Just north of Borough Hall, past the statue of Columbus and a bust of Robert Kennedy, is the **New York State Supreme Court.** The building lies at the southern end of **Cadman Plaza Park,** a long stretch of greenery extending from Columbus Park to the Brooklyn Bridge. As Cadman Plaza Park ends at the entrance to the Brooklyn Bridge, Cadman Plaza West becomes Old Fulton St. and runs down to the **waterfront,** where you can catch a lovely view of Manhattan. Old Fulton St. runs down to the base of the Broolyn Bridge and ends at **Fulton Ferry Landing** where one can marvel at breathtaking views of the Brooklyn Bridge and lower Manhattan. Don't look now, but behind you stands one of the Watchtower Buildings, world headquarters of the Jehovah's Witness organization. If the awe of God has made you hungry, stop by **Grimaldi's** (see **Restaurants,** p. 94) for a pizza (not sold by the slice) and consider boarding the **stationary barge** docked by the Landing for a first-rate chamber music concert. *(718-624-4061. Concerts are Su 4pm, Th-Sa 7:30pm. $23, students $15, seniors $20.)*

BROOKLYN HEIGHTS

Subway: N, R or 2, 3 or 4, 5 to Court St./Borough Hall and follow Court.

Before the Brooklyn Bridge, there was the steamboat. Its 1814 invention made the development of Brooklyn Heights possible. Rows of posh Greek Revival and Italianate houses sprang up, creating New York's first suburb. In 1965, shady-laned Brooklyn Heights became New York's—and the nation's—first official historic district. The picturesque Heights were home to a number of notable writers back in the 1940s and 50s, among them Arthur Miller and W.H. Auden. Today its 19th-century brownstones house mainly the young, upwardly mobile, and white, while Atlantic Ave. has a large Middle Eastern community.

PROMENADE. The view of lower Manhattan from this waterfront walkway is, very simply, one of *the* New York sights to see—even if it doubles as the roof of the toxic Brooklyn-Queens Expressway (BQE). To the left, Lady Liberty can be seen peeping from behind Staten Island. In fair weather, Ellis Island appears in full view, to the right of Liberty Island. During the day, many commuters walk from here to jobs in Manhattan, saving money, getting exercise, and experiencing the sublime all at once (see **Brooklyn Bridge,** p. 203). *(Spans from Remsen to Orange St.)*

MONTAGUE STREET. Brooklyn Heights' main commercial drag has the feel of a college town main street, with cafes, mid-priced restaurants, and overpriced "fashion" franchises like The Gap. One of its more impressive landmarks is the **St. Ann and the Holy Trinity Episcopal Church** (718-834-8794), on the corner of Clinton St., Saint Ann's contains over 4000 sq. ft. of stained glass, sparkling clean after an extensive restoration in 1998. An alternative and illustrious private school operates on the church grounds, as does the **Arts at St. Ann's** acoustically superb cultural center (718-858-2424), which attracts performers like Lou Reed and Marianne Faithfull.

BROOKLYN HISTORICAL SOCIETY. This striking building lined with spooky gargoyle-busts of Shakespeare, Beethoven, and others, houses both the very informative society and a museum. The research library is closed to the public while undergoing renovations. *(718-624-0890. 128 Pierrepont St. Take a right on Clinton St. to get to Pierrepont St., parallel to Montague St. and Remsen St. Open M, Th-Sa noon-5pm.)*

PLYMOUTH CHURCH OF PILGRIMS. Before the Civil War, this simple red-brick church was part of the underground railroad and the center of New Yorker abolitionist sentiments. Its courageous first minister and head abolitionist was Henry Ward Beecher, brother of *Uncle Tom's Cabin* author Harriet Beecher Stowe. Beecher's statue sits in the courtyard alongside a bas-relief of Abraham Lincoln, who visited the church. *(718-624-4743. Orange St., off Willow St.)*

OTHER SIGHTS. To see the Heights' potpourri of 19th-century styles, explore the Federal-style **Willow Street** between Clark and Pierrepont St. Numbers 155-159 were the earliest houses here (c. 1825), with dormer windows punctuating the sloping roofs. Walking south through the Brooklyn Heights historic district, you will arrive at **Hicks Street,** the heart of historic Brooklyn. A few blocks down, **Grace Church,** 254 Hicks St., at Grace Ct. is bedecked with Tiffany windows depicting the life of Christ. Continuing southward will bring you to **Atlantic Avenue,** Brooklyn's renowned stretch of Middle Eastern restaurants and stores. If you work your way back from the water to Court St., making a left and then a right on Schermerhorn, you will reach the **Transit Museum** (see **Museums,** p. 248).

CARROLL GARDENS AND RED HOOK

*To get to **Carroll Gardens** and **Cobble Hill** take subway F, G to Carroll St. or Bergen St. To **Red Hook** take subway A, C, F or 2, 3 or 4, 5 to Jay St./Borough Hall; or M, N, R to Court St. and then pick up bus B61 at the corner of Court St. and Atlantic Ave.*

Just south of Atlantic Ave. lies the quiet Italian neighborhood of **Cobble Hill** whose gorgeous brownstone-lined sidestreets quickly segue into **Carroll Gardens.** The large Italian population here is evidenced by the numerous pasta and pastry shops and the old *padrones* who sit out front in lawn chairs to chew the fat in their native tongue. Check out the **Cammareri Bros. Bakery,** 502 Henry St. (718-745-0848), where Nicholas Cage lost his hand, seduced Cher, and found the sensitive side to his anger in *Moonstruck.* Much of the movie was filmed in this area.

While the neighborhood does betray a heavy Italian influence, the busy parallels **Court St.** and **Smith St.,** which run perpendicular to Atlantic Ave., reflect the influence of SoHo boutique design and ethnic menageries. Thrift stores, antique vendors, small design boutiques, artist cooperatives, and craft shops crowd in the spaces between restaurants; this area makes a perfect place for some leisurely, Brooklyn-paced browsing. Look for the *Smith St.* pamphlet in some area boutiques that lists shops and eateries of note. **Carroll Park,** a tiny postage stamp of a park, overflows with frolicking children on Court St. between President and Carroll St.

To the west, on the other side of the Brooklyn-Queens Expressway (BQE), is the industrial waterfront area of **Red Hook,** home to wonderful views, occasional cobblestoned streets, and many a warehouse. For a marvelous view of the Statue of Liberty, head west on Atlantic Ave. toward the docks, or if you're not in the mood for a hike, grab bus B61. At the Union St. stop are two excellent eateries—Ferdinando's and the Latticini-Barese (see **Restaurants,** p. 96). The bus (or you on your weary feet) continues south on Columbia St. over trolley tracks and cobblestones; one block west it picks up Van Brunt, heading southwest. Get off at the southernmost stop on Van Brunt, right where the bus turns around. At the end of the street is a long pier with former warehouses that have been converted into studios. The view of the harbor and the Statue of Liberty is second only to the view from the park at the end of Coffey St. Walking a few blocks up Van Brunt, take a left on Coffey and walk west (toward the harbor); you will come to the small **Coffey St. Park** and its serene pier. Aside from the occasional fisherman and the odd kayaker, you'll be left on your own to enjoy the breathtaking view of Lady Liberty (from here she's facing you, not in profile as from Manhattan) and the bottom of Manhattan. Here, as throughout Red Hook, the lack of tall buildings combine with a west-facing waterfront to create a golden light, especially in the late afternoon and early evening.

Farther northwest, Conover St.—running perpendicular to Coffey St.—ends at another pier, which, besides its own impressive view, boasts the **Waterfront Museum,** a barge that holds maritime artifacts, a kinetic sculpture, and some sea-oriented photographs. The museum's most interesting showpiece is the small barge itself, which was restored singlehandedly by the man who currently runs it; it is the only operational wooden barge surviving in the New York Harbor. The museum hosts a music series in the summer as well as titillating programming for kids, including a small circus on Sundays in June. (See **Museums,** p. 249.) Following Bay St. east from Columbia St. for several blocks will bring you to a **football field** that draws young crowds for pickup soccer and white-clad Haitian immigrants for cricket. The enormous Red Hook housing projects are just north of here. Avoid these sidestreets at night.

NEIGHBORHOODS

UNDERGROUND DA VINCIS AND URBAN MICHELANGELOS

As the night shadows begin to lighten, the inspired artist puts the finishing touches on his canvas—he sprays some more paint on the rundown brick building, then sprints down an alley to avoid early morning police patrols. Graffiti is illegal and its practitioners must work invisibly. Using spray paint and urban resourcefulness, graffiti writers make art that reflects the city's vitality: colorful, intricate, fantastic, a mix of words and images painted on a wall, truck, or any available surface. Name "tags" are common, and the more accomplished artists can transform a dingy wall into a virtuoso masterwork. Storefronts decorated by local talent abound in Brooklyn and the Bronx. Graffiti isn't meant to stay forever inside a museum, though New York artists Jean-Michel Basquiat and Keith Haring began their careers as graffiti writers and became famous for techniques learned on city walls.

NORTH BROOKLYN

*Subway: To **Greenpoint,** take G train to Greenpoint Ave. To **Hassidic Williamsburg,** take J, M, Z train to Marcy Ave. To **artsy Williamsburg,** take L train to Bedford Ave. (For **walking tours** of the area contact the Williamsburg Art and Historical Society at 718-486-7372; see **Galleries,** p. 255.) To **Bedford-Stuyvesant** take G train to Bedford-Nostrand Ave. To **Bushwick** take M train to Myrtle Ave. To **Crown Heights** take #3 or 4 train to Utica Ave./Eastern Pkwy.*

On Brooklyn's northern border with Queens, **Greenpoint** is home to a large Polish community. **Manhattan Avenue,** the heart of the neighborhood's business district, intersects Greenpoint Ave. at the subway station. Just west of Manhattan Ave. is the **Greenpoint Historic District,** bounded by Java St. to the north, Meserole St. to the south, and Franklin St. to the west. The Italianate and Grecian houses were built in the 1850s, when Greenpoint was home to a booming shipbuilding industry. The Union's ironclad **Monitor,** which stalemated the Confederacy's *Merrimac,* was built here.

If you take Manhattan Ave. south to Driggs Ave., make a right, and go through **McCarren Park,** you'll find yourself under the copper-covered domes and triple-slashed crosses of the **Russian Orthodox Cathedral of the Transfiguration of Our Lord** at N. 12th St. Four blocks up is Kent Ave., which runs through a seedy industrial zone and under the **Williamsburg Bridge** to the monstrous **Brooklyn Naval Yard.**

South of Greenpoint is **Williamsburg,** a large neighborhood home to a thriving Hassidic Jewish population, Latino communities, and in the past decade a percolating arts scene. The **Hassidic** community is concentrated mostly in the south side of town in the area around Broadway, Heyward, and Wythe St. and along Bedford Ave. by Lee and Marcy St. Men wear long black coats and hats—dress which dates to early modern Eastern Europe and imitates the garb of the Polish nobility of that time. North of Broadway is a primarily Hispanic neighborhood.

Since the 1980s artists have been migrating to Williamsburg to find shelter from the heavy financial burdens of Manhattan. Today, Williamsburg, for blocks around the Bedford Ave. L subway stop, looks like a homey recreation of the East Village. Along **Bedford Ave.** trendy restaurants make sure young artists get their vegan patties served up just right, and funky thrift, music, and book stores vie for browsers' attention. Nervous hipsters check over newly signed leases in real estate storefronts and homemade paint supply stores carefully dole out their powdered hues.

Williamsburg sports quite a few underground, eternally shifting **galleries,** best located by asking around at local establishments. The foremost among them is **Galapagos.** This bar/performance space can be reached by going south along Bedford and then west along N. 6th St. (see **Nightlife,** p. 284). To reach the **Brooklyn Brewery** that produces the Brooklyn Lager and Brooklyn Brown Ale on tap at all the local bars, head farther down Bedford and turn onto N. 11th. (718-486-7422. 118 N. 11th St. Tastings F 6-10pm, free tours Sa noon-4:30pm.) Continuing down Bedford will bring you to Broadway, below the newly renovated **Williams-**

burg Bridge and the **Williamsburg Art and Historical Center,** 195 Bedford Ave. (718-486-7372), the cultural mecca of this vibrant community (see **Galleries,** p. 254). The Williamsburg Bridge's walkway, the **Skywalk,** makes for a pleasant stroll into the Lower East Side.

Those venturing southeast into the neighborhoods of **Bushwick, Bedford-Stuyvesant (Bed-Stuy),** and **Brownsville** should be cautious. Low public funding, high unemployment, and inadequate public works have created burnt-out buildings, patches of undeveloped land, and stagnant commercial zones. Still, social consciousness and political activism emerge from every pothole in these neglected streets. Wall murals portraying Malcolm X, slogans urging patronage of black businesses, Puerto Rican flags, and leather Africa medallions all testify to a growing sense of racial and cultural empowerment. Spike Lee's explosive *Do the Right Thing* was filmed on the streets of Bed-Stuy. Bed-Stuy also boasts an historic district called **Stuyvesant Heights,** containing, you guessed it, beautiful brownstones.

Every year on the Fourth of July weekend, an African cultural celebration is held in Brownsville on the grounds of the **Boys and Girls School,** 1700 Fulton St. From noon to midnight for several days, you can hear the solid bass of reggae bands and the slamming beats of local rap musicians. The Boys and Girls School is a community-controlled public school that grew out of the 1969 attempt to hand over control of the Ocean Hill-Brownsville School District to the community; the plan was derailed by a teachers' strike. The school's formation and subsequent problems were featured in the award-winning documentary *Eyes on the Prize.*

At 770 Eastern Pkwy. in **Crown Heights** is the world headquarters of **ChaBad,** a Hassidic Jewish sect whose Grand Rebbe, Menachem Mendel Shneerson, died in 1994. His followers believed he was the Messiah, and even after his death some claimed he would rise again. They now face the possibility of schism as some hold onto the Rebbe's divinity while others insist upon his mortality. Be aware that you may feel conspicuous or even unwelcome here unless you dress conservatively and, if you are male, wear a yarmulke or some other head covering.

INSTITUTE PARK

Subway: #2, 3 to Eastern Parkway/Brooklyn Museum.

Brooklyn's official cultural nexus, Institute Park lies between Flatbush Ave., Eastern Parkway, and Washington Ave.

THE BROOKLYN BOTANIC GARDEN. This 52-acre fairyland was founded in 1910 on a reclaimed waste dump by the Brooklyn Institute of Art and Sciences. If you've gotten over that traumatic bee stinging in grade school, the **Fragrance Garden for the Blind** is an olfactory carnival—with mint, lemon, violet, and more appetizing aromas. The more formal **Cranford Rose Garden** crams in over 100 blooming varieties of roses. Every spring, visitors can take part in the **Sakura Matsuri** (Japanese cherry blossom festival) at the Cherry Walk and Cherry Esplanade. The woodsy **Japanese Garden** contains weeping willows and a viewing pavilion over a pond. The artificial scenery's authenticity fools the many water birds that flock to the site. The **Shakespeare Garden** displays 80 plants mentioned in Will's works. Toward the rear of the gardens two cement pools blossom with lily pads. You should not miss the 100 varieties of tropical water-lilies and sacred lotus that radiate in the summer in the **Lily Pool Terrace,** as well as the rainbow assortment of flowering annuals in the **Annual Border**—both just outside of the conservatory. *(718-622-4433. 1000 Washington Ave. Open Apr.-Sept. Tu-F 8am-6pm, Sa-Su and holidays 10am-6pm; Oct.-Mar. Tu-F 8am-4:30pm, Sa-Su and holidays 10am-4:30pm. $3, students and seniors $1.50, ages 5-15 50¢. Free Tuesdays.)*

THE BROOKLYN PUBLIC LIBRARY. Its striking Art Deco main branch building stands majestically on the Grand Army Plaza. The library has spawned 53 branches and contains 1,600,000 volumes. There are changing exhibitions on the second floor. *(718-780-7700. The corner of Eastern Pkwy. and Flatbush Ave. Open M 10am-6pm, Tu-Th 9am-8pm, F-Sa 10am-6pm, Su 1-5pm; closed Sundays June-Sept.)*

NEIGHBORHOODS

THE BROOKLYN MUSEUM. Its large permanent collection, particularly of ancient artifacts, and its special exhibitions manage to draw Manhattanites out of their cushy borough. See **Museums,** p. 243.

PARK SLOPE AND PROSPECT PARK

*Subway: To **Park Slope**, take F train to Seventh Ave./Park Slope. To **Prospect Park**, take #2, 3 to Grand Army Plaza.*

Park Slope's attitude, more than its sights and architecture, sets it apart from other New York City areas. The neighborhood's extraordinary level of ethnic diversity seems exempt from the tensions of other Brooklyn neighborhoods. Professionals, academics, and families—or some combination thereof—inhabit its charming brownstones on east-west streets like Carroll St. Restaurants and stores line the north-south avenues, especially **Seventh Avenue.**

Just east of Park Slope, adjoining the southern border of Institute Park, is **Prospect Park.** From the Grand Army Plaza subway stop, head toward **Memorial Arch,** built in the 1890s to commemorate the North's Civil War victory. The charioteer atop the arch is an emblem of the maiden Columbia, the symbol of the victorious Union. Visitors may climb to the top of the arch on weekends. (718-965-8951. Sa-Su noon-4pm. Free.)

Enter Prospect Park's northern corner through **Grand Army Plaza.** Frederick Law Olmsted and Calvert Vaux designed the park in the mid-1800s and supposedly liked it better than their little Manhattan project, Central Park. Many Brooklynites share this opinion of the 526-acre urban oasis, although it's not quite clear why. If you have limited time to spend, skip the drier historical sites and head directly to **Prospect Lake,** south of Long Meadow, or **Lookout Hill** for peaceful views of glacial pools and the manmade lake below.

The park's largest area is the sweeping 90-acre **Long Meadow.** The **Friends Cemetery,** a Quaker burial ground dating from 1846, remains intact in the western section of the park.

In the eastern part of the park, at Flatbush and Ocean Ave., you can see old Brooklyn preserved in **Leffert's Homestead,** a Dutch farmhouse burned by George Washington's troops and rebuilt in 1777. The **Children's Historic House Museum** is located inside the homestead. (718-965-6505. Open Sa-Su and holidays noon-5pm. Free.) Nearby, saddle a horse taken from Coney Island's 1912 **carousel,** which plays an odd version of the Beatles' "Ob-La-Di, Ob-La-Da." (Open summer Th-F noon-4pm, Sa-Su noon-6pm. 75¢.)

The recently reopened **Prospect Park Wildlife Center** features live animal exhibits aimed mainly at children. (Open daily 10am-5pm. $2.50, seniors $1.25, ages 3-12 50¢.) In late summer, concerts are held at the **bandshell** in the northwestern corner of the park. (Events hotline 718-965-8999; park tours 718-287-3400.) Both paddle boats and horses are available for rent at **Wollman Rink.** (718-972-4588. Daily noon-5pm. Boats $10 per hr. Horses $25-30 per hr.)

FLATBUSH

Subway: D to Church Ave.; or #2 or 5 to Flatbush Ave./Brooklyn College

Just southeast of Prospect Park is the neighborhood of Flatbush, where Manhattan's turn-of-the-20th-century aristocracy maintained summer homes. You can wander around Argyle St. and Ditmas Ave. to see some of their old mansions. The area's socio-economic well-being, however, has long since deteriorated. Once a predominantly Jewish immigrant neighborhood, Flatbush carries on its legacy of shifting immigrant identities, as home to significant Jamaican and other West Indian populations. Reggae music and exotic fruit stands fill major thoroughfares, such as Church Ave., Nostrand Ave., and Ave. J on summer days. Any of these avenues will yield some of the best jerk chicken ya evah ate.

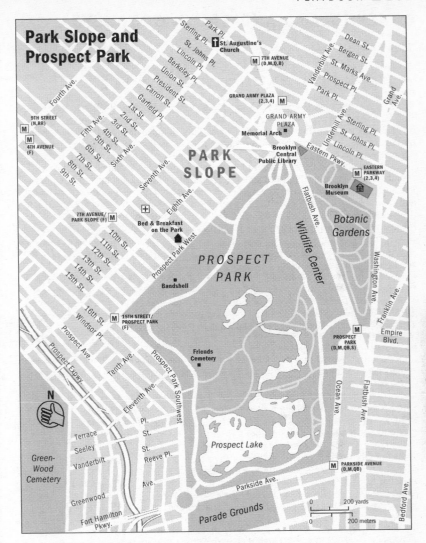

Park Slope and Prospect Park

PARK SLOPE

PROSPECT PARK

Park Pl.
Sterling Pl.
St. Johns Pl.
Lincoln Pl.
Berkeley Pl.
Union St.
President St.
Carroll St.
Garfield Pl.
1st St.
2nd St.
3rd St.
4th St.
5th St.
6th St.
7th St.
8th St.
9th St.
10th St.
11th St.
12th St.
13th St.
14th St.
15th St.
16th St.

Fourth Ave.
Fifth Ave.
Sixth Ave.
Seventh Ave.
Eighth Ave.

St. Augustine's Church

7TH AVENUE (D,M,Q,B)

GRAND ARMY PLAZA (2,3,4)

GRAND ARMY PLAZA
Memorial Arch

Brooklyn Central Public Library

Dean St.
Bergen St.
St. Marks Ave.
Prospect Pl.
Park Pl.
Vanderbilt Ave.
Underhill Ave.
Sterling Pl.
St. Johns Pl.
Lincoln Pl.

Grand Ave.

Eastern Pkwy.

EASTERN PARKWAY (2,3,4)

Brooklyn Museum

9TH STREET (N,RR)

4TH AVENUE (F)

7TH AVENUE/ PARK SLOPE (F)

Bed & Breakfast on the Park

Prospect Park West

Bandshell

15TH STREET/ PROSPECT PARK (F)

Windsor Pl.

Prospect Ave.

Prospect Expwy.

Tenth Ave.

Eleventh Ave.

Prospect Park Southwest

Friends Cemetery

Terrace Pl.
Seeley St.
Vanderbilt St.
Greenwood
Reeve Pl.
Ave.

Fort Hamilton Pkwy.

Green-Wood Cemetery

Prospect Lake

Wildlife Center

Botanic Gardens

Washington Ave.

Franklin Ave.

Empire Blvd.

PROSPECT PARK (D,M,QB,S)

Ocean Ave.

Flatbush Ave.

PARKSIDE AVENUE (D,M,QB)

Parkside Ave.

Parade Grounds

Bedford Ave.

Flatbush Ave.

N

0   200 yards
0   200 meters

In this run-down yet historic district, the long-mourned Brooklyn Dodgers once played at **Ebbets Field** (now demolished). At Flatbush and Church Ave. stands the second-oldest high school in North America, **Erasmus Hall Academy,** whose illustrious alumni include Barbra Streisand and the New York Jets' football great Joe Namath. Not a single brick can be moved from the school's center building or, according to some antiquated charter, the neighboring Dutch Reformed Church will repossess it. Founding fathers of the United States—Aaron Burr, John Jay, and Alexander Hamilton—all contributed to the school's construction.

Nearby is Brooklyn College, which was founded in 1930. The college includes the prestigious **Brooklyn Center for the Performing Arts** (718-951-4522), which often holds musical and dramatic performances (see p. 266).

CONEY ISLAND AND SOUTH BROOKLYN

*Subway: To **Greenwood Cemetery** take N, R to 25th St. To **Midwood** take D, Q to Kings Hwy.; to **Coney Island** take B, D, F, N to Stillwell Ave.; to **Brighton Beach** take D, Q to Brighton Beach; to **Sheepshead Bay** take D, Q to Sheepshead Bay.*

In the early 1900s, only the rich could afford the trip here. Mornings, they bet on horses at the racetracks in Sheepshead Bay and Gravesend; nights, they headed to the seaside for $50 dinners. The introduction of nickel-fare subway rides to Coney Island made the resort accessible to the entire population. Millions jammed the amusement parks, beaches, and restaurants on summer weekends. By the late 1940s, the area became a bit run-down. Widespread car ownership allowed people to get even farther away from the city, and a few devastating fires in Coney Island soon cleared the way for urban housing projects throughout the area. While a bit dilapidated today, Coney Island still provides the afternoon amusement captured in the watercolors of painter and *The New York Times Book Review* cartoonist David Levine. During the summer, the beach is usually crowded, and it's always fun to explore the boardwalk.

CONEY ISLAND AMUSEMENT. Some vestiges of Coney Island's golden era remain. The **Cyclone,** built in 1927, is more than the most terrifying roller coaster ride in the world—couples have been married upon it and it's included on the National Register as an historic place. Enter its 100-second-long screaming whirl over nine hills of rickety wooden tracks. *(718-266-3434. 834 Surf Ave. and W. 10th St. Open daily mid-June to Sept. noon-midnight; Easter weekend to mid-June F-Su noon-midnight. $4.)* The 1920 **Wonder Wheel** ($3), in Astroland on Surf Ave., was the world's tallest at 150 feet when it opened and has a special twist that surprises everyone; make sure you get in a colored car. The **El Dorado bumper car** ($3), 1216 Surf Ave., still plays 1970s disco tunes and invites you to "bump, bump, bump your ass off!" The **Ghost Hall** ($2.50), on 12th St. between Bowery and the boardwalk, is about as scary as a *Munsters* rerun, but has some fun, campy moments.

Your best bet for experiencing the spirit of Coney Island culture is to visit the **Coney Island Circus Sideshow,** on 12th St. at Surf Ave., a vestige of the old Coney Island with sword swallowers, snake charmers, jugglers, and the occasional "freak." *(718-371-5159. Open F 2-10pm, Sa-Su 1pm-midnight. $3, children $2.)* The sideshow also hosts **Burlesque Shows** (June-Aug. Sa 9pm-midnight; $8) and the spirited **Coney Island Mermaid Parade** (usually the last Saturday in June), a huge kitsch-heavy costume-and-float parade with prizes at the end; Queen Latifah was the Mermaid Queen in 1999. Come watch, or even register from 10am to noon on the day of the parade at **Steeplechase Park.** Next door to the sideshow, the **Coney Island Museum** documents the history of this amusement mecca with memorabilia. *(1208 Surf Ave. Open Sa-Su noon-sundown. Admission 99¢. The Sideshow also offers walking tours of the area on Sundays at 11am; $10; call for reservations.)*

Head west on Surf Ave. or take the boardwalk to the corner of W. 16th St., where the deceased **Thunderbolt** coaster stands in majestic ruins—relentless greenery has grown over its base. The tall, rusted skeleton of the **Parachute Jump,** relocated to the edge of the boardwalk in 1941, once carried carts of people to the top and then dropped them for a few seconds before their parachutes opened. Once a year, on Puerto Rican National Day, a flag somehow gets tied to the top.

NEW YORK AQUARIUM. Home to the first beluga whale born in captivity, the aquarium has all the regular denizens here, from penguins and piranhas to sharks and jellyfish. They even have some coneys, the fish that gave Coney Island its name. An outdoor theater showcases dolphins. *(718-265-3474. At Surf and W. 8th St., Coney Island. Open M-F 10am-5pm, Sa-Su 10am-6pm. $8.75, ages 2-12 and seniors $4.50.)*

NATIVE SON Salvatore Stabile, a homegrown Brooklyn talent, dropped out of NYU undergraduate film studies after inheriting $5000 from his grandmother. He put the money toward making *Gravesend,* his gritty, dark 1997 comedy, not surprisingly about teenage boys from Gravesend, the Brooklyn neighborhood in which Stabile was raised. The writer/producer/director, barely out of high school, won funding at the Hamptons film festival in Long Island and subsequently signed a two-picture deal with Steven Spielberg's DreamWorks. *Gravesend,* therefore, proved no dead end.

GREENWOOD CEMETERY. This vast, hilly kingdom of ornate mausoleums and tombstones sits directly south of Park Slope and makes for a pleasant, if morbid, stroll. Samuel Morse, Horace Greeley and Boss Tweed slumber at this "Victorian Necropolis." Headstones here take the form of sinking ships, wrecked trains, empty beds and chairs, and fire hydrants in a macabre reminder of how each grave's occupant died. *(718-469-5277 for tours. Fifth Ave. and 25th St. Open daily 8am-4pm. Tours Su at 1pm; $6.)*

SUNSET PARK. The surrounding Latino neighborhood was named for this little stretch. Here you'll find a sloping lawn criss-crossed by paths (look out the for kids tearing down the incline on bikes) with an extraordinary view of Upper New York Bay, the Statue of Liberty, and Lower Manhattan. Avid consumers flock to the area's Fifth Ave., which is lined with discount stores and hybrid restaurants. If you're in a car, you can head down to First Ave. and explore the trolley-scarred streets, the setting for Uli Wedel's *Last Exit to Brooklyn.* This district has also recently begun reflecting the influences of its increasing Chinese and Middle Eastern populations. *(41st to 44th St. from Fifth to Sixth Ave.)*

BAY RIDGE. Nearby Shore Road is lined with mansions overlooking the Verrazano-Narrows Bridge and New York Harbor. Bay Ridge was the scene of John Travolta's strutting in the classic *Saturday Night Fever.* Sadly, the 2001 Odyssey disco is no longer operational. **Bensonhurst** became a household word and rallying cry in the fight against racism following the brutal murder of Yusef Hawkins in 1989. The predominantly Italian neighborhood centers around 86th St., and is chock full of Italian bakeries, pizza joints, rowdy youths, and discount stores, especially around 17th Ave. *(South of Sunset Park, Bay Ridge centers on Third Ave., also called "Restaurant Row.")*

BOROUGH PARK. This area is the largest Hassidic Jewish neighborhood in Brooklyn. In contrast to the more visible Crown Heights Lubavitchers, the Bobovers of Borough Park eschew, for the most part, the political and secular worlds, preferring to maintain an insular community. The **main synagogue** sits at 15th Ave. and 48th St. As in the other Hassidic neighborhoods of Brooklyn, visitors will feel more welcome if they are dressed conservatively. *(North of Bensonhurst and east of Sunset Park, centered around 13th Ave. north of 65th St.)*

MIDWOOD. Once the home of the largest Sephardic Jewish community outside of Israel, the neighborhood has lately seen increasing numbers of Arabs, Italians, and non-Sephardic Jews. Nonetheless, kosher eateries still dot major arteries such as Kings Hwy. and Ocean Avenue, along with *halal* markets and pizza joints. *(East of Ocean Pkwy.)*

BRIGHTON BEACH. Beyond Ocean Pkwy. lies "Little Odessa by the Sea" socalled for the steady stream of Russian immigrants who moved here in the early 1980s. Brighton Beach is home to extraordinary delis, indoor and outdoor flea

NEIGHBORHOODS

markets, and a nightlife with live Russian music from disco to folk. In late June and early July, old Eastern Europeans complaining about their bodily ailments, Spandex-clad girls listening to Top-40 music on head phones, and middle-aged couples drowning sunburns in Noxzema all gather to watch the **Blue Angels air shows** on the boardwalk. On Fourth of July weekend, parachutists land near cheering seaside crowds.

SHEEPSHEAD BAY. Emmons Ave. runs along the bay and faces **Manhattan Beach,** a wealthy residential area of doctors and *mafiosi* (shh!) just east of Brighton Beach. In Sheepshead Bay, you can go after some blues (the fish, not the music) on any of the boats docked along Emmons Ave. Traditionally, the passengers pool their bucks as a prize for the person who lands the biggest fish. *(Boats depart 6-8am; some also have evening trips leaving 5:30-6:30pm. $24-37.)*

OTHER SIGHTS. Between 41st and 44th St., you can see a graffiti piece by the infamous artist **Dare.** Similar tribute and memorial works can be viewed all over Brooklyn—some preserved intact from the early 1970s. If you have a car, you can drive east along the Belt Pkwy., which hugs Brooklyn's shores. Stop off at **Plumb Beach** for a more intimate sun-and-sand experience. At night, the parking lot fills with big green Cadillacs and loving couples. Exit the Belt at Flatbush Ave., which leads south to the **Rockaway beaches** of Queens. Turn left just before the bridge and you can drive around the immense abandoned air strips of **Floyd Bennett Field.** The **Gateway National Park** is located here, boasting plots of beautiful communal gardens. *(718-338-3687. Open daily dawn until dusk.)*

QUEENS

The borough of Queens flaunts a melting pot mentality. Immigrant populations flow into semi-suburban communities, making the whole district a crazy quilt of customs, languages, and cuisines. Queens has always warmly welcomed an exhilarating spectrum of cultures—from 17th-century Dutch and English farmers to recent Greek immigrant families—all in search of a secure place in the New World. With an over 30% foreign-born population, the establishment of ethnic communities in new areas makes for an ever-shifting demographic landscape. Formerly German and Irish locales give way to Indian and Caribbean influences. Here every color and stripe can cut a slice off the Big Apple.

This rural colony named in honor of Queen Catherine of Braganza, wife of England's Charles II, was yanked from the Algonquin Indians in 1683. At the beginning of the 19th century, small farms began to give way to industry, which in time evolved western Queens into a busy production center. Queens officially became a borough of the City of New York in 1898, and the construction of the Long Island Railroad under the East River in 1910 fostered urban growth. Between 1910 and 1930, the borough's population quadrupled to one million, as myriad immigrants came here via Ellis Island. A 1950s building boom effectively completed the urbanization of Queens.

Although New York City needs Queens for its airports, **LaGuardia** to the north and **JFK** to the south, the borough almost seems a separate city. Although rumors circulate about extending the subway line farther into the suburbs (mainly to connect the airports to the city), Queens has to struggle to bring visitors out from the world of densely packed skyscrapers to a land of sprawling rows of buildings punctuated by peaceful, green parks and gardens. The borough has a **tourism council** (800-454-1329 or 718-647-3387), but lacks a visitor center.

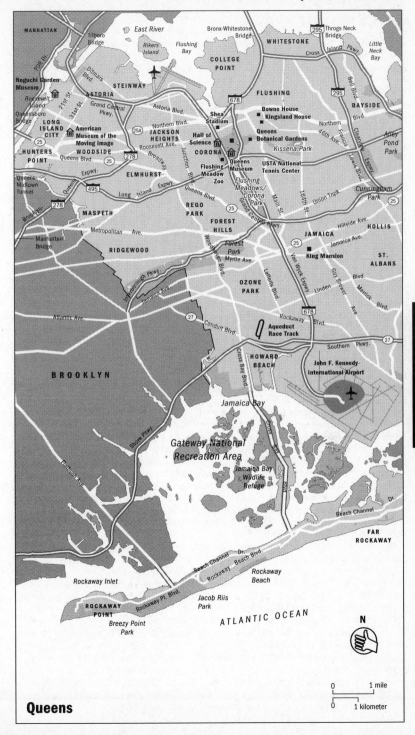

Queens

NEIGHBORHOODS

ORIENTATION

Geographically New York's largest borough, Queens comprises over a third of the city's total area. The northwest region of Queens lies just across the East River from Manhattan. The closest areas, Long Island City and **Hunter's Point,** were for many years Queens's industrial powerhouses. In the 1930s, 80% of all industry in the borough was based here; Newtown Creek saw as much freight traffic as the Mississippi River. The area has lately acquired a reputation as a low-rent artists' community, though the avant-garde seems reluctant to cross the river. North of Long Island City, Astoria, known as the Athens of New York, has by some estimates one of the largest Greek communities in the world, second only to Greece. Italian, Spanish, and Hindi are spoken alongside Greek in this middle-class area.

To the southeast, in the neighborhoods of **Woodside** and **Sunnyside,** new Irish immigrants join their established countrymen. Sunnyside, a remarkable "garden community" built in the 1920s, gained notoriety during the Great Depression when over half the original owners were evicted because they weren't able to pay their mortgages. The neighborhood now commands international recognition as a model of middle-income housing. Southeast of Sunnyside lies **Ridgewood,** a neighborhood founded by Eastern European and German immigrants a century ago. More than 2000 of the distinctively European attached-brick homes here receive protection as landmarks, securing Ridgewood a listing in the National Register of Historic Places.

East of Ridgewood, **Forest Hills, Kew Gardens,** and **Rego Park** contain some of the most expensive residential property in the city. Forest Hill's Austin Street shopping district has imported the stores of Manhattan (read: Banana Republic and the Gap), while Kew Gardens, the administrative center of Queens, has brought in big-city political bureaucracy. Originally called Whitepot, the land of Forest Hills was purchased from the Indians for some white pots—a deal almost as unreal as Peter Minuit's Manhattan purchase. The Real Good Construction Co. developed "Rego" Park—hence the name. Forest Hills and Kew Gardens offer some of the most pleasant residential strolling areas in the city with single houses, gardens, and even garages—a rarity for New York City. This pricey, upscale region showcases Tudor-style residential architecture, as well as the West Side Tennis Center, whose courts have hosted many of the sport's elite. Just north of this area, Flushing Meadows-Corona Park, site of the World's Fair in both 1939 and 1964, still attracts crowds for both its museums and its collection of world-famous, often-photographed attractions. To the west, **Corona** and **Elmhurst** have a large Hispanic population, while **Jackson Heights** is home to a large Indian community. To the east of the park, **Flushing** has become a "Little Asia," with a large Korean, Chinese, and Indian population, as well as a sizable number of Central and South American immigrants. Despite the dynamic demographic landscape, the area's elevated subway—some of the nation's oldest public transportation—preserves the flavor of early 20th-century Queens.

Bayside, east of Flushing, is a popular spot for bar-hopping. In the center of Queens, **Jamaica** is home to prosperous West Indian and African-American neighborhoods, such as **St. Albans.** Along the south shore of Queens, the site of mammoth Kennedy Airport (JFK), you can find the Jamaica Bay Wildlife Refuge. In eastern Queens **Glen Oaks, Little Neck, Douglaston** are upscale ethnic areas bordering true suburbia in Long Island's Nassau County.

The streets of Queens are neither like the orderly grid of Upper Manhattan nor the haphazard angles of those in the Village; instead, a mixed bag of urban planning techniques has resulted in a different, equally perplexing system. Streets generally run north-south and are numbered from east to west, from First St. in Astoria to 271st St. in Glen Oaks. Avenues run perpendicular to streets and are numbered from north to south, from Second Ave. to 165th Ave. The address of an establishment or residence often tells you the closest cross-street (for example, 45-07 32nd Ave. is cleverly near the intersection with 45th St.)

FLUSHING

The #7 Flushing subway line runs straight from Times Square.

Flushing began as the Dutch settlement Vlissingen, where the pure Quakers successfully fought Governor Peter Stuyvesant's 1657 ban on their religion. This victory marked the community as the supposed birthplace of religious freedom in the United States. Twenty-one historical sites comprise the Flushing **Freedom Mile** (maps and tour brochure available at Kingsland Homestead, 143-35 37th Ave.). In downtown Flushing, landmarks from before the American Revolution mingle with storefronts, food vendors, and open markets. The signs outside most establishments are written in both English and Korean.

THE KINGSLAND HOMESTEAD. Built in 1775, the Homestead was a typical home of the time, but few similar structures remain today. It holds a permanent collection of antique china and memorabilia that belonged to early trader Captain Joseph King. There is also a permanent collection of antique dolls and a fully furnished "Victorian Room," depicting the typical furnishings of a middle-class citizen of the time. As home of the **Queens Historical Society,** the Homestead displays three or four temporary exhibits each year concerning aspects of the borough's history. *(718-939-0647. 143-35 37th Ave. Open Tu, Sa-Su 2:30-4:30pm. $2, students and seniors $1. Historical Society open M-F 9:30am-5pm. Free tours. Academic adventurers can use archival and genealogical research center by appointment.)*

QUEENS BOTANICAL GARDEN. Originally an exhibition for the 1939 World's Fair in nearby Flushing Meadows-Corona Park, the garden had to move when the park was being redesigned for the 1964 World's Fair. The garden relocated to its present site, where it now boasts a 5000-bush rose garden, a 23-acre arboretum, more than nine acres of "theme gardens," and a new home compost demonstration site. On weekends, the Garden plays host to a cavalcade of wedding parties, each competing for gazebos, fountains, and the home compost demonstration site as a backdrop for commemorative photos. *(718-886-3800. Open Apr.-Oct. Tu-Su 8am-7pm; Nov.-Mar. Tu-Su 8am-4:30pm. Free. Walk from the station or take the Q44 bus toward Jamaica.)*

OTHER SIGHTS. Friends Meeting House (718-358-9636) at 137-16 Northern Blvd., built in 1696, still hosts services for local Quakers, including silent services on Sundays at 11am. Across the street the **Flushing Town Hall,** 137-35 Northern Blvd., built in 1862, has recently been restored in the Romanesque tradition. Local art and historical exhibitions await inside. *(718-463-7700. Suggested donation $3; students and seniors $2, under 12 $1.)* Live jazz and classical concerts on Fridays, except for a break in the summer; call ahead to get a schedule. *($20, students and seniors $15.)* The low, unassuming **Bowne House,** 37-01 Bowne St., built in 1661, is the oldest remaining residence in Queens and is filled with interesting antiques. Here, John Bowne defied Dutch governor Peter Stuyvesant's 1657 ban on Quaker meetings and was exiled for his efforts. *(718-359-0528. Open Tu and Sa-Su 2:30-4:30pm. $2, seniors and under 14 $1.)* **Kissena Park,** between Rose Ave. and Parsons Blvd., preserves nature on a modest scale. The Historic Grove, with its exotic foreign trees, was planted here in the 19th century as part of Parson's Nursery. As you enter from Rose Ave., down the hill you'll see beautiful Kissena Lake, circled by picnickers, cyclists, a golf course, and a few fisherfolk. Urban park rangers give walking tours and nature shows on Sundays at 2pm. *(718-353-2460. From the #7 subway stop at Main St., take the Q17 bus from in front of Modell's to Rose Ave.)* To the east of Flushing, the 600-acre **Alley Pond Park/Environmental Center (APEC),** 228-06 Northern Blvd., just off the Cross-Island Pkwy., offers miles of nature trails through the park—a green belt of wetlands, woodlands, and marshes. *(718-229-4000. Open M-Sa 9am-4:30pm. Subway: #7 to Main St., Flushing; then take the Q12 bus from Stern's department store on Roosevelt Ave. along Northern Blvd. to APEC.)* A small exhibit in the back room of the center features live snakes, snapping turtles, frogs, and guinea pigs. The park also hosts cultural enrichment programs like art exhibitions and photography classes.

NEIGHBORHOODS

FLUSHING MEADOWS-CORONA PARK

Subway: #7 from Times Square to the 111th St. elevated station or to Shea Stadium.

From the Van Wyck Expressway, motorists gaze upon the ruins of a more glamorous past. Rusting towers and half-eaten buildings punctuate the serene trees of Flushing Meadows-Corona Park, home to the 1939 and 1964 World's Fairs. The 1255-acre swamp became a huge rubbish dump until city planners decided to turn the area into fairgrounds. The remnants from the first fair are long gone, and the monuments from the second nearly gone. Yet behind the trees hide several excellent attractions, sculptured gardens, and one or two well-kept monuments. The grounds are worth a visit, not only for these hidden gems, but for the old steel and concrete dinosaurs themselves. On weekends, the park is alive again as local families come here to play frisbee and let off steam.

◼NEW YORK HALL OF SCIENCE. Futuristic when it was constructed in 1964, the hall now stands flanked by rusty rockets. Its vision of the future may not have aged well on the outside, but a recent renovation and expansion have made the exhibitions inside current and engaging. With over 150 hands-on displays demonstrating a range of scientific concepts, this museum will keep visitors of all ages occupied for hours. *(718-699-0005. 111th St. and 48th Ave. Open Sept.-June Tu-W 9:30am-2pm, Th-Su 9:30am-5pm, July-Aug. M 9:30am-2pm, Tu-Su 9:30am-5pm. $7.80, seniors and under 15 $5. Free Sept.-June Th-F 2-5pm.)*

THE QUEENS WILDLIFE CENTER AND ZOO. Features North American animals as well as more exotic species. A petting zoo features sheep, goats, cows, and other cuddly creatures. *(718-271-7761. Open M-F 10am-5pm, Sa-Su 10am-5:30pm. Tickets sold until 30min. before closing. $2.50, seniors $1.25, under 12 50¢.)*

NEW YORK STATE PAVILION. The original center of the 1964 Fair. The architect Philip Johnson probably never envisioned the towers as hide-outs for alien spacecraft as they were used in *Men In Black*. A new expansion has turned a part of the old pavilion into the new **Queens Theater in the Park** (see **Arts and Entertainment**, p. 259). South of the Pavilion, across the expressway overpass, and behind the Planet of the Apes Fountain is a restored **Coney Island carousel** (718-592-6539) that pipes out silly chipmunk tunes. *(Open daily 10:30am-8:30pm. $1 per ride.)*

THE UNISPHERE. A 380-ton steel globe tilts in retro-futuristic glory over a fountain. Constructed by the steel industry for the 1964 World's Fair, the Unisphere dramatically symbolizes "man's aspirations toward peace and his achievements in an expanding universe." Rings encircling the world represent the three manmade satellites then in orbit. On sweltering summer afternoons you may be tempted to romp around the fountain with everyone else despite the "No Wading" signs.

THE NEW YORK CITY BUILDING. The south wing of houses **World's Fair ice skating** (718-271-1996, Oct.-Mar.), the north wing the less than scintillating **Queens Museum of Art** (718-592-9700). Among the few items of interest there: "Panorama of the City of New York," the world's largest-scale model of an urban area at 9335 sq. ft. One inch on the model corresponds to 100 ft. of New York, which re-creates over 865,000 buildings in miniature. *(Open W-F 10am-5pm, Sa-Su noon-5pm. Suggested donation $4, seniors and children $2.)*

OTHER SIGHTS. While in the park, you can also cavort in a playground accessible to disabled children or try your hand at a full course of **pitch 'n' putt golf**, which has 18 par-3 holes. *(718-271-8182. Open daily 8am-7pm. Greens fee Sa-Su $7.25, M-F $8.25. Club rental $1 each.)* In the southern part of the park, **Meadow Lake** offers paddle- and row-boating, while **Willow Lake Nature Area** hosts an occasional free tour. **Shea Stadium** (718-507-8499), to the north of the park, was built for the 1964 Fair, though it is now home to the Mets (see **Sports,** p. 290). Nearby, the **USTA National Tennis Center** and **Arthur Ashe Stadium** (718-760-6200) host the U.S. Open.

ASTORIA AND LONG ISLAND CITY

Subway: N from Broadway and 34th St. in Manhattan to Broadway and 31st St. at the two areas' border.

Greek-, Italian-, and Spanish-speaking communities mingle amid the bustling shopping districts, lively neighborhood cafes and taverns of Astoria. The neighborhood lies in the upper west corner of the borough, and Long Island City—birthplace of urban poet/rapper Nas—lies just south of it. This area densely packs an average block with a few delis, a Greek bakery, and an Italian grocery. Avid shoppers head east eight blocks on Broadway to Steinway St.

THE STEINWAY PIANO FACTORY. The world-famous Steinway pianos that put this area on the map have been manufactured in the same spot, in the same way since the 1870s. The 12,000 parts of a typical Steinway include a 340 lb. plate of cast iron and tiny bits of Brazilian deer skin. Over 95% of piano performances in the U.S. are played on Steinway grands. *(718-721-2600. At 19th Rd. and 77th St.)*

THE SOCRATES SCULPTURE PARK. Sculptor Mark di Suvero created this curiosity, located just across from the building labeled "Adirondack Office Furniture." Stunning, if somewhat unnerving, 35 day-glo and rusted metal abstractions cluster on the site of what was once an illegal dump. Towering piles of rust and ribbons seem left behind by the circus. Nearby, the Sound Observatory challenges the viewer's interpretive skills; you can spend hours figuring out how to trigger rhythms and sounds on the interactive audio-sculptural apparatus. Take a trip out of Manhattan—Socrates will reward your wisdom. *(718-956-1819. At the end of Broadway, cross the intersection with Vernon Blvd. Open daily 10am-sunset. Free.)*

ISAMU NOGUCHI GARDEN MUSEUM. See **Museums**, p. 245.

KAUFMAN-ASTORIA STUDIO. The U.S.'s largest studio outside of Los Angeles sits on a 13-acre plot with 8 sound stages. Paramount Pictures used these facilities to make such major motion pictures as *Scent of a Woman* and *The Secret of My Success*. Television's *The Cosby Show* was taped here as well. The studios are closed to the public, but next door is the **American Museum of the Moving Image** (see **Museums**, p. 242).

THE INSTITUTE FOR CONTEMPORARY ART/P.S. 1. At the site of New York City's first public school, you can still see the word "Girls" cut into the stone lintel above one of the entrances. Now a part of **MoMA**, P.S. 1 presents cutting edge exhibitions and offers studio space to local artists. Long Island City offers an outstanding view of Manhattan, Roosevelt Island's ruins, and the East River. To get to the shorefront, walk toward the skyline along 45th Ave., go right on Vernon Blvd., and then take a left onto 44th Dr. Follow it to the public pier which juts into the river. To your right as you face the river lies the Queensboro Bridge, better known to Simon and Garfunkel fans as the **59th St. Bridge.** *(718-784-2084. 46-01 21st St. Galleries open W-Sa noon-6pm. Suggested donation $5, seniors and children $2.)*

CENTRAL QUEENS

*To get to **Jamaica** take subway E, J, Z to Jamaica Center. To get to **St. Albans** take subway E, J, Z to Jamaica Center; then the Q4 bus to Linden Blvd.*

Jamaica, named for the Jameco Indians, lies in the center of Queens and is the heart of the borough's black and West Indian communities. The main strip on Jamaica Ave., stretching between 150th and 168th St., constantly roars with activity. Restaurants selling succulent Jamaican beef patties, stores plying African clothing and braids, and mobs of local shoppers rushing to get a deal, crowd the brick-lined **pedestrian mall** on 165th St. After WWII, **St. Albans**, centered on Linden Blvd., just east of Merrick Blvd., became the home of newly well-off African-Americans. In the 1950s, this area recalled Harlem of the 1920s; jazz greats Count Basie, Fats Waller, and James P. Johnson as well as baseball stars like Jackie Robinson and Roy Campanella, all lived here—mostly in the Addisleigh Park area of western St. Albans. Today, wealthier blacks have moved southeast to communities like Laurelton, and West Indian bakeries and restaurants now flourish in the lively shopping district along Linden Blvd.

JAMAICA ARTS CENTER. This gallery offers changing workshops, and powerful art exhibitions by local and international artists. Recent exhibitions have included the photographic collection "The Many Faces of Queens Women," "Vietnam: From Both Sides," and a collection of quilts including patchworks made of Wonder bread and condoms. *(718-658-7400. 161-04 Jamaica Ave., at 161st St. Open M-Tu, F-Sa 9am-6pm, W-Th 9am-8pm. Free.)*

KING MANOR MUSEUM. The recently renovated colonial residence was once that of Rufus King, an early abolitionist, signer of the Constitution, one of New York's first senators, and an ambassador to Great Britain. The house, set in 11-acre **King Park,** dates back to the 1750s and combines Georgian and Federal architecture. The period rooms downstairs give you an idea of how they lived back in the day. The museum offers year-round public programs for children and adults, and the park hosts the "Jazz Under the Stars" summer concert series on Friday nights. *(718-206-0545. At Jamaica Ave. and 150th St. Open Sa-Su noon-4pm; last tour at 3:30pm. Second and last Tu of the month 12:15-2pm. $2, students and seniors $1.)*

FOREST PARK. A densely wooded area with miles of park trails, a bandshell, a golf course (718-296-0999), a carousel ($1), baseball diamonds, tennis courts, and horseback riding. If you'd like to rent horses, **Lynne's Riding School,** 88-03 70th Rd. (718-261-7679) and **Dixie Dew Riding Academy,** 88-11 70th Rd. (718-263-3500), will oblige you with a guided trail ride. *(718-235-4100, events info 718-520-5941. Subway: J, Z to Woodhaven Blvd., or the L, M to Myrtle/Wyckoff; then board the Q55 bus. Forest Park open daily 6am-9pm. Riding School and Academy open 8am-4pm and 8am-7pm, respectively. Both $20 per hr.)*

QUEENS COUNTY FARM MUSEUM. Built by Jacob and Catherine Adriance in 1772 on 50 acres of land, this is the only working farm of its era that has been restored and the oldest farm of any kind in Queens. Visitors can see a duck pond and beehives, and take home crafts made during one of many workshops. *(718-347-3276. 73-50 Little Neck Parkway in Floral Park on the border of Nassau County. Subway: E, F to Kew Gardens/ Union Turnpike; then the Q46 bus to Little Neck Pkwy. Walk 3 blocks north. Grounds open M-F 9am-5pm, Sa-Su 10am-5pm. Museum open Sa-Su 10am-5pm. Free. Hayrides Sa-Su; $2.)*

SOUTHERN QUEENS

Subway: A (marked Rockaways) to Broad Channel. Walk west along Noel Rd., which is just in front of the station, to Crossbay Blvd., then turn right and walk about one mile to the center. Or take the E, F, G, R line to 74th St./Roosevelt Ave. in Jackson Heights, then the Q53 express bus to Broad Channel, and follow the directions above.

THE JAMAICA BAY WILDLIFE REFUGE. Roughly the size of Manhattan and 10 times larger than Flushing Meadows-Corona Park, the park constitutes one of the most important urban wildlife refuges in the U.S., harboring more than 325 species of birds and small animals. Lined with benches and birdhouses, the miles of paths around the marshes and ponds resonate with the roar of planes leaving from nearby JFK airport. Beached wooden rowboats and the frequent egret or swan make the refuge a real oasis. Environmental slide shows and tours are held on weekends. *(718-318-4340. Park open daily dawn to dusk. Visitors/Nature Center open daily 8:30am-5pm. Free, but do pick up map and permit at visitors center.)*

ROCKAWAY BEACH. Immortalized by the Ramones in one of their pop-punk tributes, the 10-mile-long public beach extends from Beach 3rd St. in Far Rockaway to Beach 149th St. in the west, lined by a **boardwalk** from Beach 3rd St. all the way to Beach 126th St. Between Beach 126th St. and Beach 149th St., the beach has divisions between public and private waterfront areas; no street parking is allowed during the summer. *(718-318-4000.)*

NUDIE VIRTUE & THE PASTRAMI KING

Except for his cast-iron foam and seaweed, buff male Virtue stands completely naked. And he's stomping on two writhing, naked stone women. Yup, it's the *Civic Virtue* statue, originally installed outside Manhattan's City Hall in 1922 but banished to Queens because of an uproar surrounding its misogynist pose. *Civic Virtue* stands on the corner of Queens Blvd. and the Union Turnpike, facing the unofficial ground zero of Queens' Democratic Party—a kosher restaurant called the Pastrami King, at whose tables many a deal has been cut.

JACOB RIIS PARK. Part of the 26,000-acre Gateway National Recreation Area that extends into Brooklyn, Staten Island, and New Jersey. The park was named for Jacob Riis, a photojournalist and activist in the early 1900s. He persuaded New York City to turn this overgrown beach into a public park. Today the area is lined with its own beauteous beach and boardwalk, as well as basketball and handball courts, a golf course, and concession stands. At the eastern end of the park is the former nude beach. In the 1980s the beach decided to "clean up its act" and presently only allows you to go topless. *(718-318-4300. Just west of Rockaway Beach, separated from it by a huge chain-link fence.)*

THE BRONX

Thirty fires a night raged unchecked in the South Bronx during the 1970s (addicts torched buildings so they could collect and sell the plumbing fixtures; landlords torched buildings so they could collect insurance), and the borough seemed as far away as possible from its past of broad shopping promenades and vibrant, close-knit communities. Yet some sought creativity from within this world of negligence and decay. They reappropriated scratched-up, abandoned records, beginning the new way of life called hip-hop, that included the musical genre of rap and DJing, breakdancing, and graffiti art. This indomitable spirit drives the Bronx's ongoing resurgence from the neglect of decades past. Educational outreach programs, clean-up patrols, and citizens' advocacy groups continually spring up, as Bronx residents take charge of their condition. Furthermore, influential natives, such as Jennifer Lopez and Rosie Perez give back to the community with a message of empowerment.

While community art galleries around the borough attest to the continuation of a tradition of renewal, they also represent the Bronx's propensity to preserve everything from Revolutionary War-era homes to New York City's only virgin forest. Many only pass over the Bronx, viewing the borough's barbed buildings through the windows of elevated subways. Descending to street level, however, reveals a much less intimidating land that has persevered for generations. Until the turn of the 19th century, the area consisted largely of cottages, farmlands, and wild marshes. Then, in the 1840s, the tide of immigration swelled, bringing scores of Italian and Irish settlers. Since then, the flow of immigrants (now mostly Hispanic and Russian) has never stopped. This relentless stream has created vibrant ethnic neighborhoods (including a Little Italy to shame its Manhattan counterpart), quirky museums, a great zoo, a classic baseball stadium, lively shopping strips, and salsa/mambo dance clubs. The Bronx will give any visitor insight into the dynamics of urban life, not to mention a peak at numerous attractions.

ORIENTATION

The northern and eastern parts of the borough—made up of neighborhoods ending in "chester": Parkchester, Baychester, and Eastchester—are largely middle-class, with single-family houses and duplexes on (relatively) peaceful,

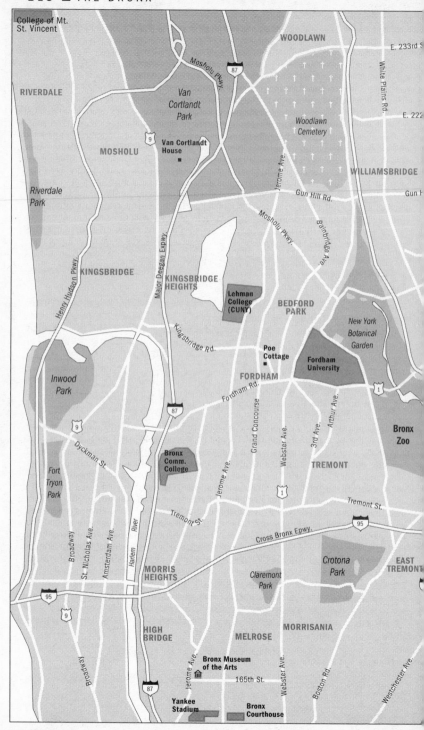

College of Mt.
St. Vincent

WOODLAWN

E. 233rd S

RIVERDALE

Mosholu Pkwy.

87

Van
Cortlandt
Park

Woodlawn
Cemetery

White Plains Rd.

E. 222

9

MOSHOLU

Van Cortlandt
House

Jerome Ave.

WILLIAMSBRIDGE

Riverdale
Park

Gun Hill Rd.

Gun H

Mosholu Pkwy.

Bainbridge Ave.

Henry Hudson Pkwy.

KINGSBRIDGE

Major Deegan Expwy.

KINGSBRIDGE
HEIGHTS

Lehman
College
(CUNY)

BEDFORD
PARK

New York
Botanical
Garden

Kingsbridge Rd.

Poe
Cottage

Fordham
University

Inwood
Park

FORDHAM

1

87

Fordham Rd.

9

Grand Concourse

Webster Ave.

3rd Ave.

Arthur Ave.

Bronx
Zoo

Dyckman St.

Bronx
Comm.
College

Jerome Ave.

TREMONT

Fort
Tryon
Park

1

Tremont St.

Tremont St.

Broadway

St. Nicholas Ave.

Amsterdam Ave.

Harlem River

Cross Bronx Epwy.

95

95

Crotona
Park

EAST
TREMONT

MORRIS
HEIGHTS

Claremont
Park

9

HIGH
BRIDGE

MELROSE

MORRISANIA

Broadway

Jerome Ave.

Bronx Museum
of the Arts

Webster Ave.

Boston Rd.

Westchester Ave.

165th St.

87

Yankee
Stadium

Bronx
Courthouse

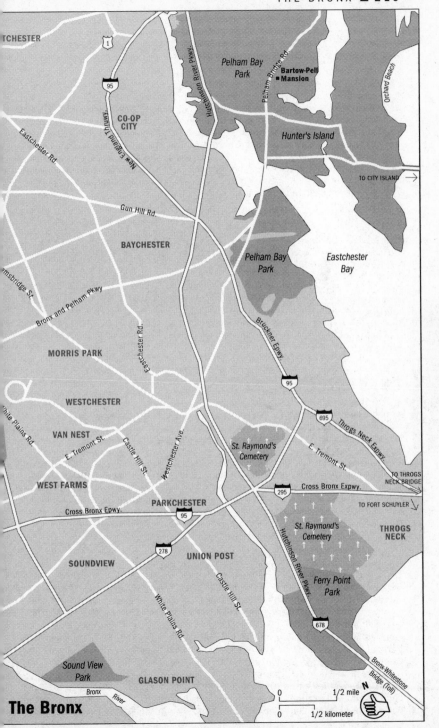

TCHESTER

1

Pelham Bay
Park

Bartow-Pell
■ Mansion

Orchard Beach

Hutchinson River Pkwy

Pelham Bridge Rd.

95

CO-OP
CITY

New England Thruway

Eastchester Rd.

Hunter's Island

TO CITY ISLAND →

Gun Hill Rd.

BAYCHESTER

Pelham Bay
Park

Eastchester
Bay

amsbridge St.

Bronx and Pelham Pkwy

Eastchester Rd.

Brückner Epwy.

MORRIS PARK

95

WESTCHESTER

695

Throgs Neck Expwy.

White Plains Rd.

VAN NEST

E. Tremont St.

Castle Hill St.

Westchester Ave.

St. Raymond's
Cemetery

E. Tremont St.

TO THROGS
NECK BRIDGE

WEST FARMS

Cross Bronx Expwy.

295

TO FORT SCHUYLER ↓

Cross Bronx Epwy.

PARKCHESTER

95

St. Raymond's
Cemetery

THROGS
NECK

278

UNION POST

Hutchinson River Pkwy.

SOUNDVIEW

Castle Hill St.

Ferry Point
Park

White Plains Rd.

678

Sound View
Park

GLASON POINT

Bronx River

Bronx-Whitestone
Bridge (Toll)

0   1/2 mile   N

0   1/2 kilometer

The Bronx

tree-lined streets. **Pelham Bay Park,** in the northeastern part of the Bronx, is the city's largest park. In the center of the borough, on the banks of the Bronx river, Bronx Park contains the **Bronx Zoo/Wildlife Conservation Park** and its plant kingdom counterpart, the equally excellent **New York Botanical Garden.** At the western edge of Bronx Park's dynamic duo sits the campus of **Fordham University** and the perpetual bazaar along Fordham Road. Below Fordham University lies the Italian neighborhood of **Belmont. Van Cortlandt Park,** in the northwest section of the borough, completes the trio of major open spaces. If you want your image of the Bronx to remain unchanged, it is recommended that you don't wander around in **Riverdale,** the posh neighborhood to the west of the park. The much-maligned **South Bronx,** taking up the southern expanse of the borough, is made up of Mott Haven, Morrisania, and Hunt's Point. The area is not a war zone, but it does demand extreme caution. Know where you're going beforehand and—women especially—do not go alone or at night.

The #1, 9, and 4 trains reach up to Van Cortlandt Park; the C and D lines serve Fordham Rd. and Bedford Park Blvd., near the Botanical Garden; the #2 and 5 skirt Bronx Park and the zoo; and the #6 stretches into Pelham Bay Park. The #4, C, and D trains whisk fans in and out of Yankee Stadium in the south of the borough. The grid that regiments Manhattan spreads into a confusing web in the Bronx, and the subway lines follow suit. The fan-like pattern of subway lines and the resulting dearth of transfer stations often make crosstown travel exasperating without a knowledge of bus lines. Thus, even the most experienced Bronx traveler knows that a good amount of travel time should be budgeted into a day of Bronx-ing. Ask for a bus map at a subway station and familiarize yourself with it: the map is also indispensable for navigating the streets on foot. Keep in mind, though, that constantly referring to a map and peering up at street signs is a good way to broadcast one's unfamiliarity with an area.

CENTRAL BRONX

BRONX ZOO/WILDLIFE CONSERVATION PARK

Telephone: 718-367-1010 or 718-220-5100. **Open:** Nov.-Mar. daily 10am-4:30pm; Apr.-Oct. M-F 10am-5pm, Sa-Su and holidays 10am-5:30pm. Parts of the zoo **close** down during Nov.-Apr. **Admission:** Apr.-Oct. $7.75, seniors and children $4; Nov.-Jan. $6, seniors and children $3; Jan.-Mar. $4, seniors and children $2. Wednesdays free. **Disabled-access Info:** 718-220-5188. **Tours:** Walking tours given weekends by the Friends of the Zoo; call 718-220-5141 three weeks in advance. **Food:** Lakeside Cafe, African Market, Flamingo Pub, and Zoo Terrace. **By Subway:** #2 or 5 to E. Tremont Ave./West Farms Sq. and walk 4 blocks north up Boston Rd. to the zoo entrance. Or take the D express to Fordham Rd., then the Bx12 bus to Southern Blvd. Walk east on Fordham Rd. to the Rainey Gate entrance. **By Bus:** Express BxM11 bus leaves from Madison Ave. in Midtown for the Bronxdale entrance to the zoo and runs back down the east side of Manhattan ($3 each way); call Liberty Lines at 718-652-8400 for details. **By Train:** Metro North runs a shuttle bus on weekends and holidays from late May to early Oct. that goes from the Metro North Fordham Rd. stop to the south entrance of the zoo, stopping in Belmont. Tickets for the shuttle can be purchased from Metro North (532-4900) as part of a $14 package that includes train fare, the shuttle, zoo admission, and a book of discounts for Belmont establishments. **By Car:** Take the Bronx River Pkwy. or (from I-95) the Pelham Pkwy.

One of the borough's biggest attractions is the Bronx Zoo/Wildlife Conservation Park, also known as the New York Zoological Society. The largest urban zoo in the United States, it provides a home for over 4000 animals. While the odd building dots the zoo, this newly environmentally conscious park prefers to showcase its stars within the 265-acre expanse of natural habitats created for each species' dwelling pleasure. The timber rattlesnake and Samantha the python (the largest snake in the U.S.) serve life in the **Reptile House,** but more benign beasts wander free in the Park's "protected sanctuary," occasionally allowing for startlingly close interaction between inhabitant and visitor. Indian elephants frolic unfettered in a **Wild Asia** while white-cheeked gibbons tree-hop in the **JungleWorld.**

Other noteworthy habitats include the **Himalayan Highlands, South America,** and the **World of Darkness.** Kids imitate animals at the hands-on **Children's Zoo,** where they can climb a spider's web or try on a turtle shell. If you tire of the kids, the crocodiles are fed Mondays and Thursdays at 2pm, sea lions daily at 3pm.

You can explore the zoo on foot or confuse the animals by traveling on the **Safari Train,** which runs between the elephant house and Wild Asia ($2). Soar into the air for a Tarzan's-eye view of the park from the **Skyfari aerial tramway** that runs between Wild Asia and the Children's Zoo ($2). The **Bengali Express Monorail** glides around Wild Asia (20min., $2). On free Wednesdays, lengthy lines for this ride accurately simulate the experience of waiting for a train in India. If you find the pace too hurried, saddle up a **camel** in the Wild Asia area ($3).

NEW YORK BOTANICAL GARDENS

Telephone: 718-817-8700. Open: Apr.-Oct. Tu-Su 10am-6pm; July-Aug. Th and Sa grounds open until 8pm. Nov.-Mar. 10am-4pm. Admission: Mar.-Oct. $3, students and seniors $2, ages 2-12 $1; Nov.-Feb. $1.50, students and seniors $1, ages 2-12 50¢; W and Sa 10am-6pm free. Certain exhibits throughout garden incur an additional charge; "passports" (Mar.-Oct. $4-10; Nov.-Feb. $2-6.50) available for all garden displays. Various tours (both paid and free) depart daily; inquire at the Visitor's Information Center. By Subway: D or #4 to Bedford Park Blvd. Walk 8 blocks east or take the Bx26, Bx12, Bx19, or Bx41 bus to the Garden. By Train: Metro-North Harlem line goes from Grand Central Station to Botanical Garden Station, which lies right outside the main gate. Call 718-532-4900. By Car: Via the Henry Hudson, Bronx River, or Pelham parkways. Parking: $4. Call 718-817-8779 for travel information.

North, across East Fordham Rd. from the zoo, sprawls the labyrinthine New York Botanical Garden. Here, urban captives cavort amid such oddities as trees, flowers, and the open sky. Snatches of forest and waterways attempt to recreate the area's original landscape. The 250-acre garden, an outstanding horticultural preserve, serves as both a research laboratory and a plant and tree museum. One can scope out the 40-acre hemlock forest kept in its natural state, the Peggy Rockefeller Rose Garden, the T.H. Everett Rock Garden and waterfall, and a hands-on children's adventure garden. Although it costs an extra few dollars to enter, the **Conservatory** deserves a visit; the gorgeous domed greenhouse contains a few different ecosystems of exquisite plant life. If you go exploring by yourself, get a garden map; it's a jungle out there. The crowded 30-minute **tram ride** ($1) skirts most of the major sights.

AROUND CENTRAL BRONX

Subway: #4, C or D to Fordham Rd.

FORDHAM UNIVERSITY. Begun in 1841 by John Hughes as St. John's College, 80-acre Fordham has matured into one of the nation's foremost Jesuit schools. Robert S. Riley built the campus in classic collegiate Gothic style in 1936—so Gothic, in fact, that *The Exorcist* was filmed here. The college's photogenic history doesn't end there—Denzel Washington matriculated here during his undergraduate years. *(718-817-1000. Webster Ave. between E. Fordham Rd. and Dr. Theodore Kazimiroff Blvd.)*

EAST FORDHAM ROAD. If you prefer urban bustle to bucolic greenery, you don't have to go far from Fordham University. This street comprises the heart of one of the largest, busiest shopping districts in New York City. Influenced mainly by black and Hispanic cultures, the strip is one long, bargain-filled marketplace. Music blaring from storefront speakers attracts customers. Street vendors vie with department and specialty stores, while wizened women dish out *helado* alongside bargain beepers and gold figurines of the Madonna. *(East Fordham Rd. from Webster Ave. to University Ave.)*

BELMONT. This uptown "Little Italy," with its two-story rowhouses and byzantine alleyways, cooks up some of the best Italian food west of Naples. **Arthur Avenue** is home to some wonderful homestyle southern Italian cooking. At **Dominick's,** between 186th and 187th St., boisterous crowds blindly put away pasta. For the same dish on three different days you may pay three different prices, but you'll never leave *triste* (see **Restaurants,** p. 92). To get a concentrated sense of the area, stop into **Arthur Avenue Retail Market,** 2334 Arthur Ave., between 186th St. and Crescent. This indoor market is indeed a Little Italy onto itself, with caffe, a butcher, a grocer, a cheese shop, and other stalls selling Italian necessities. Meanwhile, outside the **Church of Our Lady of Mt. Carmel,** 627 187th St. at Belmont Ave., stands a pair of ecclesiastical shops where you can buy a statuette of your favorite saint. The portable martyrs come in all sizes and in every color of the rainbow. The church holds high mass in Italian daily at 10:15am, 12:45, and 7:30pm. The church lights up the street and the neighborhood with its **festival** of the Lady of Mt. Carmel yearly on July 15. Across and up the street a little is the **Belmont Italian-American Playhouse,** at 2385 Arthur Ave. (718-364-4700), between 186th and 187th St. The theater also puts on Italian language productions, ranging from *Filumena* to the satires of wacky Nobel Prize-winner Dario Fo. The theater is usually closed during the summer. Recently a large **Kosovar** population has left its mark on the Arthur Ave. area; the Kosovar flag with its red background and spidery bird is hung in the window fronts of many stores, private "men's clubs," and eateries. *(Bus: Bx12 from #4 Fordham Rd. subway stop to Arthur Ave. Metro North also runs a shuttle bus on weekends and holidays which stops at the Bronx Zoo; see **Bronx Zoo,** p. 220.)*

EDGAR ALLAN POE COTTAGE. The morbid writer and his tubercular cousin/wife lived spartanly in the cottage from 1846 until 1848. The enthusiastic Bronx Historical Society now maintains the abode. Here Poe wrote *Annabel Lee, Eureka,* and *The Bells,* a tale of the neighboring Fordham bells. The museum displays a slew of Poe's manuscripts and macabrabilia. *(718-881-8900. East Kingsbridge Rd. and Grand Concourse, five blocks west of Fordham University. Subway: #4 or D to Kingsbridge Rd. Open Sa 10am-4pm, Su 1-5pm. $2.)*

HERBERT H. LEHMAN COLLEGE. Founded in 1931 as Hunter College, Lehman is a fiefdom in the CUNY empire. The U.N. Security Council met in the gymnasium building in 1946. In 1980, the Lehmans endowed the first cultural center in the Bronx, the **Lehman Center for the Performing Arts,** on the Bedford Park Blvd. side of campus. The center is a 2300-seat concert hall, experimental theater, library, dance studio, and art gallery in one. One block up through Harris Park, the **Bronx High School of Science** is a long-established center of academic excellence, as evidenced by the several Nobel Prize winners who matriculated here. *(718-960-8000. Jerome Ave. and E. 198th St. Subway: #4 to Bedford Park Blvd./Lehman College. Ticket office open Sept.-May M-F 10am-5pm; closed in summer.)*

NORTHERN BRONX

VAN CORTLANDT PARK

Subway: #1, 9 to 242nd St.

Van Cortlandt Park (718-430-1890) spreads across 1146 acres of ridges and valleys in the northwest Bronx. The slightly grungy park has two golf courses, new tennis courts, baseball diamonds, soccer, football, and cricket fields, kiddie recreation areas, a large swimming pool, and barbecue facilities. The park's **special events office** (718-430-1848) offers info about the many concerts and sports activities that take place during the warmer months. While children of all ages swarm the various ball fields, nearby Van Cortlandt Lake teems with fish. Hikers have plenty of clambering options: the **Cass Gallagher Nature Trail** in the park's northwestern section leads to rock outcroppings from the last ice age and to what is arguably the most untamed wilderness in the city; the **Old Putnam Railroad Track,** once the city's first rail link to Boston, now leads past the quarry that supplied marble for Grand Central Station. Ballplayers have a choice between the baseball and softball diamonds of the **Indian Field recreation area** (laid atop the burial grounds of pro-rebel Stockbridge Indians who were ambushed and massacred by British troops during the Revolutionary War) or the **Parade Grounds,** where you can play tennis, soccer, and cricket.

In the southwest section of the park, just below the Parade Ground, stands the **Van Cortlandt House** (718-543-3344), at 246th St., a national landmark built in 1748 by the prominent political clan of the same name. (Open Tu-F 10am-3pm, Sa-Su 11am-4pm. $2, students and seniors $1.50, under 14 free.) The house is the oldest building in the Bronx. George Washington made frequent visits here, including his 1781 meeting with Rochambeau to determine his strategy in the last days of the Revolutionary War. Washington also began his triumphal march into New York City from here in 1783. Besides featuring the oldest doll-house in the U.S., the house also sports a colonial-era garden and sundial.

WOODLAWN CEMETERY. Music lovers pay tribute at the resting places of jazz legends Miles Davis, Duke Ellington, and Lionel Hampton. Other famous individuals, such as Herman Melville, are buried here, some of them in impressive mausoleums. *(Located east of Van Cortlandt Park. Subway: #4 to Woodlawn. Open daily 9am-4:30pm.)*

MANHATTAN COLLEGE. This 139-year-old private liberal arts institution began as a high school. Starting from the corner of Broadway and 242nd St. take 242nd up, up, uphill. As you scale the mound past Irish pubs and Chinese laundromats, watch for the college's red-brick buildings and chapel. The campus sprawls over stairs, squares, and plateaus like a life-sized game of Chutes and Ladders. The second staircase on campus brings you to a sheer granite bluff crowned with a kitsch plaster Madonna, a likely kidnapping victim from a suburban garden. Hardy souls who attain the campus peaks can take in a cinemascopic view of the Bronx. In direct contrast to much of the poverty-stricken Bronx, this area features some extremely wealthy residences and a triumvirate of esteemed private schools—Fieldston School (featured in Francis Ford Coppola's short film in *New York Stories*), Horace Mann, and Riverdale. *(718-862-8000.)*

WAVE HILL. This pastoral estate in Riverdale commands a broad view of the Hudson and the Palisades. Samuel Clemens Longhorn (a.k.a. Mark Twain), Arturo Toscanini, and Teddy Roosevelt all resided in this impressive mansion. Donated to the city over 20 years ago, the estate currently offers concerts and dance amid its greenhouses and spectacular formal gardens that are free with the price of admission to the grounds. *(718-549-3200. 675 W. 252nd St. Subway: #1, 9 train to 231st St., then bus Bx7 or Bx10 to 252nd St. Walk across Parkway Bridge and turn left; walk to 249th St., turn right and walk to Wave Hill Gate. Or Metro North to Riverdale and then walk up 254th to Independence Ave., right on Independence to Wave Hill gate. Open June to mid-Oct. Tu-Th and Sa-Su 9am-5:30pm, W 9:30am-dusk; mid-Oct. to May Tu-Su 10am-4:30pm. $4, students and seniors $2. Tu free all day, Saturday free until noon.)*

VALENTINE-VARIAN HOUSE. The second-oldest building in the Bronx (built in 1758) saw light action during the Revolution. It has since become the site of the **Museum of Bronx History,** which is run by the Bronx County Historical Society. The museum, at Bainbridge Ave. and E. 208th St., functions as the borough archive. The house has retained a few period furnishings but negligible Revolutionary ambience. *(718-881-8900. Subway: D to 205th St., then walk north 2 blocks. Open Sa 10am-4pm, Su 1-5pm, otherwise by appointment. $2.)*

PELHAM BAY PARK

New York City's largest park, **Pelham Bay Park** boasts over 2100 acres of green saturated with playing fields, tennis courts, golf courses, picnic spaces, wildlife sanctuaries, a beach, and even training grounds for the city's mounted police force (see **Participatory Sports**, p. 291). The deeply knowledgeable **park rangers** lead a variety of history- and nature-oriented walks for creatures great and small (call 718-430-1890 to receive a schedule in the mail). From the **Pelham Bay stables** (718-885-0551), Shore Rd. at City Island Dr., you can take a guided ride around the park on horseback. (Open daily 8am-8pm. $20 per hr. Subway: #6 to Pelham Bay Park, then bus Bx29.) Inside the park, the **Federalist Bartow-Pell Mansion Museum** (718-885-1461), Shore Rd. opposite the golf courts, sits among a prize-winning formal herb garden landscaped in 1915. (Open W and Sa-Su noon-4pm. Closed in Aug. $2.50; students and seniors $1.25; under 12 free. Subway: #6 to Pelham Bay Park.) The interior decorator doted on the Empire/Greek Revival style. The house has a free-standing spiral staircase, an herb garden arranged around a pond complete with goldfish and spouting cherub, and an opulent bed with a strange canopy resembling a costume wig. Just down the road find **Orchard Beach,** which gets mobbed on hot summer days. Snack stands feed the sun-seeking throngs, and the lifeguards watch over them from Memorial Day to Labor Day (daily 10am-7pm).

For a whiff of New England in New York, visit **City Island,** a community of century-old houses, sailboats, and a shipyard. The **North Wind Undersea Museum** (718-885-0701) intrigues sailors and landlubbers alike. Nautical treasures include a 100-year-old tugboat cabin, antique diving gear, exotic sea shells, whale bones galore, an aquarium of local sea life, and an interactive, virtual ship's brig exhibit where fun-loving parents can incarcerate their children. Also on display is "Physty the Whale," a phantastyk life-size replica of the first beached whale ever to be saved by humankind. (Subway #6 to Pelham Bay Park; board bus #29 outside the station; get off at the first stop on City Island; the museum is on your left. Open M-F 10am-5pm, Sa-Su noon-5pm. $3, children $2.)

Aquatic life can also be viewed outside the museum in any of the many seafood restaurants lining City Island Ave.; they're pricier than those in the Bronx proper, but a careful search will yield the elusive $10 lobster. The food chain stops dead in its tracks at the nearby **Pelham Cemetery** on the west end of Reville Rd. Emblazoned on the gate is: "Lives are commemorated...deaths are recorded...love is undisguised...this is a cemetery." Hmmm. Thoughts to ponder as you wait for the #29 bus, which leaves every 30 minutes.

SOUTH BRONX

This is not the part of town to meander in search of out-of-the-way places. It does, however, offer up a few morsels to the directed traveler.

YANKEE STADIUM. Sports fans (and StairMaster freaks) will enjoy a visit to the historic arena, built in 1923. The aging stadium's frequent face-lifts have kept it on par with younger structures. The Yankees played the first night game here in 1946, and the first message scoreboard tallied runs here in 1954. Inside the 11.6-acre park (the field measures only 3.5 acres), monuments honor such Yankee greats as Lou Gehrig, Joe DiMaggio, and Babe Ruth. Besides conjuring thrills for baseball fans, Yankee Stadium injects the South Bronx's economy with much-needed income. Controversial Yankees owner George Steinbrenner has announced a possible abandonment of "The House That-Ruth Built" in the South Bronx for the more convenient and tourist-friendly confines of Midtown Manhattan. Ouch. (See **Baseball**, p. 289.) *(E. 161st St. at River Ave. Subway: #4, C, or D to 161st St.)*

HIP-HOP (R)EVOLUTION In 1973, Bronx DJ Kool Herc began prolonging songs' funky drum "break" sections by using two turntables and two copies of the same record, switching to the start of the second copy when the first one ended and then doubling back. Dancers took up the rhythm's challenge, by 1975 evolving break-dancing in response to similar turntable manipulations by Afrika Bambaataa, Grandmaster Flash, Kool, and other denizens of the 174th St. area by the Bronx River. Thus, the Bronx birthed the art of DJing, an acrobatic dance style, and a musical genre known as hip-hop/rap that would shape the sound of the new millennium. For the phatty-phat 411, hit Davey D's exhaustive web page at www.daveyd.com

THE BRONX MUSEUM OF THE ARTS. Set in the rotunda of the Bronx Courthouse, the museum's two small galleries exhibit works by contemporary masters as well as local talent, with a focus on Latino, African-American, and women artists. The museum encourages the community to create textual and visual responses to the permanent collection and mounts the (often nutty) viewer feedback alongside the original work. *(718-681-6000, ext. 141 for events. 165th St. and Grand Concourse near Yankee Stadium. Open W 3-9pm, Th-F 10am-5pm, Sa-Su noon-6pm. Suggested donation $3, students $2, seniors $1. W free admission.)*

ART AND ANTIQUE MARKET. Antiquers looking for a good deal might consider taking a look in northeastern Bronx on Bruckner Blvd., between Alexander and Willis St. The antiquer's unwilling partner(s) might want to stop by **Gallery 69,** a gallery showcasing black erotica from around the world (see p. 255). *(Subway: #6 to 3rd Ave.; walk south a few blocks to Bruckner.)*

THE LONGWOOD HISTORIC DISTRICT. A neighborhood with stately brownstones reminiscent of Harlem's Striver's Row. The **Longwood Arts Gallery,** located on the third floor of a former public school building, houses art studios and often features work by artists from its artist-in-residence program. *(Subway: #6 train to Longwood Ave., then walk two blocks away from the overpass up Longwood Ave. Open Th-F noon-5pm, Sa noon-4pm. Free. For more info call the Bronx Council on the Arts at 718-931-9500.)*

STATEN ISLAND

In 1524, 32 years after Columbus patented the New World, a Florentine named Giovanni da Verrazano sailed into New York Harbor to get some fresh water. He refilled his casks on a sizable chunk of land and unwittingly stepped into history as the godfather of Staten Island. The name (originally Staaten Eylandt) comes courtesy of Henry Hudson, who sailed through the neighboring waters while on a 1609 voyage for the Dutch East India Company.

For the first 440 years after Europeans settled it, Staten Island remained reachable only by boat. In 1713, a public ferry started running from Staten Island to the rest of the city. In spite of the new link, Staten Islanders still tended to look west to New Jersey, just a stone's throw away across the Arthur Kill ("kill" is Dutch for "channel"), rather than north and east to the city. In 1964, builder Othmar "George Washington Bridge" Ammann spanned the gap between Staten Island and Brooklyn with a 4260 ft. long suspension number, the Verrazano-Narrows Bridge. Visible from virtually everywhere on the island, the bridge has the distinction of being the world's second-longest suspension bridge, outspanned only by the Humber Bridge in England.

Although traffic now flows more easily between Manhattan and Staten Island (via Brooklyn), Staten Islanders continue unsuccessfully to lobby borough, city, and state governments for independent municipality. Many resent having to pay higher taxes to subsidize New York's poorer neighborhoods. Manhattanites tend to lump Staten Island with New Jersey; most only go there in order to ride the free ferry round-trip (without getting off) or to take driving tests (the waiting list for appointments is shorter than in Manhattan and the driving substantially less frenetic). However, the few fine attractions seem even better for their mystique, beyond the reach of swarms of disinterested ferry riders. Idyllic Snug Harbor, the serene Tibetan Museum (see p. 245), and the all-American Staten Island Mall (see p. 297) offer pleasures that most Manhattanites, sadly, have not experienced. Pick up much needed maps of Staten Island's bus routes as well as other info at the **Staten Island Chamber of Commerce,** 130 Bay St. (718-727-1900). To get there, bear left from the ferry station onto Bay St. Because of the hills and the distances (and some dangerous neighborhoods in between), it's a bad idea to *walk* from one site to the next. **Make sure to plan your excursion with the bus schedule in mind.** (Open M-F 9am-5pm. All buses depart from the ferry terminal.)

THE FERRY TERMINAL. Completely free, the ferry may very well offer the world's premier sightseeing bargain. You can take in the splendid breeze while checking out the lower Manhattan skyline, Ellis Island, the Statue of Liberty, and Governor's Island. Postcard photographers flock here for some of the most marketable views in the city. The ride is particularly exhilarating at sunset or night. *(718-390-5253 for ferry info. To get to Manhattan terminal, take the #1, 9 train to South Ferry or take the N or R to Whitehall, then walk west about 3 blocks. 30min. The ferry runs 24 hr.)*

SNUG HARBOR CULTURAL CENTER. Founded in 1801, Sailors' Snug Harbor served as the first maritime hospital and home for retired sailors in the U.S. (The iron fence that barricades it originally kept old salts from quenching their thirst at nearby bars.) Purchased by the city in 1976, it now includes 28 historic buildings scattered over wonderfully placid, unpopulated parkland—83 sprawling, green, and amazingly well-kept acres of national historic landmark. The Center provides space for contemporary art, theater, recitals, outdoor sculpture, and concerts. *(718-448-2500. 1000 Richmond Terrace. Bus: S40. Free tours of the grounds offered Sa-Su 2pm, starting at the Visitors' Center.)*

STATEN ISLAND CHILDREN'S MUSEUM. Funky, interactive exhibits at this delightful museum at the Snug Harbor Cultural Center. The "Wonder Water" exhibit so encourages the hands-on ethic it provides kid-sized rubber raincoats and rainpants for protection. The museum also features a "Walk-In Workshop" where kids can create their own art with a wide variety of materials. Outdoor performances are often held in the Center's South Meadow. *(718-273-2060. Open Tu-Su 11am-5pm. $4, under 2 free. Performance tickets $15; free family concerts Su.)*

HISTORIC RICHMOND TOWN. A huge museum complex documenting three centuries of Staten Island's culture and history. Reconstructed 17th- to 19th-century dwellings house "inhabitants" (costumed master craftspeople and their apprentices). Thanks to budget cuts, only 10 of these buildings, spread over 100 acres, remain permanently open to the public. Head for the **Voorlezer's House,** the oldest surviving elementary school in the U.S. (also a church and home), the **General Store,** and an 18th-century farmhouse. The museum rotates which buildings it opens to the public, so call in advance to find out what you can see and to get info about the summertime "living history" events. *(718-351-1611; fax 718-351-6051. 441 Clarke Ave. Bus: S74, 40min. Open July-Aug. W-F 10am-5pm, Sa-Su 1-5pm; Sept.-Dec. W-Su 1-5pm. $4, students, seniors, and 6-18 $2.50. Tours sometimes available with advance notice.)*

MORAVIAN CEMETERY. Commodore Cornelius Vanderbilt and his monied clan lie in this ornate crypt, built in 1886 by Richard Morris Hunt. Cornelius, a native Staten Islander, first ventured into business by investing in a ferry to Manhattan when he was 16 years old. Central Park creator Frederick Law Olmsted landscaped this park-like cemetery with beautiful winding paths and gentle hillsides that cry out sacrilegiously for a picnic. *(On Richmond Rd. at Todt Hill Rd. in Donegan Hills. Bus: S74 to Todt Hill Rd. Open daily 8am-6pm.)*

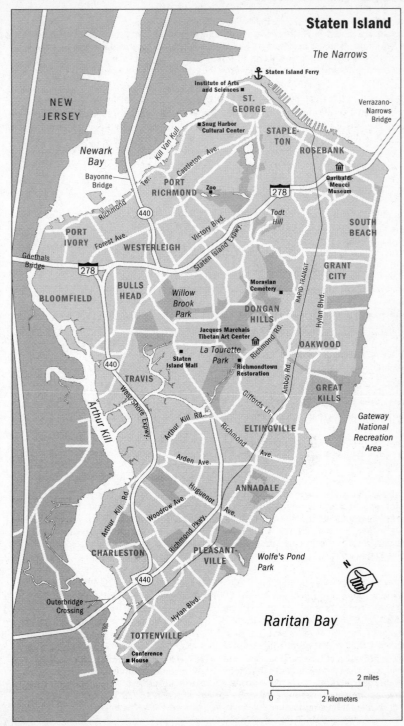

Staten Island

The Narrows

⚓ Staten Island Ferry

■ Institute of Arts and Sciences ■

ST. GEORGE

STAPLE-TON

ROSEBANK

Verrazano-Narrows Bridge

NEW JERSEY

Newark Bay

■ Snug Harbor Cultural Center

Kill Van Kull

Castleton Ave.

Bayonne Bridge

PORT RICHMOND

Zoo ■

🏛 Garibaldi-Meucci Museum

Tet.

Richmond

278

Todt Hill

SOUTH BEACH

440

PORT IVORY

Forest Ave.

WESTERLEIGH

Victory Blvd.

Staten Island Expwy.

GRANT CITY

Hylan Blvd.

Goethals Bridge

278

BLOOMFIELD

BULLS HEAD

Willow Brook Park

Moravian Cemetery ■

RAPID TRANSIT

DONGAN HILLS

Jacques Marchais Tibetan Art Center 🏛

Richmond Rd.

OAKWOOD

440

■ Staten Island Mall

La Tourette Park

■ Richmondtown Restoration

Amboy Rd.

GREAT KILLS

TRAVIS

West Shore Expwy.

Arthur Kill Rd.

Giffords Ln.

Richmond

ELTINGVILLE

Gateway National Recreation Area

Arthur Kill

Arden Ave.

Ave.

Arthur Kill Rd.

Huguenot

Ave.

ANNADALE

Woodrow Ave.

Richmond Pkwy.

CHARLESTON

PLEASANT-VILLE

Wolfe's Pond Park

N

440

Outerbridge Crossing

Hylan Blvd.

Raritan Bay

TOTTENVILLE

■ Conference House

0 ——— 2 miles

0 ——— 2 kilometers

NEIGHBORHOODS

BOROUGH HALL. The imposing Federalist building, with its clocktower and terraced garden nearby, offers an eye-widening view of the harbor (as well as an eye-deadening statue of Frank D. Paulo, depicted holding a pre-pubescent girl in a sculpture bearing the inscription, "A Public Man"). *(Just up the hill from the ferry terminal, the second street on the right is Stuyvesant Pl.; follow it as it curves upward to the right.)*

STATEN ISLAND INSTITUTE OF ARTS AND SCIENCES. Its galleries feature rotating displays pertaining to the art, science, and history of the region. The upstairs galleries host temporary exhibits whose subjects vary from the Staten Island Juried Art Exhibition to the "Fantastic World of Butterflies." *(718-727-1135. 75 Stuyvesant Pl., on the far corner of Wall St. Open M-Sa 9am-5pm, Su 1-5pm. Suggested donation $2.50; students, seniors, and under 12 $1.25.)*

ALICE AUSTEN HOUSE MUSEUM AND GARDEN. Head here for a photographic slice of turn-of-the-century Staten Island life. From 1880 to 1930 Austen took roughly 4000 photographs of her luxurious island world. After losing everything in the 1929 stock market crash, Austen languished in the city poorhouse until the Staten Island Historical Society discovered her work and published it in *Life* months before her death. This quiet museum displays many of Austen's photos and has a waterfront garden with great Verrazano-Narrows views. *(718-816-4506. 2 Hylan Blvd. Bus: S51 to Hylan Blvd. and walk one block toward the water. Open Mar.-Dec. Th-Su noon-5pm. Grounds open daily until dusk. $2, children free.)*

THE GARIBALDI-MEUCCI MUSEUM. In the mid-1800s, Giuseppe Garibaldi, an Italian patriot and mastermind of Italy's reunification, took refuge on the island following his defeat by Napoleon III. He settled in a farmhouse in Rosebank and proceeded to amass enough memorabilia to make the place a museum. He shared the house with Antonio Meucci, the less-than-celebrated inventor of the telephone (he had developed his first working model by 1851 and finally received a U.S. patent caveat in 1871, but died before being recognized as the inventor—lucky for Alexander Graham Bell). *(718-442-1608. 420 Tompkins Ave. Bus: S78 to Chestnut and Tompkins St., right in front of the museum. Open Tu-Su 1-5pm. Suggested donation $3.)*

STATEN ISLAND CONFERENCE HOUSE. The only peace conference ever held between British forces and American rebels took place here. At the summit on September 11, 1776, British commander Admiral Lord Howe met with three Continental Congress representatives—Benjamin Franklin, John Adams, and Edward Rutledge. Located at the foot of Hyland Blvd. in Tottenville, the house has become a National Historic Landmark. Inside, you can see period furnishings and refresh your knowledge of Revolutionary War minutiae. *(718-984-2086. Bus: S78 to the last stop on Craig Ave. and walk west one block farther on Hylan Blvd.; make a right on Satterlee St.; the Conference House is about 100 ft. ahead on the left. $2, seniors and under 12 $1. Guided tours by appointment F-Su 1-4pm.)*

OTHER SIGHTS. At the **Newhouse Center for Contemporary Art** you'll be privy to the work of emerging and mid-career artists working in all media *(718-448-2500, ext. 266. Open W-Su noon-5pm. Suggested donation $2.)* **High Rock Park Conservation Center** offers 72 acres adjacent to the cemetery, with miles of well-marked trails perfect for an afternoon stroll. Friendly Urban Rangers lead tours of various parts of the park on Saturday and Sunday afternoons; call for exact information. *(718-667-6042. Bus: S54 to Nevada Ave. and Rockland. Walk up the hill. Open daily 9am-5pm; grounds open dawn to dusk.)* **The Staten Island Botanical Garden,** also at the Center, tends a striking Butterfly Garden among the other beds of lilies, lilacs, sunflowers, and snapdragons on its 28 peaceful acres. *(718-273-8200. Open daily dawn to dusk. Tours by appointment.)*

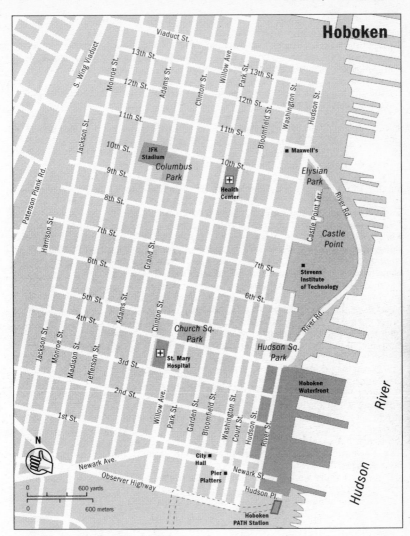

HOBOKEN, NJ

*Subway: B, D, F, N, Q, or R train to 34th St., then the PATH train ($1) to the first stop in Hoboken. The **PATH train** also leaves from the F train stations at 23rd and 14th St., and the PATH stations at 9th St./Sixth Ave., Christopher St./Greenwich Ave., and the World Trade Center. To get to Hoboken's main drag, **Washington St.,** walk along Hudson Pl. from the PATH station to Newark St., make a left, walk two blocks to Washington St., and make a right.*

Right across the Hudson River from downtown Manhattan, Hoboken's proximity to New York (10min. and $1 away via the PATH train) make its small-town charms that much more pleasant. Known primarily as a party town by outsiders, its 1.3 sq. mi. hold no fewer than 150 liquor licenses, perhaps the greatest boozing density in the nation. The thriving "scene," along with low-ish rents and a cheap commute, have drawn Big Apple yuppies in droves, as evidenced by the high proportion of

German-engineered automobiles that slide along Hoboken's streets (for a less I-bankish atmosphere and cheaper rents, try **Jersey City,** also reachable by PATH; get off at Journal Sq.). The influx of yupsters stirred conflict with Hoboken's traditional European immigrant communities, but reforming mayor and homegrown fashion-plate Anthony Russo helped to achieve some manner of consensus between the area's populations. Furthermore, all types of residents share a respect for the town's notorious history as the original home of Frank Sinatra, Jack Nicholson, and baseball.

On the far east side of the city, Frank Sinatra Dr. curves along the coast from 4th St. to 11th St. The **Hoboken City Hall,** at First and Washington, can provide you with an excellent map. Washington St. provides most of the action in Hoboken; streets around the PATH station and from 1st to 4th St. also bustle with activity. Beware pedestrian perils due to a lack of crosswalks.

On Hudson Pl., the Beaux-Arts **Erie-Lackawanna Plaza** has been featured in a number of movies (no doubt because of its spectacular view), including *On the Waterfront* and Woody Allen's *Stardust Memories*. Also along Hudson Pl., in the Hudson St. direction, bars and clubs begin their onslaught.

Before getting caught up in the alcoholic frenzy of Hoboken nightlife, you may want to indulge in charms not served in a frosty mug. If you go to the far eastern side of 8th St. to **Castle Point** (on the campus of Stevens Institute of Technology), walk up a hill and across the grass, until you reach a cannon. There, *voila*, you'll happen upon a spectacular vista of Manhattan's West Side.

Amidst the brownstones, hawked by interminable real estate agencies to young investment bankers, you'll see a handful of small parks, sporting the mayor's slogan, "More than a city…we're a neighborhood." **Church Square Park** gently interrupts Park Ave. between 4th and 5th St. with its frolicking children, relaxing seniors, and periwinkle gazebo commemorating eight classical music masters. A more recent musical monument, **Frank Sinatra Park,** sits on the eastern waterfront between 4th and 6th St. Baseball supposedly began in **Elysian Park** (along 10th and 11th St. on the eastern waterfront), in an 1846 game between the "New Yorks" and the "Knickerbockers."

Sinatra Park and Elysian Park also host a **summer concert festival,** part of Hoboken's impressive effort to showcase local culture. Meanwhile, classic movies play at the Erie-Lackawanna Plaza. (Concerts June-Aug. Elysian Park Tu 7pm; Sinatra Park Th 7pm. Movies W 9pm. Free.) Every May through September, the **Art and Music Festival** hits Washington St. with a unique Hoboken flair. For more information on these and other festivals, inquire at the **Cultural Office.** (201-420-2207. City Hall, 2nd fl.)

Last, but definitely not least, if you feel a tad too sober, you can seek refuge and refreshment at the city's many restaurants (see p. 109), many, *many* **bars** (see p. 283), or at the infamous underground rock house, **Maxwell's** (see p. 274).

MUSEUMS

Witness a culture collecting itself! Swoon under a life-sized replica of a great blue whale at the American Museum of Natural History. Control a 900 ft. aircraft carrier at the Intrepid Sea-Air-Space Museum. Slip into the world of the 2000-year-old Egyptian Temple of Dendur or of Van Gogh's 100-year-old *Café at Arles* at the Metropolitan Museum of Art. Relax alongside Monet's *Water Lilies* at the Museum of Modern Art. Or analyze the question of racialized space in the contemporary art at the Whitney. New York has accumulated more stuff in more museums than any other city in the New World. During the annual **Museum Mile Festival** in mid-June, Fifth Ave. museums keep their doors open until late at night, stage engaging exhibits, involve city kids in mural painting, and fill the streets with music. Several also sponsor film series and live concerts throughout the year (see **Arts & Entertainment,** p. 261).

THE BUDGET GUIDE TO COLLECTED CULTURE

Many New York museums request a donation instead of a fixed admission charge. No one will throw you out or even glare at you for giving less than the suggested donation; more likely, you'll feel slightly cheap and maybe guilty. Enjoy that sneaky feeling. The following museums are either downright free or request a donation: Alternative Museum, American Academy of the Arts, American Numismatic Society, Black Fashion Museum, Bronx Museum of the Arts, Brooklyn Museum, China Institute Gallery, The Cloisters, Forbes Magazine Galleries, Hall of Fame of Great Americans, Hispanic Society of America, Isamu Noguchi Museum, Maritime Industry Museum, Metropolitan Museum of Art, El Museo del Barrio, Museum of American Illustration, Museum of American Folk Art, Museum of the City of New York, Museum of Financial History, and Radio, National Museum of the American Indian, Nicholas Roerich Museum, New York Unearthed, Parsons Exhibition Center, and the Police Academy Museum.

Other museums are free or "pay-what-you-wish" during certain windows of the week—often on Tuesday or Thursday evenings. Check with the listings below to confirm when you can skimp on the following museums: American Craft Museum, Asia Society, Cooper-Hewitt Museum, Guggenheim Museum, International Center of Photography, Jewish Museum, Museum of American Folk Art, Museum of Modern Art, National Academy Museum, New Museum of Contemporary Art, Studio Museum of Harlem, and the Whitney Museum.

METROPOLITAN MUSEUM OF ART

*Located at Fifth Ave. and 82nd St. **Telephone:** General recorded info 535-7710, upcoming concerts and lectures 570-3949, group tours 570-3711. **Website:** www.metmuseum.org **Subway:** #4, 5, 6 to 86th St. **Open:** Su and Tu-Th 9:30am-5:15pm, F-Sa 9:30am-8:45pm. **Admission:** Suggested donation $10, students and seniors $5. Members and children under 12 (with an adult) free. **Disabled Access:** 535-7710. Wheelchairs at the coat-check areas. Enter through the 81st St. entrance. **Hearing-impaired Visitors:** 535-7710. **Foreign Visitors Desk:** Maps, brochures, and assistance in a number of languages; call 650-2987. **Gallery Tours:** Free, daily, in English; inquire at the main info desk for schedules, topics, and meeting places, or call 570-3930. **Key to the Met Audio Guides:** $5, $3.50 for members, discounts for groups.*

In 1866, John Jay called for the creation of a "National Institution and Gallery of Art." Eminent ex-patriots in Paris responded with ardent support. Under Jay's leadership, the New York Union League Club gained the backing of civic leaders, art collectors, and philanthropists who launched the museum in 1870. At the time, it housed only 174 Dutch and Flemish paintings from three private collections and handful of assorted antiquities. A decade later, the Metropolitan Museum settled at its present location in Central Park at Fifth Avenue and

82nd Street despite the protests of Central Park's purist designers. This once tiny project has evolved into a behemoth brimming with world treasures, spanning 1.4 million square feet and housing 3.3 million works of art (not all are on display). The Met still constantly seeks, seduces, and seizes art objects from everyone and everywhere to display them for its enormous audience.

To meet the demands of an ever-growing collection, the museum has undergone nearly constant renovation and transformation. In 1971, an extensive building improvement scheme was developed to accommodate the works. The architects Kevin Roche, John Dinkeloo, and Associates laid out a 20-year plan to make the museum more accessible to larger audiences, which included the installation of the Sackler Wing of the Temple of Dendur, the American Wing, and the Lehman Wing. The original Gothic facade designed by Calvert Vaux adorns the western side of the Lehman Wing. Recent additions include the glass-enclosed Lila Acheson Wallace Wing and the Cantor Roof Garden, which contains changing open-air sculpture exhibits. A renovated Korean collection opened in June 1998, and the new and improved Greek galleries opened this past year.

The sheer volume of superior artwork at the Met inspires awe. You'll have to save up hours, days, even weeks, to savor the collections. Don't rush the Metropolitan experience; you could camp out in here for a month—in fact, two children did live here in the children's book *From the Mixed-up Files of Mrs. Basil E. Frankweiler*. If you would like a guide around the Met, you may want to use the "Key to the Met Audio Guide" (see info above). If the Met inspires the da Vinci in you, let yourself get carried away—the museum encourages its visitors to sketch. You'll find a popular spot for this at the *Ugolino and his Sons* sculpture on the first floor.

Exhibitions through 2000: In the fall of 1999 through the winter of 2000, the Met curates a monumental collection of ancient Egyptian art and artifacts with Egyptian Art in the Age of the Pyramid and Ancient Faces; Masterpieces of Chinese Painting from the C.C. Wang Family Collection (through Jan. 9); The Nature of Islamic Ornament, Part IV: Figural Representation (through Jan. 2); Daido Moriyama: Hunter (through Jan. 2); Portraits by Ingres: Image of an Epoch (through Jan.2); Carleton Watkins: The Art of Perception (through Jan. 9); Rodin's Monument to Victor Hugo (through Jan. 2); Celebrating the American Wing: Notable Acquisitions, 1980-1999 (through Nov.); Masterpieces of the Calouste Gulbenkian Museum, Lisbon (through Feb. 27); Annual Christmas Tree and Neapolitan Baroque Creche (through Jan. 9); Icons of Rock Style, at the Costume Institute (through Mar. 26); Perfect Documents: Walker Evans and African Art, 1935 (through Sept. 3); Painters of the School of Paris (Mar.-Dec.); Japanese Art from the Mary Burke Collection (late Mar.-June 25); American Identity, at the Costume Institute (Apr. 4-Aug. 20); Subjects and Symbols in American Sculpture: Selections from the Permanent Collection (Apr. 11-Aug. 20); Art and Oracle: African Art and Rituals of Divination (Apr. 25-July 30); Iris and B. Gerald Cantor Roof Garden (May 2-late fall); American Modern: 1925-1950 (May-Oct.); A Century of Design, Part II: 1926-1950 (May-Oct.); John Singer Sargent: Beyond the Portrait Studio—Paintings and Drawings in the Met (early June-Sept. 17); Chardin (mid-June to Sept. 17).

FIRST FLOOR. The **Greek and Roman collections** receive the most traffic of all the first floor galleries. Spanning several millennia and two empires, these contain Cypriot sculptures, Greek vases, Roman busts, and wall-paintings from two villas near Mt. Vesuvius. If you can't find the giant marble limb or lewd vase you've seen in textbooks, don't worry—it may await exhibition in storage. The Greek galleries have been newly renovated for 2000.

For your wallet's sake, it's best to ignore the pricey **museum cafe** and move into the **Michael C. Rockefeller Wing,** which contains the art of **Africa,** the **Pacific Islands,** and the **Americas.** This extensive wing features one of the largest collections of non-European art in the Occident. Totem poles, boats, ceremonial masks, musical instruments, and sculptures fill this gallery. The African collection includes pieces from the Court of Benin in Nigeria and wooden sculpture by the Dogan, Bamana, and Senufo tribes of Mali. From the Pacific come artifacts from Asmat, the Sepik provinces of New Guinea, and the island groups of Melanesia and Polynesia. Inuit and Native American artifacts display alongside Aztec and Mayan art.

Next is the **Lila Acheson Wallace Wing** of 20th-century art. The Met at first resisted investing in controversial modern art; the Museum of Modern Art was built to house works that the Met would not accept (see **MoMA,** p. 235). But in 1967 the Met finally relented, establishing the **Department of 20th-Century Art,** which has since welcomed Picasso, Pollock, Warhol, Kandinsky, and others. Americans flex the most muscle here, with numerous paintings by the Modernist Stieglitz Circle, Abstract Expressionists, and color field artists. Displays from the permanent collection change every six months or so, but if you're lucky you can spot such masterpieces as Picasso's *The Blind Minstrel,* typical of his blue period, and Grant Wood's *Ride of Paul Revere,* a canvas that proves the painter of *American Gothic* was more than just a one-hit wonder.

Just between the Wrightsman Galleries and the Henry Kravis Wing lies the **European Sculpture Garden.** This sunlit courtyard provides the moment's rest for which your feet have been begging. Marble people and animals in various states of repose sit among real children and parents striking similar poses.

Across yet another threshold, you'll find the **European Sculpture and Decorative Arts** wing. Containing about 60,000 works, ranging from the early labors of the Renaissance to the early 20th century, the collection covers six media: sculpture, woodwork and furniture, ceramics and glass, metalwork and jewelry, tapestries and textiles, and mathematical instruments. Note the impressive vases and tapestries created in honor of Napoleon, Catherine the Great, and other European dignitaries who had money to burn. **The Jack and Belle Linsky Collection,** within the European Sculpture and Decorative Arts Galleries, flaunts expensive-looking, heavily adorned pieces. Highlights include canvases by Lucas Cranach the Elder, Rubens, and Boucher, more than 200 Rococo porcelain figures from such renowned factories as Meissen and Chantilly, and gaudy 18th-century French furniture. Nearby, **Medieval Art** lurks in dark and appropriately damp environs, featuring church paraphernalia such as paintings, stained glass, and a huge choir screen. The bulk of the Medieval collection, however, resides in **The Cloisters,** the towering Washington Heights branch of the Met (see p. 241).

From the north end of the Medieval gallery, exit the old Met and enter the **Robert Lehman Wing.** Opened to the public in 1975, it showcases an extraordinary collection assembled by the acquisitive Lehman clan. Italian paintings from the 14th and 15th centuries face canvases by Rembrandt, El Greco, and Goya. Nineteenth- and 20th-century French painters include Ingres, Renoir, Chagall, and Matisse.

From here, head back through Medieval Art, swing over to the left, and start humming the "Star-Spangled Banner." The **American Wing** houses one of the nation's largest and finest collections of American paintings, sculptures, and decorative crafts. The paintings cover almost all phases of American art history, from the early days of West and Trumbull to Sargent and Hopper. Celebrate early America, as you admire Gilbert Stuart's regal portraits of America's founding father, Bingham's pensive *Fur Traders Descending the Mississippi,* and the heroic *George Washington Crossing the Delaware* by Emanuel Gottlieb Leutze. Some of the more noteworthy 19th-century paintings include Sargent's *Madame X,* a stunning portrait of the notorious French beauty Mme. Gautreau, and several breathtaking Hudson River School landscapes.

MUSEUMS

Twenty-five period rooms document the history of American interior design and decorative art. Note the sinuously curved Victorian *tête-à-tête*—a naughty, "S"-shaped love seat. Art Nouveau fans will gush at the ample selection of Louis Comfort Tiffany's glasswork, while admirers of American Modernism can pay their respects in the Frank Lloyd Wright Room. The room ingeniously corresponds to the world outside the windows—a prime example of Wright's concept of "total design."

If your brain feels full, take a break and romp around in the **Arms and Armor** collection, just off the American collection. The armor collection contains a huge number of swords, rapiers, daggers, and other sharp, pointy objects. Select suits of armor built to accommodate substantial midriffs may provide a touch of comic relief in this otherwise menacing hall of warfare.

Around the corner, the **Department of Egyptian Art** occupies the entire northeast wing of the main hall, spanning thousands of years—from 3100 BC to the Byzantine Period (AD 700)—and containing a galaxy of artifacts, from earrings to whole temples (that you can enter!). Egypt gave the incredible **Temple of Dendur** to the United States in 1965 in recognition of an American campaign to save Nubian landmarks from destruction. Preserved in its entirety, the temple (c. 15 BC) even retains old graffiti, not from unruly museum visitors, but from long-dead hooligans (French soldiers during the Napoleonic occupation of Egypt). Elsewhere in the wing, mummies provide spooky fun for kids, young and old.

SECOND FLOOR. Returning to the Great Hall, you can go up the huge staircase, around the gift shop, and past the statue of Perseus to examine an extensive collection of Chinese ceramics lining the Great Hall Balcony. To one side, you'll see more Greek and Roman art; on the other, the **Department of Ancient Near Eastern and Islamic Art.** The collection of Ancient Near Eastern Art features artwork from ancient Mesopotamia, Iran, Syria, Anatolia, and a smattering of other lands, all produced during the period from 6000 BC to the Arab conquest in AD 626. Behind, in the Islamic Art room, you can see an intact 14th-century Iranian *mihrab* (a mosque's niche, pointing toward Mecca) covered entirely in blue glazed ceramic tiles.

To the right of the Great Hall Balcony lies the **Asian Art** department, with the best collection outside of Asia. Walk through to the new South Asian gallery, the **Florence and Herbert Irving Galleries for the Arts of South and Southeast Asia,** which features the colossal contortionist sculptures of Buddhas and *bodhissatvas*. Chronicling art from the entire Southeast Asian peninsula from antiquity to the present, the gallery even showcases a Cambodian Khmer courtyard. The **Ancient Chinese** gallery runs parallel, with a Han-dynasty funeral statuary. Make sure to check out the newly completed space on the **Arts of Korea** with 100 pieces from all major media. Down the hall, you can either go straight to examine one of the most extensive collections of Chinese painting in the world or turn left for Japanese paintings, woodblock prints, sculpture, ceramics and textiles (please don't miss the *ukiyo-e* prints), or shop at yet another kiosk.

The second floor also features the Met's "jewel in the crown," the Italian, Flemish, Dutch, and French schools of the **European Paintings** collection. British and Spanish works make cameo appearances. The Italian collection shows particularly strongly in early Renaissance paintings. Amid the plethora of Madonnas and beatific baby Jesuses, look for gems by Titian and Caravaggio. The Spaniards appear in less force, but you will see some El Greco, Goya, and Velázquez.

The Flemish quarters contain Van Eyck's *Crucifixion* and macabre *Last Judgment*. The enigmatic Hieronymus Bosch also makes a rare American appearance with his *Adoration of the Magi*. The Dutch make a strong showing, led by Rembrandt, whose most emblematic canvases converge at the Met: *Flora*, *The Toilet of Bathsheba*, *Aristotle with a Bust of Homer*, and

REST YER BONES If you aim to see the Met in its entirety, you'll need a place to rest. Many charming courts and gardens offer a romantic setting for foot relief. Try the Charles Engelhardt court in the American Wing, or the European Sculpture Garden between the Wrightsman Galleries and the Kravis Wing. Do a little meditating in the Astor Court, a Chinese scholar's garden complete with goldfish in the Asian art wing. The Temple of Dendur also offers an area upon which you can sit like a Nubian bird on a wire, while enormous windows grant a splendid view of Central Park and a ponderous stone offers a bed of sorts beside mummies of yore. On cool summer days, the Gerald and Iris B. Cantor Roof Garden (6th floor) allows you suntan amidst sculpture, while a view of the skyline proves that most gardens in the world lack a little altitude.

Self-Portrait. The Met is also one of the foremost repositories for the works of the Dutch master of light, Johannes Vermeer. Of fewer than 40 widely acknowledged Vermeer canvases, the Museum can claim five, including the celebrated *Young Woman with a Water Jug*.

The rich collection of Impressionism and Post-Impressionism reads like an art history textbook: George Seurat's *Circus Sideshow* and Vincent van Gogh's *Self-Portrait with a Straw Hat* are perhaps the most recognizable. Degas's renowned ballet canvases and Monet's views of Rouen Cathedral also figure prominently. If you come at the right time, you may see the **Annenberg Collection of Impressionist and Post-Impressionist** works, displayed for six months each year beginning in early November.

GROUND FLOOR. All the way downstairs the **Costume Institute,** reflects the cultural evolution of our times with an extraordinary fashion chronicle. Recent exhibitions have showcased Chanel suits through the years and a tribute to the late Gianni Versace.

MUSEUM OF MODERN ART (MOMA)

708-9400; info and film schedules 708-9480; www.moma.org. 11 W. 53rd St., between Fifth and Sixth Ave. Subway: E, F to Fifth Ave./53rd St.; or B, D, Q to 50th St. $9.50, students and seniors $6.50, under 16 free. Pay what you wish F 4:30-8:30pm. Extra fee for some special exhibitions; audio guide rental $4. Open Sa-Tu and Th 10:30am-6pm, F 10:30am-8:30pm. Free brochures and film tickets at information desk.

MoMA 2000 looks at some of the 20th century's most powerful art. Installed throughout the entire museum, works in all media will be presented "in innovative, multidisciplinary ways," including film and educational programs. Scheduled: Alfred Hitchcock: Behind the Silhouette; Automobiles for the Next Century; The Un-Private House (an architectural exhibit), and Fame after Photography.

Hipper than the Met but more traditional than the Whitney, the MoMA commands one of the world's most impressive collections of post-Impressionist, late 19th- and 20th-century art. Founded in 1929 by scholar Alfred Barr in response to the Met's refusal to display cutting-edge work, the museum's first exhibit, held in a Fifth Avenue office building, displayed then unknowns Cézanne, Gauguin, Seurat, and van Gogh. But as the ground-breaking works of 1900 to 1950 moved from cult to masterpiece status, MoMA, in turn, shifted from revolution to institution. This year the museum reclaims its innovative edge by commissioning award-winning Japanese architect Yoshio Taniguchi to expand and renovate the museum—a 650-million-dollar project lasting until 2005. The newly renovated second floor collection will extend across the entire museum, along with many new works—all part of **MoMA 2000,** a survey of the last 100 years in art. The sculpture garden will be restored to its larger original design, as will the celebrated Goodwin and Stone facade. Temporary exhibits partially compensate for the interim closure of parts of the permanent collection. Whatever its state of outward polish, however, MoMA always promises to stun and inspire the visitor with one of the most impressive art collections in the world.

FIRST FLOOR. Past the admission desk lies the **Abby Aldrich Rockefeller Sculpture Garden,** an expansive patio with a fountain, drooping willows, and a world-class assemblage of modern sculpture, often featuring works by Matisse, Picasso, and Henry Moore, as well as temporary exhibitions. **Summergarden,** a museum tradition in which Juilliard School affiliates use the garden to present free avant-garde music, occurs here Fridays and Saturdays at 8:30pm during July and August (for schedule info call 708-9491, visit the website, or see **Classical Music,** p. 271).

To the left of the sculpture garden, the **Education Center** presents films, hosts gallery talks, and features educational computer games for children. Downstairs, you can see temporary shows in the **Theater Gallery** or foreign and domestic art films in the **Roy and Niuta Titus Theaters** (see **Movies,** <u>p. 262</u>).

Next to the Center, a gallery features various changing displays. One recent exhibit: an interactive computer installation brought to you by those brains from the Massachusetts Institute of Technology. Just past the entrance and to the right, you will see the newly reopened **Abby Aldrich Rockefeller Print Collection,** a gallery filled with the lucky lady's private print collection.

SECOND FLOOR. Once home to a vastly impressive permanent display of paintings and sculptures, MoMA's second floor will look completely new as of October 1999 (see **MoMA 2000,** above). The galleries here housed such awe-inspiring and diverse works as Rodin's *John the Baptist;* van Gogh's *The Starry Night;* Duchamp's dadaist *To Be Looked at (from the Other Side of the Glass) with One Eye, Close To, for Almost an Hour; White on White* by the Russian Constructivist Malevich; Henri Matisse's *Dance (First Version);* Dalí's *Retrospective Bust of a Woman;* Monet's vibrant *Japanese Footbridge;* as well as numerous works by Picasso and surrealists, such as Max Ernst and Jean Miró.

THIRD FLOOR. The nine third-floor galleries track American and European painting from the end of World War II to the late 1960s. They feature works by Mark Rothko, Jackson Pollock, Jasper Johns, and pop-art icon Andy Warhol. European and American works from the 1940s reside in **Galleries 18** and **19.** Giaccometti's determined yet vulnerable *Man Pointing* captures post-WWII isolation. Jean Dubuffet's works also line the walls, their "primitive" child-like styles reflecting post-war disillusionment. **Gallery 20** holds works by early mid-century artists such as Edward Hopper, Georgia O'Keefe, and Andrew Wyeth. Jackson Pollock and Willem de Kooning appear in **Galleries 21** and **22.** Pollock created his giant "all-over" canvases by lying them on the floor and flinging cheap paint on the surface in a creative frenzy. **Galley 23** contains abstract work with orange lines and slashes by Barnett Newman and Ad Reinhardt. Mark Rothko's *Red, Brown, and Black,* was intended to be viewed in near darkness. Pop art stars in **Galleries 25** and **26,** where works by Frank Stella, Roy Lichtenstein, and Jasper Johns hang beside more abstract pieces by Cy Twombly and Robert Rauschenberg. New York sensation Andy Warhol's gold *Marilyn Monroe* is mounted near his world-famous *Campbell Soup Cans.* Across the room resides Claes Oldenburg's bean-baggish ice cream replica, *Floor Cone.*

MoMA owns much more 20th-century art than it will ever have space to display, even after its expansion. An ever-changing assortment of works lurks behind the third-floor stairwell, in a chamber full of the museum's recent acquisitions. The selection here also changes rapidly, but there's always something of interest. To the right of the exit from the contemporary art room is a small, dark room containing video compositions of varying degrees of quality. On the third floor MoMA's **prints and illustrated books department** frequently rotates its features. A "reading room" lets you investigate old catalogs and defunct exhibitions.

FOURTH FLOOR. The museum's fourth floor summit houses the architecture and design collections. Scale models by notables such as Frank Lloyd Wright and Buckminster Fuller sit beside blueprints for impressive buildings and accompany up-to-date displays of elegant furniture, political posters, tableware, appliances, and enough chaise longues to accommodate every psychoanalyst in New York.

MOMA, THE CAPITALIST. The **bookstore** on the first floor (708-9702) sells art books, postcards, and cool posters (open Sa-Th 11am-5:45pm, F 11am-8:45pm). The **MoMA Design Store,** across the street at 44 W. 53rd St., sells high-priced objects of contemporary design, along with interesting housewares—environmentally sound bowls, plates, and glasses stitched together from tropical leaves (open M-Th and Sa 10am-6pm, F 10am-9pm, Su 11am-8pm).

AMERICAN MUSEUM OF NATURAL HISTORY

*Located on Central Park West, 79th to 81st St. **Telephone:** 769-5100. **Website:** www.amnh.org. **Subway:** B, C to 81st St. **Bus:** M10, M7, or M11 to 79th St. **Open:** Su-Th 10am-5:45pm, F-Sa 10am-8:45pm. **Suggested Donation:** $8, students and seniors $6, under 12 $4.50. **Highlight Tours:** 6 times a day, usually leaving at 15 minutes past the hour. Call 769-5200 to reserve. **Imax Theater:** 769-5034. **Combo-ticket** (Museum and Imax): $12, students and seniors $8.50, ages 2-12 $6.50. **Double Feature:** F-Sa at 6pm $16, students and seniors $12, ages 2-12 $9. Excellent **wheelchair access.** Video displays **captioned** for hearing-impaired.*

You're never too old for the Natural History Museum, one of the city's most exhilarating sights. This, one of the largest science museums in the world, both chronicles natural environments and cultural histories. Its opening on December 22, 1877, amidst marshy land and brambly vegetation, proved the city's social event of the decade. Until the elevated train came up Columbus Avenue in 1879, however, few regular visitors came its way. Since the transportation revolution, the museum has received droves of enamored children toting tired parents, lovers on dates recounting their paleontology-loving childhoods, and students sketching marsupials.

The exhibits sparkle with mounted gems, spook with dioramas of taxidermied animals, and startle with their interactive displays on ecological threats to our planet. The walls, mounted with 5-foot crustaceans, 2-inch iridescent butterflies, and a blue whale suspended high overhead, barely scratch the surface of the museum's vast collections. Although the focus of the complex is *natural* history, numerous rooms are devoted entirely to the trappings of human cultures from all over the world. Some 32 million cultural artifacts and scientific specimens share this prestigious residence. An active, world-renowned learning and research facility, the Museum of Natural History sends out over 100 expeditions of scientists and explorers throughout the world each year.

The museum's greatest draw, its **dinosaur halls,** reopened with much fanfare in the summer of 1995. While most museums display lightweight casts of fossils (virtually indiscernible from the real ones, and much easier to mount), the Museum of Natural History insists on using real fossils in 85% of its displays. In the first few weeks after it opened, the fourth-floor exhibit attracted 50% more visitors than did the entire museum in all of 1994. Take the crowds into account when planning a visit.

The other halls, just as interesting, thankfully attract smaller crowds. On the first floor, you'll find the particularly fascinating **Hall of Meteorites, Hall of Gems, Hall of Minerals, North American Mammals, Hall of Biodiversity,** and the new

Hall of Planet Earth, which chronicles geophysical processes past and present. The famous 90-foot whale floats above the cafeteria. Exhibits on the second floor deal mostly with peoples and cultures from around the world, occasionally interrupted by a bird exhibit. The third floor displays birds, reptiles, amphibians, and specimens from New York.

The **Alexander White Natural Science Center,** the museum's only room holding *live* animals, explains the ecology of New York City to kids, while the **Discovery Room** gives them artifacts they can touch. (Hours hover around Tu-F 2-4:30pm, Sa-Su 1-4:30pm; closed Sept.; call ahead to check.) During the academic year, **The People Center,** open weekends only, schedules scholarly talks and demonstrations of various cultures' folk arts. The museum also houses an **Imax** cinematic extravaganza on one of New York's largest movie screens—four stories high and 66 ft. wide. The museum will turn its eyes heavenward as it reopens the **Hayden Planetarium** in 2000.

GUGGENHEIM MUSEUM

Located at 1071 Fifth Ave. and 89th St. Telephone: Recording 423-3500, human being 423-3662, TDD 423-3607. Website: www.guggenheim.org. Subway: #4, 5, 6 to 86th St. Open: Su-W 10am-6pm, F-Sa 10am-8pm. Admission: $12, students and seniors $7, under 12 free; F 6-8pm "pay-what-you-wish." Another Branch: Guggenheim Museum SoHo (see p. 241). Exhibits for 2000 (scheduled): Francesco Clemente (through Jan. 2000); Nam June Paik (Feb. 10 to Apr. 29); 1900: At the Crossroads (May-Sept.); Wheelchair accessible; call 423-3539.

The Guggenheim's most famous exhibit? The building itself, surely. Frank Lloyd Wright designed a permanent space for Solomon R. Guggenheim's art collection. New York can claim the subsequent smooth, spiraling, neo-futurist construction as one of its only edifices by the acclaimed architect. Until Wright designed a space of a higher standard, the works originally resided across the street from the MoMA—in active protest of the larger museum's reliance on portraiture. To create the aesthetic of the new museum, Wright flipped the ziggurat upside-down, so that the spiral became increasingly smaller toward the base. Additionally, he designed an elaborate system for hanging the pictures with rows of windows for natural light, a huge glass roof, and an adjoining home/office for Guggenheim's great influence, eccentric painter/curator, Hilla Rebay.

Under Rebay's guidance, Guggenheim amassed a large collection of abstract, ultra-modern, non-objective paintings. However, with blueprints for the building well underway, he died, leaving the original collection to his brother. The new proprietor fired Rebay and, when Frank Lloyd Wright died in 1959, removed the roof observatory and Rebay's home, while adding a large freight elevator to the spiral. Solomon's pragmatic brother also allowed rotating exhibitions. From 1990 to 1992, the museum shut down for restoration and expansion. Offices moved out of the spiral, skylights and windows were replaced, and a new 10-story "tower gallery" sprouted behind the original structure, nearly doubling potential exhibit space. When the Guggenheim reopened in the summer of 1992, critics compared the new building to a Modernist toilet, while the *Village Voice* blasted the museum's fundraising methods. Gallery-goers, however, negate the criticism, mobbing the museum every day it's open.

Each spin of the museum's spiral holds one sequence or exhibit, while the newly constructed **Tower Galleries** will probably exhibit a portion of the **Thannhauser Collection** of 19th- and 20th-century works, including several by Picasso, Matisse, van Gogh, and Cézanne. The rest of the permanent collection features much cerebral, geometric art, including that of Mondrian and his Dutch De Stijl school, the Bauhaus experiments of German Josef Albers, and the Russian modernists. The collection also holds several Degas sculptures and works by German Expressionists Kirchner, Beckman, and Marc.

WHITNEY MUSEUM

Located at 945 Madison Ave. at 75th St. *Telephone:* 570-3676. *Website:* www.whitney.org. *Subway:* #6 to 77th St. *Open:* Tu-W and F-Su 11am-6pm, Th 1-8pm. *Admission:* $12.50, students and seniors $10.50, children under 12 free; first Th of every month 6-8pm "pay what you wish." Check *"This Week at the Whitney,"* posted on a kiosk near the entrance, or call about special events, lectures, and guided tours. *Tours:* Daily; call for schedule. *Exhibitions for 2000* (scheduled): American Century II: 1950-2000 (through Feb.), advance ticket purchase recommended; Biennial 2000 (Mar.-June); Barbara Kruger (July-Oct.). *Another branch* is located in the Philip Morris building, 120 Park Ave. (917-663-2453), at 42nd St., where a sculpture court features a changing array of installation pieces. Admission and frequent gallery talks free. *Wheelchair accessible.*

When the Metropolitan Museum of Art declined a donation of over 600 works from Gertrude Vanderbilt Whitney in 1929, the wealthy patron and sculptor formed her own museum. Opened on 8th Street in 1931, the Whitney has since moved twice, most recently in 1966 to a forbidding, futuristic Upper East Side fortress designed by Bauhaus boy Marcel Breuer. In 2000, the second part of the Whitney's exciting *American Century* will painstakingly chronicle the art and culture of this century through films, paintings, dance clips, advertisements, commercial designs, and songs. A sure-to-be-controversial **Biennial Show** of works by cutting edge and emerging artists will follow.

The Whitney has assembled the largest collection of 20th-century American art in the world. Its American masterworks include Ad Reinhardt's *Abstract Painting, Number 33*, Jasper John's *Three Flags*, Frank Stella's *Brooklyn Bridge*, Robert Rauschenberg's *Satellite*, Willem De Kooning's *Woman on Bicycle*, and Georgia O'Keefe's Flower Collection and are usually on display in the **fifth floor galleries.** With the comprehensive *American Century*, however, the fifth floor as well as the rest of the museum is occupied with the exhibit.

COOPER-HEWITT NATIONAL DESIGN MUSEUM

Located at 2 E. 91st St. at Fifth Ave. *Telephone:* 849-8400. *Website:* www.si.edu/ndm. *Subway:* #4, 5, 6 to 86th St. *Open:* Tu 10am-9pm, W-Sa 10am-5pm, Su noon-5pm. *Admission:* $5, students and seniors $3, under 12 free. Tu 5-9pm free. *Library:* Open by appointment until 5:30pm daily; call 849-8330 for details. To view the *permanent collection* call 849-8330 or 849-8331 for appointment. *Exhibits for 2000* (scheduled): The Work of Charles and Ray Eames: A Legacy of Invention (through Jan.); National Design Museum Triennial (Mar.-Aug.); 100 Masterpieces from the Vitra Museum (Oct. 2000 to Mar. 2001). *Wheelchair accessible;* call 849-8404.

Since 1976, Andrew Carnegie's regal Georgian mansion has housed the Smithsonian Institution's **National Design Museum.** Exhibitions at the Cooper-Hewitt titillate and provoke. In the past, the museum has staged such offerings as a display of doghouses and a photographic excursion through the landscape of Latino Los Angeles.

The Whitney itself stands as one of the more impressive designs on site. Cast-iron archways alternate with intricately carved ceilings and an operatic staircase, bathing in the muted glow of gilded candelabras. You can see the bagpipe homage to Carnegie's Scottish heritage carved into the music-room-turned-gift-shop's moldings. An unusually low doorway leads to what was once the 5'2" west library. Now, with over two million volumes, the museum's **library** contains of America's largest and most accessible design resources. The outside **garden** is worth a visit in the summer.

The collection dates to 1859, when Peter Cooper founded the Cooper Union for the Advancement of Science and Art (see p. 156). Cooper's granddaughters subsequently opened a museum in 1897; in 1963, the Smithsonian received it as a donation; in 1972, the Carnegie mansion became its new home. The largest group of holdings contains drawings and prints, primarily of architecture and design. Glass, furniture, porcelain, metalwork, stoneware, and textiles complete the catalog, along with remarkable knick-knacks, such as a post-Revolution Russian chess set that pits red Communist pieces against pawn workers trapped in chains.

FRICK COLLECTION

Located at 1 E. 70th St. at Fifth Avenue. Telephone: 288-0700. Website: www.frick.org. Subway: #6 to 68th St. Open: Tu-Sa 10am-6pm, Su 1-6pm. Admission: $7, students and seniors $5. No children under 10 admitted; children under 16 must be accompanied by an adult. Group visits by appointment only. Free audio guides. Wheelchair accessible.

Upon his death, Pittsburgh steel magnate and 19th-century industrial baron Henry Clay Frick secured his immortality by leaving his mansion and comprehensive art collection to the city. The house showcases old masters and decorative arts in an intimate setting, juxtaposing the old with the new as Frick saw fit—a refreshing break from the art factory atmosphere of New York's larger museums. Although the mansion once seemed a tangled maze of paintings from different periods, the addition of free, electronic audioguides will help you find the right path.

Some of the world's finest Old Masters are display here, not to mention exquisite vases, sculptures, bronzes, and furniture. Two of the 35 existing Vermeers hang in the South Hall, *Officer and Laughing Girl* and *Girl Interrupted at Her Music.* Also in the hall: Monsieur Boucher's flirtatious portrait of his Madame and an early mother-and-child by Renoir. The nearby **Octagon Room** features a 15th-century altarpiece by Fra Filippo Lippi, while the anteroom showcases works by Van Eyck, El Greco, and Brueghel the Elder.

Moving through the numbered galleries, stop by Rococo foolishness in the **Fragonard Room.** Here, one can view Fragonard's masterpiece, *Progress of Love.* In the **Living Hall,** El Greco's *St. Jerome* clasps his Latin translation of the Bible next to Titian's pensive *Portrait of a Man in a Red Cap,* Holbein's determined classic *Sir Thomas More,* and Giovanni Bellini's extraordinary 15th-century masterpiece *St. Francis in the Desert.* In the next room, the **Library** walls display Gainsborough and Reynolds portraits, a Constable landscape, a Turner seascape, a Gilbert Stuart likeness of George Washington, and a portrait of Henry Clay Frick surveying his domain. In the **North Hall,** on the way to the next room, the defiantly level-eyed Ingres portrait of the *Contesse d'Hausonville* stares at you.

The largest room in the Frick, the stunningly sky-lit **West Gallery,** has three works by Rembrandt: the mysterious *Polish Rider; Nicholaes Ruts,* one of Rembrandt's earliest portrait commissions; and his sensitive *Self-Portrait.* Also note the works by Van Dyck, Vermeer, and Velázquez. Goya's depiction of blacksmiths at work in *The Forge* seems strangely out-of-place in this predominantly upper-class portraiture collection. Over at the head of the West Gallery, the **Enamel Room** contains a collection of Limoges enamels from the 16th and 17th centuries, as well as a penetrating evocation of Satan in Duccio di Buoninsegna's 1308 *The Temptation of Christ on the Mountain.*

The **Oval Room** features the averted gazes of two Gainsborough women and two Van Dycks. Also note the frisky and irreverent bronze *Diana* cast in 1776 by Jean-Antoine Houdon. The **East Gallery** holds several Whistlers with characteristically hue-centered names: *Symphony in Flesh Color and Pink, Harmony in Pink and Grey,* and *Arrangement in Black and Brown.* A fine Goya portrait of a young *Officer* also pouts here.

After walking through the least exhausting museum in New York, you can relax in the cool **Garden Court** and watch fountains of water burble up from the mouths of little stone frogs. Recordings of Henry Clay's favorite organ music sometimes play to lighten your spirits.

PIERPONT MORGAN LIBRARY

685-0610. 29 E. 36th St. at Madison Ave. Subway: #6 to 33rd St. Open Tu-F 10:30am-5pm, Sa 10:30am-6pm, Su noon-6pm. $7, students and seniors $5, under 12 free. The library gift shop sells books about Morgan's empire, cards or calendars of featured artists' works, or that 11-inch set of Picasso plates you've been pining for at $40 a pop.

The Pierpont Morgan Library contains a stunning collection of rare books, sculptures, and paintings gathered by the banker J.P. Morgan and his son. Even if you're not a bibliophile, the breathtaking building and courtyard alone merit a visit. This Low Renaissance-style *palazzo* was constructed with white marble bricks laid without mortar. Completed in 1907, the library remained private until 1924, when J.P. Morgan opened it to the public. In 1991, the museum doubled its size with the acquisition of Morgan's former townhouse. Its permanent collection, not always on display, includes drawings and prints by Blake and Dürer, illuminated Renaissance manuscripts, a copy of the Louisiana Purchase, Napoleon's love letters to Josephine, a manuscript copy of Dickens's *A Christmas Carol*, and sheet music handwritten by Beethoven and Mozart.

Down the hall from admissions and to the right stretches a long narrow hall lined with changing exhibitions that feature works by Salvador Dalí, Pablo Picasso, Henry Matisse, Georgia O'Keefe, and Diego Rivera. Once you've finished gawking at the breathtaking artwork and magnificent interior, head into the **West Room** at the end of the hallway and to the right. Morgan Sr.'s sumptuous and very red former office has a carved ceiling made during the Italian Renaissance and stained glass from 15th- and 17th-century Switzerland. Two dour Morgans stare down from the walls, as if sentinels protecting the red velvet sofas from wayward hands.

As you exit this room, spin through the magnificent **Rotunda,** the site of the original library. Walking through the rotunda leads you to the heart of the library, the **East Room.** This book lover's paradise features stacks of mahogany-toned, hand- bound volumes. With two balconies encircling it, this room provides a stunning site for frequent exhibitions, including a permanent display of archival documents pertaining to the life and times of J.P. Morgan. Among the more notable items in the room: one of three existing likenesses of John Milton; a fabulous 12th-century jewel-encrusted triptych believed to contain fragments from the Cross; and one of 11 surviving copies of the Gutenberg Bible, the first printed book.

If you have time for a spot of tea ($2.50), you can travel back in time in the enclosed marble courtyard of the Morgan Court Café, with its vaulting sun roof and graceful trees...or just rest your feet for free by the fountain.

OTHER MAJOR COLLECTIONS

ABIGAIL ADAMS SMITH MUSEUM. Although the house bears her name, Abigail never lived here; this building was actually her stable. Nine refurbished rooms filled with 18th-century articles, including a letter from George Washington. *(838-6878. 421 E. 61st St. between York and First Ave. Subway: #4, 5, 6 to 59th St.; or N, R to Lexington Ave. Open Tu-Su 11am-4pm. $3, students and seniors $2, under 12 free.)*

ALTERNATIVE MUSEUM. Founded and operated by established local artists for their less recognized counterparts, the museum advertises itself as "ahead of the times and behind the issues." New visions and social critique are the name of the game, with an emphasis on the international, the unusual, and the socially conscious. All upcoming exhibitions center around emerging contemporary artists. *(966-4444. 594 Broadway, 4th fl., near Houston and Prince St. in SoHo. Subway: B, D, F, Q to Broadway/Lafayette St. or N, R to Prince St. Open Tu-Sa 11am-6pm. Closed in Aug. Suggested donation $3.)*

MUSEUMS

THE ASIA SOCIETY. Exhibitions of Asian art, in addition to symposia, musical performances, film screenings, and an acclaimed "Meet the Author" series. The art spans the entire Asian continent, from Iran to Japan, from Yemen to Mongolia, and even includes Asian America. Scheduled for 2000: *China: 50 Years Inside the People's Republic* (photos; through Jan.) and *Sheer Realities: Clothing and Power in 19th Century Philippines* (Feb.-Apr.). The latter exhibit will appear at Grey Art Galleries, 100 Washington Sq. East while the Society renovates. *(517-ASIA or 288-6400. 725 Park Ave. at 70th St. Open Tu-W and F-Sa 11am-6pm, Th 11am-8pm, Su noon-5pm. $3, students and seniors $1; Th 6-8pm free. Tours Tu-Sa 12:30pm, Th also at 6:30pm, Su 2:30pm.)*

AMERICAN CRAFT MUSEUM. Not the old-fashioned quilts and Shaker furniture you might expect. No wooden *chachkas* here—this museum redefines the concept of crafts. Features modern pieces in wood, glass, metal, clay, plastic, paper, and fabric. Frequent ingenious exhibitions on particular subjects in diverse media. Upcoming shows include 20th-century Italian glass and Judy Chicago's painted and needlework images. Three floors of exhibits change every 3 months. *(956-3535. 40 W. 53rd St. Across from the MoMA. Subway: E, F to Fifth Ave./53rd St.; or B, D, Q to 50th St. Open Tu-W and F-Su 10am-6pm, Th 10am-8pm. $5, students and seniors $2.50; Th 6-8pm is pay-what-you-wish.)*

AMERICAN MUSEUM OF THE MOVING IMAGE. Unfortunately, this museum isn't half as exciting as it sounds. The best it has to offer is on the third floor where you can create your own digitally animated film sequence, dub your voice into scenes from *Shawshank Redemption* and *Taxi Driver*, or alter sound effects from clips of movies like *Terminator 2*. Also of interest: the old-school video games, like Pac-Man and Ms. Pac-Man, on the first floor…when they are not broken. The screening room downstairs plays vintage films on the weekends. *(718-784-0077, travel directions 718-784-4777; www.ammi.org. 35th Ave. at 36th St., Astoria, Queens. Subway: N to Broadway in Astoria. Walk along Broadway to 36th St., turn right, go to 35th Ave.; museum at right. Open Tu-F noon-5pm, Sa-Su 11am-6pm. $8.50, students and seniors $5.50, children $4.50, under 4 free. Screening tickets free with admission.)*

AUDUBON TERRACE MUSEUM GROUP. Once part of John James Audubon's estate and game preserve, the terrace now contains the following museums and societies: **Hispanic Society of America,** 613 W. 155th St., between Broadway and Riverside, devoted to Spanish and Portuguese arts and culture, including mosaics, ceramics, and paintings by El Greco, Velázquez, and Goya. Students of Hispanic culture will enjoy the 100,000-volume research library. *(926-2234. Open M-Sa 10am-4:30pm, Su 1-4pm. Free.)* The **American Numismatic Society** presents…the fascinating history of the penny! (Who knew?) An extraordinary collection of coinage and paper money from prehistoric times to the present, some of which is on display in the exhibition room. *(234-3130. Open Tu-Sa 9am-4:30pm, Su 1-4pm. Free.)* The **American Academy of Arts and Letters** honors American artists, writers, and composers. Offers occasional exhibits of manuscripts, paintings, sculptures, and first editions. Call for current exhibition details and times. *(368-5900. Subway: #1 to 157th St.)*

BLACK FASHION MUSEUM. Founded in 1979, the BFM maintains a permanent collection and mounts two yearly exhibits devoted to garments designed, sewn, or worn by black men and women from the 1860s to the present. Alongside the creations of contemporary black designers you'll find two slave dresses, a dress made by Rosa Parks, costumes from such musicals as *The Wiz*, and a tribute to Ann Lowe, who designed Jackie O's wedding dress. *(666-1320. 157 W. 126th St., between Adam Clayton Powell Jr. Blvd. and Lenox/Malcolm X Blvd. Subway: #2 or 3 to 125th St. Open by appointment M-F noon-6pm and the occasional Sa; for reservations call at least 1 day in advance. Suggested donation $3, students, seniors, and under 12 $2.)*

BRONX MUSEUM OF THE ARTS. Set in the rotunda of the Bronx Courthouse, this museum focuses on young talent, collecting works on paper by minority artists and sponsoring twice-yearly seminars for local artists, which culminate in group showings. *(718-681-6000. 1041 Grand Concourse, at 165th St. Subway: C, D to 167th St. and south 3 blocks along Grand Concourse. Open W 3-9pm, Th-F 10am-5pm, Sa-Su noon-6pm. Suggested donation $3, students and seniors $2, under 12 free.)*

BROOKLYN MUSEUM. For lovers of all things ancient, the Metropolitan Museum of Art's sibling merits a trip to Brooklyn. You'll find outstanding Ancient Greek, Roman, Middle Eastern, and Egyptian galleries on the third floor; only London's British Museum and Cairo's Egyptian Museum itself have larger Egyptian collections. Crafts, textiles, and period rooms on the fourth floor tell the story of American upper class interiors from the 17th to the 19th centuries, including the Moorish Room, a lush bit of exotica from John D. Rockefeller's Manhattan townhouse. John Singer Sargent and the Hudson River School grace the American Collection on the fifth floor. Nearby, the contemporary gallery contains noteworthy work by Alfredo Jaar and Francis Bacon. European art from the early Renaissance to Post-Impressionism, including works by Rodin, Renoir, and Monet also appear on the fifth floor. Meanwhile, multi-media Asian art fills the second floor. The enormous Oceanic and New World art collection takes up the central two-story space on the first floor—the towering totem poles covered with human/animal hybrids could fit nowhere else. The impressive African art collection here was the first of its kind in an American museum when it opened in 1923. Galleries downstairs put on temporary exhibits and weekend talks. *(718-638-5000. 200 Eastern Pkwy. at Washington Ave. Subway: #2, 3 to Eastern Pkwy. Open W-F 10am-5pm, Sa 10am-9pm, Su 11am-6pm. Suggested donation $4, students $2, seniors $1.50, under 12 free.)*

THE CHILDREN'S MUSEUM OF MANHATTAN. Founded in 1973 by Harlem and Upper West Side artists and educators in response to the elimination of music and cultural programs in public schools. This museum contains a sound studio, media center, and Dr. Seuss interactive theater. A funky "giant ear" jungle gym offers the best in educational art. Check out the new "Body Odyssey" exhibit that allows you and your child to crawl through, climb on, and pedal through the gears of creaky machines. *(721-1223. 212 W. 83rd St. off Amsterdam Ave. Subway: #1, 9 to 86th St. Open Tu-Su 10am-5pm; winter W-F 1:30-5:30pm, Sa-Su 10am-5pm. $6, seniors $3, babies under 1 free. Wheelchair accessible.)*

CHINA INSTITUTE GALLERY. This minute gallery within the China Institute showcases a broad spectrum of Chinese art, including calligraphy, ceramics, and bronzes, as well as occasional cultural-anthropological exhibits. Look for the lions guarding the red doors. *(744-8181. 125 E. 65th St. between Park and Lexington Ave. Subway: #6 to 68th St. Open M-W, F-Sa 10am-5pm, Tu-Th 10am-8pm, Su 1-5pm. $3, students and seniors $2, under 12 free; Tu, Th 6-8pm free.)*

⬛THE CLOISTERS. Charles Collen brought the High Middle Ages to Manhattan in 1938 by erecting this tranquil branch of the Met largely from pieces of 12th- and 13th-century French and Spanish monasteries. John D. Rockefeller donated the site (now Fort Tryon Park) and many of the works that make up the Cloisters' incredibly rich collection of medieval art. During the summer, retreat to the air-conditioned Treasury to admire the most fragile offerings, including incredibly intricate work in bookmaking, carving in miniature, and metalwork. Enjoy the sublimely detailed work of the world-famous Unicorn Tapestries, and rest in either of two small gardens planned according to the symbolism and aesthetic sensibilities of medieval horticulture. *(923-3700. Fort Tryon Park in Washington Heights. Subway: A to 190th St.; then follow Margaret Corbin Dr. 5 blocks north. Or take bus #4 from Madison Ave. to the Cloisters' entrance. Open Mar.-Oct. Tu-Su 9:30am-5:15pm; Nov.-Feb. Tu-Su 9:30am-4:45pm. Museum tours Mar.-Oct. Tu-F at 3pm, Su at* *noon; Nov.-Feb. W at 3pm. Suggested donation $8, students and seniors $4. Includes same-day admission to the Metropolitan Museum's main building in Central Park.)*

FORBES MAGAZINE GALLERIES. Just one more multi-millionaire financier who turned over his personal collection to the public. The late Malcolm Forbes's irrepressible penchant for the offbeat permeates this collection of eclectic exhibits. Some of the most fascinating include a rotating exhibit of Presidential paraphernalia, the world's largest private collection of Fabergé *objets d'art* and a Monopoly exhibit featuring versions of the game in its various stages of evolution. See also the rotating exhibitions in the Fine Arts gallery. *(206-5548; 206-5549. 62 Fifth Ave. at 12th St. Open Tu-Sa 10am-4pm; hours subject to change. Free admission; children under 16 must be accompanied by an adult. Thursday is reserved for group tours; call in advance.)*

FRAUNCES TAVERN MUSEUM. Features two period rooms, along with the room where George Washington said goodbye to his troops after the Revolutionary War. The 3rd floor has changing exhibits on the culture of early America. *(425-1778. 54 Pearl St., 2nd and 3rd fl. Subway: #4, 5 to Bowling Green; or #1, 9 to South Ferry; or N, R to Whitehall St. Open M-F 10am-4:45pm, Sa-Su noon-4pm. $2.50, students, children and seniors $1.)*

■**GUGGENHEIM MUSEUM SOHO.** This branch of the Guggenheim occupies two spacious floors of a historic 19th-century building with selections from the museum's mammoth permanent collection of modern and contemporary works. The neighborhood and the breezy, stylish layout lends the place a gallery atmosphere. The current exhibit "Andy Warhol: The Last Supper" is expected to continue indefinitely and is free. The **gallery store** (423-3615) peddles artsy trinkets and is a nice place to meet a friend downtown. *(423-3500. 575 Broadway at Prince St. Open Th-M 11am-6pm. Wheelchair accessible.)*

HALL OF FAME FOR GREAT AMERICANS. Located on the grounds of City University of New York in the Bronx, this poignant yet decrepit hall features over 100 bronze busts of America's immortals solemnly whiling away the years, among them Alexander Graham Bell, Abraham Lincoln, Booker T. Washington, and the Wright brothers. *(718-289-5100. 181st St. and Martin Luther King Jr. Blvd. Subway: #4 to Burnside Ave. Walk 6 blocks west along Burnside Ave. as it becomes 179th St., then walk a block north. Open daily 10am-5pm. Free.)*

INTERNATIONAL CENTER OF PHOTOGRAPHY. Housed in a landmark town-house built in 1914 for *New Republic* founder Willard Straight. The foremost exhibitor of photography in the city and a gathering place for its practitioners. Historical, thematic, and contemporary works, running from fine art to photo-journalism to celebrity portraits. The bookstore sells bi-monthly *Photography in New York*, a comprehensive guide to what is shown and where ($3). The ICP also offers myriad photography workshops; pamphlets offer complete listings and prices. *(860-1777. 1130 Fifth Ave. at 94th St.Open Tu-Th 10am-5pm, F 10am-8pm, Sa-Su 10am-6pm. $6, students and seniors $4, under 12 $1.)*

INTREPID SEA-AIR-SPACE MUSEUM. One ticket admits you to the veteran World War II and Vietnam War aircraft carrier *Intrepid*, the Vietnam War destroyer *Edson*, the only publicly displayed guided-missile submarine *Growler*, and the lightship *Nantucket*. Pioneer's Hall displays models, antiques, and film shorts of flying devices from the turn of the century to the 1930s. You can also climb aboard the Intrepid's 900 ft. flight deck to view old and new warbirds—including a declassified CIA A-12 Blackbird, the world's fastest spy plane. Don't miss the Iraqi tanks parked near the gift shop; they were captured in the Gulf War. There are a number of guided tours of the museum and its different attractions, which range from 10min. to 3hr. in length. The museum offers a schedule of temporary and new exhibits and events; call for details. New exhibits in 2000: "Flying Machines," in which you may participate in simulations of the first machines of aviation. *(245-0072. Pier 86 at 46th St. and 12th Ave. Subway: Subway to 42nd St., then take bus M42 or M50 to W. 46th St. Open May 1-Sept. 30 M-F 10am-5pm, Sa-Su 10am-6pm; Oct. 1-Apr. 30 W-Su 10am-5pm. Last admission 1hr. before closing. $10, seniors, students, and veterans $7.50, children 6-11 $5, active duty servicemen, and children under 2 free, wheelchair patrons half price.)*

ISAMU NOGUCHI GARDEN MUSEUM. Fourteen galleries, established in 1985 next door to Isamu Noguchi's studio. His breathtaking sculptures in the picturesque garden stand around *The Well*, its water shimmering down stone. The world-renowned sculptor also conceived *Sculpture to Be Seen From Mars*, a 2-mile-long face carved in the dirt next to Newark International Airport as a monument to man in the post-atomic age. *(718-721-1932; www.noguchi.org. 32-37 Vernon Blvd., Long Island City, Queens, at 10th St. and 33rd Rd. Subway: N to Broadway in Astoria. Walk along Broadway towards Manhattan until the end; turn left on Vernon Blvd. On weekends a $5 **shuttle bus** leaves from the Asia Society at 70th St. and Park Ave. in Manhattan, every 30min. 11:30am-3:30pm; return trips every hour noon-5pm. Museum open Apr.-Oct. W-F 10am-5pm, Sa-Su 11am-6pm. Suggested donation $4, students and seniors $2. A lengthy free tour kicks off at 2pm. Wheelchair accessible.)*

JAPAN SOCIETY. The first example of contemporary Japanese design in New York City. The designer, Junzo Yoshimura, sought to integrate Western with Asian style and the result is a half-Japanese, half-American amalgamation— Western on the outside but completely Asian on the inside. In the spirit of a traditional Japanese home, there is an interior pool garden on the first floor, complete with stones and bamboo trees, while a gallery on the second floor exhibits traditional and contemporary Japanese art. Dedicated to bringing the people of Japan and America closer together, the Society sponsors Japanese language courses, lectures, meetings with notable leaders, a film series, and performances. *(832-1155. A few blocks north of the U.N. at 333 E. 47th St. and First Ave. Society open Tu, Th, Sa, Su 11am-6pm, W, F 11am-6:30pm Gallery open Sept.-June May M-F 11am-6pm. Suggested donation $5.)*

JACQUES MARCHAIS MUSEUM OF TIBETAN ART. One of the largest private collections of Tibetan art in the West, worth the nearly 2-hour trip from Manhattan. Bronzes, paintings, and sculpture from Tibet and other Buddhist cultures this hilltop museum, fashioned after a Tibetan mountain temple. Its terraced sculpture gardens look down on the distant Lower Bay. Sunday programs on Asian culture ($3 over regular admission) cover topics ranging from origami "made easy" to Tibetan chanting. Call for current schedule. *(718-987-3500. 338 Lighthouse Ave., Staten Island. Take bus S74 from Staten Island Ferry to Lighthouse Ave., then turn right and walk up the fairly steep hill as it winds to the right. Open Apr.-Nov. W-Su 1-5pm; Dec.-Mar. call ahead to schedule a visiting time. $3, seniors $2.50, under 12 $1.)*

THE JEWISH MUSEUM. The permanent collection of over 14,000 works details the Jewish experience throughout history, ranging from ancient Biblical artifacts and ceremonial objects to contemporary masterpieces by Marc Chagall, Frank Stella, and George Segal. Rotating exhibits fill the first 2 floors, while the permanent exhibition on the third and fourth floors, *Culture and Continuity: The Jewish Journey*, examines Jewish history through art and artifact. *(423-3200; www.thejewishmuseum.org. 1109 Fifth Ave. at 92nd St. Open Su-M and W-Th 11am-5:45pm, Tu 11am-8pm. $8, students and seniors $5.50, under 12 free; Tu 5-9pm free and live music. Free audio tour. Wheelchair access info: 423-3225.)*

▓LOWER EAST SIDE TENEMENT MUSEUM. The museum's visitor center (open Tu-Su 11am-5pm) offers exhibits and photographs documenting Jewish life on the Lower East Side. At 97 Orchard St. stands a preserved Lower East Side tenement, built in 1863 and used until the 1930s. The tenement tour views one apartment in ruin and three others meticulously restored to recreate specific moments in the lives of three immigrant families who actually lived there: the Gumpertzes in the 1870s, the Rogarshevskys in 1918, and the Baldizzis in 1939. The tenement inspires tourists to share their own families' immigrant experiences. Tours of the "Confino Family Apartment" are geared toward families with children. All tours leave from the visitors center and make for a unique and emotional museum experience. The museum also offers walking tours of the neighborhood. *(431-0233. 97 and 90 Orchard St. near Broome St. Subway: F to Delancey St.; or J, M, or Z to Essex St. From Delancey St., walk 4 blocks east to Orchard St. and 1 block south. From Essex St., walk 2 blocks west to Orchard and 1 block south. Tours of the tenement Tu-F at 1, 2, 3 and 4pm, Th 6 and 7pm, Sa-Su every 30min. 11am-4:30pm; 1hr. Tours of the Confino Apartment Sa-Su noon, 1, 2, and 3pm; 45min. Walking tours Sa-Su 1:30 and 2:30pm; 1hr. Tickets for one exhibit $8, students and seniors $6; for two exhibits $14, students and seniors $10; for both exhibits and walking tour $20, students and seniors $14.)*

MARITIME INDUSTRY MUSEUM. This former fort houses a large collection of marine artifacts from the Vikings until today, including some dredged up from the Andrea Doria. Also houses exhibits on the great passenger liners of this century and a scale model of the Brooklyn naval yard in the 1940s. Tours of a 565ft. training ship available by appointment. *(718-409-7218. Fort Schuyler, on the campus of SUNY Maritime College at the foot of the Throgs Neck Bridge. Subway: #6 to Westchester Square/East Tremont Ave., then take bus Bx40 to Fort Schuyler, the last stop. Open M-Sa 10am-4pm, Su noon-4pm. Free.)*

EL MUSEO DEL BARRIO. This is the only museum in the U.S. devoted exclusively to the art and culture of Puerto Rico and Latin America. Begun in an East Harlem classroom, the project has blossomed into a permanent museum that features video, painting, sculpture, photography, theater, and film. Permanent collection includes pre-Columbian art and Santos de Palo, hand-crafted wooden saint-figures from Latin America. Rotating exhibits often involve contemporary Latin American artists confronting the issues affecting the Hispanic-American community. *(831-7272. 1230 Fifth Ave., at 104th St. Subway: #6 to 103rd St. Open W-Su 11am-5pm, May-Sept. W and F-Su 9am-5pm, Th noon-7pm. Suggested contribution $4, students and seniors $2.)*

THE MUSEUM FOR AFRICAN ART. The museum has recently expanded to feature two major exhibits a year along with several smaller exhibitions of stunning African and African-American art, often with special themes, such as storytelling, magic, religion, or mask-making. Objects on display span centuries, from ancient to contemporary, and come from all over Africa. Saturday afternoon mural painting sessions free with admission; many hands-on family-oriented workshops on African culture (make your own African instrument!) offered. *(966-1313. 593 Broadway, between Houston and Prince St. in SoHo. Subway: N, R to Prince and Broadway. Open Tu-F 10:30am-5:30pm, Sa-Su noon-6pm. $5, students and seniors $2.50.)*

MUSEUM OF AMERICAN FOLK ART. Three bright, white rooms devoted to crafts, from European-influenced quilts, needlepoint, and folk portraits to Navajo rugs and Mexican wooden animals. The museum has special programs such as crafts demonstrations, often enlivened by folk dancers and storytellers (call 977-7170 for info). *(595-9533. 2 Lincoln Square on Columbus Ave. between 65th and 66th St. Subway: #1, 9 to 66th St. Open Tu-Su 11:30am-7:30pm. Free. Wheelchair access.)*

MUSEUM OF AMERICAN ILLUSTRATION. Changing exhibitions of illustrations from such diverse fields as *Mad Magazine*, children's books, and advertising. *(838-2560. 128 E. 63rd St. between Park and Lexington Ave. Open Tu 10am-8pm, W-F 10am-5pm, Sa noon-4pm. Free.)*

MUSEUM OF BRONX HISTORY. Run by the Bronx Historical Society on the premises of the landmark Valentine-Varian House, this small museum, as the name indicates, concerns itself with the history of the city's northernmost borough, from the pre-revolutionary era to the sometimes troubled present. Exhibits change every Apr. and Oct. *(718-881-8900. At Bainbridge Ave. and 208th St. Subway: D to 205th St., or #4 to Mosholu Pkwy. Walk 4 blocks east on 210th St. and then south a block. Open Sa 10am-4pm, Su 1-5pm, or by appointment. $2.)*

MUSEUM OF THE CITY OF NEW YORK. This fascinating museum details the history of the Big Apple, from the construction of the Empire State Building to the history of Broadway theater. Collections include an extensive photography exhibit documenting the evolution of New York in the first half of the 20th-century, an exhibit on the consolidation of the boroughs in 1898, a toy gallery, and a variety of changing exhibits. *(534-1672; www.mcny.org. 1220 5th Ave. at 103rd St. in East Harlem, across the street from El Museo del Barrio. Subway: #6 to 103rd St. Open W-Sa 10am-5pm, Su noon-5pm. Suggested contribution $5, students, children, and seniors $4. Wheelchair accessible.)*

MUSEUM OF FINANCIAL HISTORY. Displays an interesting array of early newspapers, records of the Financial District, and archaic stock exchange equipment. Gives you a chance to sit in a New York Stock Exchange seat. *(908-4110. 28 Broadway, located in the former Standard Oil building, next to the statue of the Bull. Open M-F 11:30am-3:30pm. Suggested donation $2.)*

MUSEUM OF JEWISH HERITAGE:
A LIVING MEMORIAL TO THE HOLOCAUST. A simultaneously painful and uplift-ing tribute to the Jewish people. Housed in a sleek, new 6-sided building evoca-tive of the 6-sided star of David. Collection of poignant personal artifacts combined with hours of personal narratives captured on video only begin to present a larger picture of Jewish life. While the exhibits on the Holocaust are inherently upsetting, they are tempered by the final exhibits which present a hopeful future. *(968-1800. 18 First Pl. Subway: #4, 5 to Bowling Green; #1, 9 to South Ferry; or N, R to Whitehall St. Open Su-W 9am-5pm, Th 9am-8pm, F 9am-2pm, closed on Jewish holidays. $7, students and seniors $5. Under 5 free.)*

⬛MUSEUM OF TELEVISION AND RADIO. 25 W. 52nd St. (621-6600, daily activity schedule 621-6800), between Fifth and Sixth Ave. Subway: B, D, Q to Rockefeller Center; or E, F to 53rd St. Despite its monumental title, this museum might better fit the description of an archive. With a collection of more than 95,000 TV and radio programs, the museum's library has a specially designed computerized cataloging system that allows you to find, say, every program starring Michael J. Fox in the database. Request an episode from a librarian, and privately watch or listen to it at one of the 96 TV and radio consoles. Enjoy early episodes of *I Love Lucy* or the pilot from *The Facts of Life*. Serious scholars can request programs from the museum/library's archives held in a nuke-proof safe in upstate NY. Hosts a number of film series that focus on topics of social, historical, popular, or artistic interest (read: *Monty Python* marathons); daily schedule at the front counter. Acquaint yourself with the museum by tour, free with admission—inquire at the desk. Special screenings can be arranged for large groups. *(Open Tu-W and F-Su noon-6pm, Th noon-8pm. Hours extended until 9pm on Friday for theaters only. Suggested donation $6, students $4, under 13 and seniors $3.)*

MUSEUMS

NATIONAL ACADEMY MUSEUM. Founded in 1825 to advance the "arts of design" in America: painting, sculpture, architecture, and engraving. Currently the academy hosts exhibits, trains young artists, and serves as a fraternal organization for distinguished American artists. Such notables as Winslow Homer, Frederic Edwin Church, John Singer Sargent, and Thomas Eakins represent the 19th century in the permanent collection. The annual exhibit in 2000 is a juried show open to the public—so get your portfolios ready. *(369-4880. 1083 Fifth Ave. between 89th and 90th St. Open W-Su noon-5pm, F 10am-8pm. $8, seniors $4.50, students over 11 $4.25, under 12 free. F 5-6pm, pay-as-you-wish. Wheelchair access at 3 E. 89th St.)*

NATIONAL MUSEUM OF THE AMERICAN INDIAN. Housed in the stunning Beaux-Arts Customs House, this excellent museum exhibits the best of the Smithsonian's vast collection of Native American artifacts, in galleries and exhibitions designed by Native American artists and craftsmen, who add beautiful personal strokes. The galleries are organized thematically, not by geographical area, and focus on personal stories and accounts. The museum has changing exhibitions, often featuring contemporary work as a means of bringing Native American culture into the present and the future. *(668-6624. 1 Bowling Green Subway: #4, 5 to Bowling Green. Open daily 10am-5pm, Th closes at 8pm. Free.)*

NEW MUSEUM OF CONTEMPORARY ART. The New Museum is new again, with a greatly expanded and refurbished home. Second floor galleries, a split-level entrance, and a large bookstore are some of the most noticeable improvements. Dedicated to the roles "art" plays in "society," the New Museum supports the hottest, the newest, and the most controversial. Interactive exhibits and video tricks are to be found en masse. Many works deal with issues of identity—sexual, racial, and ethnic. Most major exhibitions are complemented by "Gallery Talks" in which the artist holds court at the museum to discuss the work and answer questions. *(219-1222. 583 Broadway between Prince and Houston St. Subway: N, R to Prince; or B, D, F, Q to Broadway/Lafayette.Open W and Su noon-6pm, Th-Sa noon-8pm. $5; artists, seniors, and students $3. Under 18 free; Th 6-8pm free.)*

NEW YORK CITY FIRE MUSEUM. Housed in a renovated 1904 firehouse, this museum is for all those kids who wanted to be firemen when they grew up. Equipment on display ranges from a hand-pulled truck dating back to when George Washington was a volunteer NYC firefighter to current models. Many of the staff are actual NYC firemen. Upstairs, placards detail great moments in New York fire history, such as the P.T. Barnum Museum fire, in which several firemen were injured while rescuing the 400lb. fat lady. *(691-1303. 278 Spring St., between Varick and Hudson St. Subway: #1, 9 to Houston; or C, E to Spring St. Open Tu-Su 10am-4pm. $4, students and seniors $2, Under 12 $1.)*

■**NEW YORK HISTORICAL SOCIETY.** Fascinating exhibits centering on the history of New York City. In 2000, look for exhibits on drawings and watercolors from the past 200 years, the physical structure of the Society itself, a "bird's eye view" of Manhattan, the over-475-year history of Italians in New York, and "$24: Manhattan's Myth of Origin," an exhibit debunking and retelling the story of Manhattan's acquisition (oops). Kids should visit the permanent "Kid City" installation that chronicles the history of New York. *(873-3400; www.nyhistroy.org. 2 W. 77th St. at Central Park West. Library and gallery Tu-Su 11am-5pm; summer library hours Tu-F 11am-5pm. Suggested donation $5, children and seniors $3. Library free.)*

NEW YORK TRANSIT MUSEUM. Housed in a defunct subway station, this little museum describes the birth and evolution of every aspect of New York's mass transit system, from subway maps to turnstiles to the trains themselves. *(718-*

243–8601. 130 Livingston St., at Schermerhorn and Borough St. Subway: #2, 3,4, M, N, or R to Borough Hall-Court St., then walk down to Schermerhorn and take a left. Open Tu-F 10am-4pm, Sa-Su noon-5pm. Admission $3; children and senior citizens $1.50; seniors free on W afternoons. Wheelchair accessible.)

NEW YORK UNEARTHED. Subway: #1 or 9 to South Ferry. Excavators discovered most of the items here during preparations for new construction in the downtown area. The small collection of Manhattan artifacts runs from clay pipes dated AD 1250 to "Lunch at the Counter, ca. 1950." In the basement you can observe archaeologists working in a glass-walled laboratory or hop inside the rumbling "Systems Elevator," a pre-virtual journey to a dig. *(748-8628. 17 State St., across from the South Ferry. Open M-Sa noon-6pm; closed Sa Jan.-Mar. Free.)*

OLD MERCHANTS HOUSE. Subway: #4, 5, or 6 to Bleecker St. Walk 3 blocks north up Lafayette St. and a block east. New York City's only preserved 19th-century family home. Built in 1832, the house was owned by prosperous merchant Seabury Tredwell, whose family's furniture, clothing, and memorabilia is faithfully preserved. *(777-1089. 29 E. 4th St., between Lafayette St. and the Bowery. Open Su-Th 1-4pm or by appointment. $3, seniors and students $2.)*

PARSONS EXHIBITION CENTER. A variety of exhibitions, many of student and faculty work, including photography, computer art, painting, and sculpture. *(229-8987. 2 W. 13th St. at Parsons School of Design on Fifth Ave. Subway: #4, 5, 6, or L, N, or R to 14th St. Open M-F 9am-6pm, Sa 10am-6pm. Free.)*

POLICE ACADEMY MUSEUM. On the second floor of the city's police academy. An esoteric and somewhat perplexing collection of crime-related artifacts. Intriguing displays of counterfeit money and firearms, including Al Capone's personal machine gun. Interspersed throughout are intimidatingly posed mannequins in uniform, as well as old trophies that the police squad's various sports leagues have won. *(477-9753. 235 E. 20th St., near Second Ave. Subway: #6 to 23rd St.Open M-F 9am-3pm. Free.)*

▨NICHOLAS ROERICH MUSEUM. A close collaborator on Stravinsky's *Rite of Spring*, Roerich also painted, philosophized, archaeologized, studied things Slavic, and founded an educational institution to promote world peace through art. Located in a stately old townhouse, the museum brims with Roerich's landscape paintings, books, and pamphlets on art, culture, and philosophy. The museum also hosts a classical music series from Oct.-May on most Sundays at 5pm. *(864-7752; fax 864-7704. 319 W. 107th St., between Broadway and Riverside Dr. Subway: #1, 9 to 110th St. Open Tu-Su 2-5pm. Free. No wheelchair access.)*

STUDIO MUSEUM IN HARLEM. Founded in 1967 at the height of the Civil Rights movement and dedicated to the collection and exhibition of works by black artists. Two exhibitions a years are culled from the photographs, paintings, and sculptures in the museum's collection. *(864-4500. 144 W. 125th St. between Adam Clayton Powell Jr. Blvd. and Lenox/Malcolm X Ave. Subway: #2, 3 to 125th St. Open W-F 10am-5pm, Sa-Su 1-6pm. $5, students and seniors $3, children $1; free on first Sa of month. Tours Sa 1, 2, 2:30, and 4pm.)*

UKRAINIAN MUSEUM. This tiny upstairs museum exhibits late 19th- and early 20th-century Ukrainian folk art, including hand-carved candelabra, traditional embroidered ceremonial clothing, and *pisanki* (painted ritual eggs). Also hosts special shows, such as the recent exhibition of art by Ukrainian New

Yorkers. Seasonal exhibits on Christmas and Easter crafts as well as numerous courses in Ukrainian embroidery, baking, and Christmas ornament-making. *(228-0110. 203 Second Ave. between 12th and 13th St. Subway: 14th St./Union Sq. Open W-Su 1-5pm. $3, students and seniors $2, children under 12 free.)*

WATERFRONT MUSEUM. This is not your typical museum. First, it's located on a barge floating in the New York Harbor. Second, the focus of the museum is the barge, the pier, the stunning view, and the waterfront area instead of the exhibits themselves. Sharps, the man who runs the museum, pulled the barge out of a muddy bank himself and took years to restore it to its present state; currently, it is the only functional wooden barge left in the New York Harbor. Mr. Sharps uses the barge-museum as a way to both educate about maritime history and draw visitors to this industrial waterfront area. The museum hosts a great **Sunset Concert Series** on Saturday evenings July-Aug. (free) and **Circusundays** in June when jugglers and acrobats come to entertain Red Hook's kids (free). Call to find out what's happening at the barge and when. *(718-624-4719; www.myplanetnet.net/waterfrontmuseum. Barge #79, 209 Conover St., in Red Hook, Brooklyn. Subway: A, C, F or 2, 3 or 4, 5 to Jay St./Boro Hall; or M, N, R to Court St. Then take bus B61 to the Beard St. stop; walk a block in the opposite direction that the bus is going. Make a left onto Conover St. and walk two blocks to the waterfront. The red barge is docked to your right. There is a free shuttle bus from surrounding Brooklyn neighborhoods.)*

MUSEUMS

GALLERIES

While New York's museums flaunt art history, New York galleries are where art *happens*. Contemporary art, such as it is, ascends, trades hands, and all too often goes belly-up in these spaces. Don't worry about how expensive it all is—the owners don't really expect you, gentle traveler, to buy anything. You'll encounter the newest of the new without paying a cent. Galleries are the ultimate free culture.

To get started, pick up a free copy of *The Gallery Guide* at any major museum or gallery; it lists the addresses, phone numbers, and hours of virtually every showplace in the city and comes equipped with several handy maps to orient you on your art odyssey. Extensive gallery info can also be found in the "Choices" listings of the free *Village Voice*, the "Art" section of *Time Out* and *New York* magazines, and in *The New Yorker*'s "Goings On About Town."

SoHo is gallery wonderland, with a particularly dense concentration of more than 40 different establishments lining Broadway between Houston and Spring St. Cutting-edge outposts of contemporary art have recently emerged in **Chelsea,** in reclaimed industrial spaces centered around West 22nd St. between Tenth and Eleventh Ave. **Madison Avenue** between 70th and 84th has a generous sampling of ritzy showplaces, and another group of galleries festoons **57th St.** between Fifth and Sixth Ave. The outer borough gallery scene extends every day, often dwelling on local themes. Most galleries are open from Tuesday to Saturday, from 10 or 11am to 5 or 6pm. In the summer, galleries often close on Saturdays and many are open by appointment only from late July through early September, as gallery owners head to the Hamptons.

Nearly all galleries host **"openings"** for their exhibitions; these are sometimes open to the public, offering the chance to drink wine, eat cheese, and pose, pose, pose. Stumbling upon an installation-in-progress can provide comic relief, as artsy types paint walls, erect bulky structures, and sweat from all the physical exertion.

SOHO

SoHo galleries not only open and close with amazing rapidity, but many of them have had to cut their losses and sell what they call "bread and butter" art—a landscape that goes well with a sofa or a sunset dangerously verging on airbrush. Still, the truly avant-garde does make a stand here—even if it is a motorized cow submerged in formaldehyde. The most cutting edge offerings have trouble nuzzling into the ground-level, commercial galleries that line West Broadway, so explore the second or third floors of gallery-packed buildings if you want to see SoHo's more experimental art. The following is a sampling of the different gallery types in the neighborhood.

AMERICAN PRIMITIVE. This small space shows only works by folk or self-taught American artists of the 19th and 20th centuries, focusing on antique folk art. Only here can you get a piece of art dedicated to baseball hero Cal Ripken made entirely out of the thread from socks. Proudly and aggressively out of the art scene—so uncool they're cool. *(966-1530. 594 Broadway, 2nd fl., between Prince and Houston St. Open M-Sa 11am-6pm; closed Sa July-Aug.)*

▓ARTISTS SPACE. Another non-profit, non-stuffy gallery. This one stresses performance: experimental theater, video art, and sculpture. Slide file of unaffiliated artists gives those without backing a chance to shine. *(226-3970. 38 Greene St., 3rd fl., at Grand St. Open Tu-Sa 10am-6pm; summer hours Tu-Sa 11am-6pm. Slide file open by appointment, usually F-Sa. Frequent free evening performances.)*

GAVIN BROWN'S ENTERPRISE. Literally and figuratively as far left as you'd want to get without a map, this tiny gallery specializes in fun, interesting contemporary work. Japanese art, Steve Pippen (the bathroom artist), and other *über*-contemporary stuff. Not much artwork, but the artwork-to-crap ratio is much higher than in most galleries. *(558 Broome St., just west of Sixth Ave. Open M-Sa noon-6pm; in summer W-F noon-6pm. Closed Aug.)*

DRAWING CENTER. Specializing exclusively in unique works on paper, this non-profit space manages to set up reliably high-quality exhibits. Both historical and contemporary works are on show—everything from Picasso to tattoo art. *(219-2166. 35 Wooster St. Open Tu-F 10am-6pm, Sa 11am-6pm; closed Aug.)*

EXIT ART. A fun and happening "transcultural" and "transmedia" non-profit space, featuring experiments in the presentation of visual art, theater, film, and video. The **Café Cultura** (open F noon-8pm, Sa noon-6pm), lets you grab a beer while absorbing the culture. About as friendly and young as it gets in the NYC art scene. *(966-7745. 548 Broadway, between Prince and Spring St., 2nd fl. Open Tu-Th 10am-6pm, F 10am-8pm, Sa 11am-6pm; closed Aug.)*

FEATURE. Daring, straightforward selections of contemporary art. Don't miss their back showroom when you visit. *(941-7077. 76 Greene St., 2nd fl., between Broome and Spring St. Open Sept.-June Tu-Sa 11am-6pm; July Tu-F 11am-6pm; closed Aug.)*

HOLLY SOLOMON GALLERY. This SoHo matriarch is an excellent place to start a tour of downtown galleries. 3 or 4 artists are always showing in this multi-floored space, providing newcomers with an accessible array of avant-garde art. Strengths include upper-tier video, illustration, photography, and installation art; unlike other galleries, Solomon's has a sense of humor. Nam June Paik, William Wegman, and Peter Hutchinson represent here. *(941-5777. 172 Mercer at Houston St. Open Sept.-June Tu-Sa 10am-6pm; July-Aug. Tu-F 10am-5pm.)*

PACE GALLERY. This famous gallery run by the Wildenstein family has two locations in the city. Its SoHo branch displays the works of biggies like Robert Irwin, Julian Schnabel, Claes Oldenburg. Exhibitions rotate every 4 weeks. *(431-9224. 142 Greene St., between Prince and Houston St. Open Sept.-June Tu-Sa 10am-6pm; June-July M-Th 10am-5:30pm, F 10am-4pm; closed in Aug. Other location: 32 E. 57th St., between Park and Madison.)*

PRINTED MATTER, INC. And you thought you knew what a "book" was. Featuring the best artist books and magazines in the biz, this non-profit bookshop/gallery makes a fascinating reading list any day of the year. Artists like John Baldessari, Cindy Sherman, and Kiki Smith are all associated with this place, but it is the commitment to displaying books by unknowns that makes Printed Matter such a valuable resource. Perpetual exhibitions and installations—always free, always fascinating. *(925-0325. 77 Wooster St. Open Tu-F 10am-6pm, Sa 11am-7pm.)*

⊠SHAKESPEARE'S FULCRUM. This is a gallery like no other; the owner wears transparent vixen-like clothing and slides down a fire pole to come down to the lower level; and the walls *breathe* with living art. Much of the work here concerns the dynamic processes of nature whether set in actual beehives, a tank of NYC tap water, or a diormama of crawling hermit crabs. Be sure to pick up their complimentary packet on the mission and gestalt of the gallery. *(966-6848. 480 Broome St. at Wooster St. Open Tu-Sa 11am-6pm, Su 1-6pm.)*

SONNABEND. This prominent gallery shows contemporary paintings by well-known American and European artists. Jeff Koons, John Baldessari, and Robert Rauschenburg top the bill. *(966-6160. 420 W. Broadway, 3rd fl. Open Tu-Sa 10am-6pm. Often closed July-Aug.)*

DAVID ZWIRNER. A small gallery that pulls together excellent, elegant one-person shows with a strong conceptual punch. Some of the smartest contemporary art around ends up on Zwirner's gracefully curated walls. *(966-9074. 43 Greene St. at Grand St. Open Tu-Sa 10am-6pm, summer hours M-Sa 10am-6pm.)*

CHELSEA

Be sure to check out the building at 529 W. 20th St. between Tenth and 11th Ave.: with eleven floors and over 20 galleries; it is a treasure trove of contemporary art. The I-20 is on the top floor of this building.

I-20. High quality, daringly original photography and video art displayed in a beautiful 11th-floor space. Textural art that includes folded fabric sculptures and other indescribable treasures. Also commands an exhilarating view of the river and piers below. *(645-1100. 529 W. 20th St., between Tenth and Eleventh Ave. Open Tu-Sa 10:30am-6pm.)*

KIM FOSTER. Specializing in emerging and contemporary art. Look out for their "Elbow Room" show in June and July of 2000 dedicated to public spaces in Manhattan and curated by an editor of *Art in America*. *(966-9024. 529 W. 20th St., between Tenth and Eleventh Ave. Open Tu-Sa 11am-6pm. Closed Aug.)*

DIA CENTER FOR THE ARTS. Sized like a museum but with a gallery's sensitivity to the pulse of current art, the 4-story Dia is reliably, irrepressibly cool. Each floor features changing exhibits/installations by a single contemporary artist, and the collection covers a balanced range of media and styles. Don't leave without stopping by the permanent installation on the roof. *(989-5566. 548 W. 22nd St., between Tenth and Eleventh Ave. $6, students; $3 seniors $3. Open W-Su noon-6pm. Closed July-Aug.)*

STUART PARR. Newcomer to the gallery scene has elegant shows of 20th century furniture and design. Expanding to photos and prints in 2000. *(206-6644. 532 W. 20th St., between Tenth and Eleventh Ave. Open June-Aug. M-F 10am-7pm, Sept.-May Tu-Sa 10am-7pm.)*

MAX PROTECH. Having started as an exhibition space for architectural drawings, Protech now hosts impressive and intelligent contemporary shows of painting, sculpture, and all things in between. Represents New York and a few Chinese artists. *(633-6999. 511 W. 22nd St., between Tenth and Eleventh St. Open Tu-Sa 10am-6pm; summer M-F 10am-6pm. Wheelchair access.)*

D'AMELIO TERRAS. Primarily sculptural, with a light formal twist that makes this small gallery go down nice and smooth (but not without a playful kick). Located on Chelsea's hot spot gallery block. *(352-9460. 525 W. 22nd., between Tenth and Eleventh Ave. Open Tu-Sa 10am-6pm; summer M-F 10am-6pm.)*

57TH STREET

FULLER BUILDING. Stylish Art Deco building harbors 12 floors of galleries. Contemporary notables such as Robert Miller, André Emmerich, and Susan Sheehan; collectors of ancient works like Frederick Schultz; and several galleries handling modern works. The **André Emmerich Gallery** (752-0124), on the 5th floor, features important contemporary work by Hockney et al. *(41 E. 57th St., between Madison and Park Ave. Subway: #4, 5, 6 to 59th St. Most galleries in the building open M-Sa 10am-5:30pm, but call ahead to make sure; Oct.-May most are closed Mondays.)*

PACE GALLERY. Four floors dedicated to the promotion of widely disparate forms of art. On the 10th floor Pace Masterprints (421-3237) and Pace Modern Masters specializes in prints; and the Pace African Art Gallery (421-3688). Pace Wildenstein-MacGill (759-7999) on the 9th floor has photography; Pace Wildenstein (421-3292) on the 2nd floor has contemporary prints. *(421-3292. 32 E. 57th St., between Park and Madison Ave. Subway: #4, 5, 6 to 59th St. Open June-Sept. M-Th 9:30am-6pm, F 9:30am-4pm; Oct.-May Tu-Sa 9:30am-6pm.)*

UPPER EAST SIDE

SOTHEBY'S. One of the most respected auction houses in the city, offering everything from Degas to Disney. Auctions open to anyone, but some require a ticket for admittance (first come, first serve). Call for displays. *(606-7000; ticket office 606-7171. 1334 York Ave. at 72nd St. Both open M-Sa 10am-5pm, Su 1-5pm. Closed Sa-Su in summer.)*

CHRISTIE'S. Flaunts its collection of valuable wares. Like Sotheby's, auctions are open to the public. *(636-2000. 20 Rockefeller Plaza at 49th St., between Fifth and Sixth Ave. Open M-Sa 10am-5pm, Su 1-5pm.)*

M. KNOEDLER & CO., INC. One of the oldest and most respected galleries in the city, it shows Abstract Expressionists like Olitski and Motherwell. Contemporary trends have infiltrated the time-honored institution, which now mounts shows like "Robert Rauschenberg: Bicyclords, Urban Bourbons & Eco-Echo." *(794-0550. 19 E. 70th St. between Madison and Fifth Ave. Open M-Th 9:30am-5pm; summer M-F 9:30am-5pm.)*

HIRSCHL AND ADLER GALLERIES. A wide variety of 18th- and 19th-century European and American art. Upstairs, at **Hirschl and Adler Modern,** more contemporary works are displayed. *(535-8810. 21 E. 70th St. between Fifth and Madison Ave. Open Tu-F 9:30am-5:15pm, Sa 9:30am-4:45pm; summer M-F 9:30am-4:45pm.)*

ACQUAVELLA. This majestic building houses exhibitions specializing in post-Impressionism, with big names such as Picasso, Degas, Cézanne, and Giacometti. *(734-6300. 18 E. 79th St. at Madison Ave. Open M-F 10am-5pm. Open Sa-Su for larger shows.)*

AMERICAS SOCIETY. Powerful exhibits dealing with subjects from all over the Americas. *(249-8950. 680 Park Ave. at 69th St. Open Tu-Su noon-6pm. Donation $3.)*

OTHER CULTURAL INSTITUTES. See **Upper East Side,** p. 175.

BROOKLYN

Mostly located in artistically vibrant **Williamsburg,** Brooklyn's galleries often provide space for cutting-edge artists who have yet to break into the commercialized world of downtown Manhattan. As a result, the art here is sometimes uneven, but always fresh.

⬛PIEROGI 2000. Though it has shown bigger-name artists like Amy Sillman and Tom Nozkowski, what sets this Williamsburg gem apart are its "front files," hundreds of affordable works by emerging artists. The files are kept on shelves and are meant to be perused by visitors. *(718-599-2144. 177 N. 9th St., between Bedford and Driggs St. Subway: L to Bedford Ave. Open Sept.-June Sa-M noon-6pm, in summer by appointment.)*

⬛THE WILLIAMSBURG ART AND HISTORICAL CENTER, The official center of the Williamsburg arts scene. Exhibits local artists, and hosts experimental theater, international poetry, avant-garde music, and a chamber orchestra. Also sponsors **walking tours** of the area. *(718-486-7372. 135 Broadway, between Bedford and Driggs. Subway: J, M, Z to Marcy Ave. and walk 3 blocks west on Broadway; or the L to Bedford Ave., walk down Bedford to Broadway. Open Sa-Su noon-6pm.)*

SIDESHOW. Don't expect any bearded ladies or contortionists here—this sideshow limits itself to a mix of emerging, bigger-name (e.g. Larry Poons, Larry Hamilton) works. *(718-486-8180. 319 Bedford Ave., between S. 2nd and S. 3rd St. Subway: L to Bedford Ave. Open F-Su 1-7pm.)*

FLIPSIDE. This gallery tends to show a lot of locals (which, considering the number of artists living in the neighborhood, could keep easily it occupied), but often branches out to non-Brooklynite work as well. Greg Stone has shown here, and Nurit Newman has both shown and curated. *(718-389-7108. 84 Withers St., between Leonard and Lorimer St., 3rd fl. Subway: L to Lorimer St. Open Sept.-May Su 1-6pm or by appointment.)*

MWMWM. *(718-599-9411. 65 Hope St., between Metropolitan and Roebling.)*

EYEWASH. This little gem specializes in site-specific installations of photo work, painting, and other media. *(718-387-2714. 143 N. 7th St. 3rd and 4th fl., between Bedford and Henry St. Subway: L to Bedford Ave., then walk ½ block from subway stop to N. 7th St. Open Sa-Su 1-6pm and by appointment; in July by appointment only.)*

THE BRONX

The community-oriented galleries here often showcase local talent and/or address issues of neighborhood and ethnic identity.

LEHMAN ART GALLERY. Housed in a building designed by Marcel Breur, the gallery's past exhibitions have included showings from a contemporary Russian surrealist, artifacts from Papua New Guinea, and a series of paintings commemorating Puerto Rican victims of domestic violence. Every June, Lehman holds a children's show displaying art made by local youngsters who have visited the museum. *(718-960-8732. 250 Bedford Park Blvd. West. On the campus of Herbert Lehman College in the Fine Arts Building. Subway: #4 or D to Bedford Park. Open approximately Tu-Sa 11am-4pm, but subject to change.)*

THE LONGWOOD ARTS GALLERY. Located on the second floor of a former public school building, this gallery often showcases the work of the those in its artist-in-residence program, which has nursed talents such as Michael Bramwell and Esperanza Cortes. There is no running in the hall. *(718-931-9500. 965 Longwood Ave. Subway: #6 to Longwood Ave.; walk away from the overpass up Longwood Ave. Open M-F 9am-5pm; Sa by appointment, so call ahead.)*

GALLERY 69. A gallery in the heart of Mott Haven's antique district that contains a large collection of black erotic art from around the world. No, the name of the gallery comes from the address. *(718-518-4242. 69 Bruckner Ave., between Willis and Alexander. Subway: #6 to 3rd Ave.; walk south a few blocks along Alexander until you reach Bruckner, then turn right. Open W-Su 11am-6pm.)*

ARTS & ENTERTAINMENT

In Manhattan, every flat surface is a potential stage and every inattentive waiter an unemployed, possibly unemployable, actor.

—Quentin Crisp

New York teems with cultural options. Choosing from among the city's dizzyingly broad array of entertainment and cultural activity is, like, one of life's great trials. The theaters, halls, clubs, and hundreds of other independent venues responsible for New York's cultural hegemony over the rest of the country compete fiercely with each other for popular attention and critical credibility. *Let's Go* lists New York's more essential venues and hot spots, but be sure to check local sources to find out about other places and get the scoop on present offerings. A number of publications print daily, weekly, and monthly entertainment calendars: try *Time Out: New York*, the *Village Voice*, *New York* magazine, and *The New York Times* (particularly the Sunday edition). The monthly *Free Time* calendar ($1.25) lists free cultural events throughout Manhattan. Try the NYC Parks Department's **entertainment hotline** (360-3456; 24hr.) for the lowdown on special events in parks throughout the city. Call the **NYC/ON STAGE hotline** (768-1818) for a comprehensive listing of theater, dance, and music events taking place each week.

THEATER

A massive revival of the stage has occurred in recent years. After a downswing in popularity, theaters have risen from the dead, attracting the masses back to Times Square. Ticket sales and prices now boom, as mainstream musicals increase in popularity. Warhorses like *The Phantom of the Opera* and *Les Misérables* have ushered armies of tourists, senior citizens, and suburbanites through the theater doors for interminable runs. Furthermore, the resurrection of Broadway has triggered an equally vibrant theater scene throughout the city—off-Broadway, off-off-Broadway, in dance and studio spaces, museums, cafes, parks, even in parking lots—cheaper and more accessible than anything along Shubert Alley.

INFORMATION. For listings of Broadway, off-Broadway, and off-off-Broadway shows, see *Listings*, a weekly guide to entertainment in Manhattan ($1). For info on shows in any of the five boroughs as well as ticket availability, you can also call the **New York City On Stage Hotline** at 768-1818. The **NYC Department of Cultural Affairs Arts Hotline** (956-2787; staffed M-F 9am-5pm) offers an actual person to advise you.

DISCOUNT TICKETS. Though Broadway tickets usually run upwards of $50, many money-saving schemes exist. Some theaters have $20 seats in the farthest reaches of the balcony, though these seats are hard to come by. **TDF Vouchers** (Theatre Development Fund) is the nation's largest nonprofit service organization for the performing arts and offers discount vouchers for off-off-Broadway productions and other events sponsored by small, independent production companies. For those eligible—students, teachers, performing-arts professionals, retirees, union and armed forces members, and clergy—it's a great deal. *($28 buys four vouchers redeemable at the box office of any participating organization. 221-0885.)*

TKTS sells tickets at a 25-50% discount on the day of the performance of many Broadway and some larger off-Broadway shows. The board near the front of the line for each TKTS booth posts the names of the shows with available tickets. Expect a $2.50 service charge per ticket, and have cash or traveler's checks for payment. The lines begin to form an hour or so before the booths opens, but move fairly quickly. More tickets become available as showtime approaches, so you may find fewer possibilities if you go too early. *(768-1818. Duffy Square, at 47th St. and Broadway. Tickets sold M-Sa 3-8pm for evening performances; W and Sa 10am-2pm for matinees; and Su 11am-7pm for matinees and evening performances. Less competitive lines form downtown, where TKTS has a branch in the mezzanine of 2 World Trade Center. Open M-F 11am-5:30pm, Sa 11am-3:30pm; Sunday matinee tickets sold on Saturday.)*

You can get a similar discount with a **"twofer"** (i.e., two for the price of one) ticket coupons available at bookstores, libraries, and the Times Square Visitors Center. As they apply mostly to old Broadway standards that have been running strong for a very long time, you should never have to pay full price to see *Cats*. For more info on how to get cheap tickets, see **Cheap Seats,** p. 260.

You may reserve full-price tickets over the phone and pay by credit card through: **Tele-Charge** (239-6200 or outside NYC 800-432-7250; 24hr.) for Broadway shows; **Ticket Central** (279-4200; open daily 1-8pm) for off-Broadway shows; **Ticketmaster** (307-4100 or outside NYC 800-755-4000; 24hr.) for all types of shows. All three services assess a per-ticket service charge; ask before purchasing. You can avoid these fees if you buy tickets directly from the box offices.

BROADWAY

Most Broadway theaters are located north of Times Square, between Eighth Ave. and Broadway, in what is also known as the "Great White Way." Broadway theaters are open only when a play is in production, and most don't have phones; often phone numbers given for a theater box office are in fact handled by a larger ticket broker agency. Here's a list of some current Broadway blockbusters.

Annie Get Your Gun, Marquis Theatre, 1535 Broadway. A revival of an old show starring the inimitable Bernadette Peters as crack shot cowgirl/showgirl Annie Oakley.

Cabaret, Kit Kat Club (in The Henry Miller's Theater), 124 W. 43rd St. Box office at the Roundabout Theater's Criterion Center, 1530 Broadway at 45th St. A daring revival of this powerful story of art and escapism in a Berlin shifting from one troubled era to another. Was the hottest ticket on Broadway in the summer of 1998. Alan Cummings has left the cast, however.

Chicago, Shubert Theater, 225 W. 44th St. An excellent revival of the often humorous portrait of Chicago's gangster era. The choreography by Anne Reinking is well worth the price of admission. $20 tickets are available at the box office at 10am on the day of the performance; 1 per person.

Death of a Salesman, Eugene O'Neill Theater, 230 W. 49th St. Brian Dennehy stars in a contemporary reworking of Arthur Miller's classic American tragedy.

Fosse, Broadhurst Theater, 235 W. 44th St. Choreographed by Chet Walker and *Chicago*'s Ann Reinking, this 1999 Tony-Award-winning Bob Fosse tribute recreates the biggest numbers of the legendary choreographer's career.

Rent, Nederlander Theater, 208 W. 41st St. A modern update of *La Bohème*. They sing, they dance, they talk about love with wireless mikes strapped to their heads. Still going strong. $20 tickets available after a 5:30pm line-up for a 6pm lottery at the box office for evening performances Tu-F; 2 tickets per person, cash only.

The Lion King, New Amsterdam Theater, Broadway and 42nd St. A show where spectacle overpowers all. The intricate costumes in this elaborate show combine an actor's body movements with those of the animal he controls. $20 rush tickets available at 10am on the day of the performance. Tickets $25-80. Expect long lines.

Opening at the end of 1999: *Dame Edna—the Royal Tour; Epic Proportions; Fame; Saturday Night Fever.*

ARTS & ENTERTAINMENT

OFF-BROADWAY AND OFF-OFF-BROADWAY

Off-Broadway theaters, by definition, feature less mainstream presentations for crowds of 499 or fewer. Runs are generally short; however, they occasionally jump to Broadway houses (as in the case of *Rent*). Many of the best off-Broadway houses huddle in the Sheridan Square area of the West Village. Eugene O'Neill got his break at the Provincetown Playhouse, and Elisa Loti made her American debut at the Actors Playhouse. **Playwrights Horizons,** 416 W. 42nd St. (279-4200), between Ninth and Tenth Ave., and **Manhattan Theater Club,** 131 W. 55th St. (399-3000 or 581-1212), for instance, rank among the most prestigious launching pads for new American plays. Off-Broadway tickets cost $15-45; TKTS sells tickets to the larger off-Broadway houses. You may see shows for free by arranging to usher; this usually entails dressing neatly and showing up at the theater around 45 minutes ahead of curtain, helping to seat ticket-holders, and then staying for 10 minutes after the performance to help clean up. Call the theater after 5pm and speak with the house manager far in advance.

The category of off-off-Broadway may include more adventurous offerings in still smaller theaters, such as **The Ontological Hysteric Theater** at St. Mark's Church (see **Neighborhoods,** p. 258). Check out the Hysteric's *Blueprint Series* in July for a respected taste of new and emerging talent.

Many of the theaters listed below offer variety and eclecticism, and many host several different companies each year. Listings and reviews appear the first Wednesday of every month in **Simon Says,** a *Village Voice* guide tailored to unconventional theater happenings around the city. Other publications with theater listings include *New York* magazine, the *New York Press*, the *New Yorker*, *Time Out: New York*.

SHAKESPEARE IN THE PARK. The renowned series, founded by the same Joseph Papp who founded the Joseph Papp Public Theater (see below), is an unmissable New York summer tradition. Two Shakespeare plays run from late June through August. For free tickets, wait in line at the **Delacorte Theater** in Central Park. The glorious outdoor amphitheater overlooks Belvedere Lake and its darling castle. Top-notch directors—plus the opportunity to perform Shakespeare in the great outdoors—attract the most important actors around. Recent performances have included *Richard III* with Denzel Washington, *The Tempest* with Patrick Stewart, and many other plays featuring, to name a few, Jeff Goldblum, Gregory Hines, Mary Elizabeth Mastrantonio, Michelle Pfeiffer, and Vanessa Redgrave. A graduate of Juilliard's first year of actors, Kevin Kline serves as the festival's artistic director and has played Hamlet in the park. *(861-7277. 539-8750 for outer-borough ticket distribution. Near the 81st St. entrance on the Upper West Side, just north of the 79th St. Transverse. Tickets available from 1pm; try to get there by 11:30am. Standby line forms at 6:30pm. Also available 1-3pm at the Public Theater at 425 Lafayette St. downtown. Limit 2 tickets per person. Doors open Tu-Su at 7:30pm; shows start at 8pm.)*

THE JOSEPH PAPP PUBLIC THEATER. From 1957 until 1991, when Joseph Papp died, his theater epitomized its founder's determination and bold originality. Today, theater impresario and Tony-winning director of *Angels in America* on Broadway, George C. Wolfe, runs the show, so to speak. The Public's six venues present a wide variety of productions and have hosted a decade-long marathon of Shakespeare's every last work, right down to *Timon of Athens*. *(539-8750. 425 Lafayette St. Ticket prices subject to change.)*

ETHNIC THEATERS. Repertorio Español, currently housed in the Gramercy Arts Theater, 138 E. 27th St. (889-2850), presents many Spanish productions (tickets $20-35). The **Negro Ensemble Company** (582-5860) rents out space to perform works by and about African-Americans (tickets $15-20). The **Pan Asian Repertory Theater,** 47 Great Jones St. (505-5655), is the nation's largest Asian-American theater (tickets $40). The **Irish Arts Center,** at 553 W. 51st St. (757-3318), presents contemporary and classic Irish and Irish-American plays (tickets $20-25).

ALTERNATIVE THEATER. Whether it be an improvised opera, performance art, stand-up comedy, political commentary, theatrical monologue, music, dance, or video art, alternative theater thrives throughout the city. Quality venues include the **Brooklyn Academy of Music's** famous Next Wave festival in the spring; **The Kitchen,** 512 W. 19th St. (255-5793); **Franklin Furnace,** 112 Franklin St. (766-2606); and **Performance Space 122 (P.S. 122),** 150 First Ave. (477-5288). **La Mama,** 74A E. 4th St. (254-6468), the most venerable of the lot, helped Sam Shepard, Andre Serban, and Elizabeth Swados get their respective (and respected) starts.

Here's a listing of some other, no less important, off-Broadway theaters and outdoor venues:

Actors Playhouse, 100 Seventh Ave. (463-0060). Tickets $35-45. Box office open noon-8pm on show days.

American Place Theater, 111 W. 46th St. (840-2960 for a schedule, 840-3074 for the box office). *Wonderland*, Julia Dahl's compelling, sharply written story of the rich and unhappy, started here summer '99.

Astor Place Theater, 434 Lafayette St. (254-4370). Home of long-running hit *Blue Man Group*, an exciting, humorous performance art/percussion show. Tickets $45-50. Box office open noon-7:30pm.

Cherry Lane, 38 Commerce St. (989-2020), at Grove St. Has hosted such American premieres as Beckett's *Waiting for Godot* and plays by Ionesco and Albee. Tickets $45. Box office open Tu-F 4-8pm, Sa-Su noon-8pm.

Douglas Fairbanks Theatre, 432 W. 42nd St. (239-4321). The drama *Bash* opened to sold-out audiences in the summer of '99. Tickets $45. Box office open noon-7:30pm.

Ensemble Studio, 549 W. 52nd St. (247-4982), at Eleventh Ave. Tickets range from free to $15. For shows with suggested donations, reservations accepted 10am-6pm. For shows with actual ticket prices, box office open noon-6pm.

Here, 145 Sixth Ave. (647-0202). Experimental musical, poetic, dramatic, even puppetry performances. Tickets $5-25.

John Houseman Theater, 450 W. 42nd St. (967-9077). Home to Studio Theater, Studio Too, The New Group, Houseman Theater Co., and Gotham City Improv. Tickets $45. Box office open 12:30-6:30pm.

Lamb's, 130 W. 44th St. (997-1780 or 575-0300). One 349-seater, one 29-seater host family-oriented plays and musicals. Tickets $25-35.

Lucille Lortel, 121 Christopher St. (924-8782). Tickets $45-55.

Minetta Lane Theater, 18 Minetta Ln. (420-8000). Hosting the high-energy "*Thwak*" in 1999. Tickets $25-45. Student tickets 5min. before show $15-20. Performance times Tu-F 8pm, Sa 7 and 10pm, Su 3pm.

New York Theatre Workshop, 79 E. 4th St. (780-9037). Box office (460-5475) open Tu-Sa 1-6pm.

Orpheum, 126 Second Ave. (477-2477), between 7th and 8th St. Scored major success with Mamet's *Oleanna*. Currently playing the infectious, rhythmic, *Stomp*. Tickets $30-50. Box office open daily 1-6pm.

Pan Asian Repertory, 47 Great Jones St. (505-5655). Tickets $40.

Playhouse 91, 316 E. 91st St. (831-2000). Currently hosts the Jewish Repertory Theater.

Primary Stages, 354 W. 45th St. (333-4052), between Eighth and Ninth Ave. Has fostered the works of David Ives since 1989. Box office open M-Sa noon-6pm.

Promenade Theatre, 2162 Broadway (580-1313). Recently performed the bawdy Manhattanite comedy, *Things You Shouldn't Say Past Midnight*. Tickets $50.

Queens Theater in the Park (718-760-0064), in Flushing Meadows-Corona Park. A film and performing arts center that hosts an annual Latino arts festival, among other events.

CHEAP SEATS
To the budget traveler, the Great White Way's major theatrical draws may seem locked away in gilded Broadway cages. Never fear, however, *Let's Go's* here! Er, that is to say, you can find cheap tickets, compadre. Should Ticketmaster (307-4100; outside NYC 800-755-4000) not work, other options exist to help you sit pretty when the curtain rises. For one, you can consult ye olde standby ticket distributor, **TKTS** (see p. 256). If choice B fails too, then still more avenues remain open to you.

Rush Tickets: Some theaters distribute them on the morning of the performance; others make student rush tickets available 30 minutes before showtime. Lines can be extremely long, so get there *early*.

Cancellation Line: No rush luck? Some theaters redistribute returned or unclaimed tickets several hours before showtime. You might have to sacrifice your afternoon—but, come on, Dame Edna is worth it!

Hit Show Club: 630 Ninth Ave. (581-4211), between 44th and 45th St. This free service distributes coupons redeemable at the box office for 1/3 or more off regular ticket prices. Call for coupons via mail or pick them up them up at the club office.

Audience Extras (989-9550): A little-known program with a lot of leftover tickets (many for prime house seats) to theater shows, concerts, and dance performances. You must pay a one-time membership fee of $130; after that, however, each ticket will only cost you $3. Most tickets sold on a day-of-show basis.

High 5 Tickets to the Arts (445-8587): Through this program any junior high or high school student between the ages of 13 and 18 can attend theater shows, concerts, and museum exhibitions for only $5. Tickets are sold at all New York Ticketmaster locations; proof of age is required, and tickets must be purchased at least one day prior to the performance. For more details and a listing of available shows, see High 5's website.

Kids' Night on Broadway (563-2929): This annual program, sponsored by TDF and the League of American Theatres, gives children ages 6 to 18 free admission (with the purchase of one regularly priced ticket) to Broadway shows on four specified nights. Kids' Night debuted in New York last year and was so successful that it has expanded to 20 cities nationwide. Tickets start selling in October; performances Jan.-Feb.

CareTix: (840-0770, ext. 230): Sponsored by Broadway Cares/Equity Fights AIDS, CareTix sells house seats for sold-out Broadway and off-Broadway shows, and for some non-theatrical events. Tickets are twice the regular box-office price, but you can claim one-half of what you pay as a tax-deductible charitable contribution to BC/EFA.

Sold-out Shows: Even if a show is sold out to the general public, theaters reserve prime house seats, usually in the first few rows, for VIPs. However, house seats frequently remain unclaimed, in which case they are sold to the general public—for full price—on the day of the show. House seats can go on sale as early as the box office opens or as late as one hour before curtain, so call the individual theater for details.

Standing-room Only: Sold on the day of show, tend to be around $15 or $20. Call first, as some theaters can't accommodate standing room.

Samuel Beckett Theater, 410 W. 42nd St. (594-2826), between Ninth and Tenth Ave. Artsy productions of contemporary drama, sometimes including post-performance discussions with members of the cast. Tickets $45, students and seniors $35. Box office open 5-8pm.

Sanford Meisner Theater, 164 Eleventh Ave. (358-3481). Opera productions to psychological dramas. Small space hosts queer-themed company. Tickets $12-15.

travel

Travel helps you remember who you forgot to be.....

Council *Travel*

SoHo Repertory Theatre, 46 Walker St. (941-8632; fax 941-7148), between Broadway and Church St. Tickets $10.

SoHo Think Tank Ohio Theater, 66 Wooster St. (966-4844), between Grand and Broome St. A theater that puts on deliberately intellectual and provoking pieces combining theater, performance art, dancing, sketch comedy, and music. In the summer of 1999 the theater hosted *The Ice Factory.* "Cafe Ohio" opens before shows at 6pm for "drinks and conversation." Shows usually W-Sa at 7pm. $10.

Sullivan Street Playhouse, 181 Sullivan St. (674-3838). Home to *The Fantasticks,* the longest running show in U.S. history. The city has renamed that section of road "Fantasticks Lane." Grab a twofer pass. All seats $36.50, on weekends $39. Shows Tu-F 8pm, Sa 3 and 7pm, Su 3 and 7:30pm. Box office open noon-showtime Tu-Su.

Theater for the New City, 152 First Ave. (254-1109), in the East Village. New avant-garde productions. Productions Th-Su 8pm. Tickets around $10. Dispatches a roving theater troupe throughout the city that performs in parks and streets (late July-Sept.). Check the *Village Voice* for details. Office open M-F 10am-6pm.

Union Square Theatre, 100 E. 17th St. (505-0700). In summer '99, this respectable off-Broadway theater housed *Wit,* the Pulitzer Prize-winning play about an iron-willed academic facing terminal ovarian cancer; a beautiful use of John Donne. Tickets $15-50.

Vineyard Theater Company's Dimson Theatre, 108 E. 15th St. (353-3366, ext. 12), between Union Sq. and Irving Pl. Premiered such marvels as Paula Vogel's 1998 Pulitzer Prize-winning *How I Learned to Drive.* Parking $5 parking.

Wooster Group, in the Performing Garage, 33 Wooster St. (966-3651; www.thewoostergroup.org), between Grand and Broome St. Founders include Willem Dafoe and Spalding Gray. Puts on all ilks of experimental theater. Shows Th-Su 8pm. $12.

FILM

If Hollywood is *the* place to make films, New York City is *the* place to see them. Most movies open in New York weeks before they're distributed across the country, and the response of Manhattan audiences and critics can shape a film's success or failure nationwide. Dozens of revival houses show classics year-round, and independent filmmakers from around the reel world come to New York to flaunt their celluloid. Big-screen aficionados should check out the cavernous **Ziegfeld,** 141 W. 54th St. (765-7600), between Sixth and Seventh Ave., one of the largest screens left in America, showing first-run films. Consult local newspapers for complete listings. Tickets run $9.50 for adults and $6 for seniors and under 11. **MoviePhone** (777-FILM/3456) allows you to reserve tickets for most major movie houses and pick them up at showtime from the theater's automated ticket dispenser; you charge the ticket price plus a $1.50 fee over the phone.

MUSEUMS AND OTHER VENUES

American Museum of the Moving Image, 35th Ave. at 36th St., Astoria, Queens (718-784-0077; see **Museums**). Three full theaters showing everything from silent classics to retrospectives of great directors. Recent programs have ranged from 50s *Father of the Bride* to *Fast Cars and Women.* Free with admission to museum: $8.50, seniors and students $5.50, children under 12 $4.50. Screenings Sa-Su; call for hours.

The Asia Society, 725 Park Ave. (288-6400), at 70th St. Subway: #6 to 68th St. Films from or about Asia. Ticket prices $7-10.

China Institute, 125 E. 65th St. (744-8181), at Lexington Ave. Sponsors Chinese and Chinese-American film series. Call for a schedule. $5-7.

French Institute/Alliance Française, in Florence Gould Hall, 55 E. 59th St. (355-6100). Francophiles can satisfy their Godard craving. Screenings Tu. $7, students $5.50.

Goethe Institute, 1014 Fifth Ave. (439-8688), between 82nd and 83rd St. Shows German films (usually with English subtitles) each week at locations around the city. Ticket prices vary.

Iris and B. Gerald Film Center, 36 E. 8th St. (998-4100), between University and Greene. Generally for student screenings; sometimes it shows off-beat films that are open to the public and free. Check outside or call for schedule.

Japan Society, 333 E. 47th St. (752-0824; see **Museums,** p. 245.) Mounts yearly retrospectives of the greatest Japanese achievements in film. Schedule can be obtained by visiting the society or by calling. $7, students, seniors, and members $5.

Metropolitan Museum of Art (535-7710; see **Museums,** p. 231). The Met posts a schedule of performances covering the spectrum from traditional Japanese music and Russian balalaika to all-star classical music recitals. Chamber music in the bar and piano music in the cafeteria on Friday and Saturday evenings, free with museum admission; other concerts may cost $15 and up. Call 535-3949 for info.

Museum of Modern Art: Roy and Niuta Titus Theaters, 11 W. 53rd St. (708-9480; see **Museums,** p. 235). The MoMA serves up an unbeatable diet of great films daily in its 2 lower-level theaters. The film department holds what it claims to be "the strongest international collection of film in the United States," and it's hard to doubt them. Film tickets are included in the price of admission and are available upon request. Also ask about screenings in the video gallery on the 3rd floor.

New York Public Libraries: For a real deal, check out a library, any library. All show free films: documentaries, classics, and last year's blockbusters. Screening times may be a bit erratic, but you can't beat the price. (For complete info on New York libraries, see **Essentials,** p. 74.)

Symphony Space, 2537 Broadway (box office 864-5400), at 95th St. Subway: #1, 9 or 2, 3 to 96th St. Primarily a live performance space, but every July the Foreign Film Festival showcases the expanding canon of quality foreign films. $8. Box office open daily noon-7pm.

Walter Reade Theater, at Lincoln Center (875-5600; box office 875-5601; www.film-link.com). Subway: #1, 9 to 66th St. New York's performing arts octopus flexes yet another cultural tentacle with this theater in the Rose Building next to the Juilliard School. Foreign and critically acclaimed American independent films dominate; also hosts the **New York Film Festival** in July. $8.50. Box office open daily 30min. before the start of the first film and closes 15min. after start of last show.

REVIVAL AND INDEPENDENT FILM HOUSES

Angelika Film Center, 18 W. Houston St. (995-2000; box office 995-2570), at Mercer St. Subway: #6 to Bleecker St.; or B, D, F, Q to Broadway/Lafayette. "K" is for *Kultur:* 8 screens of alternative, independent, and foreign cinema. Show up early on weekends; tickets frequently sell out many shows in advance. $9, seniors and under 12 $5.50. Pricey cafe upstairs.

Anthology Film Archives, 32 Second Ave. (505-5181), at E. 2nd St. Subway: F to Second Ave. A forum for independent filmmaking, focusing on the contemporary, offbeat, and avant-garde chosen from U.S. and foreign production. Hosts the annual **New York Underground Film Festival** (Mar.) and the annual **Mix Festival** (Nov.) a les-bi-gay film festival. $8, students and seniors $5.

Bryant Park Film Festival, Bryant Park (512-5700), at 42nd St. and Sixth Ave. Subway: B, D, F, Q, N, R, S or #1, 2, 3, 7, 9 to 42nd St. Running from late June to August, this free outdoor series features classic revivals such as *Mr. Smith Goes to Washington, Citizen Kane,* and *The Sound of Music.* Movies begin Mondays at sunset; rain date Tuesday nights.

Cinema Village, 22 E. 12th St. (924-3363), at University Pl. Subway: N, R, L or #4, 5, 6 to Union Sq. Features independent documentaries and hard-to-find foreign films. Great seats that lean back. $8, students $6, and seniors $5.

Film Forum, 209 W. Houston St. (727-8110; box office 727-8112), near Sixth Ave. and Varick St. Subway: C, E to Spring St.; or #1, 9 to Houston St. Three theaters with a strong selection in classics, foreign films, and independent films. $8.50, seniors $4.50 (M-F before 5pm).

The Kitchen, 512 W. 19th St. (255-5793), between Tenth and Eleventh Ave. Subway: C, E to 23rd St. World-renowned showcase for offbeat happenings. Features experimental and avant-garde film and video, as well as concerts, dance performances, and poetry readings. Most shows are from New York-based struggling artists. Season runs Sept.-May, but a summer talk series ($10 each talk) hosts such avant-luminaries as Lori Anderson and Philip Glass. Call for info. Ticket prices vary by event.

Millennium Film Workshop, 66 E. 4th St. (673-0090), between Bowey and Second Ave. Subway: F to Second Ave. More than just a theater, this media arts center presents an extensive program of experimental film and video from Sept. to June and offers classes and workshops. Also has equipment available for use. $7.

NY Video Festival, 165 W. 65th St. (875-5600; www.filminc.com.), sponsored by the Film Society of Lincoln Center, it runs in mid July at the Walter Reade theater. Tickets $8.50, seniors $4.50 at weekday matinees. Check out their website to find info on all kinds of festivals in NY.

LIVE TELEVISION

Bring your TV fantasies to life in the city of dreams. Here, you can ask Ricki Lake's guest that burning question or decide for yourself what really *is* Andy and Conan's relationship. It's best to order your tickets two to three months in advance, although standby tickets often crop up. Read on for a sampler of what deals the big names offer and how to get on the ticket.

Late Show with David Letterman (CBS) at the Ed Sullivan Theater, 1697 Broadway (975-1003), at 53rd St. The cuddly-yet-acerbic host performs his antics in front of a studio audience. If you are lucky enough to get tickets, bring a sweater—the studio is notoriously cold. Order tickets for his *Late Show* well in advance by writing: Late Show Tickets, 1697 Broadway, NY, NY 10019. For standby tickets on the day of the show, call 247-6497 at 11am on tape days (M-Th). Tickets are no longer given out at the theater.

Late Night with Conan O'Brien (NBC) (664-3057) at the G.E. Building in Rockefeller Center. Tapings Tu-F 5:30-6:30pm. To order in advance call or send a postcard to NBC Tickets, 30 Rockefeller Plaza, NY, NY 10012. You may receive up to 5 tickets at a time, but must book a month and a half in advance. Standby tickets also available the day of the show at 9am at the 49th St. entrance, but you must show up at 4:15pm to see if there is enough room. Active in summer. Must be 16 or older.

The Montel Williams Show (WFOX), 356 58th St. (989-8880). Tapings M-W 10am, 1, and 3pm. Request tickets by calling or writing to The Montel Williams Show Tickets, 353 W. 57th St., Box 184, NY, NY 10019. Must be 16 or older.

Regis and Kathie Lee (WABC) (456-3537). Send a postcard with name, address, phone number, and your request for up to 4 tickets to: Live Tickets, Ansonia Station, P.O. Box 777, NY, NY 10023. Expect a year-long wait. For standby tickets, line up at the corner of 67th St. and Columbus Ave. at 8am or earlier on weekdays. Must be 10 or older.

Ricki Lake Show (WWOR) (352-8600). Tapings W-F 3:30 and 5:30pm. Write to Ricki Lake, 401 Fifth Ave., NY, NY 10016, or go in person at least an hour before a taping.

Rosie O'Donnell (NBC) (664-3056). Send postcards March-June to NBC Tickets at Rockefeller Plaza (see **Conan,** above). A completely random lottery cares not for your desired dates or number of tickets. Standby tickets, available at 7:30am the day of taping, are also based on a lottery (read: you don't have to break your neck to get in line by 4am) from 30 Rockefeller Plaza. Ages 6-16 must be accompanied by adult.

Saturday Night Live (NBC) (664-3056). *SNL* goes on hiatus June-Aug. and only accepts ticket requests in Aug. Order tickets by sending a postcard to Rockefeller Plaza (see **Conan,** above). Warning: they don't accept requests for a specific date or quantity of tickets. Standby: get in line on the mezzanine level of Rockefeller Center (49th St. side) at 9am the morning of the show. You must be at least 16. P.S. Don't hold your breath.

The View (ABC) (456-1000). Brainchild of brazen Barbara Walters, this new hit talk sow brings together 4 opinionated women (not including Barbara's occasional appearances) from different worlds to dish the dirt. Send a request for tickets at least 2-3 months in advance to Ticket Coordinator, 320 W. 66th St., NY, NY 10023. Standby tickets available at same address. Best to show up around 9am, as filming begins at 11am every weekday.

OPERA

Lincoln Center (875-5000) has more cultural events than even the most fervent devotee could attend. Telephone or drop a line to Lincoln Center Plaza, New York, NY 10023 (rather than stopping by the currently metamorphosing Performing Arts Library) for a full schedule and a press kit as long as the *Ring* cycle. (See **Neighborhoods,** p. 189 for more info and directions.)

THE METROPOLITAN OPERA COMPANY. North America's premier opera outfit, plays on a stage as big as a football field. Regular tickets run as high as $210, so go for the upper balcony at around $42—the cheapest seats have an obstructed view. You can stand in the orchestra ($16) along with the opera freakazoids who've brought along the score, or all the way back in the Family Circle ($12). *(362-6000. Metropolitan Opera House, Lincoln Center. Regular season runs Sept.-Apr. M-Sa; box office open M-Sa 10am-8pm, Su noon-6pm. In the summer, call the ticket line at 362-6000 for info on free park concerts.)*

NEW YORK CITY OPERA. Perpendicular to "the Met," this company has come into its own under the direction of Christopher Keene, general director since 1989. "City" now has a split season (Sept.-Nov. and Mar.-Apr.) and keeps its ticket prices low year-round ($20-90). Call on Mondays to check the availability of $10 rush tickets, then wait in line the next morning. *(870-5570. New York State Theater, Lincoln Center. Open M-Sa at 10am.)*

SMALLER COMPANIES. Look for the **New York Grand Opera's** free performances at the Central Park Summerstage, every Wednesday night in July (360-2777; www.summerstage.org). Check the papers for performances of old warhorses by the **Amato Opera Company,** 319 Bowery (228-8200; Sept.-May) or the **Regina Opera Company** (718-232-3555), 65th St. and Twelfth Ave., in Brooklyn (which welcomes opera lovers to its 30th season in 2000). Music schools often stage opera (see p. 266).

DANCE

Always a kinetic city, New York is blessed with myriad burgeoning and established, cutting-edge and classical dance companies, troupes, and collectives. Your best bet to find good dance is to look through the listings in *The New Yorker, Time Out,* or *The Village Voice;* the search-engine **www.citysearch.com** can also provide you with some more off-the-beaten-path options.

FESTIVALS AND SEASONAL EVENTS

■ **Lincoln Center Out-of-Doors** (875-5108), events throughout Lincoln Center and Dam-rosch Park. This is New York at its best. For 3 weeks in August Lincoln Center sponsors a completely free performance arts festival. Among the stupendous dance offerings in 1999 were the Trocadero Ballet, Greek line-dancing instruction, and Peruvian dance.

■ **Dancing in the Park** (219-3910), on Battery Park's Great Lawn, usually late Aug. New York's only free dance festival has drawn thousands of eager fans for the past 18 years to witness some of the best classical, international, and contemporary dance in the city.

■ **Hudson River Festival** (528-2733; www.worldfinancialcenter.com), along the Hudson from Chambers St. to the South Ferry. Sponsored by the World Financial Center, this summer-long free indoor and outdoor performing arts festival hosts some stellar dance performances yearly. In 1999 Elizabeth Streb premiered a work here.

■ **Central Park Summerstage** (360-2777; www.SummerStage.org), at the Rumsey Play-field in Central Park, at 72nd St. All summer long Summerstage hosts spectacular free cultural events; the occasional dance offerings are real gems.

Dances for Wave Hill (718-549-3200), at Wave Hill, W. 249th St. and Independence Ave., Bronx. On Wednesdays and Sundays a group of dancers puts on performances of dances inspired by the Wave Hill landscape. Free with admission to Wave Hill.

Circus Amok (477-5829, ext. 317), in parks throughout Manhattan and the boroughs. In June this wacky circus hauls jugglers, acrobats, and sundry fabulous folk to various parks in New York to put on completely free circus shows. Call for dates and performance times.

THEATERS, VENUES, AND COMPANIES

New York City Ballet (NYCB) (870-5570; www.nycballet.com), at the New York State Theater (NYST), in Lincoln Center. George Balanchine's company celebrated their 50th anniversary in 1999 with special tribute performances and an exhibit at the New York Historical Society. The company's most critically acclaimed works have been the more modern pieces like *Serenade and Apollo,* but they are most famous for that New York December tradition—**The Nutcracker.** Tickets go fast for this classic, so reserve early. Regular season Nov.-Feb. and May-June. Tickets $12-65, standing room $12. Tickets can be purchased at the NY State Theater (see **Lincoln Center,** p. 266).

American Ballet Theater (477-3030, box office 362-6000), at the Metropolitan Opera House, Lincoln Center. Puts on the opulent classics of ballet such as *Swan Lake* and *Sleeping Beauty;* also does some more contemporary works by established modern choreographers like Twyla Tharp. Tickets $15-100. Tickets available at the box office.

Brooklyn Academy of Music (BAM), 30 Lafayette Ave. (718-636-4100), between Felix and Ashland Pl., in Brooklyn. America's oldest performing arts venue still hosts some of the highest quality dancing in New York; high profile companies from around the world have short seasons at BAM. See p. 269.

City Center, W. 55th St. (581-7907). This ornate Moorish theater is the venue for the granddads of modern dances' New York seasons. Among other dance luminaries **Alvin Ailey** (767-0940) brings its extraordinarily popular season here in Dec., as does **Paul Taylor** (431-5562) at the end of Feb. through the first week of Mar. Tickets generally $15-55. Box office open 11am-8pm.

■ **Joyce Theater,** 175 Eighth Ave. (242-0800), between 18th and 19th St. Subway: #1, 9 to 18th St. *The* place to go for modern dance, the Joyce runs energetic, eclectic pro-gramming year-round. If you are in the city for a while it may be worth it to become a member (membership just means you buy a certain number of tickets) to get serious discounts on tickets. Companies like Feld Ballets, Zvi Gotheiner, Jose Limon, and Pilobolus have all been known to stage stints at the Joyce. Tickets generally $20-40.

Danspace, at St. Mark's Church in the Bowery, 131 E. 10th St. (674-8194), at Second Ave. Since the 1920s Danspace has provided a venue for emerging dancers and exper-imental styles of movement: Isadora Duncan has danced in this space. Tickets $10-15.

ARTS & ENTERTAINMENT

Brooklyn Center for Performing Arts (718-951-4500 or 951-4522), 1 block west of the junction of Flatbush and Nostrand Ave. on the campus of Brooklyn College. Subway: #2 or 5 to Flatbush Ave. The Brooklyn Center for Performing Arts at Brooklyn College (BCBC) prides itself on presenting many exclusive events each year. In recent years it has showcased the Russian National Dance Company, André Watts, the kiddie-friendly Famous People Players, and the Garth Fagan Dance Company with Wynton Marsalis. Season Oct.-May. Tickets $20-40.

Dance Theater Workshop, 219 W. 19th St. (924-0077), between Seventh and Eighth Ave., in Chelsea. Subway: #1, 9 to 18th St. Supports emerging dancers and puts up contemporary dance throughout the year. Box office open M-F 10am-6pm. Works in conjunction with the **Cunningham Studio,** 55 Bethune St., at Washington St., to keep modern dance alive.

Young Dancers in Repertory Center for Dance Studies, 231 60th St. (718-567-9620), in Sunset Park, Brooklyn. Subway: N, R to 59th St./Fourth Ave. and then walk 3 blocks west (toward the water). This dance school/performance space often offers free concerts. Call for schedule.

Thalia Spanish Theater, 41-17 Greenpoint Ave. (718-729-3880), between 41st and 42nd St., in Sunnyside, Queens. Subway: #7 to 40th St./Lowery St.; take the local for Friday shows. This Queens theater is dedicated to the arts of Spanish-speaking cultures. Their dance seasons are exquisite and have been showcasing these dance forms long before they became outrageously popular. The fall-winter (mid-Nov. to Feb.) season sees **flamenco** with Andrea del Conte Danza company. In the spring and summer Thalia heats it up with Raoul Jaurena on the *bandoneon* for **Tango Tango.** Throughout the year Thalia also puts on Mexican folklore pieces featuring **folklorico** dance. Shows usually F at 8pm. $18, students $15.

Theater East, 211 E. 60th St. (838-9090), between Second and Third Ave. **Flamenco** shows from Th-Su. Cover $15.

PARTICIPATORY DANCE

🖾 **Midsummer Night Swing,** (875-5766), Lincoln Center Plaza, outdoors. For 10 years some of the best names in jazz, big band, and swing have been coming to play for this exuberant happenin' from late June to late July. Just come with or without a partner to dance the night away and see some great couples swishing around you. If access to the plaza dance floor is sold out, you can strut your stuff (along with other hapless dancing feet) anywhere on the plaza. Tickets go on sale at the plaza at 6pm, but the line often begins at 5pm. Dancing 8:15-11pm; free lessons 6:30pm. $11; 6-night pass $62.

Dancing on the Plaza, the Arsenal (360-3444), Central Park, at Fifth Ave. and E. 64th St. Free ballroom dancing in Aug. on Th 6-8:30pm. The first 30min. are devoted to lessons for the toe-tied.

Dancing Through Sunset Parks (718-567-9620), throughout Brooklyn parks. Run by the Young Dancers in Repertory Center for Dance Studies this annual series offers twice weekly dance classes for kids and teenagers in local parks in the mornings. July-Aug. Call for details.

CLASSICAL MUSIC

Musicians advertise themselves vigorously in New York City, so you should have no trouble finding the notes. Free recitals are common. Just look in *Time Out* and *The Free Time* calendar ($2) for listings of priceless classical events. Remember that many events, such as outdoor music, depend on the season.

Lincoln Center (546-2656; www.lincolncenter.org) remains the great depot of New York's Classical music establishment. Its regular tickets cost a lot, but student and rush rates exist for select performances; some festivals and outdoor events are free. You can buy all Lincoln Center tickets through **CenterCharge** (721-6500; open M-Sa 10am-8pm, Su noon-8pm). **Alice Tully Hall** box office hours are daily 11am to 6pm (opens at noon on Sunday) and 30 minutes after the start of every performance. **Avery Fisher Hall** box office hours are daily 10am to 6pm (opens at noon on Sunday) and 30 minutes after the start of every performance.

Chamber Symphony Orchestra, at Alice Tully Hall (262-6927) in Lincoln Center. Season runs from Nov.-May. Almost all regular tickets $35. Some $25 student discount tickets available.

Concerts in the Park (875-5709; www.newyorkphilharmonic.org), in parks throughout the five boroughs and Long Island. The Philharmonic does us all a service, playing magnificent outdoor concerts in parks during July. Concerts followed by fireworks. Absolutely free.

Great Performers Series, at Alice Tully and Avery Fisher Halls in Lincoln Center (875-5937). Or call Avery Fisher Hall (875-5020; after 3pm 875-5030). From Oct.-May, Great Performers hosts a series of performances by names such as Yo-Yo Ma, Itzhak Perlman, Simon McBurney, Ton Koopman, and James Galway. Watch especially for the New Visions program in Sept. 2000. Tickets run from $35 and up for a series.

Juilliard School of Music, at Lincoln Center (769-7406; www.julliard.edu), is one of the world's leading factories of classical musicians. Juilliard's **Paul Recital Hall** hosts free student recitals almost daily during the school year Sept.-May; Alice Tully Hall holds larger student recitals, also free, most Wednesdays from September to May at 1pm. Orchestral recitals, faculty performances, chamber music, and dance and theater events take place regularly at Juilliard and never cost more than $10—you may see the next generation's Yo-Yo Ma for a third of the cost of seeing this one's. Call for a complete schedule.

Lincoln Center Festival, at Lincoln Center (875-5928). Cutting edge and ethnic events throughout the great Lincoln Center complex in the middle of July. Tickets $20-55. Ask for student discounts at the Avery Fisher Hall box office.

Mostly Mozart, at Alice Tully and Avery Fisher Halls in Lincoln Center (875-5766). In its 34th season in 2000, this summer festival (July-August) festival is a NY staple. Tickets $15-50. A few free events. Ask for student discounts at the Avery Fisher Hall box office.

National Chorale, at Avery Fisher Hall (333-5333), in Lincoln Center. Choral music to make your soul soar. At the end of 1999 the Chorale puts on Handel's *Messiah;* look also for Mozart, Bach, and Schubert requiems in 2000. Tickets from $21.

New York Philharmonic, at Avery Fisher Hall (875-5656; www.newyorkphilharmonic.org), in Lincoln Center. Begins its regular season in mid-September. Tickets range $10-60. On the day of select performances students can get $10 tickets. Come early or call ahead. Box office open M-Sa 10am-6pm, Su noon-6pm, and 30min. after the start of every performance.

MUSIC SCHOOLS

Visiting a music school promises low cost and high quality music—a panacea for a weary budget traveler's soul. Except for opera and ballet productions ($5-12), concerts at the following schools are free and frequent (especially Sept.-May): the **Juilliard School of Music,** Lincoln Center (see above); the **Mannes College of Music,** 150 W. 85th St. (580-0210), between Columbus and Amsterdam Ave.; the **Manhattan School of Music,** 122 Broadway (749-2802); and the **Bloomingdale School of Music,** 323 W. 108th St. (663-6021), near Broadway.

OTHER HALLS AND VENUES

Carnegie Hall (247-7800), Seventh Ave. at 57th St. Subway: N, R to 57th St., or B, D, or E to Seventh Ave. The New York Philharmonic's original home was saved from demolition in the 60s by Isaac Stern and is still the favorite coming-out locale of musical debutantes. Top soloists and chamber groups are booked regularly. Box office open Mon.-Sat. 11am-6pm, Sun. noon-6pm; tickets $10-60. See **Carnegie Hall,** p. 169, for more about the hall.

92nd Street Y, 1395 Lexington Ave. (996-1100). The Upper East Side's cultural mecca. The Y's Kaufmann Concert Hall seats only 916 people and offers an intimate setting unmatched by New York's larger halls, with flawless acoustics and the oaken ambience of a Viennese salon. Once home to the **New York Chamber Symphony** under the fiery direction of Gerard Schwartz, the Y still plays host to a panoply of world-class visiting musicians. A distinguished artists series dating back to the late 1930s has featured all the big names from Segovia and Schnabel to Yo-Yo Ma, Alfred Brendel, and Schlomo Mintz. Other notable series include Jazz in July, Chamber Music at the Y, Lyrics and Lyricists, Keyboard Conversation, and Young Concert Artists. Also hosts an ongoing series of literary readings at the Poetry Center and some of the most engaging lectures in New York. Readings $8-15, lectures $18, concerts $15-40.

Merkin Concert Hall, 129 W. 67th St. (362-8719), between Broadway and Amsterdam Ave. Subway: #1, 9 to 66th St. Quartered in Abraham Goodman House, this division of the Hebrew Arts School offers diverse genres of music. A typical week at the Merkin might include love songs spanning 400 years, classical and modern Chinese music, or a gay chorus. Merkin specializes in traditional Jewish and 20th-century classical music. One of New York's best spaces for chamber music, this intimate theater is known as "the little hall with the big sound." Season Sept.-June. Tickets $8-50.

Symphony Space, 2537 Broadway (864-5400; www.symphonyspace.org) at 95th St. Subway: #1, 9 to 96th St. The misleadingly named Symphony Space hosts more than just one type of cultural event. The performance season (Sept.-June) offers classical and traditional ethnic musical performances, plays, dance, and the "Selected Shorts" program of fiction read by famous actors. Sponsors an ambitious program of old and new foreign films. Open Tu-Sa 1-7pm. Tickets by phone Th-Sa noon-6pm. Most movies $8, other events range from free to $45.

Town Hall, 123 W. 43rd St. (840-2824), between Sixth Ave. and Broadway. Subway: #1, 2, 3, 9, or N, R to 42nd St. This landmark is an elegant pavilion with excellent acoustics. Tenacious trio McKim, Mead, & White designed the place in 1921; it has since hosted a wide variety of cultural events, including lectures by luminaries such as Sandra Bernhard, jazz festivals, and concerts of all kinds. Joan Sutherland made her debut here. The building has a seating capacity of 1495. Box office open M-Sa noon-6pm, open until showtime on day of show.

Museum of Modern Art (708-9491; for more info see **Museums,** p. 235). "Summergarden," an contemporary classical music series, features Juilliard students performing in the museum's Sculpture Garden. July and Aug. F-Sa at 8:30pm. On most weekends in July and Aug., Enter through the (normally locked) back gate at 14 W. 54th St. between 6 and 10pm. Free.

Nicholas Roerich Museum (see **Museums,** p.248)

Frick Collection (see p. 240). From Sept. through May, the Frick Collection hosts free classical music concerts Su 5pm (summer concerts once each in July and Aug.). Tickets limited to 2 per applicant; written requests must be received by the third Monday before the concert, or show up to an hour before the show and try to steal seats of no-shows.

Cooper-Hewitt Museum (see p. 239). Free Cross-currents concert series brings everything from classical to soul to hip-hop in the garden of the Cooper-Hewitt Museum from late June through July Tu 6:30-8pm.

Cathedral of St. John the Divine, 1047 Amsterdam Ave. (662-2133), at 112th St. Subway: #1, 9 to 110th St. An impressive array of classical concerts, art exhibitions, lectures, plays, movies, and dance events (see **Neighborhoods,** p. 192). Prices vary.

St. Paul's Chapel (602-0874 or 602-0747), on Broadway between Church and Fulton St. Subway: A, C to Broadway/Nassau St. Seasonal music concert series at Manhattan's only surviving pre-Revolutionary church includes summer classical festival (Th 1pm) and noon concert series (Sept.-June M and Th) held in conjunction with Trinity Church. Suggested donation $2.

Trinity Church, 74 Trinity Pl. (602-0800), at Wall St. Subway: #4 or 5 to Wall St. With St. Paul's Chapel, Trinity Church presents the Sundays at 4 classical concert series Sept.-June, in addition to other-concerts throughout the year. Tickets $15-20, students and seniors can reserve standard seating for $10. The church also has a summer concert series, which is often free. In 1999, they hosted a 10-week Beethoven Festival every Thursday at 1pm. (See **Neighborhoods,** p. 135.)

World Financial Center (945-0505 or 528-2733, www.worldfinancialcenter.com), Battery Park City. Subway: C or E to World Trade Center. The Hudson River Festival presents free performances daily throughout the summer in the Winter Garden (the Center's main atrium) the Esplanade, and various locations throughout the Center and Battery Park City. The festival features dynamic theatre, dance, art exhibitions, and world music events such as West African Storytelling and Dance, A Midsummer Night's Dream, A Jewish Portraits exhibition, and Latin Big Band. Other free dance and music concerts appear at the nearby World Trade Center. (See **Neighborhoods,** p. 134.)

🎭 **Brooklyn Academy of Music,** 30 Lafayette St. (718-636-4100; www.bam.org), between Felix and Ashland Pl. Subway: #2, 3 or 4, 5 or D, Q to Atlantic Ave.; or B, M or N, R to Pacific St. The oldest performing arts center in the country, the Brooklyn Academy of Music (BAM) has compiled a colorful history of magnificent performances: here Pavlova danced, Caruso sang, and Sarah Bernhardt played Camille. Now, it focuses on new non-traditional, multicultural programs—with the occasional classical music performance. Jazz, blues, performance art, opera, and dance take this stage. Late spring brings Dance Africa, featuring West African dancing as well as crafts. BAM's annual **Next Wave Festival,** Sept.-Dec., features contemporary music, dance, theater, and performance art; it helped start talent like Mark Morris and Laurie Anderson. Call about student rush. The **Brooklyn Philharmonic Orchestra,** which performs here Nov.-Mar. and hosts a brief opera season Feb.-June. Orchestra and opera tickets $30-50. Manhattan Express Bus ("BAM bus") departs round-trip from 120 Park Ave. at 42nd St. for each performance ($5, round-trip $10). **BAM Rose Cinemas** features American and foreign films, retrospectives, documentaries, and special film festivals on its 4 large screens throughout the year. Call 636-4157 for info. ($8.50, children and seniors $5). Accepts V, MC. Wheelchair access. **Brooklyn Center for Performing Arts** (718-951-4500 or 951-4522), 1 block west of the junction of Flatbush and Nostrand Ave. on the campus of Brooklyn College. Subway: #2 or 5 to Flatbush Ave. The Brooklyn Center for Performing Arts at Brooklyn College (BCBC) prides itself on presenting many exclusive events each year. In recent years it has showcased the Russian National Dance Company, André Watts, the kiddie-friendly Famous People Players, and the Garth Fagan Dance Company with Wynton Marsalis. Season Oct.-May. Tickets $20-40.

Colden Center for the Performing Arts, 65-30 Kissena Blvd. (718-793-8080), at Queens College in Flushing, Queens. Subway: #7 to Main St., Flushing, then bus Q17 or Q25-34 to the corner of Kissena Blvd. and the Long Island Expressway. The Colden Center has a beautiful, 2143-seat theater, which hosts an excellent program of jazz, classical, and dance concerts Sept.-May. Special efforts made to feature emerging artists whose works reflect the borough's cultural diversity. Call for schedule and prices. Accepts AmEx, V, MC. Wheelchair access.

Ukrainian Bandura Ensemble of New York, 84-82 164th St. (718-658-7449) in Jamaica, Queens. This ensemble keeps the 62-stringed bandura alive, playing at parades, festivals, and various other events around the city as the occasion arises. Season Sept.-June.

JAZZ

Since its beginnings in the early part of this century, jazz has played a pivotal role in New York's music scene. Uptown at Minton's, Charlie Parker, Dizzy Gillespie, and Thelonious Monk overthrew traditional swing; the Five-Spot in the East Village set the stage for Monk's legendary gig with John Coltrane. From Big Band orchestras and traditional stylists to free, fusion, and avant-garde artists, jazz in all its forms thrives in venues across the city. You can check out one of the many hazy dens that bred lingo like "cat" and "hip" (a "hippie" was originally someone on the fringes of jazz culture who talked the talk but was never really in the know), or more formal shows at Lincoln Center. Summer means open-air (often free) sets in parks and plazas. Throughout the year, many museums offer free jazz in their gardens and cafes. Check the papers to find listings of jazz venues around the city.

JAZZ CLUBS

Expect high covers and drink minimums at the legendary jazz spots. Most of them crowd tables together and charge $6-9 per drink. While hearing the jazz gods costs an arm and a leg, a few bars supply reliable no-names free of charge. And, although some "classier" joints take credit cards, you might want to take cash, just in case.

Apollo Theatre, 253 W. 125th St. (749-5838, box office 864-0372), between Frederick Douglass Blvd. and Adam Clayton Powell Blvd. Subway: #1, 9, 2, 3 to 125th St. This historic Harlem landmark has heard Duke Ellington, Count Basie, Ella Fitzgerald, Lionel Hampton, Billie Holliday, and Sarah Vaughan. A young Malcolm X shined shoes here. The Apollo is now undergoing a resurgence in popularity. Ticket prices vary; order through Ticketmaster (307-7171). A big draw is Wednesday's legendary Amateur Night, where acts are either gonged (ouch!) or rated "regular," "show-off," "top dog," or "super top dog." Tickets $10-18 for Amateur Night.

Birdland, 315 W. 44th St. (581-3080), between Eighth and Ninth Ave. Subway: #1, 2, 3, 9; or N, R to 42nd St.; or A, C, E to Times Square. A dinner club serving decent cajun food and top jazz. It's easy to see the stage in the comfy, neon-accented, nouveau setting, and the music is smoked-out-and-splendid. Blue Note makes recordings here. Appetizers $5-9, entrees $10-16, sandwiches $8-10. Su-W $15 cover, $10 min. food/drink; Th-Sa $15-25 cover, $20-25 min. food/drink. Add $5 for min. at bar. Open daily 5pm-2am. First set nightly at 9pm, 2nd at 11pm. Reservations recommended. Accepts AmEx, Discover, MC, V.

Blue Note, 131 W. 3rd St. (475-8592; www.bluenote.net), near MacDougal St. Subway: A, C, E, F, B, D, Q to Washington Sq. The legendary jazz club is now a commercialized concert space with crowded tables and a tame audience. But the Blue Note still brings in many of today's all-stars, such as Take 6. Cover for big-name performers $20 and way up, $5 food/drink min. Students get half off the cover Su-Th 11:30pm set only. More reasonable Sunday jazz brunch includes food, drinks, and jazz for $18.50 (noon-6pm, shows at 1 and 3:30pm; reservations recommended). Other sets daily 9 and 11:30pm. Accepts AmEx, Diner's Club, JCB, MC, V.

Cotton Club, 656 W. 125th St. (663-7980), on the corner of Riverside Dr. Subway: #1, 9 to 125th St. More tourists than regulars at this jazz hall of the greats. Cover for brunch and Gospel Shows $25; jazz shows $30; no minimum, and may include dinner. Call ahead for reservations and information. Accepts MC, V.

Detour, 349 E. 13th St. (533-6212), between First and Second Ave. Subway: N, R or #4, 5, 6 to Union Sq. Great nightly jazz and no cover—perfect together. One-drink min. Happy hour M-F 4-7pm, drinks are 2-for-1. Spoken word Sunday nights at 8pm. No food, but with a bevy of local restaurants' menus, they encourage you to order take-out. Open daily 3pm-3am. Accepts AmEx, MC, V. Wheelchair accessible.

Fez, 380 Lafayette St. (533-2680), behind Time Café. Subway: #6 to Astor Pl. This lushly appointed, Moroccan-decorated club draws an extremely photogenic crowd, especially on Thursday nights when the Mingus Big Band holds court (sets at 9 and 11pm; reservations suggested). Other nights vary: music ranges from jazz to alt-pop, hip hop, and spoken word. Cover ranges from $8-20; 2-drink minimum. Student and group discounts. Kitchen open 8:30 to around midnight. Accepts MC, V.

■ **Knitting Factory,** 74 Leonard St. (219-3055), between Broadway and Church St. Subway: #1, 9 or 2, 3 or 6 or A, C, E to Canal. Walk up Broadway to Leonard St. Free-thinking musicians anticipate the apocalypse with a wide range of edge-piercing performances complemented by great acoustics. Several shows nightly. Sonic Youth played here every Thursday for years (alas, no more). The Factory also hosts a summertime **jazz festival.** Cover $5-20; entry to the cozy bar up front is always free. Box office open M-F 10am-11pm, Sa-Su 2-11pm. Bar open M-F 4:30pm-2am, Sa-Su 6pm-2am. All ages shows. Free live music every night in tap bar at 11pm.

Lenox Lounge, 288 Lenox Ave. (427-0253), between 124th and 125th St. Subway: #2, 3 to 125th. You'll appreciate the rich ambience and history that make this small club, with its frayed edges, "one of the hidden treasures of Harlem." A legend in the days when Ella graced the stage, this lounge is intimate and intense. Jazz F, Sa, and M nights. M free; 1-drink min. Open daily noon-4am.

■ **Small's,** 183 W. 10th St. (929-7565), at Seventh Ave. Subway: #1, 9 to Christopher St. Yes, it's got some of the best up-and-comers performing night after night with the occasional visit from luminaries. Yes, the fact that it doesn't serve alcohol allows it to stay open all night, often providing a late, late night showcase for musicians who still have chops left over from performances at other clubs. Cover $10. Free non-alcoholic beverages. Open daily 10-8am. Call ahead for info about early bird specials (read: no cover).

Showman's Café, 2321 Frederick Douglass Blvd. (864-8941), between 124th and 125th St. Subway: #1, 9 to 125th St. Largely local crowd flocks to hear excellent jazz at this friendly Harlem joint W-Sa. $10 drink min. Open until 4am.

St. Nick's Pub, 773 St. Nicholas Ave. (283-9728), between 148th and 149th St. Subway: A, B, C, D to 145th St. A small, comfy bar with a dedicated crowd and great jazz. Bar opens at 12:30pm, jazz shows M-Sa 9pm until 3 or 4am, or just "til." Sunday evening soul quartet show 6pm-midnight. Monday nights especially notable: Patience Higgins and the Sugar Hill Jazz Quartet host a laid-back jam session. Cover $3, or 2 people for $5 with 2-drink minimum. If you're lucky enough to visit on the right day (usually Mondays), soul food is free. Cash only.

Swing 46, 349 W. 46th St. (262-9554), between Eighth and Ninth Ave. Subway: C, E to 50th St. Formerly the home of Red Blazer Too, this place has jumped on the big band wagon and delivers all kinds of smooth grooves like Swingtime Mondays, Jump Tuesdays, and Big Band Thursdays. Pink and palmy decor helps get you in the Ipanema mood. Cover Su-W $7, Th-Sa $12 with 2-drink minimum (drinks $10-16). Dinner ($12-22) served daily 5pm-midnight. Swing lessons at 9:15pm, sets begin at 10pm. No smoking in main room. Accepts AmEx, MC, V.

■ **Village Vanguard,** 178 Seventh Ave. (255-4037), between W. 11th St. and Greenwich. Subway: #1, 2, 3, 9 to 14th St. A windowless, wedge-shaped cavern, as old and hip as jazz itself. The walls are 65-years-thick with memories of Lenny Bruce, Leadbelly, Miles Davis, and Sonny Rollins. Every Monday the Vanguard Orchestra unleashes its torrential Big Band sound on sentimental journeymen at 9:30 and 11:30pm. Cover on M-Sa $15 plus $10 min. Sets Su-Th 9:30 and 11:30pm, F-Sa 9:30, 11:30pm, and 1am. Reservations recommended. Cash and traveler's checks only.

Sweet Basil, 88 Seventh Ave. (242-1785), between Bleecker and Grove St. Subway: #1, 9 to Christopher St./Sheridan Sq. Serves mostly traditional jazz with dinner. Lots of tourists, some regulars. Occasional star sets. Cover $17.50 plus $10 min. No cover for jazz brunch (Sa-Su 2-6pm). Shows M-Th 9 and 11pm, Sa-Su 9, 11pm, and 12:30am. Open daily noon-2am. Accepts AmEx, MC, V. Wheelchair accessible.

A PRETTY SWEET FRUIT Many a folklorist has wondered the origin of the "Big Apple" moniker. Some would tell you that a happy marriage between jazz and capitalism produced this popular name for New York. In the 1920s and 30s when jazz musicians bragged about playing New York, they'd say they were playing "the Big Apple," meaning they had reached the height of success. Charles Gillett, the past president of the New York Convention and Visitors Bureau, popularized the name with his Big Apple Campaign in 1971. His P.R. ploy hit onto something inexplicably catchy.

OTHER JAZZ VENUES

Guggenheim Museum (423-3500; see **Museums,** p. 238). Live jazz, Brazilian, and world beat music in its rotunda on Fridays and Saturdays from 5-8pm. Museum admission required, but F 6-8pm pay-what-you-wish.

Museum of Modern Art (708-9480; see **Museums,** p. 235). From September to May MoMA features jazz in its Garden Cafe on Fridays from 5:30 to 7:45pm. Museum admission is required, but Friday 4:30-8:30pm is pay-what-you-wish.

Radio City Music Hall (247-4777; see **Neighborhoods,** p. 173) boasts a bill of great performers that reads like an invitation list to the Music Hall of Fame; Ella Fitzgerald, Frank Sinatra, Ringo Starr, Linda Ronstadt, and Sting, among others, have all performed at the legendary venue. Box office at 50th St. and Sixth Ave. Open M-Sa 10am-8pm, Su 11am-8pm.

◪ **Saint Peter's,** 619 Lexington Ave. (935-2200; see p. 172), at 52nd St. On Sundays, jazz vespers sound at 5pm, usually followed at 7 or 8pm by a full-fledged jazz concert ($5-10 donation for the concert). Informal jazz concerts often held on Wednesday afternoons. On October 10, the annual All Night Soul session rocks from 5pm to 5am. In addition, the hippest ministry in town brings you art openings and exhibits, theater, lectures, and more. Call ahead for a current schedule of St. Peter's offerings. Dale R. Lind, Pastor to the Jazz Community, oversees all tuneful good deeds.

SUMMER JAZZ AND FESTIVALS

The **JVC Jazz Festival** blows into the city in June. All-star performances of past series have included Elvin Jones, Ray Charles, Tito Puente, and Mel Torme. Tickets go on sale in early May, but many events take place outdoors in the parks and are free. **Bryant Park** hosts a large number of these concerts, as does **Damrosch Park** at Lincoln Center. Call 501-1390 in the spring for info, or write to: JVC Jazz Festival New York, P.O. Box 1169, New York, NY 10023. Annual festivals sponsored by major corporations bring in local talent as well as giants on the forefront of innovation. These concerts take place throughout the city (some free) but are centered at TriBeCa's **Knitting Factory.** Call 219-3055 in the spring.

Central Park Summerstage (360-2777; www.centerstage.org), at 72nd St. in Central Park, divides its attention among many performing arts, including jazz, opera, rock, and folk. Call or pick up Central Park's calendar of events, available at the Dairy in Central Park (see **Neighborhoods,** p. 180). The free concerts run mid-June to early August.

The **World Financial Center Plaza** (945-0505) infrequently hosts free concerts between June and September, featuring jazz styles ranging from Little Jimmy Scott to the Kit McClure Big Band, an all-female jazz orchestra. The **World Trade Center** (435-4170), on Church St. at Dey St., hosts free lunchtime jazz concerts in its plaza each Wednesday during July and August. Two performers are featured each week, one performing at noon and the other at 1pm. The **South Street Museum** (732-7678) sponsors a series of outdoor concerts from July to early September at Pier 17, Ambrose Stage, and the Atrium. Head to **Lincoln Center Plaza** and Damrosch Park's **Guggenheim Bandshell** to hear free jazz, salsa, and Big Band delights. **Alice Tully Hall,** also at Lincoln Center, presents a summer jazz series (875-5299). Guest soloist Wynton Marsalis trumpeted the inaugural season.

ROCK, POP, PUNK, FUNK

Combine the grit, heady anonymity, and super self-consciousness of New York with the rhythmic rattle of the subway and you have arrived at the perfect tincture for musical inspiration. Music has serenaded New York City through its modern growing pains: the Velvet Underground crooned to New York as the city flirted with heroin, languor, and insipid conversation, and Public Enemy fought the power that could never extinguish their measured, syncopated rage. Music (along with the self-important distinctions between genre) is what stitches together myriad New York scenes. So check the comprehensive listings in the *Village Voice* or *Time Out: New York* magazine, keep your amp turned on high, and explore the amazing wealth of kickin' options that pulse through New York's veins.

Music festivals are also hot tickets and provide the opportunity to see tons of bands at a (relatively) low price. The **CMJ Music Marathon** (516-498-3150; fax 516-466-7161; www.cmj.com) runs for four nights in the fall and includes over 400 bands and workshops on alternative music culture and college radio production. The **Digital Club Festival** (677-3530), a newly reconfigured indie-fest visits New York in late July. The **Macintosh New York Music Festival** presents over 350 bands over a week-long period. For more electronic experimental sounds, check out Creative Time's **Music in the Anchorage,** a June concert series happening in the massive stone chambers in the base of the Brooklyn Bridge. Call 206-6674, ext. 252 for info, or stop by **Other Music** (see **Record Stores,** p. 300) for tickets and a brochure.

If **arena rock** is more your style, check out **Madison Square Garden** (465-6000), at Seventh Ave. and W. 33rd St., perhaps America's premier entertainment facility. MSG hosts over 600 events and nearly 6,000,000 spectators every year. Apart from rock concerts, regular offerings include exhibitions; trade shows; boxing matches; rodeos; monster trucks; dog, cat, and horse shows; circuses; tennis games; and the odd presidential convention (tickets $20-50). **Radio City Music Hall** (247-4777) and New Jersey's **Meadowlands** (201-935-3900) also stage high-priced performances. From June to early September the **Coca-Cola Concert Series** (516-221-1000) brings rock, jazz, and reggae concerts to **Jones Beach.** Tickets cost $15-40 (see **Long Island,** p. 325).

Beacon Theatre, 2124 Broadway (496-7070), between 74th and 75th St. Subway: #1, 9, 2, 3 to 72nd St. Mid-sized concert hall featuring mid-sized alternative rock names, as well as world-beat concerts and multi media performance events. Call for schedule; there's something almost every weekend. Tickets $25-100.

The Bitter End, 147 Bleecker St. (673-7030), between Thompson St. and LaGuardia St. Subway: A, C, E or B, D, F, Q to W. 4th St.; or #6 to Bleecker St. Small space hosts sweet-sounding folk and country music; they claim artists like Billy Joel, Stevie Wonder, Woody Allen, and Rita Rudner all got their starts here. Look for their likenesses in the gaudy mural behind the bar. Call for show times. Cover $5-10. Open Su-Th 7:30pm-2am, F-Sa 7:30pm-4am.

Bottom Line, 15 W. 4th St. (228-7880 or 228-6300), at Mercer St. Subway: A, C, E, F, or B,D, Q to W. 4th St. A somber, loft-like space where rainbows weave across the walls against a black background. If you can't find a seat, you can sit at the bar (even without ordering a drink) surrounded by old show photos. A mixed bag of music and entertainment—from jazz to kitsch to country to theater to old-time rock-and-roll by over-the-hill singers. Recent shows include Buster Poindexter, the Jazz Mandolin Project, and Joan Baez. Double proof of age (21+) required, or come with a parent or guardian. Some all-ages performances. Cover $15-30. Shows nightly 7:30 and 10:30pm.

CBGB/OMFUG (CBGB's), 315 Bowery (982-4052), at Bleecker St. Subway: #6 to Bleecker St. The initials have stood for "country, bluegrass, blues, and other music for uplifting gourmandizers," since 1973, but this club has always been about punk rock. Generations of New Yorkers have come to CB's to rock out. *Blondie* and the *Talking Heads* got their starts here, and the club continues to be *the* place to see great alternative rock. CB's has adjusted to the post-punk 90s with more diverse offerings, including a website (www.cbgb.com), but the punk spirit lives on in the famously narrow, cavernous interior, the multi-colored layers of graffiti, and the wistful eyes of the clientele. Shows nightly around 8pm. Cover $3-10. Next door's **CB's Gallery** (677-0455) also offers live music.

Continental, 25 Third Ave. (529-6924; www.nytrash.com/continental), between St. Mark's Pl. and Stuyvesant. A dark club that hosts the loud set nightly. Come for noise, rock, and local punk. Iggy Pop, Debbie Harry, and Patti Smith have all played here. Check lamp posts and fliers for shows and times. Happy hour daily half-price drinks. Shot of anything $2 with a beer; 5 shots of anything $10. Cover generally $3-6.

■ **The Cooler,** 416 W. 14th St. (229-0785), at Greenwich St. Subway: #1, 2, 3 or A, C, E to 14th St. In the heart of the meat-packing district. The Cooler showcases non-mainstream alternative, dub, electronica, and illbient by some of the town's smartest DJs in a huge vault of a room. Meat hooks and scales on gory display. Cover varies. Free Mondays. Doors open Su-Th 8pm, F-Sa 9pm.

Irving Plaza, 17 Irving Pl. (777-6800 or 777-1224 for concert info), at 15th St., between Third Ave. and Union Sq. Subway: #4, 5, 6 or L or N, R to 14th St./Union Sq. A midsized club decorated in a puzzling chinoiserie style. Features rock, comedy, performance art, and other entertainment in its enormous space. Must purchase tickets in advance for the bigger shows. Cover varies. Doors generally open at 8pm. Box office open M-F noon-6:30pm.

Knitting Factory, 74 Leonard St. (219-3055), between Broadway and Church St. Subway: #1, 2, 3, 6, 9, A, C, or E to Canal. Walk up Broadway to Leonard St. Free-thinking musicians anticipate the apocalypse with a wide range of edge-piercing performances complemented by great acoustics. Several shows nightly. Sonic Youth played here every Thursday for years (alas, no more). The Factory hosts summertimes' **What is Jazz** festival, an open-ended exploration of the musical form. Cover, usually $10, shows $20-30 for entrance to the back room/performance space only; entry to the cozy bar up front is always free. Box office open M-F 10am-11pm, Sa-Su 2-11pm. Bar open M-F 4:30pm-2am, Sa-Su 6pm-2am.

Maxwell's, 1039 Washington St. (201-798-0406), at 11th St. in Hoboken, NJ. Subway: B, D, F, Q, or N, R to 34th St., then PATH train ($1) to Hudson Pl. the first stop in Hoboken. Once there, walk along Hudson Pl. to Hudson St., up 1 block to Newark St., left 2 blocks to Washington St., and right 10 blocks to 11th St. Strong underground acts have plied their trade in the back room of this Hoboken restaurant for about 15 years (see **Hoboken,** p. 229). New Order played its first U.S. show here. Recent visitors include Superchunk, Stereolab, and Domestic Room. Hosts open-mic poetry readings and an occasional free concert. Cover $5-15. Shows occasionally sell out, so get tix in advance from Maxwell's or TicketMaster. Open Tu-Su 5pm-whenever.

Mercury Lounge, 217 E. Houston St. (260-4700), at Ave. A (between Essex and Ludlow St.). Subway: F to Second Ave./E. Houston St. Once a gravestone parlor, the Mercury has attracted an amazing number of big-name acts to its fairly small-time room, running the gamut from folk to pop to noise. Past standouts have included spoken-word artist Maggie Estep, Morphine, and 10,000 Maniacs. Music nightly. Box office open M-F 11-7, Sa 12-7. Cover varies.

■ **Roseland,** 239 W. 52nd St. (245-5761), at Eighth Ave. and Broadway. Subway: C, E to 50th St. Decently priced concert club featuring major-label alt-rock, with forays into large rave events and Mötley Crüe-type territory. Tickets $15-25

■ **Sounds of Brazil (SOB's),** 204 Varick St. (243-4940), at Houston St. (See p. 286.)

Wetlands Preserve, 161 Hudson St. (386-3600), near Laight St. in TriBeCa. Subway: #1, 9 or A, C, E to Canal St. A giant Summer of Love mural in the back room sets the tone, a Volkswagen bus curio shop swims in tie-dyes, and mood memorabilia harkens back to Woodstock in this 2-story whole-earth spectacular. An often-changing weekly program has included Deadcenter, a weekly Grateful Dead tribute; Breaking Point with hip-hop, drum 'n' bass, and electro; and rock-underground-alternative-whatever. Cover $7-10. Shows usually kick off at 9 or 10pm.

RADIO

In New York City, the radio spectrum serves up everything from soulless elevator instrumentals (WLTW 106.7 FM) to pirate radio broadcasts of underground sounds and community activism. As with most American radio, the lower on the dial, the less-commercial (and more innovative) the sounds will be. WFMU 91.1, for example, is a college radio station without a college—Upsala College collapsed in 1994 and the acclaimed high-quality eclecticism of FMU enabled it to continue as the college's only surviving department. FMU broadcasts genre-defying free-form music to devoted listeners and is strongest in obscure guitar-based music from the 1920s to the present day. Another college radio gem is Columbia's WKCR 89.9 FM—playing everything but rock. KCR's "Out to Lunch" weekdays from noon to 3pm airs a spectrum of jazz and is knowledgeable about the current scene. For independent hip-hop and underground rap, check out Stretch and Bobbito's show on KCR (Th 1-5am). WQHT 97.1 FM sends out more commercial styles, beginning each weekday with Dr. Dre and Ed Lover's morning show of phat beats, dope rhymes, and fast-paced talk. In the evenings QHT brings in DJs to cut, scratch, and mix on the last major label wax.

The following stations are FM unless otherwise noted:

Classical: WNYC 93.9, WQXR 96.3

Jazz: WBGO 88.3, WCWP 88.1, WQCD 101.9

College/Indie/Alternative/Popular: WNYU 89.1, WKCR 89.9, WSOU 89.5, WFMU 91.1, WDRE 92.7, WHTZ 100.3, WAXQ 104.3, WXRK 92.3 102.7,

Classic Rock: WQXR 104.3, WNEW 102.7

Top 40: WPSC 88.7, WRKS 98.7, WPLJ 95.5, WRCN 103.9, WMXV 105.1

Hip-Hop/R&B/Soul: WQHT 97.1, WBLS 107.5, WWRL 1600AM

Oldies: WRTN 93.5, WCBS 101.1

Foreign-Language Programming: WADO 1280AM, WWRV 1330AM, WKDM 1380AM, WZRC 1480AM, WNWK 105.9

News: WABC 770AM, WCBS 880AM, WINS 1010AM, WBBR 1130AM

Public Radio: WNYC 93.9, WNYC 820AM, WBAI 99.5

Sports: WFAN 660AM

Pirate: 103.9 (Sunday in Williamsburg), 88.7 Steal This Radio (Lower East Side)

NIGHTLIFE

A city like this one makes me dream tall and feel in on things.
—Toni Morrison, *Jazz*

When that insomniac empress, Gotham, loosens her corset, takes down her hair, and retires her bustle, so should you. See performance art; witness avant-garde comedy; hear live hip-hop; sip a highball; work it at a drag show; and absolutely learn to salsa. Do whatever, so long as you keep up with your hungry hostess, the city herself. In New York's night kitchen, you could easily cook up a different feast for the senses every evening of your life and never repeat. Whether you prefer Times Square's blinding lights or a Harlem jazz club, a smoky Borough bar or a Lower East Side be-seen-ery, allow yourself to succumb to the city's dark side. At the end of it all, a 4:30am cab ride home through empty streets with the windows down will inevitably make your spirits soar. A number of publications print daily, weekly, and monthly nightlife calendars; try *Time Out: New York*, the *Village Voice*, *New York* magazine, *The New York Free Press*, and *The New York Times* (particularly the Sunday edition). The monthly *Free Time* calendar ($1.25) lists free cultural events throughout Manhattan. You can also tap endlessly knowledgeable salespeople at record stores (see p. 300) for cultural information about music scenes in New York; if *Let's Go* doesn't list it, ask them to help you find that one club that spins "Cubo-funk-trip-indie-ambient" on a Tuesday evening. For gay and lesbian nightlife options see **The Queer Apple**, p. 309.

BARS

Since one of New York City's most attractive features is its "never sleeps" quality, do take advantage of its chic and/or charmingly divey bars' late hours. Every major street has a couple of dark holes where the locals burrow on weeknights. Most keep prices tied down and music pumped up. The following listings focus on conversing and imbibing. Of course, *Let's Go* researchers are not allowed to drink while on duty, lest ramble they be gin to ?drinking much merry, vodka be good.

SOHO AND TRIBECA

Naked Lunch Bar and Lounge, 17 Thompson St. (343-0828), at Grand St. Adorned with the roach-and-typewriter motif found in the novel and movie of the same name. The after-work crowd has no qualms about dancing in the aisle alongside the bar. If you join in, no one will judge you. Unbeatable martinis like the Tanqueray tea ($7). Live Latin jazz Wednesday. All beers $5. Sometimes a small cover. Prices drop for happy hour Tu-F 5-8pm. Open Tu-F 5pm-4am, Sa 8pm-4am.

Double Happiness, 173 Mott St. (941-1282), between Broome and Grand St. Recently opened by the owners of the toxically hip Orchard Bar, this downstairs spot takes advantage of a dual downtown fetish—all things Asian and minimalist. Abacuses adorn the walls and an appropriately chinoiserie-meets-Calvin-Klein-meets-Nike crowd decorates the dance floor. Happy hour Su-Th 6-7:30pm. Open Su-Th 6pm-3am, F-Sa 6pm-4am.

Milady's, 160 Prince St. (226-9069), at Thompson. A rough in the overbearing diamond mine that is SoHo. Down-to-earth neighborhood haunt that claims the only pool table in SoHo (not exactly accurate) and a cast of affable regulars. Milady's is a fun joint to shuck off local pretense and have a good time. Everything (even martinis) under $6. If you're lucky, the bartender will pick up the fourth drink. Good, inexpensive food also served. Open daily 1pm-4am.

OCR SOHO AND TRIBECA ■ 277

NV and 289 Lounge, 289 Spring St. (929-6868), near Varick St. Gothic playground meets post-industrialism results in a web of ceiling pipes over the curtain-laden, sconce-enhanced chambers. Deep blues, pinks, golds, and greens set the mood in two bars and dance floors. As long as the club is up 'n' coming, you can enter the iron gates without too much bouncer inspection. Mixed drinks are club priced ($7-8) and the cover ($10-20) could be much more substantial for a night of pure fun. You will find each of the following in decreasing proportion: themed nights, DJs, and celebs. Open W-Su 10pm-4am, happy hour W-Th 6-10pm.

Lucky Strike, 59 Grand St. (941-0772), at W. Broadway. The people here are beautiful, but don't let that stop you. The enlivened crowd is too secure to be exclusive or pretentious, so all are welcome. Lovely food and divine drinks ($4-8). The vanilla shanti ($7.50) tastes like a carnival in a martini glass. Open Su-W noon-3am, Th-Sa noon-4am.

MercBar, 151 Mercer St. (966-2727), between Prince and Houston St. A fine standby with a good crowd of nice lookers. Although many stop here on their way to other, trendier spots, a few more intelligent bar-goers rest on the cozy couches for the night. The spotlights allow you to see the warm, hunting lodge decor—canoe and all. Beers on tap ($5), mixed drinks ($6-7). Open M-Sa 5pm-4am, Su 6pm-4am.

Red Bench Bar, 107 Sullivan St. (274-9120), between Prince and Spring St. The small, dark interior of the Red Bench oozes a retro sensibility of intimacy, chandeliers, and mirrored bars. The local crowd seems justifiably protective of this neighborhood secret. Drink prices hover between $5-7. Open daily 5pm-4am.

Match, 160 Mercer St. (343-0220), between Prince and Houston St. Chic bar/restaurant with famed pick up scene. Drinks are expensive, as is the food, but for half-price sushi available daily 5-7pm. Open Su-W 11:30am-2am, Th-Sa 11:30am-4am.

Circa Tabac, 32 Watt St. (941-1781), between Sixth Ave. and Thompson. Claims to be the first and perhaps only cigarette lounge in the world. As the war against smoking has become entrenched even in downtown New York, Circa Tabac renews that nasty little habit's illicit class. Enhancing its atmosphere of taboo, Tabac's decor recalls a Prohibition-era speakeasy, with protective curtains and Art Deco pieces. State-of-the-art air purifiers and odor killers keep the air clear and sweet-smelling. 160 different kinds of nicotine candy sticks ($5-12). Beers $5; "champagne cocktails" $6-12. Open Su-W 5pm-2am, Th-Sa 5pm-4am.

X-R Bar, 128 Houston St. (674-4080), at Sullivan St. Comfortable joint sports couches and glowing marble behind a bar pumping true blues. Su-W quality live music focusing on acoustic sound with a gospel/bluesey lining; Th-Sa DJ. Beers $4; drinks $4-6. Open daily 3pm-4am.

Cafe Noir, 32 Grand St. (431-7910). Cool in so many ways—the patrons, the bartenders, and the large street-front windows (open in summer), all provide the Noir with a classy but unpretentious feel. Draft beers $4-5. Open daily 11am-4am.

The Ear Inn, 326 Spring St. (226-9060), near the Hudson River. Built in 1817 as the home for an aide of George Washington (who lived down the street), this spot has a humorous history. After Prohibition, the bar had no name and was known as "the green door." When they decided to give the space a name in the 1970s, instead of fighting with the landmark commission for a new sign, the owners decided to paint over part of the neon "Bar" sign and rename it "Ear." Appetizers and salads $3-7, dinner $6-10, specials and entrees $5-9. Pint of domestic beer $4-4.75; bottled beers cheaper. Food served daily noon-4:30pm and M-W 6pm-2am, Th-Sa 6pm-3am, Su 6pm-1am. Bar open until 4am. Happy hour M-F 4:30-7pm.

Fanelli's, 94 Prince St. (226-9412), at Mercer St. Established in 1872 in a beautiful building of black cast iron. A casual neighborhood hangout, where it always feels like it's late. Standard bar fare, cheap brew ($3.50 for domestic drafts, $4 for imports and microbrews), and a quick-witted waitstaff. Pick up a complimentary copy of their official history by the door. Open M-Th 10am-2am, F-Sa 10am-3am, Su 11am-2am.

GREENWICH VILLAGE

Bar d'O, 29 Bedford St. (627-1580). Sultry lounge with drag performances (see **Gay and Lesbian Life,** p. 310).

Bar 6, 502 Sixth Ave. (691-1363), between 12th and 13th St. Subway: #1, 2, 3 to 14th St.; or A, E or B, D to Sixth Ave./8th St. French-Moroccan bistro by day, sizzling bar by night. Live DJ spins (primarily house) every night but Monday. Beers on tap ($4-5 per pint) usually from local Brooklyn Brewery. Kitchen open weekdays noon-2am, weekends noon-3am; bar stays open later.

The Village Idiot, 355 W. 14th St. (989-7334), between Eighth and Ninth Ave. No Dostoevksy here. New York's infamous honky-tonk bar has reopened in the Village, and the beer is still cheap ($1.25 mugs of Miller Genuine Draft), the music still loud (and still country, by God), and the ambience still as close to a roadhouse as this city gets. If watching the customers' drunken antics isn't interesting enough, you can purchase a goldfish from the tank and feed it to one of the snapping turtles. Open daily noon-4am.

Automatic Slims, 733 Washington St. (645-8660), at Bank St. Simple bar with an excellent selection of blues and soul. Decorated with pictures of the Velvet Underground. 20-somethings sit at tables with classic vinyls under glass. Weekends pack a more diverse crowd. American cooking served 6pm-midnight. Entrees $7-18. Open Tu-Sa 6pm-4am.

The Whitehorse Tavern, 567 Hudson St. (243-9260), at W. 11th St. Dylan Thomas drank himself to death here, pouring 18 straight whiskies through an already tattered liver. Boisterous students and locals pay homage to the poet. Great jukebox. Outdoor patio. Beer $3-5. Open Su-Th 11am-2am, F-Sa 11am-4am.

Julius, 159 W. 10th St. (929-9672), at Waverly Pl., between Sixth and Seventh Ave. A hot spot for gay men since 1966, after a protest against laws denying service to homosexuals (see **Gay and Lesbian Life,** p. 309). Things have quieted down since then; Julius is now a low-key, friendly neighborhood gay bar. M-Th 8pm-2am, F-Sa 8pm-4am.

The Slaughtered Lamb Pub, 182 W. 4th St. (627-5262), at Jones St. A somewhat sinister-looking, if tacky, English pub dedicated to the werewolf, from medieval lore to Michael Jackson's *Thriller*. More than 150 types of beer ($5-25 per bottle), yards of ale, and darts and billiards downstairs in the "dungeon." Skeleton at the front door. Open Su-W noon-3am, Th-Sa noon-4am.

Rose's Turn, 55 Grove St (366-5438). Mixed piano bar with open mic and perhaps the most musically talented barstaff in New York. Full F-Sa; Sunday provides a small-to-medium crowd for a pleasant balance of liveliness and intimacy. Come F-Su to hear singer Terri White (who also tends bar)—her voice is one of the city's undiscovered wonders. Beer $4.50-5.50. Drinks $5-6. Open daily 4pm-4am.

Nell's, 246 W. 14th St. (675-1567), between Seventh and Eighth Ave. Declining legendary hot spot; the faithful hang on for mellow schmoozing and soulful music upstairs and phat beats below. Racially diverse crowd. Cover Su-W $10, Th-Sa $15. Open M 7pm-1am, W 9pm-3am, other nights 10pm-4am. Free comedy Monday nights. No sneakers or jeans.

EAST VILLAGE AND LOWER EAST SIDE

Subway: *For Lower East Side, take F to Delancey St. or Second Ave., or J, M, or Z to Essex St; for East Village, take the #6 to Astor Pl.*

Baby Jupiter, 170 Orchard St. (982-2229). Everything you could want in a single locale—including a light-up American flag and a metal shark. Delicious food with a Southern flair, like the blackened catfish ($13). Entrees $12+. Bar hosts music, comedy, and performance art. Comfy couches in the back room let you curl up as you digest. Occasional $5 cover. Open Su-Th 11am-midnight, F-Sa 11am-1am; shows start at 8pm.

The Bank, 225 E. Houston St. (505-5033), at Essex St. A stately bank converted into a gritty club, with a heavy Goth-boy and chain concentration. Clear sight-lines make it great for live music; underground vault a great spot for the wee hours. Cover usually $8-12. Call for schedule.

Bbar (Bowery Bar), 40 E. 4th St. (475-2220), at the Bowery. Bbar has long held court on Bowery as a flagship of cooler-than-thou-ness. While other outposts may have trumped its cachet, this bar—with its pleasant outdoor lounge (complete with pool table) and dining area—has still got enough attitude to give you a healthy sense of self-worth for going there. Tuesday night is "Beige," promoter Erich Conrad's wonderfully flamboyant gay party. Open Su-Th 11:30am-3am, F-Sa 11:30am-4am.

Beauty Bar, 231 E. 14 St. (539-1389), between Second and Third Ave. This bar used to be a hair parlor—and they haven't touched a thing. People leave the primping for bathroom mirrors and settle here to quaff $3.50-4.50 beers and take in the funky decor. Crowded with East Village natives any night of the week. Open Su-Th 5pm-4am, F-Sa 7pm-4am.

bOb Bar, 235 Eldridge St. (777-0588), between Houston and Stanton St. Comfy and laid-back, with a hip-hop-inclined crowd and DJs that spin anything they can get their hands on. Happy hour Friday 7-10pm for $2 beers. Open daily 7pm-4am.

Bowery Ballroom, 6 Delancey St. (533-2111), between Bowery and Christy St. Rockin' music club with indie friendly roots and sentiment. Box office open M-F 11am-7pm, Sa-Su noon-7pm. Cover $10-20. Usually 18+. Open 7pm-4am.

Brownie's, 169 Ave. A (420-8392). Small club is the indie mecca of Manhattan. Come to commune with your favorite effete pop stars and the bespectacled geek-chic-ers who love them. Bands M-Th 8-11pm, cover $6; F-Su 8pm-1am, cover $7. DJs after band until closing around 4am.

Chez Es Saada, 42 E. 1st St. (777-5617), between Fist and Second Ave. With fountains in the walls and rose petals strewn on the floor, the basement caverns in this Moroccan restaurant are the perfect place to sample the huge list of cocktails. The drinks are expensive ($9-12!) and the food is forgettable, but you'll be hard-pressed to find a more luxurious spot. Open Su-Th 6pm-2am, F-Sa 6pm-3am.

d.b.a., 41 First Ave. (475-5097), between 2nd and 3rd St. It could mean "drink better ale" or "don't bother asking," depending on whom you consult. With 19 premium beers on tap, well over 100 bottled imports and microbrews, and 45 different tequilas, this extremely friendly, out-of-the-way bar lives up to its motto—"drink good stuff." Beers debut here, and tastings are held monthly. Older crowd. Outdoor beer-garden open until 10pm. Open daily 1pm-4am.

Doc Holliday's, 141 Ave. A (979-0312), at 9th St. Before you go to Doc Holliday's, you should know what not to expect: first, a velvet rope with a supercilious bouncer; second, a cosmopolitan-drinking crowd; and, third, any hope of hearing yourself think. What you can expect is a raucous clientele, cheap beer ($1.75 cans of Pabst Blue Ribbon), lots of cowboy boots affixed to the walls and ceiling and country music blaring from the jukebox. Great promo nights including Monday when ladies drink free Bud Light and Busch until 11pm, Tuesday "Beer Bust" $5 all you can drink Bud Light and Busch, Sunday $2 Rolling Rock. Daily happy hour 5-8pm (Tu 2-8pm) 2 for 1 drinks. Open daily noon-4am.

Drinkland, 339 E. 10th St. (228-2435), between Ave. A and B. A young, downtown crowd soaks in the Jetsons-meets-trip-hop decor. Beers $4. Mixed drinks $4-8. DJs spin everything from breakbeat to classic funk. Open daily 6pm-4am.

Global 33, 93 Second Ave. (477-8427), between 5th and 6th St. Bar with a James Bond feel; sleek decor, replete with retro globes and airplanes in flight render Global 33 the hub of the Second Ave. set. Great cocktails like the "sidecar" (brandy, lemon juice, triple sec in a sugar-coated glass) warrant the $6.50 tag because they're served in a large shaker. Martini $7.50. Sake $6-11. Ample sized tapas $3.50-11. DJ nightly. Kitchen open Su-Th 6pm-midnight, F-Sa 6pm-2am. Bar open daily 6pm-4am.

NIGHTLIFE

Holiday Lounge, 75 St. Mark's Pl. (777-9637), between First and Second Ave. East Village staple with beautiful horseshoe bar, lively crowd, and a great room in the back with diner-like booths. Strong mixed drinks ($2.50) keep local art-school graduates from giving up. Open daily 5pm-1am.

Idlewild, 145 Houston St. (477-5005), between Eldridge and Forsythe St. This recently opened Lower East Side spot takes JFK airport's former name and runs with it, lifting the theme bar to new heights (get it?) with a fuselage-shaped interior, reclining airplane seats with tray tables, and a boarding ramp. Beer $4-5. Drinks $7-10. Open Su-W 8pm-3am, Th-Sa 8pm-4am.

The International Bar, 120½ First Ave. (777-9244), between 7th St. and 8th St. Mark's Pl. Grimy and authentic East Village. This long and skinny bar has only 2 tables in the back, but the large, friendly counter seats many. Christmas lights and yellow sponge-painted walls give this bar a fiery glow. With domestic beers priced at $2.75, it's the "most reasonably priced bar on the Ave.," and a good scene at night. Clientele includes immigrants, lost youths, and college kids. Open M-Th noon-4am, F-Su 2pm-4am.

Joe's Bar, 520 E. 6th St. (473-9093), between Ave. A and B. Young and eclectic neighborhood crowd makes up most of the regulars. Very laid-back and unpretentious. Great jukebox. Pilsner, Bass, and Fosters on tap. Beers $2-3 a mug. Serious pool on Monday nights. Open daily noon-4am.

KGB, 85 E. 4th St. (505-3360), at Second Ave. Formerly a meeting place for the Ukrainian Communist Party, this dark red hangout for literati and Slavophiles retains its original furnishings, including the Lenin propaganda banner and candle-illuminated photos of factories. Occasional readings. Over 20 different kinds of Stoli ($3 per shot). Open daily 7:30pm-4am.

Korova Milk Bar, 200 Ave. A (254-8838), between 12th and 13th St. A tribute to the recently deceased Kubrick's twisted vision, this mockup of little Alex's "moloko plus" bar in *A Clockwork Orange* is replete with sultry mannequins, luscious couches, and psychedelic adverts. Live DJs and trippy decor warrant $3.50-4.50 beers and $5 mixed drinks. Tuesday Gothic; every other Friday Britpop; Saturday Old Skool Disco, after midnight, $2 cover. Open daily 5pm-4am.

La Linea, 15 First Ave. (777-1571), between 1st and 2nd St. A long narrow bar with three different environments. The first room opens onto the street and is a friendly, lantern-laden bar room. The middle room is a comfortable lounge area, and the back room is a blue grotto that has the decided feel of an adolescent "make-out lounge" of truth-or-dare infamy (without the adolescents). Great place for a chill drink. Beer $4. Happy hour (daily 3-9pm) $1 off. Mondays $3 margaritas after 9pm. Open daily 3pm-4am.

The Living Room, 84 Stanton St. (533-7237), at the corner of Allen. Low-key and laid back, like your own living room—though *you* may not have live music nightly at 8pm. All types of live music from jazz and ethnic tunes. A decent selection of food (burgers $7.50; burritos $8.50) and a fine brunch (Sa-Su 11am-4pm). Bar serves wine and beer only. Daytime restaurant open M-F 10am-6pm.

Lucky Cheng's, 24 First Ave. (473-0516), between 1st and 2nd St. One of New York's better-known drag clubs, this one throws in an Asian twist. Upstairs restaurant and downstairs bar serviced by gorgeous "girls." Friday night "trans-fem-ation" party: "girls" $10, boys $15. Bar Open Su-Th 6pm-midnight, F-Sa 6pm-3am.

Mars Bar, 25 1st St. (473-9842), on Second Ave. A proud dive with bright, gritty decor. Working class peeps, musicians, and transient folk mix with the occasional hipster local or the still-less-frequent tourist. Great jukebox with hard stuff, indie, and blues. Cheap drinks: bottled beer, $2.50-3; mixed drinks, max. $3.50. Open daily noon-4am.

Max Fish, 178 Ludlow St. (529-3959), at Houston St. Aggressively hip bar draws big crowds of cool people on Thursday to Saturday, and small crowds of cool people on other days. Decidedly avant and colorful decor: found objects, original cartoons, and the like. Easily the best jukebox in town, playing everything from the Fugees to the Stooges. Beer $2.75. Open daily 5:30pm-4am.

McSorley's Old Ale House, 15 E. 7th St. (473-9148), at Third Ave. Their motto is, "We were here before you were born," and unless you're 147 years old, they're right. Since its 1854 opening, McSorley's has played host to such luminaries as Abe Lincoln, the Roosevelts (Teddy and Frankie), and John Kennedy; women were not allowed in until 1970. Nowadays the crowd is decidedly more collegiate, especially on Friday and Saturday, but the sense of history pervades. Only 2 beers: light and dark. Two-fisters take note: mugs come 2 at a time ($3 for 2). Open M-Sa 11am-1am, Su 1pm-1am.

M&R Bar, 264 Elizabeth St. (226-0559), between Houston and Prince St. This NoLIta haunt works the comfortable-neighborhood-bar-with-just-a-little-bit-of-attitude angle. Sandwiches $9-12, appetizers $6. Open S-Th 5pm-midnight, F-Sa 5pm-4am.

Orchard St. Bar, 200 Orchard St. (673-5350), between Houston and Stanton St. A long, narrow, haunt lined with softly glowing sconces, stone seats and the hip faces of the Lower East Side scene. The lack of a sign out front should clue you in to the fact that you needn't mention that you read about the place in a travel guide. DJ after 10 on some weekend nights. Beer $4-5. Other drinks $5-6. Open daily 6pm-4am.

Sake Bar Decibel, 240 E. 9th St. (979-2733), off Second Ave. All things Japanese have become seriously fashionable in the East Village, and *sake* (Japanese rice wine) is no exception. Gorgeous downstairs bar made from hewn logs stands beside a narrow passageway strewn with pebbles. Other room has intimate, wooden booths. Very hip and very Japanese clientele. Over 60 kinds of *sake* $4-6 per glass. Snacks such as marinated seaweed $3; *shio kara* (sauce pickled squid) $3. Open M-Sa 8pm-3am, Su 8pm-1am.

Sofie's, 507 E. 5th St. (228-5680), between Ave. A and Ave. B. Stools, tables, TV, jukebox, and East Villagers drowning out their roommate difficulties. Sofie's is a classic in that anonymous, cheap-drinks way that its student clientele savors. Open daily noon-4am.

Tenth Street Lounge, 212 E. 10th St. (473-5252), between First and Second Ave. A SoHo-esque bar east of Fifth Ave. Mahogany bar and fresh-squeezed juices almost merit the $4-5 cost of beer at this chic village hangout. A very expensive-looking club, with a clientele to match. Gorgeous place for an early-evening drink—the front bar is open to the street until 9pm. Occasional $10 cover F-Sa evenings; no cover in summer. Call ahead to be put on the guest list. Open M-Sa 5pm-3am, Su 3pm-2am.

Tribe, 132 First Ave. (979-8965), at St. Mark's Pl. Behind the frosted glass windows lies a chic, friendly bar with colorful ambient back lighting. DJ nightly: Tuesday salsa/Latin, Thursday-Friday Old Skool 1970s and 1980s, Monday live music with DJ. Beer $5; cocktails $5-10. Open daily 5pm-4am.

MIDTOWN AND CHELSEA

Hungry pool sharks should check out the cavernous **Billiard Club,** 220 W. 19th St. (206-7665; pool alone $7-12 per hr.).

Coffee Shop Bar, 29 Union Sq. West (243-7969), facing Union Sq. Park. A chic diner for fashion victims, owned by 3 Brazilian models whose gorgeous friends serve updated cuisine from the homeland. Sure, it's a bar and restaurant, but more importantly, it's a spectacle. Waifs abound, but Twiggy figures aren't a likely result of the delicious food like tasty *media noche* sandwich ($9). Good for dessert ($5-6), a very late dinner ($8-17), or to watch others have dinner. Beers $4-6. Open daily 6am-5am. AmEx, V, MC.

Heartland Brewery, 35 Union West (645-3400), at 17th St. Packed, loud, and friendly brew pub with a "down home" American menu that contrasts with the after-work corporate crowd. Daytime family feel gives way to swinging singles scene at night. Beers on tap $5. "Aunt Bee's" chocolate mud cake with lightly whipped cream $5. Open M-Th noon-11pm, F-Sa noon-midnight, Su noon-10pm; bar closes 2 hours later. Accepts AmEx, V, MC, Transmedia. Other location: 1285 Ave. of the Americas (6th Ave.) at 51st St. (582-8244).

Old Town Bar and Grill, 45 E. 18th St. (529-6732), between Park Ave. and Broadway. A quiet 104-year-old hideaway with wood, brass, and a mature clientele to match. Seen on the old "Late Night with David Letterman" opening montage. The consensus among many New Yorkers is that these are the best burgers in the city. Beware of perpetual after-work and weekend mobs. Beer on tap $4, Heineken $3.75, domestics $3. Open M-Sa 11:30am-1am, Su 3pm-midnight. Accepts AmEx, V, MC.

Live Bait, 14 E. 23rd St. (353-2492), between Madison and Broadway. Subway: #6 or N, R to 23rd St. Run by the same folks as the Coffee Shop Bar and **Luna** (475-8464), the Union Sq. Park restaurant open only in the summer. Live Bait reels in an eclectic and raucous crowd of locals, tourists, and business people to frolic amidst the self-consciously tacky decor. Relatively good Cajun menu, including beer-steamed shrimp ($9) and fried calamari with marinara ($8). Live music occasionally in the fall; call for info. Open M-W 11am-11pm, Th-F 11am-midnight, Sa-Su noon-midnight (closed on Sundays in the summer). Accepts AmEx, Diner's Club, MC, Transmedia, V.

O'Flaherty's, 334 W. 46th St. (246-8928), between Eighth and Ninth Ave. Subway: A, C, E to 50th St. Although located on ritzy Restaurant Row, this small bar manages to keep the feel of a true neighborhood pub. Summer parties in garden, a coffee gallery, and actors' night on Wednesday. Great selection of beers on tap, including Murphy's ($4 per pint). Live music every night at 10:30pm ranges from rock-and-roll to blues unplugged to bluegrass.

Peter McManus, 152 Seventh Ave. (929-9691 or 463-7620), at 19th St. Made famous by a *New York Times* article on the timeless appeal of ordinary bars, of which this is the epitome. Ordinary drinks, ordinary clientele, ordinary prices, and ordinary bathrooms. The carved mahogany bar and leaded glass windows add to the charm. A smattering of video games and a jukebox. $2-4.50 drafts. Open daily 10:30am-4am.

UPPER WEST SIDE
AND MORNINGSIDE HEIGHTS

The Evelyn Lounge, 380 Columbus Ave. (724-0276), on the corner of 78th St. Swanky, multi-decor bar for the after-work set. Great live music Tu-Th. Drinks are a bit pricey but cover the cost of comfy couches colonized by cultured cliques. Open daily 6pm-4am.

Hi-Life Bar and Grill, 477 Amsterdam Ave. (787-7199), at 83rd St. Step into the 1930s at this sleek retro hangout. Often crowded. Friendly waitstaff and a late-night menu are a big draw. Sushi and raw bar half-price M and Tu, DJ on Th-Sa. Open M-F 4:30pm-late, Sa-Su 10:30am-4pm for brunch and 4:30pm-late.

Merchants, 521 Columbus Ave. (721-3689), between 85th and 86th. Intimate tables by the fireplace in winter and a happening sidewalk scene in the summer makes Merchants perennially popular. Swank singles scene. Drafts $5; cocktails $5-9. Open daily 11:30am-4am.

▨ **Tap-A-Keg Bar,** 2731 Broadway (749-1734), between 104th and 105th St. Relaxed, diverse local group chat it up with the friendliest darn bartenders around. Happy hour fills you with $2-3 pints (2-9pm; weekends noon-7pm). Open daily 2pm-4am.

▨ **Yogi's,** 2156 Broadway (873-9852), at 76th St. Three attributes place this bar in the booze stratosphere: a constant stream of Elvis and country faves from the jukebox; bartenders' and customers' predilection to dance on the bar; and, most importantly, seriously cheap beer. Pitchers $5; shots $2.50. Open daily noon-4am.

UPPER EAST SIDE

▨ **Ozone,** 1720 Second Ave. (860-8950), between 89th and 90th St. Dim and elegant, Ozone's front room holds a classy bar, while the back has a carnival-esque tent. Wear black and fit right in. Large selection of imported beers. Cigar menu available. Happy Hour daily 4-7pm; live DJ Th-Sa. Open daily 4pm-4am.

Match, 33 E. 60th St. (906-9177), between Madison and Park Ave. Sleek bar in this nouveau-Asian restaurant touted as the best pickup scene in *New York* magazine's "Best Of 1999" issue. Leave the baby oil and pickup lines at home though; this place is classy. Beer $5, cocktails $7-8, dim sum rack $9.50. Open M 11am-midnight, Tu-Sa 11am-1am, Su 5-11pm.

J.L. Sullivan's, 1715 First Ave. (831-7419), between 88th and 89th. Raucous Irish bar with tons of drink specials and games for all in addition to a small pool table. Th-F nights the scene is packed with budgeteers and the HI crowd because of their 6-10pm $10 unlimited draft offer. Sa 8-11pm $15 open bar. Open M-F 9:30am-4am, Sa-Su noon-4am.

Mo's Caribbean Bar and Grille, 1454 Second Ave. (650-0561; www.college-pride.com/nycbars), at 76th St. Lively, friendly bar with the island touch. Big screen TV invites raucous and rapt attention to sporting events and other visual bonding activities. Sign onto website for 2 free drinks. Draft beer $3.50-4. Happy Hour 4-7pm. M-F 4pm-4am, Sa-Su noon-4am.

Auction House, 300 E. 89th St. (427-4458), near Second Ave. Watch cultural elite mingle and drink. Rooms of ornately carved wood chairs, gilt oil paintings of naked women, and crimson velvet curtains. Even the bathroom soap matches the deep red accents. Drink prices standard—neither exorbitant nor cheap. Open daily 8pm-4am.

American Trash, 1471 First Ave. (988-9008), between 76th and 77th St. Cavernous barroom hung with "trash" (read: twisted metal bits) from NASCAR go-carts to Molly Hatchet posters. Have a wild 'n' crazy time celebrating lowbrow culture. Drink specials change every night. Live music Sundays (JJ and the All-American-Trash band); live DJ Mondays. Happy hour M-F noon-7pm, Sa-Su 5-7pm. Women drink at Happy Hour prices Tu 4pm-midnight. Open daily noon-4am.

HOBOKEN, NEW JERSEY

The bars here are *everywhere*. For info on how to get to Hoboken see p. 283.

Scotland Yard, 72 Hudson St. (201-222-9273). From the PATH station, walk along Hudson Pl. to Hudson St. and up 2 blocks. A spacious wood-paneled bar is the centerpiece of this English pub. British memorabilia covers the walls—perfect for Anglophiles and expatriates. Beers $3-6.50. Open M-Tu 4pm-2am, W-Th 1pm-2am, F-Sa 2pm-3am, Su 6pm-2am. Live music Sa-Tu afternoon.

Miss Kitty's Saloon and Dance Hall Floozies, 94-98 Bloomfield St. (201-792-0041), at 1st St. From the Hoboken PATH station, walk along Hudson Pl. to Hudson St., up 3 blocks to 1st St., then left 4 blocks to Bloomfield St. Yuppie-filled spacious Wild West-style saloon. Beers $3-5. Open M-Th 4pm-2am, F 4pm-3am, Sa 6pm-2am, Su 6pm-2am.

BROOKLYN

Montero's Bar & Grill, 73 Atlantic Ave. (718-624-9799), at Hicks St. in Brooklyn Heights. Subway: #2, 3, 4, 5, M, N, or R to Borough Hall, then 4 blocks on Court St. to Atlantic Ave. Heavily bedecked with all manner of nautical knick-knacks, Montero's still looks very much like the longshoremen's bar it once was. A brief perusal of the impressive array of vintage photos on the walls and a couple of $3 beers will have you reminiscing noisily with all the old-timers. Open M-Sa 8am-4am, Su noon-4pm.

Frank's Cocktail Lounge, 606 Fulton St., at S. Elliot Pl. Subway: C to Lafayette Ave. Dark, dog-eared, and intimate. Frank presides over it all, and it's hard to imagine a friendlier host. Weekend nights often feature first-rate jazz and blues performances. Open 4pm-4am.

Peter's Waterfront Ale House, 155 Atlantic Ave. (718-522-3794), between Henry and Clinton St. Subway: #2, 3, 4, 5, M, N, or R to Borough Hall, then walk 4 blocks on Court St. to Atlantic Ave. Friendly neighborhood bar and eatery is a great spot to go for beer and burgers. 15 beers on tap change seasonally, and the burgers ($7) are large and in charge. Specials like mussels in a *weiss* beer broth broaden the definition of pub grub. Family eatery by day, Pete's offers live blues on Wednesday nights and live jazz on Thursday nights from 10:30pm. Open daily noon-11pm, bar open until 3 or 4am.

Galapagos, 70 N 6th St. (718-782-5188), in Williamsburg. Subway: L to Bedford; go south along Bedford and then west along N. 6th St. No finches here—Galapagos is a bar in a renovated warehouse with futuro-sleek decor that hosts a film series, performances by its own theater troupe, and art exhibitions. Call for info.

Teddy's (718-384-9787), at N. 8th St. and Berry St., in Greenpoint. Subway: L to Bedford Ave. and 1 block west. The *artiste* crowd starts drinking here, and only you can find out where they wind up. Cheap drinks ($1-3). Occasional 1970s lounge nite. Jazz on Thursday from Nov.-Mar. Open daily 11:30am-midnight.

Mugs Ale House, 125 Bedford Ave., in Greenpoint. Subway: L to Bedford Ave. Quiet neighborhood pub serves reasonably priced beers, dark ales, and lagers ($2-5) to local artists and younger residents. Open daily 3pm-3am.

Montague Street Saloon, 122 Montague St. (718-522-6770), near Court St. Subway: #2 or 3 to Clark St.; take Henry St. to Montague. Young wanna-be yuppies congregate to eat, drink, and be merry on this fashionable street in Brooklyn Heights. Open M-F 11:30am-1am, Sa-Su 11:30am-2am.

Johnny Macks, 1114 Eighth Ave. (718-832-7961), in Park Slope. Subway: F to Seventh Ave.-Park Slope; walk east 1 block to Eighth Ave., then south 3 blocks. College grads frequent this dark-wood-panelled bar, which prides itself on its selection of microbrews ($3 on tap). Open daily noon-4am.

THE BRONX

The Boat Livery, Inc., 663 City Island Ave. (718-885-1843), at Bridge St. Subway: #6 to Pelham Bay Park, then bus Bx29 to City Island Ave. and Kilroe. The place to come if you want cheap beer, bloodworms, or fishing tackle. This is the real deal, the sort of place you can only find on City Island. You can even rent a skiff ($20 per hr.). But if you don't have any luck, just bury yourself in this comfortable, friendly bar for a $1 glass of Bud. Boat rental open 5am-4:30pm. Bait shop open 5am-8:30pm. Bar open 5am-midnight.

STATEN ISLAND

Adobe Blues, 63 Lafayette Ave. (718-720-2583), at Fillmore St. Take the Staten Island Ferry, then the S44 bus to Lafayette Ave. A lively mix of beer- and chili-lovers fill this bar, styled after old Western saloons. More than 230 beers to choose from. Lunch $6-7, dinner $8-13. Live jazz or blues W, F, and Sa. No cover. Open Su-Th 11:30am-midnight, F-Sa 11:30am-2am. Kitchen open until 1am F-Sa.

WELCOME TO THE JUNGLE Early in the 90s, black Londoners spawned jungle, a frantic urban music style that has adapted well to New York City. NYC is the original urban jungle, although here the crowd is comprised mostly of white post-ravers. Jungle incorporates the slow, dubby basslines of reggae with sped-up hip-hop breakbeats and recombinant sampling strategies, stewed thick and fast with inflections of techno. The result is edgy, experimental, and futuristic. New York now offers about four jungle club nights a week. Konkrete Jungle (604-4224) is the most established, while Jungle Nation (802-7495) throbs with a more serious crowd. DJs to look for include Dara, Delmar, Soulslinger, DB, Cassien, and Peshay.

DANCE CLUBS

A wilderness of human flesh
Crazed with avarice, lust and rum
New York, thy name's Delirium.

—Byron R. Newton, "Ode to New York"

Carefree crowds, hype music, unlimited fun, massive pocket book damage—these foundations of the New York club scene make it an unparalleled institution of boogie. Trying to guess the clubs most worthy of your financial sacrifice can prove tragic. The simplest route to fabulosity entails asking around record stores (especially the smaller ones), where salespeople are usually in the know and often have flyers for discount admission. In the East Village, for one, flyer-toting teens abound on the street, especially in front of record stores—but size up the source of your info before embarking on a night of madness with a slew of others like him. Some of the best parties stay underground, advertised only by word of mouth, or by flyer. Many clubs move from space to space each week, but hardcore clubbers know where to find them.

The rules are simple. Door people, the clubs' fashion police, forbid anything drab or conventional. Like, don't wear khaki shorts and a purse across your chest, for crying out loud. Above all, just look confident—attitude is at least half the battle. Come after 11pm unless you crave solitude. In fact, you're pretty uncool if you show up before 1 or 2am. A few after-hours clubs keep gettin' busy until 5-6am, or even later. Careful, though: even the best clubs are only good on one or two nights a week.

For a change of tempo, try out Lincoln Center's **Midsummer Night Swing Dancextravaganza,** held from late June until late July. Every night from Wednesday to Saturday, Lincoln Center invites couples and singles to tango, swing, shimmy, or foxtrot under the stars. For the price of admission the center provides a dance floor, a cafe, and live music (dancing W-Sa 8:15pm, lessons W-Th 6:30pm).

Let's Go has ranked the following dance clubs according to fun and value. The suggestions could well have changed by the summer of '00, as New York hip is an elusive commodity. Call ahead to make sure that you know what (and whom) you'll find when you arrive.

Arlene Grocery, 95 Stanton St. (358-1633; www.arlenegrocery.com), between Ludlow and Orchard St. Subway: F to Second Ave. Every night Arlene Grocery puts on at least 5 (Sa-Su 7) rock, punk, indie, or hip-hop bands back-to-back. Big names like Bob Dylan are known to come by and play in this intimate space. No cover. Doors open at 7pm. Stop by next door at the **Butcher Bar** where the bands sometimes play an impromptu acoustic set; they've also got a functioning fireplace in winter.

The Bank, 225 E. Houston St. (505-5033), at Essex St. Subway: F to Delancey St. A stately bank converted into a gritty club, with a heavy Goth-boy and chain concentration. Clear sight-lines make it great for live music; underground vault a great spot for the wee hours. Call for schedule. Cover usually $8-12.

China Club, 2130 Broadway (398-3800), at 75th St. Subway: #1, 2, 3, or 9 to 72nd St. Rock-and-roll hot spot where Bowie and Jagger used to come on their off nights. Models and long-haired men make it a great people-watching spot. Pudgy, rich men trying to get by the doorman make it a great people-mocking spot. Monday night is for the "beautiful people" crowd. Be well-dressed or you won't get in. Go elsewhere for great dancing. Cover around $20. Opens daily at 10pm.

Club Las Vegas, 179 Dyckman St. (942-1516), between Sherman and Vermilyea St. This uptown (and we do mean uptown) Latin disco sports a young, attractive Hispanic crowd and pounding, infectious dance music. Not many bridge-and-tunnel folk find their way up here. Cover $10 (cash only). Call for hours.

Nell's, 246 W. 14th St. (675-1567), between Seventh and Eighth Ave. Subway: #1, 2, 3, or 9 to 14th St. A legendary hot spot past its heyday; the faithful hang on for mellow shmoozing and soulful music upstairs and phat beats below. Racially diverse crowd. Cover M $5. Tu-W, Su $10, Th-Sa $15. Open daily 10pm-4am.

■ **Mother,** 432 W. 14th St. (366-5680; www.mothernyc.com), at Washington St., in the Meat Packing District. Subway: A, C, E to 14th St. Mother is the mother of all underground clubs in NY. Each night here features a different theme, usually centering around some fetish or another. Nights of note include **Jackie 60** (Tu), **Long Black Veil and the Vampyre** (Th), **Clit Club** (F), and **Click+Drag** (Sa). It's best to check their website for the ever-changing schedule of events, dress codes, and cover charges. Cover is usually $10 or under. Open times vary. (See **Clit Club,** p. 310.)

■ **Sounds of Brazil (SOB's),** 204 Varick St. (243-4940), at the corner of Seventh Ave. and Houston St. in the Village. Subway: #1, 9 to Houston. Celebrating 18 years of making the world beat, this luncheonette-turned-dance-club presents bopping musicians playing the sounds of Brazil, Africa, Latin America, and the Caribbean amidst an appropriately diverse crowd. Cover $10-18; free before 7pm. Saturday sees live samba with free admission before 9pm (before 8pm in winter). First Thursday of each month get down to the Indian hip-hop/jungle/pop of *Basement Bhangra,* one of the city's most energetic dance parties; cover $15. Open for dining Tu-Th 7pm-2:30am, F-Sa 7pm-4am. Most shows M-Th 8 and 10pm; F-Sa 9, 11pm, 1am or 10pm, midnight, and 2am.

Tunnel, 220 Twelfth Ave. (695-7292 or 695-4682), at 27th St. Subway: #1, 9, or C, E to 23rd St. The premier scene in the late 80s and early 90s, this warehouse of a club has seen better days, but is still a popular spot attracting anyone and everyone. With five rooms, lounges, glass-walled live shows, and cages for dancing, this party attracts a diverse crowd including celebrities, drag queens, and hip-hop heads alike. With massive crowds of about 3000 to control, along with increasing police drug raids on the club circuit, it's no wonder security is so tight. Friday and Saturday are regular party nights featuring techno, house, R&B, hip-hop, and other genres. Sundays are reserved for hip hop night. Dress clean and casual. Cover $20 for women, $25 for men. State-issued ID required. Open F-Su 10pm-4am.

Twilo, 530 W. 27th St. (268-1600). Subway: #1 or 9 to 28th St., or C or E to 23rd St. A crowded scene early in the night, with meaty shirtless glam boys and the occasional 8 ft. tall drag queen cavorting alongside straight, suburban types. Later, the music gets deeper and the crowd more serious. If you stay past the 4am clearout, expect to remain until breakfast time. Cover $20-25. Doors open around midnight.

Webster Hall, 125 E. 11th St. (353-1600), between Third and Fourth Ave. Subway: #4, 5, 6, N, or R or L to Union Sq.-14th St. 3 blocks south and a block east. Popular club offers a rock/reggae room and a coffeeshop in addition to the main, house-dominated dance floor. **Psychedelic Thursdays** often feature live bands and $2.50 beers. F-Sa see the motto of "4 floors, 5 eras, 4 DJs...and 40,000 sq. ft. of fun" put into effect. Open Th-Sa 10pm-4am. Cover $15-20, though promotions like "Ladies' Night Out" and time-limited freebies ease the cost.

MISCELLANEOUS HIPSTER HANGOUTS

New York is a sucked orange.

—Ralph Waldo Emerson

A New York night is filled with attractions and events that defy categorization, from performance art to renegade parties and shows to poetry slams. Many hot spots don't have defined locations: mobile parties like **Giant Step** and **Soul Kitchen** move from club to club with an ardent crowd of followers, drawn in by the innovative amalgamations of jazz, funk, and hip-hop beats. The cover varies from show to show. Check the papers for upcoming locations.

ABC No Rio, 156 Rivington St. (254-3697; schedule info 539-6089), near Clinton St. Subway: B, D, Q to Essex St. Walk a block north and then 3 blocks east. The art out front explains their mantra: "No SoHo, No dinero, No Rio." A non-profit, community-run space featuring lots of hardcore and punk-related genres, as well as occasional poetry readings, art exhibitions, etc. No alcohol served. All ages. Cover $2-5.

The Anyway Café, 34 E. 2nd St. (473-5021), at Second Ave. Sample Russian-American culture at this dark, relaxed, leopard-spotted hangout. Numerous literary readings during the week, as well as jazz on Friday and Saturday nights, and Russian folk on Sunday. Every night of the week, there's some kind of music. All begin at 9pm. Friendly and free of the smoky pretension which all-too-often plagues such venues. Also a great place to kick back with homemade sangria and sample some gourmet Russian specialties ($8-12). Open M-Th 5pm-2am, F-Sa 5pm-4am, Su noon-1am.

Bowlmor, 110 University Pl. (255-8188), near 13th St. Subway: #4, 5, 6, or L, or N, R to Union Sq. Proof that New York is the greatest city in the world. It's an after-hours lights-out bowling alley with glowing pins where DJs spin jungle, trip-hop, and house. $4.25 per person/per game, after 5pm $5.45, F-Su $6. Shoe rental $3. Beer $2.50. Open M and F 10am-4am, Tu-W 10am-1am, Sa 11am-4am, Su 11am-1am. (See **Sports,** p. 292.)

Collective Unconscious, 145 Ludlow St. (254-5277), south of Houston St. A performance space collectively (and unconsciously) run by 15 local artists who put up their own shows and provide a venue/studio/rehearsal/you-name-it space for the Village artistic community. Frequent open-mic events, including, but not limited to, Wednesday nights. Call for events schedule. Friendly, artsy people and usually something interesting. No alcohol or other refreshments served, but BYOB is A-OK. Cover $3-9.

Mission Café, 82 Second Ave. (505-6616), between 4th and 5th St. This theater hot spot every week hosts astrologers giving cheap tarot readings. Features a different artist on the wall every month. Steamed eggs, made on the espresso machine every morning with jack cheese, scallions, and tomato with a bagel ($3.50). Coffee and juices (including specialty drinks) 85¢-$3.25. Open M-F 8am-9pm, Sa 9am-11pm, Su 9am-8pm.

Nuyorican Poets Café, 236 E. Third St. (505-8183), between Ave. B and Ave. C. Subway: F to Second Ave. Walk 3 blocks north and 3 blocks east. New York's leading joint for "poetry slams" and spoken-word performances; several regulars have been featured on MTV. A mixed bag of doggerel and occasional gems. If you don't like the poets, don't worry—there's likely to be a heckler in the house. Workshops for your inner poet, DJ-enhanced parties, and occasional risque acts like "Erotic words en Español." Cover $5-10.

Our Name is Mud, 3 locations: 1566 Second Ave. (570-6868), between 81st and 82nd St.; 506 Amsterdam Ave. (579-5575), between 84th and 85th St.; and 59 Greenwich St. (647-7899; www.ournameismud.com), at Seventh Ave. At these

NIGHTLIFE

quirky pottery stores you can mudsling to your heart's content by making your own ceramic creations ($5 for 30min.). Thursdays (5-10pm) and Fridays (6-9pm) are bring your own booze and food nights. Check their website for special promos. Open M-W and Sa 11:30am-8pm, Th 11:30am-10pm, F 11:30am-9pm, Su 11:30am-7pm.

The Point, 940 Garrison Ave. in the Bronx (718-542-4139), at the corner of Manida in Hunt's Point. Subway: #6 to Hunts Point. On the fringe of one of New York's poorest neighborhoods, The Point houses a growing artistic community and is the homebase of dancer/choreographer Arthur Aviles. Monthly Latin jazz and hip-hop performances are offered, as well as studio facilities, a theater, and classes in art and self-defense. Community based efforts like the South Bronx Film and Video Festival enable Hunt's Point to call itself "the artistic capital of the Bronx." Call for schedule of events.

Soundlab (726-1724). Locations vary. Cultural alchemy in the form of an illbient happening, nomadic style. Expect a smart, funky, racially mixed crowd absorbing smart, funky, radically mixed sound. Call the number to find where the next Lab goes down; past locales include the base of the Brooklyn Bridge, the 15th floor of a Financial District skyscraper, and outdoors in a Chinatown park.

Tenth Street (Russian and Turkish) Baths, 268 E. 10th St. (674-9250), between First Ave. and Ave. A. Expert masseur Boris runs this co-ed bathhouse that offers all conceivable legal bodily services—oak-leaf massages, salt scrubs, oil massages, and black-mud treatments. Conventional services are also provided, such as saunas, steam rooms, and an ice-cold pool. Admission $20. Open daily 9am-10pm; Th and Su men-only, W women-only.

COMEDY CLUBS

Comic Strip Live, 1568 Second Ave. (861-9386), between 81st and 82nd St. Sunday comics' characters Dagwood and Dick Tracy line the 4-color walls of this well-established pub-style club. Former regulars include just about everyone in the post-SNL pantheon. Shows Su-Th around 8pm, additional shows on weekends. $9 drink min. every night. Su and Tu-Th $10 cover; F-Sa $14 cover. Make reservations, especially for weekends.

Dangerfield's, 1118 First Ave. (593-1650), between 61st and 62nd St. Rodney's respectable comic launching pad is celebrating its 30th year of humor. Rising stars from throughout the country perform here, and HBO specials featuring the likes of Roseanne Barr and Jerry Seinfeld have all been taped at the club. Be prepared for a surprise—the line-up is only available the day of the show, and unannounced guest comedians appear occasionally. Cover Su-Th $12.50, F-Sa $15, Sa 10:30pm show $20. Su-Th shows at 8:45pm, F shows at 9 and 11:15pm, Sa shows at 8, 10:30pm, and 12:30am. Doors open 1hr. before 1st show.

The Original Improvisation, 346 W. 46th St. (265-8133), between Eighth and Ninth Ave. This classic comedy spot recently relocated and is now in **Danny's Skylight Room,** the site a quarter-century of comedy—acts from Saturday Night Live, Johnny Carson, and David Letterman. Richard Pryor and Robin Williams got started here. A bit off the beaten path but worth the trip for comedy diehards. Cover F $7.50, Sa $10, plus $9 drink or food min. Shows F-Sa at 10:45pm.

Uptight Citizens Brigade Theater, 161 W. 22nd St. (366-9176), between Sixth and Seventh Ave. Offbeat sketch and improvisational comedy. Tickets range from free to $10.

SPORTS

While most cities would be content to field a major league team in each big-time sport, New York opts for the Noah's Ark approach: two baseball teams, two NHL hockey teams, two NFL football teams (although the Giants and Jets are now quartered across the river in New Jersey), an NBA basketball team, a WNBA basketball team, and an MLS soccer squad. In addition to local teams' regularly scheduled season games, New York hosts a number of celebrated world-class events such as the New York Marathon and tennis' U.S. Open. The city papers overflow with info on upcoming events.

SPECTATOR SPORTS

BASEBALL. The newly revived national pastime thrives from late March to early October, when two high-exposure teams make their exploits off the field almost as melodramatic as those on it. The legendary **New York Yankees,** the team of Joe DiMaggio, Babe Ruth, and Lou Gehrig and the winners of more championships than any other team in American sports, play ball at **Yankee Stadium** (718-293-6000) in the Bronx. In 1998, the Yankees won the most games in baseball history and overcame the San Diego Padres in the World Series, thus regaining their stature as the best team around. Now, the Yankees grapple with controversy surrounding the trade of David Wells (who pitched a perfect game in 1998) for legendary former Red Sox pitcher Roger Clemens (who started out rocky in '99). For the first time in 35 years, 1999 saw both the Mets and Yankees achieve first place in their respective divisions—although *Let's Go* won't know how the teams ended up until after we publish in November '99. Tickets are usually available the day of the game, ranging from $12 to $21; you can also find them on the web at www.tix.com. If you're lookin' to start some trouble, root for the other team, particularly if it's Boston… some burly guy from Queens will throw batteries at you.

For the second year in a row (1997, 1998), the Yankees dominated New York's other baseball team, the **Mets** (short for the "Metropolitans"), during the interleague "Subway Series." Created in 1962 to replace the much-mourned Giants and Dodgers, the Mets set the still-unbroken major league record for losses in a season during their first year. In 1969, only seven years later, the "Miracle Mets" captured the World Series. Although the Mets won again in 1986, they quickly wound up deep in the cellar, spawning a David Letterman catchphrase: "We're so close to spring you can almost hear the Mets suck." However, the recent acquisitions of sluggers Mike Piazza and Robin Ventura have brought the Mets back to their winning form. Watch them go to bat at **Shea Stadium** (718-507-6387) in Queens (subway: #7 to Willets Point/Shea Stadium). (Tickets range from $10 for bleacher seats to $45 for lower box seats.)

BASKETBALL. Though they've been unable to regain the heights of their 1969 Championship Season, the New York Knickerbockers (usually referred to as the **Knicks**) are once again a force in the NBA. In 1999, the Knicks shocked the basketball world by becoming the worst regular season team to reach the championship series. Despite an injury to aging star Patrick Ewing, the team, led by infamous choker Latrell Sprewell and castaway Marcus Camby, upset the Miami Heat and Indiana Pacers before finally losing to the San Antonio Spurs in the finals. The Knicks do their dribbling at **Madison Square Garden** (465-5867) from November to late April. Tickets, which start at $22, are fairly hard to come by unless you order well in advance. On the collegiate level, the Garden plays host to Big East Conference contender St. John's Red Storm during the winter and the NIT and Big East tournaments in March.

Also playing at the Garden are the **New York Liberty** (564-9622) of the Women's National Basketball Association (WNBA). Star players Rebecca Lobo, Teresa Weatherspoon, and Sophia Witherspoon, have led the Liberty to the top of the league standings in each of the last three seasons, creating excitement among NY fans and attracting record crowds for women's basketball. The WNBA take the court June through August, and tickets are fairly easy to get (tickets start at $8).

FOOTBALL. Though both New York teams once battled in the trenches at Shea Stadium, nowadays they play across the river at **Giants Stadium** in East Rutherford, New Jersey. The **Jets** (516-560-8200), led by charismatic coach Bill Parcells, resurrected quarterback Vinny Testaverde, and loudmouth wideout Keyshawn Johnson, have New Yorkers abuzz with talk of bringing home a third Super Bowl ring to the Big Apple. Tickets start at $25 (cash only at the Meadowlands box office). After a disappointing 1998 season, the **Giants** (201-935-8222) rebuilt their squad in an attempt to challenge their division rivals, the Dallas Cowboys. Tickets are nigh impossible to get—season ticket holders have booked them all for the next 40 years. See *Let's Go: New York City 2039* for details. Try any local sports bar for the best view of the action you're likely to get.

HOCKEY. In a town known for its speed and turbulence, it's not hard to understand why New Yorkers attend hockey games with such fervor. The **New York Rangers** play at **Madison Square Garden** (MSG 465-6741, Rangers 308-6977) from late fall to late spring. After enduring 54 championship-less years, the Rangers finally captured the Stanley Cup in June 1994. However, New Yorkers may have to wait another 54 years; the Rangers rack up losses while mourning the 1999 retirement of hockey's greatest player ever, Wayne Gretzky. Tickets start at $12; reserve well in advance. Similarly, the **New York Islanders,** after winning four consecutive Stanley Cups in the early 1980s, are one of the few teams worse than the Rangers. They hang their skates at the **Nassau Coliseum** (516-794-9300) in Uniondale, Long Island. Tickets range $19-60 (season runs Sept.-Apr.).

SOCCER. Buoyed by swelling youth interest and the 1994 World Cup in New York, soccer has undergone a meteoric rise in popularity in the past few years, culminating in the start of a new American league, **Major League Soccer (MLS).** Since the league's inception in 1996, New Yorkers have wasted no time learning what the rest of the world has known for decades—no other sport can compare to *futbol*. With talents like star midfielder Tab Ramos, the **New York/New Jersey Metrostars** often spice up their losses with five-minute spurts of sheer brilliance. Fans keep turning out to curse the 'Stars after these moments of brilliance are over. The Metrostars kick off at **Giants Stadium** (888-4-METROTIX/463-8768) late March through September (tickets $15-35).

TENNIS. Tennis enthusiasts who get their tickets three months in advance can attend the prestigious **U.S. Open,** one of tennis' four Grand Slam events, held in late August and early September at the United States Tennis Association's (USTA) Tennis Center in Flushing Meadows Park, Queens (718-760-6200). Tickets are $22-82 and can be purchased by calling 888-673-6849. The **Virginia Slims Championship,** featuring the world's top women players, comes to Madison Square Garden (465-6741) in mid-November. Tickets for the opening rounds start at $25.

HORSERACING. Forsake the rat race for some equine excitement. Thoroughbred fans can watch the stallions go at **Belmont Park** (718-641-4700) every day except Monday and Tuesday, from May through late July and from September to mid-October, and may even catch a grand slam event. The **Belmont Stakes,** run the first Saturday in June, is one leg in the Triple Crown. The "Belmont Special" train leaves from Penn Station twice per day ($8 round-trip, including $1 off admission). Meanwhile, **Aqueduct Racetrack** (718-641-4700), next to JFK Airport, has races from late October to early May, every day except Monday and Tuesday. (Subway: A to Aqueduct.) Grandstand seating at both tracks costs $2. Racing in New York is suspended during the month of August, when the action goes upstate to Saratoga.

PEOPLERACING. On the first Sunday in November, two million spectators line rooftops, sidewalks, and promenades to cheer 22,000 runners in the **New York City Marathon** (16,000 racers actually finish). The race begins on the Verrazano Bridge and ends at Central Park's Tavern on the Green.

PARTICIPATORY SPORTS

Whether trying to slim down at the health club or commuting to work via bicycle, endless amateur and recreational athletes twist and flex in New York. Although space in much of the city is at a premium, the **City of New York Parks and Recreation Department** (360-8111 or 800-201-PARK/7275) for a recording of park events) manages to maintain numerous playgrounds and parks in all boroughs, for everything from baseball and basketball to croquet and shuffleboard.

SWIMMING: BEACHES AND POOLS

Coney Island Beach and Boardwalk (2½ mi.), on the Atlantic Ocean, from W. 37th St. to Corbin Pl., in Brooklyn (718-946-1350). Subway: B, D, F, or N to Coney Island (last stop).

Jones Beach State Park, on the Atlantic Ocean in Nassau County (516-785-1600). Take LIRR to Freeport or Wantaugh, and catch a shuttle to the beach.

Long Beach, on the Atlantic Ocean in Nassau County. Take LIRR to Long Beach.

Manhattan Beach (¼ mi.), on the Atlantic Ocean, from Ocean Ave. to Mackenzie St. in Brooklyn (718-946-1373). Subway: D train to Brighton Beach then bus B1.

Orchard Beach and Promenade (1¼ mi.), on Long Island Sound in Pelham Bay Park, Bronx (718-885-2275). Subway: #6 to Pelham Bay Park, then bus #12 to Orchard Beach.

Rockaway Beach and Boardwalk (7½ mi.), on the Atlantic Ocean. From Beach 1st St., Far Rockaway, to Beach 149th St., Neponsit, Queens (718-318-4000). Lifeguards on duty Memorial Day-Labor Day daily 10am-6pm. Subway: A to "Broad Channel," then take the "S" shuttle to Rockaway Park.

Staten Island: South Beach, Midland Beach, and **Franklin D. Roosevelt Boardwalk** (2½ mi.), on Lower New York Bay. From Fort Wadsworth to Miller Field, New Dorp. Take bus #51 from the ferry terminal.

POOLS. Public pools are scattered throughout all the boroughs of New York, but they can be dangerous, since isolated incidents of sexual assault have occurred in the past couple years. The NYC Parks Department has added security and is considering segregating some pools by sex. If you can find the few pools that aren't in troubled neighborhoods, you'll have a cheap way to escape from the sweltering summer heat. Some of the nicer pools include **John Jay Pool** (794-6566), east of York Ave. at 77th St., and **Asser Levy Pool** (447-2020), at 23rd St. and Asser Levy Pl. (next to the East River). All outdoor pools are open from early July through Labor Day from 11am to 7 or 8pm, depending on the weather. Both pools listed above are free, although the latter's heated indoor pool is open only to members. Call the Parks Aquatic Information Line at 800-201-PARK/7275 or 718-699-4219.

Indoor pools can be somewhat safer than outdoor pools and tend to be open year-round, but most require some sort of annual membership fee of $10 or more.

BASKETBALL. Basketball is one of New York's favorite pastimes. Courts can be found in parks and playgrounds all over the city, and most are frequently occupied. **Pickup basketball** games can also be found in various parts of the city, each with its own rituals, rulers, and degree of intensity. **The Cage,** at W. 4th and Sixth Ave., is home to some of the city's best amateur players: rumor has it that scouts for college and pro teams occasionally drop by incognito to ferret out new talent. Other pickup spots worth checking out (if you're any good) include courts at **Central Park, 96th and Lexington Ave.,** and **76th and Columbus Ave.**

HELL ON WHEELS The in-line skating craze has hit New York hard.

Messengers careen through crowded streets on their skates, oblivious to the flow of traffic around them, and park paths are often clogged with talented (and not-so-talented) bladers. The type of skating varies from space to space; some areas have slalom courses and half-pipes set up similar to skateboarding courses. **New York Skateout** offers both in-line skating lessons and tours. Call them at 486-1919 for more information. The following open stretches feature good views and a skate-happy crowd:

Battery Park: try skating from the tip of Manhattan through Battery Park City on the west side of the island. Great view of the harbor and skyline; extremely flat skating surface.

West Street: the city has blocked off about ten blocks stretching from Christopher to Horatio St. Big crowd of heavy-duty skaters; view of the Hudson.

Chelsea Piers: roller rink in a massive sports and entertainment complex on the Hudson, at 23rd St. and 12th Ave. Very popular with in-line hockey players.

East River Promenade: Slightly narrow boardwalk running from 81st to 60th St. The path is very low and close to the river; great views of Roosevelt Island.

Central Park: The park has several roller-zones, including the self-descriptive Outer Loop and a slalom course near Tavern on the Green (67th St.).

BICYCLING. From spring to fall, daily at dawn and dusk and throughout the weekend, packs of dedicated (and fashion-conscious) cyclists dressed in biking shorts navigate the trails and wide roads of **Central Park.** (Bike rental: 517-3623. Apr.-Sept. daily 10am-5pm, in good weather. $8 per hr. for 3-speeds, $10 per hr. for 10-speeds, $15 per hr. for tandems. Credit card, ID, or $100 deposit required for all bikes.) The circular drive is car-free M-Th 10am-3pm and 7-10pm, and F 10am-3pm and 7pm until M 6am; see Jogging below for tips on where to ride in Central Park. On the West Side, along the Hudson bank, **Riverside Park** between 72nd and 110th St. draws more laid-back riders. Other excellent places to cycle weekends include the deserted **Wall Street** area, or the unadorned roads of Brooklyn's **Prospect Park.** For quick same-day excursions, plenty of bike shops around Central Park rent out two-wheelers by the hour. (For more info on biking in New York City, see **Essentials**, p. 68.)

JOGGING. When running in **Central Park** during no-traffic hours (see **Bicycling,** above), stay in the right-hand runners' lane to avoid being mowed down by some reckless pedal-pusher. **Stay in populated areas and stay out of the park after dark.** Recommended courses include the 1.58 mi. jaunt around the Reservoir and a picturesque 1.72 mi. route starting at Tavern on the Green along West Drive, heading south to East Drive, and then circling back west up 72nd St. to where you started. Another beautiful place to run is **Riverside Park,** which stretches along the Hudson River bank from 72nd to 116th St.; for safety's sake, don't stray too far north.

BOWLING. Bowlmor, 110 University Pl. (255-8188), near 13th St. Expect an effortlessly hip, mixed crowd. A recent trip turned up bowling diehards getting clumsy with the $2.50 beer, big-name NYC jungle DJs playing pinball, and Japanese breakdancers nailing strikes (for info see **Nightlife,** p. 287). **Tennis** courts (989-2300) are on the higher floors; call to reserve a space (courts $38-72 per hr.).

GOLF. Although New York golf courses don't measure up to those at Pebble Beach, New Yorkers remain avid golfers, jamming all of the 13 well-manicured city courses during the weekends. Most are found in the Bronx or Queens, including **Pelham Bay Park** (718-885-1258), **Van Cortlandt Park** (718-543-4595), and **Forest Park** (718-296-0999). Greens fees are approximately $23-25 during the week and $25-30 Saturdays and Sundays for non-NYC residents. Reservations for summer weekends are suggested 7 to 10 days in advance.

ICE SKATING. The first gust of cold winter air brings out droves of aspiring Paul Wylies and Tara Lipinskys. While each of the rinks in the city has its own character, nearly all have lockers, skate rentals, and a snack bar. The most popular and expensive is the famous sunken plaza in **Rockefeller Center,** Fifth Ave. and 50th St. (332-7654), which doubles as the chic American Festival Cafe during the spring and summer months. The Rockefeller rink is always crowded during the winter months, and throngs of spectators stand around the outside edges, observing the skating below. You can glide in circles at **Wollman Memorial Rink** (517-4800), located in a particularly scenic section of Central Park near 64th St. ($15 for 2hr., $25 all day; includes helmet and pads; $100 deposit required.) **Sky Rink** (336-6100), at W. 21st St. and the Hudson River, boasts two full-sized Olympic rinks. Call for hours, prices, and skate rental fees.

HORSEBACK RIDING. Horseback riding in Central Park, for those well-versed in English saddle, operates out of **Claremont Stables** (724-5100), 175 W. 89th St. (Open M-F 6am-10pm, Sa-Su 6am-6pm. $35 per hr. Make reservations.) In Queens, **Dixie Do Stables** (718-263-3500) gives guided trail rides through Forest Park (Open 9am-5pm. $20 per hr.).

CRICKET AND CROQUET. You won't see Ian Botham swinging his chunk of willow, but you can turn a few overs of off-spin at **cricket fields** throughout the boroughs. Fields include **Flushing Meadows-Corona Park** in Queens (call 718-520-5932; permits $8 per 2hr.) and **Canarsie Beach Park** in Brooklyn (718-965-8919). During the summer, weekend permits are nearly impossible to come by. All parks welcome spectators, and Flushing Meadows-Corona Park has added three new fields.

For a dose of mallet and wicket, head to the croquet lawn in Central Park, north of Sheep Meadow (call 360-8134 for $30 permits; open mid-Apr. to early Nov.).

CLIMBING. You can climb to your heart's content in the center of Manhattan at the **ExtraVertical Climbing Center,** in the Harmony Atrium, 61 W. 62nd St. (586-5382; www.extravertical.com). No experience necessary. (Day pass $16, students $12, challenge climbs $9 for 2, equipment rental $7; lessons $55-110; passes $75-650. Open M 5-10pm, Tu-F 1-10pm, Sa 10am-10pm, Su noon-8pm.)

ROWBOATS. You can rent them at the **Loeb Boathouse** in Central Park. (517-2233. Open daily Apr.-Sept. 10:30am-4:30pm, weather permitting. $10 per hr.; refundable $30 deposit.)

SHOPPING

If it exists, you can buy it somewhere in New York City. While the city has more ritzy department stores than even Ivana, the former Mrs. Trump, could handle on a given day, its shopping scene caters to every desire—from the boutiques on Fifth and Madison Ave. to the hole-in-the-wall record stores of St. Mark's Place. The streets too, serve as a venue for vendors hawking their perfumed oils, art books, hats, and odd shoes. Beware: there's a reason that "Rolex" is so cheap—it's either *very* fake or *very* stolen. For hard-core mall shopping, see **Shopping in Long Island**, p. 309.

CLOTHING AND DEPARTMENT STORES

DOWNTOWN

Andy's Chee-pee's, 16 W. 8th St. (460-8488), between Fifth and Sixth Ave., in Greenwich Village. Subway: N, R to 8th St. Not really cheap at all, but worth a peek, if only for that vintage clothing aroma. Open M-Th 11am-8pm, F-Sa 11am-8:30pm, Su noon-7pm. Also at 691 W. Broadway (420-5980), near W. 4th St. Open M-Sa 11am-8pm, Su noon-7pm.

Anna Sui, 113 Greene St. (941-8406), between Spring and Prince St., in SoHo. Funky, beautiful, pricey designs. Open M-Sa 11:30am-7pm, Su noon-6pm.

Antique Boutique, 712 Broadway (460-8830), near Astor Pl., in Greenwich Village. Blares better techno than many clubs, and sells both stunning vintage clothing and interesting (but expensive) new designs. As with most outfitters of club gear, expect a lot of shiny plastics and outrageous attitudes. Check the basement for overlooked marked-down gems. 10% discount for students with ID. Open M-Th 11am-9pm, F-Sa 11am-10pm, Su noon-8pm.

⬛ **Canal Jean Co.,** 504 Broadway (226-3663), between Prince and Broome St., in SoHo. This original and enormous home of surplus bargains brims with neon ties, baggy pants, alterna-tees, and silk smoking jackets. Artsy hipsters can buy their black slim-fitting jeans here. Poke around bargain central in the basement. Open Su-Th 10:30am-8pm, F-Sa 10:30am-9pm. Open in summer daily 9:30am-9pm.

⬛ **Century 21,** 22 Cortlandt St. (227-9092), between Broadway and Church St., by the World Trade Center. A shopper's dream—department store with *very* discounted designer wares. Sift through the bargain basement duds to find that Armani suit you could never afford. Open Su 11am-6pm, M-W 7:45am-7:30pm, Th 7:45am-8:30pm, F 7:45am-8pm, Sa 10am-7:30pm.

Cheap Jack's, 841 Broadway (777-9564 or 995-0403), between 13th and 14th St., in Greenwich Village. Subway: L, N, R or #4, 5, 6 to Union Sq. Yet another vintage store using the word "cheap" a bit too loosely. Jack, whoever he is, sells racks and racks of worn jeans, old flannels, leather jackets, and other vintage "gems." Open Tu-Su 11:30am-7pm. Accepts AmEx, V, MC.

Cynthia Rowley, 112 Wooster St. (334-1144), in SoHo. A queen bee of SoHo women's fashion, combining sweet and elegant looks. Open M, W, and Sa 11am-7pm, Th-F 11am-8pm, Su noon-6pm.

Language, 238 Mulberry St. (431-5566; www.language-nyc.com), between Prince and Spring St. Exquisite (and unaffordable) clothing and furniture—some designed inhouse, some unbelievably vintage. Perhaps the most gracefully original urban gear around. Open M-W, Sa 11am-7pm, Th 11am-8pm, Su noon-6pm.

Nassau St. Pedestrian Mall, located west of City Hall, stores here offer discounted clothing, often for $10 or less. It's well worth the rummage, but don't head here past 6pm.

Pearl River, 277 Canal St. (431-4770), at Broadway. This Chinese department store sells all the basic necessities, along with a few hard-to-find luxuries. Cheap clothes, paper lanterns, the miraculous Japanese buckwheat pillow, and soft-core "male model" playing cards. All for cheap, all under one roof. Open daily 10am-730pm.

Patricia Field, 10 E. 8th St. (254-1699), near Fifth Ave. Fabulous array of costly, kinky, hip gear; the fabric of choice is vinyl and the colors are neon. Perpetual "ho" sale dealing in G-strings, rubber skirts ($30), and S&M hoods ($60). Extensive selection of "pasties" (nipple tassles, $12-18). Open M-Sa noon-8pm, Su 1-7pm. Sister store **Hotel Venus** at 38 W. Broadway (966-4066).

La Petite Coquette, 51 University Pl. (473-2478), between 9th and 10th St., in Greenwich Village. The fulfillment of your bordello fantasies. This small shop offers all things beaded, embroidered, laced, fringed, and tied to add intrigue to your evenings and perfume your drawers. Celebrity photos on the walls testify that La Petite Coquette will elude your budget, but they won't drive away the true lingerie enthusiast. Come for their post-Valentine's Day sale (mid- to late Feb.) when most items are 40% off. Open M-W and Sa 11am-7pm, Th 11am-8pm, Su noon-6pm.

Religious Sex, 7 St. Marks Pl. (477-9037; www.religioussex.com), between Second and Third Ave., in Greenwich Village. Specializing in the "beautiful and the unusual," Religious Sex supplies vinyl corsets, plush tigerskin cowboy hats, opulent boas, and tulle and sequined tutus to Village fetishists and luminaries such as Prince, Drew Barrymore, and Aerosmith. Amazing array of kinky outerwear that delights in the outlandish and dabbles in the gothic. Leave mom at home. 4" vinyl spike heels $125. Open M-W noon-8pm, Th-Sa noon-9pm, Su 1-8pm.

Reminiscence, 50 W. 23rd St. (243-2292), between Fifth and Sixth Ave. in Chelsea. Happily stuck in a 1970s groove. But now it's even cheaper—a few items cost under $10. Open M-F 10:30am-7:30pm, Sa 11am-7:30pm, Su noon-7pm.

Sephora, 555 Broadway (625-1309), between Spring and Prince St. An overwhelming array of cosmetic products carefully designed to elicit your secret vanity. The tantalizing rainbow arrangements and the sheer magnitude of perfumes, powders, and exfoliaters at Sephora could convince even Snow White that she needed Sheseido's help. Prices range the gamut from very reasonable to quite absurd. Open Sa and M-W 10am-8pm, Th-F 10am-9pm, Su noon-7pm.

SoHo Flea Market, western end of Canal St. Find honest-to-goodness antiques in the midst of the usual funky junk. Open on weekends during the day.

So What!, 153 Prince St. (505-7615), off Broadway. It must have been here that the Pilgrims got their $24 worth of bauble to buy Manhattan, because only So What! can make the seriously cheap seem seriously attractive. Descend into this underground lair of accessorizing to see covetous girls of all ages trying on, oggling at, and salivating over every kind of hair clip, boa, jeweled item, make-up, purse, or tiara that is currently in style. These things are inexpensive—but beware, those sparkly bobby pins and glittered bangles do add up. Almost everything is under $10. Open Su-Th 10am-10pm, F-Sa 10am-midnight.

Uncle Sam's Army Navy, 37 W. 8th St. (674-2222), between Fifth and Sixth Ave., in Greenwich Village. Eclectic and funky supply of military garb from around the world (we're talkin' *East* German uniform pants). Also houses good selection of less official wear for when you're at ease. Carries Carhart, Dickies, and Leatherman. Official German tank tops $5. Italian dress uniform pants $20. Trooper work pants $8. Very gay friendly. Open M-F 10am-9pm, Sa 10am-10pm, Su 11am-8pm.

World Trade Center (435-4170), at West and Liberty St. Located in the concourse, this "mall" provides a sufficient variety of 40 shops and restaurants, its biggest drawback is its "basement" feel. Shops open M-F 7:30am-6:30pm, Sa 10am-5pm (see p. 131).

MIDTOWN

Bergdorff-Goodman, 745 and 754 Fifth Ave. (753-7300), between 57th and 58th St. Subway: #4, 5, 6 to 59th St. The legendary mansion of clothing. Those lounging in the lap of luxury get up to buy pricey jewelry and swank outfits by the crystal light of Bergdorff's chandeliers. Open M-W and F 10am-7pm, Th 10am-8pm, Sa 10am-6pm.

Bloomingdale's, 1000 Third Ave. (705-2000), at 59th St. Subway: #4, 5, 6 to 59th St. Affectionately known as "Bloomie's," this behemoth of a store dedicates 9 floors to decadence. Sidestep the eternal tango between casual shoppers and perfume spritzers on the 1st floor, and dodge the throngs of foreign tourists buying up the Clinique counter. There's something for everyone here, but most exceeds our peasant budgets. Just remember: there are bathrooms on floors 2, 7, and 8, and soft, cushy chairs in the fur salon for when your friend takes too long with her stoles. Open M-F 10am-8:30pm, Sa 10am-7pm, Su 11am-7pm.

Brooks Brothers, 346 Madison Ave. (682-8800), at E. 44th St. Subway: #6 to Grand Central. Every day is Father's Day at Brooks Brothers: striped oxfords, tasteful ties, and all types of male accoutrements. Open M-W and F-Su noon-6pm, Th 9am-8pm.

Dollar Bills, 32 E. 42nd St. (867-0212), between Madison and Fifth Ave. Subway: #4, 5, 6, or S to Grand Central; or #1, 2, 3, 9, or N, R to Times Sq. and walk east on 42nd St. Great bargains on normally expensive designer clothes. It's hit or miss, but when you hit, you hit big. Armani, Fendi, and other chic European designers can all be found here with careful sifting and a little luck. Open M-F 8am-7pm, Sa 10am-6pm, Su noon-5pm.

Lord and Taylor, 424 Fifth Ave. (391-3344), between 38th and 39th St. Subway: B, D, F to 42nd St.; or N, R to 34th St. Courtly and claustrophobic. Features 10 floors of fashion frenzy. Scores of New Yorkers come to be shod at the acclaimed shoe department and treated like lords—caring service and free early morning coffee. Lord and Taylor also offers legendary Christmas displays. The first in history to use the picture window as a stage for anything other than merchandise, the store began this custom in 1905 during an unusually balmy December that failed to summon the appropriate meteorological garnish; Lord and Taylor filled its windows with mock blizzards, reviving the Christmas spirit for gloomy city-dwellers. Open M-Tu and Sa 10am-7pm, W-F 10am-8:30pm, Su 11am-7pm.

Macy's, 151 W. 34th St. (695-4400), between Broadway and Seventh Ave. Subway: #1, 2, 3, 9 to Penn Station; or B, D, F, N, Q, or R to 34th St. The world's "finest" department store can be the most exhilarating or the most frustrating experience, depending on your mood. Within its 2.1 million square feet you can purchase a book, grab either a snack or an all-out meal, get a facial and a haircut, mail a letter, have your jewelry appraised, exchange currency, purchase theater tickets, and get lost. The visitors center, located on the 1st floor balcony, is the place you'll most likely want to go for assistance of any kind (494-3027). Open M-Sa 10am-8:30pm, Su 11am-7pm.

Manhattan Mall (465-0500), at Sixth Ave. and 33rd St. Subway: N, R to 34th St. The flashy colored lights and fantasy-land exterior of the mall appear to herald an amusement park. Inside, at **Stern's Department Store** and many smaller chain stores, you can ascend to 8 different levels of commodity heaven. You'll find fashion, toys, electronics, and hard-to-find items. The building is twisted into a doughnut shape to focus shoppers' attention toward the goods and away from real life on the streets outside. The top level, called "Taste of the Town," is an entire floor of homogenized, multi-cultured fast food. Open M-Sa 10am-8pm, Su 11am-6pm.

Saks Fifth Avenue, 611 Fifth Ave. (753-4000), between 49th and 50th St. Subway: B, D, F, Q to 50th St. Subdued and chic. This institution has aged well and continues to combine inflated prices with smooth courtesy. Open M-W and F 10am-7pm, Th 10am-8pm, Sa 10am-6:30pm, Su noon-6pm.

Tiffany & Co., 727 Fifth Ave. (755-8000), between 56th and 57th St. Subway: #1, 9 to 50th St./Broadway; or #4, 5, 6 to 50th St./Lexington Ave. The window displays entice even the most determinedly oblivious passersby. Give in and enter to aah over the massive diamonds, giggle at nervous couples picking out rings, and smirk at the "you can't afford that" side of your nature. Do head up to the 3rd floor to see which famous people have registered for what, dahling. The workers here are trained in the Tiffany secret—signature white bows tied without knots. New York-related window exhibits show regularly, especially around Christmas. Open M-W and F-Sa 10am-6pm, Th 10am-7pm.

Trump Tower (832-2000), at 57th St. and Fifth Ave., gleams with garish pink marble and gold along with a painfully dated 80s interior. Inside, a fountain of plenty flows down the walls of a 6-story atrium jam-packed with upscale boutiques and restaurants. Boutiques open M-Sa 10am-6pm. Atrium open daily 8am-10pm.

UPTOWN

Allan and Suzi, 416 Amsterdam Ave. (724-7445), at 80th St. RuPaul, Courtney Love, and Annie Lennox shop here. From new Gaultier Madonna-wear at 70% off to original Pucci dresses, this store is fashion discount (though still expensive) chaos. A large assortment of platform shoes surrounds the melée. Men's clothing includes Armani and Versace suits. Open daily noon-7pm.

Barneys New York (826-8900), Madison Ave. and 61st St. Same shtick as its downtown counterpart (see above), but this one features a chi-chi **cafe,** a great place to spot celebrity shoppers sipping skinny lattes as they rest their weary legs and bag-laden arms. Open M-F 10am-8pm, Sa 10am-7pm; Sept.-June also Su noon-6pm.

Diesel, 770 Lexington Ave. (308-0055), at 60th St. Diesel's "Style-Lab" has scientifically procured the hippest urban gear around. This Diesel has a DJ and cafe to make shopping a well-rounded experience. Open M-Sa 10am-8pm, Su noon-6pm.

Encore, 1132 Madison Ave., 2nd fl. (879-2850), at 84th St. Second-hand designer clothes. Open M-W and F 10:30am-6:30pm, Th 10:30am-7:30pm, Sa 10:30am-6pm, Su noon-6pm. Closed Su July-Aug.

Michael's, 1041 Madison Ave., 2nd fl. (737-7273), between 79th and 80th St. Also peddles designer second-hand threads. Open M-W and F-Sa 9:30am-6pm, Th 9:30am-3pm. Closed Sa July-Aug.

OUTER BOROUGHS

Staten Island Mall, off Richmond Rd., near the center of the island. Bus: S44 from the ferry terminal, and ride for about 45min. All the big, boring names of mall-dom are here. Open M-Sa 10am-9:30pm, Su noon-6pm.

Domsey's, 431 Kent Ave. (718-384-6000), Williamsburg, Brooklyn. Subway: J, M, or Z to Marcy. Poorly paid Manhattanites and hipsters alike head to Domsey's, the best vintage clothing store in the city. Astounding bargains await the diligent shopper in this sprawling warehouse. The selection is vast in one of the few stores in the city where used clothing is actually cheap. Open M-F 8am-5:30pm, Sa 8am-6:30pm, Su 11am-5:30pm.

SPECIALTY STORES

Adorned, 47 Second Ave. (473-0007), between Second and Third St. Comfortable, safe, and friendly place to add bauble to your body. They won't do anything outlandish or hard core (no surface pierces or face/hand tattoos) unless you're seriously covered already. As they see it, they're here to "make you beautiful, not mutilated." Custom work available. Nose pierce $15; navel $20. Jewelry not included. Skilled, traditional henna work (hands and feet) $20 and up. Tattoos $75 and up. Open Su-Th noon-8pm, F-Sa noon-10pm.

Astor Place Hair Stylists, 2 Astor Pl. (475-9854) at Broadway. Complement your new Village wardrobe with a distinctive trim at the largest haircutting establishment in the world, famed for its low-priced production-line approach to style. One observer noted, "It's like Club MTV with clippers." If you want, you can get a haircut here that emulates much of the local graffiti art. Don't shy away by the constant drone of mechanical clippers—this is no salon, but you can get a decent haircut. Q-Tip, Adam Sandler, and Joan Rivers represent just some of the celeb clientele that frequent this establishment. One hundred-ten people (including a DJ) work in this 3-story complex. Short hair cuts $11; long hair cuts $13; Su $2 extra. Open M-Sa 8am-8pm, Su 9am-6pm.

BJ Discount Pet Shop, 151 E. Houston St. (982-5310). Good things come in small cages at this pet store, which specializes in bizarre petite pets. Yet, their animals have made it big. The Madagascar hissing roaches appeared in *Men In Black,* a millipede in a Showtime movie, and many other species on David Letterman. Despite their serious business sense, the owners have a warm sense of humor, evident in the South American Boa cage with a sign reading, "Hug me." Open M-Sa 10am-6:30pm.

Condomania, 351 Bleecker St. (691-9442), near W. 10th St. Subway: #1, 9 to Christopher St. "America's first condom store" is basically just condoms, dental dams, and lube. Pick up some XXX-rated fortune cookies or a box of "Penis Pasta" with your order. Friendly staff answers all questions and gives safe-sex tips. Open Su-Th 11am-11pm, F-Sa 11am-midnight.

The Counter Spy Shop, 444 Madison Ave. (688-8500), between 49th and 50th St. Subway: #6 to 51st St. James Bond fans and clinical paranoids will love this store, devoted to the technology of subterfuge and deception. Bullet-proof vests, hidden cameras, and domestic lie detectors share the racks with false-bottom cans ($20) and junior spy t-shirts ($10). One useful title: *How To Get Even with Anybody, Anytime.* Open M 9am-6pm, Tu-F 9am-7pm, Sa 10am-4pm, Su 11am-4pm. Accepts AmEx, V, MC, Discover.

Hammacher Schlemmer, 157 E. 57th St. (421-9000), between Third and Lexington Ave. Subway: #4, 5, 6 to 59th St. If the name doesn't set you rolling, leave it to the smorgasbord of bizarre merchandise inside. This store is a gadget-fancier's delight. Marvel at such essential items as a self-cleaning litter box, a pedal-powered swan boat, and a singing, dancing Elvis telephone. More redeemingly, Hammacher's zeal for automated convenience has also provided the world with the steam iron, the electric razor, and the pressure cooker. Open M-Sa 10am-6pm. Accepts AmEx, MC, V.

■ **K. Trimming,** 519 Broadway (431-8829), between Spring and Broome St. A cavernous warehouse of every kind of sewing product you could ever want: doilies, swaths of colored fabrics, sequins, embroidered trimmings, pom-poms, ribbons, buttons, and more. It's a tempting sartorial jungle where amateur and aspiring SoHo designers come to find their wares. Open Su-Th 9am-7:30pm, F 9am-3pm.

Kate's Paperie, 561 Broadway (941-9816), between Prince and Spring St. A decadent array of all things relating to stationery. Bring back the art of letter writing in style with designer paper ranging from $1-30 a sheet. **Also at:** 8 W. 13th St. (633-0570). Open M-Th 10:30am-7pm, F-Sa 10:30am-8pm, Su 11am-7pm.

The Leather Man, 111 Christopher St. (243-5339), between Bleecker and Hudson St. Subway: #1, 9 to Christopher St. What a window display! Not for the timid—chains, leather, and, in the basement, all manner of sex toys, etc. Plenty of stuff for your folks...nudge, nudge, wink, wink. Friendly staff, helpful to all genders and orientations. Gift certificates available. Open M-Sa noon-11pm, Su noon-8pm.

Little Rickie, 49½ First Ave. (505-6467), at 3rd St. Subway: F to Second Ave. A store for kids raised on TV. Pee Wee Herman decals, Madonna tapestries, and Elvis lamps, as well as marionettes of the Pope and Indonesian penis dolls. Open M-Sa 11am-8pm, Su noon-7pm.

Maxilla & Mandible, 451 Columbus Ave. (724-6173), between 81st and 82nd St. Subway: #1 or 9 to 79th St. Shelves and boxes of well-displayed shells, fossils, eggs, preserved insects, and—most of all—bones from every imaginable vertebrate (including *Homo sapiens*). A giant walking-stick insect under glass and an 11ft. alligator skeleton stand out prominently among the merchandise. "Dinosaur dung" for the little ones ($3). Open Tu-Sa 11am-7pm.

Nike Town, 6 E. 57th (891-6453), between Fifth and Madison Ave. Subway: #4, 5, 6 to 59th St. Enter through the tower or on 57th St. to visit Nike's latest advance toward world domination. Part sports museum, part athletic department store, this Nike mecca has 5 heavenly white floors dedicated to every conceivable athletic activity. Open M-F 10am-8pm, Sa 10am-7pm, Su 11am-6pm.

The Pop Shop, 292 Lafayette St. (219-2784), at Houston St. 1980s pop artist Keith Haring's cartoonish, socially conscious artwork can be found on posters and post-cards all over the city, but where else could you find Haring-decorated umbrellas ($40), t-shirts ($20), and practically anything else? You can get a full-sized Keith Haring poster for anywhere from $5 to $40. Opened in 1985, the shop was hand-painted by the late artist in his distinctive style, and all proceeds benefit the Keith Haring Foundation, which supports a range of social causes. Open Tu-Sa noon-7pm, Su noon-6pm.

Rita Ford Music Boxes, 19 E. 65th St. (535-6717), between Madison and Fifth Ave. Not just plastic pop-up boxed ballerinas; all kinds of music boxes are sold, from 19th-century antiques to plastic clown and fire truck models. Expensive (some upwards of $12,000), but well worth a peek. Open M-Sa 9am-5pm.

Schoepfer Studios, 138 W. 31st St. (736-6939), between Sixth and Seventh Ave. Subway: N, R to 34th St. A gallery-store of great breadth in the realm of stuffed and mounted dead animals. Buy a genuine rattlesnake (from $100), or just buy the earrings ($18). Open M-F 10am-4pm.

Tender Buttons, 143 E. 62nd St. (758-7004), near Lexington Ave. A treasure trove of billions of buttons. If you carelessly lost the button on your favorite Renaissance doublet, you will find a replacement here. Also has cuff links and buckles. The ladies-who-lunch shop here. Open M-F 11am-6pm, Sa 11am-5:30pm.

Warner Bros. Studio Store, 1 E. 57th St. (754-0300), at Fifth Ave. Subway: B, Q to 57th St./Sixth Ave.; or N, R to 57th St./Seventh Ave. A 9-story shrine to Warner Bros.' most profitable icons, from the Looney Tunes to Batman and Robin. Find Bugs Bunny, the Tasmanian Devil, Elmer Fudd, and Yosemite Sam emblazoned on every conceivable item, from hats to housewares. That's *not* all folks...you can even buy clothing from Acme, the generic brand to beat all others. Open M-Sa 10am-8pm, Su noon-8pm. Accepts AmEx, Discover, MC, V.

COMPUTERS AND ELECTRONICS

Nobody Beats the Wiz, locations include: 871 Sixth Ave. (594-2300), at 31st St.; and 17 Union Sq. West (741-9500), at 15th St. Long-held promise to beat any other store's price. If you bring in an advertisement for an item which is priced lower than N.B.T.W., they will discount the item 10% for you. Both open M-Sa 10am-8pm, Su11am-7pm.

J & R Music World, 23 Park Row (732-8600 or 238-9000), near City Hall. Subway: N, R, 4, 5, or 6 to City Hall. Will also meet most of your electronics needs with competitive prices. Open M-W and F-Sa 9am-7pm, Th 9am-7:30pm, Su 10:30am-6:30pm.

Willoughby's, 50 E. 42nd St. (681-7844), between Park and Madison Ave. Discounted electronics. Open M-F 8:30am-7:30pm, Sa-Su 10am-7pm.

RECORD STORES

The largest labels are available at HMV and Tower Records (see below). For music enthusiasts on the lookout for more obscure titles or labels, at least a dozen smaller stores can be found east of Broadway in the East Village, and round about Bleecker St. in the West Village. Lacking the commercial bloat, these knowledgeable places specialize in hard-to-find alternative and electronic releases, imports, dance remixes, rare oldies, and vinyl records. Several of the smaller stores also sell used music at bargain prices. Perseverance pays off in this city; if you can't find what you want here, you're not looking hard enough.

Accidental, 131 Ave. A (995-2224), between St. Marks and 9th St. If after clubbing you crave the eerie lyric of that gritty DJ, stop by Accidental to find it—this place *never* closes. More-than-reasonable prices and an exponentially growing selection in this cluttered store. CDs, vinyl, cassettes, kitschy videos, and posters. Open always.

Ayo's Multi Kulti, 218 Thompson St. (979-1872), near W. 3rd St. Subway: A, C, E, or B, D, F, Q to W. 4th St. For those interested in non-Western music. Ayo and staff will help you find what you want, whether it be tunes of Rajasthani desert nomads or Haitian voodoo-jazz. Open M-Sa 12:30-10pm, Su 12:30-7:30pm.

Bleecker St. Records, 239 Bleecker St. (255-7899). Subway: A, B, C, D, E, F, or Q to W. 4th St. The walls of this vintage shop are decorated with old vinyl platters. Heavy concentration of jazz LPs complement a formidable selection of old rock, blues, country, and soul. Open M-Th 11am-10pm, F-Sa 11am-1am, Su noon-10pm.

Colony Records, 1619 Broadway (265-2050), at 49th St. Subway: #1, 9 to 50th St.; or N, R to 49th St. You really can't miss the big neon sign, not even camouflaged in its Times Square locale. Mind-blowing selection of all forms of new and used music on CD, tape, and vinyl—from rock to Japanese Imperial Court music. Check out the vintage sheet music and the selection of autographs, memorabilia, and movie scripts. Open daily 10am-midnight.

Disc-O-Rama, 186 W. 4th St. (206-8417), between Sixth and Seventh Ave. All CDs $10 or below. Strong alternative section in addition to more standard Top 40 choices. The CDs aren't in order, so be prepared for a search (only the top 200 are organized). Open M-Th 10:30am-10:30pm, F 10:30am-11:30pm, Sa 10am-12:30am, Su 11:30am-8pm.

Downtown Music Gallery, 211 E. 5th St. (473-0043), between Second and Third Ave. Subway: #6 to Astor Pl.; or N, R to 8th St. Dense and diverse, the selection of CDs and records should please most non-mainstream music enthusiasts. The gallery's "downtown, prog, avant, and japanoise" section is very strong—virtually all of John Zorn's many musical projects are available. The staff knows the music well and happily dispenses advice upon request. Open Su-Th noon-9pm, F-Sa noon-11pm.

Earwax, 204 Bedford Ave. (718-218-9608), in Williamsburg, Brooklyn. Subway: L to Bedford Ave. Wax for the ears. Come here to get your Wordsound and avant-garde weirdness, from Sub Dub to Morton Subotnick. Eclectic electronica and vinyl selection should keep the DJs busy. Stocks flyers announcing underground Brooklyn art and sound events. Open daily noon-8pm.

Generation Records, 210 Thompson St. (254-1100), between Bleecker and 3rd St. All kinds of alternative and underground rock on CD and vinyl; the hardcore and industrial/experimental selection is especially impressive. Fairly low prices (CDs $11-13) and the best assortment of hard-to-find imports in the Village. Great deals on used merchandise downstairs. Open M-Th 11am-10pm, F-Sa 11am-1am, Su noon-10pm.

Gryphon Record Shop, 233 W. 72nd St. (874-1588), just off Broadway. Subway: #1, 9 or 2, 3 to 72nd St. Wall-to-wall shelves of classical, Broadway, and Jazz LPs, many rare or out of print. Real collector atmosphere; proprietor has the knowledge to match. Open M-Sa 11am-7pm, Su 12:30-6:30pm. Student Advantage card discounts.

HMV, 1280 Lexington Ave. (348-0800), at 86th St. "Music superstore," looking like dad's study filled with CDs and large posters of the newest Big Thing. His Master's Voice provides a wide range of classical, jazz, new age, show tunes, and pop schlock. Other locations: 565 Fifth Ave., at 46th; 57 W. 34th St.; and Broadway and 72nd St. All open M-Sa 9am-11pm, Su 10am-10pm.

Jammyland, 60 E. 3rd St. (614-0185), between First and Second Ave. Subway: #6 to Bleecker St. Wide selection of reggae, dub, dancehall, ska, and other Jamaican innovations, along with a decent world music supply. Helpful staff lets you listen before you buy. Come also to find out what's up in the NY reggae scene. Open M-Sa noon-midnight, Su noon-10pm.

▩ Kim's Video and Audio, 6 St. Mark's Pl. (598-9985). This is the mothership of Kim's outposts. Upstairs holds new and used vinyl and a tremendous video showcase specializing in independent and foreign films; downstairs has a startlingly strong selection of independent and import CDs for reasonable prices. The supply of experimental beats—from 1970s Jamaican dub to avant jazz to futuristic jungle—is exhaustive. The other Kim's locations (144 Bleecker St., 350 Bleecker St. and 85 Ave. A.; 387-8250, 675-8996, and 529-3410, respectively) offer smaller music departments with the same quality. Open daily 9am-midnight.

Liquid Sky/Temple, 241 Lafayette St. (343-0532). Subway: #6 to Spring St. or N, R to Prince St. Closed for renovations at time of writing; opening a new store Sept. 1, 1999; call for hours. Post-rave record and clothing shop. Since this is a store for techno DJs (and DJ-wannabees), most of the music is on vinyl, but there is a decent selection of pricey CDs and mix tapes. Good location to find discount flyers for underground clubs and rave events.

Midnight Records, 263 W. 23rd St. (675-2768), between seventh and eighth Ave. Subway: #1, 9 or C, E to 23rd St. A mail-order and retail store specializing in hard-to-find rock records. Posters plaster the walls; every last nook is crammed with records—over 10,000 in stock. Prices aren't cheap, but if you're looking for the Prats' album *Disco Pope*, this may be the only place to find it. Lots of 1960s and 70s titles. Most LPs $9-20. Open Tu-Sa noon-6pm.

Ordered Chaos/Japan Music Shop, 170 Ave. B (598-4888), between 10th and 11th St. Small section at the back of this New Age gift store deals in Japanese alternative music (CD and vinyl) and Asian pop culture items. Friendly owner is knowledgeable about all things Japanese; look for her "De-i Productions" label carrying Japanese artists. Open Tu-Su 1-8pm.

▩ Other Music, 15 E. 4th St. (477-8150), across from Tower Records. Subway: F, B, D, Q to Broadway and Lafayette St.; or N, R to 8th St. Specializing in the alternative and avant-garde. Obscure stuff abounds, but you can avoid steep import prices with the sizeable used CD section. Posters and flyers keep the clientele updated on where to see their favorite performers. Open M-Th noon-9pm, F-Sa noon-10pm, Su noon-7pm.

Rock and Soul, 462 Seventh Ave. (695-3953), between 35th and 36th St. Behind all the hi-fi electronics and DJ equipment is the place to find any of the tracks you hear thumping in the clubs. Specializing in the newest releases as well as the old-school classics, digging through these crates of reggae, R&B, house, and underground hip-hop LPs and CDs is a soulful music-lover's dream. Open M-Sa 9:30am-7pm. Accepts AmEx, V, MC.

Second Coming Records, 235 Sullivan St. (228-1313), near W. 3rd St. Subway: A, B, C, D, E, F, or Q to W. 4th St. Vinyl, and lots of it. An especially strong selection of underground 7-inches. Thanks to a recent expansion, the CD stock now accommodates a wide range of alternative and popular releases, both new and used. Also good for alternative imports and oddities. Open daily 11am-7pm.

Sounds, 20 St. Mark's Pl. (677-3444), between 2nd and 3rd Ave. Subway: #6 to Astor Pl. Good, fair-priced selection of alternative, dance music, and jazz. Used CD folders offer the best values, but be prepared to search. Racks of used LPs. New CDs from $9, used from $0.88. For used CDs, they'll pay (in cash) up to 50% of their resale value. **CD & Cassette Annex** at 16 St. Mark's Pl. (677-2727). Open M-Th noon-10:30pm, F-Sa noon-11:30pm, Su noon-9pm.

Throb, 211 E. 14th St. (533-2328), between 2nd and 3rd Ave. Jungle, trip-hop, house, loungecore, and more, Throb caters to folks who are serious about their beats. Wax for the DJs, CD for the audiophiles, and a (cute) staff to assist the confused. Lots of flyers here that will direct you to some phat parties. Open M-Sa noon-9pm, Su 1pm-9pm.

Tower Records, 692 Broadway (505-1500), at E. 4th St. Subway: F, B, D, Q to Broadway and Lafayette St.; or N, R to 8th St. One-stop music emporium, nearly a block long with 4 full floors of merchandise. Gadgets like the music-video computer let you preview select songs before purchasing them, while a touch-screen store directory makes tracking down that elusive album by your favorite mainstream artist a cinch. Uptown locations: 1535 3rd Ave., at 86th St., and 2107 Broadway, at 74th St. Open daily 9am-midnight.

BOOKSTORES

Whether your taste runs to esoteric cosmology or Third World revolution, whether you seek the newest *Let's Go* guide or a first-edition copy of Joyce's *Dubliners*, Manhattan is the island for you. Chains like **Barnes and Noble** (807-0099), **B. Dalton** (674-8780), and **Waldenbooks** (269-1139) discount current best-sellers, while New York's wealth of smaller bookstores deserve exploration.

Coliseum Books, 1771 Broadway (757-8381), at 57th St. Subway: #1, 9, or A, B, C, D to 59th St. This alternative to big chain stores is just a stone's throw from Lincoln Center and Carnegie Hall. It has a fine selection of drama and music, in addition to its main stock of new releases and poetry. Open M 8am-10pm, Tu-Th 8am-11pm, F-Sa 8am-11:30pm, Su noon-8pm.

Corner Bookstore, 1313 Madison Ave. (831-3554), at 93rd St. Careful selection and a friendly staff make this cozy neighborhood bookstore a treasure for Upper East Side book lovers. Note the antique cash register and the *zafdik* cat named Murphy. Open M-Th 10am-8pm, F 10am-7pm, Sa-Su 11am-6pm.

Crawford Doyle Booksellers, 1082 Madison Ave. (288-6300), between 81st and 82nd St. Synthesizes computer technology and old-fashioned customer care to serve all your bookstore needs. Open M-Sa 10am-6pm, Su noon-5pm.

Gotham Book Mart, 41 W. 47th St. (719-4448). Subway: B, D, F, Q to 50th St. Legendary and venerable, Gotham's renowned selection of new and used volumes of 20th-century writing has long made it a favorite among the New York literati. This little renegade store smuggled censored copies of works by Joyce, Lawrence, and Miller to America. Then-unknown LeRoi Jones and Allen Ginsberg once worked here as clerks. The store boasts first edition Edward Gorey. An upstairs gallery features changing exhibits. Open M-F 9:30am-6:30pm, Sa 9:30am-6pm.

Shakespeare and Company, 716 Broadway (529-1330), at Washington Pl. Subway: N, R to 8th St.; or #6 to Astor Pl. A New York institution. Shakespeare & Co. carries high-quality literature, high-brow journals, a great selection of vintage crime, art, and theater books, and a huge periodical section. Open Su-Th 10am-11pm, F-Sa 10am-midnight.

St. Mark's Bookshop, 31 Third Ave. (260-7853), at 9th St. Subway: #6 to Astor Pl. The ultimate East Village bookstore. Excellent selection, with an emphasis on current literary theory, fiction, and poetry. Helpful staff. Open daily 10am-midnight.

SHOPPING

▨ **Strand,** 828 Broadway (473-1452), at 12th St. Subway: #4, 5, 6, or L, or N, R to 14th St. The world's largest used bookstore. A must-see, with 8 mi. of shelf space that holds nearly 2 million books including rare titles and first editions. 50% off review copies and paperbacks. Vast collection of art books. Check the outdoor carts for extreme bargains. Staffers will search out obscure titles at your bidding. Ask for a catalog, or better yet, get lost in the shelves on your own. Open M-Sa 9:30am-9:20pm, Su 11am-9:20pm.

SPECIALTY BOOKSTORES

Applause Theater and Cinema Books, 211 W. 71st St. (496-7511), between Broadway and West End Ave. Subway: #1, 9 or 2, 3 to 72nd St. Great selection of scripts, screenplays, and books on everything from John Wayne to tap dancing. Over 4000 titles. Look out for their intermittent $1 sale and the odd celebrity. Knowledgeable staff. Open M-Sa 10am-8pm, Su noon-6pm.

Argosy Bookstore, 116 E. 59th St. (753-4455), between Park and Lexington Ave. Subway: #4, 5, 6 to 59th St.; or N, R to Lexington Ave. Buys and sells rare, used, and out-of-print books, along with autographed editions, Americana, and some truly swell maps. Extremely helpful staff and a friendly clientele to boot. Many racks of $1 books. Open M-F 10am-6pm; Oct.-May also Sa 10am-5pm. Accepts AmEx, Visa, MC. Wheelchair accessible.

Asahiya Bookstore, 52 Vanderbilt Ave. (883-0011), at E. 45th St. Subway: #4, 5, 6, 7, or S to 42nd St. Japanese books and periodicals. Origami, some stationery, and a few English-language books on Japan for the *gaijín* among us. Open daily 10am-8pm. Accepts AmEx, MC, V. Wheelchair accessible.

Biography Bookstore, 400 Bleecker St. (807-8692), at W. 11th St. Subway: #1 or 9 to Christopher St. Let us sit upon the ground and tell sad tales of the deaths of kings, presidents, rock idols, and other personalities. Biography-browsing at its best. Very strong gay/lesbian section, as well as bestsellers. Open M-Th 11am-10pm, F-Sa 11am-midnight, Su 11am-7pm.

Black Out Books, 50 Ave. B (777-1967; www.panix.com/~blackout), between 3rd and 4th St. A self-described "meeting place/clearinghouse for activists and ideas," Black Out serves as a haven for East Village anarchists, activists, and those who love them. Sections on "Art as Resistance," "Imprisonment," and, surprisingly, "Erotica" share the small store with tracts such as The Complete Manual of Pirate Radio. Check windows and inside for community political and social activities. Open daily 11am-10pm.

Books of Wonder, 16 W. 18th St. (989-3270), between fifth and sixth Ave. Subway: #1, 9 to 18th St.; or F to 16th and 6th. New York City's largest children's bookstore. The used book section is worth exploring. Storytelling on Sunday at 11:45am, only for ages 3-7. Open M-Sa 11am-7pm, Su noon-6pm.

The Complete Traveller Bookstore, 199 Madison Ave. (685-9007), at 35th St. Subway: #6 to 32nd St. Possibly the widest selection of guidebooks on the Eastern Seaboard. New addition of travel guides for the elderly. Most importantly, the store carries a full assortment of *Let's Go* guidebooks (priceless). Open M-F 9am-7pm, Sa 10am-6pm, Su 11am-5pm. Accepts AmEx, Visa, MC, Discover. Wheelchair accessible.

▨ **The Drama Book Shop,** 723 Seventh Ave. (944-0595; fax: 730-8739; www.drama-bookshop.com), at the corner of 48th St. Subway: #1, 9 or 2, 3 or N, R to Times Square. Take the elevator to the second floor. If it ever appeared onstage, you'll find it in print here. Find half the aspiring actors in the city and the monologues they seek, all in one compact location. A necessary stop for any theater, film or plain ol' performing arts buff. Accepts AmEx, MC, V. Open M-F 9:30am-7pm, W 9:30am-8pm, Sa 10:30am-5:30pm, Su noon-5pm.

■ **Forbidden Planet,** 840 Broadway (473-1576), at 13th St. Subway: N, R, or L or #4, 5, 6 to Union Sq./14th St. An amazing repository of all things sci-fi—the mecca of the Trekkie world. New and used comic books, D&D figurines, a section of V.C. Andrews books, and a shelf about serial killers at this large sci-fi/fantasy warehouse. Unhealthily skinny boys and the death-goth girls who love them congregate here. Here's where to get all those missing back issues of *Cerebus the Aardvark.* Open daily 10am-8:30pm.

Hacker Art Books, 45 W. 57th St. (688-7600), between Fifth and Sixth Ave. Subway: B, Q to 57th St. Five flights up from the rumble of the street, Hacker's volumes comprise one of the best art book selections anywhere. Catalogs of Picasso's ceramics stand alongside how-to crafts books and the work of cutting-edge theorists. The selection here should satisfy art historians, birdhouse builders, and fans of prehistoric stoneware alike. Accepts MC, V. Open M-F 9:30am-6pm.

Kate's Paperie, 561 Broadway (941-9816), between Prince and Spring St. A decadent array of stationery. Bring back the art of letter writing in style with designer paper ranging from $1-30 a sheet. Open M-Th 10:30am-7pm, F-Sa 10:30am-8pm, Su 11am-7pm. **Also at:** 8 W. 13th St. (633-0570), with slightly shorter hours.

Liberation Bookstore, 421 Lenox Ave. (281-4615), at 131st St. Subway: #2, 3 to 135th St. This small store houses a great selection of African and African-American history, art, poetry, and fiction. Open Tu-F 3-7pm, Sa noon-4pm. Cash only.

Murder Ink, 2486 Broadway (362-8905), between 92nd and 93rd St. Subway: #1, 9 or 2, 3 to 96th St. Decorated in the official colors of murder (red and black), this store is loaded with enough whodunits to have you looking over your shoulder for a lifetime. New, used, and happily cluttered.

A Photographer's Place, 133 Mercer St. (431-9358), between Prince and Spring St. Subway: R to Prince St. Small, quiet store contains photography books aplenty—new, rare, and out of print—as well as a great postcards collection. Open M-Sa 11am-8pm, Su noon-6pm.

■ **Printed Matter, Inc.,** 77 Wooster St. (925-0325). And you thought you knew what a "book" was. Featuring the best artist books and magazines in the biz, this non-profit bookshop/gallery makes a fascinating reading list any day of the year. Artists like John Baldessari, Cindy Sherman, and Kiki Smith are all associated with this place, but the store's commitment to displaying books by unknowns makes Printed Matter such a valuable resource. Perpetual exhibitions and installations—always free, always fascinating. Also a great place to find out about local **internships** and events in the arts. Open Tu-F 10am-6pm, Sa 11am-7pm.

Revolution Books, 9 W. 19th St. (691-3345), between Fifth and Sixth Ave. Subway: #4, 5, 6, L, N, R to 14th St. Books on radical struggles from around the world. Large collection of works on Marx, Mao, and Malcolm X. Not-for-profit and mostly staffed by very clued-in volunteers. Open M-Sa 10am-7pm, Su noon-5pm.

See Hear, 59 E. 7th St. (505-9781), between First and Second Ave. Subway: N, R to Astor Pl. A small store dedicated to books, comics, 'zines, and rock mags, mostly of the underground variety. Open daily noon-8pm.

Universal News and Cafe Corp., 484 Broadway (965-9042), between Broome and Grand St. Over 7000 magazine titles (both foreign and domestic) covering everything from fashion to fishing to politics. Cafe and sitting area so you can munch and relax while you read. Open daily 7am-midnight.

Untitled, 159 Prince St. (982-2088), between Broadway and Thompson St. Fine arts store specializing in design and typography. Veritable library of postcards, catalogued for your convenience (each 75¢). Open M-Sa 10am-10pm, Su 11am-9pm.

Zakka, 510 Broome St. (431-3961), between W. Broadway and Thompson. Subway: C or E to Spring St. If Japanese pop/punk teen culture is what you crave, you won't want to miss this boutique/bookstore/toy store/video palace, which stocks all the latest paraphernalia pertaining to androgynous Asian pop-eyed anime. All kinds of hip Tokyo magazines, and a decent collection of cutting-edge design and photography books. Open W-M noon-8pm.

POSTERS AND COMICS

Anime Crash, 13 E. 4th St. (254-4670), between Broadway and Lafayette St. Subway: #1, 2, 3, 9 to Christopher St.; or N, R to 8th St.; or #4, 5, 6 to Bleecker St. Japanese pop culture, from Akira to Zandor. Import comics, model sets, huge posters, and cool miscellany. CDs, videos, and laser discs also on sale. Open M-Th 11am-9pm, F-Sa 11am-10pm, Su noon-7pm.

Village Comics, 214 Thompson St. (777-2770), between Bleecker and W. 3rd St. Subway: A, B, C, D, E, F, or Q to W. 4th St. The requisite comics jostle for space amidst collectible figurines, sci-fi trinkets, horror-movie doodads, and, in the back, porn movies and magazines. For kids who love D&D and adults who've never stopped playing. Open M-Tu 10:30am-7:30pm, W-Sa 10:30am-8:30pm, Su 11am-7pm.

TOYS AND GAMES

F.A.O. Schwarz, 767 Fifth Ave. (644-9400), at 58th St. Subway: #4, 5, 6 to 59th St.; walk 1 block west and 1 block south. A child's fantasy world: everything that whirs, flies, or begs to be assembled appears in this huge hands-on toy store. Promotional displays invite kids and teenagers on first dates to frolic to their heart's content. Nintendo has a super station where you can "test out" video games and Barbie has her own pink annex. As close to Willy Wonka as the real world comes. Open M-W 10am-7pm, Th-Sa 10am-8pm, Su 11am-6pm. Accepts AmEx, Visa, MC.

Game Show, 1240 Lexington Ave. (472-8011), at 83rd St. Everything from Monopoly and Pictionary to the ever-lovin' Kosherland, the original Hüsker Dü (Bob Mould not included), and a discreet section of "adult" games like Talk Dirty to Me. Open M-W and F-Sa 11am-6pm, Th 11am-7pm; Sept.-May also Su noon-5pm. Other location: 474 Ave. of the Americas (633-6328), between 11th and 12th St. Open M-W and F-Sa noon-7pm, Th noon-8pm, Su noon-5pm.

Star Magic, 1256 Lexington Ave. (988-0300), at 85th St. Specializing in "space age gifts," this store carries everything from telescopes to dried astronaut ice cream to tarot decks. Get some crystal or holographic jewelry to impress your New Age friends. Ravers can pick up glow-sticks and other luminous apparel. Also at 745 Broadway (228-7770), at 8th St. Open M-Sa 10am-8pm, Su 11am-7pm.

Village Chess Shop, 230 Thompson St. (475-9580), between Bleecker and W. 3rd St. Subway: A, B, C, D, E, F, or Q to W. 4th. St. The Village's keenest intellects square off in rigorous strategic combat while sipping coffee ($1) and juice ($1.50). Play is $1 or $1.60 for clocked play per hour per person. Don't !@%*# swear or you'll be penalized 25¢. Novices can get their game analyzed for $3. The shop also showcases several breathtaking antique chess sets, as well as more recent models based on Tolkien's *Lord of the Rings*, the *Simpsons*, Shakespearean characters, and the Civil War. Open daily noon-midnight.

THE QUEER APPLE

New York has been a major center for American gay life since the 19th century, when an open bohemian lifestyle flourished in Greenwich Village. During the 1920s and 30s, the fledgling community found its way uptown to Harlem where the clubs were more tolerant and the scene vibrant and creative. Still marginalized, the gay community was slowly building a confident internal support structure that resulted in the formation of the first gay student organization at Columbia in 1966; it was soon followed in 1967 by a similar group at NYU. Tensions erupted, however, in 1969; clashes between homosexuals and police ensued after a raid on the Stonewall Inn in the Village. The incident (New Yorker's just celebrated its thirty-year anniversary) has since become known as the **Stonewall Riot,** and is often credited as the inspiration for the gay rights movement.

In 1981, in the face of AIDS and the frustration associated with an excess of media hype and a lack of helpful action, gay New Yorkers developed the **Gay Men's Health Crisis (GMHC),** the first medical organization dedicated to serving those with AIDS (see below). When the political and medical establishment persisted in its silence about AIDS, activists formed **ACT-Up,** the first gay militant group, which continues to stage political events throughout the city and nation. The group organized a 25th anniversary rally of the Stonewall Riot on the Great Lawn of Central Park; estimates of attendance at the 1994 event range from 100,000 to 500,000. Since then, in late June every year, gay pride is celebrated at the **Pride Parade** through Greenwich Village (on June 25 in 2000). This ecstatic event is jam-packed with juggling drag queens, vans trailing rainbow streamers, and jubilant confetti-tossers.

Today gay and lesbian communities thrive in New York. An established contingent clusters around **Christopher Street** in the West Village, while an edgier, often younger, group rocks out in the East Village on First and Second Ave., south of E. 12th St. (see **Greenwich Village,** p. 149). Their gentrified neighbors have moved onto **Chelsea,** giving the word "guppie" (short for "gay urban professional" who sculpts his tanned body in Chelsea's gyms) a whole new scope and meaning. Here rainbow flags fly in dry cleaners and taxi dispatch centers, and buff boys waltz from juice-bar to gym to juice-bar again. The large lesbian community in **Park Slope** has lent the neighborhood the moniker "Dyke Slope" (see **Park Slope,** p. 207).

FURTHER READING: BISEXUAL, GAY, AND LESBIAN TRAVELERS.

Spartacus International Gay Guide. Bruno Gmunder Verlag ($33).

Damron Men's Guide, Damron Road Atlas, Damron's, and *The Women's Traveller.* Damron Travel Guides ($14-19). For more information, call 415-255-0404 or 800-462-6654 or check their website (www.damron.com).

Ferrari Guides' Gay Travel A to Z, Ferrari Guides' Men's Travel in Your Pocket, Ferrari Guides' Women's Travel in Your Pocket, and *Ferrari Guides' Inn Places.* Ferrari Guides ($14-16). For more information, call 602-863-2408 or 800-962-2912 or check their website (www.q-net.com).

The Gay Vacation Guide: The Best Trips and How to Plan Them, Mark Chesnut. Citadel Press ($15).

Gayellow Pages ($16). Call 212-674-0120, email gayellow@banet.net or check the website (gayellowpages.com).

BEFORE YOU LEAVE HOME

Gay, lesbian, and bisexual travelers should have no trouble having a great time in New York. The following is a list of resources to help plan your trip.

Gay's the Word, 66 Marchmont St., London WC1N 1AB (tel. (020) 278 7654; email gays.theword@virgin.net; www.gaystheword.co.uk). The largest gay and lesbian bookshop in the U.K. Mail-order service available. No catalogue of listings, but they will provide a list of titles on a given subject.

Giovanni's Room, 345 S. 12th St., Philadelphia, PA 19107 (tel. 215-923-2960; fax 923-0813; email giophilp@netaxs.com). An international feminist, lesbian, and gay bookstore with mail-order service which carries the publications listed here.

International Gay and Lesbian Travel Association, 4331 N. Federal Hwy., 304, Fort Lauderdale, FL 33308 (tel. 954-776-2626 or 800-448-8550; fax 954-776-3303; email IGLTA@aol.com; www.iglta.com). An organization of over 1350 companies serving gay and lesbian travelers worldwide. Call for lists of travel agents, accommodations, and events.

International Lesbian and Gay Association (ILGA), 81 rue Marché-au-Charbon, B-1000 Brussels, Belgium (tel./fax 32 2 502 24 71; email ilga@ilga.org; www.ilga.org). Not a travel service. Provides political information, such as homosexuality laws of individual countries.

RESOURCES AND SHOPS

A great first stop for any les/bi/gay traveler should be the **Lesbian and Gay Community Center,** 208 W. 13th St. (620-7310; www.gaycenter.org), between Seventh and Eighth Ave. (Subway: F or L to 14th St. Open daily 9am-11pm.) The center provides information and referral services and hosts myriad programs, groups, and social activities. Among their most noteworthy events are bi-monthly dances ($8, with membership $6) and the lesbian movie night on the last Friday and second Tuesday of every month (usually $6). The center also houses the **National Museum and Archive of Lesbian and Gay History** (open W 6-9pm, or call the Center for an appointment).

There are numerous publications dedicated to the gay and lesbian community of New York. *HomoXtra* (*HX* and *HX for Her)* and *Next* both have listings of nightlife and activities, and are available free at the center and at bars around the city. The free *LGNY* (no, that's not *Let's Go NY*, but *Lesbian-Gay NY*) also provides listings, and is distributed throughout the boroughs. The nationally distributed *Advocate* magazine has a New York section; also check the *Village Voice*, which details events, services, and occasional feature articles of interest to gays and lesbians. In addition some websites will give you info that the printed rags don't reveal. Check out www.gmad.org, a resource for gay men of African descent, and www.pridelinks.com, a no-holds-barred **queer search engine.**

The amazingly helpful **Gayellow Pages,** P.O. Box 533, Village Station, New York, NY 10014 (674-0120; fax 420-1126; email gayellow@banet.net; gayellowpages.com), has a special New York edition ($16) which lists accommodations, organizations, and services in the city.

HEALTH AND SUPPORT SERVICES

Callen-Lorde Community Health Center, 356 W. 18th St. (271-7200), between Eighth and Ninth Ave. Health services, as well as a walk-in sexually transmitted disease clinic and counseling (M-Tu 7-9pm). Lesbian Health Program (M-W 7-8:30pm).

Gay Men's Health Crisis (GMHC), 119 W. 24th St. (367-1000), between 6th and 7th Ave. Subway: #1, 9 or F, N, R, C to 23rd St. Health care and counseling for men and women with HIV and AIDS. Walk-in counseling M-F 11am-8pm. **Hotline:** 800-243-7692 or 807-6655 (open M-F 10am-9pm, Sa noon-3pm).

THE QUEER APPLE

Gay and Lesbian Switchboard, 989-0999. Peer counseling or referrals for the gay or lesbian traveler. Open M-F 6-10pm, Sa noon-5pm. 24hr. recording.

Bookstores

A Different Light, 151 W. 19th St. (989-4850), at Seventh Ave. Subway: #1, 9 to 18th St. This fabulous bookstore offers an amazing selection of lesbian and gay readings—everything from the latest queer sci-fi thriller to anthologies of transgender theory. The store really shines with its near-daily readings by prominent names in lesbigay literary circles. Stop by for a schedule of the free Sunday movie series. Open daily 10am-midnight.

Oscar Wilde Gay and Lesbian Bookshop, 15 Christopher St. (255-8097), near Sixth Ave. Subway: #1, 9 to Christopher St. This cozy little shop has the distinction of being the world's first gay and lesbian bookstore. Usual readings in queer literature, and a number of rare and first edition books. Open daily noon-8pm.

Religious Services

Church of St. Paul and St. Andrew, On 86th St. (362-3179) at West End Ave. Dates from 1897. Check out the octagonal tower and the angles in the spandrels. Gay-friendly services Su 11am.

Congregation Beth Simchat Torah, 57 Bethune St. (929-9498; www.cbst.org). Synagogue catering to the NY lesbian and gay community.

Metropolitan Community Church of New York, 446 W. 36th St. (629-7440), between 9th and 10th St. Subway: #1, 2, 3, 9 to 34th St. Christian Church of the gay and lesbian community.

ACCOMMODATIONS

If you're moving to New York and want help finding a gay, lesbian, bi- or transsexual roommate, it might be worthwhile to pay a visit to **Rainbow Roommates,** 268 W. 22nd St. (627-8612; www.gayroommate.com), near Eighth Ave. For $150 Rainbow Roommates provides you with a four-month subscription to personalized listings matching the roommate criteria you have requested. You may also want to try the **DG Neay Realty Group,** 57 W. 16th St. (627-4242; fax 989-1207), on the corner of Sixth Ave., which hosts **"G.R.I.N."**—the Gay Roommate Information Network. (Registration fee $39. Open M-Th 11am-7pm, F-Su 10:30am-6pm.) Most hotels and hostels in New York are friendly to gay and lesbian travelers; the **Gershwin Hotel** and the **Washington Square Hotel** both have scenes which can be fun for the queer traveler. Here are some more B,G, L,T options:

Chelsea Pines Inn, 317 W. 14th St. (929-1023; fax 620-5646; email cpiny@aol.com), between Eighth and Ninth Ave. Subway: A, C, E to 14th St. For the ultimate in fabulous stays. Friendly, amenity-laden haven of cozy rooms decorated with vintage film posters. Gorgeous garden and "greenhouse" out back. A/C, cable TV, refrigerator, and washing facilities in all rooms. Rooms with private showers but shared toilet: full-size bed $89-109, queen-size bed $99-119. Rooms with private bath: queen-size bed $109-129, queen-size bed with breakfast area $119-139. $20 for extra person. 3-day min. stay on weekends. Continental breakfast included, including fresh homemade bread. Reservations are essential.

Colonial House, 318 W. 22nd St. (800-689-3779 or 243-9669; fax 633-1612; www.colonialhouseinn.com), between 8th and 9th Ave., in Chelsea. Very comfortable, inviting bed 'n' breakfast housed in a classy Chelsea brownstone. All rooms have cable TV, A/C, and phone, some with bath and fireplace. Sun deck with a "clothing optional" area. 24hr. desk and concierge service. Breakfast (8am-noon) included. Double bed "economy" room $80-99; queen-size bed with shared bath $99-125; queen-size bed with private bath $125-145. Check-in 3pm. Check-out noon. Reservations are encouraged and require one night's deposit within 10 days of stay.

HANGOUTS AND RESTAURANTS

For general restaurant information see **Restaurants,** p. 87.

Big Cup, 228 8th Ave. (206-0059), between 21st and 22nd St. Bright, campy colors and comfy velvet chairs make this a great place to curl up with a cup of joe ($1.20) and cruise for cute Chelsea boys who will happily wink back. Offers creative coffee flavors ($1.40-2.45) and daring sandwich combinations ($5.50-6.50). Tarot readings Tuesday nights at 8pm. Open M-Th 7am-1am, F 7am-2am, Sa 8am-2am, Su 8am-2am. **$**

The Viceroy, 160 Eighth Ave. (633-8484), at 18th St. Although consistently tasty, food is hardly the lure to this swanky cafe, bar, restaurant, and hub of the Chelsea gay scene. Cute boys pick at the American-Mediterranean cuisine, while waiters glide by against a backdrop of Art Deco elegance. The food is expensive here; your best bet is the Sa-Su breakfast (9-11:30am) for a piddling $9. Bloody Marys $5.50; espresso $2. Open Su-W 11:30am-midnight, Th-Sa 11:30am-1am. **$$-$$$**

B.M.W. Gallery and Coffee Magic Espresso Bar, 199 Seventh Ave. (229-1807), between 21st and 22nd St. Friendly, small cafe/bar/performance space/living room. Good selection of wines, microbrews, and gay magazines. Beers $3-6; coffee $1.25-2.25; Mochaccino $2.50-3.50. Live music nightly, and if you bring in your favorite CD, they'll play it for 10min. (longer if they like it). Open 24hr.

Caffe Raffaella, 134 Seventh Ave. (929-7247), north of Christopher St., in Greenwich Village. Predominantly gay, male clientele. Intimate, unpretentious atmosphere with a touch of subdued, Old World decadence. Sip steamed milk with *orzata* (sweet almond syrup, $2.50) while reclining in the embrace of an overstuffed chair, or cool off outside with a Caffe Raffaella (double espresso with vanilla ice cream and fresh whipped cream, $3.75). Open Su-Th 10am-2am, F-Sa 10am-3am.

Negril, 362 W. 23rd St. (807-6411), between Eighth and Ninth Ave. The Jamaican fare served in this colorful, if overzealous, gay-friendly haunt is light, yet incredibly spicy. *Bon Appetit* magazine once printed the recipe for their ginger lime chicken ($8.50). Beans or jerk chicken comes with rice or grilled banana and steamed vegetables ($7.50). Sandwiches $6.50-7.50, "light meals" (salads, etc.) $3.50-7.50, and entrees $6.50-8.50. Spicy ginger beer $3.50. Festive Sunday brunch with live band 11am-4pm. Open M-F 11am-midnight, Sa-Su 11am-4pm and 5pm-2am, F-Sa bar open until 4am. Wheelchair accessible. See **Restaurants,** p. 99. **$**

NIGHTLIFE

Following is a list of clubs (some of them dance-oriented, others geared towards conversation and drinking) at the center of gay and lesbian nightlife. Some of these clubs are geared exclusively towards lesbians or gay men, and may frown on letting in hopefuls of the opposite sex. If you and a friend of the opposite sex want to go to any of these clubs together, it might be wise to avoid behaving like a heterosexual couple, especially in front of the bouncer. The website www.mansco.com/lf2/ref/NEWYOR~1.HTM has a good list of gay and lesbian clubs in New York. To find out where the next dykerrific dance party is being held, lesbians should call the **Sheescape Danceline** (686-5665). **Hershee Bar** (631-1093 or 631-1102) also throws female fetes; call to find out the current location. Also keep in mind **Hot: The Ninth Annual NYC Celebration of Queer Culture,** Vineyard 26, 309 E. 26th St. (532-1535; www.dixonplace.org), at Dixon Pl. Every July after Pride warms everyone up, Hot steps in to fill the gay culture void (like there could ever be one) with artsy performances and off-beat happenings. (Subway: #6 to 28th St.)

THE QUEER APPLE

🎵 **Aspara,** at the Gemini Lounge, 221 Second Ave. (330-8615), between 13th and 14th St. A seriously sexy party with gorgeous ladies each trying to outdo themselves on the wild side. Come to dance hard, play hard, and strut your stuff. Every other Su 10pm-4am. Cover $8, with flyer $6.

Barracuda, 275 W. 22nd St. (645-8613), at Eighth Ave. Subway: C, E to 23rd St. Brimming with ripped Chelsea boys of all shapes and sizes. 1950s decor, complete with sofas, a pool table, and a dazzling collection of kitsch furniture, makes for a cozy hangout in the back, while the determined mobs in the front seem to have something else on their minds entirely. Most drinks $4-7. Open daily 4pm-4am.

Bar d'O, 29 Bedford St. (627-1580). The coziest lounge with the most sultry lighting in the city. Superb performances by drag divas Joey Arias and Raven O (Tu and Sa-Su nights, 10:30pm, $5). Even without the fine chanteuses, this is a damn fine place for a drink. Women's night on Monday packs a glam night of drag kings. Go early for the atmosphere, around midnight for the performances, and 2am to people-watch/gender-guess (is that a boy or a girl?). Don't try to leave in the middle of a show, or you'll be in for a nasty tongue-lashing. Doors open around 7pm.

Bbar (Bowery Bar), 40 E. 4th St. (475-2220), at the Bowery. Formerly the place to go downtown to ape the city's celebs, this bar has still got enough attitude to give you a healthy sense of self-worth for going there. Tuesday night is "Beige," promoter Erich Conrad's wonderfully flamboyant gay party. Open daily 11:30am-4am.

Boiler Room, 86 E. 4th St. (254-7536), between First and Second Ave. Hip East Village hangout that sees a mixed crowd with a strong dyke contingent. Drag kings nightly. Open daily 4pm-4am.

Café Con Leche, 124 W. 43rd St. (330-9061), by Broadway. Throbs with Latin house jams while men dance among their admirers. Predominantly for gay men of color, but the enthusiastic crowd is mixed and open, so all are welcome. Cover $10. Open daily 11am-4am.

Clit Club, 432 W. 14th St. (529-3300), at Washington St. Subway: A, C, E to 14th St. Friday nights in the Bar Room. The grandmother of NY dyke clubs, the Clit still draws one of the younger and more diverse crowds around. This is *the* place to be for young, beautiful, queer grrls. Host Julie throws a burning hot party, with go-go dancers, house music, and babes galore. Hit on the femme of your dreams at the pool table, or just chill out in the video room. Women only. Cover $3 before 11pm, $7 after 11pm. Doors open at 9:30pm. Tuesday nights the same space becomes **Jackie 60** (366-5680). Drag queens work it while the (sometimes) celebrity crowd eggs them on to even more fabulous feats of glamour; unfortunately, Jackie 60 will have closed at the end of 1999, so get it while it's hot if it's not too late. Frequent theme nights, such as "Transylvania 6060," a transvestite horror fest. Performances around 11:30pm. Cover $10. Doors open at 10pm.

Crazy Nanny's, 21 Seventh Ave. South (366-6312), near LeRoy St. Subway: 1, 9 to Houston St. Glamour dykes and the women who love them come here to shoot some pool and just hang out. Dancing nightly. Happy hour (M-Sa 4-7pm) spells 2-for-1 drinks. Open daily 4pm-4am.

The Cubbyhole, 281 W. 12th St. (243-9041), at W. 4th St. Subway: A, C, E, or L to 14th St. Yes, these 2 streets do intersect in the non-Euclidean West Village near Eighth Ave. Piano bar provides a relaxed scene for lesbians. Very low-key, but definitely queer. No cover. Happy hour until 7pm M-Sa. Open M-F 4pm-4am, Sa 2pm-4am, Su 3pm-4am.

Flamingo East, 219 Second Ave. (533-2860), between 13th and 14th St. Subway: L to Third Ave.; or #4, 5, 6 to Union Sq. Swank, kinky, hip. This place transcends lounge kitsch and takes you to the next level. Try Sunday nights for splendid Hawaiian lounge at *The 999999's.* A good place for your fabbest duds—nothing is too vintage or too outrageous. Open Su-Th 5:30pm-2:30am, F-Sa 5:30pm-4:30am.

g, 223 W. 19th St. (929-1085), between Seventh and Eighth Ave. Subway: #1, 9 or 2, 3 to 18th St. Once a meeting place for the über-cool, this Chelsea hangout's heyday has noticeably come to a close. Despite a humbling erosion of interest among hipsters, however, g still manages to attract a respectable guppie crowd with its glitzy decor and juice bar. With its cute crowd and famous frozen Cosmos, g undoubtedly has several good years left of stardom. Open daily 4pm-4am.

The Hangar, 115 Christopher St. (627-2044). Subway: #1, 9 to Christopher St. Queer locals and out-of-towners gather to enjoy the half-price happy hour M-F 3-9pm. 2-for-1 Tu, $100 pool tournament W, and similar lures continue throughout the week. Open Su-W noon-3am, Th-Sa noon-4am.

Henrietta Hudson, 438 Hudson St. (924-3347), between Morton and Barrow St. Young, clean-cut lesbian crowd. Mellow in the afternoon, packed at night and on the weekends. Try the Henrietta Girlbanger or the Girl Scout ($6.50). Happy hour (2 for 1) M-F 5-7pm. No cover. Open daily 3pm-4am.

Julius, 159 W. 10th St. (929-9672), at Waverly Pl., between Sixth and Seventh Ave. Subway: A, C, E to 14th St. This bar and restaurant has been a hot spot for gay men since 1966, when a protest was staged against the laws denying service to homosexuals. Today commemorative plaques explain the event while older, more conservative men drink legally amid the rainbow flags. Happy hour M-Sa 4-9pm, drinks half price. Open daily noon-2am.

King, 579 Sixth Ave. (366-5464), at 16th St. Cruisy place with bartenders who are refreshingly low on bad attitude. Weekends are a good bet. Beer $4. Drinks $4-7. Open daily 4pm-4am.

Kurfew, W. 27th St. (888-4-KURFEW), between Eleventh and Twelfth Ave. Saturdays at the Tunnel's mid-block entrance. Kurfew is New York's best party for the gay 18-25 set. Fun music, friendly folks, and lots of very cute boys. Cover $20; with ad $15; with student ID and an ad/invite $10. Doors open 11pm.

La Nueva Escuelita, 301 W. 39th St. (631-0588), at Eighth Ave. Subway: A, C, E to 42nd St. Queer Latin dance club that throbs with merengue, salsa, soul, hip-hop, and drag shows. Their **Spicy Fridays** party is a lesbian dreamscape with go-go girls galore. Largely Latin crowd. Open Th-Su 10pm-5am. Cover Th $3, F $10, Sa $15, Su $8.

Lovergirl, at Opera, 539 W. 21 St. (631-1000), between Tenth and Eleventh Ave. Subway: C, E to 23rd St. Female dance party has taken up residence at the Opera Club in Chelsea with DJs and go-go girls vying for your attention. Open Sa 10pm-4am. Cover $8 before midnight, $10 after.

The Lure, 409 W.13th St. (741-3919). One of the world's great leather bars, managed by retired (and still beautiful) porn legend Kyle Brandon. Wednesday night is Pork, voted NYC's best bar night of 1999 by *HX* magazine. Pork is more diverse, less uniformly leather, than the Lure's other nights—and each Pork Wednesday has a new theme for the evening. A great time, especially later. Opens at 10pm. Cover $5. Open M-Sa 8pm-4am, Su 5pm-4am.

Meow Mix, 269 E. Houston St. (254-1434), at Suffolk St. A major party scene Tu-Su nights for East Village lesbians. Especially hot on Saturday. Lots of events, including comedy, readings, performances, and the occasional *Xena: Warrior Princess* swordfight. Friendly staff. Call for schedule. Cover usually $2-5.

The Monster, 80 Grove St. (924-3558), at 4th St. and Sheridan Sq. Subway: #1, 9 to Christopher St. Look for the snarl of Christmas lights above the door. Cabaret-style piano bar with downstairs disco; heats up F-Sa. Crazy singles scene amid decadently lush vegetation. Cover after 10pm F-Sa $5. Open daily 4pm-4am.

The Roxy, 515 W. 18th St. (645-5156). Currently *the* place to be on Saturday nights. Hundreds of gay men dance, lounge, and drink in the Roxy's gigantic, luxurious space. Upstairs lounge/bar provides a different DJ and more intimate setting. Downstairs, high ceilings and a beautiful dance floor and lounge space give hedonists plenty of room to play. Busy nights boast beautiful go-go boys. Beer $5. Drinks $6+. Cover $20.

Splash, 50 W. 17th St. (691-0073). One of the most popular mega-bars. Enormous bar complex on two floors, packed on weekends with muscular boys who love to flirt. Cool, almost sci-fi decor provides a sleek backdrop for a very crowded scene, with a dance floor that completes the evening. Cover varies, peaking at $7. Beer $4; drinks $5-6.

The Spike, 120 Eleventh Ave. (243-9688), at W. 20th St. Subway: C, E to 23rd St. Caters to an adventurous crowd of leather-clad men (and some women) who know how to create a spectacle. Drink specials F-Sa 9pm-midnight. Open daily 9pm-4am.

Uncle Charlie's, 56 Greenwich Ave. (255-8787), at Perry St. Subway: #1, 9 to Christopher St. Biggest and best-known gay bar and club in the city. Mainstream and preppy, with guppies galore. It's still fun, if a bit crowded on the weekends. Women are welcome, but few come. No cover. Open daily 3pm-4am.

Wonder Bar, 505 E. 6th St. (777-9105). On a strip crowded with bars, Wonder Bar stands out. Done up in zebra chic and laid back neutrals, and frequented by a chill bohemian crowds and the occasional curious breeder. Open W-Sa 10pm-4am.

DAYTRIPPING TO FIRE ISLAND

*For transportation info, see **Daytrips**, p. 325.*

A countercultural enclave during the 1960s and home to a thriving 1970s disco scene, Fire Island heads into the millennium partying loud and queer. Two prominent Fire Island resort hamlets, **Cherry Grove** and **The Pines,** host largely gay communities. Queer-filled streets border spectacular Atlantic Ocean beaches, and the fabulous scene rages late into the night. Weekdays provide an excellent opportunity to enjoy the beauty and charm of the island in a low-key setting, with Thursdays and Sundays offering an ideal balance of sanity and scene—whereas Friday and Saturday prices climb with crowd size.

Most vacationers buy a summer share, a Long Island tradition of sardine-esque accommodation. Meanwhile, both towns host establishments which advertise themselves as "guest houses." Be aware that some of these may not be legally accredited (due to such things as fire code violations), and that some may not be lesbian-friendly. **The Cherry Grove Beach Hotel** (516-597-6600) is a good bet, located on the Main Walk of Cherry Grove and close to the beach. Rooms feature double beds, kitchenettes, and balconies, and start at $40 (but can cost up to $400 for the best rooms during peak seasons). Weekday prices are lower (full price the first night and $30 each additional night). Reservations are required. The hotel is open May to October. Other options: **Carousel Guest House** (516-597-6612) and **Holly House** (516-597-6911). Both are located on the Holly Walk, right behind the Ice Palace, and offer beds in clean rooms for reasonable prices (unless it's the weekend and peak season). For real luxury, try the **Belvedere** (516-597-6448). Themed rooms and a beautiful building make this all-male establishment a popular place. Even at its cheapest, however, expect to pay at least $100 for a night.

Fire Island's restaurant life generally entails unspectacular eats at astounding prices. One pretty good option is **Rachel's at the Grove** (516-597-4174), on Ocean Walk at the beach. Patio seating overlooks the Atlantic. A standard American meal will cost you $9-12. Reservations are recommended for dinner. *(*Open daily 10am-4pm, kitchen closes 11pm.)*

CHERRY GROVE. This more commercial of the two resort towns offers a cornucopia of rainbow-flagged restaurants and souvenir shops around the ferry slip. Narrow, raised boardwalks line the roadless area. These paths lead to small, uniformly shingled houses that generally overflow with men, though lesbian couples come here too. You can disco till dawn at the **Ice Palace** (516-597-6600), attached to the Cherry Grove Beach Hotel. Sip on a fruit smoothie ($6) while the piano bar boogies from 4 to 8pm, followed by disco until 4am. Check the billboard by the entry ramp for details about special weekend shows.

THE PINES. 10-minute walk up the beach from Cherry Grove, the Pines has traditionally looked down its nose at its uninhibited neighbor. Here, naughtiness cloaks itself in darkness. You see, the daring have been known to cruise a forest nook known as the "Meat Rack." Those who prefer not to go bump in the night, however, opt for the beach walk—by far the more beautiful *and safer-in-every-way* choice. Houses here are spacious and often stunningly modern, with an asymmetric aesthetic and huge windows. You may want to bring along a flashlight to navigate the often poorly lit boardwalks here. The Pines' active, upscale nighttime scene, unfortunately has a bit of a secret club feel to it—all-male secret club. Try The Island Club and Bistro (516-597-6001) at select times for a fairly busy scene. The Pines moves by an undeniably fixed, circuit-like schedule: one club will be busy for half an hour, and then all the men will disappear to private parties or their own homes for one hour, and then another spot will be busy for one hour, and so on. Don't be afraid to strike out on your own—the beach at night is truly breathtaking. *(For more information on Fire Island, see Daytripping, p. 325.)*

THE QUEER APPLE

DAYTRIPPING FROM NYC

This city drives me crazy, or, if you prefer, crazier; and I have no peace of mind or rest of body till I get out of it.

—Lafcadio Hearn, 1889 (he later fled to Tokyo)

LONG ISLAND

Long Island's nose (tactfully shaved off by a local plastic surgeon) nuzzles the tip of Manhattan. Technically, this 120 mile-long island includes the boroughs of Queens and Brooklyn. Looking beyond geography, however, deep into the island soul, you'll see that the true Long Islander (natives would say "Lawn-GUY-lander") would happily let piggybacking boroughs sink into the Atlantic—as long as their bridges to Manhattan remained intact. Largely a land of sport utility vehicles and carpools, landscape "artists" and snow-blowers, boob-jobs and climate control, Long Island's voice is nasal, irritating, yet strangely comforting. Despite its profusion of big hair and Avon products, "Strong Island" has drawn millions of city expatriates eastward in search of a little bit of grass, space, and fresh air.

Long Island *is* a pleasant place to visit and deserves a daytrip if you want to find out how a population flourishes with Kool Aid flowing through its veins. Stereotypes aside, one quickly learns that the gestalt of Long Island refracts through its numerous and ever-multiplying communities. There's new money, old money, and no money spread across the island from Hicksville (no joke) to the Hamptons.

Miles of sandy beaches, scenic harbors, and lush, green parks brought New York millionaires, who built country homes on the rocky north shore. Thus arose the exclusive "Gold Coast" captured in its 1920s heyday by F. Scott Fitzgerald's *The Great Gatsby*. Later emigrés moved farther east to the picturesque resort towns of Montauk and the Hamptons. The 1950s brought a turning point for the island: cars became more affordable, and young couples enjoying postwar prosperity sought dream houses for their baby-boom families. Most importantly, new Long Island neighborhoods like Levittown provided a safe, wholesome environment in which to raise children. This comfortable ideal, however, appears dimmer through the lenses of artists such as David Lynch, Eric Fischl, and John Cheever.

Much of the land is firmly developed today. Resort towns continue to prosper; the small offshore islands provide warmth and relaxation; parks and preserves grow larger and greener. For years, the Long Island Railroad (LIRR) provided the only major connection from these attractions into the city. During the 1950s, the Island's main artery, the Long Island Expressway (LIE, officially called State Highway 495), grew to include 73 exits on the 85-mile stretch from Manhattan to Riverhead. Even with the development of new transportation channels, traffic clogs the expressway during rush hour (7am to midnight). While many have rooted all facets of their lives on the Island, others commute to Manhattan by train.

PRACTICAL INFORMATION AND ORIENTATION

Area Code: A slanted and enchanted 516.

Visitor Information: Long Island Convention and Visitors Bureau (516-951-2423). Information on how to order free brochures and maps for Long Island and the Hamptons. Tourist offices are located on the eastbound side of the Long Island Expwy. between Exits 51 and 52, the eastbound side of the Southern State Pkwy. between Exits 13 and 14 (in Valley Stream), and in Tanger Outlet Mall in Riverhead. Open daily 9am-7pm.

Trains: Long Island Railroad (LIRR) (automated info 718-217-5477 or 516-822-5477; TDD hearing impaired 718-558-3022; lost and found 212-643-5228; open daily 7:20am-7:20pm). Long Island's main public transportation trains leave from Penn Station in Manhattan (34th St. at Seventh Ave.; subway: #1, 2, 3, 9 or A, C, E) and meet in Jamaica, Queens (subway: E, J, Z) before proceeding to "points east." LIRR also connects in Queens at the #7 subway Hunters' Point Ave., Woodside, Jamaica, and Main St. Flushing stations; in Brooklyn, at the Flatbush Ave. station (subway: #2, 3 or 4, 5 or D, Q to Atlantic; or B, M, N, R to Pacific). Most Long Island towns are served by LIRR; call for info. Fares vary daily and by "zone." Rush hour "peak" tickets (Manhattan-bound 5am-9am, outbound 4-8pm) cost $4.75-15.25. Off-peak fares are up to $5 cheaper. Tickets can be purchased aboard trains, but you will be surcharged if the station ticket office is open. The LIRR offers various tours May-Nov.

Taxis: Many local cab companies have cars waiting at the train stations. At stations where this is not the case or at other places, consult a phone book or call 411. As in New York City, Long Island taxis are expensive, but sometimes necessary. Many companies ask you to pay double the metered fare, because the drivers must spend time and money on the return trip.

BUSES

MTA Long Island Bus (516-766-6722; open M-F 7am-6pm, Sa 8am-5pm). Daytime bus service in Queens, Nassau, and western Suffolk. Service runs along major highways, but the routes are complex and irregular—confirm your destination with the driver. Some buses run every 15min., others every hr. Fare $1.50; crossing into Queens from Nassau County costs an additional 50¢; transfers 25¢. Disabled travelers and senior citizens pay half fare. Services Jones Beach daily during summer, connecting with the LIRR in Freeport. Buses also run in summer from the LIRR station in Babylon to Robert Moses State Park on Fire Island ($1.75 each way). Call for current schedule.

Suffolk Transit (516-852-5200; open M-F 8am-4:30pm). Runs from Lindenhurst to the eastern end of Long Island. The 10a, 10b, and 10c lines make frequent stops along the South Fork. No service Sunday. Fare $1.50; seniors and the disabled 50¢; transfers 25¢; under 5 free.

Hampton Jitney (800-936-0440 or 516-283-4600). The luxury bus. Two lines servicing destinations in the Hamptons. More expensive, but more comfortable and comprehensive than other buses or the LIRR. Schedule and fares vary daily. Departs from various Manhattan locations. One-way fares $22, round-trip $40. Reservations required; call in advance, especially on weekends.

Sunrise Express (800-527-7709, in Suffolk 516-477-1200). "NY Express" runs a few times daily from Manhattan to the North Fork ($15, round-trip $29). Call for schedule. Buses go directly to Riverhead, then stop at almost all villages on the North Fork to Greenport. Catch buses on the southwest corner of 44th St. and Third Ave. or in Queens (LIE Exit 24 to Kissena Blvd., in front of Queens College's Colden Ctr. at the Q88 bus stop). Bicycles ($10) and pets ($5) allowed. Kids (ages 1-5) on laps ride free. Reservations recommended. Cash only.

DAYTRIPS

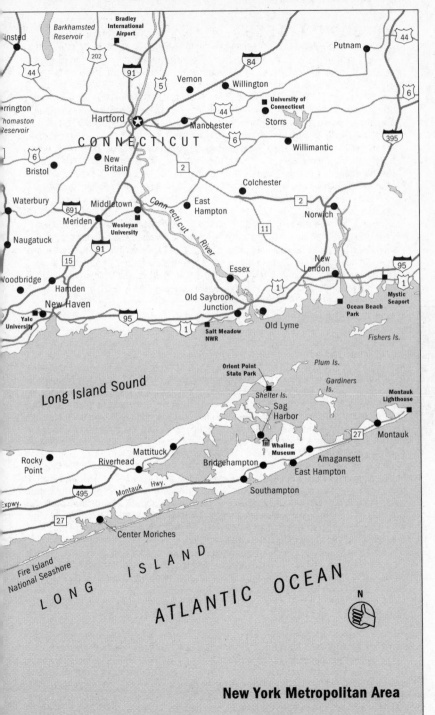

New York Metropolitan Area

GO DOWN MOSES Robert Moses, New York's (and perhaps the world's) most influential modern builder, executed his first projects on the barren sandbars and tightly-held domains of Long Island. Through his efforts, Moses freed up huge areas of land for public recreation and established the park-centered power base from which he would eventually build $27 billion worth of public works. Before Moses took over the Long Island Parks Commission, New Yorkers had nowhere to take their coveted first automobiles—only a few strips of beach lay open to them, and it took up to four dust-choked hours to get there from downtown Manhattan. Moses, full of lofty ideals, finagled $14 million from a graft-ridden state budget, built tree-lined highways (Northern State and Southern State Parkways), and developed the giant southern sandbar of Long Island into Jones Beach, a model recreation area with lavish facilities and a Disney-like attention to detail. To wrest right-of-way and parkland from its owners, Moses attacked the rich landowners who owned most of the island; failing their cooperation, he rerouted his plans to seizing the small holdings of independent farmers. To keep his beaches "clean," he had the bridges over the parkways built too low to accommodate city buses, blocked the Long Island Railroad from building a stop, and made it nearly impossible for charter companies carrying African-Americans to get permits to go to Jones Beach. Those who could not pay the parking fees were directed to "poor lots" far from the beach. Thus, in Long Island, a precedent was set for the grand public works projects, accommodation of a large and mobile middle class, and institutional racism and classism with which Moses would revolutionize public building.

SHOPPING IN LONG ISLAND

If the iridescent lighting and chrome trimmings of the Manhattan Mall have got you craving that suburban sprawl (and the nearest Betsey Johnson boutique), hightail it out of Daffy-land to the mecca of malls, Long Island. The first landing of the fashion plane is at **Roosevelt Field Shopping Center** (516-742-8000), a former airstrip where Amelia Earhart began her famous voyage (open M-Sa 10am-9:30pm, Su 11am-7pm). Too bad she didn't go down in style, in digs from the Armani Exchange with shoes by Steve Madden. The mall has hundreds of stores and five anchors (Macy's, Bloomingdales, Nordstrom, Stern's, and J.C. Penney) for the best in one-stop shopping. Roosevelt Field has its own exit (M2) off the Meadowbrook Parkway just south of the Northern State Parkway.

Those with more time than money should head straight for **Tanger Outlet Centers,** at the very end of the LIE. They have everything from Adidas to Wok and Roll at this sprawling discount outlet. Stock up on designer duds at Off Fifth Avenue (Saks), Corningware at Corning Revere, boxers at Calvin Klein, orange socks at the Gap Outlet, and cross trainers at Nike. (516-369-2732 or 369-6255. Accessible with Sunrise Express buses. Open Apr.-Dec. M-Sa 10am-9pm, Su 10am-7pm; Jan.-Mar. Su-Th 10am-7pm, F-Sa 10am-9pm.)

Save enough money for the drive back and enough space in the car for goods from the newly expanded **Walt Whitman Mall.** A brand-spanking new Saks Fifth Avenue and Bloomingdales will put this mall on the designer map. (516-271-1741. On Rte. 110. Open M-Sa 10am-9:30pm, Su 11am-7pm.)

NASSAU COUNTY

Nassau County, the western half of the island, is a tale of two identities—the North "fro-yo is less fattening" Shore and the South "yo, I like gold chains" Shore with a neatly ordered web of sprawling suburbia in between. The South Shore is the Land of young-lovin' Joey Buttafuoco, iridescent jogging suits, and muscled men with rattails dusting their necks and parrots gracing their shoulders. In the North Shore daughters wear U. Penn sweatshirts, talk on the Lexus car phone, and smoke slim cigarettes, the healthy alternative. Both shores suf-

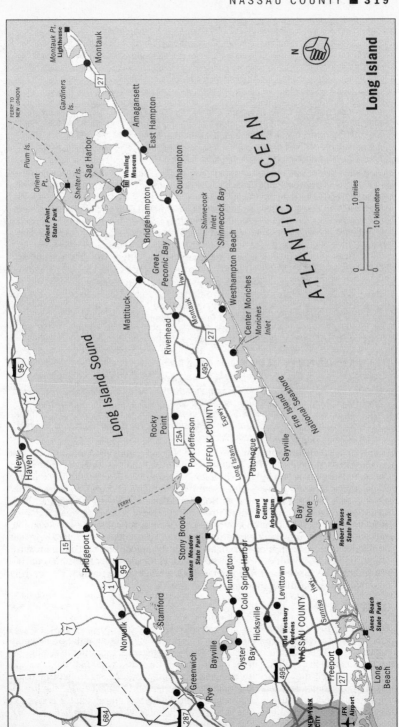

N

Long Island

Montauk Pt. Lighthouse

Montauk

27

Amagansett

East Hampton

Gardiners Is.

FERRY TO NEW LONDON

Plum Is.

Orient Pt.

Shelter Is.

Sag Harbor

Whaling Museum

Orient Point State Park

Southampton

Bridgehampton

Shinnecock Inlet

Shinnecock Bay

Westhampton Beach

Great Peconic Bay

Mattituck

Riverhead

Center Moriches

Moriches Inlet

27

495

ATLANTIC OCEAN

Long Island Sound

95

1

New Haven

Rocky Point

25A

Port Jefferson

SUFFOLK COUNTY

Long Island Expwy.

Patchogue

Sayville

Fire Island National Seashore

FERRY

15

Bridgeport

95

1

Stony Brook

Sunken Meadow State Park

Bayard Cutting Arboretum

Bay Shore

Robert Moses State Park

Huntington

Cold Spring Harbor

Levittown

7

Stamford

Norwalk

Bayville

Oyster Bay

Hicksville

Old Westbury Gardens

NASSAU COUNTY

495

Sunrise Hwy.

Jones Beach State Park

Greenwich

Rye

684

287

Freeport

27

Long Beach

NEW YORK CITY

✈ **JFK Airport**

10 miles

10 kilometers

0

0

DAYTRIPS

fer a surplus of dermatologists and orthodontists. Amid the frequent strip malls and cookie-cutter residential architecture, Nassau offers numerous peaceful spots to unwind, with abundant beaches, quiet garden estates, historical preserves, and a taste of small-town life. The LIRR and buses access the following sites (call ahead since bus schedules vary daily).

JONES BEACH

Information: 516-785-1600. *Directions:* LIRR to Freeport; shuttle bus stops every 30min. In the summer, the LIRR runs a package deal for the trip ($11 from Manhattan, June 29 to Sept. 7). Both the Meadowbrook Parkway and the Wantagh Parkway lead directly to Jones Beach; if you drive, you will have to pay for parking ($7; M-F 8am-4pm, Sa-Su 6am-6pm). *Hours:* Park closes at midnight, except for those with special fishing permits.

When New York State Parks Commissioner Robert Moses discovered Jones Beach in 1921, it was a barren spit of land off the Atlantic shore of Nassau County. Within 10 years, he had bought up the surrounding land, imported tons of sand, planted beach grass to preserve the new dunes, and completed dozens of buildings for purposes as diverse as diaper-changing and archery. His industrious efforts created 6½ miles of popular public beaches. Although the water is not the bluest nor the sun the strongest, **Jones Beach State Park** still attracts a small army of beach-goers, due to its wealth of attractions and proximity to Manhattan. The dozen or so parking fields accommodate 23,000 cars, and there are nearly 2500 acres of beachfront here with eight different public beaches on the rough Atlantic Ocean and the calmer Zachs Bay. Only 40 minutes from the city, Jones Beach becomes a sea of umbrellas and blankets with barely a patch of sand showing in the summertime. Along the 1½-mile **boardwalk** you can find two Olympic-sized pools, softball fields, roller-skating, mini-golf, a fitness course, basketball, and nightly dancing. Additionally, the **Marine Theater** inside the park often hosts big-name rock concerts.

NASSAU COUNTY MUSEUM OF ART

Located at One Museum Dr., Roslyn Harbor. *Telephone:* 516-484-9338. *By Train:* LIRR to Roslyn Station (50min., round-trip $9; from there take a taxi. *By Car:* LIE to Exit 39N (Glen Cove Rd. North); go 2 mi. to Northern Blvd. (Rte. 25A), and turn left. At the second light, turn right into the museum. *Admission:* $4, students and children $2, seniors $3. *Open:* Tu-Su 11am-5pm. *Tours* given free Tu-Su at 2pm. Admission to the **Tee Ridder Miniatures Museum** included; same hours as main museum.

Located in the quaint town of Roslyn, the Nassau County Museum of Art is a perfect daytrip from the city. The museum's rich collection of traditional and contemporary art is housed in a Georgian mansion that was previously a house of the Frick family's Long Island estate. While the permanent collection contains works from masters such as Bonnard, Braque, Rauschenberg, and Vuillard, changing exhibitions like the recent "Contemporary American Masters: The 1960s" keep the museum exciting with fashion relics, space memorabilia, and pop art. Probably most exceptional are the gorgeous 145-acre **grounds** that double as a living exhibit of extraordinary landscape design and an impressive **sculpture park** with works from Botero and Calder among others. Also on the grounds is the fascinating **Tee Ridder Miniatures Museum,** which boasts tiny intricate representations of our designed world.

OYSTER BAY

SAGAMORE HILL. Perhaps the most precious jewel in the crown of Oyster Bay is this estate on Sagamore Hill Rd. off Cove Neck Rd. Once the summer presidential residence of Theodore Roosevelt, this National Historic Site reflects the importance of nature and wildlife in the philosophy of the conservationist President. In 1905, Roosevelt met here with envoys from Japan and Russia to set in motion negotiations that would lead to the Treaty of Portsmouth, which ended the Russo-Japanese War. The house is jam-packed with "Teddy" memorabilia; the collection of antlers reflects his interests in "preserving" wildlife. *(Recorded info 516-922-4447;*

human being 922-4788. LIRR to Oyster Bay and call a taxi. Take the LIE to Exit 41 North, take the road toward Oyster Bay and follow signs to Sagamore Hill. Visitors Center open daily 9:30am-4pm; off-season W-Su 9:30am-4pm. $5, under 16 free. Tours of the house every 30min. Come early; only 200 tickets are available each day.)

PLANTING FIELDS ARBORETUM. Nestled among the sportscar-filled grounds of Oyster Bay affluence, the massive arboretum consists of 409 acres of some of the most valuable real estate in the New York area. Two huge greenhouses, covering 1½ acres, contain the largest camellia collection in the Northeast. The flowers burst into bloom during the unlikely months of December, January, and February, when most city-dwellers have begun to forget what flora looks like. Other quirky highlights include a "synoptic garden" of plants obsessively alphabetized according to their Latin names (every letter is represented except J and W). The **Fall Flower Show,** held for two weeks in early October, attracts huge crowds every year. The arboretum hosts a summer concert series; past seasons have seen Joan Baez and the Indigo Girls. Call for a concert schedule. *(516-922-9200. LIRR to Oyster Bay or Locust Valley, then call a taxi. By Car: North Hempstead Tpke. to Mill River Hollow Rd.; take a left on Glen Cove Rd. and another left on Planting Fields Rd. Parking on the grounds 9am-5pm; $5. Main greenhouse open daily 9am-5pm. Admission free.)*

Insurance magnate William Robertson Coe once counted his coins at **Coe Hall** on the grounds of the arboretum. Constructed in 1921 in the Tudor Revival style, the mansion has rows upon rows of mind-boggling windows. Unfortunately, only eight decorated rooms are open to the public; the inside is better left to the interior-design enthusiast. *(516-922-0479. Open daily Apr.-Sept. noon-3:30pm; $5, students and seniors $3.50, 7-12 $1.)*

OLD WESTBURY GARDENS

Information: 516-333-0048. Directions: LIRR to Westbury and then call a taxi. By Car: Take the LIE to Exit 39S, Glen Cove Rd. Take a left on Willets Rd. Drive east until reaching Old Westbury Rd. The entrance to the gardens is up to the left. Open: W-M 10am-5pm. Last ticket sold 4pm. Admission: $6, ages 6-12 $3, seniors $5. House and garden $10, ages 6-12 $6, seniors $8.

Now obscured by car dealerships and chain restaurants, the ghost of a luxury lifestyle is preserved at the Old Westbury Gardens. Once the home of a Gold Coast millionaire, the huge, elegant manor house roosts comfortably amid acres of formal, flower-filled gardens. Two nearby lakes are ornamented by sculptures, gazebos, and water lilies. A vast rose garden adjoins a number of theme gardens such as the Grey Garden, which contains only plants in shades of silver and deep purple. Children will love the full-sized **playhouse** in the Cottage Garden. Sunday afternoon classical concerts are occasionally performed by Juilliard students in May, June, September, and October (free with regular admission).

WALT WHITMAN'S BIRTHPLACE

Information: 516-427-5240. Located at 246 Old Walt Whitman Rd., South Huntington. Directions: Take the LIRR to Huntington and catch the S1 bus to Amityville; get off at the Walt Whitman Mall. The museum is diagonally across from the Mall. The S1 does not run on Sunday. Open: Summer M-W and Th-F 11am-4pm, Sa-Su noon-5pm; winter W-F 1-4pm, Sa-Su noon-4pm. Admission: $3, students and seniors $2, ages 7-12 $1, under 7 free.

Walt Whitman's Birthplace State Historic Site and Interpretive Center is a simple memorial to the flashy American poet whose 1855 *Leaves of Grass* introduced a free-verse style infused with a democratic spirit that revolutionized poetry. The small, weathered farmhouse was built in 1816 by Walt Whitman, Sr., a carpenter and the father of the self-proclaimed "Walt Whitman, a cosmos, of Manhattan the son" who less pompously called himself "The Old Gray Poet." The Whitmans moved to Brooklyn when the poet-to-be was only four years old, and the house they left behind provides interesting commentary on his life. A new visitor's center has a unique retrospective of the oft-photographed poet, one of the first editions of *Leaves of Grass*, and a copy of the only known recording of Whitman.

THE AMERICAN MERCHANT MARINE MUSEUM

*Located on Steamboat Rd. in King's Point. **Directions:** LIRR to Great Neck, then board the Nassau Country Bus bound for "Middle Neck Road/Academy," which stops at the LIRR station and runs directly to the Academy. **Telephone:** Human being 516-773-5515; recording 773-5000. **Open:** Aug.-June Tu-F 10am-3:30pm, Sa-Su 1-4:30pm. **Donation** requested.*

The museum nestles in the bosom of the U.S. Merchant Marine Academy and houses exhibits on the history and past glories of the Merchant Marines. The surrounding town of **King's Point**—a decidedly private community—is the exclusive niche of the already posh Great Neck. Amble down the shaded tree-lined roads to see how the other one millionth live. It's a lovely place to bring a picnic.

SUFFOLK COUNTY

The eastern half of Long Island, reaching to its two long forks and small offshore islands, makes up Suffolk County. Far from the frenzied hubbub of Manhattan, the peaceful communities are so small and quaint that many are self-proclaimed villages or hamlets. Residents proudly hang American flags from the porches of paint-chipped white farmhouses with thick shingles, and weekend activity is characterized by antique shopping and barn sales galore. In this rural atmosphere, the latest action movie at the local theater is about as fast-paced as it gets.

THE HAMPTONS

The most famous region of Suffolk County is the cluster of communities along the South Fork collectively known as The Hamptons, the Malibu of the east and a prized location for a vacation house. It is home to wealthy summering Manhattanites, modern-day Gatsbys, and displaced West Coast stars. Artists (most notoriously Jackson Pollock) and writers have made the serene and sufficiently sexy Hamptons their home for decades. The area jams in July, when traffic backs up for miles (and hours) on Highway 27. The rich and famous often bypass this line-up by helicoptering into their monstrous, tree-lined estates.

Each special Hampton has its own stereotype: Westhampton is new money, Southampton is old money, and East Hampton is artists. Bridgehampton, appropriately enough, connects the two communities of Southampton and East Hampton. All of the communities have main streets with rows of resort-style stores (read: beachware, art galleries, corner groceries, and glazed pottery vendors). By investigating the side streets, you will find myriad castle-like complexes on the water. It's difficult to find an entrance to the quiet, perfect beach which borders the Hamptons because residents have stacked their well-guarded pleasure palaces in a tight row along the ocean. Reaching the beach, therefore, is easier from less pretentious nearby towns like Amagansett and Montauk.

SOUTHAMPTON AND WATER MILL

From the Southampton LIRR station, head right out of the parking lot along Railroad Plaza to North Main St.; turn left onto N. Main and walk to the stop sign; bear left and keep walking as N. Main becomes Main St. and takes you to the center of town (about a half-mile altogether).

Southampton has several museums and homes worth visiting, making it a nice daytrip. Most of the sites lie within walking distance of each other. Established in 1640 as the first English colony in the future New York State, Southampton is a beautiful town of vast 19th-century houses which grow larger closer to the ocean. While wandering through Southampton's residential sections, look over the hedges and gates to glimpse houses designed by Stanford White and other luminaries of the late 19th-century architectural scene. Continue walking down Main St. until it bends and becomes Dune Rd. and peer through the rows of hedges and enormous, ornate gates. Behind them, you can almost glimpse the beachfront mansions of some of the town's wealthiest. Most beaches are difficult to reach, and the few open to the public (look for signs) lack changing facilities and bathrooms.

STARGAZING? Some famous faces you might see in the Hamptons: Billy Joel (singer/songwriter), Kim Basinger and Alec Baldwin (acting duo), Tom Wolfe (*Bonfire of the Vanities* author), Jann Wenner (*Rolling Stone* publisher), Steven Spielberg (auteur), Donna Karan (fashion designer), Geraldine Ferraro (vee-pee contenda'), and Barbra Streisand (Babs).

Perched at the corner of Main and Meeting House Ln. is the **Southampton Historical Museum,** where you'll find a collection of buildings and exhibits, including a one-room schoolhouse, whaling and farming equipment, and local Native American artifacts. (516-283-2494. Open June 12 to Sept. 15 Tu-Su 11am-5pm. Call in winter for an appointment. $3, seniors $2, children $1.) Across Main St. on the corner of Jobs Ln. is the **Rogers Memorial Library** (516-283-0774), a whimsical red brick building sporting ivy and turrets. The Venetian-style **Parrish Art Museum** lies next door. Here, a modern gallery houses a permanent collection concentrating on American artists, particularly those (like William Merritt Chase and Fairfield Porter) who lived and worked near Southampton. Temporary exhibitions also focus on the town. The Parrish is surrounded by a picturesque **garden** showcasing a police line-up of reproduction Roman busts presided over by Caesar Augustus. (516-283-2118. Museum open June-Sept. M-Sa 11am-5pm, Su 1-5pm. Suggested donation $2, seniors $1, students free. Wheelchair accessible.)

Just outside of Southampton at the intersection of Hwy. 27 and Old Mill Rd., the tiny community of **Water Mill** hosts the original mill that was built "to supply the necessities of the towne" in 1644. The **Water Mill Museum** has been in its present location since 1726, and is open for tours. (516-726-4625. Open late May to late Sept. M-Sa 10am-5pm, Su 1-5pm. $2, seniors $1.50, children free.)

EAST HAMPTON AND AMAGANSETT

East Hampton is fast becoming the playground of the area's elite. The center of town is home to more art galleries, clothing stores, and colonial memorabilia outlets than one would care to imagine, but the town is great for strolling, window-shopping, and whiling away the hours. Many artists have found inspiration and refuge here—most prominently Jackson Pollock. The studio/home he shared with Lee Krasner has since been dubbed the **Pollock-Krasner House and Study Center,** a museum of sorts. Don't expect to see Pollock's *Full Fathom Five*—none of the artists' major works is on display. Visitors must tread around the home in foam slippers, so as not to damage any of the paint splotches on the floor. (516-324-4929. 830 Fireplace Rd. Open by appointment May-Oct. Th-Sa 11am-4pm. $5.)

Nearby **Amagansett** is little more than a tiny Main St. that offers some great live music. **The Stephen Talkhouse** hosts performers such as Marianne Faithfull and Judy Collins, as well as lesser-known acts. (516-267-3117; www.stephentalkhouse.com. 161 Main St. Performances begin at 8pm. Tickets from $5.)

SAG HARBOR

The LIRR does not stop at Sag Harbor, but the town is accessible via Suffolk County Transit bus: take the LIRR to the Southampton station and catch the S92, which runs 9 times a day.

Out of the South Fork's north shore droops Sag Harbor, one of the diamonds in the rough of Long Island. Founded in 1707, this port used to be more important than New York Harbor as its deep waters made for easy navigation. At its peak, this winsome village was the world's fourth-largest whaling port. James Fenimore Cooper began his first novel, *Precaution*, in a Sag Harbor hotel in 1824. And to round off Sag Harbor's dazzling and captivating history: during Prohibition the harbor served as a major meeting-place for smugglers and rum-runners from the Caribbean.

In the past few years, an increasing number of tourists have returned to the quiet, tree-lined streets of salt-box cottages and Greek Revival mansions. The legacy of Sag Harbor's former grandeur survives in the second-largest collection of

DAYTRIPS

Colonial buildings in the U.S. and in the cemeteries lined with the gravestones of Revolutionary soldiers and sailors. Check out the **Sag Harbor Whaling Museum** in the town's Masonic Temple at the corner of Main St. and Garden St. A huge whale rib arches over the front door. Note the antique washing-machine, made locally in 1864, and the excellent scrimshaw collection. (516-725-0770. Open May-Sept. M-Sa 10am-5pm, Su 1-5pm. $3, ages 6-13 $1, seniors $2. Tours by appointment; $2.) The equally intriguing **Custom House,** across the street, features an extensive collection of period furniture and trivial keepsakes. (516-725-0250. Open June and Sept. Sa-Su 10am-5pm; July-Aug. Tu-Su 10am-5pm. $3, ages 7-14 and seniors $1.50.)

MONTAUK

Take the LIRR to Montauk and head to the right out of the train station along the 4-lane road. This is Edgemere Rd.; it leads straight to the village green, a 10-15min. walk. There is no city-bound afternoon train service during the week, which makes getting there much easier than leaving. M-F the only trains back to the city leave at 10:36pm and 12:52am, Sa-Su there are several afternoon trains; the Hampton Jitney makes several trips per day.

As the easternmost point of the South Fork, Montauk offers an unobstructed view of the Atlantic Ocean. Despite the slightly commercialized tourist/hotel areas and the three-hour trip, the peaceful salty air is worth the effort. The **Montauk Point Lighthouse and Museum** is at the island's edge. The 110-foot structure went up in 1796 by special order of President George Washington. The first public works project in the newly formed United States, it helped to guide many ships into the harbor, including the schooner *La Amistad.* Back then, the lighthouse was 297 feet off the shoreline, but thanks to the wonders of geology, it's now fully attached, surrounded by the Montauk Point State Park. If your lungs are willing, you should definitely climb the 137 spiraling steps to the top to look out over the seascape across the Long Island Sound to Connecticut and Rhode Island. Try to spot the *Will o' the Wisp,* a ghostly clipper ship sometimes sighted on hazy days under full sail with a lantern hanging from its mast. Experts claim that the ship is a mirage resulting from the presence of phosphorus in the atmosphere, but what do they know? (516-668-2544. Open M-F and Su 10:30am-6pm, Sa 10:30am-7:30pm; Oct. daily 10am-4pm; other times call for info. $4, seniors $3, under 12 $2.50.)

If tower climbing has made you hungry, stop off at the world famous **Lobster Roll** (516-267-3740), on Hwy. 27 (the Montauk Pkwy.), in the Napeague Stretch. The restaurant's featured dish, a flaky, lobster salad-stuffed treat ($10.75), is worth every *drachma, rubel, shekel,* or the currency of your international hotspot of choice. Bring the kids; the owners keep a cabinet full of Fisher Price toys. (Open daily 11:30am-10pm.)

If you prefer to catch your own chicken of the sea, try a half-day fluke-fishing cruise with **Viking** (516-668-5700; $27 includes all equipment; departs 8am, 1, and 2pm; less frequent cruises for striped bass and other fish) or **Lazybones'** (516-668-5671; $25 includes all equipment; departs 7am and 1pm). Viking also runs whale-watching cruises. **Hither Hills State Park,** accessible from the village green in Montauk via bus 10C, offers lovely vistas, swimming, and picnicking spots. (516-668-2554. Open 8am-9pm.)

LONG BEACH

Getting There: Take the LIRR (orange line) to Long Beach, the last stop; you may have to transfer at Jamaica. Round-trip: $9.50-14, 50min. Beach: Follow the crowds heading straight south for about 5 blocks. Beach pass $5 per day; 10-pass $25. Combination Ticket (LIRR and beach pass): $12; must be purchased at either Penn Station in Manhattan or at Flatbush Station in Brooklyn.

Each summer the sleepy suburb of Long Beach transforms into a blissful beach town. Teenagers wax up their surf boards and whip out the peroxide; mothers pop open the iced tea mix; local drugstores run out of flip-flops and sunscreen. If you feel confined by the skyscrapers or humidity of Manhattan in the summer, you'll love breezy Long Beach. The wide and sandy beaches entice you to an ocean friendly to swimmers and well-surveyed by lifeguards. Since going topless in New York is now legal for both sexes, you can work on eradicating that sickly farmer's tan. Most city folk head straight to **National Beach,** the beach directly parallel to the train station. If you head either east (left) or west (right) when you reach the **boardwalk,** you'll see the less crowded beaches. **Volleyball** nets cluster on National, Edwards, and Riverside Beaches, all of which host both tournaments and impromptu matches.

Long Beach celebrates an idyllic **July 4.** The city offers no official fireworks show of its own, but if you stroll along the boardwalk in the evening you can see amateur pyrotechnics galore, as well as displays from adjacent towns, as small hordes of happy families dance, swim, and soak in the warm night.

If you desire an out-of-the-sun lunch, Long Beach offers many options. Quality restaurants cluster around **Park Street,** parallel to the beach and across from the train station. **Gino's Pizzeria** (516-432-8193), across from the train station on Park St., sells great pizza to the swarms of sandy, sunburnt folk who flock here. Regular slices cost $1.50 and gourmet slices like the fresh mozzarella, basil, and tomato on foccacia cost $2.35. (Open M-Th, Su 11am-midnight, F-Sa 11am-1am.) A down-to-earth local scene thrives nightly in the many **bars** that dot the small streets of Long Beach's west end. Regularly packed, **The Inn,** 943 W. Beech St. (516-432-9220), at Tennessee Ave., bustles with Irish sing-along on Tuesday nights and live music on Wednesday, Friday, and Saturday nights. (Kitchen open until 11pm. Open M-Sa 11am-4am, Su noon-4am.) To get to the west end from the train station, head toward the beach to Beech St.; make a right onto Beech, and walk about eight blocks. Residential homes will give way to bars, restaurants, and small delicatessens. If you want to stay and drink in Long Beach, make sure to check the train schedule beforehand; the LIRR runs with limited service as the night wears on.

FIRE ISLAND

Rolling sandy beaches, azure ocean, and relative seclusion have sent visitors scurrying from their day jobs in Manhattan to the pristine, quiet towns that dot Fire Island. This, southern Long Island's barrier against the temperamental Atlantic, developed in the early 20th-century, when middle-income families began to acquire beachfront property en masse. Some towns retain their original layout of closely packed bungalows without yards. Residents have done much to fend off the bright lights of the tourist industry, even as their property values have increased. The amazingly influential urban planner Robert Moses himself could not build a road across the island because citizens fought so fiercely to retain their quiet plots of land. Since then, the state has protected most areas of Fire Island by declaring them either a state park or a federal "wilderness area."

This lack of infrastructure insures both peace and inconvenience; visitors must often climb aboard water taxis to make the journey to another town. Still, 17 summer communities have managed to forge distinct niches on Fire Island. The separation has made the towns diverse—providing homes for middle-class clusters, openly gay communities (see **Gay and Lesbian Life,** p. 306), and pockets of vacationing Hollywood stars.

GETTING THERE

Traveling from Fire Island from Manhattan involves multiple modes of transportation. **Trains** from Penn Station depart almost every hour to one of the three ports that will lead you to the island. However, sometimes you must transfer trains to get there. After your train arrives at **Bay Shore** ($9.50) or **Sayville** ($9.50), you must take a taxi to the port. The train to **Patchogue** ($10.75) takes longer and only leads to several of the ports on Fire Island but does not necessitate a taxi. Ferries from Bay Shore (516-665-3600), go to Kismet, Saltaire, Fair Harbor, Atlantic, Dunewood, Ocean Beach, Seaview, and Ocean Bay Park (round-trip $11.50, under 12 $5.50). Ferries from Sayville (516-589-8980) go to Sailors' Haven, Cherry Grove, and Fire

DAYTRIPS

Island Pines (round-trip $11, under 12 $5). Ferries from Patchogue (516-475-1665) go to Davis Park and Watch Hill (round-trip $10, under 12 $5.50). To get from one town to the other, call one of many water taxi companies like the aptly named **Water Taxi** (516-665-8885). Prices range from a couple of bucks to $35 depending on how far you are going.

BEACHES AND COMMUNITIES

The largest community on Fire Island, **Ocean Beach** is naturally the most publicly accessible. Small town virtues, such as kindness and respect, appear this close to New York City. Signs throughout the city warn visitors that they too must act respectfully: no drinking in public; no walking around town without a shirt; no "discourteous" public displays. Stick to these rules and you'll enjoy a peaceful stay on glistening beach. Ocean Beach's main street is lined with gray wooden buildings with thick shingles, restaurants, small groceries, and beachware shops. You can grab a delightful bite to eat at **Michael's Pizzeria** (sandwiches $5-8, pizza and pasta $10-14; open M-F 8am-midnight, Sa-Su 6am-noon), or you can make your own lunch from the **Ocean Beach Trader** (open M-Th 7am-8pm, F 7am-10:30pm, Sa 7am-9:30pm), one of three grocery stores on the strip. Here, you can also pick up a list of services and phone numbers, a map, and a brief history of the island, in the *Fire Island News* or the *Fire Island Tide*. Save enough money for a soft, chewy oatmeal raisin cookie ($1.75), one of many gigantic desserts from **Rachel's Bakery** (open daily 7am-10pm). **The Alligator** (516-583-8896) is a barely adorned bar that concentrates instead on drinks ($2-5) and a big-screen TV (F-Sa cover $5; open daily noon-4am).

Take any side street (perpendicular to the main drag) all the way across the island to arrive at miles and miles of coastline. Once there, you can walk along the shore to see the beachfront homes that grow larger as you travel either way down the beach. The largest homes are located about two miles away in posh **Saltaire** (a completely residential community), followed closely by the up-and-coming town of **Fair Harbor.** If you walk in the other direction just over 2½ mi., you will arrive at the private bungalows and raised boardwalks of **Cherry Grove** and the colossal homes of **Fire Island Pines,** two predominantly gay communities (for more on Cherry Grove and The Pines, see **Gay and Lesbian Life,** p. 306).

Those in the know travel by water taxi to nearby **Ocean Bay Park,** a community that grew tired of the restrictions in nearby Ocean Beach and so created Ocean Bay Park as a haven for those of the rule-bending ilk. **Flynns** (516-583-5000) proves the local lore nightly. In addition to serving lunch and dinner, the bar rocks the island every weekend (open M-Th noon-11pm, F-Su noon-3am). The affluent residential town of **Seaview** lies between Ocean Beach and Ocean Bay Park.

Ferries run late into the night, but if you want to spend the night, shack up at **Glegg's Hotel,** which has clean rooms and a friendly, knowledgeable staff. Room prices vary according to season, number of vacancies, and days of the week. Doubles can cost anywhere from $60 on a weekday to $220 on a peak-season weekend.

PARKS AND SIGHTS

The **Fire Island National Seashore** (516-289-4810 for the headquarters in Patchogue) is the official moniker for the stretches of coastline that hug the island. This is Fire Island's biggest draw, and the daytime hotspot for summertime fishing, clamming, and guided nature walks. The **Fire Island Lighthouse Visitor Center** (516-661-4876; small museum open daily 9:30am-5pm) houses the only monument on the isle. The facilities at **Sailor's Haven** (just west of the Cherry Grove community) include a marina, a nature trail, and a famous beach. Similar facilities at **Watch Hill** (516-597-6455) include a 20-unit campground, where reservations are required. **Smith Point West,** on the eastern tip of the island, has a small visitors center and a nature trail with disabled access (516-281-3010; center open daily 9am-5pm). Here you can spot horseshoe crabs, white-tailed deer, and monarch butterflies, which flit across the country every year to winter in Baja California.

The **Sunken Forest,** so called because of its location behind the dunes, is another of the island's natural wonders. Located directly west of Sailor's Haven, its soil supports an unusual and attractive combination of gnarled holly, sassafras, and poison ivy. Some of the forest's specimens are over 200 years old. From the summit of the dunes, you can see the forest's trees laced together in a hulky, uninterrupted mesh.

ATLANTIC CITY, NJ

The geography of Atlantic City has been etched in the collective psyche of generations of Americans. For over 50 years, board-gaming strategists have vied for control of this coastal city from opposite sides of the *Monopoly* board. When *Monopoly* came out, Atlantic City was *the* beachside hotspot among resort towns. The opulence faded first into neglect and then into a deeper shade of tackiness. With the legalization of gambling in 1976, casinos soon rose from the rubble of the Boardwalk. Today, velvet-lined temples of schmaltz (each with a dozen restaurants and big-name entertainment) blight the beach and draw all kinds of tourists, from international jet-setters to local seniors. The "Gamblor" can hardly be contained once spawned; Atlantic City continues to grow with high-rollers Arnold Schwarzenegger and Donald Trump as prime investors. But only a few blocks from this indulgence lies an impoverished and crime-ridden community. Glitz and glamour no longer thrive on Baltic Ave. and the only people vying for control of Atlantic Ave. are pawnshoppers, peep-show owners, and pickpockets. One local resident embraces the grit, saying, "Atlantic City is a dump, but we have the best cheese steaks in the world."

ORIENTATION AND PRACTICAL INFORMATION

Atlantic City, halfway down New Jersey's coast, is accessible via the **Garden State Parkway** and the **Atlantic City Expressway,** or easily reached by bus from New York.

The city's attractions cluster on and around the **Boardwalk,** which runs east-west along the Atlantic Ocean. All but two of the casinos (the Trump Castle and Harrah's) overlook this paradise of soft-serve ice cream and fast food. Running parallel to the Boardwalk, **Pacific** and **Atlantic Avenues** offer cheap restaurants, hotels, convenience stores, and 99¢ emporiums. Atlantic Ave. can be dangerous after dark, and any street farther out can be dangerous even by day.

Getting around Atlantic City is easy on foot. When your winnings become too heavy to carry, have someone push you around in a **Rolling Chair,** quite common along the Boardwalk ($10 plus gratuity for 14 blocks, $20 for 24 blocks). On the streets, catch a **jitney** ($1.50), which runs 24 hours up and down Pacific Ave. (call 344-8642 for frequent rider and senior citizen passes), or a NJ Transit Bus ($1) covering Atlantic Ave.

Airport: Atlantic City International (645-7895 or 800-892-0354). Located just west of Atlantic City in Pamona with service to Washington, D.C., Philadelphia, and New York (around $50 one-way). Served by Spirit, U.S. Airways, and Thai Aviation.

Buses: Greyhound (609-340-2000 or 800-231-2222). Buses travel every 30min. between Port Authority (NYC) and most major casinos (approx. 2½hr., ask for casino drop-off rates and pay around $27 round-trip). Many casinos, in addition to the round-trip discounts, will give gamblers between $15 and $20 in coins upon arrival. (Trump Plaza offers $20 for starting your gambling spree at their casino.) **New Jersey Transit** (in-state 800-582-5946, 215-569-3752) offers hourly service between NYC and the transit station on Atlantic Ave. between Michigan and Ohio St. ($23, seniors $9.60 each way). **Gray Line Tours** (800-669-0051) offers several daytrips to Atlantic City (3hr.; $21 on weekdays, $23 on weekends). Your ticket receipt is redeemable for cash, chips, or food from a casino when you arrive. Tropicana and the Sands offer the most at $20 per person. The bus drops you at the casino and picks you up later the same day. Call for nearest NYC bus pickup locations. Call 800-995-8898 for info about economical overnight packages. Terminal open 24hr.

Parking: You can park your car at Merv Griffin's Resort International (see **Casinos**, p. 331); $3 self-park to stay as long as you want. At hotels, parking $2-7.

Visitor Information: Atlantic City Convention Center and Visitors Bureau, 2314 Pacific Ave. (449-7130). The "Old Convention Center" is currently closed during its transformation into a sports venue. However, it will remain home of the Miss America Pageant. A new visitors center will be built just outside of the city on the Expressway. Information is not yet available on when it will open. Call ahead for information.

Bookstore: Atlantic City News and Book Store (344-9444), 101 S. Illinois Ave., at the intersection with Pacific Ave. Carries a comprehensive collection of strategic gambling literature. Open 24hr.

Pharmacy: Parkway, 2838 Atlantic Ave. (345-5105), one block from TropWorld. Delivers locally and to the casinos. Open M-F 9am-6:30pm, Sa 9am-5:30pm. Automated phone system available 24hr. to place refill orders or to leave a message.

Hospital: Atlantic City Medical Center (344-4081), 1925 Pacific Ave. at the intersection with Michigan Ave.

Rape and Abuse Hotline: 646-6767; 24hr. counseling, referrals, and accompaniment.

Emergency: 911.

Area Code: 609.

ACCOMMODATIONS AND CAMPING

Large, red-carpeted beachfront hotels have bumped smaller operators a few streets back. Smaller hotels along **Pacific Avenue,** a block from the Boardwalk, have rooms that run about $60-95 in the summer. Rooms in the city's guest houses are reasonably priced, though facilities can be dismal. Reserve ahead, especially on weekends, as rooms go quickly. Many hotels lower their rates mid-week. Winter is slow in Atlantic City, as water temperature, numbers of gamblers, and hotel rates all drop significantly. **Campsites** closest to the action cost the most; the majority close September through April. Reserve ahead if you plan to visit in July or August.

Since budget bargains get booked quickly in the summer, if you have a car it pays to stay in Absecon, about 8 mi. from Atlantic City. Exit 40 from the Garden State Parkway will take you to Rte. 30, which is lined with great deals. The **American Lodge,** 232 E. White Horse Pike (800-452-4050), ½ mi. east from the parkway at Exit 40, offers large rooms with king-size beds, cable, refrigerators, and A/C (rooms $45-95; jacuzzi $20 extra; 4-person max. with no charge).

Inn of the Irish Pub, 164 St. James Pl. (344-9063; www.theirishpub.com), near the Ramada Tower, just off the Boardwalk. Big, clean rooms, decorated with antiques. No TVs, phone, or A/C, but in the summer the breeze from the beach keeps things cool. Some rooms have a sea view. Plush lobby with TV and pay phone. Porch sitting area complete with rocking chairs. Coin-op laundry in hotel next door. Adjoining restaurant offers a $2 lunch special and a $6 dinner special. Su-Th special: private shower/twin beds $27.50. Single with shared bath $29, with private bath $40.20 weekdays and $62.20 on weekends; double with shared bath $60, with private bath $75; quad with shared bath $60. Prices include tax; rates are stable all year. Key deposit $5. Accepts AmEx, V, MC.

Comfort Inn, 154 South Kentucky Ave. (888-247-5337 or 609-348-4000; www.comfort-inn.com). Near the Sands. All rooms feature king size or 2 queen size beds, private bath, and jacuzzi. Rate includes "Deluxe" continental breakfast, free on-site parking, and access to outdoor heated pool. 10% discount for AAA, AARP, military, corporate groups, and government. Prices: Mar.-May $59, June $69, July $79, Aug. $89, early Sept. $69, late Sept. $59. Rooms with ocean views are an additional $20, but come with fridge, microwave, and a bigger jacuzzi. Call well in advance for summer weekends and holidays. Rates are subject to change. Accepts AmEx, V, MC.

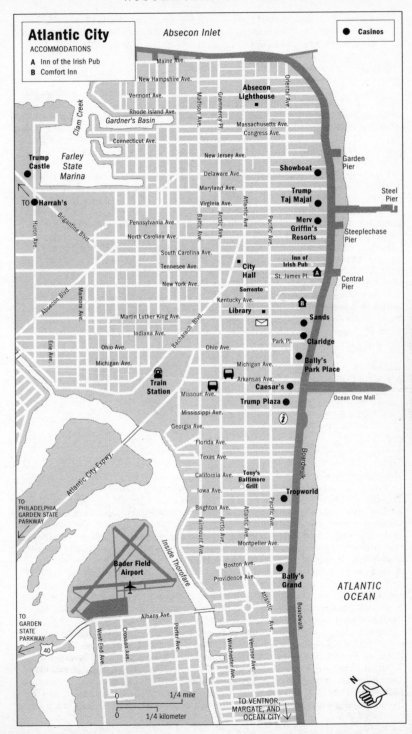

Atlantic City

ACCOMMODATIONS
A Inn of the Irish Pub
B Comfort Inn

● Casinos

Absecon Inlet

DAYTRIPS

Maine Ave.
New Hampshire Ave.
Vermont Ave.
Rhode Island Ave.
Gardner's Basin
Connecticut Ave.

Oriental Ave.
Absecon
Lighthouse
Massachusetts Ave.
Congress Ave.

Clam Creek

Farley State Marina

Trump
Castle

TO ● Harrah's

Huron Ave.

Brigantine Blvd.

Madison Ave.
Grammercy Pl.
Atlantic Ave.
Baltic Ave.
Arctic Ave.
Pacific Ave.

New Jersey Ave.
Delaware Ave.
Maryland Ave.
Virginia Ave.
Pennsylvania Ave.
North Carolina Ave.
South Carolina Ave.
Tennesee Ave.
New York Ave.

Absecon Blvd.
Mamora Ave.
Erie Ave.

Martin Luther King Ave.
Indiana Ave.
Ohio Ave.

Bacharach Blvd.

Ohio Ave.
Michigan Ave.

City
Hall

Sorrento
Kentucky Ave.
Library

Park Pl.

Inn of
Irish Pub
St. James Pl.

B

Michigan Ave.
Arkansas Ave.
Missouri Ave.
Mississippi Ave.
Georgia Ave.

Train
Station

Caesar's
Trump Plaza

ⓘ

Showboat
Trump
Taj Majal
Merv
Griffin's
Resorts

Garden
Pier

Steel
Pier

Steeplechase
Pier

Central
Pier

Sands
Claridge
Bally's
Park Place

Ocean One Mall

Florida Ave.
Texas Ave.
California Ave.
Iowa Ave.
Brighton Ave.

Tony's
Baltimore
Grill

Tropworld

Boardwalk
Pacific Ave.
Atlantic Ave.
Arctic Ave.
Fairmount Ave.

Montpelier Ave.
Boston Ave.
Providence Ave.

Bally's
Grand

*ATLANTIC
OCEAN*

TO
PHILADELPHIA,
GARDEN STATE
PARKWAY

Atlantic City Expwy.

Inside Thorofare

Bader Field
Airport

TO
GARDEN
STATE
PARKWAY

40

Albany Ave.
West End Ave.
Crossan Ave.
Porter Ave.
Winchester Ave.
Ventnor Ave.

0   1/4 mile

0   1/4 kilometer

N

TO VENTNOR,
MARGATE, AND
OCEAN CITY

Birch Grove Park Campground (641-3778), Mill Rd. in Northfield. About 6 mi. from Atlantic City, off Rte. 9. 50 sites. Attractive and secluded. Sites $18 for 2; with two-way hookup $21; 4-way hookup $24. Sites available Apr.-Oct. Cash or check only.

FOOD

The food in Atlantic City is, for the most part, fairly reasonable. 75¢ hotdogs and $1.50 pizza slices crowd the Boardwalk. After cashing in your chips, you can visit a casino buffet (lunch about $6-7, dinner $10). Beyond the boardwalk, the town itself has better restaurants. For a complete rundown of local dining, pick up a copy of *Shorecast Insider's Guide At the Shore* or *Whoot* (both free) from a hotel lobby, restaurant, or local store, or hang around casino gambling dens and score free pretzels, coffee, cookies, juice, and even yogurt provided to high rollers.

Your best bet for cheap sit-down dining in Atlantic City is the **Inn of the Irish Pub,** at 164 St. James Pl. (345-9613), which serves hearty, modestly priced dishes like deep-fried crab cakes ($4.75) and Dublin beef stew ($5). The lunch special (M-F 11:30am-2pm) includes a pre-selected sandwich and cup of soup for $2. This oaky, inviting pub has a century's worth of Joycean élan and Irish memorabilia draped on the walls. Mugs of domestic draft cost $1. (Open 24hr.)

Pacific Avenue is cramped with steak, sub, and pizza shops. Celebrity supporters of the **White House Sub Shop,** 2301 Arctic Ave. (345-1564 or 345-8599), include Bill Cosby, Johnny Mathis, and the late Frank Sinatra. Ol' Blue Eyes was rumored to have had these immense subs ($4-9) flown to him while he was on tour. (Open M-Th 10am-11pm, F-Sa 10am-midnight, Su 11am-11pm.) For the best pizza in town, hit **Tony's Baltimore Grille,** 2800 Atlantic Ave. (345-5766), at Iowa Ave. Sit in one of the large booths and twiddle the knobs on your own personal jukebox (pasta $4-6, pizza $6-7; open daily 11am-3am; bar open 24hr.). Many pizza joints offer large slices of aged pizza, especially later in the day; beware of these rubber slices and search for fresher options at places like **Sbarro** ($2), near Bally's. For a traditional and toothsome oceanside dessert, try custard ice cream ($2) or saltwater taffy ($6 per pound), both available at vendors along the Boardwalk. **Custard and Snack House** (345-5151), between South Carolina and Ocean Ave., makes 37 flavors of soft-serve ice cream and yogurt, ranging from peach to tutti-frutti (cones $2.25; open Su-Th 10am-midnight, F-Sa 10am-3am).

CAINO

You don't have to spend a penny to enjoy yourself in Atlantic City's casinos, but you deserve a prize if you can help it. Vast, plush interiors and spotless marble bathrooms could entertain a resourceful and voyeuristic budget traveler for hours. You can watch the blue-haired old ladies with vacant, zombie-like stares shove quarter after quarter in the slot machines. You can gaze in admiration at the fat, 70-something men dressed in polyester, trying to act like Bond at the blackjack tables. As a matter of fact, you're not the only one watching—hidden behind one-way mirrors, cameras monitor the heavy bid tables, and suited men politely observe all aspects of the games, from dealers to players.

Thousands of square feet of flashing lights stupefy the gaping crowds. The non-stop rattling of chips, clicking of slot machines, clacking of coins, and shouts of joy (or more likely defeat) are enough to expose most to "the fever." Once you catch it, it's hard to stop. In case you do find yourself chained to a slot machine or blackjack table, avoid reloading at an ATM at all costs.

There certainly are plenty of places to indulge, as the casinos on the Boardwalk all fall within a dice toss of one another. The farthest south is **The Grand** (347-7111), between Providence and Boston Ave., and the farthest north is **Showboat** (343-4000), at Delaware Ave. and Boardwalk. If you like Disney-fied representations of sacred Indian culture, you'll love the Donald Trump's **Taj Mahal**, 1000 Boardwalk (449-1000). Here, you can eat at the "Gobi Dessert" or "The Delhi Deli." It will feel like *Monopoly* when you realize Trump owns three other hotel casinos in the city:

Trump Plaza (441-6100) and **Trump World's Fair** (441-6000) on the Boardwalk, and **Trump Castle** (441-2000) at the not-quite-fun-yet Marina.

The Atlantic City version of **Caesar's Boardwalk Resort and Casino** (348-4411) at Arkansas Ave. pales in comparison to the Las Vegas Palace; however, it makes a valiant effort to resemble an ancient Roman palace. **The Sands** (441-4000) at Indiana Ave. stands big and ostentatious with its pink-and-green seashell motif.

Other casinos worth exploring: **Bally's Park Place** (340-2000); **Harrah's Marina Hotel** (441-5000); the **Claridge** (340-3400) at Indiana Ave.; **Showboat** (343-4000) at States Ave.; **TropWorld Casino** (340-4000) at Iowa Ave.; and **Bally's Grand** (347-7111) at Georgia Ave. Check out the celebrity handprints at the main entrance to Merv Griffin's **Resorts International** (344-6000) at North Carolina Ave. and Boardwalk.

Open nearly all the time, casinos lack windows and clocks, denying you the cues that signal hours slipping away. Free drinks (coffee and juice) keep you peppy and satisfied. A book like John Scarne's *New Complete Guide to Gambling* will help you plan an intelligent strategy, but keep your eyes on your watch or you might spend five hours and five digits before you know what hits you. To curb inevitable losses, stick to the cheaper games: blackjack, slot machines, and the low bets in roulette and craps. Minimum bets go up in the evenings and on weekends. Stay away from the cash machines. If you're on a tight budget, play the 5¢ slots available only at Trump Plaza, TropWorld, Bally's Grand, and Taj Mahal. You can gamble for hours on less than $10. If you don't know the finer points of multiple action blackjack, *chemin de fer*, or *pai gow* poker, pick up a free *Gaming Guide* at any of the casinos—a guard can point you to this complete listing of rules and odds.

The minimum gambling age of 21 is strictly enforced. Even if you sneak by the bouncers at the doors, you cannot collect winnings if you are underage. When a young gambler hit a $200,000 jackpot, claiming his father had won, the casino reviewed videos to discover the kid had pulled the lever.

BEACHES AND BOARDWALK

There's something for everyone at Atlantic City, thanks to the **Boardwalk.** Those under 21 (or those tired of the endless cycle of winning money and losing more) gamble for prizes at one of the many arcades that line the Boardwalk. That cute teddy bear in the window is easier to get than the $2 million grand prize at a resort. Those tired of spending money can take a swim at the **beach.** For quieter sands, you can head west to adjacent Ventnor City.

The **Steel Pier,** in front of the Taj Mahal, is a typical amusement park with cotton candy, a ferris wheel, kiddie rides, and plenty of carnival games lining the entrance. ($2-3 each ride. Open daily noon-midnight in the summer. Call the Taj Mahal for winter hours.) Ride the Go-Carts at **Schiff's Central Pier,** off St. James Pl. ($6 includes one adult and one child.)

If the Guinness Book Museum in the Empire State Building wasn't enough, Atlantic City offers skeptical consumers the over-priced **Ripley's Believe It or Not Museum** (347-2001) at New York Ave. and Boardwalk. If willing to pay the price you can see wonders like a roulette table made of jelly beans and the world's largest rubber tire. (Open Su-Th 10am-10pm, F-Sa 10am-10pm. $9, children $7.) If the price of admission is too steep, take a peek in the gift shop where you may still find fascinating facts and mind-boggling puzzles. If you have a car—or extreme wanderlust—head down Atlantic Ave. five miles or so to the intersection with Decatur St. and check out **Lucy the Elephant** (823-6473), a former real estate office built in 1881 in the shape of an elephant—now a national landmark. Like her Asian and African counterparts, Lucy's future is uncertain, so your $3 admission fee (children $1) will go toward the "Save Lucy the Elephant" fund. (Open mid-June to Labor Day M-Th 10am-8pm, F-Sa 10am-5pm; Apr.-May and Sept.-Oct. Sa-Su 10am-4:30pm.)

DAYTRIPS

COOPERSTOWN, NY

To an earlier generation, Cooperstown evoked images of James Fenimore Cooper's frontiersman hero, Leatherstocking, who roamed the woods around the gleaming waters of Lake Otsego. But now, as more of a shrine than a tourist attraction, tiny Cooperstown recalls a different source of American legend and myth—baseball. Tourists file through the Baseball Hall of Fame, buy baseball memorabilia, eat in baseball-themed restaurants, and sleep in baseball-themed motels. Fortunately for the tepid fan, baseball's mecca is surrounded by a charming village, rural beauty and some of New York state's best rural tourist attractions.

PRACTICAL INFORMATION. Cooperstown is accessible from I-90 and I-88 via Rte. 28. Street parking is rare in Cooperstown; your best bets are the free parking lots just outside of town on Rte. 28 south of Cooperstown, on Glen Ave. at Maple St., and near the Fenimore House. From these parking lots, it's an easy 10-minute walk to Main St. **Trolleys** make the short trip from these lots, dropping off riders at the Hall of Fame, the Farmer and Fenimore museums, Doubleday Field, the Chamber of Commerce, and downtown. (Runs late June to mid-Sept. daily 8:30am-9pm; early June and Sept.-Oct. Sa-Su 8:30am-6pm. All-day pass $2, children $1.) **Pine Hall Trailways** (800-858-8555) picks up visitors at Clancy's Deli on Rte. 28 and Elm St. twice daily for New York City (5½hr., $40). The **Cooperstown Area Chamber of Commerce**, 31 Chestnut St. (547-9983), on Rte. 28 near Main St., offers info for accommodations and "free/inexpensive things to do in Cooperstown" (generally open daily 9am-5pm, but hrs. vary; call ahead). **Post office:** 40 Main St. (547-2311; open M-F 8:30am-5pm, Sa 8:30am-noon). **ZIP code:** 13326. **Area code:** 607.

ACCOMMODATIONS AND FOOD. Summertime lodging in Cooperstown seems to require the salary of a Major Leaguer, and during peak tourist season (late June to mid-Sept.), many accommodation-seekers strike out. Fortunately, there are alternatives to endless arbitration. The **Mohican Motel,** 90 Chestnut St. (547-5101), offers more comforts than Natty Bumppo ever needed. Large beds, cable TV, and A/C provide hints of modernity. (Late June to early Sept. doubles $72-87; triples $92-97; quads $98-103; Sa $25 extra; in spring and fall $51-56/$60/$64/Sa $15 extra.) **Glimmerglass State Park** (547-8662), 7 mi. north of Cooperstown on Rte. 31 (a.k.a. Main St. in Cooperstown) on the east side of Lake Otsego, has 43 pristine campsites in a gorgeous lakeside park. Daytime visitors can swim, fish, and boat (for $6 per vehicle) from 11am to 7pm. (Showers, dumping station; no hookups. Register 11am-9pm. Sites $13; $2 registration fee. Call 800-456-2267 for reservations and a heinous $7.50 service charge.) The closest campground to the Hall of Fame is **Cooperstown Beaver Valley Campground** (293-8131 or 800-726-7314), off Rte. 28, 10 minutes south of Cooperstown. Spacious wooded sites include a pool and recreation area, with boat and canoe rentals available. (Sites $24, with hookup $27.)

The **Doubleday Café,** 93 Main St. (547-5468), scores twice with a $6-8 Mexican dinner menu and pints of Old Slugger beer on tap for $2.75 (open Su-Th 7am-10pm, F-Sa 7am-11pm; bar open 2hr. after kitchen). For elegant but affordable dining, check out the **Hoffman Lane Bistro** (547-7055), on Hoffman Ln., off Main St. across from the Hall of Fame. Light, airy rooms with white tablecloths welcome the picky but budget-conscious, with lunch options like the quiche of the day ($6) or clams over linguini ($6; call for hours). A Cooperstown institution, **Schneider's Bakery,** 157 Main St. (547-9631), has been feeding locals since 1887 with delicious 41¢ "old-fashioneds" (donuts less sweet and greasy than their conventional cousins), and equally spectacular onion rolls (30¢; open M-Sa 6:30am-5:30pm, Su 7:30am-1pm).

TAKE ME OUT TO. The **National Baseball Hall of Fame and Museum** (547-7200), on Main St., is an enormous monument to America's favorite pastime. In addition to memorabilia from the immortals—featuring everything from the bat with which Babe Ruth hit his famous "called shot" home run in the 1932 World Series to the infamous jersey worn by 65 lb. White Sox midget Eddie Gaedel—the museum displays a moving multimedia tribute to the sport, a detailed display on the African-

American Baseball Experience, and a history tracing baseball to ancient Egyptian religious ceremonies. As one exhibit reads, "In the beginning, shortly after God created Heaven and Earth, there were stones to throw and sticks to swing." You'll have to fight the crowds to see all this, of course: the daily turnstile count at the museum in the summer exceeds the town population. (Open May-Sept. daily 9am-9pm; Oct.-Apr. 9am-5pm. $9.50, seniors $8, ages 7-12 $4.)

The **annual ceremonies** for new inductees, free to the public, will takes place in late July on the field adjacent to the **Clark Sports Center** on Susquehanna Ave., a 10-minute walk from the Hall. During the weekend of the ceremonies, fans scramble for a bit of contact with the many Hall of Famers who sign autographs (at steep prices) along Main St. **Free baseball games** are played on Saturday and Monday at 2pm in the delightfully intimate Doubleday Field. Plan accordingly—over 40,000 visitors are expected. Rooms must be reserved months in advance.

Nearby, the **Fenimore Art Museum** (547-1400 or 888-547-1450), Lake Rd./Rte. 80, features Native American art, photos, Hudson River School paintings, and James Fenimore Cooper memorabilia. (Open daily 9am-6pm; Sept.-Oct. 10am-5pm; call for hrs. Apr.-June and Nov.-Dec. $9, ages 7-12 $4.) Across the Street, the **Farmer's Museum** (547-1450 or 547-1500) offers exhibits on 19th-century rural life, with a still-operating farmstead. (Open Apr.-May Tu-Su 10am-4pm; June-Sept. daily 10am-5pm; Oct.-Nov. 10m-4pm. Combination tickets with Hall of Fame and Fenimore Art Museum $22, ages 7-12 $9.50.)

If you're looking for culture beyond the museums, the **Glimmerglass Opera Company**, 8 Chesnut St. (547-1257), is a world-renowned but tiny outfit. Shows are held at the historic Alice Busch Opera Theater; call for times and shows. *(Opera Festival yearly July-Aug. Tickets M-Tu and Th $20-$70, F-Su $40-80.)*

CATSKILLS

The Catskills, home of Rip Van Winkle's century-long repose, remained in a happy state of somnambulent obscurity for centuries. After the purple haze of Woodstock jolted the region to life in 1969, the Catskills had to undergo an extensive detox period. Barring the occasional flashback, such as the 1994 and 1999 repetitions of the rock festival, the state-managed Catskill Forest Preserve has regained its status as a nature-lover's dreamland, offering pristine miles of hiking and skiing trails, adorably dinky villages, and crystal-clear fishing streams. Traveling from I-87, the region is most easily explored by following Rt. 28 W.

Adirondack/Pine Hill Trailways provides excellent service through the Catskills. The main stop is in **Kingston**, 400 Washington Ave. (331-0744 or 800-858-8555; ticket office open M-F 5:45am-11pm, Sa-Su 6:45am-11pm), on the corner of Front St. Buses run to New York City (2hr.; 10 per day; $18.50, M and W-Su same-day round-trip $35, Tu-Th $25). Other stops in the area include Woodstock, Pine Hill, Saugerties, and Hunter; each connects with New York City, Albany, and Utica. Four stationary **tourist cabooses** dispense info, including the extremely useful *Ulster County: Catskills Region Travel Guide*, at the traffic circle in Kingston, on Rt. 28 in Shandaken, on Rt. 209 in Ellenville, and on Rt. 9 W in Milton (open May-Oct. 9am-5pm; hrs. vary depending on volunteer availability). Rest stop **visitors centers** along I-87 can advise you on area sights and distribute excellent, free maps of New York State. **Area code:** 914, unless otherwise noted.

CATSKILL FOREST PRESERVE. The 250,000-acre **Catskill Forest Preserve** contains many small towns and outdoor adventure opportunities. Ranger stations distribute free permits for backcountry camping, necessary for stays over 3 days. Still, most of the **campgrounds** listed below sit at gorgeous trail heads that make great day-long jaunts. Reservations are vital in summer, especially weekends. (800-456-2267. Sites $9-12; $2 1st day registration fee; phone reservation fee $7.50; $2 more for partial hookup. Open May-Sept.) The **Office of Parks** (518-474-0456) distributes brochures on the campgrounds. Required permits for **fishing** (non-NY residents $20 for 5 days) are available in sporting goods stores and at many campgrounds. Winter **ski** season tends to run from Nov. to mid-Mar., with popular slopes down numerous mountainsides along Rt. 28 and Rt. 23A. Although hiking trails are maintained, some lean-to's are dilapidated and crowded. For more info, call the **Dept. of Environmental Conservation** (256-3000). **Adirondack Trailways** buses from Kingston service most trail heads—drivers will let you out along secondary bus routes.

WOODSTOCK. The signs advertising "Tie-Dyed T-shirts" and "Last incense for 20mi. sold here" might suggest to you that Woodstock, between Phoenicia and Kingston, is *the* place to be for aging hippies. Although the famed 1969 concert was actually held in Saugerties, Woodstock has been a haven for artists and writers since the turn of the century. The tie-dyed legacy has faded, and Woodstock has become an expensive, touristed town. Still, neo-hippie hipsters operate out of the **Woodstock School of Art** on Rt. 212, accessible from Rt. 28 via Rt. 375. (679-2388. Open M-Sa 9am-3pm.) In addition to art classes, the school houses a gallery that pays homage to Woodstock's artistic tradition.

MT. TREMPER. Kaleidoworld, located on Rt. 28, fiercely competes with mother nature for the title of most spectacular attraction in the Catskills. (688-5328. Open daily 10am-7pm; mid-Oct. to July closed Tu. $10, seniors $8, kids under 4 ft. 6 in. $8.) The two largest kaleidoscopes in the world are proudly displayed here, with the largest (56ft) leaving Woodstock-era veterans muttering, "I can see the music!" The adjacent Crystal Palace (included in admission) features wicked cool, hands-on, interactive kaleidoscopes. Chant your mantra at the **Zen Mountain Monastery,** on S. Plank Rd., 10mi. from Woodstock off Rt. 212 from Mt. Tremper. (688-2228. $5 includes lunch; weekend and week-long retreats from $195.) The 8:45am Sun. services include an amazing demonstration of zazen meditation.

    Kenneth L. Wilson, on Wittenburg Rd. 3.7mi. from Rt. 212 (make a hard right onto Wittenburg Rd.), has well-wooded **campsites** showers, and a family atmosphere. The pond-front beach has a gorgeous panorama of surrounding mountains staring into the looking-glass lake (hey there, Narcissus). Canoe rentals, fishing, and hiking round out the options. (679-7020. Sites $12, plus a $2.50 service charge. Registration 8am-9pm. Day use $5, seniors free M-F. Canoes ½-day $10, full-day $15.)

PHOENICIA. Phoenicia is another fine place to anchor a trip to the Catskills. The **Esopus Creek,** to the west, has great trout **fishing,** and **The Town Tinker** rents inner-tubes for summertime river-riding. (10 Bridge St. 688-5553. Inner-tubes $7 per day, with seat $10. Driver's license or $50 deposit required. Tube taxi transportation $3. Life jackets $2. Open mid-May to Sept. daily 9am-6pm; last rental 4:30pm.) If tubes don't float your boat, the wheezing steam-engine of the 100-year-old **Catskill Mountain Railroad** can shuttle you for 6 scenic mi. from Bridge St. to Mt. Pleasant. (40min., late May to early Sept. Sa-Su 1 per hr., 11am-5pm. $4, round-trip $6, under 12 $2.) At the 65 ft. high **Sundance Rappel Tower,** off Rt. 214, visitors climb up and return to earth the hard way. (688-5640. 4 levels of lessons; beginner 3-4hr., $22. Lessons only held when a group of 8 is present. Reservations 1 week in advance required.) For a trip to the Preserve's peak, head to Woodland Valley campground (below), where a 9.8mi. hike to the 4204 ft. summit of **Slide Mt.** lends a view of New Jersey, Pennsylvania, and the Hudson Highlands.

    The somewhat primitive **Woodland Valley** campground, off High St. 7mi. southeast of Phoenicia, has flush toilets and showers, and is accessible to many hiking trails (688-7647; sites $9, plus a $2.50 service charge. Open late May-early Oct.). The **Cobblestone Motel,** is surrounded by mountains on Rt. 214 and under friendly new management. It has a family atmosphere, an outdoor pool, and clean, newly renovated rooms, most with a fridge. (688-7871. Doubles $44, large doubles $55, with kitchenette $65; 1-bedroom cottages $70, 3-room cottages with kitchen $95.)

PINE HILL. Pine Hill is nestled near **Belleayre Mt.,** which offers hiking trails and ski slopes. (254-5000 or 800-942-6904. Ski lift, lesson, and rental package M-F $50, Sa-Su $60; children $40/$50.) **Belleayre Hostel** is a lodging bargain; follow Rt. 28 past Big Indian, making a left on Main St. at the big white "Pine Hill" sign, then another left into the second parking lot. Bunks and private rooms in a rustic setting near Phoenicia. Amenities include a recreational room, kitchen access, laundry ($2), a picnic area, and sporting equipment. (254-4200. Bunks in summer $10, in winter $13; private rooms $25/$30; cabins for up to 4 $40/$50.)

HUNTER MT. AND HAINES FALLS. From Rt. 28, darting north on Rt. 42 and then east onto Rt. 23A leads through a gorgeous stretch along **Hunter Mt.,** one of the most popular **skiing** areas on the east coast (ski info 518-263-4223, accommodations 800-775-4641). Hunter Mt. offers **Skyride,** the longest, highest chairlift in the Catskills, during festivals held throughout the summer and fall ($7, ages 3-12 $3.50, under 6 $1; $1 off with festival admission). Motels and outdoor stores dot the highway. Past Hunter Mt., **North Lake/South Lake campground** in Haines Falls has 219 campsites near two lakes, a waterfall, and hiking. (518-589-5058. $16, plus a $2.50 service charge, reserve 2 days in advance. Day use $5. Canoe rental $15.)

INDEX

B

ABOUT LET'S GO

FORTY YEARS OF WISDOM

As a new millennium arrives, *Let's Go: Europe*, now in its 40th edition and translated into seven languages, reigns as the world's bestselling international travel guide. For four decades, travelers criss-crossing the Continent have relied on *Let's Go* for inside information on the hippest backstreet cafes, the most pristine secluded beaches, and the best routes from border to border. In the last 20 years, our rugged researchers have stretched the frontiers of backpacking and expanded our coverage into Asia, Africa, Australia, and the Americas. We're celebrating our 40th birthday with the release of *Let's Go: China*, blazing the traveler's trail from the Forbidden City to the Tibetan frontier; *Let's Go: Perú & Ecuador*, spanning the lands of the ancient Inca Empire; *Let's Go: Middle East*, with coverage from Istanbul to the Persian Gulf; and the maiden edition of *Let's Go: Israel*.

It all started in 1960 when a handful of well-traveled students at Harvard University handed out a 20-page mimeographed pamphlet offering a collection of their tips on budget travel to passengers on student charter flights to Europe. The following year, in response to the instant popularity of the first volume, students traveling to Europe researched the first full-fledged edition of *Let's Go: Europe*, a pocket-sized book featuring honest, practical advice, witty writing, and a decidedly youthful slant on the world. Throughout the 60s and 70s, our guides reflected the times. In 1969 we taught travelers how to get from Paris to Prague on "no dollars a day" by singing in the street. In the 80s and 90s, we looked beyond Europe and North America and set off to all corners of the earth. Meanwhile, we focused in on the world's most exciting urban areas to produce in-depth, fold-out map guides. Our new guides bring the total number of titles to 48, each infused with the spirit of adventure and voice of opinion that travelers around the world have come to count on. But some things never change: our guides are still researched, written, and produced entirely by students who know first-hand how to see the world on the cheap.

HOW WE DO IT

Each guide is completely revised and thoroughly updated every year by a well-traveled set of over 250 students. Every spring, we recruit over 180 researchers and 70 editors to overhaul every book. After several months of training, researcher-writers hit the road for seven weeks of exploration, from Anchorage to Adelaide, Estonia to El Salvador, Iceland to Indonesia. Hired for their rare combination of budget travel sense, writing ability, stamina, and courage, these adventurous travelers know that train strikes, stolen luggage, food poisoning, and marriage proposals are all part of a day's work. Back at our offices, editors work from spring to fall, massaging copy written on Himalayan bus rides into witty, informative prose. A student staff of typesetters, cartographers, publicists, and managers keeps our lively team together. In September, the collected efforts of the summer are delivered to our printer, which turns them into books in record time, so that you have the most up-to-date information available for your vacation. Even as you read this, work on next year's editions is well underway.

WHY WE DO IT

We don't think of budget travel as the last recourse of the destitute; we believe that it's the only way to travel. Living cheaply and simply brings you closer to the people and places you've been saving up to visit. Our books will ease your anxieties and answer your questions about the basics—so you can get off the beaten track and explore. Once you learn the ropes, we encourage you to put *Let's Go* down now and then to strike out on your own. You know as well as we that the best discoveries are often those you make yourself. When you find something worth sharing, please drop us a line. We're Let's Go Publications, 67 Mount Auburn St., Cambridge, MA 02138, USA (email: feedback@letsgo.com). For more info, visit our website, http://www.letsgo.com.

Next time, make your *own* hotel arrangements.

Yahoo! Travel

READER QUESTIONNAIRE

Name: _____

Address: _____

City: _____ State: _____ Country: _____

ZIP/Postal Code: _____ E-mail: _____ How old are you? ____

And you're...?   in high school   in college   in graduate school

                    employed   retired   between jobs

Which book(s) have you used? _____

Where have you gone with Let's Go? _____

Have you traveled extensively before?   yes   no

Had you used Let's Go before?   yes   no   **Would you use it again?**   yes   no

How did you hear about Let's Go? friend   store clerk   television

                                  review   bookstore display

                                  ad/promotion   internet   other: _____

Why did you choose Let's Go?   reputation   budget focus   annual updating

                                  wit & incision price   other: _____

Which guides have you used?   Fodor's   Footprint Handbooks Frommer's $-a-day

                               Lonely Planet   Moon Guides   Rick Steve's

                               Rough Guides   UpClose   other: _____

Which guide do you prefer? Why? _____

Please rank the following in your Let's Go guide: (1=needs improvement, 5=perfect)

packaging/cover	1 2 3 4 5	food	1 2 3 4 5	maps	1 2 3 4 5
cultural introduction	1 2 3 4 5	sights	1 2 3 4 5	directions	1 2 3 4 5
"Essentials"	1 2 3 4 5	entertainment	1 2 3 4 5	writing style	1 2 3 4 5
practical info	1 2 3 4 5	gay/lesbian info	1 2 3 4 5	budget resources	1 2 3 4 5
accommodations	1 2 3 4 5	up-to-date info	1 2 3 4 5	other: _____	1 2 3 4 5

How long was your trip?   one week   two wks.   three wks.   a month   2+ months

Why did you go? sightseeing   adventure travel   study abroad   other: _____

What was your average daily budget, not including flights? _____

Do you buy a separate map when you visit a foreign city?   yes   no

Have you used a Let's Go Map Guide?   yes   no   **If you have, which one?** _____

Would you recommend them to others?   yes   no

Have you visited Let's Go's website?   yes no

What would you like to see included on Let's Go's website? _____

What percentage of your trip planning did you do on the web? _____

What kind of Let's Go guide would you like to see? recreation (e.g., skiing)   phrasebook

                     spring break   adventure/trekking   first-time travel info   Europe altas

Which of the following destinations would you like to see Let's Go cover?

            Argentina   Brazil   Canada   Caribbean   Chile   Costa Rica   Cuba

            Morocco   Nepal   Russia   Scandinavia   Southwest USA   other: _____

Where did you buy your guidebook?   independent bookstore   college bookstore

            travel store   Internet   chain bookstore   gift   other: _____

Please fill this out and return it to **Let's Go, St. Martin's Press,** 175 Fifth Ave., New York, NY 10010-7848. All respondents will receive a free subscription to **The Yellow-jacket,** the Let's Go Newsletter. You can find a more extensive version of this survey on the web at http://www.letsgo.com.

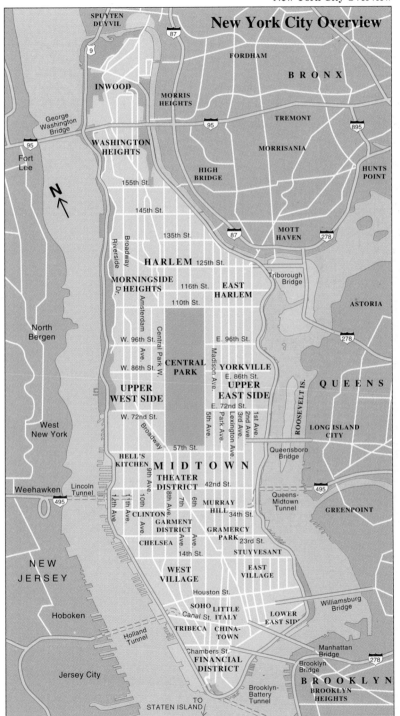

New York City Subways

Subways

Stops are not served by all trains at all times.
Refer to Transit Authority map for descriptions of express, local, and limited service.

Times Sq/42 St

Shuttle

Grand Central

57 St
49 St
47-50 Sts
42 St
7 Av
50 St
42 St/42 St
5 Av
Herald Sq/34 St
32 St
28 St
23 St
34 St
28 St
23 St

L 14 St/8 Av
Christopher St/Sheridan Sq
W 4 St/6 Av
Houston St
Spring St
Canal St
Franklin St
Chambers St
World Trade Center
Cortlandt St
Rector St
Wall St
Bowling Green

23 St
14 St/Union Sq
3 Av
1 Av
Astor Pl
8 St NYU
Lafayette/Bleecker
Bowery
Grand St
Spring St
Prince St
Canal St

Broadway/Lafayette
2 Av
Essex St/Delancey St
E Broadway

Chambers St/Brooklyn Br/City Hall
Fulton St
Broad St/J,Z
Wall St
Whitehall St/South Ferry

1,9 South Ferry

York St
High St/Bklyn Br
Jay St/Borough Hall
Court St/Borough Hall
Hoyt St/Fulton Mall
Hoyt St
Lawrence St
DeKalb Av
Pacific St/Atlantic Av
Nevins St
Hoyt St
Schermerhorn St
Bergen St
4 Av/9 St

Pelham Bay Park 6

Dyre Av 5
Baychester Av
Nereid Av
238 St
233 St
225 St
219 St
Gun Hill Rd
Pelham Pkwy
Morris Pk

241 St 2,5

Woodlawn 4
Mosholu Pkwy
Bedford Pk
Burke Av
Allerton Av
Pelham Pkwy
Bronx Pk

C Pk D 205 St

Buhre Av
Middletown Rd
Westchester Sq/E Tremont Av
Zerega Av
Castle Hill Av
St Lawrence Av
Parkchester
Morrison Av/Soundview Av
Elder Av
Whitlock Av
E 177 St
E 180 St

242 St/Van Cortlandt Pk 1,9
238 St
231 St
225 St/Marble H
215 St
207 St A
200 St
Kingsbridge Rd
Fordham Rd
182-183 St
Tremont Av
174-175 St
170 St
167 St
161 St/Yankee St
149 St/Concourse
138 St/Concourse
3rd Av/149 St

Bedford Pk
Kingsbridge Rd
Fordham Rd
182-183 St
Burnside
176 St
Mt Eden
170 St
167 St
161 St/Yankee St
149 St
Freeman St
Simpson St

Hunts Pt Av
Intervale Av/163 St
Prospect Av
Jackson Av
E 149 St
E 143 St/St Marys St

Cypress Av
Brook Av
3rd Av/138 St

190 St
181 St
168 St B
157 St
145 St
137 St/City College
125 St
116 St/Columbia
110 St/Cathedral Pkwy
103 St
96 St
86 St
79 St
72 St
66 St/Lincoln Cir
59 St/Columbus Cir

163 St/Amsterdam
155 St
145 St
136 St
125 St
116 St
110 St
103 St
96 St
86 St
81 St
72 St

145 St 3
135 St
125 St
116 St
110 St
103 St
96 St
86 St
77 St
68 St/Hunter
59 St
51 St
Lexington
Grand Central
42 St

7 Av
50 St
42 St/42 St
34 St
Herald Sq
23 St

Main St/Roosevelt Av/LIRR 7
Willets Pt/Shea Stadium
103 St/Corona Plaza
Junction Blvd
90 St
82 St
74 St/Broadway
69 St
65 St
Northern Blvd
46 St
Steinway
36 Av/Washington
30 Av/Grand Av
Astoria Blvd/Hoyt Av

Ditmars Blvd N

Queensboro Plaza
Queens Plaza

Roosevelt Av
Woodside
59 St
Jackson Hts/Roosevelt Av

Grand Av
12 St

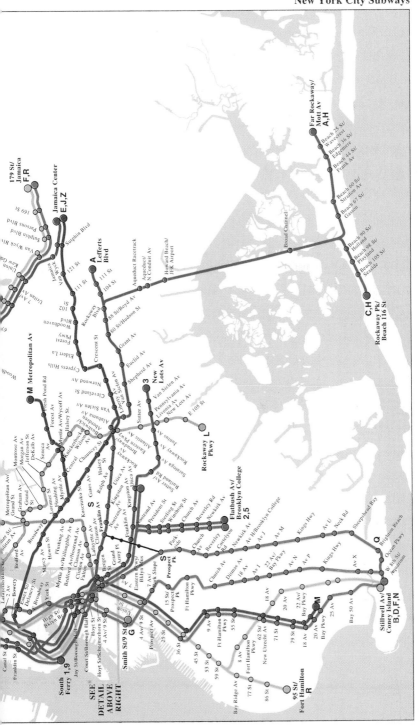

Downtown Manhattan

Midtown Manhattan

East River

Queensboro Bridge

Queens-Midtown Tunnel

FDR Dr.

First Ave.

E. 56th St.
E. 55th St.
E. 54th St.
E. 53rd St.
E. 52nd St.
E. 51st St.
E. 50th St.
E. 49th St.
E. 48th St.
E. 47th St.
E. 46th St.
E. 45th St.
E. 44th St.
E. 43rd St.

TURTLE BAY

United Nations

Second Ave.

Third Ave.

Citicorp Center

Lexington Ave.

E. 42nd St.
E. 41st St.
E. 40th St.
E. 39th St.
E. 38th St.
E. 37th St.
E. 36th St.
E. 35th St.
E. 34th St.
E. 33rd St.
E. 32nd St.

Second Ave.

Third Ave.

Park Ave..

Park Ave..

Madison Ave.

Grand Central Terminal

New York Public Library

MURRAY HILL

Empire State Building

Fifth Ave.

Rockefeller Center

Museum of Modern Art

Bryant Park

W. 40th St.

E. 60th St.
E. 59th St.
E. 58th St.
E. 57th St.

Grand Army Plaza

Park South

Central

Carnegie Hall

Broadway

B.D.F.Q.7

GARMENT DISTRICT

HERALD SQUARE

Seventh Ave.

TIMES SQUARE

Eighth Ave.

Eighth Ave.

COLUMBUS CIRCLE

A,B,C,D,
1,2,3,9

New York Convention & Visitors Bureau

C,E

A,C,E

A,C,E

Port Authority Bus Terminal

General Post Office

Ninth Ave.

Ninth Ave.

W. 60th St.
W. 59th St.
W. 58th St.
W. 57th St.
W. 56th St.
W. 55th St.
W. 54th St.
W. 53rd St.
W. 52nd St.
W. 51st St.
W. 50th St.
W. 49th St.
W. 48th St.
W. 47th St.
W. 46th St.
W. 45th St.
W. 44th St.
W. 43rd St.
W. 42nd St.
W. 41st St.
W. 39th St.
W. 38th St.
W. 37th St.
W. 36th St.
W. 35th St.
W. 34th St.
W. 33rd St.

Dyer Ave.

Tenth Ave.

Tenth Ave.

HELL'S KITCHEN

Eleventh Ave.

Lincoln Tunnel

Twelfth Ave.

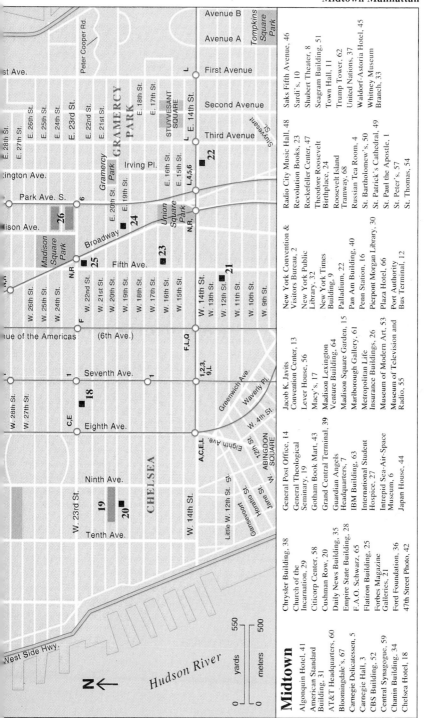

Uptown

American Museum of Natural History, 53
The Ansonia, 55
The Arsenal, 25
Asia Society, 14
Belvedere Castle, 36
Bethesda Fountain, 33
Blockhouse No. 1, 42
Bloomingdale's, 22
Bridle Path, 30
Cathedral of St. John the Divine, 47
Central Park Zoo, 24
Chess and Checkers House, 28
Children's Museum of Manhattan, 51
Children's Zoo, 26
China House, 19

Cleopatra's Needle, 38
Columbia University, 46
Conservatory Garden, 2
Cooper-Hewitt Museum, 7
The Dairy, 27
Dakota Apartments, 56
Delacorte Theater, 37
El Museo del Barrio, 1
Fordham University, 60
Frick Museum, 13
Gracie Mansion, 10
Grant's Tomb, 45
Great Lawn, 39
Guggenheim Museum, 9
Hayden Planetarium (at the American Museum of Natural History), 53
Hector Memorial, 50
Hotel des Artistes, 57

Hunter College, 16
International Center of Photography, 5
Jewish Museum, 6
The Juilliard School (at Lincoln Center), 59
Lincoln Center, 59
Loeb Boathouse, 34
Masjid Malcolm Shabazz, 43
Metropolitan Museum of Art, 11
Mt. Sinai Hospital, 4
Museum of American Folk Art, 58
Museum of American Illustration, 21
Museum of the City of New York, 3
National Academy of Design, 8
New York Convention & Visitors Bureau, 61

New York Historical Society, 54
New York Hospital, 15
Plaza Hotel, 23
Police Station (Central Park), 40
Rockefeller University, 20
7th Regiment Armory, 17
Shakespeare Garden, 35
Soldiers and Sailors Monument, 49
Strawberry Fields, 32
Studio Museum in Harlem, 44
Symphony Space, 48
Tavern on the Green, 31
Temple Emanu-El, 18
Tennis Courts, 41
Whitney Museum of American Art, 12
Wollman Rink, 29
Zabar's, 52